Database Concepts

Brief Contents

Contents

Colin Johnson is a production supervisor for a small manufacturer in Seattle. Several years ago, Colin wanted to build a database to keep track of components in product packages. At the time, he was using a spreadsheet to perform this task, but he could not get the reports he needed from the spreadsheet. Colin had heard about Microsoft Access, and he tried to use it to solve his problem. After several days of frustration, he bought several popular Microsoft Access books and attempted to learn from them. Ultimately, he gave up and hired a consultant who built an application that more or less met his needs. Over time, Colin wanted to change his application, but he did not dare try.

Colin was a successful businessperson who was highly motivated to achieve his goals. A seasoned Windows user, he had been able to teach himself how to use Microsoft Excel, Microsoft PowerPoint, and a number of production-oriented application packages. He was flummoxed at his inability to use Microsoft Access to solve his problem. "I'm sure I could do it, but I just don't have any more time to invest," he thought. This story is especially remarkable because it has occurred tens of thousands of times over the past decade to many other people.

Microsoft, Oracle, IBM, and other database management system (DBMS) vendors are aware of such scenarios and have invested millions of dollars in creating better graphical interfaces, hundreds of multipanel wizards, and many sample applications. Unfortunately, such efforts treat the symptoms and not the root of the problem. In fact, most users have no clear idea what the wizards are doing on their behalf. As soon as these users require changes to database structure or to components such as forms and queries, they drown in a sea of complexity for which they are unprepared. With little understanding of the underlying fundamentals, these users grab at any straw that appears to lead in the direction they want. The consequence is poorly designed databases and applications that fail to meet the users' requirements.

Why can people like Colin learn to use a word processor or a spreadsheet product yet fail when trying to learn to use a DBMS product? First, the underlying database concepts are unnatural to most people. Whereas everyone knows what paragraphs and margins are, no one knows what a relation is. Second, it seems as though using a DBMS product ought to be easier than it is. "All I want to do is keep track of something. Why is it so hard?" people ask. Without knowledge of the relational model, breaking a sales invoice into five separate tables before storing the data is mystifying to business users.

This book is intended to help people like Colin understand, create, and use databases in a DBMS product, whether they are individuals who found this book in a bookstore or students using this book as their textbook in a class.

NEW TO THIS EDITION

Students and other readers of this book will benefit from new content and features in this edition. These include the following:

- Mircosoft Office 2013, and particularly Microsoft Access 2013, is now the basic software used in the book and is shown running on Microsoft Windows 8.1.
- DBMS software coverage has been updated to include Microsoft SQL Server 2014 Express Edition and Oracle MySQL 5.6 Community Server.

- New material to illustrate the concepts of SQL joins has been added to Chapter 3 to make this material easier for students to understand.
- New material on SQL programming via SQL/Persistent Stored Modules (SQL/PSM) has been added to Appendix E to provide a better organized discussion and expanded discussion of this material, which had previously been spread among other parts of the book. This material also provides a discussion of importing Microsoft Excel worksheet data in to a database.
- Material on *Big Data* and the evolving *NoSQL movement* is now briefly introduced in Chapter 1, while the main, expanded discussion of this material is in Chapter 8 and the new Appendix K, "Big Data" Big Data remains the theme for Chapter 8, which includes the material on the development of nonrelational data stores (such as Cassandra and HBase) and the Hadoop Distributed File System (HDFS) first introduced in DBC e06. Appendix K, "Big Data"—has been added to provide additional, more detailed material on the NoSQL databases used in Big Data setups for those instructors who still want to cover this topic in depth.
- The Oracle NetBeans IDE is used in Chapter 7 in place of the Eclipse PDT IDE. Since an integrated downloadable installation file for both the Java JDK and NetBeans is available, this results in a much easier software installation of these products in Appendix I. The NetBeans IDE is also arguably easier to use then the Eclipse PDT, which will make it easier for students to create the HTML and PHP Web pages used in Chapter 7.

We kept all the main innovations included in DBC e06, including:

- The coverage of Web database applications in Chapter 7 now includes data input Web form pages. This allows Web database applications to be built with both data-input and data-reading Web pages.
- The coverage of Microsoft Access 2013 now includes Microsoft Access switchboard forms (covered in Appendix H, "The Access Workbench—Section H—Microsoft Access 2013 Switchboards"), which are used to build menus for database applications. Switchboard forms can be used to build database applications that have a user-friendly main menu that users can use to display forms, print reports, and run queries.
- Each chapter now features an independent Case Question set. The Case Question sets are problem sets that generally do not require the student to have completed work on the same case in a previous chapter (there is one intentional exception that ties data modeling and database design together). Although in some instances the same basic named case may be used in different chapters, each instance is still completely independent of any other instance.
- Support for Oracle Database Express Edition 11*g* Release 2 is maintained. Appendix B, "Getting Started with Oracle Database Express Edition 11*g* Release 2," shows you how to use the product and the Oracle SQL Developer GUI utility. The appendix provides the basic knowledge, and Oracle SQL Developer screenshots in the text are used to illustrate specific concepts.

THE NEED FOR ESSENTIAL CONCEPTS

With today's technology, it is impossible to utilize a DBMS successfully without first learning fundamental concepts. After years of developing databases with business users, we believe that the following database concepts are essential:

- Fundamentals of the relational model
- Structured Query Language (SQL)
- Data modeling
- Database design
- Database administration

And because of the increasing use of the Internet, the World Wide Web, commonly available analysis tools, and the emergence of the NoSQL movement, four more essential concepts need to be added to the list:

- Web database processing
- Data warehouse structures
- Business intelligence (BI) systems
- Nonrelational structured data storage

Users like Colin—and students who will perform jobs similar to his—need not learn these topics to the same depth as future information systems professionals. Consequently, this textbook presents only essential concepts—those that are necessary for users like Colin who want to create and use small databases. Many of the discussions in this book are rewritten and simplified explanations of topics that you will find fully discussed in David M. Kroenke and David J. Auer's *Database Processing: Fundamentals, Design, and Implementation*.[1] However, in creating the material for this text, we have endeavored to ensure that the discussions remain accurate and do not mislead. Nothing here will need to be unlearned if students take more advanced database courses.

TEACHING CONCEPTS INDEPENDENT OF DBMS PRODUCTS

This book does not assume that students will use any particular DBMS product. The book does illustrate database concepts with Microsoft Access, SQL Server Express edition, Oracle Database Express Edition, and MySQL Community Server so that students can use these products as tools and actually try out the material, but all the concepts are presented in a DBMS-agnostic manner. When students learn the material this way, they come to understand that the fundamentals pertain to any database, from the smallest Microsoft Access database to the largest Microsoft SQL Server or Oracle Database database. Moreover, this approach avoids a common pitfall. When concepts and products are taught at the same time, students frequently confound concepts with product features and functions. For example, consider referential integrity constraints. When they are taught from a conceptual standpoint, students learn that there are times when the values of a column in one table must always be present as values of a column in a second table. Students also learn how this constraint arises in the context of relationship definition and how either the DBMS or the application must enforce this constraint. If taught in the context of a DBMS—say in the context of Microsoft Access—students will only learn that in some cases you check a check box and in other cases you do not. The danger is that the underlying concept will be lost in the product feature.

All this is not to say that a DBMS should not be used in this class. On the contrary, students can best master these concepts by applying them using a commercial DBMS product. This edition of the book was written to include enough basic information about Microsoft Access, SQL Server Express edition, Oracle Database Express Edition, and MySQL so that you can use these products in your class without the need for a second book or other materials. Microsoft Access is covered in some depth because of its popularity as a personal database and its inclusion in the Microsoft Office Professional suite of applications. However, if you want to cover a particular DBMS in depth or use a DBMS product not discussed in the book, you need to supplement this book with another text or additional materials. Pearson provides a number of books for Microsoft Access 2013 and other DBMS products, and many of them can be packaged with this text.

---

[1]David M. Kroenke and David J. Auer, *Database Processing: Fundamentals, Design, and Implementation*, 13th edition (Upper Saddle River, NJ: Pearson/Prentice Hall, 2014).

THE ACCESS WORKBENCH

This new edition of the text continues using "The Access Workbench," a feature first introduced in the third edition. Because Microsoft Access is widely used in introductory database classes, we feel it is important to include specific information on using Microsoft Access. Each chapter has an accompanying section of "The Access Workbench," which illustrates the chapter's concepts and techniques using Microsoft Access. "The Access Workbench" topics start with creating a database and a single table in Chapter 1 and move through various topics, finishing with Web database processing against a Microsoft Access database in Chapter 7 and using Microsoft Access (together with Microsoft Excel) to produce PivotTable OLAP reports in Chapter 8. This material is not intended to provide comprehensive coverage of Microsoft Access, but all the necessary basic Microsoft Access topics are covered so that your students can learn to effectively build and use Microsoft Access databases.

KEY TERMS, REVIEW QUESTIONS, EXERCISES, CASES, AND PROJECTS

Because it is important for students to apply the concepts they learn, each chapter concludes with sets of key terms, review questions, exercises (including exercises tied to "The Access Workbench"), Case Question sets, and three projects that run throughout the book. Students should know the meaning of each of the key terms and be able to answer the review questions if they have read and understood the chapter material. Each of the exercises requires students to apply the chapter concepts to a small problem or task.

The first of the projects, Garden Glory, concerns the development and use of a database for a partnership that provides gardening and yard maintenance services to individuals and organizations. The second project, James River Jewelry, addresses the need for a database to support a frequent-buyer program for a retail store. The third project, The Queen Anne Curiosity Shop, concerns the sales and inventory needs of a retail business. These three projects appear in all of the book's chapters (although the actual text of the James River Jewelry project is found in online Appendix D). In each instance, students are asked to apply the project concepts from the chapter. Instructors will find more information on the use of these projects in the instructor's manual and can obtain databases and data from the password-protected instructor's portion of this book's Web site (**www.pearsonhighered .com/kroenke**).

SOFTWARE USED IN THE BOOK

Just as we have treated our discussions in a DBMS-agnostic way, whenever possible, we have selected software to be as operating system independent as possible. It is amazing how much excellent software is available online. Many major DBMS vendors provide free versions of their premier products (for example, Microsoft's SQL Server Express edition, Oracle Corporation's Oracle Database Express Edition, and MySQL Community Server). Web editors and integrated development environments (IDEs) are also available (for example, Eclipse, NetBeans, and Visual Studio Express edition). PHP, considered the fourth most commonly used programming language, is downloadable for use with many operating systems and Web servers.

So although the examples in this book were created using a Microsoft operating system, SQL Server 2014 Express edition, Microsoft Access 2013, Microsoft Excel 2013, and the IIS Web Server, most of them could just as easily be accomplished using Linux, MySQL Server Community edition, Apache OpenOffice Base, Apache OpenOffice Calc, and the Apache Web server. Some software products used in the book, such as PHP and NetBeans, are available for multiple operating systems.

Over the past 30-plus years, we have found the development of databases and database applications to be an enjoyable and rewarding activity. We believe that the number, size, and importance of databases will increase in the future and that the field will achieve even greater prominence. It is our hope that the concepts, knowledge, and techniques presented in this book will help students to participate successfully in database projects now and for many years to come.

CHANGES FROM THE SIXTH EDITION

The most significant change in this edition is the coverage of the rapidly evolving use of *Big Data* and the associated *NoSQL movement*. The need to be able to store and process extremely large datasets is transforming the database world. Although these developments leave the database fundamentals covered in this book unchanged, they do require us to put the relational databases that are the core of this text into the context of the overall database picture and to provide the reader with an understanding of the nonrelational structured storage used in the Big Data environment. Therefore, Chapter 8 is now organized around the topic of Big Data, and the topics of data warehouses, clustered database servers, distributed databases, and an introduction to business intelligence (BI) systems find a natural home in that chapter. To provide additional coverage of Big Data, Appendix K has been added to allow a discussion in more depth than the page limitations of the book allow. For those wanting the same coverage of BI found in the previous edition of *Database Concepts*, we have moved BI material that no longer fit in Chapter 8 to Appendix J.

Finally, we have maintained the chapter-independent Case Question sets we added in the sixth edition. Although the chapter projects tie the topics in each chapter together, the case questions do not require the student to have completed work on the same case in a previous chapter or chapters. There is one intentional exception that spans Chapters 4 and 5 that ties data modeling and database design together, but each of these chapters also includes a standalone case. Although in some instances the same basic named case may be used in different chapters, each instance is still completely independent of any other instance, and we provide needed Microsoft Access 2013 database and SQL scripts at the text Web site at **www.pearsonhighered.com/kroenke**.

We have, of course, also updated information on all the other products in the book. In particular, we cover the newly released Microsoft SQL Server 2014 and MySQL 5.6 Community Server.

We have kept and improved upon several features introduced in earlier editions of the book:

- The use of "The Access Workbench" sections in each chapter to provide coverage of Microsoft Access fundamentals now includes Microsoft Access switchboards (Appendix H, "The Access Workbench—Section H—Microsoft Access 2013 Switchboards," available online).
- Introductions to the use of Microsoft SQL Server 2014 Express Edition (Appendix A, "Getting Started with Microsoft SQL Server 2014 Express Edition," available online), Oracle Database Express Edition 11*g* Release 2 (Appendix B, "Getting Started with Oracle Database Express Edition 11*g* Release 2," available online) and Oracle MySQL 5.6 Community Server (Appendix C, "Getting Started with MySQL 5.6 Community Server," available online).
- The use of fully developed datasets for the three example databases that run throughout various portions of the book—Wedgewood Pacific Corporation, Heather Sweeney Designs, and Wallingford Motors.
- The use of the PHP scripting language, now used in the NetBeans IDE, in the Web database processing topics now includes code for Web page input forms.
- Coverage of the dimensional database model is maintained in the restructured Chapter 8, together with coverage of OLAP.

In order to make room for this new material, we have had to move some valuable material previously found in the book itself to online appendices. This includes the James River Jewelry set of project questions, which is now in online Appendix D, "James River Jewelry Project Questions," the material on SQL Views is now in online Appendix E, "SQL Views, SQL/PSM, and Importing Data" with additional material on SQL Persistent Stored Modules (SQL/PSM) and how to import Microsoft Excel data. The business intelligence systems material on reporting systems and data mining is now in online Appendix J "Business Intelligence Systems."

BOOK OVERVIEW

This textbook consists of 8 chapters and 11 appendices (all of which are readily available online at **www.pearsonhighered.com/kroenke**). Chapter 1 explains why databases are used, what their components are, and how they are developed. Students will learn the purpose of databases and their applications, as well as how databases differ from and improve on lists in spreadsheets. Chapter 2 introduces the relational model and defines basic relational terminology. It also introduces the fundamental ideas that underlie normalization and describe the normalization process.

Chapter 3 presents fundamental SQL statements. Basic SQL statements for data definition are described, as are SQL SELECT and data modification statements. No attempt is made to present advanced SQL statements; only the essential statements are described. Online Appendix E adds coverage of SQL views.

The next two chapters consider database design. Chapter 4 addresses data modeling, using the entity-relationship (E-R) model. This chapter describes the need for data modeling, introduces basic E-R terms and concepts, and presents a short case application (Heather Sweeney Designs) of E-R modeling. Chapter 5 describes database design and explains the essentials of normalization. The data model from the case example in Chapter 4 is transformed into a relational design in Chapter 5.

In this edition, we continue to use the more effective discussion of normalization added in an earlier edition. We have presented a prescriptive procedure for normalizing relations through the use of a four-step process. This approach not only makes the normalization task easier, it also makes normalization principles easier to understand. Therefore, this approach has been retained in this edition. For instructors who want a bit more detail on normal forms, short definitions of most normal forms are included in Chapter 5.

The last three chapters consider database management and the uses of databases in applications. Chapter 6 provides an overview of database administration. The case example database is built as a functioning database, and it serves as the example for a discussion of the need for database administration. The chapter surveys concurrency control, security, and backup and recovery techniques. Database administration is an important topic because it applies to all databases, even personal, single-user databases. In fact, in some ways this topic is more important for those smaller databases because no professional database administrator is present to ensure that critical tasks are performed.

Chapter 7 introduces the use of Web-based database processing, including a discussion of Open Database Connectivity (ODBC) and the use of the PHP scripting language. It also discusses the emergence and basic concepts of Extensible Markup Language (XML).

Chapter 8 discusses the emerging world of Big Data and the NoSQL movement. Business intelligence (BI) systems and the data warehouse architectures that support them are discussed, but many details of BI systems have been moved to online Appendix J. Chapter 8 also discusses dimensional databases. The chapter also walks through how to build a dimensional database for Heather Sweeney Designs and then use it to produce a PivotTable Online Analytical Processing (OLAP) report. Chapter 8 also provides a discussion of distributed databases and object-relational databases.

Appendix A provides a short introduction to Microsoft SQL Server 2014 Express Edition, Appendix B provides an introduction for Oracle Database Express Edition 11*g*

Release 2, and Appendix C provides a similar introduction for MySQL 5.6 Community Server. Microsoft Access is covered in "The Access Workbench" sections included in each chapter. Appendix D now contains the James River Jewelry project questions, and the material on SQL views is located in Appendix E. Appendix F provides an introduction to systems analysis and design and can be used to provide context for Chapter 4 (data modeling) and Chapter 5 (database design)—although in this book we focus on databases, databases are used in applications. Appendix F describes the application development process in more detail. Appendix G is a short introduction to Microsoft Visio 2013, which can be used as a tool for data modeling (Chapter 4) and database design (Chapter 5). Another useful database design tool is the MySQL Workbench, and this use of the MySQL Workbench is discussed in Appendix C. Appendix H extends Chapter 5's section of "The Access Workbench" by providing coverage of Microsoft Access 2013 switchboards. Appendix I provides detailed support for Chapter 7 by giving detailed instructions on getting the Microsoft IIS Web server, PHP, and the NetBeans IDE up and running. Appendix J provides additional material on business intelligence (BI) systems to supplement and support Chapter 8 by giving details on report systems and data mining. Finally, Appendix K provides additional material on Big Data and NoSQL databases to supplement and support Chapter 8.

KEEPING CURRENT IN A RAPIDLY CHANGING WORLD

In order to keep *Database Concepts* up to date between editions, we post updates on the book's Web site at **www.pearsonhighered.com/kroenke** as needed. Instructor resources and student materials are also available on the site, so be sure to check it from time to time.

ACKNOWLEDGMENTS

We would like to thank the following reviewers for their insightful and helpful comments:

Namjoo Choi, University of Kentucky
David Chou, Eastern Michigan University
Geoffrey Decker, Northern Illinois University
Deena Engel, New York University
Marni Ferner, University of North Carolina, Wilmington
Jean Hendrix, University of Arkansas at Monticello
Malini Krishnamurthi, California State University, Fullerton
Rashmi Malhotra, Saint Joseph's University
Gabriel M. Petersen, North Carolina Central University
Eliot Rich, University at Albany, State University of New York
Liz Thiry, Pennsylvania State University
Bond Wetherbe, Texas Tech University
Diana Wolfe, Oklahoma State University–Oklahoma City

We would like to thank Nicole Sam, our editor; Denise Vaughn, our program manager; and Ilene Kahn, our project manager, for their professionalism, insight, support, and assistance in the development of this project. We would also like to thank Robert Mills, Robert Yoder, and Scott Vandenberg for their detailed comments on the final manuscript. Finally, David Kroenke would like to thank his wife, Lynda, and David Auer would like to thank his wife, Donna, for their love, encouragement, and patience while this project was being completed.

David Kroenke
Seattle, Washington

David Auer
Bellingham, Washington

About the Authors

David M. Kroenke entered the computing profession as a summer intern at the RAND Corporation in 1967. Since then, his career has spanned education, industry, consulting, and publishing.

He has taught at the University of Washington, Colorado State University, and Seattle University. Over the years, he has led dozens of teaching seminars for college professors. In 1991 the International Association of Information Systems named him Computer Educator of the Year.

In industry, Kroenke has worked for the U.S. Air Force and Boeing Computer Services, and he was a principal in the startup of three companies. He was also vice president of product marketing and development for the Microrim Corporation and was chief technologist for the database division of Wall Data, Inc. He is the father of the semantic object data model. Kroenke's consulting clients include IBM Corporation, Microsoft, Computer Sciences Corporation, and numerous other companies and organizations.

His text *Database Processing: Fundamentals, Design, and Implementation*, first published in 1977, is now in its 13th Edition (coauthored with David Auer for the 11th, 12th, and 13th editions). He introduced *Database Concepts* (now in the seventh edition that you are reading) in 2003. Kroenke has published many other textbooks, including the classic *Business Computer Systems* (1981). Recently, he has authored *Using MIS* (7th Edition), *Experiencing MIS* (5th Edition), *MIS Essentials* (4th Editon), *Processes, Systems and Information: An Introduction to MIS* (2nd Edition) (coauthored with Earl McKinney), and *Essentials of Processes, Systems and Information* (coauthored with Earl McKinney).

An avid sailor, Kroenke also wrote *Know Your Boat: The Guide to Everything That Makes Your Boat Work*. Kroenke lives in Seattle, Washington. He is married and has two children and three grandchildren.

Since 1994, **David J. Auer** has been the director of Information Systems and Technology Services at Western Washington University's College of Business and Economics (CBE) and a lecturer in CBE's Department of Decision Sciences. Since 1981, he has taught CBE courses in quantitative methods, production and operations management, statistics, finance, and management information systems. Besides managing CBE's computer, network, and other technology resources, he also teaches management information systems courses. He has taught the Principles of Management Information Systems and Business Database Development courses, and he was responsible for developing CBE's network infrastructure courses, including Computer Hardware and Operating Systems, Telecommunications, and Network Administration. He has coauthored several MIS-related textbooks.

Auer holds a bachelor's degree in English literature from the University of Washington, a bachelor's degree in mathematics and economics from Western Washington University, a master's degree in economics from Western Washington University, and a master's degree in counseling psychology from Western Washington University. He served as a commissioned officer in the U.S. Air Force, and he has also worked as an organizational development specialist and therapist for an employee assistance program (EAP).

Auer and his wife, Donna, live in Bellingham, Washington. He has two children and four grandchildren.

PART 1 Database Fundamentals

Part I introduces fundamental concepts and techniques of relational database management. Chapter 1 explains database technology, discusses why databases are used, and describes the components of a database system. Chapter 2 introduces the relational model and defines key relational database terms. It also presents basic principles of relational database design. Chapter 3 presents Structured Query Language, an international standard for creating and processing relational databases.

After you have learned these fundamental database concepts, we will focus on database modeling, design, and implementation in Part II. Finally, we will discuss database management, Web database applications, Big Data, and business intelligence (BI) systems in Part III.

CHAPTER 1 Getting Started

CHAPTER OBJECTIVES

- Identify the purpose and scope of this book
- Know the potential problems with lists
- Understand the reasons for using a database
- Understand how using related tables helps you avoid the problems of using lists
- Know the components of a database system
- Learn the elements of a database
- Learn the purpose of a database management system (DBMS)
- Understand the functions of a database application
- Introduce nonrelational databases

Knowledge of database technology increases in importance every day. Databases are used everywhere: They are key components of e-commerce and other Web-based applications. They lay at the heart of organization-wide operational and decision support applications. Databases are also used by thousands of work groups and millions of individuals. It is estimated that there are more than 10 million active databases in the world today.

The purpose of this book is to teach you the essential relational database concepts, technology, and techniques that you need to begin a career as a database developer. This book does not teach everything of importance in relational database technology, but it will give you sufficient background to be able to create your own personal databases and to participate as a member of a team in the development of larger, more complicated databases. You will also be able to ask the right questions to learn more on your own.

In this first chapter, we investigate the reasons for using a relational database. We begin by describing some of the problems that can occur when using lists. Using a series of examples, we illustrate how using sets of related tables helps you to avoid those problems. Next, we describe the components of a database system and explain the elements of a database, the purpose of the database management system (DBMS), and the functions of a database application. Finally, we introduce nonrelational databases.

WHY USE A DATABASE?

A database is used to help people keep track of things. You might wonder why we need a special term (and course) for such technology when a simple **list** could serve the same purpose. Many people do keep track of things by using lists, and sometimes such lists are valuable. In other cases, however, simple lists lead to data inconsistencies and other problems.

In this section, we examine several different lists and show some of these problems. As you will see, we can solve the problems by splitting lists into tables of data. Such tables are the key components of a database. A majority of this text concerns the design of such tables and techniques for manipulating the data they contain.

Problems with Lists

Figure 1-1 shows a simple list of student data, named the Student List,[1] stored in a spreadsheet. The Student List is a very simple list, and for such a list a spreadsheet works quite well. Even if the list is long, you can sort it alphabetically by last name, first name, or email address to find any entry you want. You can change the data values, add data for a new student, or delete student data. With a list like the Student List in Figure 1-1, none of these actions is problematic, and a database is unnecessary. Keeping this list in a spreadsheet is just fine.

Suppose, however, we change the Student List by adding adviser data, as shown in Figure 1-2. You can still sort the new Student with Adviser List in a number of ways to find an entry, but making changes to this list causes **modification problems**. Suppose, for example, that you want to delete the data for the student Chip Marino. As shown in Figure 1-3, if you delete the seventh row you not only remove Chip Marino's data, you also remove the fact that there is an adviser named Tran and that Professor Tran's email address is Ken.Tran@ourcampus.edu.

Similarly, updating a value in this list can have unintended consequences. If, for example, you change AdviserEmail in the eighth row, you will have inconsistent data. After the change, the fifth row indicates one email address for Professor Taing, and the eighth row indicates a different email address for the same professor. Or is it the same professor? From this list, we cannot tell if there is one Professor Taing with two inconsistent email addresses or whether there are two professors named Taing with different email addresses. By making this update, we add confusion and uncertainty to the list.

	A	B	C
1	LastName	FirstName	Email
2	Andrews	Matthew	Matthew.Andrews@ourcampus.edu
3	Brisbon	Lisa	Lisa.Brisbon@ourcampus.edu
4	Fischer	Douglas	Douglas.Fischer@ourcampus.edu
5	Hwang	Terry	Terry.Hwang@ourcampus.edu
6	Lai	Tzu	Tzu.Lai@ourcampus.edu
7	Marino	Chip	Chip.Marino@ourcampus.edu
8	Thompson	James	James.Thompson@ourcampus.edu

	A	B	C	D	E
1	LastName	FirstName	Email	AdviserLastName	AdviserEmail
2	Andrews	Matthew	Matthew.Andrews@ourcampus.edu	Baker	Linda.Baker@ourcampus.edu
3	Brisbon	Lisa	Lisa.Brisbon@ourcampus.edu	Valdez	Richard.Valdez@ourcampus.edu
4	Fischer	Douglas	Douglas.Fischer@ourcampus.edu	Baker	Linda.Baker@ourcampus.edu
5	Hwang	Terry	Terry.Hwang@ourcampus.edu	Taing	Susan.Taing@ourcampus.edu
6	Lai	Tzu	Tzu.Lai@ourcampus.edu	Valdez	Richard.Valdez@ourcampus.edu
7	Marino	Chip	Chip.Marino@ourcampus.edu	Tran	Ken.Tran@ourcampus.edu
8	Thompson	James	James.Thompson@ourcampus.edu	Taing	Susan.Taing@ourcampus.edu

---

[1]In order to easily identify and reference the lists being discussed, we capitalize the first letter of each word in the list names in this chapter. Similarly, we capitalize the names of the database tables associated with the lists.

FIGURE 1-3

Modification Problems in the Student with Adviser List

		A	B	C	D	E
Deleted row—too much data lost	1	LastName	FirstName	Email	AdviserLastName	AdviserEmail
	2	Andrews	Matthew	Matthew.Andrews@ourcampus.edu	Baker	Linda.Baker@ourcampus.edu
	3	Brisbon	Lisa	Lisa.Brisbon@ourcampus.edu	Valdez	Richard.Valdez@ourcampus.edu
	4	Fischer	Douglas	Douglas.Fischer@ourcampus.edu	Baker	Linda.Baker@ourcampus.edu
Changed row—inconsistent data	5	Hwang	Terry	Terry.Hwang@ourcampus.edu	Taing	Susan.Taing@ourcampus.edu
	6	Lai	Tzu	Tzu.Lai@ourcampus.edu	Valdez	Richard.Valdez@ourcampus.edu
	7	Marino	Chip	Chip.Marino@ourcampus.edu	Tran	Ken.Tran@ourcampus.edu
Inserted row—data missing	8	Thompson	James	James.Thompson@ourcampus.edu	Taing	Sue.Taing@ourcampus.edu
	9	???	???	???	Green	George.Green@ourcampus.edu

Finally, what do we do if we want to add data for a professor who has no advisees? For example, Professor George Green has no advisees, but we still want to record his email address. As shown in Figure 1-3, we must insert a row with incomplete values, called **null values**, in the database field. In this case, the term *null value* means a missing value, but there are other meanings of the term *null value* that are used when working with databases. We will discuss the problems of null values in detail in the next chapter, where we will show that null values are always problematic and that we want to avoid them whenever possible.

Now, what exactly happened in these two examples? We had a simple list with three columns, added two more columns to it, and thereby created several problems. The problem is not just that the list has five columns instead of three. Consider a different list that has five columns: the Student with Residence List shown in Figure 1-4. This list has five columns, yet it suffers from none of the problems of the Student with Adviser List in Figure 1-3.

In the Student with Residence List in Figure 1-4, we can delete the data for student Chip Marino and lose only data for that student. No unintended consequences occur. Similarly, we can change the value of Residence for student Tzu Lai without introducing any inconsistency. Finally, we can add data for student Garret Ingram and not have any null values.

An essential difference exists between the Student with Adviser List in Figure 1-3 and the Student with Residence List in Figure 1-4. Looking at those two figures, can you determine the difference? The essential difference is that the Student with Residence List in Figure 1-4 is all about a *single thing*: All the data in that list concern *students*. In contrast, the Student with Adviser List in Figure 1-3 is about *two things*: Some of the data concern *students* and some of the data concern *advisers*. In general, whenever a list has data about two or more different things modification problems will result.

To reinforce this idea, examine the Student with Adviser and Department List in Figure 1-5. This list has data about three different things: *students*, *advisers*, and *departments*. As you can see in the figure, the problems with inserting, updating, and deleting data just get worse. A change in the value of AdviserLastName, for example, might

FIGURE 1-4

The Student with Residence List

		A	B	C	D	E
Inserted row—data OK	1	LastName	FirstName	Email	Phone	Residence
	2	Andrews	Matthew	Matthew.Andrews@ourcampus.edu	301-555-2225	123 15th St Apt 21
	3	Brisbon	Lisa	Lisa.Brisbon@ourcampus.edu	301-555-2241	Dorsett Room 201
	4	Fischer	Douglas	Douglas.Fischer@ourcampus.edu	301-555-2257	McKinley Room 109
Changed row—no inconsistent data	5	Hwang	Terry	Terry.Hwang@ourcampus.edu	301-555-2229	McKinley Room 208
	6	Ingram	Garrett	Garett.Ingram@ourcampus.edu	301-555-2223	Dorsett Room 218
	7	Lai	Tzu	Tzu.Lai@ourcampus.edu	301-555-2231	McKinley Room 115
Deleted row—no data loss	8	Marino	Chip	Chip.Marino@ourcampus.edu	301-555-2243	234 16th St Apt 32
	9	Thompson	James	James.Thompson@ourcampus.edu	301-555-2245	345 17th St Apt 43

FIGURE 1-5

The Student with Adviser and Department List

> If Adviser **Baker** is changed to **Taing**, we need to change *AdviserEmail* as well. If changed to **Valdez**, we need to change *AdviserEmail*, *Department*, and *AdminLastName*.

	A	B	C	D	E	F	G
1	LastName	FirstName	Email	AdviserLastName	AdviserEmail	Department	AdminLastName
2	Andrews	Matthew	Matthew.Andrews@ourcampus.edu	Baker	Linda.Baker@ourcampus.edu	Accounting	Smith
3	Brisbon	Lisa	Lisa.Brisbon@ourcampus.edu	Valdez	Richard.Valdez@ourcampus.edu	Chemistry	Chaplin
4	Fischer	Douglas	Douglas.Fischer@ourcampus.edu	Baker	Linda.Baker@ourcampus.edu	Accounting	Smith
5	Hwang	Terry	Terry.Hwang@ourcampus.edu	Taing	Susan.Taing@ourcampus.edu	Accounting	Smith
6	Lai	Tzu	Tzu.Lai@ourcampus.edu	Valdez	Richard.Valdez@ourcampus.edu	Chemistry	Chaplin
7	Marino	Chip	Chip.Marino@ourcampus.edu	Tran	Ken.Tran@ourcampus.edu	InfoSystems	Rogers
8	Thompson	James	James.Thompson@ourcampus.edu	Taing	Susan.Taing@ourcampus.edu	Accounting	Smith
9	???	???	???	???	???	Biology	Kelly

> Deleted row—Student, Adviser, and Department data lost

> Inserted row—both Student and Adviser data missing

necessitate a change in only AdviserEmail, or it might require a change in AdviserEmail, Department, and AdminLastName. As you can imagine, if this list is long—for example, if the list thousands of rows—and if several people process it, the list will be a mess in a very short time.

Using Relational Database Tables

The problems of using lists were first identified in the 1960s, and a number of different techniques were developed to solve them. Over time, a methodology called the **relational model** emerged as the leading solution, and today almost every commercial database is based on the relational model. We will examine the relational model in detail in Chapter 2. Here, however, we introduce the basic ideas of the relational model by showing how it solves the modification problems of lists.

Remember your eighth-grade English teacher? He or she said that a paragraph should have a single theme. If you have a paragraph with more than one theme, you need to break it up into two or more paragraphs, each with a *single theme.* That idea is the foundation of the design of relational databases. A **relational database** contains a collection of separate tables. A **table** holds data about one and only one theme in most circumstances. If a table has two or more themes, we break it up into two or more tables.

BTW

A table and a *spreadsheet* (also known as a *worksheet*) are very similar in that you can think of both as having rows, columns, and cells. The details that define a table as something different from a spreadsheet are discussed in Chapter 2. For now, the main differences you see are that tables have column names instead of identifying letters (for example, *Name* instead of *A*) and that the rows are not necessarily numbered.

A Relational Design for the Student with Adviser List The Student with Adviser List in Figure 1-2 has two themes: *students* and *advisers*. If we put this data into a relational database, we place the student data in one table named STUDENT and the adviser data in a second table named ADVISER.

BTW

In this book, table names appear in all capital, or uppercase, letters (STUDENT, ADVISER). Column names have initial capitals (Phone, Address), and where column names consist of more than one word the initial letter of each word is capitalized (LastName, AdviserEmail).

We still want to show which students have which advisers, however, so we leave AdviserLastName in the ADVISER table. As shown in Figure 1-6, the values of AdviserLastName now let us link rows in the two tables to each other.

Now consider possible modifications to these tables. As you saw in the last section, three basic **modification actions** are possible: **insert**, **update**, and **delete**. To evaluate a design, we need to consider each of these three actions. As shown in Figure 1-7, we can insert, update, and delete in these tables with no modification problems.

For example, we can insert the data for Professor Bill Yeats by just adding his data to the ADVISER table. No student references Professor Yeats, but this is not a problem. Perhaps a student will have Professor Yeats as an adviser in the future. We can also update data values without unintended consequences. The email address for Professor Susan Taing can be changed to Sue.Taing@ourcampus.edu, and no inconsistent data will result because Professor Taing's email address is stored just once in the ADVISER table. Finally, we can delete data without unintended consequences. For example, if we delete the data for student Chip Marino from the STUDENT table, we lose no adviser data.

A Relational Design for the Student with Adviser and Department List We can use a similar strategy to develop a relational database for the Student with Adviser and

---

FIGURE 1-6

The Adviser and Student Tables

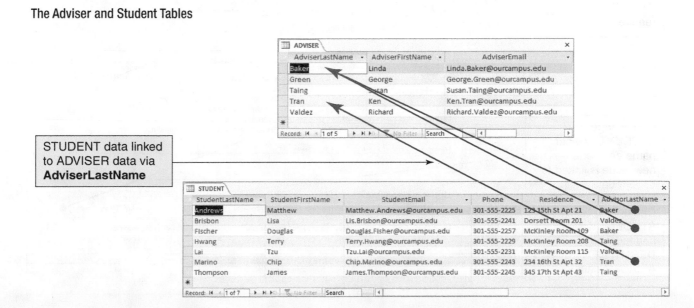

STUDENT data linked to ADVISER data via **AdviserLastName**

FIGURE 1-7

Modifying the Adviser and Student Tables

Changed data—data remains consistent

Inserted data—no STUDENT data required

Deleted data—no ADVISER data lost

ADVISER		
AdviserLastName	AdviserFirstName	AdviserEmail
Baker	Linda	Linda.Baker@ourcampus.edu
Green	George	George.Green@ourcampus.edu
Taing	Susan	Sue.Taing@ourcampus.edu
Tran	Ken	Ken.Tran@ourcampus.edu
Valdez	Richard	Richard.Valdez@ourcampus.edu
Yeats	Bill	Bill.Yeats@ourcampus.edu

Record: 3 of 6   No Filter   Search

STUDENT					
StudentLastName	StudentFirstName	StudentEmail	Phone	Residence	AdvisorLastName
Andrews	Matthew	Matthew.Andrews@ourcampus.edu	301-555-2225	123 15th St Apt 21	Baker
Brisbon	Lisa	Lis.Brisbon@ourcampus.edu	301-555-2241	Dorsett Room 201	Valdez
Fischer	Douglas	Douglas.Fisher@ourcampus.edu	301-555-2257	McKinley Room 109	Baker
Hwang	Terry	Terry.Hwang@ourcampus.edu	301-555-2229	McKinley Room 208	Taing
Lai	Tzu	Tzu.Lai@ourcampus.edu	301-555-2231	McKinley Room 115	Valdez
Marino	Chip	Chip.Marino@ourcampus.edu	301-555-2243	234 16th St Apt 32	Tran
Thompson	James	James.Thompson@ourcampus.edu	301-555-2245	345 17th St Apt 43	Taing

Record: 6 of 7   No Filter   Search

Department List shown in Figure 1-5. This list has three themes: *students*, *advisers*, and *departments*. Accordingly, we create three tables, one for each of these three themes, as shown in Figure 1-8.

As illustrated in Figure 1-8, we can use AdviserLastName and Department to link the tables. Also, as shown in this figure, this set of tables does not have any modification problems. We can insert new data without creating null values, we can modify data without

FIGURE 1-8

The Department, Adviser, and Student Tables

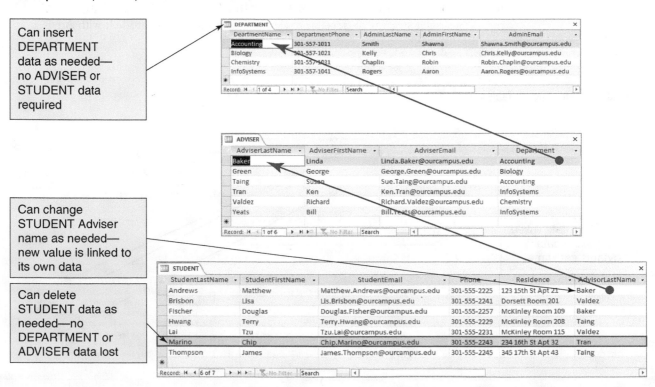

Can insert DEPARTMENT data as needed—no ADVISER or STUDENT data required

Can change STUDENT Adviser name as needed—new value is linked to its own data

Can delete STUDENT data as needed—no DEPARTMENT or ADVISER data lost

creating inconsistencies, and we can delete data without unintended consequences. Notice in particular that when we add a new row to DEPARTMENT we can add rows in ADVISER, if we want, and we can add rows in STUDENT for each of the new rows in ADVISER, if we want. However, all these actions are independent. None of them leaves the tables in an inconsistent state.

Similarly, when we modify an AdviserLastName in a row in STUDENT, we automatically pick up the adviser's correct first name, email address, and department. If we change AdviserLastName in the first row of STUDENT to Taing, it will be connected to the row in ADVISER that has the correct AdviserFirstName, AdviserEmail, and Department values. If we want, we can also use the value of Department in ADVISER to obtain the correct DEPARTMENT data. Finally, notice that we can delete the row for student Marino without a problem.

As an aside, the design in Figure 1-8 has removed the problems that occur when modifying a list, but it has also introduced a new problem. Specifically, what would happen if we deleted the first row in ADVISER? Students Andrews and Fischer would have an invalid value of AdviserLastName because Professor Baker would no longer exist in the ADVISER table. To prevent this problem, we can design the database so that a deletion of a row is not allowed if other rows depend on it, or we can design it so that the dependent rows are deleted as well. We are skipping way ahead here; however, we will discuss such issues in later chapters.

A Relational Design for Art Course Enrollments   To fix in your mind the ideas we have been examining, consider the Art Course List in Figure 1-9, which is used by an art school that offers art courses to the public. This list has modification problems. For example, suppose we change the value of CourseDate in the first row. This change might mean that the date for the course is changing, in which case the CourseDate values should be changed in other rows as well. Alternatively, this change could mean that a new Advanced Pastels (Adv Pastels) course is being offered. Either is a possibility.

As with the previous examples, we can remove the problems and ambiguities by creating a separate table for each theme. However, in this case the themes are more difficult to determine. Clearly, one of the themes is *customer* and another one is *art course*. However, a third theme exists that is more difficult to bring to light. The customer has paid a certain amount toward a course. The amount paid is not a property of the customer because it varies depending on which course the customer is taking. For example, customer Ariel Johnson paid $250 for the Advanced Pastels (Adv Pastels) course and $350 for the Intermediate Pastels (Int Pastels) course. Similarly, the amount paid is not a property of the course because it varies with which customer has taken the course. Therefore, the third theme of this list must concern the *enrollment* of a particular student in a particular class. Figure 1-10 shows a design using three tables that correspond to these three themes—we name this set of three tables the *Art Course Database*.

Notice that the *Art Course Database* design assigns an **ID column** named CustomerNumber that assigns a unique identifying number to each row of CUSTOMER;

FIGURE 1-9

The Art Course List with Modification Problems

	A	B	C	D	E	F	G
1	CustomerLastName	CustomerFirstName	Phone	CourseDate	AmountPaid	Course	Fee
2	Johnson	Ariel	206-567-1234	10/1/2015	$250.00	Adv Pastels	$500.00
3	Green	Robin	425-678-8765	9/15/2015	$350.00	Beg Oils	$350.00
4	Jackson	Charles	360-789-3456	10/1/2015	$500.00	Adv Pastels	$500.00
5	Johnson	Ariel	206-567-1234	3/15/2015	$350.00	Int Pastels	$350.00
6	Pearson	Jeffery	206-567-2345	10/1/2015	$500.00	Adv Pastels	$500.00
7	Sears	Miguel	360-789-4567	9/15/2015	$350.00	Beg Oils	$350.00
8	Kyle	Leah	425-678-7654	11/15/2015	$250.00	Adv Pastels	$500.00
9	Myers	Lynda	360-789-5678	10/15/2015	$0.00	Beg Oils	$350.00

How to enter the fee for a new course?

Consequences of changing this date?

Consequences of deleting this row?

FIGURE 1-10

The Art Course Database Tables

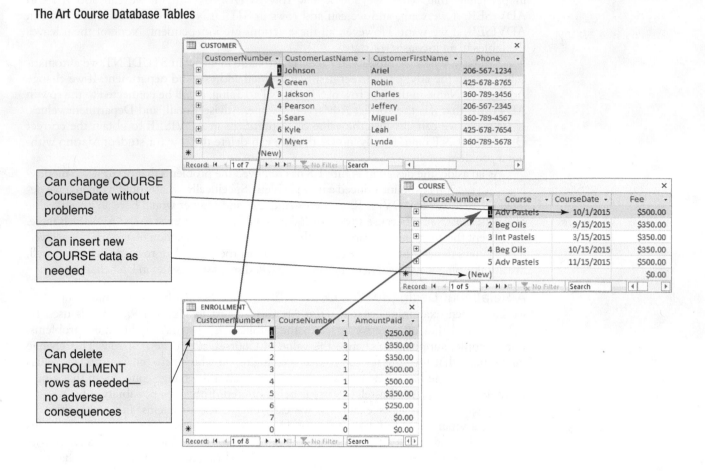

this is necessary because some customers might have the same name. Another ID column, named CourseNumber, has also been added to COURSE. This is necessary because some courses have the same name. Finally, notice that the rows of the ENROLLMENT table show the amount paid by a particular customer for a particular course and that the ID columns CustomerNumber and CourseNumber are used as linking columns to the other tables.

A Relational Design for Parts and Prices Now let's consider a more complicated example. Figure 1-11 shows a spreadsheet that holds the Project Equipment List used by a housing contractor named Carbon River Construction to keep track of the parts that it buys for various construction projects.

The first problem with this list concerns modifications to the existing data. Suppose your job is to maintain the Project Equipment List, and your boss tells you that customer Elizabeth Barnaby changed her phone number. How many changes would you need to make to this spreadsheet? For the data in Figure 1-11, you would need to make this change 10 times. Now suppose the spreadsheet has 5,000 rows. How many changes might you need to make? The answer could be dozens, and you need to worry not only about the time this will take but also about the possibility of errors—you might miss her name in a row or two and fail to properly update her phone number in these rows.

Consider a second problem with this list. In this business, each supplier agrees to a particular discount for all parts it supplies. For example, in Figure 1-11 the supplier NW Electric has agreed to a 25 percent discount. With this list, every time you enter a new part quotation, you must enter the supplier of that part, along with the correct discount. If

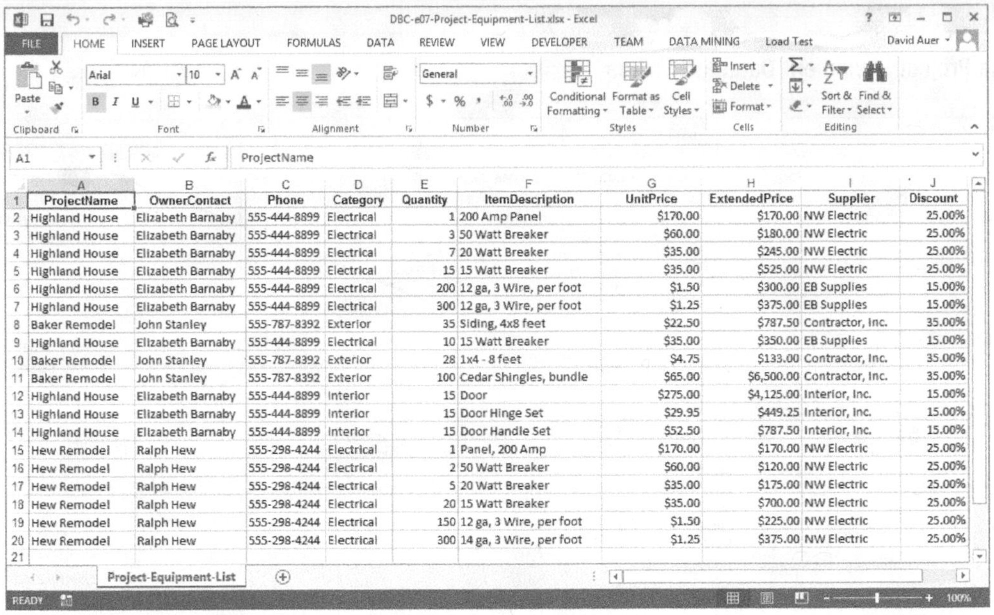

ProjectName	OwnerContact	Phone	Category	Quantity	ItemDescription	UnitPrice	ExtendedPrice	Supplier	Discount
Highland House	Elizabeth Barnaby	555-444-8899	Electrical	1	200 Amp Panel	$170.00	$170.00	NW Electric	25.00%
Highland House	Elizabeth Barnaby	555-444-8899	Electrical	3	50 Watt Breaker	$60.00	$180.00	NW Electric	25.00%
Highland House	Elizabeth Barnaby	555-444-8899	Electrical	7	20 Watt Breaker	$35.00	$245.00	NW Electric	25.00%
Highland House	Elizabeth Barnaby	555-444-8899	Electrical	15	15 Watt Breaker	$35.00	$525.00	NW Electric	25.00%
Highland House	Elizabeth Barnaby	555-444-8899	Electrical	200	12 ga, 3 Wire, per foot	$1.50	$300.00	EB Supplies	15.00%
Highland House	Elizabeth Barnaby	555-444-8899	Electrical	300	12 ga, 3 Wire, per foot	$1.25	$375.00	EB Supplies	15.00%
Baker Remodel	John Stanley	555-787-8392	Exterior	35	Siding, 4x8 feet	$22.50	$787.50	Contractor, Inc.	35.00%
Highland House	Elizabeth Barnaby	555-444-8899	Electrical	10	15 Watt Breaker	$35.00	$350.00	EB Supplies	15.00%
Baker Remodel	John Stanley	555-787-8392	Exterior	28	1x4 - 8 feet	$4.75	$133.00	Contractor, Inc.	35.00%
Baker Remodel	John Stanley	555-787-8392	Exterior	100	Cedar Shingles, bundle	$65.00	$6,500.00	Contractor, Inc.	35.00%
Highland House	Elizabeth Barnaby	555-444-8899	Interior	15	Door	$275.00	$4,125.00	Interior, Inc.	15.00%
Highland House	Elizabeth Barnaby	555-444-8899	Interior	15	Door Hinge Set	$29.95	$449.25	Interior, Inc.	15.00%
Highland House	Elizabeth Barnaby	555-444-8899	Interior	15	Door Handle Set	$52.50	$787.50	Interior, Inc.	15.00%
Hew Remodel	Ralph Hew	555-298-4244	Electrical	1	Panel, 200 Amp	$170.00	$170.00	NW Electric	25.00%
Hew Remodel	Ralph Hew	555-298-4244	Electrical	2	50 Watt Breaker	$60.00	$120.00	NW Electric	25.00%
Hew Remodel	Ralph Hew	555-298-4244	Electrical	5	20 Watt Breaker	$35.00	$175.00	NW Electric	25.00%
Hew Remodel	Ralph Hew	555-298-4244	Electrical	20	15 Watt Breaker	$35.00	$700.00	NW Electric	25.00%
Hew Remodel	Ralph Hew	555-298-4244	Electrical	150	12 ga, 3 Wire, per foot	$1.50	$225.00	NW Electric	25.00%
Hew Remodel	Ralph Hew	555-298-4244	Electrical	300	14 ga, 3 Wire, per foot	$1.25	$375.00	NW Electric	25.00%

FIGURE 1-11

The Project Equipment List as a Spreadsheet

dozens or hundreds of suppliers are used, there is a chance that you will sometimes enter the wrong discount. If you do, the list will have more than one discount for one supplier—a situation that is incorrect and confusing.

A third problem occurs when you enter data correctly but inconsistently. The first row has a part named 200 Amp panel, whereas the 15th row has a part named Panel, 200 Amp. Are these two parts the same item, or are they different? It turns out that they are the same item, but they were named differently.

A fourth problem concerns partial data. Suppose you know that a supplier offers a 20 percent discount, but Carbon River has not yet ordered from the supplier. Where do you record the 20 percent discount?

Just as we did for the previous examples, we can fix the Project Equipment List by breaking it up into separate tables. Because this list is more complicated, we need to use more tables. When we analyze the Project Equipment List, we find data about four themes: *projects*, *items*, *price quotations*, and *suppliers*. Accordingly, we create a database with four tables and relate those four tables using linking values, as before. Figure 1-12 shows our four tables and their relationships—we will name this set of tables the *Project Equipment Database*.

In Figure 1-12, note that the QUOTE table holds a unique quote identifier (QuoteID), a quantity, a unit price, an extended price (which is equal to [quantity * unit price]), and three ID columns as linking values: ProjectID for PROJECT, ItemNumber for ITEM, and SupplierID for SUPPLIER.

Now if Elizabeth Barnaby changes her phone number we need to make that change only once—in the PROJECT table. Similarly, we need to record a supplier discount only once—in the SUPPLIER table.

Processing Relational Tables

By now, you may have a burning question: It may be fine to tear the lists up into pieces in order to eliminate processing problems, but what if the users want to view their data in the format of the original list? With the data separated into different tables, the users will have to jump from one table to another to find the information they want, and this jumping around will become tedious.

FIGURE 1-12

The Project Equipment Database Tables

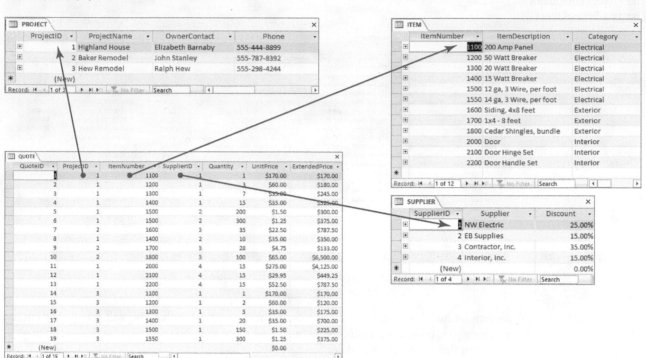

This is an important question and one that many people addressed in the 1970s and 1980s. Several approaches were invented for combining, querying, and processing sets of tables. Over time, one of those approaches, a language called **Structured Query Language (SQL)**, emerged as the leading technique for data definition and manipulation. Today, SQL is an international standard. Using SQL, you can reconstruct lists from their underlying tables; you can query for specific data conditions; you can perform computations on data in tables; and you can insert, update, and delete data.

Processing Tables by Using SQL   You will learn how to code SQL statements in Chapter 3. However, to give you an idea of the structure of such statements, let's look at an SQL statement that joins the three tables in Figure 1-10 to produce the original Art Course List. Do not worry about understanding the syntax of this statement, just realize that it produces the result shown in Figure 1-13, which contains all the Art Course List data (although in a slightly different row order[2]).

```
SELECT   CUSTOMER.CustomerLastName,
         CUSTOMER.CustomerFirstName, CUSTOMER.Phone,
         COURSE.CourseDate, ENROLLMENT.AmountPaid,
         COURSE.Course, COURSE.Fee
FROM     CUSTOMER, ENROLLMENT, COURSE
WHERE    CUSTOMER.CustomerNumber = ENROLLMENT.CustomerNumber
  AND    COURSE.CourseNumber = ENROLLMENT.CourseNumber;
```

---

[2]We will discuss how to sort data to control the row order in Chapter 3.

FIGURE 1-13

Results of the SQL Query to Recreate the Art Course List

Art Course List						✕
CustomerLastName ▾	CustomerFirstName ▾	Phone ▾	CourseDate ▾	AmountPaid ▾	Course ▾	Fee ▾
Johnson	Ariel	206-567-1234	10/1/2015	$250.00	Adv Pastels	$500.00
Johnson	Ariel	206-567-1234	3/15/2015	$350.00	Int Pastels	$350.00
Green	Robin	425-678-8765	9/15/2015	$350.00	Beg Oils	$350.00
Jackson	Charles	360-789-3456	10/1/2015	$500.00	Adv Pastels	$500.00
Pearson	Jeffery	206-567-2345	10/1/2015	$500.00	Adv Pastels	$500.00
Sears	Miguel	360-789-4567	9/15/2015	$350.00	Beg Oils	$350.00
Kyle	Leah	425-678-7654	11/15/2015	$250.00	Adv Pastels	$500.00
Myers	Lynda	360-789-5678	10/15/2015	$0.00	Beg Oils	$350.00

Record: ◄ ◄ 1 of 8 ► ►I ► No Filter Search

As you will learn in Chapter 3, it is also possible to select rows, to order them, and to make calculations on row data values. Figure 1-14 shows the result of the SQL statement:

```
SELECT    CUSTOMER.CustomerLastName,
          CUSTOMER.CustomerFirstName, CUSTOMER.Phone,
          COURSE.Course, COURSE.CourseDate, COURSE.Fee,
          ENROLLMENT.AmountPaid,
          (COURSE.Fee-ENROLLMENT.AmountPaid) AS AmountDue
FROM      CUSTOMER, ENROLLMENT, CUSTOMER
WHERE     CUSTOMER.CustomerNumber = ENROLLMENT.CustomerNumber
    AND   COURSE.CourseNumber = ENROLLMENT.CourseNumber
    AND   (COURSE.Fee - ENROLLMENT.AmountPaid) > 0
ORDER BY  CUSTOMER.CustomerLastName;
```

This SQL statement joins the Art Course Database tables together, computes the difference between the course Fee and the AmountPaid, and stores this result in a new column named AmountDue. The SQL statement then selects only rows for which AmountDue is greater than zero and presents the results sorted by CustomerLastName. Compare the data in Figure 1-13 with the results in Figure 1-14 to ensure that the results are correct.

FIGURE 1-14

Results of the SQL Query to Compute Amount Due

Amount Due Query							✕
CustomerLastName ▾	CustomerFirstName ▾	Phone ▾	Course ▾	CourseDate ▾	Fee ▾	AmountPaid ▾	AmountDue ▾
Johnson	Ariel	206-567-1234	Adv Pastels	10/1/2015	$500.00	$250.00	$250.00
Kyle	Leah	425-678-7654	Adv Pastels	11/15/2015	$500.00	$250.00	$250.00
Myers	Lynda	360-789-5678	Beg Oils	10/15/2015	$350.00	$0.00	$350.00
*							

Record: ◄ ◄ 1 of 3 ► ►I ► No Filter Search

WHAT IS A DATABASE SYSTEM?

As shown in Figure 1-15, a database system has four components: users, the database application, the database management system (DBMS), and the database.

Starting from the right of Figure 1-15, the **database** is a collection of related tables and other structures. The **database management system (DBMS)** is a computer program used to create, process, and administer the database. The DBMS receives requests encoded in SQL and translates those requests into actions on the database. The DBMS is a large, complicated program that is licensed from a software vendor; companies almost never write their own DBMS programs.

A **database application** is a set of one or more computer programs that serves as an intermediary between the user and the DBMS. Application programs read or modify database data by sending SQL statements to the DBMS. Application programs also present data to users in the format of forms and reports. Application programs can be acquired from software vendors, and they are also frequently written in-house. The knowledge you gain from this text will help you write database applications.

Users, the fourth component of a database system, employ a database application to keep track of things. They use forms to read, enter, and query data, and they produce reports.

Of these components, we will consider the database, the DBMS, and database applications in more detail.

The Database

In the most general case, a database is defined as a self-describing collection of related records. For all relational databases (the majority of databases today and the primary type considered in this book), this definition can be modified to indicate that a database is a self-describing collection of related tables.

The two key terms in this definition are **self-describing** and **related tables**. You already have a good idea of what we mean by *related tables.* One example of related tables consists of the ADVISER and STUDENT tables, which are related by the common column AdviserName. We will build on this idea of relationships further in the next chapter.

Self-describing means that a description of the structure of the database is contained within the database itself. Because this is so, the contents of a database can always be determined just by looking inside the database itself. It is not necessary to look anywhere else. This situation is akin to that at a library, where you can tell what is in the library by examining the catalog that resides within the library.

Data about the structure of a database are called **metadata**. Examples of metadata are the names of tables, the names of columns and the tables to which they belong, properties of tables and columns, and so forth.

All DBMS products provide a set of tools for displaying the structure of their databases. For example, Figure 1-16 shows a diagram produced by Microsoft Access that

FIGURE 1-15

Components of a
Database System

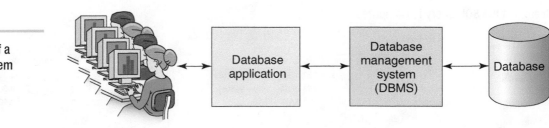

Users

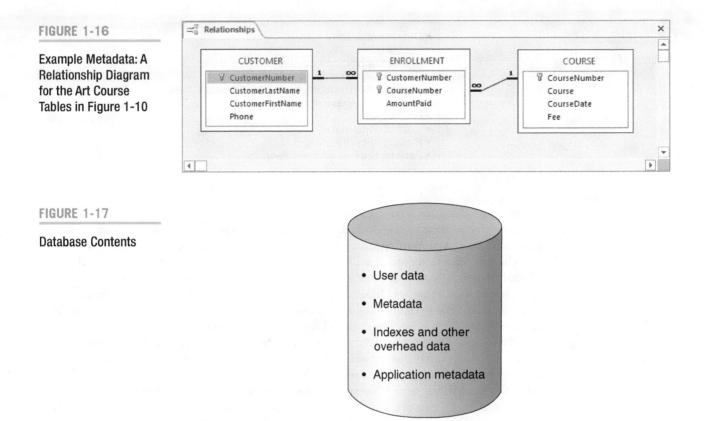

FIGURE 1-16

Example Metadata: A
Relationship Diagram
for the Art Course
Tables in Figure 1-10

FIGURE 1-17

Database Contents

displays the relationships between the Art Course database tables shown in Figure 1-10. Other tools describe the structure of the tables and other components.

The contents of a database are illustrated in Figure 1-17. A database has user data and metadata, as just described. A database also has indexes and other structures that exist to improve database performance, and we will discuss such structures in later chapters. Finally, some databases contain application metadata; these are data that describe application elements, such as forms and reports. For example, Microsoft Access carries application metadata as part of its databases.

The DBMS

The purpose of a DBMS is to create, process, and administer databases. A DBMS is a large, complicated product that is almost always licensed from a software vendor. One DBMS product is Microsoft Access. Other commercial DBMS products are:

- Microsoft SQL Server
- Oracle Corporation's MySQL
- Oracle Corporation's Oracle Database
- IBM's DB2

Dozens of other DBMS products exist, but these five have the lion's share of the market.

Figure 1-18 lists the functions of a DBMS. A DBMS is used to create a database and to create tables and other supporting structures inside that database. As an example of the latter, suppose that we have an EMPLOYEE table with 10,000 rows and that this table includes a column, DepartmentName, that records the name of the department in which an employee works. Furthermore, suppose that we frequently need to access employee data by DepartmentName. Because this is a large database, searching through the table to find, for example, all employees in the accounting department would take a long time.

FIGURE 1-18

Functions of a DBMS

- Create database
- Create tables
- Create supporting structures (e.g., indexes)
- Read database data
- Modify (insert, update, or delete) database data
- Maintain database structures
- Enforce rules
- Control concurrency
- Provide security
- Perform backup and recovery

To improve performance, we can create an index (akin to the index at the back of a book) for DepartmentName to show which employees are in which departments. Such an index is an example of a supporting structure that is created and maintained by a DBMS.

The next two functions of a DBMS are to read and modify database data. To do this, a DBMS receives SQL and other requests and transforms those requests into actions on the database files. Another DBMS function is to maintain all the database structures. For example, from time to time it might be necessary to change the format of a table or another supporting structure. Developers use a DBMS to make such changes.

With most DBMS products, it is possible to declare rules about data values and have a DBMS enforce them. For example, in the Art Course database tables in Figure 1-10, what would happen if a user mistakenly entered a value of 9 for CustomerID in the ENROLLMENT table? No such customer exists, so such a value would cause numerous errors. To prevent this situation, it is possible to tell the DBMS that any value of CustomerID in the ENROLLMENT table must already be a value of CustomerID in the CUSTOMER table. If no such value exists, the insert or update request should be disallowed. The DBMS then enforces these rules, which are called **referential integrity constraints**.

The last three functions of a DBMS listed in Figure 1-18 have to do with database administration. A DBMS controls **concurrency** by ensuring that one user's work does not inappropriately interfere with another user's work. This important (and complicated) function is discussed in Chapter 6. Also, a DBMS contains a security system that is used to ensure that only authorized users perform authorized actions on the database. For example, users can be prevented from seeing certain data. Similarly, users' actions can be confined to making only certain types of data changes on specified data.

Finally, a DBMS provides facilities for backing up database data and recovering it from backups when necessary. The database, as a centralized repository of data, is a valuable organizational asset. Consider, for example, the value of a book database to a company such as Amazon.com. Because the database is so important, steps need to be taken to ensure that no data will be lost in the event of errors, hardware or software problems, or natural or human catastrophes.

Application Programs   Figure 1-19 lists the functions of database application programs. First, an application program creates and processes forms. Figure 1-20 shows a typical form for entering and processing customer data for the Art Course application.

Notice that this form hides the structure of the underlying tables from the user. By comparing the tables and data in Figure 1-10 to the form in Figure 1-20, we can see that

FIGURE 1-19

Functions of Database Application Programs

- Create and process forms
- Process user queries
- Create and process reports
- Execute application logic
- Control application

FIGURE 1-20

Example Data Entry Form

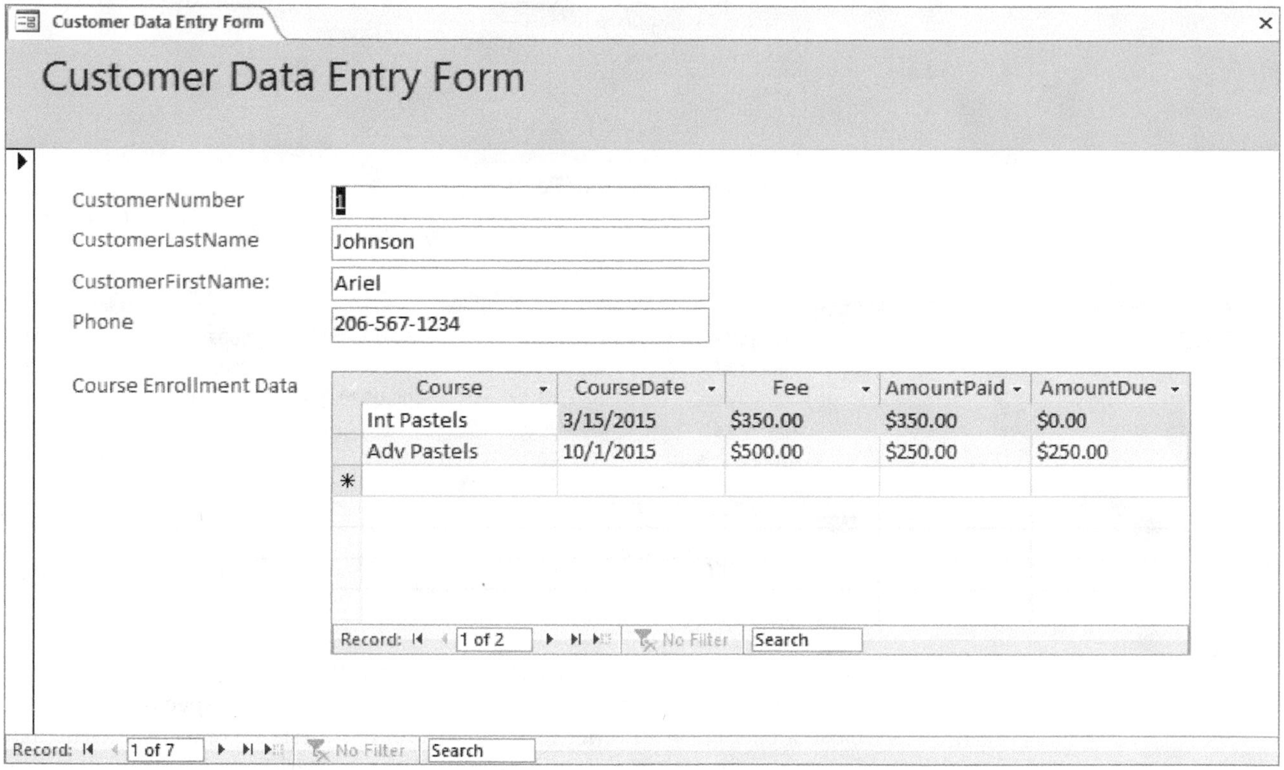

data from the CUSTOMER table appear at the top of the form, whereas data from the ENROLLMENT and the COURSE tables are combined and presented in a tabular section labeled Course Enrollment Data.

The goal of this form, like that for all data entry forms, is to present the data in a format that is useful for the users, regardless of the underlying table structure. Behind the form, the application processes the database in accordance with the users' actions. The application generates an SQL statement to insert, update, or delete data for any of the three tables that underlie this form.

The second function of application programs is to process user queries. The application program first generates a query request and sends it to the DBMS. Results are then formatted and returned to the user. Figure 1-21 illustrates this process in a query of the Art Course database in Figure 1-10.

In Figure 1-21(a), the application obtains the name or part of a name of a course. Here the user has entered the characters *pas.* When the user clicks OK, the application constructs an SQL query statement to search the database for any course containing these characters. The result of this SQL query is shown in Figure 1-21(b). In this particular case, the application queried for the relevant course and then joined the ENROLLMENT and CUSTOMER data to the qualifying COURSE rows. Observe that the only rows shown are those with a course name that includes the characters *pas.*

The third function of an application is to create and process reports. This function is somewhat similar to the second because the application program first queries the DBMS for data (again using SQL). The application then formats the query results as a report. Figure 1-22 shows a report that displays all the Art Course database enrollment data in order by course. Notice that the report, like the form in Figure 1-20, is structured according to the users' needs and not according to the underlying table structure.

FIGURE 1-21

Example Query

(a) Query Parameter Form

CustomerLastName ▾	CustomerFirstName ▾	Course ▾	CourseDate ▾	Fee ▾	AmountPaid ▾	Amount Due ▾
Jackson	Charles	Adv Pastels	10/1/2015	$500.00	$500.00	$0.00
Johnson	Ariel	Int Pastels	3/15/2015	$350.00	$350.00	$0.00
Johnson	Ariel	Adv Pastels	10/1/2015	$500.00	$250.00	$250.00
Kyle	Leah	Adv Pastels	11/15/2015	$500.00	$250.00	$250.00
Pearson	Jeffery	Adv Pastels	10/1/2015	$500.00	$500.00	$0.00

Record: I◄ ◄ 1 of 5 ► ►I ►☒ No Filter | Search

(b) Query Results

In addition to generating forms, queries, and reports, the application program takes other actions to update the database in accordance with application-specific logic. For example, suppose a user using an order entry application requests 10 units of a particular item. Suppose further that when the application program queries the database (via the DBMS) it finds that only eight units are in stock. What should happen? It depends on the logic of that particular application. Perhaps no units should be removed from inventory and the user should be notified, or perhaps the eight units should be removed and two more placed on back order. Perhaps some other action should be taken. Whatever the case, it is the job of the application program to execute the appropriate logic.

FIGURE 1-22

Example Report

Course Enrollment Report

Course	CourseDate	CustomerLastName	CustomerFirstName	Phone	Fee	AmountPaid	AmountDue
Adv Pastels							
	10/1/2015						
		Jackson	Charles	360-789-3456	$500.00	$500.00	$0.00
		Johnson	Ariel	206-567-1234	$500.00	$250.00	$250.00
		Pearson	Jeffery	206-567-2345	$500.00	$500.00	$0.00
	11/15/2015						
		Kyle	Leah	425-678-7654	$500.00	$250.00	$250.00
Beg Oils							
	9/15/2015						
		Green	Robin	425-678-8765	$350.00	$350.00	$0.00
		Sears	Miguel	360-789-4567	$350.00	$350.00	$0.00
	10/15/2015						
		Myers	Lynda	360-789-5678	$350.00	$0.00	$350.00
Int Pastels							
	3/15/2015						
		Johnson	Ariel	206-567-1234	$350.00	$350.00	$0.00

Finally, the last function of application programs listed in Figure 1-19 is to control the application. This is done in two ways. First, the application needs to be written so that only logical options are presented to the user. For example, the application may generate a menu with user choices. In this case, the application needs to ensure that only appropriate choices are available. Second, the application needs to control data activities with the DBMS. The application might direct the DBMS, for example, to make a certain set of data changes as a unit. The application might tell the DBMS to either make all these changes or none of them. You will learn about such control topics in Chapter 6.

Personal Versus Enterprise-Class Database Systems

Database technology can be used in a wide array of applications. On one end of the spectrum, a researcher might use database technology to track the results of experiments performed in a lab. Such a database might include only a few tables, and each table would have, at most, several hundred rows. The researcher would be the only user of this application. This is a typical use of a **personal database system**.

At the other end of the spectrum, some enormous databases support international organizations. Such databases have hundreds of tables with millions of rows of data and support thousands of concurrent users. These databases are in use 24 hours a day, 7 days a week. Just making a backup of such a database is a difficult task. These databases are typical uses of **enterprise-class database systems**.

Figure 1-23 shows the four components of a personal database application. As you can see from this figure, Microsoft Access (or another personal DBMS product) takes on the role of both the database application and the DBMS. Microsoft designed Microsoft Access this way to make it easier for people to build personal database systems. Using Microsoft Access, you can switch between DBMS functions and application functions and never know the difference.

By designing Microsoft Access this way, Microsoft has hidden many aspects of database processing. For example, behind the scenes Microsoft Access uses SQL just as all other relational DBMS products do. You have to look hard, however, to find it. Figure 1-24 shows the SQL statement that Microsoft Access used for the query in Figure 1-13. As you examine this figure, you might be thinking, "I'm just as glad they hid it—it looks complicated and hard." In fact, it looks harder than it is, but we will leave that topic for Chapter 3.

Figure 1-25 shows the Microsoft Access query results (the same results shown in Figure 1-13) in Microsoft Access 2013. Microsoft Access 2013 is a commonly used personal DBMS and is available as part of the Microsoft Office 2013 suite. We will introduce you to Microsoft Access 2013 in this book using a section in each chapter called "The Access Workbench." By the time you have completed all the sections of "The Access Workbench," you will have a solid understanding of how to use Microsoft Access 2013 to create and use databases.

The problem with database technology being hidden (and with using lots of *wizards* to accomplish database design tasks) is that you do not understand what is being done on your behalf. As soon as you need to perform some function that the Microsoft Access team

FIGURE 1-23

Personal Database System

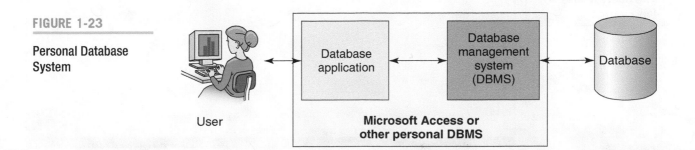

User

Microsoft Access or other personal DBMS

FIGURE 1-24

SQL Generated by Microsoft Access Query

> The SQL has been arranged to make it easy to read

Art Course List

```
SELECT  CUSTOMER.CustomerLastName,
        CUSTOMER.CustomerFirstName,
        CUSTOMER.Phone,
        COURSE.CourseDate,
        ENROLLMENT.AmountPaid,
        COURSE.Course,
        COURSE.Fee
FROM    CUSTOMER, ENROLLMENT, COURSE
WHERE (((CUSTOMER.CustomerNumber)=[ENROLLMENT].[CustomerNumber])
    AND ((COURSE.CourseNumber)=[ENROLLMENT].[CourseNumber]));
```

did not anticipate, you are lost. Therefore, to be even an average database developer you have to learn what is behind the scenes.

Furthermore, such products are useful only for personal database applications. When you want to develop larger database systems, you need to learn all the hidden technology. For example, Figure 1-26 shows an enterprise-class database system that has three different applications, each of which has many users. The storage of the database itself is spread over many different disks—perhaps even over different specialized computers known as *database servers*.

FIGURE 1-25

Microsoft Access 2013

> The database name **Art-Course-Database**

> The table object **CUSTOMER** is displayed under the All Access Objects

> The query object Art Course List stores the query itself

> The query results in table format

Art-Course-Database : Database- C:\Users\Auer\Documents\Art-Course-Database.accdb (Access 2007 - 2013 file format) - Ac...

FILE   HOME   CREATE   EXTERNAL DATA   DATABASE TOOLS

All Access Objects

Tables
- COURSE
- CUSTOMER
- ENROLLMENT

Queries
- Amount Due Query
- Art Course List
- Course Enrollment
- Course Enrollment Data
- Course Parameter Query

Forms
- Course Enrollment Data Entry Su...
- Customer Data Entry Form

Reports
- Course Enrollment Report

Art Course List

CustomerLastName	CustomerFirstName	Phone	CourseDate	AmountPaid	Course	Fee
Johnson	Ariel	206-567-1234	10/1/2015	$250.00	Adv Pastels	$500.00
Johnson	Ariel	206-567-1234	3/15/2015	$350.00	Int Pastels	$350.00
Green	Robin	425-678-8765	9/15/2015	$350.00	Beg Oils	$350.00
Jackson	Charles	360-789-3456	10/1/2015	$500.00	Adv Pastels	$500.00
Pearson	Jeffery	206-567-2345	10/1/2015	$500.00	Adv Pastels	$500.00
Sears	Miguel	360-789-4567	9/15/2015	$350.00	Beg Oils	$350.00
Kyle	Leah	425-678-7654	11/15/2015	$250.00	Adv Pastels	$500.00
Myers	Lynda	360-789-5678	10/15/2015	$0.00	Beg Oils	$350.00

Record: 1 of 8   No Filter   Search

CUSTOMER Last Name

FIGURE 1-26

Enterprise-Class
Database System

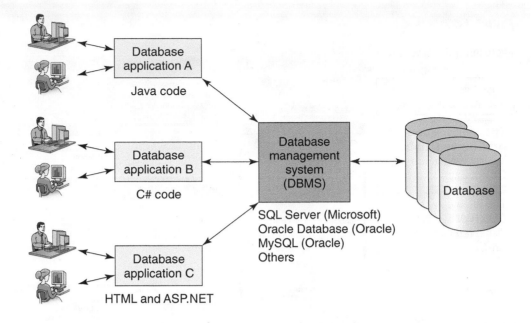

Notice that in Figure 1-26 the applications are written in three different languages: Java, C#, and a blend of HTML and ASP.NET. These applications call on an industrial-strength DBMS product to manage the database. No wizards or simple design tools are available to develop a system like this; instead, the developer writes program code using standard tools, such as those in integrated development environments. To write such code, you need to know SQL and other data access standards.

Although hidden technology and complexity are good in the beginning, business requirements will soon take you to the brink of your knowledge, and then you will need to know more. To be a part of a team that creates such a database application, you will need to know everything in this book. Over time, you will need to learn more. We will close this chapter with three examples of enterprise-class DBMS products.

Microsoft SQL Server 2014 Figure 1-27 shows the same SQL query used to produce the query results in Figure 1-13 and the associated query results when the SQL is executed in the **Microsoft SQL Server 2014** DBMS. We are actually running the query in the **Microsoft SQL Server 2014 Management Studio**, which is the user client interface to Microsoft SQL Server 2014.

Further, we are using the freely downloadable **Microsoft SQL Server 2014 Express Edition**. This version is a great learning tool, and it can also be used for smaller databases. For more information, see Appendix A, "Getting Started with Microsoft SQL Server 2014 Express Edition."

Note that in Figure 1-27 we are using exactly the same SQL statement we used previously, but now you can see how it is entered into a text editor window in the Microsoft SQL Server 2014 Management Studio and how the Execute button is used to execute the SQL statement against the Art-Course-Database tables. You can also see how the query results, which match those shown in Figure 1-13 but are sorted in a different order, are displayed in a separate Results window. This illustrates the importance of SQL—it is essentially the same in all DBMS products, and thus it is vendor and product independent (although there are some differences in SQL syntax between various DBMS products).

Oracle Database Express Edition 11*g* Release 2 Figure 1-28 shows the same SQL query used to produce the query results in Figure 1-13 and the associated query results when the SQL is executed in the **Oracle Database Express Edition 11*g* Release 2**

FIGURE 1-27

Microsoft SQL Server 2014

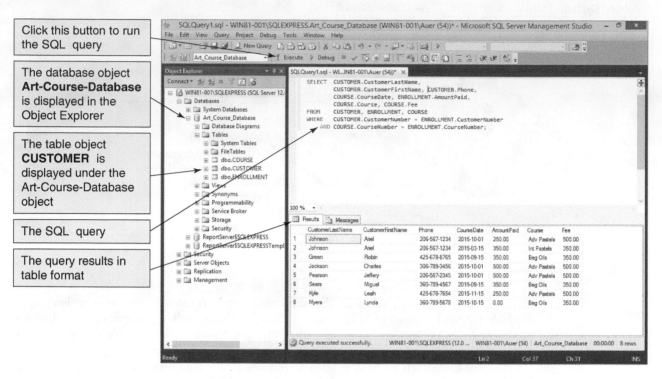

DBMS. We are using **Oracle SQL Developer** as user client interface to Oracle Database 11*g* Release 2.

Oracle, like Microsoft with SQL Server 2014, makes an express edition of the DBMS available for free download, and for Oracle this is the Oracle Database Express Edition 11*g* Release 2. Also like Microsoft SQL Server 2014 Express Edition, the Express Edition version of Oracle Database is a great learning tool, and it can also be used for smaller databases. For more information, see Appendix B, "Getting Started with Oracle Database Express Edition 11*g* Release 2."

Note that in Figure 1-28 we are again using exactly the same SQL statement we used previously, but now you can see how it is entered into a text editor window in Oracle SQL Developer and how to click a button to run the SQL statement against the Art Course Database tables (the COURSE, CUSTOMER, and ENROLLMENT table objects). You can also see how the query results, which match those shown in Figure 1-13 but are sorted in a different order, are displayed in a separate Query Result window.

Oracle MySQL 5.6 Community Server   Figure 1-29 shows the same SQL query used to produce the query results in Figure 1-13 and the associated query results when the SQL is executed in the **Oracle MySQL 5.6 Community Server** DBMS. We are again actually running the query in the user client interface to MySQL 5.6, which is the **MySQL Workbench**.

The MySQL 5.6 Community Server edition, like the Microsoft SQL Server 2014 Express Edition, can be downloaded for free. There is one significant difference between these two products because the MySQL 5.6 Community Server edition is a standard, full-strength edition of MySQL. However, if you want the full product support package, you have to purchase MySQL 5.6 Enterprise Edition from Oracle. MySQL is a popular

FIGURE 1-28

Oracle Database Express Edition 11*g* Release 2

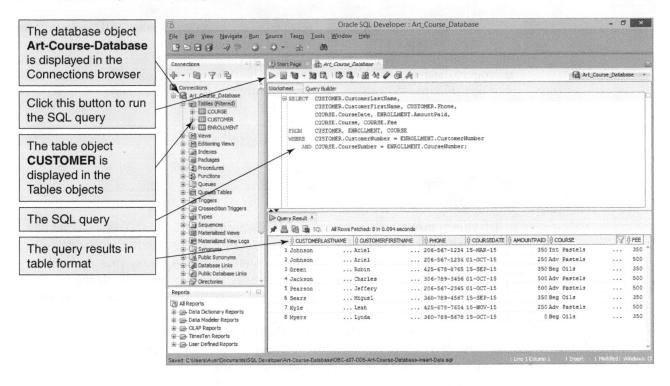

The database object **Art-Course-Database** is displayed in the Connections browser
Click this button to run the SQL query
The table object **CUSTOMER** is displayed in the Tables objects
The SQL query
The query results in table format
Oracle SQL Developer : Art_Course_Database
SELECT CUSTOMER.CustomerLastName,
CUSTOMER.CustomerFirstName, CUSTOMER.Phone,
COURSE.CourseDate, ENROLLMENT.AmountPaid,
COURSE.Course, COURSE.Fee
FROM CUSTOMER, ENROLLMENT, COURSE
WHERE CUSTOMER.CustomerNumber = ENROLLMENT.CustomerNumber
AND COURSE.CourseNumber = ENROLLMENT.CourseNumber;

FIGURE 1-29

MySQL 5.6

Click this button to run the SQL query
The SQL query
The database object **art_course_database** is displayed in the Object Browser
The table object **CUSTOMER** is displayed under the art-course-database object
The query results in table format
MySQL Workbench
SELECT CUSTOMER.CustomerLastName,
CUSTOMER.CustomerFirstName, CUSTOMER.Phone,
COURSE.CourseDate, ENROLLMENT.AmountPaid,
COURSE.Course, COURSE.Fee
FROM CUSTOMER, ENROLLMENT, COURSE
WHERE CUSTOMER.CustomerNumber = ENROLLMENT.CustomerNumber
AND COURSE.CourseNumber = ENROLLMENT.CourseNumber;

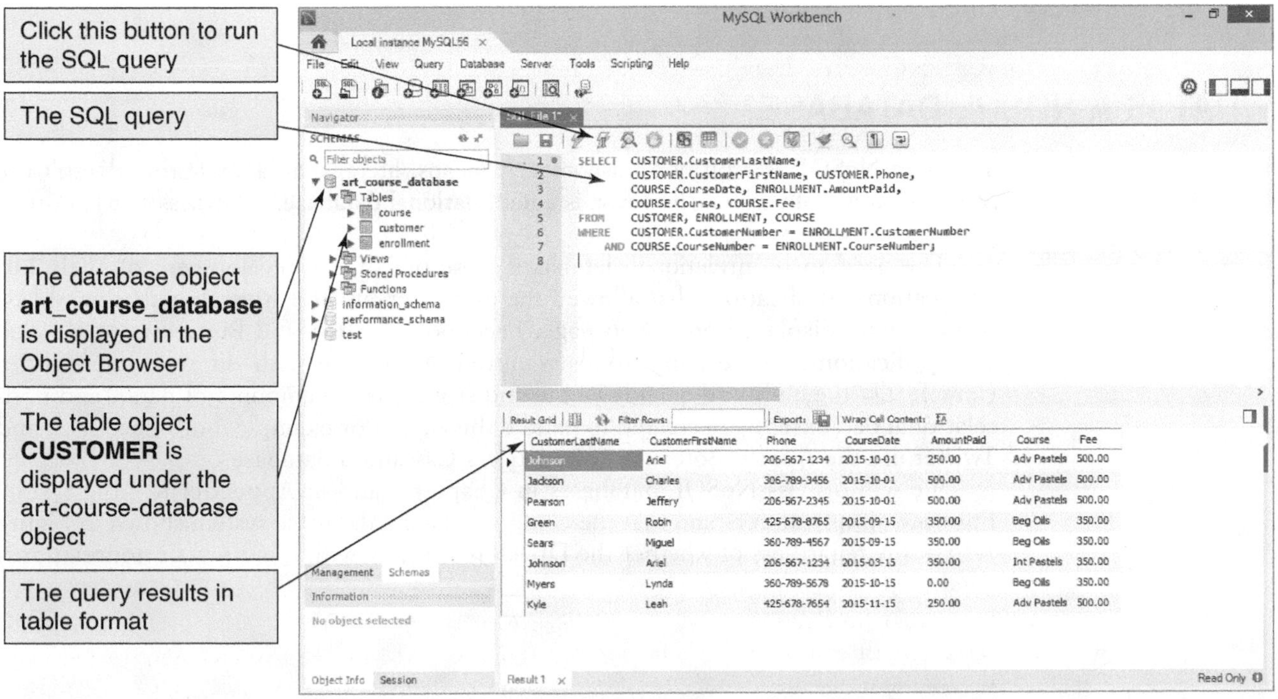

open-source product and is widely used for Web database applications (see our discussion of Web database applications in Chapter 7). This version is a great learning tool, and more information can be found in Appendix C, "Getting Started with Oracle MySQL 5.6 Community Server Edition."

Note that in Figure 1-29 we are again using exactly the same SQL statement we used previously, but now you can see how it is entered into a text editor window in the MySQL Workbench and which button to click to run the SQL query against the art-course-database tables. You can also see how the query results, which match those shown in Figure 1-13 but are sorted in a different order, are displayed in a separate Results window.

BTW

Of these three enterprise-class DBMS products, Oracle Database, while perhaps the most powerful DBMS product of the three, is the most difficult to master. If you are studying Oracle Database in a class, your instructor will know how to introduce Oracle Database topics to you to ease the learning process, as well as the appropriate order of topics to make sure you learn the material in an orderly fashion. Oracle Database is widely used in industry, and your efforts to learn about it will be a good investment.

However, if you are working through this book on your own, we believe you will find is easier to start with Microsoft SQL Server 2014 (which is the DBMS we use to illustrate most topics in the text) or Oracle MySQL 5.6 Community Server. Both of these products are relatively easy to download, install, and start using. Both are also widely used and will be good investments of your time and energy.

WHAT IS A NOSQL DATABASE?

The term **NoSQL** is a bit of a misnomer. It means, literally, a database that doesn't use SQL. What it really means, however, is a **nonrelational database**, regardless of what query language is used.

The need for nonrelational databases arose out of the development of **Web 2.0**[3] applications, applications that allowed the user to create and store data that would be subsequently displayed on a Web page. Facebook, Twitter, and Pinterest are all Web 2.0 applications. These applications required a database with different capabilities (specifically the ability to quickly create and store massive amounts of data), and nonrelational databases were created to handle this data. For example, both Facebook and Twitter use the Apache Software Foundation's Cassandra database.

We will discuss NoSQL databases in Chapter 8 and in Appendix K, "Big Data." For now, simply understand that the components of a database system shown in Figure 1-15 apply regardless of whether the DBMS is working with relational or nonrelational databases.

---

[3]See the Wikipedia article on **Web 2.0**.

THE ACCESS WORKBENCH

Section 1

Getting Started with Microsoft Access

"The Access Workbench" is designed to reinforce the concepts you learn in each chapter. In addition, you will learn many Microsoft Access skills by following along on your computer. In this chapter's section of "The Access Workbench," we will review some database basics from Chapter 1 as we walk through the basic steps necessary to build and use Microsoft Access database applications.

As discussed in this chapter, Microsoft Access is a personal database that combines a DBMS with an application generator. The DBMS performs the standard DBMS functions of database creation, processing, and administration, and the application generator adds the abilities to create and store forms, reports, queries, and other application-related functions. In this section, we will work with only one table in a database; in Chapter 2's section of "The Access Workbench" you will expand this to include two or more tables.

We will begin by creating a Microsoft Access database to store the database tables and the application forms, reports, and queries. In this section, we will work with basic forms and reports. Microsoft Access queries are discussed in Chapter 3's section of "The Access Workbench."

The Wallingford Motors Customer Relations Management System

Our Microsoft Access database will be used by a car dealership named Wallingford Motors, which is located in the Wallingford district of Seattle, Washington. Wallingford Motors is the dealer for a new line of hybrid cars named Gaea.[4] Instead of using only a gasoline or diesel engine, hybrid cars are powered by a combination of energy sources, such as gasoline and electricity. Gaea produces the following four models:

1. **SUHi**   The sport-utility hybrid (Gaea's answer to the SUV)
2. **HiLuxury**   A luxury-class four-door sedan hybrid
3. **HiStandard** A basic four-door sedan hybrid
4. **HiElectra** A variant of the HiStandard that uses a higher proportion of electrical power

Interest in hybrid cars—and specifically in the Gaea product line—is increasing. The sales staff at Wallingford Motors needs a way to track its customer contacts. Therefore, our database application will be a simple example of what is known as a **customer relationship management (CRM) system**. A CRM is used by sales staff to track current, past, and potential customers as well as the sales staff's contacts with these customers (among other uses). We will start out with a personal CRM used by one salesperson and expand it into a companywide CRM in later sections.[5]

Creating a Microsoft Access Database

We will name our Microsoft Access application and its associated database **WMCRM**. Our first step is to create a new Microsoft Access database.

---

[4]Gaea, or Gaia, was the Greek goddess of the Earth.

[5]Many CRM applications are available in the marketplace. In fact, Microsoft has one: Microsoft Dynamics CRM.

(Continued)

The Microsoft Access 2013 Tile

The Microsoft Access 2013 tile on the Windows 8.1 Start screen— click this tile to start Microsoft Access 2013

Right-click the Microsoft Access 2013 tile, and then click Pin to Taskbar to place the Microsoft Access 2013 button on the Desktop Toolbar

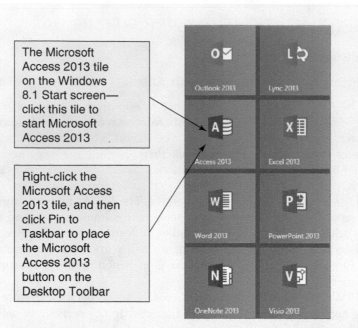

Creating the Microsoft Access Database WMCRM

1. Click Access tile on the Windows 8.1 Start screen as shown in Figure AW-1-1.
   - **NOTE:** The same command works for Windows 8. For Windows 7, select **Start | All Programs | Microsoft Office | Microsoft Access 2013**.
   - **NOTE:** We recommend that you pin a Microsoft Access 2013 button to the Windows Desktop Taskbar for ease of use. To do this, right-click the **Microsoft Access 2013 tile** on the Start screen to open a shortcut menu, and then click the **Pin to Taskbar** command.
   - **NOTE:** The menu commands, icon locations, and file locations used in "The Access Workbench" are those found when using Microsoft Access 2013 in the Microsoft Windows 8.1 operating system. If you are using the Microsoft **Windows 7** or **Microsoft Windows 8** operating systems, the exact operating system terminology may vary somewhat, but these variations will not change the required actions.
   - **NOTE:** Microsoft Access 2013 is used in these sections, and the wording of the steps and appearance of the screenshots reflect its use. If you have a different version of Microsoft Access, there will be some differences in the step details and in what you see onscreen. However, the basic functionality is the same, and you can complete "The Access Workbench" operations using any version of Microsoft Access.
2. The Microsoft Access 2013 Splash Screen appears, as shown in Figure AW-1-2. This screen displays the names of database files that have been recently used, an Open Other Files command, and template buttons for various types of databases and database applications.
3. Click the **Blank desktop database** template button to open the Blank desktop database dialog box as shown in Figure AW-1-3.
   - **NOTE:** By default, in Windows 8.1 the database will be created in the *Documents* folder on This PC. Note that this is a major difference and is new to Windows 8.1. In Windows 8 and Windows 7, the database will be created in the *My Documents* folder in the *Documents* library folder. The *Documents* library folder contains both a *My Documents* folder and a *Public Documents* folder.

FIGURE AW-1-2

The Microsoft Access 2013 Splash Screen

The **Recent** list—this is empty because we haven't opened any files

The **Open Other Files** button

The **Blank desktop database** template button—use this to create a new database on the computer itself

The **Microsoft Access 2013** button on the Desktop Taskbar

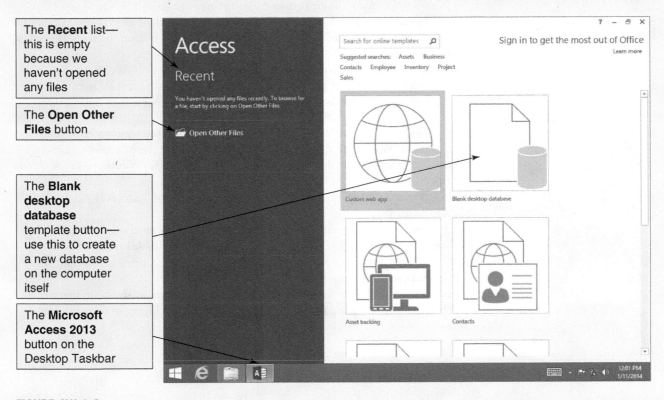

FIGURE AW-1-3

The Blank Desktop Database Dialog Box

The **Blank desktop database** dialog box

Type the database file name **WMCRM.accdb** here

The database will be created in this file location

The **Open** button—use this button to browse to a different file location if needed

Click the **Create** button after you have typed in the database file name

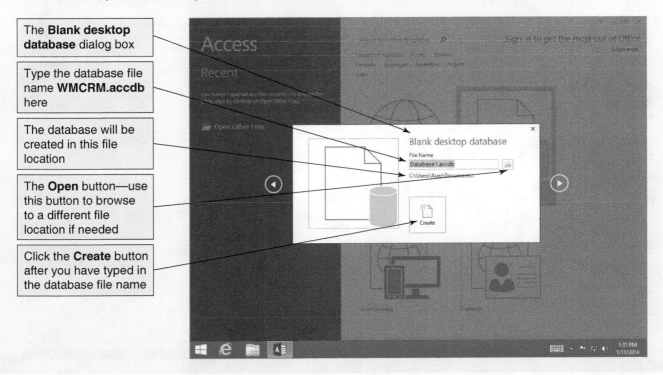

(Continued)

4. Type in the database name **WMCRM.accdb** in the **File Name** text box, and then click the **Create** button.

   - **NOTE:** If you clicked the Open button to browse to a different file location, use the File New Database dialog box to create the new database file. Once you have browsed to the correct folder, type the database name in the File Name text box of the File New Database dialog box, and then click the OK button to create the new database.

5. The new database appears, as shown in Figure AW-1-4. The Microsoft Access window itself is now named (in full—only part may be visible) **WMCRM : Database – C:\Users\Auer\ Documents\WMCRM.accdb (Access 2007-2013 file format) – Access** to include the database name.

   - **NOTE:** The reference to Microsoft Access 2007-2013 in the window name indicates that the database is stored as an **.accdb* file, which is the Microsoft Access database file format introduced with Microsoft Access 2007. Prior versions of Microsoft Access used the **.mdb* file format. Microsoft Access 2013 does not introduce a new database file format but continues to use the Microsoft Access 2007 **.accdb* file format.

6. Note that because this is a new database Microsoft Access has assumed that you will want to immediately create a new table. Therefore, a new table named **Table1** is displayed in Datasheet view in the document window. We do *not* want this table open at this time, so click the **Close** document button shown in Figure AW-1-4.

7. The Microsoft Access 2013 window with the new database appears, as shown in Figure AW-1-5. You can see most of the features of the Microsoft Office Fluent user interface in this window.

FIGURE AW-1-4

The New Microsoft Access Database

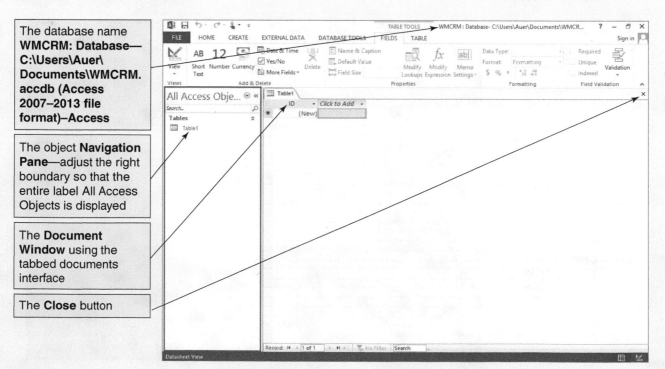

The database name **WMCRM: Database— C:\Users\Auer\ Documents\WMCRM. accdb (Access 2007–2013 file format)–Access**

The object **Navigation Pane**—adjust the right boundary so that the entire label All Access Objects is displayed

The **Document Window** using the tabbed documents interface

The **Close** button

FIGURE AW-1-5

The Microsoft Office Fluent User Interface

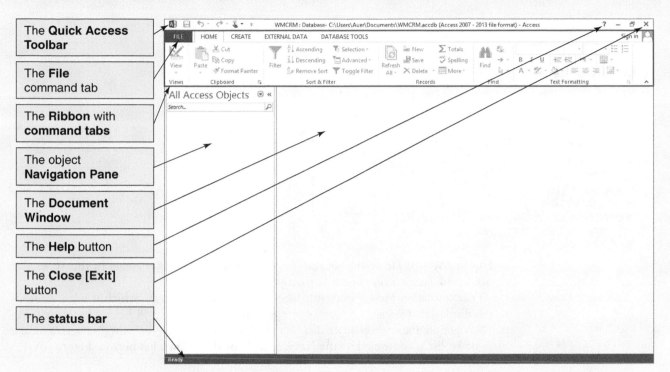

The **Quick Access Toolbar**	
The **File** command tab	
The **Ribbon** with **command tabs**	
The object **Navigation Pane**	
The **Document Window**	
The **Help** button	
The **Close [Exit]** button	
The **status bar**	

The Microsoft Office Fluent User Interface

Microsoft Access 2013 uses the **Microsoft Office Fluent user interface** found in most (but not all) of the Microsoft Office 2007 and Office 2013 applications. The major features of the interface can be seen in Figure AW-1-5. To illustrate its use, we will modify some of the default settings of the Microsoft Access database window.

The Quick Access Toolbar

First, we will modify the Quick Access Toolbar shown in Figure AW-1-5 to include a Quick Print button and a Print Preview button.

Modifying the Microsoft Access Quick Access Toolbar

1. Click the **Customize Quick Access Toolbar** drop-down arrow button shown in Figure AW-1-5. The Customize Quick Access Toolbar drop-down list appears, as shown in Figure AW-1-6.
2. Click **Quick Print**. The Quick Print button is added to the Quick Access Toolbar.
3. Click the **Customize Quick Access Toolbar** drop-down button. The Customize Quick Access Toolbar drop-down list appears.
4. Click **Print Preview**. The Print Preview button is added to the Quick Access Toolbar.
5. The added buttons are visible in the figures shown later in this section of "The Access Workbench," such as Figure AW-1-7.

Database Objects and the Navigation Pane

Microsoft uses the term **object** as a general name for the various parts of a Microsoft Access database. Thus, a *table* is an object, a *report* is an object, a *form* is an object, and so on. Microsoft Access objects are displayed in the Microsoft Access **Navigation Pane**, as shown

(Continued)

FIGURE AW-1-6

The Quick Access Toolbar

The **Quick Access Toolbar**

The **Customize Quick Access Toolbar** drop-down arrow button

The **Customize Quick Access Toolbar drop-down list**—click an item to add it to the toolbar

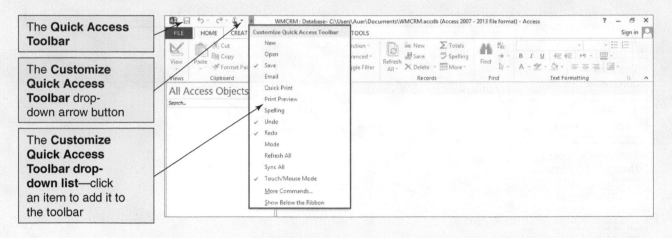

in Figure AW-1-3. However, because you have not created any objects in the WMCRM database, the Navigation Pane is currently empty.

The Navigation Pane is currently labeled as *All Access Objects*, which is what we want to see displayed. We can, however, select exactly which objects will be displayed by using the **Navigation Pane drop-down list**. As shown in Figure AW-1-7, the Navigation Pane drop-down list is controlled by the **Navigation Pane drop-down list button**. Figure AW-1-6

FIGURE AW-1-7

The Navigation Pane Drop-Down List

The **Quick Print** button

The **Print Preview** button

The **Navigation Pane** drop-down list button

The **All Access Objects** drop-down list

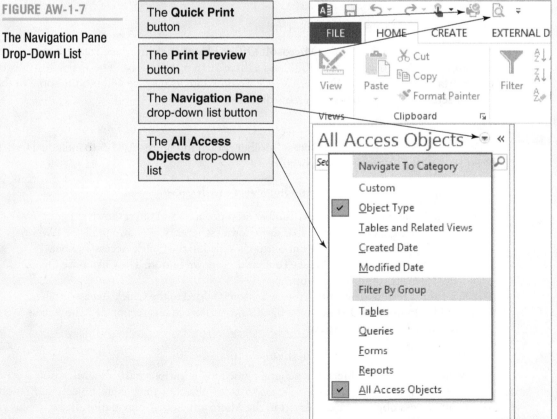

FIGURE AW-1-8

The Empty Navigation Pane

Use the **Shutter Bar Open/Close** button to hide or display the Navigation Pane

The Navigation Pane is empty because we have not created any objects for this database

shows the empty Navigation Pane and the **Shutter Bar Open/Close button**. We can hide the Navigation Pane if we want to by clicking the Shutter Bar Open/Close button, which is displayed as a left-facing double-chevron button on the upper-right corner of the Navigation Pane in Figure AW-1-8. If we click the button, the Navigation Pane shrinks to a small band labeled *Navigation Pane* on the right side of the Microsoft Access 2013 window. The band will then display the Shutter Bar Open/Close button as a right-facing double-chevron button that we can click to restore the Navigation Pane when we want to use it again.

Closing a Database and Exiting Microsoft Access

The *Close* button shown in Figure AW-1-5 is actually a *close and exit button*. You can click it to close the active database and then exit Microsoft Access. Note that Microsoft Access actively saves most changes to a database, and it prompts you with *Save* command requests when they are needed. For example, when you close a table with modified column widths Microsoft Access asks if you want to save the changes in the table layout. Therefore, you do not need to save Microsoft Access databases the way you save Microsoft Word documents and Microsoft Excel workbooks. You can simply close a database, knowing that Microsoft Access has already saved all critical changes since you opened it.

Closing a Database and Exiting Microsoft Access

1. Click the **Close** button. The database closes, and you exit Microsoft Access.

BTW

Instead of clicking the Close button, you can simultaneously close the database and exit Microsoft Access by clicking the File command tab, and then clicking the Exit command. To close just the database while leaving Microsoft Access open, select the File command tab, and then click the Close Database command.

(Continued)

Opening an Existing Microsoft Access Database

Earlier in this section of "The Access Workbench" we created a new Microsoft Access database for the Wallingford Motors CRM (WMCRM.accdb), modified some Microsoft Access settings, and closed the database and exited Microsoft Access. Before we can continue building this database, we need to start Microsoft Access and open the WMCRM.accdb database.

When we open an existing database, Microsoft Access 2013 (like Microsoft Access 2007 and Microsoft Access 2010 before it) gives us the option of using Microsoft Access security options to shut down certain Microsoft Access 2013 features in a database to protect ourselves against harm not only from viruses but also from other possible problems. Unfortunately, the Microsoft Access 2013 security options also shut down significant and needed operational features of Microsoft Access. Therefore, we will normally enable the features that the Microsoft Access 2013 security warning warns us about when we open an existing database.

Opening a Recently Opened Microsoft Access Database

1. Open Microsoft Access 2013 by clicking the **Microsoft Access 2013** button on the Windows Start screen (or on the Windows Taskbar if you pinned it there as suggested). Microsoft Access 2013 is displayed with the splash screen open, as shown in Figure AW-1-9
2. The **Recent list** is displayed on the splash screen, and the database file WMCRM.accdb is now listed there.
3. Note that if the database has been used very recently it will be available in the Recent file list. You may make the file a permanent part of the Recent file list, by right-clicking the file name to display a shortcut menu, and then clicking the *Pin to list* command. Similarly, you can remove a file from the Recent list by using the *Remove from list* command on the shortcut menu.
4. Click the **WMCRM.accdb** file name in the **Recent file list** to open the database. A **Security Warning** bar appears with the database, as shown in Figure AW-1-10.

FIGURE AW-1-9

The Recent File List

The **WMCRM.accdb** database in the Recent list—click the file name to open the file. Right-clicking the file name displays a shortcut menu with options to (1) remove this file from the Recent list and (2) pin it to the list permanently.

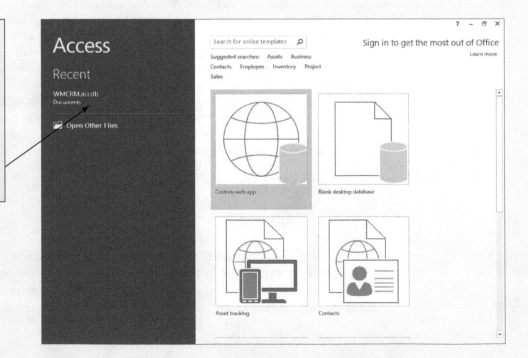

FIGURE AW-1-10

The Security Warning Bar

The **Security Warning** bar

The **Click for more details** link

Click the **Enable Content** button

5. At this point, we have the option of clicking the Security Warning bar's **Click for more details** link, which will display a detailed version of the warning together with security options. However, for our purposes in this text, we simply need to enable the active content, so click the **Enable Content** button.

- **NOTE:** At some point, you should select the **Click for more details** link and explore the available security settings.

- **NOTE:** In Microsoft Access 2007, the Security Warning bar appeared every time the database was reopened (although from a *nontrusted location*—see Chapter 6's section of "The Access Workbench" for a discussion of *trusted locations*). In Microsoft Access 2010 and Microsoft Access 2013, the Security Warning bar is only displayed the first time you reopen a database, and your choice of options is remembered from that point on.

Creating a Microsoft Access Database Table

At this point in the development of the WMCRM database application, the database will be used by one salesperson, so we need only two tables in the WMCRM database—CUSTOMER and CONTACT. We will create the CUSTOMER table first. The CUSTOMER table will contain the columns and characteristics shown in the table in Figure AW-1-11. The column characteristics are type, key, required, and remarks.

Type refers to the kind of data the column will store. Some possible Microsoft Access data types are shown in Figure AW-1-12. For CUSTOMER, most data are stored as **short text** data which can store up to 255 characters (also commonly called **character** data, this data type was previously called just **text**—**long text** now refers to a data type previously called **memo**, which can store up to 65,535 characters), which means we can enter strings of letters, numbers, and symbols (a space is considered a symbol). The number behind the word *Text* indicates how many characters can be stored in the column. For example, customer last names may be up to 25 characters long. The only **number**, or **numeric**, data column in the CUSTOMER table is CustomerID, which is listed as **AutoNumber**. This indicates that Microsoft Access will automatically provide a sequential number for this column for each new customer that is added to the table.

Key refers to table identification functions assigned to a column. These are described in detail in Chapter 2. At this point, you simply need to know that a **primary key** is a column value used to identify each row; therefore, the values in this column must be unique.

(Continued)

FIGURE AW-1-11

Database Column Characteristics for the CUSTOMER Table

Column Name	Type	Key	Required	Remarks
CustomerID	AutoNumber	Primary Key	Yes	Surrogate Key
LastName	Text (25)	No	Yes	
FirstName	Text (25)	No	Yes	
Address	Text (35)	No	No	
City	Text (35)	No	No	
State	Text (2)	No	No	
ZIP	Text (10)	No	No	
Phone	Text (12)	No	Yes	
Fax	Text (12)	No	No	
Email	Text (100)	No	No	

FIGURE AW-1-12

Microsoft Access 2013 Data Types

Name	Type of Data	Size
Short Text	Characters and numbers	Maximum 255 characters
Long Text	Large text	Maximum 65,535 characters
Number	Numeric data	Varies with Number type
Date/Time	Dates and times from the year 100 to the year 9999	Stored as 8-byte double-precision integers
Currency	Numbers with decimal places	One to four decimal places
AutoNumber	A unique sequential number	Incremented by one each time
Yes/No	Fields that can contain only two values	Yes/No, On/Off, True/False, etc.
OLE Object	An object embedded in or linked to a Microsoft Access table	Maximum 1 GB
Hyperlink	A hyperlink address	Maximum 2,048 characters in each of three parts of the hyperlink address
Attachment	Any supported type of file may be attached to a record	Independent of Microsoft Access
Calculated	Results of a calculation based on data in other cells	Varies depending on values used in calculation
Lookup Wizard...	A list of possible data values located in a value list	Varies depending on the values in the value list

This is the reason for using the AutoNumber data type, which automatically assigns a unique number to each row in the table as it is created.

Required refers to whether the column must have a data value. If it must, a value must be present in the column. If not, the column may be blank. Note that because CustomerID is a primary key used to identify each row it *must* have a value.

Remarks contains comments about the column or how it is used. For CUSTOMER, the only comment is that CustomerID is a **surrogate key**. Surrogate keys are discussed in Chapter 2. At this point, you simply need to know that surrogate keys are usually computer-generated unique numbers used to identify rows in a table (that is, a primary key). This is done by using the Microsoft Access AutoNumber data type.

Creating the CUSTOMER Table

1. Click the **Create** command tab to display the **Create** command groups.
2. Click the **Table Design** button, as shown in Figure AW-1-13.
3. The **Table1** tabbed document window is displayed in **Design** view, as shown in Figure AW-1-14. Note that along with the **Table1** window a contextual tab grouping named **Table Tools** is displayed and that this tab grouping adds a new command tab named **Design** to the set of command tabs displayed.
   - **NOTE:** It seems like now would be a good time to name the new table CUSTOMER. With Microsoft Access, however, you do not name a table until you save it the first time, and you cannot save a table until you have at least one column defined. So, we will define the columns, and then we will save and name the table. If you want, save the table after you have defined just one column. This will close the table, so you will have to reopen it to define the remaining columns.
4. In the **Field Name** column text box of the first line, type the column name **CustomerID** and then press the **Tab** key to move to the **Data Type** column. (You can also click the Data Type column to select it.)
   - **NOTE:** The terms *column* and *field* are considered synonyms in database work. The term *attribute* is also considered to be equivalent to these two words.
5. Select the **AutoNumber** data type for CustomerID from the **Data Type** drop-down list, as shown in Figure AW-1-15.
6. If you like, an optional comment may be stored in the Description column. To do so, move to the Description column by pressing the **Tab** key or clicking in the **Description** text box.

FIGURE AW-1-13

The Table Design Button

| The **Create** tab |
| The **Table Design** button |
| When the mouse is held over the Table Design button, a **tool tip** for the button that shows that a new table object will be created will be displayed below the button. |

FIGURE AW-1-14

The Table1 Tabbed Document Window

The **TABLE TOOLS** contextual command tab is displayed along with the set of command tabs that comprise Table Tools

The **DESIGN** command tab and its command groups are displayed

The **Table1** tabbed document window in Design view

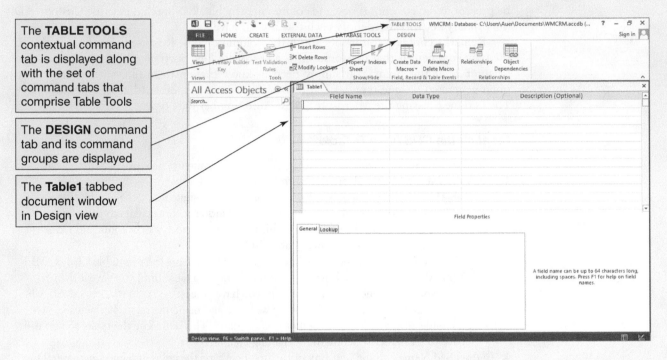

FIGURE AW-1-15

Selecting the Data Type

The **Data Type** drop-down list arrow button

The **Data Type** drop-down list

Select **AutoNumber**

FIGURE AW-1-16

The Completed CustomerID Column

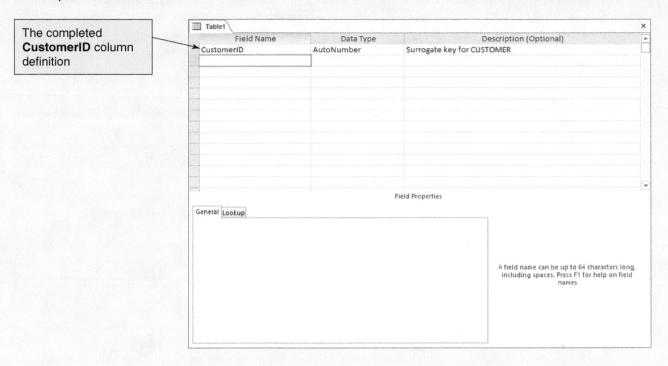

The completed **CustomerID** column definition

Type the text **Surrogate key for CUSTOMER** and then press the **Tab** key to move to the next row. The **Table1** tabbed document window now looks as shown in Figure AW-1-16.

- ■ **NOTE:** The Remarks column in the set of database column characteristics shown in Figure AW-1-11 is *not* the same as the table Description column shown in Figure AW-1-16. Be careful not to confuse them. The Remarks column is used to record technical data, such as facts about table keys and data default values that are necessary for building the table structure. The Description column is used to describe to the user the data stored in that field so that the user understands the field's intended use.

7. The other columns of the CUSTOMER table are created using the sequence described in steps 4 through 6—at this point you should add each of the remaining columns shown in Figure AW-1-9 to the CUSTOMER table while following those steps.

- ■ **NOTE:** See Figure AW-1-19 for the Description entries.

8. To set the number of characters in text columns, edit the **Data Type Field Size** property text box, as shown in Figure AW-1-17. The default value for Field Size is 255, which is also the maximum value for a text field.

9. To make a column required, click anywhere in the column **Data Type Required** property text box to display the **Required** property drop-down list arrow button, then click the button to display the Required property drop-down list, as shown in Figure AW-1-18, and then select **Yes** from the Required property drop-down list. The default is No (not required), and Yes must be selected to make the column required.[6]

---

[6]Microsoft Access has an additional Data Type property named Allow Zero Length. This property confounds the settings necessary to truly match the SQL constraint NOT NULL discussed in Chapter 3. However, the discussion of Allow Zero Length is beyond the scope of this book. See the Microsoft Access Help system for more information.

(Continued)

FIGURE AW-1-17

Editing the Text Field Size

Edit this number to set the number of characters

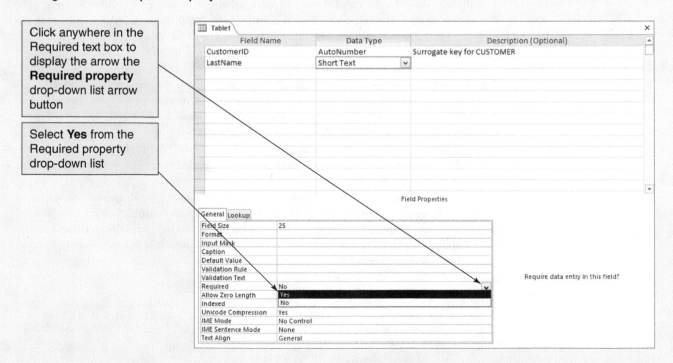

FIGURE AW-1-18

Setting the Column Required Property Value

Click anywhere in the Required text box to display the arrow the **Required property** drop-down list arrow button

Select **Yes** from the Required property drop-down list

Now we need to set a primary key for the CUSTOMER table. According to Figure AW-1-11, we need to use the CustomerID column as the primary key for this table.

Setting the CUSTOMER Table Primary Key

1. Move the mouse pointer to the **row selector column** of the row containing the CustomerID properties, as shown in Figure AW-1-19. Click to select the row.
2. Click the **Primary Key** button in the Tools group of the Design tab, as shown in Figure AW-1-20. CustomerID is selected as the primary key for the CUSTOMER table.

We have finished building the CUSTOMER table. Now we need to name, save, and close the table.

Naming, Saving, and Closing the CUSTOMER Table

1. To name and save the CUSTOMER table, click the **Save** button in the Quick Access Toolbar. The **Save As** dialog box appears, as shown in Figure AW-1-21.
2. Type the table name **CUSTOMER** into the **Save As** dialog box's Table Name text box and then click **OK**. The table is named and saved. The table name CUSTOMER now appears on the document tab, and the CUSTOMER table object is displayed in the Navigation Pane, as shown in Figure AW-1-22.
3. To close the CUSTOMER table, click the **Close** button in the upper-right corner of the tabbed documents window, as shown in Figure AW-1-22. After the table is closed, the CUSTOMER table object remains displayed in the Navigation Pane, as shown in Figure AW-1-23.

FIGURE AW-1-19

Selecting the CustomerID Row

The **row selector column**—move the mouse pointer into this column to select a specific row

Move the mouse pointer here and click to select the CustomerID row

Field Name	Data Type	Description (Optional)
CustomerID	AutoNumber	Surrogate key for CUSTOMER
LastName	Short Text	Customer's last name
FirstName	Short Text	Customer's first name
Address	Short Text	Customer's street address, including apartment or unit number
City	Short Text	Customer's city
State	Short Text	Customer's state using standard two-letter abbreviations
ZIP	Short Text	Customer's ZIP code using ZIP+4
Phone	Short Text	Customer's phone number including area code
Fax	Short Text	Customer's fax number including area code
Email	Short Text	Customer's email address

Field Properties

General | Lookup

Field Size	Long Integer
New Values	Increment
Format	
Caption	
Indexed	Yes (Duplicates OK)
Text Align	General

A field name can be up to 64 characters long, including spaces. Press F1 for help on field names.

(Continued)

FIGURE AW-1-20

Setting the Primary Key

Click the **Primary Key** button in the Tools group of the Design tab to set CustomerID as the primary key

A *key symbol* here indicates that CustomerID is the primary key of the table

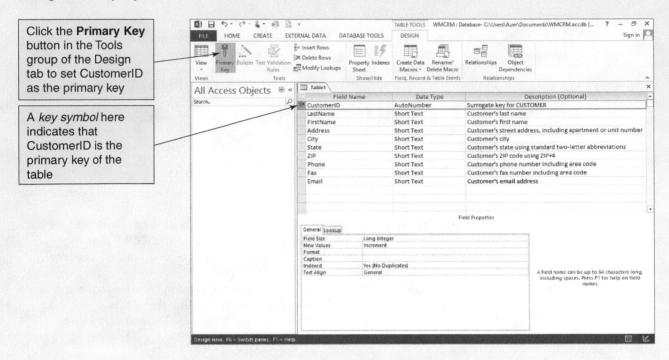

FIGURE AW-1-21

Naming and Saving the CUSTOMER table

Click the **Save** button in the Quick Access Toolbar to display the **Save As** dialog box

Type the table name **CUSTOMER** in the Table Name text box

The **OK** button

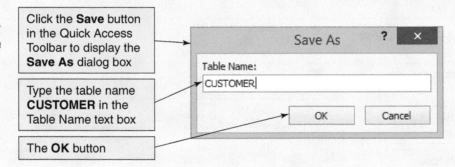

Inserting Data into Tables: The Datasheet View

There are three commonly used methods for adding data to a table. First, we can use a table as a **datasheet**, which is visually similar to and works like a Microsoft Excel worksheet. When we do this, the table is in **Datasheet view**, and we enter the data cell by cell. Second, we can build a **data entry form** for the table and then use the form to add data. Third, we can use SQL to insert data. This section covers the first two of these methods; we will use the SQL method in Chapter 3's section of "The Access Workbench."

In Microsoft Access 2013, we can also use Datasheet view to create and modify table characteristics. When we open a table in Datasheet view, the Table Tools contextual tab includes a Datasheet command tab and ribbon with tools to do this. We do *not* recommend this; it is better to use Design view, as previously discussed in this section, for creating and modifying table structures.

FIGURE AW-1-22

The Named CUSTOMER Table

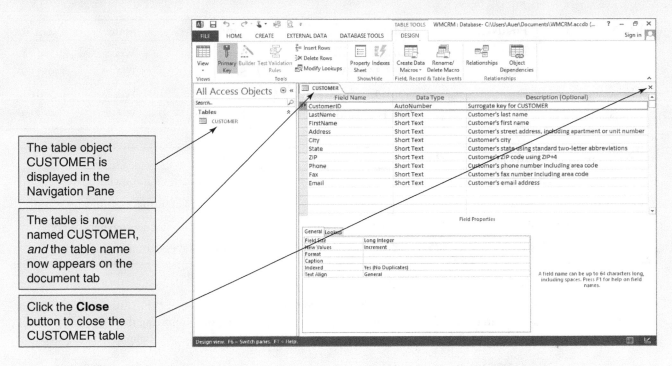

The table object CUSTOMER is displayed in the Navigation Pane

The table is now named CUSTOMER, *and* the table name now appears on the document tab

Click the **Close** button to close the CUSTOMER table

FIGURE AW-1-23

The CUSTOMER Table Object

The table object CUSTOMER is displayed in the Navigation Pane

However, at this point we do not need to modify the table structure—we simply need to put some data into the CUSTOMER table. Figure AW-1-24 shows some data for Wallingford Motors customers.

Adding Data to the CUSTOMER Table in Datasheet View

1. In the Navigation Pane, double-click the **CUSTOMER** table object. The CUSTOMER table window appears in a tabbed document window in Datasheet view, as shown in

(Continued)

CUSTOMER Data

LastName	FirstName	Address	City	State	Zip
Griffey	Ben	5678 25th NE	Seattle	WA	98178
Christman	Jessica	3456 36th SW	Seattle	WA	98189
Christman	Rob	4567 47th NW	Seattle	WA	98167
Hayes	Judy	234 Highland Place	Edmonds	WA	98210

LastName	FirstName	Phone	Fax	Email
Griffey	Ben	206-456-2345		Ben.Griffey@somewhere.com
Christman	Jessica	206-467-3456		Jessica.Christman@somewhere.com
Christman	Rob	206-478-4567	206-478-9998	Rob.Christman@somewhere.com
Hayes	Judy	425-354-8765		Judy.Hayes@somewhere.com

Figure AW-1-25. Note that some columns on the right side of the datasheet do not appear in the window, but you can access them by scrolling or minimizing the Navigation Pane.

- **NOTE:** As in a worksheet, the intersection of a row and column in a datasheet is called a *cell*.

2. Click the **Shutter Bar Open/Close** button to collapse the Navigation Pane. This makes more of the CUSTOMER datasheet visible, as shown in Figure AW-1-26.

The CUSTOMER Table in Datasheet View

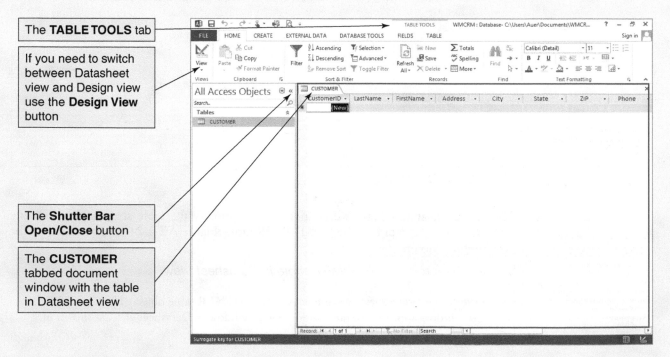

The **TABLE TOOLS** tab

If you need to switch between Datasheet view and Design view use the **Design View** button

The **Shutter Bar Open/Close** button

The **CUSTOMER** tabbed document window with the table in Datasheet view

FIGURE AW-1-26

The Collapsed Navigation Pane

The **Shutter Bar Open/Close** button

The collapsed **Navigation Pane**

The **CUSTOMER** tabbed document window with the table in Datasheet view

3. Click the **CUSTOMER** document tab to select the CUSTOMER table in Datasheet view.
4. Click the cell in the CustomerID column with the phrase **(New)** in it to select that cell in the new row of the CUSTOMER datasheet.
5. Press the **Tab** key to move to the LastName cell in the new row of the CUSTOMER datasheet. For customer Ben Griffey, type **Griffey** in the LastName cell. Note that as soon as you do this the AutoNumber function puts the number 1 in the CustomerID cell and a new row is added to the datasheet, as shown in Figure AW-1-27.

FIGURE AW-1-27

Entering Data Values for Ben Griffey

This row has been autonumbered as CustomerID 1

A new, blank row is added to the datasheet

(Continued)

FIGURE AW-1-28

The Completed Row of Data Values

Column widths can be adjusted by using the mouse to drag the column border to the desired width

6. Using the **Tab** key to move from one column to another in the CUSTOMER datasheet, enter the rest of the data values for Ben Griffey.
7. The final result is shown in Figure AW-1-28. Note that the width of the Email column was expanded using the mouse to move the border of the column—just as you would in a Microsoft Excel worksheet.
   - **NOTE:** If you make a mistake and need to return to a cell, click the cell to select it and Microsoft Access will automatically shift into Edit mode. Alternatively, you can use **Shift-Tab** to move to the right in the datasheet and then press **F2** to edit the contents of the cell.
   - **NOTE:** Remember that LastName, FirstName, and Phone *require* a data value. You will not be able to move to another row or close the table window until you have a value in each of these cells.
   - **NOTE:** Figure AW-1-28 shows a column labeled *Click to Add* to the right of the Email column. This is a table tool in Datasheet view that you can use to create or modify table structures. We do not recommend using these tools—we prefer to use Design view instead!
8. Use the **Tab** key to move to the next row of the CUSTOMER datasheet and enter the data for Jessica Christman, as shown in Figure AW-1-29.

FIGURE AW-1-29

The Completed CUSTOMER Datasheet

Many column widths had to be adjusted to get all the data to show in one window—use the mouse to drag the column borders to the desired widths

Click the **Close** button to close the CUSTOMER datasheet

9. Adjust the datasheet column widths so that you can see the contents of the datasheet in one screen. The final result is shown in Figure AW-1-29.

10. We are adding only the data for Jessica Christman at this point, and we will add the remaining CUSTOMER data later in this section of "The Access Workbench." Click the **Close** button in the upper-right corner of the document window to close the CUSTOMER datasheet. A dialog box appears that asks if you want to save the changes you made to the layout (column widths). Click the **Yes** button.

11. Click the **Shutter Bar Open/Close** button to expand the Navigation Pane. This makes the objects in the Navigation Pane visible.

Modifying Data in Tables: The Datasheet View

After entering data into a table, you can modify or change the data by editing the data values in the Datasheet view. To illustrate this, we will temporarily change Jessica Christman's phone number to 206-467-9876.

Modifying Data in the CUSTOMER Table in Datasheet View

1. In the Navigation Pane, double-click the **CUSTOMER** table object. The CUSTOMER table window appears in a tabbed document window in Datasheet view.

2. Click the **Shutter Bar Open/Close** button to collapse the Navigation Pane.

3. Click the **cell** that contains Jessica Christman's phone number to select it. Microsoft Access automatically puts the cell into Edit mode.
   - **NOTE:** If you instead use the **Tab** key (or **Shift-Tab** to move to the left in the datasheet) to select the cell, press the **F2** key to edit the contents of the cell.

4. Change the phone number to **206-467-9876**.
   - **NOTE:** Remember that Phone has a field size of 12 characters. You have to delete characters before you can enter new ones.

5. Press the **Enter** key or otherwise move to another cell to complete the edit. The CUSTOMER datasheet appears as shown in Figure AW-1-30.

6. Because we really do not want to change Jessica Christman's phone number, edit the Phone value back to its original value of **206-467-3456**. Complete the edit and click the **Save** button on the Quick Access Toolbar to save the changes.

7. Click the **Close** button in the upper-right corner of the document window to close the CUSTOMER datasheet.

8. Click the **Shutter Bar Open/Close** button to expand the Navigation Pane.

FIGURE AW-1-30

The Modified CUSTOMER Datasheet

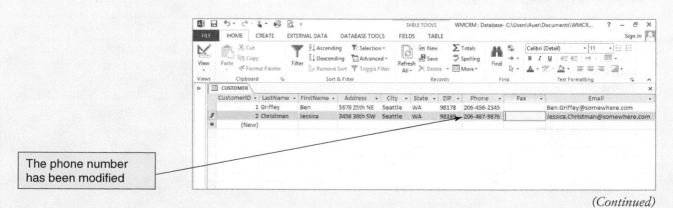

The phone number has been modified

(Continued)

Deleting a Row in the CUSTOMER Datasheet

Click a cell in this column to select an entire row—a left-click will simply select the row, while a right-click will select the row and display a shortcut menu

The **Delete Record** command in the shortcut menu

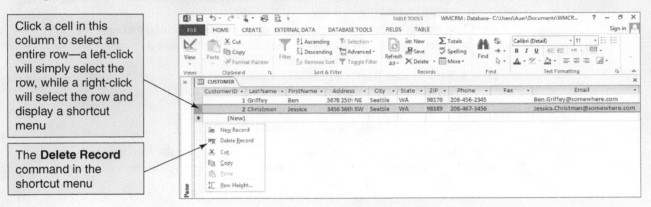

Deleting Rows in Tables: The Datasheet View

After the data have been entered into a table, you can delete an entire row in Datasheet view. To illustrate this, we will temporarily delete Jessica Christman's data.

Deleting a Row in the CUSTOMER Table in Datasheet View

1. In the Navigation Pane, double-click the **CUSTOMER** table object. The CUSTOMER table window appears in a tabbed document window in Datasheet view.
2. Click the **Shutter Bar Open/Close** button to collapse the Navigation Pane.
3. Right-click the **row selector cell** on the left side of the CUSTOMER datasheet for the row that contains Jessica Christman's data. This selects the entire row and displays a shortcut menu, as shown in Figure AW-1-31.
   - **NOTE:** The terms *row* and *record* are synonymous in database usage.
4. Click the Delete Record command in the shortcut menu. As shown in Figure AW-1-32, a Microsoft Access dialog box appears, warning you that you are about to permanently delete the record.
   - **NOTE:** As also shown in Figure AW-1-32, Microsoft Access 2013 with default settings performs the visual trick of actually removing the row! However, the row is not permanently deleted until you click the **Yes** button in the Microsoft Access dialog box. If you click the **No** button, the row reappears.

The Microsoft Access Deletion Warning Dialog Box

The row with Jessica Christman's data has already been visually removed!

Click the **Yes** button to actually delete the row

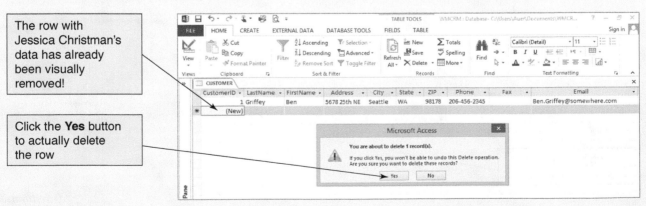

5. Click the **Yes** button to complete the deletion of the row.
   - ■ **NOTE:** Alternatively, you can delete the row by clicking the **row selector cell** and then pressing the **Delete** key. The same Microsoft Access dialog box shown in Figure AW-1-32 then appears.
6. Because we do not want to really lose Jessica Christman's data at this point, add a new row to the CUSTOMER datasheet that contains Jessica's data. As shown in Figure AW-1-33, the CustomerID number for Jessica Christman is now 3 instead of 2. In an autonumbered column, each number is used only once.
7. Click the **Close** button in the upper-right corner of the document window to close the CUSTOMER datasheet.
8. Click the **Shutter Bar Open/Close** button to expand the Navigation Pane.

Inserting Data into Tables: Using a Form

Now, we will create and use a **form** to insert data into a table. A form provides a visual reference for entering data into the various data columns, and Microsoft Access has a form generator as part of its application generator functions. We could build a form manually in Form Design view, but instead we can take the easy route and use the **Form Wizard**, which will take us through a step-by-step process to create the form we want.

Creating a Data Entry Form for the CUSTOMER Table

1. Click the **Create** command tab to display the Create command tab and its command groups, as shown in Figure AW-1-34.
2. Click the **Form Wizard** button shown in Figure AW-1-34. The Form Wizard appears, as shown in Figure AW-1-35.
3. The CUSTOMER table is already selected as the basis for the form, so we only have to select which columns we want to include on the form. We can choose columns one at a time by highlighting a column name and clicking the right-facing single-chevron button. Or we can choose all the columns at once by clicking the right-facing double-chevron button. We want to add all the columns in this case, so click the **right-facing double-chevron** button to add all the columns and then click the **Next** button.
   - ■ **NOTE:** In a real-world situation, we might not want to display the CustomerID value. In that case, we would deselect it by highlighting it and clicking the left-facing single-chevron button.

FIGURE AW-1-33

The New CustomerID Number

The row with the reentered Jessica Christman data now has a CustomerID of 3—AutoNumber numbers are sequential and are used only once!

(Continued)

FIGURE AW-1-34

The Create Command Tab and Form Wizard Button

The **CREATE** command tab

The **Form Wizard** button

The **Forms** command group

4. When asked, "What layout would you like for your form?" click the **Next** button to select the default **Columnar** layout.

5. When asked, "What title do you want for your form?" type the form title **WMCRM Customer Data Form** into the text box and then click the **Finish** button. As shown in Figure AW-1-36, the completed form appears in a tabbed document window and a WMCRM Customer Data Form object is added to the Navigation Pane.

   ■ **NOTE:** The WMCRM Customer Data Form is properly constructed and sized for our needs. Sometimes, however, we might need to make adjustments to the form design. We can make form design changes by switching to form Design view. To switch to form Design view, click the **Design View** button in the View gallery.

   Now that we have the form we need, we can use the form to add some data to the CUSTOMER table.

FIGURE AW-1-35

The Form Wizard

The **Form Wizard**

The CUSTOMER table is already selected

The **right-facing single chevron** button

Click the **right-facing double chevron** button to select all of the fields in the table

The **Next** button

FIGURE AW-1-36

The Completed WMCRM Customer Data Form

Inserting Data into the CUSTOMER Table Using a Form

1. Click the **New Record** button. A blank form appears.
2. Click the **LastName** text box to select it. Enter the data for Rob Christman shown in Figure AW-1-24. You can either use the **Tab** key to move from text box to text box or you can click the text box you want to edit.
3. When you are done entering the data for Rob Christman, enter the data for Judy Hayes shown in Figure AW-1-24. After you have entered the data for Judy Hayes, your form will look as shown in Figure AW-1-37.
4. Click the **Close** button in the upper-right corner of the document window to close the WMCRM Customer Data Form.

Modifying Data and Deleting Records: Using a Form

Just as we can modify data and delete rows in Datasheet view, we can edit data and delete records by using a form. Editing data is simple: Move to the record you want to edit by using the **record navigation buttons** (First Record, Previous Record, etc.) shown in Figure AW-1-37, click the appropriate field text box, and then edit the contents. Deleting a record is also simple: Move to the record you want to edit by using the record navigation buttons and then click the *Delete Record* button in the Delete drop-down list of the Records group of the Home command tab, as shown in Figure AW-1-38. However, you will not use these capabilities at this time.

Creating Single-Table Microsoft Access Reports

One common function of an application is to generate printed reports. Microsoft Access 2013 has a report generator as part of its application generator functions. Just as with forms, we could build a form manually, or we can take the easy route and use the **Report Wizard**.

(Continued)

FIGURE AW-1-37

The WMCRM Customer Data Form for Customer Judy Hayes

| The WMCRM Customer Data Form with the data for Judy Hayes |
| The **Close** button |
| The **Last Record** button |
| The **Next Record** button |
| The **Previous Record** button |
| The **First Record** button |

FIGURE AW-1-38

The Delete Record Button

| The **HOME** command tab |
| The **Records** command group |
| The **Delete** drop-down list arrow button |
| The **Delete Record** button |

FIGURE AW-1-39

The Create Command Tab and Report Wizard Button

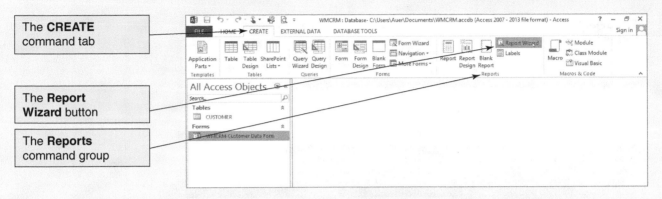

The **CREATE** command tab

The **Report Wizard** button

The **Reports** command group

Creating a Report for the CUSTOMER Table

1. Click the **Create** command tab to display the Create command groups, as shown in Figure AW-1-39.
2. Click the **Report Wizard** button shown in Figure AW-1-39. The Report Wizard appears, as shown in Figure AW-1-40.
3. The CUSTOMER table is already selected as the basis for the report, so we only have to select which columns we want on the form. Just as with the Form Wizard, we can choose columns one at a time by highlighting the column name and clicking the right-facing single-chevron button. We can also choose all the columns at once by clicking the right-facing double-chevron button. In this case, we want to use only the columns **LastName**, **FirstName**, **Phone**, **Fax**, and **Email**. Click each column name in the Available Fields list

FIGURE AW-1-40

The Report Wizard

The **Report Wizard**

The CUSTOMER table is already selected

The **Available Fields** list

Click the **right-facing single chevron** button to select the highlighted field in the table

The **Next** button

> Report Wizard
>
> Which fields do you want on your report?
>
> You can choose from more than one table or query.
>
> Tables/Queries
>
> Table: CUSTOMER
>
> Available Fields:
> - CustomerID
> - LastName
> - FirstName
> - Address
> - City
> - State
> - ZIP
> - Phone
>
> Selected Fields:
>
> Cancel   < Back   Next >   Finish

(Continued)

The Completed Column Selection

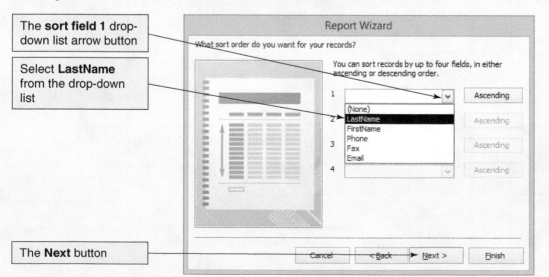

The **Selected Fields** list

The **Next** button

to select it and then click the **right-facing single-chevron** button to move each column to Selected Fields. The completed selection looks as shown in Figure AW-1-41.

- **NOTE:** You can select only one column at a time. The usual technique of selecting more than one column name at a time by pressing and holding the **Ctrl** key while clicking each additional column name does *not* work in this case.

4. Click the **Next** button.
5. Microsoft Access now asks, "Do you want to add any grouping levels?" Grouping can be useful in complex reports, but we do not need any groupings for this simple report that lists customers. Instead, we can use the default nongrouped column listing, so click the **Next** button.
6. As shown in Figure AW-1-42, we are now asked, "What sort order do you want for your records?" The most useful sorting order in this case is by last name, with sorting by first name

Choosing the Sort Order

The **sort field 1** drop-down list arrow button

Select **LastName** from the drop-down list

The **Next** button

FIGURE AW-1-43

The Finished Report

The **Wallingford Motors Customer Report** print preview window

The **Reports** section of the Navigation Pane

The **Wallingford Motors Customer Report** object

The report is sorted by LastName and then FirstName

The **Close** button

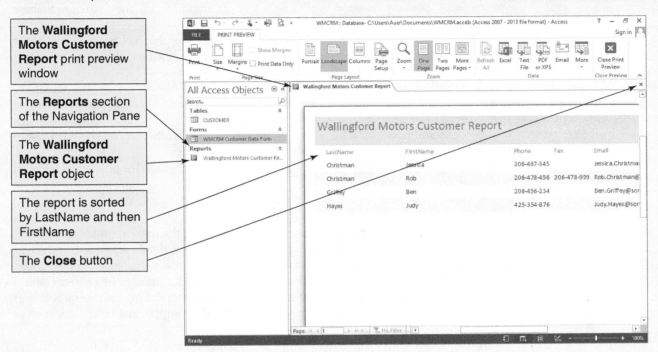

for identical last names. For both sorts, we want an *ascending* sort (from A to Z). Click the **sort field 1** drop-down list arrow and select **LastName**. Leave the sort order button set to **Ascending**.

7. Click the **sort field 2** drop-down list arrow and select **FirstName**, leave the sort order button set to **Ascending**, and click the **Next** button.

8. We are now asked, "How would you like to lay out your report?" We will use the default setting of **Tabular Layout**, but click the **Landscape Orientation** radio button to change the report orientation to landscape. Click the **Next** button.

9. Finally, when we are asked, "What title do you want for your report?" we edit the report title to read **Wallingford Motors Customer Report**. Leave the **Preview the report** radio button selected. Click the **Finish** button. As shown in Figure AW-1-43, the completed report appears in a tabbed document window, a Reports section has been added to the Navigation Pane, and the Wallingford Motors Customer Report object appears in this section.

10. Click the **Close** button in the upper-right corner of the document window.

Closing a Database and Exiting Microsoft Access 2013

We have finished all the work we need to do in this chapter's "The Access Workbench." We have learned how to create a database; how to build database tables, forms, and reports; and how to populate a table with data by using Datasheet view and a form. We finish by closing the database and Microsoft Access.

Closing the WMCRM Database and Exiting Microsoft Access 2013

1. To close WMCRM: Database and exit Microsoft Access 2013, click the **Close** button in the upper-right corner of the Microsoft Access 2013 window.

(Continued)

SUMMARY

The importance of database processing increases every day because databases are used in information systems everywhere—and increasingly so. The purpose of this book is to teach you essential database concepts and to help you get started using and learning database technology.

The purpose of a database is to help people keep track of things. Lists can be used for this purpose, but if a list involves more than one theme modification problems will occur when data are inserted, updated, or deleted.

Relational databases store data in the form of tables. Almost always, the tables are designed so that each table stores data about a single theme. Lists that involve multiple themes need to be broken up and stored in multiple tables, one for each theme. When this is done, a column needs to be added to link the tables to each other so that the relationship from a row in one table to a row in another table can be shown.

Structured Query Language (SQL) is an international language for processing tables in relational databases. You can use SQL to join together and display data stored in separate tables, create new tables, and query data from tables in many ways. You can also use SQL to insert, update, and delete data.

The components of a database system are the database, the database management system (DBMS), one or more database applications, and users. A database is a self-describing collection of related records. A relational database is a self-describing collection of related tables. A database is self-describing because it contains a description of its contents within itself, which is known as metadata. Tables are related by storing linking values of a common column. The contents of a database are user data; metadata; supporting structures, such as indexes; and sometimes application metadata.

A database management system (DBMS) is a large, complicated program used to create, process, and administer a database. DBMS products are almost always licensed from software vendors. Specific functions of a DBMS are summarized in Figure 1-18.

The functions of database applications are to create and process forms, to process user queries, and to create and process reports. Application programs also execute specific application logic and control the application. Users provide data and data changes and read data in forms, queries, and reports.

DBMS products for personal database systems provide functionality for application development and database management. They hide considerable complexity, but at a cost: Requirements unanticipated by DBMS features cannot be readily implemented. Enterprise-class database systems include multiple applications that might be written in multiple languages. These systems may support hundreds or thousands of users.

An example of a personal database system is Microsoft Access 2013, which is discussed in this book in chapter sections titled "The Access Workbench." These sections cover all the basic knowledge that you need to create and use databases in Microsoft Access 2013.

Examples of enterprise-class DBMS products include Microsoft SQL Server 2014, Oracle MySQL 5.6, and Oracle Database Express Edition 11*g* Release 2. Information about these DBMS products is provided in Appendix A, "Getting Started with Microsoft SQL Server 2014 Express Edition"; Appendix B, "Getting Started with Oracle Database Express Edition 11*g* Release 2"; and Appendix C, "Getting Started with Oracle MySQL 5.6 Community Server."

NoSQL refers to nonrelational databases used in Web 2.0 applications such as Facebook and Twitter. NoSQL databases are discussed in Chapter 8 and Appendix K, "Big Data."

KEY TERMS

concurrency
database
database application
database management system
  (DBMS)
delete
enterprise-class database system
ID column
insert
list
metadata
Microsoft SQL Server 2014
Microsoft SQL Server 2014 Express
  Edition

Microsoft SQL Server 2014
  Management Studio
modification action
modification problem
MySQL Workbench
nonrelational database
NoSQL
null value
Oracle Database Express
  Edition 11*g* Release 2 Express
  Edition
Oracle MySQL 5.6
  Community Server
Oracle SQL Developer

personal database system
referential integrity
  constraint
related tables
relational database
relational model
self-describing
Structured Query Language
  (SQL)
table
update
user
Web 2.0

REVIEW QUESTIONS

1.1 Why is the study of database technology important?

1.2 What is the purpose of this book?

1.3 Describe the purpose of a database.

1.4 What is a modification problem? What are the three possible types of modification problems?

1.5 Figure 1-30 shows a list that is used by a veterinary office. Describe three modification problems that are likely to occur when using this list.

1.6 Name the two themes in the list in Figure 1-30.

1.7 What is an ID column?

1.8 Break the list in Figure 1-30 into two tables, each with data for a single theme. Assume that owners have a unique phone number but that pets have no unique column. Create an ID column for pets like the one created for customers and courses for the Art Course database tables in Figure 1-10.

1.9 Show how the tables you created for question 1.8 solve the problems you described in question 1.5.

1.10 What does SQL stand for, and what purpose does it serve?

1.11 Another version of the list used by the veterinary office is shown in Figure 1-31. How many themes does this list have? What are they?

FIGURE 1-30

The Veterinary Office List—Version One

	A	B	C	D	E	F	G	H
1	PetName	PetType	PetBreed	PetDOB	OwnerLastName	OwnerFirstName	OwnerPhone	OwnerEmail
2	King	Dog	Std. Poodle	27-Feb-12	Downs	Marsha	201-823-5467	Marsha.Downs@somewhere.com
3	Teddy	Cat	Cashmier	1-Feb-11	James	Richard	201-735-9812	Richard.James@somewhere.com
4	Fido	Dog	Std. Poodle	17-Jul-13	Downs	Marsha	201-823-5467	Marsha.Downs@somewhere.com
5	AJ	Dog	Collie Mix	5-May-13	Frier	Liz	201-823-6578	Liz.Frier@somewhere.com
6	Cedro	Cat	Unknown	6-Jun-10	James	Richard	201-735-9812	Richard.James@somewhere.com
7	Woolley	Cat	Unknown	???	James	Richard	201-735-9812	Richard.James@somewhere.com
8	Buster	Dog	Border Collie	11-Dec-09	Trent	Miles	201-634-7865	Miles.Trent@somewhere.com
9	Jedah	Cat	Abyssinian	1-Jul-06	Evans	Hilary	210-634-2345	Hilary.Evans@somewhere.com

FIGURE 1-31

The Veterinary Office List—Version Two

	A	B	C	D	E	F	G	H	I	J	K
1	PetName	PetType	PetBreed	PetDOB	OwnerLastName	OwnerFirstName	OwnerPhone	OwnerEmail	Service	Date	Charge
2	King	Dog	Std. Poodle	27-Feb-12	Downs	Marsha	201-823-5467	Marsha.Downs@somewhere.com	Ear Infection	17-Aug-14	$ 65.00
3	Teddy	Cat	Cashmier	1-Feb-11	James	Richard	201-735-9812	Richard.James@somewhere.com	Nail Clip	5-Sep-14	$ 27.50
4	Filo	Dog	Std. Poodle	17-Jul-13	Downs	Marsha	201-823-5467	Marsha.Downs@somewhere.com			
5	AJ	Dog	Collie Mix	5-May-13	Frier	Liz	201-823-6578	Liz.Frier@somewhere.com	One year shots	5-May-14	$ 42.50
6	Cedro	Cat	Unknown	6-Jun-10	James	Richard	201-735-9812	Richard.James@somewhere.com	Nail Clip	5-Sep-14	$ 27.50
7	Woolley	Cat	Unknown	???	James	Richard	201-735-9812	Richard.James@somewhere.com	Skin Infection	3-Oct-14	$ 35.00
8	Buster	Dog	Border Collie	11-Dec-09	Trent	Miles	201-634-7865	Miles.Trent@somewhere.com	Laceration Repair	5-Oct-14	$ 127.00
9	Jedah	Cat	Abyssinian	1-Jul-06	Evans	Hilary	210-634-2345	Hilary.Evans@somewhere.com	Booster Shots	4-Nov-14	$ 111.00

1.12 Break the list in Figure 1-31 into tables, each with a single theme. Create ID columns as you think necessary.

1.13 Show how the tables you created for question 1.12 solve the three problems of lists identified in this chapter.

1.14 Describe in your own words and illustrate with tables how relationships are represented in a relational database.

1.15 Name the four components of a database system.

1.16 Define the term *database*.

1.17 Why do you think it is important for a database to be self-describing?

1.18 List the components of a database.

1.19 Define the term *metadata*, and give some examples of metadata.

1.20 Describe the use of an index.

1.21 Define the term *application metadata*, and give some examples of application metadata.

1.22 What is the purpose of a DBMS?

1.23 List the specific functions of a DBMS.

1.24 Define the term *referential integrity constraint.* Give an example of a referential integrity constraint for the tables you created for question 1.8.

1.25 Explain the difference between a DBMS and a database.

1.26 List the functions of a database application.

1.27 Explain the differences between a personal database system and an enterprise-class database system.

1.28 What is the advantage of hiding complexity from the user of a DBMS? What is the disadvantage?

1.29 Summarize the differences between the database systems in Figure 1-23 and Figure 1-26.

1.30 What is a *NoSQL* database? What are *Web 2.0* applications, and why can't these applications use a relational database?

EXERCISES

The following spreadsheets form a set of named spreadsheets with the indicated column headings. Use these spreadsheets to answer exercises 1.31 through 1.33.

A. Name of spreadsheet: EQUIPMENT
   Column headings:
   Number, Description, AcquisitionDate, AcquisitionPrice

B. Name of spreadsheet: COMPANY
   Column headings:
   Name, IndustryCode, Gross Sales, OfficerName, OfficerTitle

C. **Name of spreadsheet:** COMPANY
   Column headings:
   Name, IndustryCode, Gross Sales, NameOfPresident

D. **Name of spreadsheet:** COMPUTER
   Column headings:
   SerialNumber, Make, Model, DiskType, DiskCapacity

E. **Name of spreadsheet:** PERSON
   Column headings:
   Name, DateOfHire, DeptName, DeptManager, ProjectID, NumHours,
   ProjectManager

1.31   For each of the spreadsheets provided, indicate the number of themes you think
the spreadsheet includes and give an appropriate name for each theme. For some
of them, the answer may depend on the assumptions you make. In these cases, state
your assumptions.

1.32   For any spreadsheet that has more than one theme, show at least one modification
problem that will occur when inserting, updating, or deleting data.

1.33   For any spreadsheet that has more than one theme, break up the columns into tables such that each table has a single theme. Add ID columns if necessary, and add
a linking column (or columns) to maintain the relationship between the themes.

ACCESS WORKBENCH KEY TERMS

AutoNumber (data type)
character (data type)
customer relationship management
  (CRM) system
data entry form
datasheet
Datasheet view
form
Form Wizard
key
long text (data type)
memo (data type)
Microsoft Office Fluent user interface
Navigation Pane
Navigation Pane drop-down list

Navigation Pane drop-down list
  button
number (data type)
numeric (data type)
object
primary key
record navigation buttons
remarks
Report Wizard
required
short text (data type)
Shutter Bar Open/Close button
surrogate key
text (data type)
type

ACCESS WORKBENCH EXERCISES

The Wedgewood Pacific Corporation (WPC), founded in 1957 in Seattle, Washington,
has grown into an internationally recognized organization. The company is located
in two buildings. One building houses the Administration, Accounting, Finance, and
Human Resources departments, and the second houses the Production, Marketing,
and Information Systems departments. The company database contains data about

(Continued)

FIGURE 1-32

Database Column Characteristics for the EMPLOYEE Table

EMPLOYEE

Column Name	type	Key	Required	Remarks
EmployeeNumber	AutoNumber	Primary Key	Yes	Surrogate Key
FirstName	Text (25)	No	Yes	
LastName	Text (25)	No	Yes	
Department	Text (35)	No	Yes	
Phone	Text (12)	No	No	
Email	Text (100)	No	Yes	

employees; departments; projects; assets, such as computer equipment; and other aspects of company operations.

A.   Create a Microsoft Access database named WPC in a Microsoft Access file named WPC.accdb.

B.   Figure 1-32 shows the column characteristics for the WPC EMPLOYEE table. Using the column characteristics, create the EMPLOYEE table in the WPC database.

C.   Figure 1-33 shows the data for the WPC EMPLOYEE table. Using Datasheet view, enter the data for the first three rows of data in the EMPLOYEE table shown in Figure 1-33 into your EMPLOYEE table.

FIGURE 1-33

Wedgewood Pacific Corporation EMPLOYEE Data

Employee Number	FirstName	LastName	Department	Phone	Email
[AutoNumber]	Mary	Jacobs	Administration	360-285-8110	Mary.Jacobs@WPC.com
[AutoNumber]	Rosalie	Jackson	Administration	360-285-8120	Rosalie.Jackson@WPC.com
[AutoNumber]	Richard	Bandalone	Legal	360-285-8210	Richard.Bandalone@WPC.com
[AutoNumber]	Tom	Caruthers	Accounting	360-285-8310	Tom.Caruthers@WPC.com
[AutoNumber]	Heather	Jones	Accounting	360-285-8320	Heather.Jones@WPC.com
[AutoNumber]	Mary	Abernathy	Finance	360-285-8410	Mary.Abernathy@WPC.com
[AutoNumber]	George	Smith	Human Resources	360-285-8510	George.Smith@WPC.com
[AutoNumber]	Tom	Jackson	Production	360-287-8610	Tom.Jackson@WPC.com
[AutoNumber]	George	Jones	Production	360-287-8620	George.Jones@WPC.com
[AutoNumber]	Ken	Numoto	Marketing	360-287-8710	Ken.Numoto@WPC.com
[AutoNumber]	James	Nestor	InfoSystems		James.Nestor@WPC.com
[AutoNumber]	Rick	Brown	InfoSystems	360-287-8820	Rick.Brown@WPC.com

D. Create a data input form for the EMPLOYEE table and name it WPC Employee Data Form. Make any adjustments necessary to the form so that all data display properly. Use this form to enter the rest of the data in the EMPLOYEE table shown in Figure 1-33 into your EMPLOYEE table.

E. Create a report named Wedgewood Pacific Corporation Employee Report that presents the data contained in your EMPLOYEE table sorted first by employee last name and second by employee first name. Make any adjustments necessary to the report so that all headings and data display properly. Print a copy of this report.

SAN JUAN SAILBOAT CHARTERS CASE QUESTIONS

San Juan Sailboat Charters (SJSBC) is an agency that leases (charters) sailboats. SJSBC does not own the boats. Instead, SJSBC leases boats on behalf of boat owners who want to earn income from their boats when they are not using the boats themselves, and SJSBC charges the owners a fee for this service. SJSBC specializes in boats that can be used for multiday or weekly charters. The smallest sailboat available is 28 feet in length, and the largest is 51 feet in length.

Each sailboat is fully equipped at the time it is leased. Most of the equipment is provided at the time of the charter. The majority of the equipment is provided by the owners, but some is provided by SJSBC. Some of the owner-provided equipment is attached to the boat, such as radios, compasses, depth indicators and other instrumentation, stoves, and refrigerators. Other owner-provided equipment is not physically attached to the boat, such as sails, lines, anchors, dinghies, life preservers, and equipment in the cabin (dishes, silverware, cooking utensils, bedding, and so on). SJSBC provides consumable supplies such as charts, navigation books, tide and current tables, soap, dish towels, toilet paper, and similar items. The consumable supplies are treated as equipment by SJSBC for tracking and accounting purposes.

Keeping track of equipment is an important part of SJSBC's responsibilities. Much of the equipment is expensive, and those items not physically attached to the boat can be easily damaged, lost, or stolen. SJSBC holds the customers responsible for all of the boat's equipment during the period of their charter.

SJSBC likes to keep accurate records of its customers and charters, and customers are required to keep a log during each charter. Some itineraries and weather conditions are more dangerous than others, and the data from these logs provides information about the customer experience. This information is useful for marketing purposes, as well as for evaluating a customer's ability to handle a particular boat and itinerary.

Sailboats need maintenance (two definitions of *boat* are: (1) "break out another thousand" and (2) "a hole in the water into which one pours money"). SJSBC is required by its contracts with the boat owners to keep accurate records of all maintenance activities and costs.

A. Create a sample list of owners and boats. Your list will be similar in structure to that in Figure 1-30, but it will concern owners and boats rather than owners and pets. Your list should include, at a minimum, owner name, phone, and billing address, as well as boat name, make, model, and length.

B. Describe modification problems that are likely to occur if SJSBC attempts to maintain the list in a spreadsheet.

C. Split the list into tables such that each has only one theme. Create appropriate ID columns. Use a linking column to represent the relationship between a boat and an owner. Demonstrate that the modification problems you identified in part B have been eliminated.

D. Create a sample list of owners, boats, and charters. Your list will be similar to that in Figure 1-31. Your list should include the data items from part A as well as the charter date, charter customer, and the amount charged for each charter.

E. Illustrate modification problems that are likely to occur if SJSBC attempts to maintain the list from part D in a spreadsheet.

F. Split the list from part D into tables such that each has only one theme. Create appropriate ID columns. Use linking columns to represent relationships. Demonstrate that the modification problems you identified in part E have been eliminated.

GARDEN GLORY PROJECT QUESTIONS

Garden Glory is a partnership that provides gardening and yard maintenance services to individuals and organizations. Garden Glory is owned by two partners. They employ two office administrators and a number of full- and part-time gardeners. Garden Glory will provide one-time garden services, but it specializes in ongoing service and maintenance. Many of its customers have multiple buildings, apartments, and rental houses that require gardening and lawn maintenance services.

A. Create a sample list of owners and properties. Your list will be similar in structure to that in Figure 1-30, but it will concern owners and properties rather than owners and pets. Your list should include, at a minimum, owner name, phone, and billing address, as well as property name, type, and address.

B. Describe modification problems that are likely to occur if Garden Glory attempts to maintain the list in a spreadsheet.

C. Split the list into tables such that each has only one theme. Create appropriate ID columns. Use a linking column to represent the relationship between a property and an owner. Demonstrate that the modification problems you identified in part B have been eliminated.

D. Create a sample list of owners, properties, and services. Your list will be similar to that in Figure 1-31. Your list should include the data items from part A as well as the date, description, and amount charged for each service.

E. Illustrate modification problems that are likely to occur if Garden Glory attempts to maintain the list from part D in a spreadsheet.

F. Split the list from part D into tables such that each has only one theme. Create appropriate ID columns. Use linking columns to represent relationships. Demonstrate that the modification problems you identified in part E have been eliminated.

JAMES RIVER JEWELRY PROJECT QUESTIONS

The James River Jewelry project questions are available in online Appendix D, which can be downloaded from the textbook's Web site: **www.pearsonhighered.com/kroenke**.

THE QUEEN ANNE CURIOSITY SHOP PROJECT QUESTIONS

The Queen Anne Curiosity Shop sells both antiques and current-production household items that complement or are useful with the antiques. For example, the store sells antique dining room tables and new tablecloths. The antiques are purchased from both individuals and wholesalers, and the new items are purchased from distributors. The store's customers include individuals, owners of bed-and-breakfast operations, and local interior designers who work with both individuals and small businesses. The antiques are unique, although some multiple items, such as dining room chairs, may be available as a set (sets are never broken). The new items are not unique, and an item may be reordered if it is out of stock. New items are also available in various sizes and colors (for example, a particular style of tablecloth may be available in several sizes and in a variety of colors).

A. Create a sample list of purchased inventory items and vendors and a second list of customers and sales. The first list should include inventory data, such as a description, manufacturer and model (if available), item cost, and vendor identification and contact data you think should be recorded. The second list should include customer data you think would be important to The Queen Anne Curiosity Shop, along with typical sales data.

B. Describe problems that are likely to occur when inserting, updating, and deleting data in these spreadsheets.

C. Attempt to combine the two lists you created in part A into a single list. What problems occur as you try to do this?

D. Split the spreadsheets you created in part A into tables such that each has only one theme. Create appropriate ID columns.

E. Explain how the tables in your answer to part D will eliminate the problems you identified in part B.

F. What is the relationship between the tables you created from the first spreadsheet and the tables you created from the second spreadsheet? If your set of tables does not already contain this relationship, how will you add it into your set of tables?

CHAPTER 2 The Relational Model

CHAPTER OBJECTIVES

- Learn the conceptual foundation of the relational model
- Understand how relations differ from nonrelational tables
- Learn basic relational terminology
- Learn the meaning and importance of keys, foreign keys, and related terminology
- Understand how foreign keys represent relationships
- Learn the purpose and use of surrogate keys
- Learn the meaning of functional dependencies
- Learn to apply a process for normalizing relations

This chapter explains the relational model, the single most important standard in database processing today. This model, which was developed and published in 1970 by Edgar Frank Codd, commonly referred to as E. F. Codd,[1] then an employee at IBM, was founded on the theory of relational algebra. The model has since found widespread practical application, and today it is used for the design and implementation of every commercial relational database worldwide. This chapter describes the conceptual foundation of this model.

---

[1]E. F. Codd, "A Relational Model of Data for Large Shared Databanks," *Communications of the ACM* (June 1970): 377–387. A downloadable copy of this paper in PDF format is available at **http://dl.acm.org/citation.cfm?id=362685**

RELATIONS

Chapter 1 states that databases help people keep track of things and that relational DBMS products store data in the form of tables. Here we need to clarify and refine those statements. First, the formal name for a "thing" that is being tracked is **entity**, which is defined as something of importance to the user that needs to be represented in the database. Further, it is not entirely correct to say that DBMS products store data in tables. DBMS products store data in the form of relations, which are a special type of table. Specifically, a **relation** is a two-dimensional **table** consisting of **rows** and **columns** that has the following characteristics:

1. Each row of the table holds data that pertain to some entity or a portion of some entity.
2. Each column of the table contains data that represent an attribute of the entity. For example, in an EMPLOYEE relation each row would contain data about a particular employee and each column would contain data that represented an attribute of that employee, such as LastName, Phone, or EmailAddress.
3. The cells of the table must hold a single value, and thus no repeating elements are allowed in a cell.
4. All the entries in any column must be of the same kind. For example, if the third column in the first row of a table contains EmployeeNumber, then the third column in all other rows must contain EmployeeNumber as well.
5. Each column must have a unique name.
6. The order of the columns within the table is unimportant.
7. The order of the rows is unimportant.
8. The set of data values in each row must be unique—no two rows in the table may hold identical sets of data values.

The characteristics of a relation are summarized in Figure 2-1.

A Sample Relation and Two Nonrelations

Figure 2-2 shows a sample EMPLOYEE table. Consider this table in light of the characteristics discussed earlier. First, each row is about an EMPLOYEE entity, and each column represents an attribute of employees, so those two conditions are met. Each cell has only one value, and all entries in a column are of the same kind. Column names are unique, and we could change the order of either the columns or the rows and not lose any information.

FIGURE 2-1

Characteristics of a Relation

```
1. Rows contain data about an entity
2. Columns contain data about attributes of the entity
3. Cells of the table hold a single value
4. All entries in a column are of the same kind
5. Each column has a unique name
6. The order of the columns is unimportant
7. The order of the rows is unimportant
8. No two rows may hold identical sets of data values
```

FIGURE 2-2

Sample EMPLOYEE Relation

EmployeeNumber	FirstName	LastName	Department	Email	Phone
100	Jerry	Johnson	Accounting	JJ@somewhere.com	834-1101
200	Mary	Abernathy	Finance	MA@somewhere.com	834-2101
300	Liz	Smathers	Finance	LS@somewhere.com	834-2102
400	Tom	Caruthers	Accounting	TC@somewhere.com	834-1102
500	Tom	Jackson	Production	TJ@somewhere.com	834-4101
600	Eleanore	Caldera	Legal	EC@somewhere.com	834-3101
700	Richard	Bandalone	Legal	RB@somewhere.com	834-3102

FIGURE 2-3

Nonrelational Table—
Multiple Entries per
Cell

EmployeeNumber	FirstName	LastName	Department	Email	Phone
100	Jerry	Johnson	Accounting	JJ@somewhere.com	834-1101
200	Mary	Abernathy	Finance	MA@somewhere.com	834-2101
300	Liz	Smathers	Finance	LS@somewhere.com	834-2102
400	Tom	Caruthers	Accounting	TC@somewhere.com	834-1102, 834-1191, 834-1192
500	Tom	Jackson	Production	TJ@somewhere.com	834-4101
600	Eleanore	Caldera	Legal	EC@somewhere.com	834-3101
700	Richard	Bandalone	Legal	RB@somewhere.com	834-3102, 834-3191

FIGURE 2-4

Nonrelational Table—
Order of Rows Matters
and Kind of Column
Entries Differs in Email

EmployeeNumber	FirstName	LastName	Department	Email	Phone
100	Jerry	Johnson	Accounting	JJ@somewhere.com	834-1101
200	Mary	Abernathy	Finance	MA@somewhere.com	834-2101
300	Liz	Smathers	Finance	LS@somewhere.com	834-2102
400	Tom	Caruthers	Accounting	TC@somewhere.com	834-1102
				Fax:	834-9911
				Home:	723-8765
500	Tom	Jackson	Production	TJ@somewhere.com	834-4101
600	Eleanore	Caldera	Legal	EC@somewhere.com	834-3101
				Fax:	834-9912
				Home:	723-7654
700	Richard	Bandalone	Legal	RB@somewhere.com	834-3102

Finally, no two rows are identical—each row holds a different set of data values. Because this table meets all requirements of the definition of *relation*, we can classify it as a relation.

Now consider the tables shown in Figures 2-3 and 2-4. Neither of these tables is a relation. The EMPLOYEE table in Figure 2-3 is not a relation because the Phone column has cells with multiple entries. For example, Tom Caruthers has three values for phone, and Richard Bandalone has two values. Multiple entries per cell are not permitted in a relation.

The table in Figure 2-4 is not a relation for two reasons. First, the order of the rows is important. Because the row under Tom Caruthers contains his fax number, we may lose track of the correspondence between his name and his fax number if we rearrange the rows. The second reason this table is not a relation is that not all values in the Email column are of the same kind. Some of the values are email addresses, and others are types of phone numbers.

Although each cell can have only one value, that value can vary in length. Figure 2-5 shows the table from Figure 2-2 with an additional variable-length Comment attribute. Even though a comment can be lengthy and varies in length from row to row, there is still only one comment per cell. Thus, the table in Figure 2-5 is a relation.

FIGURE 2-5

Relation with Variable-
Length Column Values

EmployeeNumber	FirstName	LastName	Department	Email	Phone	Comment
100	Jerry	Johnson	Accounting	JJ@somewhere.com	834-1101	Joined the Accounting Department March after completing his MBA. Will take the CPA exam this fall.
200	Mary	Abernathy	Finance	MA@somewhere.com	834-2101	
300	Liz	Smathers	Finance	LS@somewhere.com	834-2102	
400	Tom	Caruthers	Accounting	TC@somewhere.com	834-1102	
500	Tom	Jackson	Production	TJ@somewhere.com	834-4101	
600	Eleanore	Caldera	Legal	EC@somewhere.com	834-3101	
700	Richard	Bandalone	Legal	RB@somewhere.com	834-3102	Is a full-time consultant to legal on a retainer basis.

A Note on Presenting Relation Structures

Throughout this book, when we write out the relation structure of a relation that we are discussing, we use the following format:

RELATION_NAME (Column01, Column02, ..., LastColumn)

The relation name is written first, and it is written in all capital (uppercase) letters (for example, EMPLOYEE), and the name is singular, not plural (EMPLOYEE, not EMPLOYEES). If the relation name is a combination of two or more words, we join the words with an underscore (for example, EMPLOYEE_PROJECT_ASSIGNMENT). Column names are contained in parentheses and are written with an initial capital letter followed by lowercase letters (for example, Department). If the column name is a combination of two or more words, the first letter of each word is capitalized (for example, EmployeeNumber and LastName). Thus, the EMPLOYEE relation shown in Figure 2-2 would be written as:

EMPLOYEE (EmployeeNumber, FirstName, LastName, Department, Email, Phone)

> **BTW**
>
> Relation structures, such as the one shown earlier, are part of a database schema. A **database schema** is the design on which a database and its associated applications are built.

A Note on Terminology

In the database world, people generally use the terms *table* and *relation* interchangeably. Accordingly, from now on this book does the same. Thus, any time we use the term *table* we mean a table that meets the characteristics required for a relation. Keep in mind, however, that, strictly speaking, some tables are not relations.

Sometimes, especially in traditional data processing, people use the term **file** instead of *table*. When they do so, they use the term **record** for *row* and the term **field** for *column*. To further confound the issue, database theoreticians sometimes use yet another set of terms: Although they do call a table a *relation*, they call a *row* a **tuple** (rhymes with *couple*) and a *column* an **attribute**. These three sets of terminology are summarized in Figure 2-6.

To make matters even more confusing, people often mix up these sets of terms. It is not unusual to hear someone refer to a relation that has rows and fields. As long as you know what is intended, this mixing of terms is not important.

We should discuss one other source of confusion. According to Figure 2-1, a table that has duplicate rows is not a relation. However, in practice this condition is often ignored. Particularly when manipulating relations with a DBMS, we may end up with a table that

FIGURE 2-6

Equivalent Sets of Terms

Table	Row	Column
File	Record	Field
Relation	Tuple	Attribute

has duplicate rows. To make that table a relation, we should eliminate the duplicates. On a large table, however, checking for duplication can be time-consuming. Therefore, the default behavior for DBMS products is not to check for duplicate rows. Hence, in practice, tables might exist with duplicate (nonunique) rows that are still called relations. You will see examples of this situation in the next chapter.

TYPES OF KEYS

A **key** is one or more columns of a relation that is used to identify a row. A key can be **unique** or **nonunique**. For example, for the EMPLOYEE relation in Figure 2-2 EmployeeNumber is a *unique key* because a value of EmployeeNumber identifies a unique row. Thus, a query to display all employees having an EmployeeNumber of 200 will produce a single row. In contrast, Department is a *nonunique key*. It is a key because it is used to identify a row, but it is nonunique because a value of Department potentially identifies more than one row. Thus, a query to display all rows having a Department value of Accounting will produce several rows.

From the data in Figure 2-2, it appears that EmployeeNumber, LastName, and Email are all unique identifiers. However, to decide whether this is true database developers must do more than examine sample data. Instead, they must ask the users or other subject-matter experts whether a certain column is unique. The column LastName is an example where this is important. It might turn out that the sample data just happen to have unique values for LastName. The users, however, might say that LastName is not always unique.

Composite Keys

A key that contains two or more attributes is called a **composite key**. For example, suppose that we are looking for a unique key for the EMPLOYEE relation, and the users say that although LastName is not unique, the combination of LastName and Department is unique. Thus, for some reason the users know that two people with the same last name will never work in the same department. Two Johnsons, for example, will never work in accounting. If that is the case, then the combination (LastName, Department) is a unique composite key.

Alternatively, the users may know that the combination (LastName, Department) is not unique but that the combination (FirstName, LastName, Department) is unique. The latter combination, then, is a composite key with three attributes.

BTW

Composite keys, like one-column keys, can be unique or nonunique.

Candidate and Primary Keys

Candidate keys are keys that uniquely identify each row in a relation. Candidate keys can be single-column keys, or they can be composite keys. The **primary key** is the candidate key that is chosen as the key that the DBMS will use to uniquely identify each row in a relation. For example, suppose that we have the following EMPLOYEE relation:

EMPLOYEE (EmployeeNumber, FirstName, LastName, Department, Email, Phone)

The users tell us that EmployeeNumber is a unique key, that Email is a unique key, and that the composite key (FirstName, LastName, DepartmentName) is a unique key. Therefore, we have three candidate keys. When designing the database, we choose one of the candidate keys to be the primary key. In this case, for example, we use EmployeeNumber as the primary key.

BTW

It may help you to understand why the unique keys that could be used as the main identifier for the relation are referred to as candidate keys if you think of them as the "candidates" in the running to be elected "primary key"—but remember that only one candidate will win the election. Any "losing" candidate keys will still be present in the relation, and each will be known as an **alternate key**.

The primary key is important not only because it can be used to identify unique rows, but also because it can be used to represent rows in relationships. Although we did not indicate it in the Art Course Database tables in Figure 1-10 in Chapter 1, CustomerID was the primary key of CUSTOMER. As such, we used CustomerID to represent the relationship between CUSTOMER and ENROLLMENT by placing CustomerID as a column in the ENROLLMENT table to create the link between the two tables. In addition, many DBMS products use values of the primary key to organize storage for the relation. They also build indexes and other special structures for fast retrieval of rows using primary key values.

In this book, we indicate primary keys by underlining them. Because EmployeeNumber is the primary key of EMPLOYEE, we write the EMPLOYEE relation as:

EMPLOYEE (<u>EmployeeNumber</u>, FirstName, LastName, Department, Email, Phone)

Each DBMS program has its own way of creating and indicating a primary key. In Chapter 1's section of "The Access Workbench," we briefly discussed primary keys and explained how to set a primary key in Microsoft Access 2013. Figure 2-7 shows the CUSTOMER table

FIGURE 2-7

Defining a Primary Key in Microsoft Access 2013

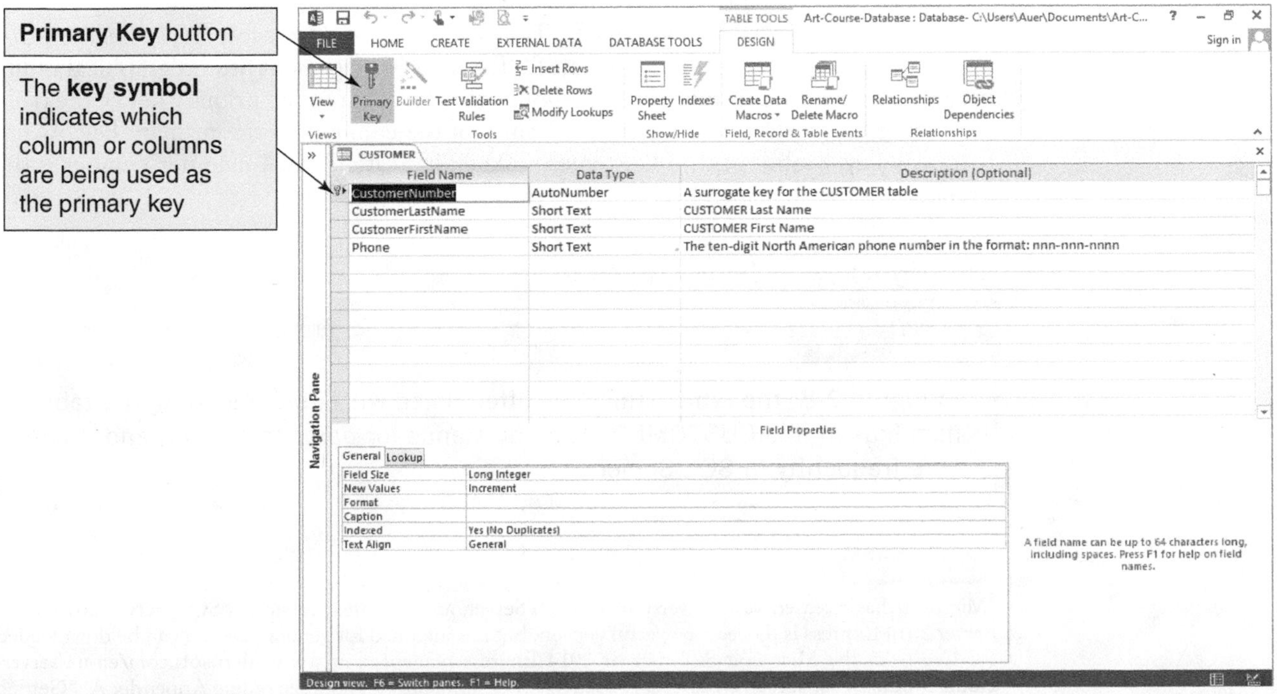

FIGURE 2-8

Defining a Primary Key in Microsoft SQL Server 2014

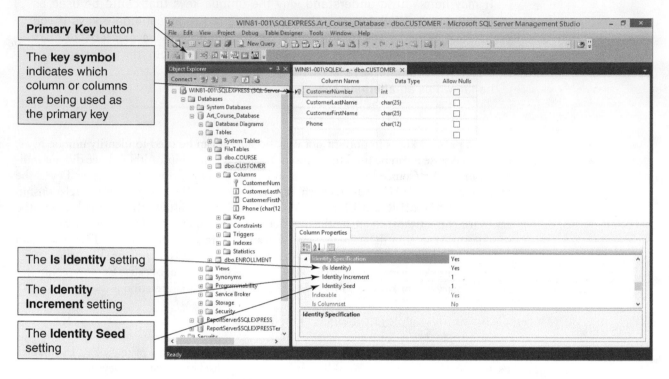

from the Art Course database in Figure 1-10 in the Microsoft Access table Design view. In table Design view, we can spot the primary key of the table by finding the key symbol next to the names of the columns in the primary key. In this case, a key symbol is located next to CustomerNumber, which means that the developer has defined CustomerNumber as the primary key for this table.

Figure 2-8 shows the same CUSTOMER table in Microsoft SQL Server 2014 Express,[2] as it appears in the Microsoft SQL Server Management Studio graphical utility program. This display is more complex, but again we can spot the primary key of the table by finding the key symbol next to the names of the columns in the primary key. Again, there is a key symbol next to CustomerNumber, indicating that CustomerNumber is the primary key for this table.

BTW

In Figure 2-8, the table names are often listed with *dbo* preceding the table name, as in dbo.CUSTOMER. The dbo stands for *database owner*, and it occurs frequently in SQL Server.

---

[2]Microsoft has released various versions of SQL Server, and the latest version is SQL Server 2014. SQL Server 2014 Express is the least powerful version, but it is intended for general use and can be downloaded for free from the Microsoft SQL Server 2014 Express homepage at **www.microsoft.com/en-us/server-cloud/products/sql-server/#fbid=LO4TSseuGs9**. For more information, see online Appendix A, "Getting Started with Microsoft SQL Server 2014 Express Edition."

FIGURE 2-9

Defining a Primary Key in Oracle Database Express Edition 11*g* Release 2

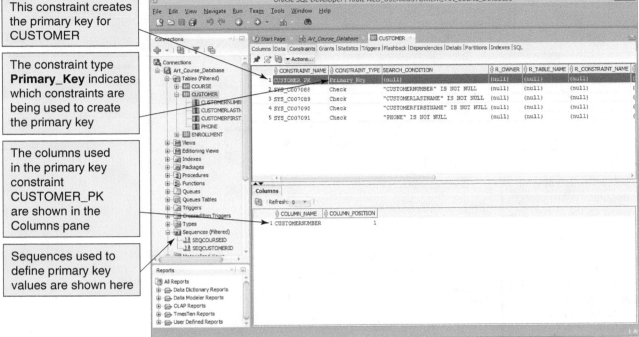

Figure 2-9 shows the same CUSTOMER table in Oracle's Oracle Database Express Edition 11*g* Release 2,[3] as seen in the Oracle SQL Developer graphical utility program. This display is more complex than Microsoft Access, but we can spot the primary key of the table by finding the row with the term Primary_Key in the CONSTRAINT_TYPE column, and then selecting that row. When we do so, the set of primary key columns is displayed in the tabbed Columns pane.

Figure 2-10 shows the same CUSTOMER table in Oracle's MySQL 5.6 Community Server,[4] as seen in the MySQL Workbench graphical utility program. This display is more

---

[3]Originally just referred to as *Oracle*, the database product is now known as Oracle Database because Oracle Corporation has grown far beyond its database product roots and now owns and sells a large range of products. These can be seen at **www.oracle.com**. As of this writing, Oracle Database 12c is the latest production version. The freely downloadable Oracle Database Express Edition 11*g* Release 2 is available at **www.oracle.com/technetwork/database/database-technologies/express-edition/downloads/index.html?ssSourceSiteId=ocomen**. Oracle Database Express Edition 11*g* Release 2 is an enterprise-class DBMS and, as such, is much more complex than Microsoft Access. For more information, see online Appendix B, "Getting Started with Oracle Database Express Edition 11*g* Release 2."

[4]On February 26, 2008, Sun Microsystems acquired MySQL from MySQL AB. On April 29, 2009, Oracle Corporation made an offer to buy Sun Microsystems, and on January 27, 2010, Oracle completed its acquisition of Sun Microsystems. For more details, see **www.oracle.com/us/sun/index.htm**. This makes Oracle the owner of both the Oracle Database and the MySQL DBMS. As of this writing, MySQL 5.6 is the latest production version of the popular MySQL DBMS. The free MySQL Community Server edition and the MySQL Workbench can be downloaded from the MySQL Web site at **http://dev.mysql.com/downloads/**. If you are running a Microsoft Windows OS, you should download and use the MySQL Installer for Windows available at **http://dev.mysql.com/downloads/windows/installer/**. Like SQL Server 2014, MySQL is an enterprise-class DBMS and, as such, is much more complex than Microsoft Access. Also like SQL Server 2014, MySQL does not include application development tools, such as form and report generators. For more information, see online Appendix C, "Getting Started with Oracle MySQL 5.6 Community Server."

FIGURE 2-10

Defining a Primary Key in Oracle MySQL 5.6 Community Server

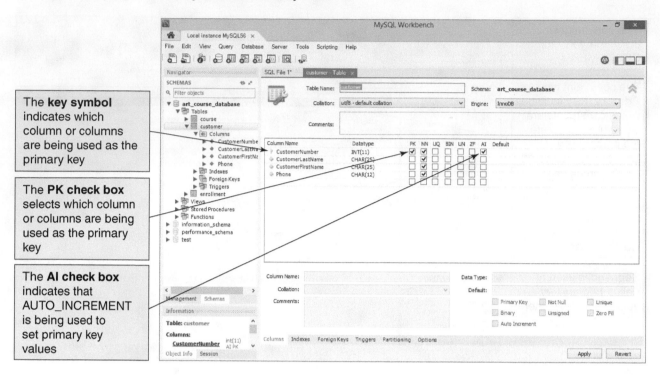

The **key symbol** indicates which column or columns are being used as the primary key

The **PK check box** selects which column or columns are being used as the primary key

The **AI check box** indicates that AUTO_INCREMENT is being used to set primary key values

complex than Microsoft Access, but we can spot the primary key of the table by finding the key symbol next to the name(s) of the primary key column(s) in the Column Name list. Again, there is a key symbol next to CustomerNumber, indicating that CustomerNumber is the primary key for this table.

A common method of specifying primary keys is to use SQL, which we briefly introduced in Chapter 1. We will see how SQL is used to designate primary keys in Chapter 3.

Surrogate Keys

A **surrogate key** is a column with a unique, DBMS-assigned identifier that has been added to a table to be the primary key. The unique values of the surrogate key are assigned by the DBMS each time a row is created, and the values never change.

An ideal primary key is short, numeric, and never changes. Sometimes one column in a table will meet these requirements or come close to them. For example, EmployeeNumber in the EMPLOYEE relation should work very well as a primary key. But in other tables, the primary key does not come close to being ideal. For example, consider the relation PROPERTY:

PROPERTY (Street, City, State, ZIP, OwnerID)

The primary key of PROPERTY is (Street, City, State, ZIP), which is long and nonnumeric (although it probably will not change). This is not an ideal primary key. In cases like this, the database designer will add a surrogate key, such as PropertyID:

PROPERTY (PropertyID, Street, City, State, ZIP, OwnerID)

Surrogate keys are short, numeric, and change—they are ideal primary keys. Because the values of the surrogate primary key will have no inherent meaning to users, they are often hidden on forms, query results, and reports.

Surrogate keys have been used in the databases we have already discussed. For example, in the Art Course Database tables shown in Figure 1-10 we added the surrogate keys CustomerNumber to the CUSTOMER table and CourseNumber to the COURSE table.

Most DBMS products have a facility for automatically generating key values. In Figure 2-7, we can see how surrogate keys are defined with Microsoft Access 2013. In Microsoft Access, Data Type is set to AutoNumber. With this specification, Microsoft Access assigns a value of 1 to CustomerNumber for the first row of CUSTOMER, a value of 2 to CustomerNumber for the second row, and so forth.

Enterprise-class DBMS products, such as Microsoft SQL Server, Oracle MySQL, and Oracle Database, offer more capability. For example, with SQL Server, the developer can specify the starting value of the surrogate key as well as the amount by which to increment the key for each new row. Figure 2-8 shows how this is done for the definition of the surrogate key CustomerNumber for the CUSTOMER table. In the Column Properties window, which is below the dbo.CUSTOMER table column details window, there is a set of **identity** specifications that have been set to indicate to SQL Server that a surrogate key column exists. The **is identity** value for CustomerNumber is set to Yes to make CustomerNumber a surrogate key. The starting value of the surrogate key is called the **identity seed**. For CustomerNumber, it is set to 1. Furthermore, the amount that is added to each key value to create the next key value is called the **identity increment**. In this example, it is set to 1. These settings mean that when the user creates the first row of the CUSTOMER table, SQL Server will give the value 1 to CustomerNumber. When the second row of CUSTOMER is created, SQL Server will give the value 2 to CustomerNumber, and so forth.

Oracle Database uses a **SEQUENCE** function to define automatically increasing sequences of numbers that can be used as surrogate key numbers. When using a SEQUENCE, the starting value can be any value (the default is 1), but the increment will always be 1. Figure 2-9 shows the existing sequences in the Art Course Database.

MySQL uses the **AUTO_INCREMENT** function to automatically assign surrogate key numbers. In AUTO_INCREMENT, the starting value can be any value (the default is 1), but the increment will always be 1. Figure 2-10 shows that CustomerNumber is a surrogate key for CUSTOMER that uses AUTO_INCREMENT (AI) to set the value of the column.

Foreign Keys and Referential Integrity

As described in Chapter 1, we place values from one relation into a second relation to represent a relationship. The values we use are the primary key values (including composite primary key values, when necessary) of the first relation. When we do this, the attribute in the second relation that holds these values is referred to as a **foreign key**. For example, in the Art Course database shown in Figure 1-10 we represent the relationship between customers and the art courses they are taking by placing CustomerNumber, the primary key of CUSTOMER, into the ENROLLMENT relation. In this case, CustomerID in ENROLLMENT is referred to as a foreign key. This term is used because CustomerNumber is the primary key of a relation that is foreign to the table in which it resides.

Consider the following two relations, where besides the EMPLOYEE relation we now have a DEPARTMENT relation to hold data about departments:

EMPLOYEE (EmployeeNumber, FirstName, LastName, Department, Email, Phone)

and:

DEPARTMENT (DepartmentName, BudgetCode, OfficeNumber, DepartmentPhone) where EmployeeNumber and DepartmentName are the primary keys of EMPLOYEE and DEPARTMENT, respectively.

Now suppose that Department in EMPLOYEE contains the names of the departments in which employees work and that DepartmentName in DEPARTMENT also contains these names. In this case, Department in EMPLOYEE is said to be a foreign key to DEPARTMENT. In this book, we denote foreign keys by displaying them in italics. Thus, we would write these two relation descriptions as follows:

EMPLOYEE (<u>EmployeeNumber</u>, FirstName, LastName, *Department,* Email, Phone)

and:

DEPARTMENT (<u>DepartmentName</u>, BudgetCode, OfficeNumber, DepartmentPhone)

Note that it is not necessary for the primary key and the foreign key to have the same column name. The only requirement is that they have the same set of values.

In most cases, it is important to ensure that every value of a foreign key matches a value of the primary key. In the previous example, the value of Department in every row of EMPLOYEE should match a value of DepartmentName in DEPARTMENT. If this is the case (and it usually is), then we declare the following rule:

Department in EMPLOYEE must exist in DepartmentName in DEPARTMENT

Such a rule is called a **referential integrity constraint**. Whenever you see a foreign key, you should always look for an associated referential integrity constraint.

Consider the Art Course database shown in Figure 1-10. The structure of this database is:

CUSTOMER (<u>CustomerNumber</u>, CustomerLastName, CustomerFirstName, Phone)
COURSE (<u>CourseNumber</u>, Course, CourseDate, Fee)
ENROLLMENT (*<u>CustomerNumber</u>*, *<u>CourseNumber</u>*, AmountPaid)

The ENROLLMENT table has a composite primary key of (CustomerNumber, CourseNumber), where CustomerNumber is a foreign key linking to CUSTOMER and CourseNumber is a foreign key linking to COURSE. Therefore, two referential integrity constraints are required:

CustomerNumber in ENROLLMENT must exist in CustomerNumber in CUSTOMER

and:

CourseNumber in ENROLLMENT must exist in CourseNumber in COURSE

Just as DBMS products have a means of specifying primary keys, they also have a way to set up foreign key referential integrity constraints. We discuss the details of setting up referential integrity constraints in this chapter's section of "The Access Workbench." Figure 2-11 shows the tables from the Art Course database in Figure 1-10 in the Microsoft Access Relationships window and with the Edit Relationships dialog box showing the details of the relationship between CUSTOMER and ENROLLMENT. Notice that the Enforce Referential Integrity check box is checked, so the referential integrity constraint between CustomerNumber in ENROLLMENT (the foreign key) and CustomerNumber in CUSTOMER (the primary key) is being enforced.

Figure 2-12 shows the same foreign key relationship between CUSTOMER and ENROLLMENT in the Microsoft SQL Server Management Studio program. Again, this display is more complex, but notice that the property Table Designer: Enforce Foreign Key Constraint is set to Yes. This means that the referential integrity constraint

FIGURE 2-11

Enforcing Referential Integrity in Microsoft Access 2013

The relationship is between CUSTOMER and ENROLLMENT— the foreign key CustomerNumber in ENROLLMENT references the primary key CustomerNumber in CUSTOMER

Use this check box to enforce referential integrity in this relationship

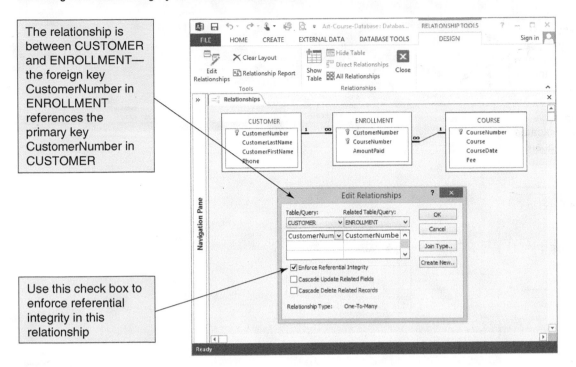

FIGURE 2-12

Enforcing Referential Integrity in Microsoft SQL Server 2014

The relationship is between ENROLLMENT and CUSTOMER

We are enforcing the foreign key constraint—which *is* the referential integrity constraint

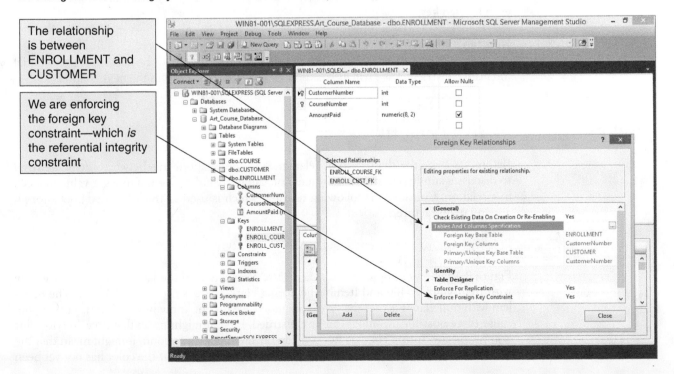

FIGURE 2-13

Enforcing Referential Integrity in Oracle Database Express Edition 11*g* Release 2

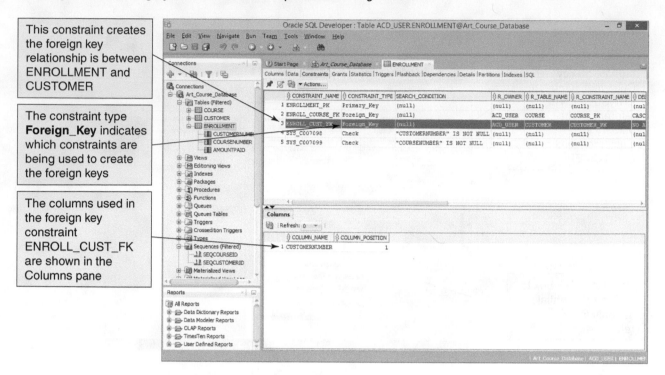

between CustomerNumber in ENROLLMENT (the foreign key) and CustomerNumber in CUSTOMER (the primary key) is being enforced.

Figure 2-13 shows foreign keys in Oracle Database Express Edition 11*g* Release 2. Here the Foreign Keys tab in the Oracle SQL Developer utility displays the properties of each foreign key.

Figure 2-14 shows foreign keys in MySQL 5.6 Community Server. Here the Foreign Keys tab in the MySQL Workbench utility displays the properties of each foreign key.

Just as SQL can be used to specify primary keys, it can also be used to set referential integrity constraints. We will look at how to use SQL to do this in the next chapter.

THE PROBLEM OF NULL VALUES

Before we leave the discussion of relations and the relationships between them, we need to discuss a subtle but important topic: null values. A **null value** is a missing value in a cell in a relation. Consider the following relation, which is used to track finished goods for an apparel manufacturer:

ITEM (<u>ItemNumber</u>, ItemName, Color, Quantity)

Figure 2-15 shows sample data for this table. Notice that in the last row of data—the row with ItemNumber 400 and ItemName Spring Hat—there is no value for Color. The problem with null values is that they are ambiguous; we do not know how to interpret them because three possible meanings can be construed. First, it might mean that no value of Color is appropriate; Spring Hats do not come in different colors. Second, it might mean that the value is known to be blank; that is, Spring Hats have a color, but the color has not yet been

FIGURE 2-14

Enforcing Referential Integrity in Oracle MySQL 5.6 Community Server

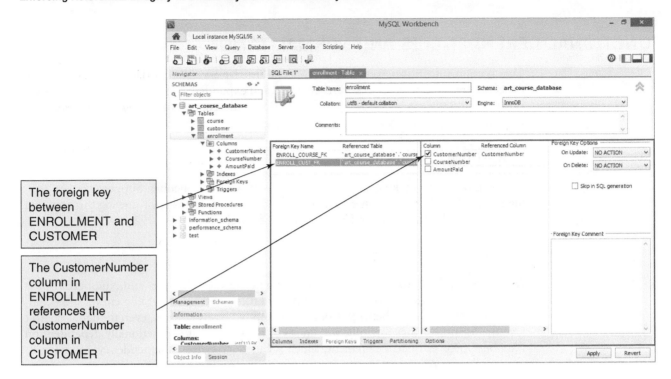

The foreign key between ENROLLMENT and CUSTOMER

The CustomerNumber column in ENROLLMENT references the CustomerNumber column in CUSTOMER

FIGURE 2-15

Sample ITEM Relation and Data

ItemNumber	ItemName	Color	Quantity
110	Small T-Shirt	Red	15
120	Small T-Shirt	Blue	5
150	Small T-Shirt	Green	7
210	Med T-Shirt	Red	8
400	Spring Hat		5

decided. Maybe the color is established by placing ribbons around the hats, but this is not done until an order arrives. Finally, the null value might mean that the hats' color is simply unknown; the hats have a color, but no one has checked yet to see what it is.

You can eliminate null values by requiring an attribute value. DBMS products allow you to specify whether a null value can occur in a column. We discussed how to do this for Microsoft Access in Chapter 1's "The Access Workbench." For Microsoft SQL Server 2014, notice the column in the dbo.CUSTOMER table column details window labeled *Allow Nulls* in Figure 2-8. A check box without a checkmark means that null values are not allowed in this column. Note that, in Figure 2-9, the Oracle SQL Developer utility for Oracle Database Express Edition 11*g* R2 is showing the data on the Constraints tab, and this tab does not indicate null values. If, however, we looked at the Columns tab, we would see whether null values are allowed in each column. For MySQL 5.6 Community Server, note that in Figure 2-10 the Column Details tab in the MySQL Table Editor shows an NN (NOT NULL) check box that indicates whether null values are allowed in the column. Regardless of the DBMS being used, if nulls are not allowed then some value must be entered for each row in the table. If the attribute is a text value, users can be allowed to enter values such as "not appropriate," "undecided," or "unknown," when necessary. If the attribute is not text, then some other coding system can be developed.

For now, be aware that null values can occur and that they always carry some ambiguity. The next chapter will show another, possibly more serious, problem of null values.

FUNCTIONAL DEPENDENCIES AND NORMALIZATION

This section introduces some of the concepts used for relational database design; these concepts are used in the next several chapters and expanded upon in Chapter 5. This book presents only the essentials. To learn more, you should consult other, more comprehensive references.[5]

Functional Dependencies

To get started, let us take a short excursion into the world of algebra. Suppose you are buying boxes of cookies, and someone tells you that each box costs $5. Knowing this fact, you can compute the cost of several boxes with the formula:

$$CookieCost = NumberOfBoxes \times \$5$$

A more general way to express the relationship between CookieCost and NumberOfBoxes is to say that CookieCost depends upon NumberOfBoxes. Such a statement tells the character of the relationship between CookieCost and NumberOfBoxes, even though it doesn't give the formula. More formally, we can say that CookieCost is **functionally dependent** on NumberOfBoxes. Such a statement, which is called a **functional dependency**, can be written as follows:

$$NumberOfBoxes \rightarrow CookieCost$$

This expression says that NumberOfBoxes determines CookieCost. The term on the left, NumberOfBoxes, is called the **determinant**.

Using another example, we can compute the extended price of a part order by multiplying the quantity of the item by its unit price:

$$ExtendedPrice = Quantity \times UnitPrice$$

In this case, we would say that ExtendedPrice is functionally dependent on Quantity and UnitPrice, or:

$$(Quantity, UnitPrice) \rightarrow ExtendedPrice$$

The composite (Quantity, UnitPrice) is the determinant of ExtendedPrice.

Now, let us expand these ideas. Suppose you know that a sack contains either red, blue, or yellow objects. Further suppose you know that the red objects weigh 5 pounds each, the blue objects weigh 5 pounds each, and the yellow objects weigh 7 pounds each. If a friend looks into the sack, sees an object, and tells you the color of the object, you can tell the weight of the object. We can formalize this in the same way as in the previous example:

$$ObjectColor \rightarrow Weight$$

---

[5]See David M. Kroenke and David J. Auer, *Database Processing: Fundamentals, Design, and Implementation*, 13th edition (Upper Saddle River, NJ: Prentice Hall, 2014); and C. J. Date, *An Introduction to Database Systems*, 8th edition (Boston: Addison-Wesley, 2004).

FIGURE 2-16

ObjectColor	Weight	Shape
Red	5	Ball
Blue	5	Cube
Yellow	7	Cube

Thus, we can say that Weight is functionally dependent on ObjectColor and that ObjectColor determines Weight. The relationship here does not involve an equation, but this functional dependency is still true. Given a value for ObjectColor, you can determine the object's weight.

In addition, if we know that the red objects are balls, the blue objects are cubes, and the yellow objects are cubes, then:

$$ObjectColor \rightarrow Shape$$

Thus, ObjectColor also determines Shape. We can put these two together and state:

$$ObjectColor \rightarrow (Weight, Shape)$$

Thus, ObjectColor determines Weight and Shape.

Another way to represent these facts is to put them into a table, as shown in Figure 2-16. Note that this table meets all the conditions in our definition of a relation, as listed in Figure 2-1, so we can refer to it as a relation. If we call it the OBJECT relation and use ObjectColor as the primary key, we can write this relation as:

OBJECT (<u>ObjectColor</u>, Weight, Shape)

Now, you may be thinking that we have just performed some trick or sleight of hand to arrive at a relation, but one can make the argument that the only reason for having relations is to store instances of functional dependencies. Consider a relation such as the CUSTOMER relation from the Art Course database in Figure 1-10:

CUSTOMER (<u>CustomerNumber</u>, CustomerLastName, CustomerFirstName, Phone)

Here we are simply storing facts that express the following functional dependency:

$$CustomerNumber \rightarrow (CustomerLastName, CustomerFirstName, Phone)$$

Primary and Candidate Keys Revisited

Now that we have discussed the concept of functional dependency, we can define primary and candidate keys more formally. Specifically, a primary key of a relation can be defined as "one or more attributes that functionally determine all the other attributes of the relation." The same definition holds for candidate keys as well.

Recall the EMPLOYEE relation from Figure 2-2 (shown without primary or foreign keys indicated):

EMPLOYEE (EmployeeNumber, FirstName, LastName, Department, Email, Phone)

As previously discussed, based on information from users, this relation has three candidate keys: EmployeeNumber, Email, and the composite (FirstName, LastName, Department). Because this is so, we can state the following:

$$EmployeeNumber \rightarrow (FirstName, LastName, Department, Email, Phone)$$

Equivalently, if we are given a value for EmployeeNumber, we can determine FirstName, LastName, Department, Email, and Phone. Similarly, we can state that:

Email → (EmployeeNumber, FirstName, LastName, Department, Phone)

That is, if we are given a value for Email, we can determine EmployeeNumber, FirstName, LastName, Department, and Phone. Finally, we also can state that:

(FirstName, LastName, Department) → (EmployeeNumber, Email, Phone)

This means that if we are given values of FirstName, LastName, and Department, we can determine EmployeeNumber, Email, and Phone.

These three functional dependencies express the reason the three candidate keys are candidate keys. When we choose a primary key from the candidate keys, we are choosing which functional dependency we want to define as the one that is most meaningful or important to us.

Normalization

The concepts of functional dependencies and determinants can be used to help in the design of relations. Recalling the concept from Chapter 1 that a table or relation should have only one theme, we can define **normalization** as the process of (or set of steps for) breaking a table or relation with more than one theme into a set of tables such that each has only one theme. Normalization is a complex topic, and it consumes one or more chapters of more theoretically oriented database books. Here we reduce this topic to a few ideas that capture the essence of the process. After this discussion, if you are interested in the topic, you should consult the references mentioned earlier for more information.

The problem that normalization addresses is as follows: A table can meet all the characteristics listed in Figure 2-1 and still have the modification problems we identified for lists in Chapter 1. Specifically, consider the following ADVISER_LIST relation:

ADVISER_LIST (AdviserID, AdviserName, Department, Phone, Office, StudentNumber, StudentName)

What is the primary key of this relation? Given the definitions of candidate key and primary key, it has to be an attribute that determines all the other attributes. The only attribute that has this characteristic is StudentNumber. Given a value of StudentNumber, we can determine the values of all the other attributes:

StudentNumber → (AdviserID, AdviserName, Department, Phone, Office, StudentName)

We can then write this relation as follows:

ADVISER_LIST (AdviserID, AdviserName, Department, Phone, Office, StudentNumber, StudentName)

However, this table has modification problems. Specifically, an adviser's data are repeated many times in the table, once for each advisee. This means that updates to adviser data might need to be made multiple times. If, for example, an adviser changes offices, that change will need to be completed in all the rows for the person's advisees. If an adviser has 20 advisees, that change will need to be entered 20 times.

Another modification problem can occur when we delete a student from this list. If we delete a student who is the only advisee for an adviser, we will delete not only the student's data but also the adviser's data. Thus, we will unintentionally lose facts about two entities while attempting to delete one.

If you look closely at this relation, you will see a functional dependency that involves the adviser's data. Specifically:

AdviserID → (AdviserName, Department, Phone, Office)

Now, we can state the problem with this relation more accurately—in terms of functional dependencies. Specifically, this relation is poorly formed because it has a functional dependency that does not involve the primary key. Stated differently, AdviserID is a determinant of a functional dependency, but it is not a candidate key and thus cannot be the primary key under any circumstances.

Relational Design Principles

From the discussion so far, we can formulate the following design principles for what we can call a **well-formed relation**:

1. For a relation to be considered well formed, every determinant must be a candidate key.
2. Any relation that is not well formed should be broken into two or more relations that are well formed.

These two principles are the heart of normalization—the process of examining relations and modifying them to make them well formed. This process is called *normalization* because you can categorize the problems to which relations are susceptible into different types called *normal forms*.

There are many defined normal forms. Technically, our well-formed relations are those that are said to be in **Boyce-Codd Normal Form (BCNF)**. For example, any relation that has the characteristics listed in Figure 2-1 is called a relation in **first normal form (1NF)**. Besides first normal form and Boyce-Codd normal form, other normal forms exist, such as second, third, fourth, fifth, and domain/key normal form. We further describe normal forms later in this chapter.

However, if we simply follow the aforementioned design principles we will avoid almost all the problems associated with non-normalized tables. In some rare instances, these principles do not address the problems that arise (see questions 2.40 and 2.41 in the Exercises section), but if you follow these principles, you will be safe most of the time.

The Normalization Process

We can apply the principles just described to formulate the following **normalization process** for normalizing relations:

1. Identify all the candidate keys of the relation.
2. Identify all the functional dependencies in the relation.
3. Examine the determinants of the functional dependencies. If any determinant is not a candidate key, the relation is not well formed. In this case:
   a. Place the columns of the functional dependency in a new relation of their own.
   b. Make the determinant of the functional dependency the primary key of the new relation.
   c. Leave a copy of the determinant as a foreign key in the original relation.
   d. Create a referential integrity constraint between the original relation and the new relation.
4. Repeat step 3 as many times as necessary until every determinant of every relation is a candidate key.

To understand this process, consider the following relation:

PRESCRIPTION (PrescriptionNumber, Date, Drug, Dosage, CustomerName, CustomerPhone, CustomerEmail)

Sample data for the PRESCRIPTION relation are shown in Figure 2-17.

FIGURE 2-17

Sample PERSCIPTION Relation and Data

PrescriptionNumber	Date	Drug	Dosage	CustomerName	CustomerPhone	CustomerEmail
P10001	10/17/2015	DrugA	10mg	Smith, Alvin	575-523-2233	ASmith@somewhere.com
P10003	10/17/2015	DrugB	35mg	Rhodes, Jeff	575-645-3455	JRhodes@somewhere.com
P10004	10/17/2015	DrugA	20mg	Smith, Sarah	575-523-2233	SSmith@somewhere.com
P10007	10/18/2015	DrugC	20mg	Frye, Michael	575-645-4566	MFrye@somewhere.com
P10010	10/18/2015	DrugB	30mg	Rhodes, Jeff	575-645-3455	JRhodes@somewhere.com

Step 1 of the Normalization Process

According to the normalization process, we first identify all candidate keys. PrescriptionNumber clearly determines Date, Drug, and Dosage. If we assume that a prescription is for only one person, then it also determines CustomerName, CustomerPhone, and CustomerEmail. By law, prescriptions must be for only one person, so PrescriptionNumber is a candidate key.

Does this relation have other candidate keys? Date, Drug, and Dosage do not determine PrescriptionNumber because many prescriptions can be written on a given date, many prescriptions can be written for a given drug, and many prescriptions can be written for a given dosage.

What about customer columns? If a customer had only one prescription, then we could say that some identifying customer column—for example, CustomerEmail—would determine the prescription data. However, people can have more than one prescription, so this assumption is invalid.

Given this analysis, the only candidate key of PRESCRIPTION is PrescriptionNumber.

Step 2 of the Normalization Process

In step 2 of the normalization process, we now identify all functional dependencies. PrescriptionNumber determines all the other attributes, as just described. If a drug had only one dosage, then we could state that:

Drug → Dosage

But this is not true because some drugs have several dosages. Therefore, Drug is not a determinant. Furthermore, Dosage is not a determinant because the same dosage can be given for many different drugs.

However, examining the customer columns, we do find a functional dependency:

CustomerEmail → (CustomerName, CustomerPhone)

To know whether functional dependency is true for a particular application, we need to look beyond the sample data in Figure 2-17 and ask the users. For example, it is possible that some customers share the same email address, and it is also possible that some customers do not have email. For now, we can assume that the users say that CustomerEmail is a determinant of the customer attributes.

Step 3 of the Normalization Process

In step 3 of the normalization process, we ask whether there is a determinant that is *not* a candidate key. In this example, CustomerEmail is a determinant and not a candidate key. Therefore, PRESCRIPTION has normalization problems and is not well formed. According to step 3, we split the functional dependency into a relation of its own:

CUSTOMER (CustomerName, CustomerPhone, CustomerEmail)

We make the determinant of the functional dependency, CustomerEmail, the primary key of the new relation.

FIGURE 2-18

Normalized
Prescription Customer
Relations and Data

CustomerName	CustomerPhone	CustomerEmail
Smith, Alvin	575-523-2233	ASmith@somewhere.com
Rhodes, Jeff	575-645-3455	JRhodes@somewhere.com
Frye, Michael	575-645-4566	MFrye@somewhere.com
Smith, Sarah	575-523-2233	SSmith@somewhere.com

PrescriptionNumber	Date	Drug	Dosage	CustomerEmail
P10001	10/17/2015	DrugA	10mg	ASmith@somewhere.com
P10003	10/17/2015	DrugB	35mg	JRhodes@somewhere.com
P10004	10/17/2015	DrugA	20mg	SSmith@somewhere.com
P10007	10/18/2015	DrugC	20mg	MFrye@somewhere.com
P10010	10/18/2015	DrugB	30mg	JRhodes@somewhere.com

We leave a copy of CustomerEmail in the original relation as a foreign key. Thus, PRESCRIPTION is now:

PRESCRIPTION (PrescriptionNumber, Date, Drug, Dosage, *CustomerEmail*)

Finally, we create the referential integrity constraint:

CustomerEmail in PRESCRIPTION must exist in CustomerEmail in CUSTOMER

At this point, if we move through the three steps, we find that neither of these relations has a determinant that is not a candidate key, and we can say that the two relations are now normalized. Figure 2-18 shows the result for the sample data.

Normalization Examples

We now illustrate the use of the normalization process with four examples.

Normalization Example 1   The relation in Figure 2-19 shows a table of student residence data named STU_DORM. The first step in normalizing it is to identify all candidate keys. Because StudentNumber determines each of the other columns, it is a candidate key. LastName cannot be a candidate key because two students have the last name Smith. None of the other columns can be a candidate key, either, so StudentNumber is the only candidate key.

Next, in step 2, we look for the functional dependencies in the relation. Besides those for StudentNumber, a functional dependency appears to exist between DormName and DormCost. Again, we would need to check this out with the users. In this case, assume that the functional dependency:

DormName → DormCost

is true and assume that our interview with the users indicates that no other functional dependencies exist.

FIGURE 2-19

Sample STU_DORM
Relation and Data

StudentNumber	LastName	FirstName	DormName	DormCost
100	Smith	Terry	Stephens	3,500.00
200	Johnson	Jeff	Alexander	3,800.00
300	Abernathy	Susan	Horan	4,000.00
400	Smith	Susan	Alexander	3,800.00
500	Wilcox	John	Stephens	3,500.00
600	Webber	Carl	Horan	4,000.00
700	Simon	Carol	Stephens	3,500.00

In step 3, we now ask if any determinants exist that are not candidate keys. In this example, DormName is a determinant, but it is not a candidate key. Therefore, this relation is not well formed and has normalization problems.

To fix those problems, we place the columns of the functional dependency (DormName, DormCost) into a relation of their own and call that relation DORM. We make the determinant of the functional dependency the primary key. Thus, DormName is the primary key of DORM. We leave the determinant DormName as a foreign key in STU_DORM. Finally, we find the appropriate referential integrity constraint. The result is:

STU_DORM (StudentNumber, LastName, FirstName, *DormName*)

DORM (DormName, DormCost)

with the constraint:

DormName in STU_DORM must exist in DormName in DORM

The data for these relations appear as shown in Figure 2-20.

Normalization Example 2   Now consider the EMPLOYEE table in Figure 2-21. First, we identify the candidate keys in EMPLOYEE. From the data, it appears that EmployeeNumber and Email each identify all the other attributes. Hence, they are candidate keys (again, with the proviso that we cannot depend on sample data to show all cases; we must verify this assumption with the users).

In step 2, we identify other functional dependencies. From the data, it appears that the only other functional dependency is:

Department → DeptPhone

Assuming that this is true, then according to step 3 we have a determinant, Department, that is not a candidate key. Thus, EMPLOYEE has normalization problems.

To fix those problems, we place the columns in the functional dependency in a table of their own and make the determinant the primary key of the new table. We leave the determinant as a foreign key in the original table. The result is the two tables:

EMPLOYEE (EmployeeNumber, LastName, Email, *Department*)

DEPARTMENT (Department, DeptPhone)

FIGURE 2-20

Normalized STU_DORM and DORM Relations and Data

StudentNumber	LastName	FirstName	DormName
100	Smith	Terry	Stephens
200	Johnson	Jeff	Alexander
300	Abernathy	Susan	Horan
400	Smith	Susan	Alexander
500	Wilcox	John	Stephens
600	Webber	Carl	Horan
700	Simon	Carol	Stephens

DormName	DormCost
Alexander	3,800.00
Horan	4,000.00
Stephens	3,500.00

FIGURE 2-21

Sample EMPLOYEE Relation and Data

EmployeeNumber	LastName	Department	Email	DeptPhone
100	Johnson	Accounting	JJ@somewhere.com	834-1100
200	Abernathy	Finance	MA@somewhere.com	834-2100
300	Smathers	Finance	LS@somewhere.com	834-2100
400	Caruthers	Accounting	TC@somewhere.com	834-1100
500	Jackson	Production	TJ@somewhere.com	834-4100
600	Caldera	Legal	EC@somewhere.com	834-3100
700	Bandalone	Legal	RB@somewhere.com	834-3100

FIGURE 2-22

Normalized EMPLOYEE
and DEPARTMENT
Relations and Data

EmployeeNumber	LastName	Department	Email
100	Johnson	Accounting	JJ@somewhere.com
200	Abernathy	Finance	MA@somewhere.com
300	Smathers	Finance	LS@somewhere.com
400	Caruthers	Accounting	TC@somewhere.com
500	Jackson	Production	TJ@somewhere.com
600	Caldera	Legal	EC@somewhere.com
700	Bandalone	Legal	RB@somewhere.com

Department	DeptPhone
Accounting	834-1100
Finance	834-2100
Legal	834-3100
Production	834-4100

FIGURE 2-23

Sample MEETING
Relation and Data

Attorney	ClientNumber	ClientName	MeetingDate	Duration
Boxer	1000	ABC, Inc	11/5/2015	2.00
Boxer	2000	XYZ Partners	11/5/2015	5.50
James	1000	ABC, Inc	11/7/2015	3.00
Boxer	1000	ABC, Inc	11/9/2015	4.00
Wu	3000	Malcomb Zoe	11/11/2015	7.00

with the referential integrity constraint:

Department in EMPLOYEE must exist in Department in DEPARTMENT

The result for the sample data is shown in Figure 2-22.

Normalization Example 3 Now consider the MEETING table in Figure 2-23. We begin by looking for candidate keys. No column by itself can be a candidate key. Attorney determines different sets of data, so it cannot be a determinant. The same is true for ClientNumber, ClientName, and MeetingDate. In the sample data, the only column that does not determine different sets of data is Duration, but this uniqueness is accidental. It is easy to imagine that two or more meetings would have the same duration.

The next step is to look for combinations of columns that can be candidate keys. (Attorney, ClientNumber) is one combination, but the values (Boxer, 1000) determine two different sets of data. They cannot be a candidate key. The combination (Attorney, ClientName) fails for the same reason. The only combinations that can be candidate keys of this relation are (Attorney, ClientNumber, MeetingDate) and (Attorney, ClientName, MeetingDate).

Let us consider those possibilities further. The name of the relation is MEETING, and we are asking whether (Attorney, ClientNumber, MeetingDate) or (Attorney, ClientName, MeetingDate) can be a candidate key. Do these combinations make sense as identifiers of a meeting? They do unless more than one meeting of the same attorney and client occurs on the same day. In that case, we need to add a new column, MeetingTime, to the relation and make this new column part of the candidate key. In this example, we assume that this is not the case and that (Attorney, ClientNumber, MeetingDate) and (Attorney, ClientName, MeetingDate) are the candidate keys.

The second step is to identify other functional dependencies. Here two exist:

ClientNumber → ClientName

and:

ClientName → ClientNumber

Each of these determinants is part of one of the candidate keys. For example, ClientNumber is part of (Attorney, ClientNumber, MeetingDate). However, being part of a candidate key is not enough. The determinant must be the same as the entire candidate key. Thus, the MEETING table is not well formed and has normalization problems.

When you are not certain whether normalization problems exist, consider the three modification operations discussed in Chapter 1: insert, update, and delete. Do problems exist with any of them? For example, in Figure 2-23 if you change ClientName in the first row to ABC, Limited, do inconsistencies arise in the data? The answer is yes because ClientNumber 1000 would have two different names in the table. This and any of the other problems that were identified in Chapter 1 when inserting, updating, or deleting data are sure signs that the table has normalization problems.

To fix the normalization problems, we create a new table, CLIENT, with columns ClientNumber and ClientName. Both of these columns are determinants; thus, either can be the primary key of the new table. However, whichever one is selected as the primary key also should be made the foreign key in MEETING. Thus, two correct designs are possible. First, we can use:

MEETING (Attorney, *ClientNumber*, MeetingDate, Duration)
CLIENT (ClientNumber, ClientName)

with the referential integrity constraint:

ClientNumber in MEETING must exist in ClientNumber in CLIENT

Second, we can use:

MEETING (Attorney, *ClientName*, MeetingDate, Duration)
CLIENT (ClientNumber, ClientName)

with the referential integrity constraint:

ClientName in MEETING must exist in ClientName in CLIENT

Data for the first design are shown in Figure 2-24.

Notice in these two designs that either the attribute ClientNumber or ClientName is both a foreign key and also part of the primary key of MEETING. This illustrates that foreign keys can be part of a composite primary key.

Note that when two attributes, such as ClientNumber and ClientName, each determine one another they are **synonyms**. They both must appear in a relation to establish their equivalent values. Given that equivalency, the two columns are interchangeable; one can take the place of the other in any other relation. All things being equal, however, the administration of the database will be simpler if one of the two is used consistently as a foreign key. This policy is just a convenience, however, and not a logical requirement for the design.

Normalization Example 4 For our last example, let us consider a relation that involves student data. Specifically:

GRADE (ClassName, Section, Term, Grade, StudentNumber, StudentName, Professor, Department, ProfessorEmail)

Given the confused set of columns in this table, it does not seem well formed, and it appears that the table will have normalization problems. We can use the normalization process to find what they are and to remove them.

FIGURE 2-24

Normalized MEETING and CLIENT Relations and Data

Attorney	ClientNumber	MeetingDate	Duration
Boxer	1000	11/5/2014	2.00
Boxer	2000	11/5/2014	5.50
James	1000	11/7/2014	3.00
Boxer	1000	11/9/2014	4.00
Wu	3000	11/11/2014	7.00

ClientNumber	ClientName
1000	ABC, Inc
2000	XYZ Partners
3000	Malcomb Zoe

First, what are the candidate keys of this relation? No column by itself is a candidate key. One way to approach this is to realize that a grade is a combination of a class and a student. In this table, which columns identify classes and students? A particular class is identified by (ClassName, Section, Term), and a student is identified by StudentNumber. Possibly, then, a candidate key for this relation is:

(ClassName, Section, Term, StudentNumber)

This statement is equivalent to saying:

(ClassName, Section, Term, StudentNumber) → (Grade, StudentName, Professor, Department, ProfessorEmail)

This is a true statement as long as only one professor teaches a class section. For now, we will make that assumption and consider the alternate case later. If only one professor teaches a section, then (ClassName, Section, Term, StudentNumber) is the one and only candidate key.

Second, what are the additional functional dependencies? One involves student data, and another involves professor data, specifically:

StudentNumber → StudentName

and:

Professor → ProfessorEmail

We also need to ask if Professor determines Department. It will if a professor teaches in only one department. In that case, we have:

Professor → (Department, ProfessorEmail)

Otherwise, Department must remain in the GRADE relation.

We will assume that professors teach in just one department, so we can confirm the following functional dependencies from our discussion above:

StudentNumber → StudentName

and:

Professor → (Department, ProfessorEmail)

If we examine the GRADE relation a bit further, however, we can find one other functional dependency. If only one professor teaches a class section, then:

(ClassName, Section, Term) → Professor

Thus, according to step 3 of the normalization process, GRADE has normalization problems because the determinants StudentNumber, Professor, and (ClassName, Section, Term) are not candidate keys. Therefore, we form a table for each of these functional dependencies. As a result, we have a STUDENT table, a PROFESSOR table, and a CLASS_PROFESSOR table. After forming these tables, we then take the appropriate columns out of GRADE and put them into a new version of the GRADE table, which we will name GRADE_1. We now have the following design:

STUDENT (<u>StudentNumber</u>, StudentName)
PROFESSOR (<u>Professor</u>, Department, ProfessorEmail)
CLASS_PROFESSOR (<u>ClassName</u>, <u>Section</u>, <u>Term</u>, *Professor*)
GRADE_1 (*<u>ClassName</u>*, *<u>Section</u>*, *<u>Term</u>*, Grade, *<u>StudentNumber</u>*)

with the referential integrity constraints:

StudentNumber in GRADE_1 must exist in StudentNumber in STUDENT
Professor in CLASS_PROFESSOR must exist in Professor in PROFESSOR
(ClassName, Section, Term) in GRADE_1 must exist in (ClassName, Section, Term)
   in CLASS_PROFESSOR

Next, consider what happens if more than one professor teaches a section of a class. In that case, the only change is to make Professor part of the primary key of CLASS_PROFESSOR. Thus, the new relation is:

CLASS_PROFESSOR_1 (ClassName, Section, Term, *Professor*)

Class sections that have more than one professor will have multiple rows in this table—one row for each of the professors.

This example shows how normalization problems can become more complicated than simple examples might indicate. For large commercial applications that potentially involve hundreds of tables, such problems can sometimes consume days or weeks of design time.

Eliminating Anomalies from Multivalued Dependencies

In the interest of full disclosure, if professors can teach more than one class in the previous example, then GRADE has what is called a **multivalued dependency**. When modification problems are due to functional dependencies, and we then normalize relations to BCNF, we eliminate these anomalies. However, anomalies can also arise from another kind of dependency—the multivalued dependency. A *multivalued dependency* occurs when a determinant is matched with a particular *set* of values.

Examples of multivalued dependencies are:

$$EmployeeName \rightarrow \rightarrow EmployeeDegree$$
$$EmployeeName \rightarrow \rightarrow EmployeeSibling$$
$$PartKitName \rightarrow \rightarrow Part$$

In each case, the determinant is associated with a set of values, and example data for each of these multivalued dependencies are shown in Figure 2-25. Such expressions are read as "EmployeeName multidetermines EmployeeDegree" and "EmployeeName multidetermines EmployeeSibling" and "PartKitName multidetermines Part." Note that multideterminants are shown with a double arrow rather than a single arrow.

Employee Jones, for example, has degrees AA and BS. Employee Greene has degrees BS, MS, and PhD. Employee Chau has just one degree, BS. Similarly, employee Jones has siblings (brothers and sisters) Fred, Sally, and Frank. Employee Greene has sibling Nikki, and employee Chau has siblings Jonathan and Eileen. Finally, PartKitName Bike Repair has parts Wrench, Screwdriver, and Tube Fix. Other kits have parts as shown in Figure 2-25.

Unlike functional dependencies, the determinant of a multivalued dependency can never be the primary key. In all three of the tables in Figure 2-25, the primary key consists of the composite of the two columns in each table. For example, the primary key of the EMPLOYEE_DEGREE table is the composite key (EmployeeName, EmployeeDegree).

Multivalued dependencies pose no problem as long as they exist in tables of their own. None of the tables in Figure 2-25 has modification anomalies. However, if $A \rightarrow \rightarrow B$, then any relation that contains A, B, and one or more additional columns will have modification anomalies. Notice that when you put multivalued dependencies into a table of their own, they disappear. The result is just a table with two columns, and the primary key (and sole candidate key) is the composite of those two columns. When multivalued dependencies have been isolated in this way, the table is said to be in **fourth normal form (4NF)**.

FIGURE 2-25

Three Examples
of Multivalued
Dependencies

EMPLOYEE_DEGREE

	EmployeeName	EmployeeDegree
1	Chau	BS
2	Green	BS
3	Green	MS
4	Green	PhD
5	Jones	AA
6	Jones	BA

EMPLOYEE_SIBLING

	EmployeeName	EmployeeSibling
1	Chau	Eileen
2	Chau	Jonathan
3	Green	Nikki
4	Jones	Frank
5	Jones	Fred
6	Jones	Sally

PARTKIT_PART

	PartKitName	Part
1	Bike Repair	Screwdriver
2	Bike Repair	Tube Fix
3	Bike Repair	Wrench
4	First Aid	Aspirin
5	First Aid	Bandaids
6	First Aid	Elastic Band
7	First Aid	Ibuprofin
8	Toolbox	Drill
9	Toolbox	Drill bits
10	Toolbox	Hammer
11	Toolbox	Saw
12	Toolbox	Screwdriver

The hardest part of multivalued dependencies is finding them. Once you know they exist in a table, just move them into a table of their own. Whenever you encounter tables with odd anomalies, especially anomalies that require you to insert, modify, or delete different numbers of rows to maintain integrity, check for multivalued dependencies.

BTW

You will get a chance to work with multivalued dependencies and 4NF in exercises 2.40 and 2.41. If you want to learn about them, see one of the more advanced texts mentioned in the footnote on page 76. In general, you should normalize your relationships so that they are either in BCNF or 4NF.

NORMAL FORMS: ONE STEP AT A TIME

A table and a spreadsheet are very similar to one another in that we can think of both as having rows, columns, and cells. Edgar Frank (E. F.) Codd, the originator of the relational model, defined three normal forms in an early paper on the relational model. He defined any table that meets the definition of a relation (see Figure 2-1 on page 63) as being in **first normal form (1NF)**.

For 1NF, ask yourself: Does the table meet the definition in Figure 2-1? If the answer is yes, then the table is in 1NF.

Codd pointed out that such tables can have anomalies (which are referred to elsewhere in the text as *normalization problems*), and he defined a **second normal form (2NF)** that eliminated some of those anomalies. A relation is in 2NF if and only if (1) it is in 1NF and (2) all nonkey attributes are determined by the entire primary key. This means that if the primary key is a composite primary key, no nonkey attribute can be determined by an attribute or attributes that make up only part of the key. Thus, if you have a relation (**A**, **B**, **N**, **O**, **P**) with the composite key (**A**, **B**), then none of the nonkey attributes—**N**, **O**, or **P**—can be determined by *just* **A** or *just* **B**.

For 2NF, ask yourself: (1) Is the table in 1NF, and (2) are all nonkey attributes determined by *only* the *entire* primary key rather than *part* of the primary key? If the answers are *yes* and *yes*, then the table is in 2NF. Note that the problem solved by 2NF can *only occur* in a table with a *composite primary key*—if the table has a single column primary key, then this problem *cannot occur* and if the table is in 1NF it will also be in 2NF.

However, the conditions of 2NF did not eliminate all the anomalies, so Codd defined **third normal form (3NF)**. A relation is in 3NF if and only if (1) it is in 2NF and (2) there are no nonkey attributes determined by another nonkey attribute. Technically, the situation described by the preceding condition is called a **transitive dependency**. Thus, in our relation (**A**, **B**, **N**, **O**, **P**) *none* of the nonkey attributes—**N**, **O**, or **P**—can be determined by **N**, **O**, or **P** or any combination of them.

For 3NF, ask yourself: (1) Is the table in 2NF, and (2) are there any nonkey attributes determined by *another* nonkey attribute or attributes? If the answers are *yes* and *no*, then the table is in 3NF.

Not long after Codd published his paper on normal forms, it was pointed out to him that even relations in 3NF could have anomalies. As a result, he and R. Boyce defined the **Boyce-Codd Normal Form (BCNF)**, which eliminated the anomalies that had been found with 3NF. As stated earlier, a relation is in BCNF if and only if every determinant is a candidate key.

For BCNF, ask yourself: (1) Is the table in 3NF, and (2) are all *determinants* also *candidate keys*? If the answers are *yes* and *yes*, then the table is in BCNF.

1NF through BCNF are summed up in a widely known phrase:

I swear to construct my tables so that all nonkey columns are dependent on the key, the whole key, and nothing but the key, so help me Codd!

This phrase actually is a very good way to remember the order of the normal forms:

I swear to construct my tables so that all nonkey columns are dependent on

- *the key,*   [This is 1NF]
- *the whole key,*   [This is 2NF]
- *and nothing but the key,*   [This is 3NF and BCNF]

so help me Codd!

Also note that all these definitions were made in such a way that a relation in a higher normal form is defined to be in all lower normal forms. Thus, a relation in BCNF is automatically in 3NF, a relation in 3NF is automatically in 2NF, and a relation in 2NF is automatically in 1NF.

There the matter rested until others discovered another kind of dependency, called a **multivalued dependency**, which is discussed earlier in this chapter and is illustrated in exercises 2-40 and 2-41. To eliminate multivalued dependencies, **fourth normal form (4NF)** was defined. To put tables into 4NF, the initial table must be split into tables such that the multiple values of any multivalued attribute are moved into the new tables. These are then accessed via 1:N relationships between the original table and the tables holding the multiple values.

For 4NF, ask yourself: (1) Have the multiple values determined by any multivalued dependency been moved into a separate table? If the answer is *yes*, then the tables are in 4NF.

A little later, another kind of anomaly involving tables that can be split apart but not correctly joined back together was identified, and **fifth normal form (5NF)** was defined to eliminate that type of anomaly. A discussion of 5NF is beyond the scope of this book.

You can see how the knowledge evolved: None of these normal forms were perfect—each one eliminated certain anomalies, and none asserted that it was vulnerable to no anomaly at all. At this stage, in 1981, R. Fagin took a different approach and asked why, rather than just chipping away at anomalies, we do not look for conditions that would have to exist in order for a relation to have no anomalies at all. He did just that and, in the process, defined **domain/key normal form (DK/NF)**, and, no, that is not a typo—the name has the slash between "domain" and "key," while the acronym places it between "DK" and "NF"! Fagin proved that a relation in DK/NF can have no anomalies, and he further proved that a relation that has no anomalies is also in DK/NF.

For some reason, DK/NF never caught the fancy of the general database population, but it should have. As you can tell, no one should brag that their relations are in BCNF—instead we should all brag that our relations are in DK/NF. But for some reason (perhaps because there is fashion in database theory, just as there is fashion in clothes), it just is not done.

You are probably wondering what the conditions of DK/NF are. Basically, DK/NF requires that all the constraints on data values be logical implications of the definition of domains and keys. To the level of detail of this text, and to the level of detail experienced by 99 percent of all database practitioners, this can be restated as follows: Every determinant of a functional dependency must be a candidate key. This is exactly where we started and what we have defined as BCNF.

You can broaden this statement a bit to include multivalued dependencies and say that every determinant of a functional or multivalued dependency must be a candidate key. The trouble with this is that as soon as we constrain a multivalued dependency in this way, it is transformed into a functional dependency. Our original statement is fine. It is like saying that good health comes to overweight people who lose weight until they are of an appropriate weight. As soon as they lose their excess weight, they are no longer overweight. Hence, good health comes to people who have appropriate weight.

For DK/NF, ask yourself: Is the table in BCNF? For our purposes in this book, the two terms are synonymous, so if the answer is yes, we will consider that the table is also in DK/NF.

So, as Paul Harvey used to say, "Now you know the rest of the story." Just ensure that every determinant of a functional dependency is a candidate key (BCNF), and you can claim that your relations are fully normalized. You do not want to say they are in DK/NF until you learn more about it, though, because someone might ask you what that means. However, for most practical purposes your relations are in DK/NF as well.

Note: For more information on normal forms, see David M. Kroenke and David J. Auer, *Database Processing: Fundamentals, Design, and Implementation*, 13th edition (Upper Saddle River, NJ: Prentice Hall, 2014): 118–151.

THE ACCESS WORKBENCH

Section 2

Working with Multiple Tables in Microsoft Access

In Chapter 1's "The Access Workbench," we learned how to create Microsoft Access 2013 databases, tables, forms, and reports. However, we were limited to working with only one table. In this section, we will:

- See examples of the modification problems discussed in Chapters 1 and 2.
- Work with multiple tables.

(Continued)

CONTACT Data

CustomerID	Date	Type	Remarks
1	7/7/2014	Phone	General interest in a Gaea.
1	7/7/2014	Email	Sent general information.
1	7/12/2014	Phone	Set up an appointment.
1	7/14/2014	Meeting	Bought a HiStandard.
3	7/19/2014	Phone	Interested in a SUHi, set up an appointment.
1	7/21/2014	Email	Sent a standard follow-up message.
4	7/27/2014	Phone	Interested in a HiStandard, set up an appointment.
3	7/27/2014	Meeting	Bought a SUHi.
4	8/2/2014	Meeting	Talked up to a HiLuxury. Customer bought one.
3	8/3/2014	Email	Sent a standard follow-up message.
4	8/10/2014	Email	Sent a standard follow-up message.
5	8/15/2014	Phone	General interest in a Gaea.

We will continue to use the WMCRM database we created in Chapter 1's section of "The Access Workbench." At this point, you have created and populated (which means you have inserted the data into) the CONTACT table. Figure AW-2-1 shows the contacts that have been made with each customer. Note that there is no customer with CustomerID 2—this is because we deleted and reentered the data for Jessica Christman.

Possible Modification Problems in the WMCRM Database

We know from the topics covered in this chapter that we really need a separate table to store the CONTACT data, but in order to illustrate the modification problems discussed in Chapter 1 let us combine it into one table with the data already in CUSTOMER. This table is available in the file WMCRM-Combined-Data.accdb, which is available at the Web site for this book (**www.pearsonhighered.com/kroenke**). We will use this database to see modification problems in non-normalized tables and then build the correctly normalized tables in the actual WMCRM database.

We will need to start Microsoft Access 2013, open the WMCRM-Combined-Data. accdb file, and take a look at the WMCRM-Combined-Data database.

Opening an Existing Microsoft Access Database

1. Select the **Microsoft Access 2013** icon on the Start screen, or click the **Microsoft Access 2013** button on the Taskbar if you pinned it there. The Microsoft Access 2013 splash screen window appears, as shown in Figure AW-2-2.
   - **NOTE:** The menu command or icon location used to start Microsoft Access 2013 may vary, depending on the operating system and how Microsoft Office is installed on the computer you are using.
2. Click the **Open Other Files** button on the Microsoft Access 2013 splash screen to open the File | Open page, as shown in Figure AW-2-3.
3. Click the **Computer** button to open the Open | Computer pane, as shown in Figure AW-2-4.
4. Click the **Browse** button to open the Open dialog box, as shown in Figure AW-2-5.

FIGURE AW-2-2

The Microsoft Access 2013 Splash Screen

The **WMCRM.aacdb** file name in the Recent list

Click the **Open Other Files** button to display the file menu Open page

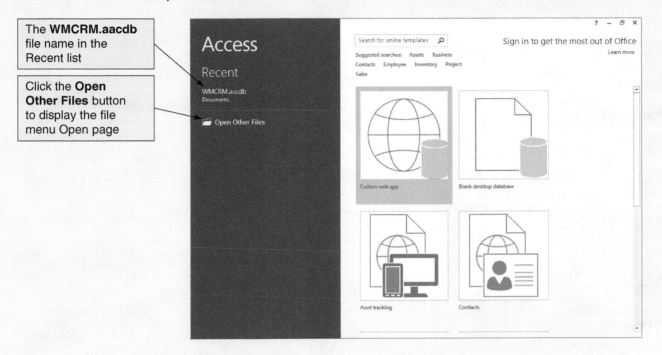

FIGURE AW-2-3

The Microsoft Access 2013 File | Open Page

The File | Open page

The Open | Recent pane is displayed with **WMCRM.aacdb** file name in the Recent list—you can click a file name to open the file

Click the **Computer** button to display the Open | Computer pane

(Continued)

FIGURE AW-2-4

The Open | Computer Page

The File | Open page

The Open | Computer pane is displayed with the Browse button— you can click this button to search for files

Click the **Browse** button to display the Open dialog box

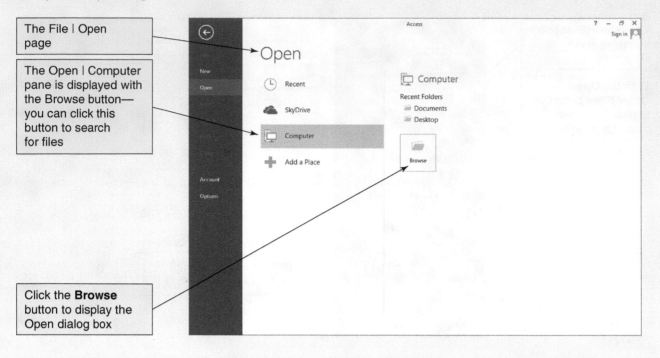

FIGURE AW-2-5

The Open Dialog Box

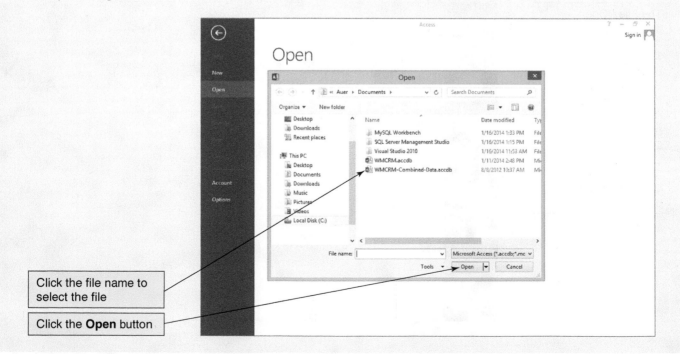

Click the file name to select the file

Click the **Open** button

FIGURE AW-2-6

The CUSTOMER_CONTACT Table

5. Browse to the **WMCRM-Combined-Data.accdb** file, click the file name to highlight it, and then click the **Open** button.
6. The **Security Warning** bar appears with the database. Click the Security Warning bar's **Enable Content** button to select this option.
7. In the Navigation Pane, double-click the **CUSTOMER_CONTACT** table object to open it.
8. Click the **Shutter Bar Open/Close** button to minimize the Navigation Pane.
9. The CUSTOMER_CONTACT table appears in Datasheet view, as shown in Figure AW-2-6. Note that there is one line for each contact, which has resulted in the duplication of basic customer data. For example, there are five sets of basic data for Ben Griffey.
10. Close the CUSTOMER_CONTACT table by clicking the document window's **Close** button.
11. Click the **Shutter Bar Open/Close** button to expand the Navigation Pane.
12. In the Navigation Pane, double-click the **Customer Contact Data Input Form** object to open it. The Customer Contact Data Input Form appears, as shown in Figure AW-2-7. Note that the form displays all the data for one record in the CUSTOMER_CONTACT table.

FIGURE AW-2-7

The Customer Contact Data Input Form

All fields from the CUSTOMER_CONTACT table appear on the form

Form browsing buttons

(Continued)

FIGURE AW-2-8

The Wallingford Motors Customer Contact Report

Contact data for each customer are grouped together and sorted by date

Wallingford Motors Customer Contact Report

CustomerID	Date	LastName	FirstName	Email	Type	Remarks
1						
	7/7/2014	Griffey	Ben	Ben.Griffey@somewhere.com	Phone	General interest in a Gaea.
	7/7/2014	Griffey	Ben	Ben.Griffey@somewhere.com	Email	Sent general information.
	7/12/2014	Griffey	Ben	Ben.Griffey@somewhere.com	Phone	Set up an appointment.
	7/14/2014	Griffey	Ben	Ben.Griffey@somewhere.com	Meeting	Bought a HiStandard.
	7/21/2014	Griffey	Ben	Ben.Griffey@somewhere.com	Email	Sent a standard follow-up message.
3						
	7/19/2014	Christman	Jessica	Jessica.Christman@somewhere.com	Phone	Interested in a SUHI, set up an appointment.
	7/27/2014	Christman	Jessica	Jessica.Christman@somewhere.com	Meeting	Bought a SUHI.
	8/3/2014	Christman	Jessica	Jessica.Christman@somewhere.com	Email	Sent a standard follow-up message.
4						
	7/27/2014	Christman	Rob	Rob.Christman@somewhere.com	Phone	Interested in a HiStandard, set up an appointment.
	8/2/2014	Christman	Rob	Rob.Christman@somewhere.com	Meeting	Talked up to a HiLuxury. Customer bought one.
	8/10/2014	Christman	Rob	Rob.Christman@somewhere.com	Email	Sent a standard follow-up message.
5						
	8/15/2014	Hayes	Judy	Judy.Hayes@somewhere.com	Phone	General interest in a Gaea.

13. Close the Customer Contact Data Input Form by clicking the document window's **Close** button.
14. In the Navigation Pane, double-click the **Wallingford Motors Customer Contact Report** to open it.
15. Click the **Shutter Bar Open/Close** button to minimize the Navigation Pane.
16. The Wallingford Motors Customer Contact Report appears, as shown in Figure AW-2-8. Note that the form displays the data for all contacts in the CUSTOMER_CONTACT table, sorted by CustomerNumber and Date. For example, all the contact data for Ben Griffey (who has a CustomerID of 1) is grouped at the beginning of the report.
17. Close the Wallingford Motors Customer Contact Report by clicking the document window's **Close** button.
18. Click the **Shutter Bar Open/Close** button to expand the Navigation Pane.

Now, assume that Ben Griffey has changed his email address from Ben .Griffey@somewhere.com to Ben.Griffey@elsewhere.com. In a well-formed relation, we would have to make this change only once, but a quick examination of Figures AW-2-6 through AW-2-8 shows that Ben Griffey's email address appears in multiple records. We therefore have to change it in every record to avoid update problems. Unfortunately, it is easy to miss one or more records, especially in large tables.

Updating Ben Griffey's Email Address

1. In the Navigation Pane, double-click the **Customer Contact Data Input Form** object to open it. Because Ben Griffey is the customer in the first record, his data is already in the form.
2. Edit the **Email** address to read *Ben.Griffey@elsewhere.com*, as shown in Figure AW-2-9.
3. Click the **Next Record** button to move to the next record in the table. Again, the record shows Ben Griffey's data, so again edit the **Email** address to read *Ben.Griffey@elsewhere.com.*
4. Click the **Next Record** button to move to the next record in the table. For the third time, the record shows Ben Griffey's data, so again edit the **Email** address to read *Ben.Griffey@elsewhere.com.*
5. Click the **Next Record** button to move to the next record in the table. For the fourth time, the record shows Ben Griffey's data, so again edit the **Email** address to read *Ben.Griffey@elsewhere.com.*

FIGURE AW-2-9

The Customer Contact Data Input Form with the Updated Email Address

The email address
has been updated

The **Next Record**
button

Customer Contact Data Input Form	✕

Customer Contact Data Input Form

CustomerID	1
LastName	Griffey
FirstName	Ben
Address	5678 25th NE
City	Seattle
State	WA
ZIP	98178
Phone	206-456-2345
Fax	
Email	Ben.Griffey@elsewhere.com
Date	7/7/2014
Type	Email
Remarks	Sent general information.

Record: I◀ ◀ 1 of 12 ▶ ▶I ▶✳ 🐾 No Filter Search

6. Click the **Next Record** button to move to the next record in the table. Finally, another customer's data (the data for Jessica Christman's contact on 7/19/2014) appears in the form, so we assume that we have made all the necessary updates to the database records.
7. Close the Customer Contact Data Input form by clicking the document window's **Close** button.
8. In the Navigation Pane, double-click the report **Wallingford Motors Customer Contact Report** to open it.
9. Click the **Shutter Bar Open/Close** button to minimize the Navigation Pane.
10. The Wallingford Motors Customer Contact Report now looks as shown in Figure AW-2-10. Note that the email addresses shown for Ben Griffey are inconsistent—we missed one record when we updated the table, and now we have inconsistent data. A modification error—in this case an update error—has occurred.
11. Close the Wallingford Motors Customer Contact Report by clicking the document window's **Close** button.
12. Click the **Shutter Bar Open/Close** button to expand the Navigation Pane.

This simple example shows how easily modification problems can occur in tables that are not normalized. With a set of well-formed, normalized tables, this problem would not have occurred.

Closing the WMCRM-Combined-Data Database

1. Click the **Close** button to close the database and exit Microsoft Access.

(Continued)

FIGURE AW-2-10

The Updated Wallingford Motors Customer Contact Report

A modification problem has occurred. Not all records were updated with the new email address, and the database records are now inconsistent

Working with Multiple Tables

The table structure for the CUSTOMER_CONTACT table in the WMCRM-Combined-Data database is:

CUSTOMER_CONTACT (CustomerID, LastName, FirstName, Address, City, State, ZIP, Phone, Fax, Email, Date, Type, Remarks)

Applying the normalization process discussed in this chapter, we will have the following set of tables:

CUSTOMER (CustomerID, LastName, FirstName, Address, City, State, ZIP, Phone, Fax, Email)

CONTACT (ContactID, *CustomerID*, ContactDate, ContactType, Remarks)

with the referential integrity constraint:

CustomerID in CONTACT must exist in CustomerID in CUSTOMER

Note that we have modified a couple of column names in the CONTACT table—we are using ContactDate instead of Date and ContactType instead of Type. We will discuss the reason for this later in this section. Our task now is to build and populate the CONTACT table and then to establish the relationship and referential integrity constraint between the two tables.

First, we need to create and populate (insert data into) the CONTACT table, which will contain the columns and column characteristics shown in the table in Figure AW-2-11.[6] The CustomerID column appears again in CONTACT, this time designated as a

---

[6]Although we are using it for simplicity in this example, a column such as Remarks (also often called Comments or Notes) can cause problems in a database. For a complete discussion, see David M. Kroenke and David J. Auer, *Database Processing: Fundamentals, Design, and Implementation*, 13th edition (Upper Saddle River, NJ: Prentice Hall, 2014).

FIGURE AW-2-11

Database Column Characteristics for the CONTACT Table

Column Name	Type	Key	Required	Remarks
ContactID	AutoNumber	Primary Key	Yes	Surrogate Key
CustomerID	Number	Foreign Key	Yes	Long Integer
ContactDate	Date/Time	No	Yes	Short Date
ContactType	Text (10)	No	Yes	Allowed values are Phone, Fax, Email, and Meeting
Remarks	Memo	No	No	

foreign key. As discussed in this chapter, the term *foreign key* designates this column as the link to the CUSTOMER table. The value in the CustomerID column of CONTACT tells which customer was contacted. All we have to do is look up the value of CustomerID in the CUSTOMER table.

Note that when we build the CONTACT table there is no "foreign key" setting. We will set up the database relationship between CUSTOMER and CONTACT after we have finished building the CONTACT table.

Note the following:

- Some new data types are being used: Number, Date/Time, and Memo.
- CustomerID must be set as a Number data type and specifically as a Long Integer data type to match the data type Microsoft Access creates for the AutoNumber data type in the CUSTOMER table.
- The Type column has only four allowed values: Phone, Fax, Email, and Meeting. For now, we can simply input only these data values. You will learn how to enforce the data restriction for this column in Chapter 3.

Creating the CONTACT Table

1. Open Microsoft Access 2013.
2. In the Recent list of database files, click **WMCRM.accdb**. The database file opens in Microsoft Access.
3. Click the **Create** command tab.
4. Click the **Table Design** button.
5. The Table1 tabbed document window is displayed in Design view. Note that along with the Table1 window a contextual tab named Table Tools is displayed and that this tab adds a new command tab and ribbon, named Design, to the set of command tabs displayed.
6. Using the steps we followed to create the CUSTOMER table in Chapter 1's section of "The Access Workbench," begin to create the CONTACT table. The following steps detail only new information that you need to know to complete the CONTACT table.
   - **NOTE:** When creating the CONTACT table, be sure to enter appropriate comments in the Description column.
7. When creating the CustomerID column, set the data type to **Number**. Note that the default Field Size setting for Number is Long Integer, so no change is necessary. Be sure to set the Required property to **Yes**.
8. After creating the ContactID column, set it as the primary key of the table.

(Continued)

FIGURE AW-2-12

The Reserved Word Warning

> The column name Date is a reserved word—do **not** use reserved words as column names

> Click the **Cancel** button and revise the column name

9. When creating the ContactDate column, start by using the column name *Date*. As soon as you enter the column name and try to move to the Data Type column, Microsoft Access displays a dialog box, warning you that Date is a reserved word, as shown in Figure AW-2-12. Click the **Cancel** button, and change the column name to **ContactDate**.

   ■ **NOTE:** Normally, you should avoid reserved words such as Date and Time. Generally, column names such as ContactDate are preferred, both to avoid reserved words and to clarify exactly which date you are referring to, and that is why we changed the column names in the CONTACT table.

10. When creating the ContactDate column, set the data type to **Date/Time** and set the format to **Short Date**, as shown in Figure AW-2-13. Be sure to set the Required property to **Yes**.

11. To name and save the CONTACT table, click the **Save** button in the Quick Access Toolbar.

12. Type the table name **CONTACT** into the Save As dialog box text box, and then click the **OK** button. The table is named and saved, and it now appears with the table name CONTACT.

13. To close the CONTACT table, click the **Close** button in the upper-right corner of the tabbed document window. The CONTACT table now appears as a table object in the Navigation Pane.

Creating Relationships Between Tables

In Microsoft Access, you build relationships between tables by using the **Relationships window**, which you access by using the **Database Tools | Relationships** command. After a relationship is created in the Relationships window, referential integrity constraints are set in the **Edit Relationships dialog box** within that window by using the **Enforce Referential Integrity check box**.

FIGURE AW-2-13

Setting the Date Format

Select the **Short Date** date format from the drop-down list

Creating the Relationship Between the CUSTOMER and CONTACT Tables

1. Click the **Database Tools** command tab to display the Database Tools command groups, as shown in Figure AW-2-14.
2. Click the **Relationships** button in the Show/Hide group. As shown in Figure AW-2-15, the Relationships tabbed document window appears, together with the Show Table dialog box. Note that along with the Relationships window, a contextual tab named Relationship Tools is displayed and that this tab adds a new command tab named Design to the set of command tabs displayed.
3. In the Show Table dialog box, the CONTACT table is already selected. Click the **Add** button to add CONTACT to the Relationships window.
4. In the Show Table dialog box, click the **CUSTOMER** table to select it. Click the **Add** button to add CUSTOMER to the Relationships window.
5. In the Show Table dialog box, click the **Close** button to close the dialog box.
6. Rearrange and resize the table objects in the Relationships window using standard Windows drag-and-drop techniques. Rearrange the CUSTOMER and CONTACT table objects until they appear as shown in Figure AW-2-16. Now we are ready to create the relationship between the tables.
   - **NOTE:** A formal description of how to create a relationship between two tables is "In the Relationships window, drag a primary key column and drop it on top of the corresponding foreign key column." It is easier to understand this after you have actually done it.
7. Click and hold the column name **CustomerID in the CUSTOMER table** and then drag it over the **column name CustomerID in the CONTACT table**. Release the mouse button, and the Edit Relationships dialog box appears, as shown in Figure AW-2-17.
   - **NOTE:** In CUSTOMER, CustomerID is the primary key, and in CONTACT, CustomerID is the foreign key.

(Continued)

FIGURE AW-2-14

The Database Tools Command Tab

The **DATABASE TOOLS** command tab

The **Relationships** button

The **Relationships** command group

8. Click the **Enforce Referential Integrity** check box.
9. Click the **Create** button to create the relationship between CUSTOMER and CONTACT. The relationship between the tables now appears in the Relationships window, as shown in Figure AW-2-18.
10. To close the Relationships window, click the **Close** button in the upper-right corner of the document window. A Microsoft Access warning dialog box appears, asking whether you want to save changes to the layout of relationships. Click the **Yes** button to save the changes and close the window.

At this point, we need to add data on customer contacts to the CONTACT table. Using the CONTACT table in Datasheet view, as discussed earlier, we enter the data shown in Figure AW-2-1 into the CONTACT table. Again, note that there is *no* customer

FIGURE AW-2-15

The Relationships Window

The **RELATIONSHIP TOOLS** contextual command tab

The **DESIGN** command tab

The **Relationships** tabbed document window

The **Show Table** dialog box

Select a table name, then click the **Add** button to add the table to the Relationships window

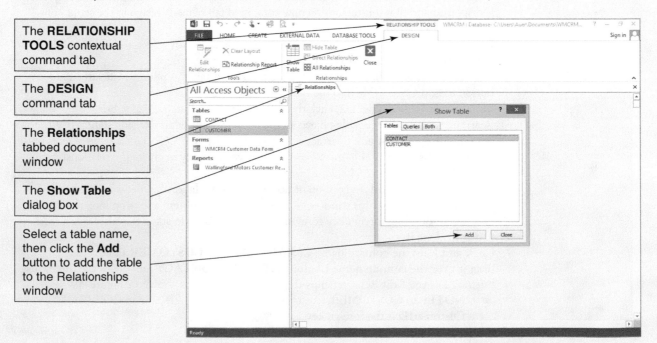

FIGURE AW-2-16

The Table Objects in the Relationships Window

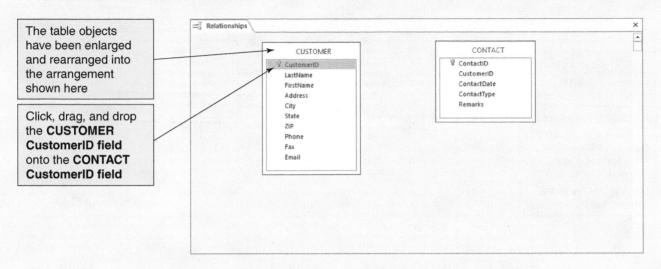

The table objects have been enlarged and rearranged into the arrangement shown here

Click, drag, and drop the **CUSTOMER CustomerID field** onto the **CONTACT CustomerID field**

with CustomerID of 2—this is because we deleted and reentered the data for Jessica Christman in Chapter 1's section of "The Access Workbench." Also note that because referential integrity is enabled, we *cannot* enter a CustomerID that does not already exist in the CUSTOMER table. The CONTACT table with the data inserted looks as shown in Figure AW-2-19. Be sure to close the table after the data have been entered.

FIGURE AW-2-17

The Edit Relationships Dialog Box

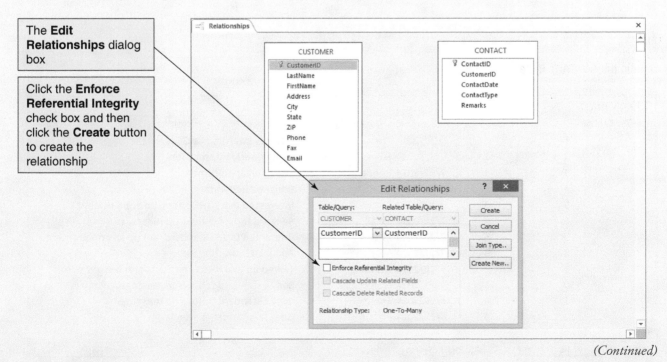

The **Edit Relationships** dialog box

Click the **Enforce Referential Integrity** check box and then click the **Create** button to create the relationship

(Continued)

FIGURE AW-2-18

The Completed Relationship

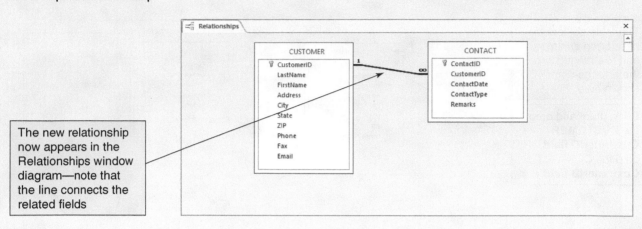

The new relationship now appears in the Relationships window diagram—note that the line connects the related fields

Using a Form That Includes Two Tables

In Chapter 1's section of "The Access Workbench," we created a data entry form for the CUSTOMER table. Now we will create a Microsoft Access form that will let us work with the combined data from both tables.

Creating a Form for Both the CUSTOMER and CONTACT Tables

1. Click the **Create** command tab.
2. Click the **Form Wizard** button in the Forms command group. The Form Wizard appears.
3. Select the **CUSTOMER** table in the Tables/Queries drop-down list. To add all the columns, click the **right-facing double-chevron** button. Do *not* click the **Next** button yet.

FIGURE AW-2-19

Data in the CONTACT Table

ContactID	CustomerID	ContactDate	ContactType	Remarks
1	1	7/7/2014	Phone	General interest in a Gaea.
2	1	7/7/2014	Email	Sent general information.
3	1	7/12/2014	Phone	Set up an appointment.
4	1	7/14/2014	Meeting	Bought a HiStandard.
5	3	7/19/2014	Phone	Interested in a SUHi, set up an appointment.
6	1	7/21/2014	Email	Sent a standard follow-up message.
7	4	7/27/2014	Phone	Interested in a HiStandard, set up an appointment.
8	3	7/27/2014	Meeting	Bought a SUHi.
9	4	8/2/2014	Meeting	Talked up to a HiLuxury. Customer bought one.
10	3	8/3/2014	Email	Sent a standard follow-up message.
11	4	8/10/2014	Email	Sent a standard follow-up message.
12	5	8/15/2014	Phone	General interest in a Gaea.
* (New)	0			

Record: 14 1 of 12 ▶ ▶I ▶▢ No Filter Search

FIGURE AW-2-20

The Completed Form for CUSTOMER and CONTACT Data

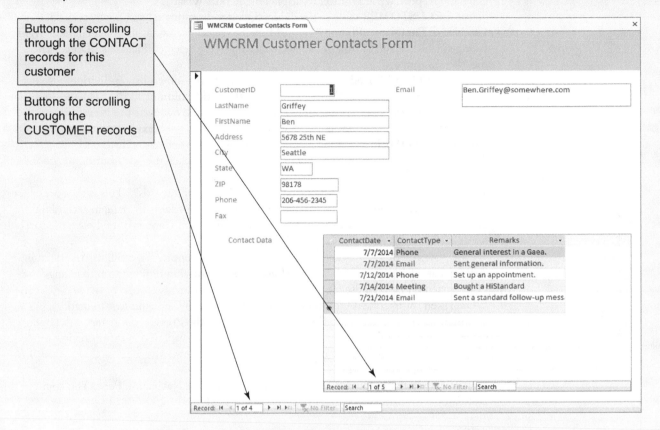

Buttons for scrolling through the CONTACT records for this customer

Buttons for scrolling through the CUSTOMER records

4. Select the **CONTACT** table in the Tables/Queries drop-down list. Individually select and add the **ContactDate, ContactType**, and **Remarks** columns to the Selected Fields list by using the **right-facing single-chevron** button. Now click the **Next** button.

   ■ **NOTE:** You have just created a set of columns from two tables that you want to appear on one form.

5. When asked "How do you want to view your data?" use the default **by CUSTOMER** selection because we want to see all contacts for each customer. Also use the selected **Forms with subforms** option to treat the CONTACT data as a subform within the CUSTOMER form. Click the **Next** button.

6. When asked "What layout would you like for your subform?" click the **Next** button to use the default Datasheet layout.

7. When asked "What titles do you want for your form?" type the form title **WMCRM Customer Contacts Form** into the Form: text box and the form title **Contact Data** into the Subform: text box. Click the **Finish** button. The completed form appears.

8. Click the **Shutter Bar Open/Close** button to minimize the Navigation Pane. The completed form is displayed as shown in Figure AW-2-20.

9. Click the **Shutter Bar Open/Close button** to expand the Navigation Pane.

10. Close the form window.

Creating a Report That Includes Data from Two Tables

In this section, we will create a report that includes data from two or more tables. This Microsoft Access report will let us use the combined data from both the CUSTOMER and CONTACT tables.

(Continued)

Creating a Report for Both the CUSTOMER and CONTACT Tables

1. Click the **Create** tab.
2. Click the **Report Wizard** button to display the Report Wizard.
3. Select the **CUSTOMER** table in the Tables/Queries drop-down list. One by one, click **LastName, FirstName, Phone, Fax**, and **Email** to select each one, and then click the **right-facing single-chevron** button to add each column to the Selected Fields list. Do *not* click the Next button yet.
4. Select the **CONTACT** table in the Tables/Queries drop-down list. Individually select and add the **ContactDate, ContactType**, and **Remarks** columns to the Selected Fields list by clicking the **right-facing single-chevron** button. Now click the **Next** button.
5. When asked "How do you want to view your data?" click the **Next** button to use the default **by CUSTOMER** selection (in order to see all contacts for each customer).
6. When asked "Do you want to add any grouping levels?" click the **Next** button to use the default nongrouped column listing.
7. We are now asked "What sort order do you want for detail records?" This is the sort order for the CONTACT information. The most useful sorting order is by date, in ascending order. Click the **sort field 1** drop-down list arrow and select **ContactDate**. Leave the sort order button set to **Ascending**. Click the **Next** button.
8. We are now asked "How would you like to lay out your report?" We will use the default setting of stepped layout, but click the **Landscape orientation** radio button to change the report orientation to landscape. Then click the **Next** button.
9. When asked "What title do you want for your report?" edit the report title to read **Wallingford Motors Customer Contacts Report**. Leave the **Preview the report** radio button selected. Click the **Finish** button. The completed report is displayed in Print Preview mode.
10. Click the **Close Print Preview** button to close Print Preview.
11. Click the **Home** command tab.
12. Click the **Shutter Bar Open/Close** button to minimize the Navigation Pane. The completed report is displayed as shown in Figure AW-2-21.

FIGURE AW-2-21

The Wallingford Motors Customer Contact Report

13. Although this may not be the best layout for the report, the Microsoft Access Form Wizard has created a usable report with all columns correctly sized to display the information (if there are any columns that are not correctly displayed use the Layout view in the view gallery to make minor adjustments—this tool can be used to make basic adjustments by simply clicking the report section you want to change). We will discuss how to use report Design view to modify reports in Chapter 5's section of "The Access Workbench."

14. Click the **Shutter Bar Open/Close** button to expand the Navigation Pane.

15. Click the document window's **Close** button to close the report window.

Closing the Database and Exiting Microsoft Access

We have finished the work we need to do in this chapter's "The Access Workbench." As usual, we finish by closing the database and Microsoft Access.

Closing the WMCRM Database and Exiting Microsoft Access

1. To close the WMCRM database and exit Microsoft Access 2013, click the **Close** button in the upper-right corner of the Microsoft Access 2013 window.

SUMMARY

The relational model is the most important standard in database processing today. It was first published by E. F. Codd in 1970. Today, it is used for the design and implementation of almost every commercial database.

An entity is something of importance to a user that needs to be represented in a database. A relation is a two-dimensional table that has the characteristics listed in Figure 2-1. In this book, and in the database world in general, the term *table* is used synonymously with the term *relation*. Three sets of terminology are used for relational structures. The terms *table, row*, and *column* are used most commonly, but *file, record*, and *field* are sometimes used in traditional data processing. Theorists also use the terms *relation, tuple*, and *attribute* for the same three constructs. Sometimes these terms are mixed and matched. Strictly speaking, a relation may not have duplicate rows; however, sometimes this condition is relaxed because eliminating duplicates can be a time-consuming process.

A key is one or more columns of a relation that is used to identify a row. A unique key identifies a single row; a nonunique key identifies several rows. A composite key is a key that has two or more attributes. A relation has one primary key, which must be a unique key. A relation may also have additional unique keys, called candidate keys. A primary key is used to represent the table in relationships, and many DBMS products use values of the primary key to organize table storage. In addition, an index normally is constructed to provide fast access via primary key values. An ideal primary key is short, numeric, and never changes.

A surrogate key is a unique numeric value that is appended to a relation to serve as the primary key. Surrogate key values have no meaning to the user and are normally hidden on forms, query results, and reports.

A foreign key is an attribute that is placed in a relation to represent a relationship. A foreign key is the primary key of a table that is different from (foreign to) the table in which it is placed. Primary and foreign keys may have different names, but they must use the same data types and sets of values. A referential integrity constraint specifies that the values of a foreign key be present in the primary key.

A null value occurs when no value has been given to an attribute. The problem with a null value is that its meaning is ambiguous. It can mean that no value is appropriate, that a value is appropriate but has not yet been chosen, or that a value is appropriate and has been chosen but is unknown to the user. It is possible to eliminate null values by requiring attribute values. (Another problem with null values will be discussed in the next chapter.)

A functional dependency occurs when the value of one attribute (or set of attributes) determines the value of a second attribute (or set of attributes). The attribute on the left side of a functional dependency is called the determinant. One way to view the purpose of a relation is to say that the relation exists to store instances of functional dependencies. Another way to define a primary (and candidate) key is to say that such a key is an attribute that functionally determines all the other attributes in a relation.

Normalization is the process of evaluating a relation and, when necessary, breaking the relation into two or more relations that are better designed and said to be well formed. According to normalization theory, a relation is poorly structured if it has a functional dependency that does not involve the primary key. Specifically, in a well-formed relation, every determinant is a candidate key.

A process for normalizing relations into BNCF is shown on page 79, and a discussion of multivalued dependencies and 4NF is found on pages 86–87. According to this process, relations that have normalization problems are divided into two or more relations that do not have such problems. Foreign keys are established between the old and new relations, and referential integrity constraints are created. For reference, a brief discussion of all normal forms is presented on pages 88–89.

KEY TERMS

alternate key	fourth normal form (4NF)	record
attribute	foreign key	referential integrity constraint
AUTO_INCREMENT	functional dependency	relation
Boyce-Codd Normal Form (BCNF)	functionally dependent	row
candidate key	identity	second normal form (2NF)
column	identity increment	SEQUENCE
composite key	identity seed	surrogate key
database schema	is identity	synonyms
determinant	key	table
domain key/normal form (DK/NF)	multivalued dependency	third normal form (3NF)
entity	nonunique key	transitive dependency
field	normalization	tuple
file	normalization process	unique key
fifth normal form (5NF)	null value	well-formed relation
first normal form (1NF)	primary key	

REVIEW QUESTIONS

2.1   Why is the relational model important?

2.2   Define the term *entity* and give an example of an entity (other than the one from this chapter).

2.3   List the characteristics a table must have to be considered a relation.

2.4   Give an example of a relation (other than one from this chapter).

2.5   Give an example of a table that is not a relation (other than one from this chapter).

2.6   Under what circumstances can an attribute of a relation be of variable length?

2.7   Explain the use of the terms *file, record*, and *field*.

2.8   Explain the use of the terms *relation, tuple*, and *attribute*.

2.9   Under what circumstances can a relation have duplicate rows?

2.10   Define the term *unique key* and give an example.

2.11   Define the term *nonunique key* and give an example.

2.12   Give an example of a relation with a unique composite key.

2.13   Explain the difference between a primary key and a candidate key.

2.14   Describe four uses of a primary key.

2.15   What is a *surrogate key*, and under what circumstances would you use one?

2.16   How do surrogate keys obtain their values?

2.17   Why are the values of surrogate keys normally hidden from users on forms, queries, and reports?

2.18   Explain the term *foreign key* and give an example.

2.19   Explain how primary keys and foreign keys are denoted in this book.

2.20   Define the term *referential integrity constraint* and give an example of one.

2.21   Explain three possible interpretations of a null value.

2.22   Give an example of a null value (other than one from this chapter) and explain each of the three possible interpretations for that value.

2.23   Define the terms *functional dependency* and *determinant*, using an example not from this book.

2.24   In the following equation, name the functional dependency and identify the determinant(s):

$$Area = Length \times Width$$

2.25   Explain the meaning of the following expression:

$$A \rightarrow (B, C)$$

Given this expression, tell if it is also true that:

$$A \rightarrow B$$

and:

$$A \rightarrow C$$

2.26   Explain the meaning of the following expression:

$$(D, E) \rightarrow F$$

Given this expression, tell if it is also true that:

$$D \rightarrow F$$

and:

$$E \rightarrow F$$

2.27   Explain the differences in your answers to questions 2.25 and 2.26.

2.28   Define the term *primary key* in terms of functional dependencies.

2.29   If you assume that a relation has no duplicate data, how do you know there is always at least one primary key?

2.30   How does your answer to question 2.29 change if you allow a relation to have duplicate data?

2.31   In your own words, describe the nature and purpose of the normalization process.

2.32   Examine the data in the Veterinary Office List—Version One in Figure 1-30 (see page 55) and state assumptions about functional dependencies in that table. What is the danger of making such conclusions on the basis of sample data?

2.33   Using the assumptions you stated in your answer to question 2.32, what are the determinants of this relation? What attribute(s) can be the primary key of this relation?

2.34 Describe a modification problem that occurs when changing data in the relation in question 2.32 and a second modification problem that occurs when deleting data in this relation.

2.35 Examine the data in the Veterinary Office List—Version Two in Figure 1-31 (see page 56) and state assumptions about functional dependencies in that table.

2.36 Using the assumptions you stated in your answer to question 2.35, what are the determinants of this relation? What attribute(s) can be the primary key of this relation?

2.37 Explain a modification problem that occurs when changing data in the relation in question 2.35 and a second modification problem that occurs when deleting data in this relation.

EXERCISES

2.38 Apply the normalization process to the Veterinary Office List—Version One relation shown in Figure 1-30 (see page 55) to develop a set of normalized relations. Show the results of each of the steps in the normalization process.

2.39 Apply the normalization process to the Veterinary Office List—Version Two relation shown in Figure 1-31 (see page 56) to develop a set of normalized relations. Show the results of each of the steps in the normalization process.

2.40 What is a multivalued dependency, and how is it resolved by 4NF? To answer these questions, consider the following relation:

STUDENT(<u>StudentNumber</u>, StudentName, <u>SiblingName</u>, Major)

Assume that the values of SiblingName are the names of all of a given student's brothers and sisters; also assume that students have at most one major.

   A. Show an example of this relation for two students, one of whom has three siblings and the other of whom has only two siblings.

   B. List the candidate keys in this relation.

   C. State the functional dependencies in this relation.

   D. Explain why this relation does not meet the relational design criteria set out in this chapter (that is, why this is not a well-formed relation).

   E. Define and discuss 4NF, and how 4NF can be used to allow a set of well-formed relations.

   F. Divide this relation into a set of relations that meet the relational design criteria (that is, that are well formed). Specify the type of final normal form for each the final relations.

2.41 What is a multivalued dependency, and how is it resolved by 4NF? To answer these questions, alter question 2.40 to allow students to have multiple majors. In this case, the relational structure is:

STUDENT (<u>StudentNumber</u>, StudentName, <u>SiblingName</u>, <u>Major</u>)

   A. Show an example of this relation for two students, one of whom has three siblings and the other of whom has one sibling. Assume that each student has a single major.

   B. Show the data changes necessary to add a second major for only the first student.

C. Based on your answer to part B, show the data changes necessary to add a second major for the second student.

D. Explain the differences in your answers to parts B and C. Comment on the desirability of this situation.

E. Define and discuss 4NF, and how 4NF can be used to allow a set of well-formed relations.

F. Divide this relation into a set of well-formed relations. Specify the type of normal form for each of the final relations.

2.42 The text states that you can argue that "the only reason for having relations is to store instances of functional dependencies." Explain, in your own words, what this means.

2.43 Consider a table named ORDER_ITEM, with data as shown in Figure 2-26. The schema for ORDER_ITEM is:

ORDER_ITEM (OrderNumber, SKU, Quantity, Price)

where SKU is a "Stocking Keeping Unit" number, which is similar to a part number. Here it indicates which product was sold on each line of the table. Note that one OrderNumber must have at least one SKU associated with it, and may have several. Use this table and the detailed discussion of normal forms on pages 88–89 to answer the following questions.

A. Define 1NF. Is ORDER_ITEM in 1NF? If not, why not, and what would have to be done to put it into 1NF? Make any changes necessary to put ORDER_ITEM into 1NF. If this step requires you to create an additional table, make sure that the new table is also in 1NF.

B. Define 2NF. Now that ORDER_ITEM is in 1NF, is it also in 2NF? If not, why not, and what would have to be done to put it into 2NF? Make any changes necessary to put ORDER_ITEM into 2NF. If this step requires you to create an additional table, make sure that the new table is also in 2NF.

C. Define 3NF. Now that ORDER_ITEM is in 2NF, is it also in 3NF? If not, why not, and what would have to be done to put it into 3NF? Make any changes necessary to put ORDER_ITEM into 3NF. If this step requires you to create an additional table, make sure that the new table and any other tables created in previous steps are also in 3NF.

D. Define BCNF. Now that ORDER_ITEM is in 3NF, is it also in BCNF? If not, why not, and what would have to be done to put it into BCNF? Make any changes necessary to put ORDER_ITEM into BCNF. If this step requires you to create an additional table, make sure that the new table and any other tables created in previous steps are also in BCNF.

FIGURE 2-26

The ORDER_ITEM Table

	OrderNumber	SKU	Quantity	Price
1	1000	201000	1	300.00
2	1000	202000	1	130.00
3	2000	101100	4	50.00
4	2000	101200	2	50.00
5	3000	100200	1	300.00
6	3000	101100	2	50.00
7	3000	101200	1	50.00

ACCESS WORKBENCH KEY TERMS

Edit Relationships dialog box   Relationships window
Enforce Referential Integrity check box

ACCESS WORKBENCH EXERCISES

In the "Access Workbench Exercises" in Chapter 1, we created a database for the Wedgewood Pacific Corporation (WPC) of Seattle, Washington, and created and populated the EMPLOYEE table. In this exercise, we will build the rest of the tables needed for the database, create the referential integrity constraints between them, and populate them.

The full set of normalized tables for the WPC database is as follows:

DEPARTMENT (<u>DepartmentName</u>, BudgetCode, OfficeNumber, Phone)

EMPLOYEE (<u>EmployeeNumber</u>, FirstName, LastName, *Department*, Phone, Email)

PROJECT (<u>ProjectID</u>, ProjectName, *Department*, MaxHours, StartDate, EndDate)

ASSIGNMENT (<u>*ProjectID*</u>, <u>*EmployeeNumber*</u>, HoursWorked)

The primary key of DEPARTMENT is DepartmentName, the primary key of EMPLOYEE is EmployeeNumber, and the primary key of PROJECT is ProjectID. Note that the EMPLOYEE table is the same as the table we have created, except that Department is now a foreign key. In EMPLOYEE and PROJECT, Department is a foreign key that references DepartmentName in DEPARTMENT. Note that a foreign key does not need to have the same name as the primary key to which it refers. The primary key of ASSIGNMENT is the composite (ProjectID, EmployeeNumber). ProjectID is also a foreign key that references ProjectID in PROJECT, and EmployeeNumber is a foreign key that references EmployeeNumber in EMPLOYEE.

The referential integrity constraints are:

Department in EMPLOYEE must exist in DepartmentName in DEPARTMENT

Department in PROJECT must exist in DepartmentName in DEPARTMENT

ProjectID in ASSIGNMENT must exist in ProjectID in PROJECT

EmployeeNumber in ASSIGNMENT must exist in EmployeeNumber in EMPLOYEE

A.   Figure 2-27 shows the column characteristics for the WPC DEPARTMENT table. Using the column characteristics, create the DEPARTMENT table in the WPC.accdb database.

FIGURE 2-27

Column Characteristics for the DEPARTMENT Table

Column Name	Type	Key	Required	Remarks
DepartmentName	Text (35)	Primary Key	Yes	
BudgetCode	Text (30)	No	Yes	
OfficeNumber	Text (15)	No	Yes	
Phone	Text (12)	No	Yes	

FIGURE 2-28

WPC DEPARTMENT Data

DepartmentName	BudgetCode	OfficeNumber	Phone
Administration	BC-100-10	BLDG01-300	360-285-8100
Legal	BC-200-10	BLDG01-200	360-285-8200
Accounting	BC-300-10	BLDG01-100	360-285-8300
Finance	BC-400-10	BLDG01-140	360-285-8400
Human Resources	BC-500-10	BLDG01-180	360-285-8500
Production	BC-600-10	BLDG02-100	360-287-8600
Marketing	BC-700-10	BLDG02-200	360-287-8700
InfoSystems	BC-800-10	BLDG02-270	360-287-8800

B. For the DEPARTMENT table, create a data input form named WPC Department Data Form. Make any necessary adjustments to the form so that all data display properly. Use this form to enter into your DEPARTMENT table the data in the DEPARTMENT table shown in Figure 2-28.

C. Create the relationship and referential integrity constraint between DEPARTMENT and EMPLOYEE. Enable enforcing of referential integrity and enable cascading of data updates, but do *not* enable cascading of deletions.

D. Figure 2-29 shows the column characteristics for the WPC PROJECT table. Using the column characteristics, create the PROJECT table in the WPC.accdb database.

E. Create the relationship and referential integrity constraint between DEPARTMENT and PROJECT. Enable enforcing of referential integrity and enable cascading of data updates, but do *not* enable cascading of deletions.

F. For the PROJECT table, create a data input form named WPC Project Data Form. Make any necessary adjustments to the form so that all data display properly. Use this form to enter into your PROJECT table the data in the PROJECT table shown in Figure 2-30.

FIGURE 2-29

Column Characteristics for the PROJECT Table

Column Name	Type	Key	Required	Remarks
ProjectID	Number	Primary Key	Yes	Long Integer
ProjectName	Text (50)	No	Yes	
Department	Text (35)	Foreign Key	Yes	
MaxHours	Number	No	Yes	Double, fixed, 2 decimal places
StartDate	Date/Time	No	No	Medium date
EndDate	Date/Time	No	No	Medium date

(Continued)

FIGURE 2-30

WPC PROJECT Data

ProjectID	ProjectName	Department	MaxHours	StartDate	EndDate
1000	2014 Q3 Product Plan	Marketing	135.00	10-MAY-14	15-JUN-14
1100	2014 Q3 Portfolio Analysis	Finance	120.00	05-JUL-14	25-JUL-14
1200	2014 Q3 Tax Preparation	Accounting	145.00	10-AUG-14	15-OCT-14
1300	2014 Q4 Product Plan	Marketing	150.00	10-AUG-14	15-SEP-14
1400	2014 Q4 Portfolio Analysis	Finance	140.00	05-OCT-14	NULL

G. When creating and populating the DEPARTMENT table, the data were entered into the table before the referential integrity constraint with EMPLOYEE was created, but when creating and populating the PROJECT table the referential integrity constraint was created before the data were entered. Why did the order of the steps differ? Which order is normally the correct order to use?

H. Figure 2-31 shows the column characteristics for the WPC ASSIGNMENT table. Using the column characteristics, create the ASSIGNMENT table in the WPC.accdb database.

I. Create the relationship and referential integrity constraint between ASSIGNMENT and PROJECT and between ASSIGNMENT and EMPLOYEE. When creating both relations, enable enforcing of referential integrity, but do *not* enable cascading of data updates or cascading of data from deleted records.

J. For the ASSIGNMENT table, create a data input form named WPC Assignment Data Form. Make any necessary adjustments to the form so that all data display properly. Use this form to enter into your ASSIGNMENT table the data in the ASSIGNMENT table shown in Figure 2-32.

K. When creating the relationships between the database tables, we allowed the cascading of data changes between some tables but not between others. (*Cascading* means that changes to data in one table are also made to the other table in the relationship.) The value of a primary key changes in this case, and that change

FIGURE 2-31

Column Characteristics for the ASSIGNMENT Table

Column Name	Type	Key	Required	Remarks
ProjectID	Number	Primary Key, Foreign Key	Yes	Long Integer
EmployeeNumber	Number	Primary Key, Foreign Key	Yes	Long Integer
HoursWorked	Number	No	No	Double, fixed, 1 decimal places

FIGURE 2-32

WPC ASSIGNMENT Data

ProjectID	EmployeeNumber	HoursWorked
1000	1	30.0
1000	8	75.0
1000	10	55.0
1100	4	40.0
1100	6	45.0
1200	1	25.0
1200	2	20.0
1200	4	45.0
1200	5	40.0
1300	1	35.0
1300	8	80.0
1300	10	50.0
1400	4	15.0
1400	5	10.0
1400	6	27.5

is then made in the values of the matching foreign key. Why did we enable cascading of related field values between (1) DEPARTMENT and EMPLOYEE and (2) DEPARTMENT and PROJECT but not for (3) EMPLOYEE and ASSIGNMENT and (4) PROJECT and ASSIGNMENT?

L. For both the DEPARTMENT and EMPLOYEE tables, create a data input form named WPC Department Employee Data Form. This form should show all the employees in each department.

M. Create a report named Wedgewood Pacific Corporation Department Employee Report that presents the data contained in your DEPARTMENT and EMPLOYEE tables. The report should group employees by department. Print out a copy of this report.

REGIONAL LABS CASE QUESTIONS

Regional Labs is a company that conducts research and development work on a contract basis for other companies and organizations. Figure 2-33 shows data that Regional Labs collects about projects and the employees assigned to them.

This data is stored in a relation (table) named PROJECT:

PROJECT (ProjectID, EmployeeName, EmployeeSalary)

ProjectID	EmployeeName	EmployeeSalary
100-A	Eric Jones	64,000.00
100-A	Donna Smith	70,000.00
100-B	Donna Smith	70,000.00
200-A	Eric Jones	64,000.00
200-B	Eric Jones	64,000.00
200-C	Eric Parks	58,000.00
200-C	Donna Smith	70,000.00
200-D	Eric Parks	58,000.00

A. Assuming that all functional dependencies are apparent in this data, which of the following are true?

1. ProjectID → EmployeeName
2. ProjectID → EmployeeSalary
3. (ProjectID, EmployeeName) → EmployeeSalary
4. EmployeeName → EmployeeSalary
5. EmployeeSalary → ProjectID
6. EmployeeSalary → (ProjectID, EmployeeName)

B. What is the primary key of PROJECT?

C. Are all the nonkey attributes (if any) dependent on the primary key?

D. In what normal form is PROJECT?

E. Describe two modification anomalies that affect PROJECT.

F. Is ProjectID a determinant? If so, based on which functional dependencies in part A?

G. Is EmployeeName a determinant? If so, based on which functional dependencies in part A?

H. Is (ProjectID, EmployeeName) a determinant? If so, based on which functional dependencies in part A?

I. Is EmployeeSalary a determinant? If so, based on which functional dependencies in part A?

J. Does this relation contain a transitive dependency? If so, what is it?

K. Redesign the relation to eliminate modification anomalies.

GARDEN GLORY PROJECT QUESTIONS

Figure 2-34 shows data that Garden Glory collects about properties and services.

A. Using these data, state assumptions about functional dependencies among the columns of data. Justify your assumptions on the basis of these sample data and also on the basis of what you know about service businesses.

B. Given your assumptions in part A, comment on the appropriateness of the following designs:

1. PROPERTY (PropertyName, PropertyType, Street, City, Zip, ServiceDate, Description, Amount)

FIGURE 2-34

Sample Data for Garden Glory

PropertyName	Type	Street	City	ZIP	ServiceDate	Description	Amount
Eastlake Building	Office	123 Eastlake	Seattle	98119	5/5/2014	Lawn Mow	$ 42.50
Elm St Apts	Apartment	4 East Elm	Lynnwood	98223	5/8/2014	Lawn Mow	$ 123.50
Jeferson Hill	Office	42 West 7th St	Bellevue	98040	5/8/2014	Garden Service	$ 53.00
Eastlake Building	Office	123 Eastlake	Seattle	98119	5/10/2014	Lawn Mow	$ 42.50
Eastlake Building	Office	123 Eastlake	Seattle	98119	5/12/2014	Lawn Mow	$ 42.50
Elm St Apts	Apartment	4 East Elm	Lynnwood	98223	5/15/2014	Lawn Mow	$ 123.50
Eastlake Building	Office	123 Eastlake	Seattle	98119	5/19/2014	Lawn Mow	$ 42.50

2. PROPERTY (PropertyName, PropertyType, Street, City, Zip, <u>ServiceDate</u>, Description, Amount)

3. PROPERTY (<u>PropertyName</u>, PropertyType, Street, City, Zip, <u>ServiceDate</u>, Description, Amount)

4. PROPERTY (<u>PropertyID</u>, PropertyName, PropertyType, Street, City, Zip, ServiceDate, Description, Amount)

5. PROPERTY (<u>PropertyID</u>, PropertyName, PropertyType, Street, City, Zip, <u>ServiceDate</u>, Description, Amount)

6. PROPERTY (<u>PropertyID</u>, PropertyName, PropertyType, Street, City, Zip, *ServiceDate*)

   and:

   SERVICE (<u>ServiceDate</u>, Description, Amount)

7. PROPERTY (<u>PropertyID</u>, PropertyName, PropertyType, Street, City, Zip, ServiceDate)

   and:

   SERVICE (<u>ServiceID</u>, *ServiceDate*, Description, Amount)

8. PROPERTY (<u>PropertyID</u>, PropertyName, PropertyType, Street, City, Zip, *ServiceDate*)

   and:

   SERVICE (<u>ServiceID</u>, ServiceDate, Description, Amount, *PropertyID*)

9. PROPERTY (<u>PropertyID</u>, PropertyName, PropertyType, Street, City, Zip)

   and:

   SERVICE (<u>ServiceID</u>, ServiceDate, Description, Amount, *PropertyID*)

C. Suppose Garden Glory decides to add the following table:

SERVICE_FEE (PropertyID, ServiceID, Description, Amount)

Add this table to what you consider to be the best design in your answer to part B. Modify the tables from part B as necessary to minimize the amount of data duplication. Will this design work for the data in Figure 2-34? If not, modify the design so that this data will work. State the assumptions implied by this design.

JAMES RIVER JEWELRY PROJECT QUESTIONS

The James River Jewelry project questions are available in online Appendix D, which can be downloaded from the textbook's Web site: **www.pearsonhighered.com/kroenke**.

THE QUEEN ANNE CURIOSITY SHOP PROJECT QUESTIONS

Figure 2-35 shows typical sales data for The Queen Anne Curiosity Shop, and Figure 2-36 shows typical purchase data.

A. Using these data, state assumptions about functional dependencies among the columns of data. Justify your assumptions on the basis of these sample data and also on the basis of what you know about retail sales.

B. Given your assumptions in part A, comment on the appropriateness of the following designs:

    1. CUSTOMER (<u>LastName</u>, FirstName, Phone, Email, InvoiceDate, InvoiceItem, Price, Tax, Total)

    2. CUSTOMER (<u>LastName</u>, <u>FirstName</u>, Phone, Email, InvoiceDate, InvoiceItem, Price, Tax, Total)

    3. CUSTOMER (LastName, FirstName, <u>Phone</u>, Email, InvoiceDate, InvoiceItem, Price, Tax, Total)

    4. CUSTOMER (<u>LastName</u>, <u>FirstName</u>, Phone, Email, <u>InvoiceDate</u>, InvoiceItem, Price, Tax, Total)

FIGURE 2-35

Sample Sales Data for The Queen Anne Curiosity Shop

LastName	FirstName	Phone	InvoiceDate	InvoiceItem	Price	Tax	Total
Shire	Robert	206-524-2433	14-Dec-14	Antique Desk	3,000.00	249.00	3,249.00
Shire	Robert	206-524-2433	14-Dec-14	Antique Desk Chair	500.00	41.50	541.50
Goodyear	Katherine	206-524-3544	15-Dec-14	Dining Table Linens	1,000.00	83.00	1,083.00
Bancroft	Chris	425-635-9788	15-Dec-14	Candles	50.00	4.15	54.15
Griffith	John	206-524-4655	23-Dec-14	Candles	45.00	3.74	48.74
Shire	Robert	206-524-2433	5-Jan-15	Desk Lamp	250.00	20.75	270.75
Tierney	Doris	425-635-8677	10-Jan-15	Dining Table Linens	750.00	62.25	812.25
Anderson	Donna	360-538-7566	12-Jan-15	Book Shelf	250.00	20.75	270.75
Goodyear	Katherine	206-524-3544	15-Jan-15	Antique Chair	1,250.00	103.75	1,353.75
Goodyear	Katherine	206-524-3544	15-Jan-15	Antique Chair	1,750.00	145.25	1,895.25
Tierney	Doris	425-635-8677	25-Jan-15	Antique Candle Holders	350.00	29.05	379.05

FIGURE 2-36

Sample Purchase Data for The Queen Anne Curiosity Shop

PurchaseItem	PurchasePrice	PurchaseDate	Vendor	Phone
Antique Desk	1,800.00	7-Nov-14	European Specialties	206-325-7866
Antique Desk	1,750.00	7-Nov-14	European Specialties	206-325-7866
Antique Candle Holders	210.00	7-Nov-14	European Specialties	206-325-7866
Antique Candle Holders	200.00	7-Nov-14	European Specialties	206-325-7866
Dining Table Linens	600.00	14-Nov-14	Linens and Things	206-325-6755
Candles	30.00	14-Nov-14	Linens and Things	206-325-6755
Desk Lamp	150.00	14-Nov-14	Lamps and Lighting	206-325-8977
Floor Lamp	300.00	14-Nov-14	Lamps and Lighting	206-325-8977
Dining Table Linens	450.00	21-Nov-14	Linens and Things	206-325-6755
Candles	27.00	21-Nov-14	Linens and Things	206-325-6755
Book Shelf	150.00	21-Nov-14	Harrison, Denise	425-746-4322
Antique Desk	1,000.00	28-Nov-14	Lee, Andrew	425-746-5433
Antique Desk Chair	300.00	28-Nov-14	Lee, Andrew	425-746-5433
Antique Chair	750.00	28-Nov-14	New York Brokerage	206-325-9088
Antique Chair	1,050.00	28-Nov-14	New York Brokerage	206-325-9088

5. CUSTOMER (<u>LastName</u>, <u>FirstName</u>, Phone, Email, InvoiceDate, <u>InvoiceItem</u>, Price, Tax, Total)

6. CUSTOMER (<u>LastName</u>, <u>FirstName</u>, Phone, Email)

   and:

   SALE (<u>InvoiceDate</u>, InvoiceItem, Price, Tax, Total)

7. CUSTOMER (<u>LastName</u>, <u>FirstName</u>, Phone, Email, *InvoiceDate*)

   and:

   SALE (<u>InvoiceDate</u>, InvoiceItem, Price, Tax, Total)

8. CUSTOMER (<u>LastName</u>, <u>FirstName</u>, Phone, Email)

   and:

   SALE (<u>InvoiceDate</u>, <u>InvoiceItem</u>, Price, Tax, Total, *LastName*, *FirstName*)

C. Modify what you consider to be the best design in part B to include surrogate ID columns called CustomerID and SaleID. How does this improve the design?

D. Modify the design in part C by breaking SALE into two relations named SALE and SALE_ITEM. Modify columns and add additional columns as you think necessary. How does this improve the design?

E. Given your assumptions, comment on the appropriateness of the following designs:

1. PURCHASE (<u>PurchaseItem</u>, PurchasePrice, PurchaseDate, Vendor, Phone)

2. PURCHASE (<u>PurchaseItem</u>, <u>PurchasePrice</u>, PurchaseDate, Vendor, Phone)

3. PURCHASE (<u>PurchaseItem</u>, PurchasePrice, <u>PurchaseDate</u>, Vendor, Phone)

4. PURCHASE (<u>PurchaseItem</u>, PurchasePrice, PurchaseDate, <u>Vendor</u>, Phone)

5. PURCHASE (<u>PurchaseItem</u>, PurchasePrice, <u>PurchaseDate</u>)

and:

VENDOR (<u>Vendor</u>, Phone)

6. PURCHASE (<u>PurchaseItem</u>, PurchasePrice, <u>PurchaseDate</u>, Vendor)

and:

VENDOR (<u>Vendor</u>, Phone)

7. PURCHASE (<u>PurchaseItem</u>, PurchasePrice, <u>PurchaseDate</u>, *Vendor*)

and:

VENDOR (<u>Vendor</u>, Phone)

F. Modify what you consider to be the best design in part E to include surrogate ID columns called PurchaseID and VendorID. How does this improve the design?

G. The relations in your design from part D and part F are not connected. Modify the database design so that sales data and purchase data are related.

CHAPTER 3 Structured Query Language

This chapter describes and discusses **Structured Query Language (SQL)**. SQL is not a complete programming language; rather, it is a **data sublanguage**. SQL consists only of constructs for defining and processing a database. To obtain a full programming language, SQL statements must be embedded in scripting languages, such as VBScript, or in programming languages, such as Java or C#. SQL statements also can be submitted interactively, using a DBMS-supplied command prompt.

SQL was developed by the IBM Corporation in the late 1970s, and successive versions were endorsed as national standards by the **American National Standards Institute (ANSI)** in 1986, 1989, and 1992. The 1992 version is sometimes referred to as SQL-92 or sometimes ANSI-92 SQL. In 1999, SQL:1999 (also referred to as SQL3), which incorporated some object-oriented concepts, was released. This was followed by the release of SQL:2003 in 2003, SQL:2006 in 2006, SQL:2008 in 2008, and, most recently, SQL:2011 in 2011. Each of these added new features or extended existing SQL features, including SQL support for **Extensible Markup Language (XML)**, which is discussed in Chapter 7, and, in SQL:2008, the SQL TRUNCATE TABLE and SQL MERGE statements. SQL has also been endorsed as a standard by the **International Organization for Standardization (ISO)** (and, no, that's not a typo—the acronym is *ISO*, not *IOS*!). Our discussion here focuses on common language features that have been in SQL since SQL-92 but does include some features from SQL:2003 and SQL:2008.[1]

---

[1]For more information about the history and development of SQL, see the Standardization section of the Wikipedia article on **SQL**. Wikipedia also has articles of some of the named versions of SQL. For example, see the article on **SQL:2008** for a discussion of the features added to SQL:2008.

SQL is text oriented. It was developed long before the **graphical user interface (GUI)** became common, and requires only a text processor. Today, Microsoft Access, Microsoft SQL Server, Oracle Database, MySQL, and other DBMS products provide GUI tools for performing many of the tasks that are performed using SQL. However, the key phrase in that last sentence is *many of*. You cannot do everything with graphic tools that you can do with SQL. Furthermore, to generate SQL statements dynamically in program code, you must use SQL.

You will learn how to use SQL with Microsoft Access in this chapter's "The Access Workbench." Access uses SQL but hides it behind the scenes, presenting a variant of the **Query by Example (QBE)** GUI for general use. Although knowledge of SQL is not a requirement for using Access, you will be a stronger and more effective Access developer if you know SQL.

SQL statements are commonly divided into categories, five of which are of interest to us here:

- **Data definition language (DDL)** statements, which are used for creating tables, relationships, and other structures
- **Data manipulation language (DML)** statements, which are used for querying, inserting, modifying, and deleting data. One component of SQL DML is SQL view, which are discussed in Appendix E. Views are used to create predefined queries.[2]
- **SQL/Persistent stored modules (SQL/PSM)** statements, which extend SQL by adding procedural programming capabilities, such as variables and flow-of-control statements, that provide some programmability within the SQL framework.
- **Transaction control language (TCL)** statements, which are used to mark transaction boundaries and control transaction behavior.
- **Data control language (DCL)** statements, which are used to grant database permissions (or to revoke those permissions) to users and groups, so that the users or groups can perform various operations on the data in the database.

In this chapter, we discuss SQL DDL and DML. Additional SQL DML (SQL views) and SQL/PSM are discussed in Appendix E, and SQL TCL and DCL are discussed in Chapter 6.

AN EXAMPLE DATABASE

The Wedgewood Pacific Corporation (WPC), founded in 1957 in Seattle, Washington, has grown into an internationally recognized organization. The company is located in two buildings. One building houses the Administration, Accounting, Finance, and Human Resources departments, and the second houses the Production, Marketing, and Information Systems departments. The company database contains data about *employees*, *departments*, *projects*, *assets* (such as computer equipment), and other aspects of company operations.

---

[2]Queries by themselves are sometimes considered to be another major category of SQL commands, but we do not make that distinction in this book. For more details, see the Wikipedia article on **SQL**.

In this chapter, we use an example database for WPC that has the following four relations:

DEPARTMENT (<u>DepartmentName</u>, BudgetCode, OfficeNumber, Phone)

EMPLOYEE (<u>EmployeeNumber</u>, FirstName, LastName, *Department*, Phone, Email)

PROJECT (<u>ProjectID</u>, ProjectName, *Department*, MaxHours, StartDate, EndDate)

ASSIGNMENT (*<u>ProjectID</u>*, *<u>EmployeeNumber</u>*, HoursWorked)

The primary key of DEPARTMENT is DepartmentName, the primary key of EMPLOYEE is EmployeeNumber, and the primary key of PROJECT is ProjectID. In EMPLOYEE and PROJECT, Department is a foreign key that references DepartmentName in DEPARTMENT. Remember that a foreign key does not need to have the same name as the primary key to which it refers. The primary key of ASSIGNMENT is the composite (ProjectID, EmployeeNumber). ProjectID is also a foreign key that references ProjectID in PROJECT, and EmployeeNumber is a foreign key that references EmployeeNumber in EMPLOYEE.

The referential integrity constraints are:

Department in EMPLOYEE must exist in Department in DEPARTMENT

Department in PROJECT must exist in Department in DEPARTMENT

ProjectID in ASSIGNMENT must exist in ProjectID in PROJECT

EmployeeNumber in ASSIGNMENT must exist in EmployeeNumber in EMPLOYEE

An illustration of these tables in Microsoft Access 2013 and the database column characteristics for these tables are shown in Figure 3-1. Sample data for these relations are shown in Figure 3-2.

FIGURE 3-1

Database Column Characteristics for the WPC Database

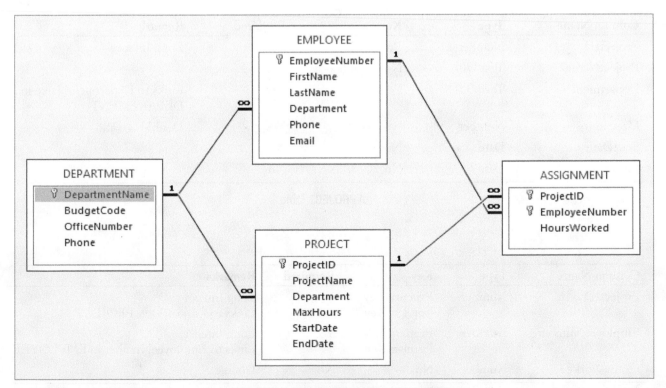

(a) The WPC Tables in Microsoft Access 2013

(continued)

FIGURE 3-1   Continued

Column Name	Type	Key	Required	Remarks
DepartmentName	Text (35)	Primary Key	Yes	
BudgetCode	Text (30)	No	Yes	
OfficeNumber	Text (15)	No	Yes	
Phone	Text (12)	No	Yes	

(b) DEPARTMENT Table

Column Name	Type	Key	Required	Remarks
EmployeeNumber	AutoNumber	Primary Key	Yes	Surrogate Key
FirstName	Text (25)	No	Yes	
LastName	Text (25)	No	Yes	
Department	Text (35)	Foreign Key	Yes	Links to DepartmentName in DEPARTMENT
Phone	Text (12)	No	No	
Email	Text (100)	No	Yes	

(c) EMPLOYEE Table

Column Name	Type	Key	Required	Remarks
ProjectID	Number	Primary Key	Yes	Long Integer
ProjectName	Text (50)	No	Yes	
Department	Text (35)	Foreign Key	Yes	Links to DepartmentName in DEPARTMENT
MaxHours	Number	No	Yes	Double
StartDate	Date	No	No	
EndDate	Date	No	No	

(d) PROJECT Table

Column Name	Type	Key	Required	Remarks
ProjectID	Number	Primary Key, Foreign Key	Yes	Long Integer Links to ProjectID in PROJECT
EmployeeNumber	Number	Primary Key, Foreign Key	Yes	Long Integer Links to EmployeeNumber in EMPLOYEE
HoursWorked	Number	No	No	Double

(e) ASSIGNMENT Table

FIGURE 3-2

Sample Data for the WPC Database

DepartmentName	BudgetCode	OfficeNumber	Phone
Administration	BC-100-10	BLDG01-300	360-285-8100
Legal	BC-200-10	BLDG01-200	360-285-8200
Accounting	BC-300-10	BLDG01-100	360-285-8300
Finance	BC-400-10	BLDG01-140	360-285-8400
Human Resources	BC-500-10	BLDG01-180	360-285-8500
Production	BC-600-10	BLDG02-100	360-287-8600
Marketing	BC-700-10	BLDG02-200	360-287-8700
InfoSystems	BC-800-10	BLDG02-270	360-287-8800

(a) DEPARTMENT Table

Employee Number	FirstName	LastName	Department	Phone	Email
1	Mary	Jacobs	Administration	360-285-8110	Mary.Jacobs@WPC.com
2	Rosalie	Jackson	Administration	360-285-8120	Rosalie.Jackson@WPC.com
3	Richard	Bandalone	Legal	360-285-8210	Richard.Bandalone@WPC.com
4	Tom	Caruthers	Accounting	360-285-8310	Tom.Caruthers@WPC.com
5	Heather	Jones	Accounting	360-285-8320	Heather.Jones@WPC.com
6	Mary	Abernathy	Finance	360-285-8410	Mary.Abernathy@WPC.com
7	George	Smith	Human Resources	360-285-8510	George.Smith@WPC.com
8	Tom	Jackson	Production	360-287-8610	Tom.Jackson@WPC.com
9	George	Jones	Production	360-287-8620	George.Jones@WPC.com
10	Ken	Numoto	Marketing	360-287-8710	Ken.Numoto@WPC.com
11	James	Nestor	InfoSystems		James.Nestor@WPC.com
12	Rick	Brown	InfoSystems	360-287-8820	Rick.Brown@WPC.com

(b) EMPLOYEE Table

ProjectID	ProjectName	Department	MaxHours	StartDate	EndDate
1000	2014 Q3 Product Plan	Marketing	135.00	10-MAY-14	15-JUN-14
1100	2014 Q3 Portfolio Analysis	Finance	120.00	05-JUL-14	25-JUL-14
1200	2014 Q3 Tax Preparation	Accounting	145.00	10-AUG-14	15-OCT-14
1300	2014 Q4 Product Plan	Marketing	150.00	10-AUG-14	15-SEP-14
1400	2014 Q4 Portfolio Analysis.	Finance	140.00	05-OCT-14	

(c) PROJECT Table

(continued)

FIGURE 3-2 Continued

ProjectID	EmployeeNumber	HoursWorked
1000	1	30.0
1000	8	75.0
1000	10	55.0
1100	4	40.0
1100	6	45.0
1200	1	25.0
1200	2	20.0
1200	4	45.0
1200	5	40.0
1300	1	35.0
1300	8	80.0
1300	10	50.0
1400	4	15.0
1400	5	10.0
1400	6	27.5

(d) ASSIGNMENT Table

In this database, each row of DEPARTMENT is potentially related to many rows of EMPLOYEE and PROJECT. Similarly, each row of PROJECT is potentially related to many rows of ASSIGNMENT, and each row of EMPLOYEE is potentially related to many rows of ASSIGNMENT.

Finally, assume the following rules, which are called **business rules**:

- If an EMPLOYEE row is to be deleted and that row is connected to any ASSIGNMENT, the EMPLOYEE row deletion will be disallowed.
- If a PROJECT row is deleted, then all the ASSIGNMENT rows that are connected to the deleted PROJECT row will also be deleted.

The business sense of these rules is as follows:

- If an EMPLOYEE row is deleted (for example, if the employee is transferred), then someone must take over that employee's assignments. Thus, the application needs someone to reassign assignments before deleting the employee row.
- If a PROJECT row is deleted, then the project has been canceled, and it is unnecessary to maintain records of assignments to that project.

These rules are typical business rules. You will learn more about such rules in Chapter 5.

"Does Not Work with Microsoft Access ANSI-89 SQL"

If you have completed the end-of-chapter "Access Workbench Exercises" for Chapters 1 and 2, you will recognize the database we're using in this chapter as the Wedgewood Pacific Corporation database from those exercises. You can use that database to try out the SQL commands in this chapter. However, be warned that not all standard SQL syntax works in Access.

As mentioned previously, our discussion of SQL is based on SQL features present in SQL standards since the ANSI SQL-92 standard (which Microsoft refers to as ANSI-92 SQL). Unfortunately, Microsoft Access defaults to the earlier SQL-89 version—Microsoft calls it ANSI-89 SQL or Microsoft Jet SQL (after the Microsoft Jet DBMS used by Access). ANSI-89 SQL differs significantly from SQL-92, and therefore some features of the SQL-92 language will not work in Access.

Microsoft Access 2013 (and the earlier Microsoft Access 2003, 2007, and 2010 versions) does contain a setting that allows you to use SQL-92 instead of the default ANSI-89 SQL. Microsoft included this option to allow Access tools such as forms and reports to be used in application development for Microsoft SQL Server, which supports newer SQL standards. To set the option, after you have opened Microsoft Access 2013, click the **File** command tab and then click the **Options** command to open the Access Options dialog box. In the Access Options dialog box, click the **Object Designers** button to display the Access Options Object Designers page, as shown in Figure 3-3.

As shown in Figure 3-3, the **SQL Server Compatible Syntax (ANSI 92)** options control which version of SQL is used in an Access 2013 database. If you check the **This database** check box, you will use SQL-92 syntax in the current database (if you open Microsoft Access without opening a database, this option is grayed out and not available). Or you can check the **Default for new databases** check box to make SQL-92 syntax the default for all new databases you create.

FIGURE 3-3

The Microsoft Access 2013 Options Object Designers Page

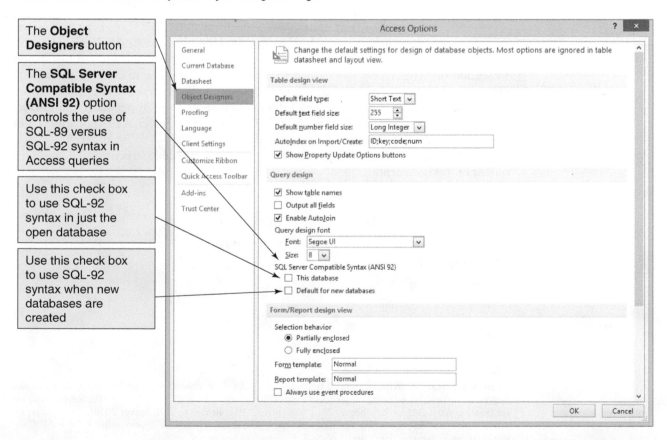

Unfortunately, very few Access users or organizations using Access are likely to set the Access SQL version to the SQL-92 option, and in this chapter, we assume that Access is running in the default ANSI-89 SQL mode. One advantage of doing so is that it will help you understand the limitations of Access ANSI-89 SQL and how to cope with them.

In the discussion that follows, we use "Does Not Work with Microsoft Access ANSI-89 SQL" boxes to identify SQL commands and clauses that do not work in Access ANSI-89 SQL. We also identify any workarounds that are available. Remember that the one *permanent* workaround is to choose to use the SQL-92 syntax option in the databases you create!

> ## BTW
>
> Different DBMS products implement SQL in slightly different ways. The SQL statements in this chapter run on Microsoft SQL Server (SQL Server 2014 Express was used to obtain the output shown in this chapter) and also run on Microsoft Access with exceptions as noted. If you are running the SQL statements on a different DBMS, you may need to make adjustments—consult the documentation for the DBMS you are using.

SQL FOR DATA DEFINITION (DDL)—CREATING TABLES AND RELATIONSHIPS

The SQL DDL is used to create and alter database structures, such as tables, and to insert, modify, and delete data in the tables.

Before creating tables, you must create a database. Although there is an SQL statement for creating a database, most developers use GUI tools to create databases. The tools are DBMS specific. Creating a database in Microsoft Access is demonstrated in Chapter 1's section of "The Access Workbench." For instructions on how to create a database in Microsoft SQL Server Express Edition, see Appendix A. For instructions on how to create a database in Oracle Database Express Edition 11*g* Release 2, see Appendix B. For instructions on how to create a database in MySQL 5.6 Community Server, see Appendix C. For all other DBMS products, consult the documentation.[3]

The **SQL CREATE TABLE statement** is used to create table structures. The essential format of this statement is:

```
CREATE TABLE NewTableName (
      three-part column definition,
      three-part column definition,
      three-part column definition,
      optional table constraints
      . . .
      );
```

---

[3] Also see David M. Kroenke and David J. Auer, *Database Processing: Fundamentals, Design, and Implementation*, 13th edition (Upper Saddle River, NJ: Prentice Hall, 2014), Chapter 10A for information on creating databases in SQL Server 2012 (which is also applicable to SQL Server 2014), online Chapter 10B for information on creating databases in Oracle Database 11*g* Release 2, and online Chapter 10C for information on creating databases in MySQL Community Server 5.6.

The parts of the three-part column definition are the column name, the column data type, and, optionally, a constraint on column values. Thus, we can restate the CREATE TABLE format as:

```
CREATE TABLE NewTableName (
    ColumnName DataType OptionalConstraint,
    ColumnName DataType OptionalConstraint,
    ColumnName DataType OptionalConstraint,
    optional table constraints
    . . .
    );
```

The column constraints we consider in this text are **PRIMARY KEY, FOREIGN KEY, NOT NULL, NULL**, and **UNIQUE**. In addition to these, there is also a **CHECK** column constraint, which is discussed with the ALTER statement at the end of this chapter. Finally, the **DEFAULT keyword** (DEFAULT is not considered a column constraint) can be used to set initial values.

Does Not Work with Microsoft Access ANSI-89 SQL

Microsoft Access ANSI-89 SQL does not support the UNIQUE and CHECK column constraints, nor the DEFAULT keyword.

Solution: Equivalent constraints and initial values can be set in the table Design view. See the discussion in this chapter's section of "The Access Workbench."

Consider the SQL CREATE TABLE statements for the DEPARTMENT and EMPLOYEE tables shown in Figure 3-4 (which includes the DEPARTMENT, EMPLOYEE and PROJECT tables, but intentionally omits the ASSIGNMENT table at this point in the discussion).

The EMPLOYEE column EmployeeNumber has an Integer (abbreviated Int) data type and a PRIMARY KEY column constraint. The next column, FirstName, uses a Character (signified by Char) data type and is 25 characters in length. The column constraint NOT NULL indicates that a value must be supplied when a new row is created. The fifth column, Phone, uses a Char(12) data type (to store separators between the area code, prefix, and number) with a column constraint of NULL. NULL indicates that null values are allowed, which means that a row can be created without a value for this column.

The fourth column, Department, uses the Char(35) data type, a NOT NULL column constraint, and the DEFAULT keyword to set the department value to the human resources department if no department value is entered when a new row is created.

The sixth and final column, Email, uses the VarChar(100) data type and the NOT NULL and UNIQUE column constraints. VarChar means a variable-length character data type. Thus, Email contains character data values that vary in length from row to row, and the maximum length of an Email address value is 100 characters. However, if an Email address value has only 14 characters, then only 14 characters will be stored.

As implied by the existence of VarChar, Char values are of fixed length. The Char(25) definition for FirstName means that 25 characters will be stored for every value of FirstName, regardless of the length of the value entered. FirstNames will be padded with blanks to fill the 25 spaces when necessary.

You might wonder, given the apparent advantage of VarChar, why it isn't used all the time. The reason is that extra processing is required for VarChar columns. A few extra bytes are required to store the length of the value, and the DBMS must go to some trouble to arrange variable-length values in memory and on disk. Vendors of DBMS products usually provide guidelines for when to use which type, and you should check the documentation for your specific DBMS product for more information.

FIGURE 3-4

SQL CREATE TABLE Statements

```
CREATE  TABLE DEPARTMENT(
        DepartmentName    Char(35)        PRIMARY KEY,
        BudgetCode        Char(30)        NOT NULL,
        OfficeNumber      Char(15)        NOT NULL,
        Phone             Char(12)        NOT NULL,
        );

CREATE  TABLE EMPLOYEE(
        EmployeeNumber    Int             PRIMARY KEY,
        FirstName         Char(25)        NOT NULL,
        LastName          Char(25)        NOT NULL,
        Department        Char(35)        NOT NULL DEFAULT 'Human Resources',
        Phone             Char(12)        NULL,
        Email             VarChar(100)    NOT NULL UNIQUE,
        );

CREATE  TABLE PROJECT (
        ProjectID         Int             PRIMARY KEY,
        ProjectName       Char(50)        NOT NULL,
        Department        Char(35)        NOT NULL,
        MaxHours          Numeric(8,2)    NOT NULL DEFAULT 100,
        StartDate         Date            NULL,
        EndDate           Date            NULL,
        );
```

The UNIQUE column constraint for Email means that there cannot be any duplicated values in the Email column. This ensures that each person has a different email address.

In the PROJECT table, the MaxHours column uses the Numeric(8,2) data type. This means that MaxHours values consist of up to eight decimal numbers, with two numbers assumed to the right of the decimal point. The decimal point is not stored and does not count as one of the eight numbers. Thus, the DBMS would display the stored value 12345 as 123.45, and the stored value of 12345678 (which uses all eight of the allowed digits) as 123456.78.

The DEFAULT keyword is used. DEFAULT 100 means that when a new row is created, if no value is provided for MaxHours, the DBMS is to provide the value 100.00. Note that the input value does not assume that the last two numbers are to the right of the decimal place.

Does Not Work with Microsoft Access ANSI-89 SQL

Although Microsoft Access supports a Number data type, it does not support the (*m,n*) extension to specify the number of digits and the number of digits to the right of the decimal place.

Solution: You can set these values in the table Design view after the column is created. See the discussion in this chapter's section of "The Access Workbench."

Also in the PROJECT table, the StartDate column uses the Date data type. This means that StartDate values will consist of dates (there is a Time data type for use with times). Various DBMS products handle date and time values in different ways, and, again, you should consult the documentation for your specific DBMS product. According to the SQL standard and as shown in Figure 3-4, every SQL statement should end with a semicolon.

Although some DBMS products do not require the semicolon, it is good practice to learn to provide it. Also, as a matter of style, we place the ending parenthesis and the semicolon on a line of its own. This style blocks out the table definitions for easy reading.

The four data types shown in Figure 3-4 are the basic SQL data types, but DBMS vendors have added others to their products. Figures 3-5(a), 3-5(b), and 3-5(c) show some of the data types allowed by SQL Server 2014, Oracle Database Express Edition 11*g* Release 2, and MySQL 5.6, respectively.

FIGURE 3-5

Data Types for Widely Used DBMS Products

Numeric Data Types	Description
Bit	1-bit integer. Values of only **0, 1** or **NULL**.
Tinyint	1-byte integer. Range is from **0** to **255**.
Smallint	2-byte integer. Range is from $-2^{(15)}$ (**–32,768**) to $+2^{(15)} -1$ (**+32,767**).
Int	4-byte integer. Range is from $-2^{(31)}$ (**–2,147,483,468**) to $+2^{(31)} -1$ (**+2,147,483,467**).
Bigint	8-byte integer. Range is from $-2^{(63)}$ (**–9,223,372,036,854,775,808**) to $+2^{(63)} -1$ (**+9,223,372,036,854,775,807**).
Decimal (p[,s])	Fixed precision (p) and scale (s) numbers. Range is from $-10^{38} +1$ to $10^{38} -1$ with maximum precision (p) of 38. Precision ranges from 1 through 38, and default precision is 18. Scale (s) indicates the number of digits to the right of the decimal place. Default scale value is 0, and scale values range from 0 to p, where 0 <= s <= p.
Numeric (p[,s])	Numeric works identically to Decimal.
Smallmoney	4-byte money. Range is from **–214,748.3646** to **+214,748.3647** with accuracy of one ten-thousandth of a monetary unit. Use decimal point to separate digits.
Money	9-byte money. Range is from **–922,337,203,685,477.5808** to **+922,337,203,685,477.5807** with accuracy of one ten-thousandth of a monetary unit. Use decimal point to separate digits.
Float (n)	n-bit storage of the mantissa in scientific floating point notation. The value of n ranges from 1 to 53, and the default is 53.
Real	Equivalent to Float (24).
Date and Time Data Types	**Description**
Date	3-bytes fixed. Default format YYYY-MM-DD. Range is from **January 1, 1** (0001-01-01) through **December 31, 9999** (9999-12-31).
Time	5-bytes fixed is default with 100 nanosecond precision (.0000000). Default format is HH:MM:SS.NNNNNNN. Range is from **00:00:00.0000000** through **23:59:59.9999999**.
Smalldatetime	4-bytes fixed. Restricted date range, and rounds time to nearest second. Range is from **January 1, 1900 00:00:00 AM** (1900-01-01 00:00:00) through **June 6, 2079 23:59.59 PM** (2079-06-06 23:59.59).

(a) Common SQL Server 2014 Data Types

(*continued*)

FIGURE 3-5   Continued

Date and Time Data Types	Description
Datetime	8-bytes fixed. Basically combines Date and Time, but spans less dates and has less time precision (rounds to .000, .003 or .007 seconds). Use DATETIME2 for more precision. Date range is from **January 1, 1753** (1753-01-01) through **December 31, 9999** (9999-12-31).
Datetime2	8-bytes fixed. Combines Date and Time with full precision. Use instead of DATETIME. Range is from **January 1, 1 00:00:00.0000000 AM** (0001-01-01 00:00:00.0000000) through **December 31, 9999 23:59.59.9999999 PM** (9999-12-31 23:59.59.9999999).
Datetimeoffset	10-byte fixed-length default with 100 nanosecond precision (.0000000). Uses 24 hour clock, based on Coordinated Universal Time (UTC). UTC is a refinement of Greenwich Mean Time (GMT), based on the prime meridian at Greenwich, England, which defines when midnight (00:00:00.0000000) occurs. Offset is the time zone difference from the Greenwich time zone. Default format is YYYY-MM-DD HH:MM:SS.NNNNNNN (+|−)HH:MM. Range is from **January 1, 1 00:00:00.0000000 AM** (0001-01-01 00:00:00.0000000) through **December 31, 9999 23:59.59.9999999 PM** (9999-12-31 23:59.59.9999999) with an **offset of −14:59 to +14:59**. Use for 24 hour time.
Timestamp	See documentation.
String Data Types	**Description**
Char (n)	n-byte fixed-length string data (non-Unicode). Range of n is from **1** through **8000**.
Varchar (n | max)	n-byte variable-length string data (non-Unicode). Range of n is from **1** through **8000**. Max creates a maximum $+2^{(31)}-1$ bytes (2 GBytes).
Text	Use VARCHAR(max). See documentation.
Nchar (n)	(n x 2)-byte fixed-length **Unicode** string data. Range of n is from **1** through **4000**.
Nvarchar (n | max)	(n x 2)-byte variable-length **Unicode** string data. Range of n is from **1** through **4000**. Max creates a maximum $+2^{(31)}-1$ bytes (2 GBytes).
Ntext	Use NVARCHAR(max). See documentation.
Binary (n)	n-byte fixed-length binary data. Range of n is from **1** through **8000**.
Other Data Types	**Description**
Varbinary (n | max)	Variable-length binary data. Range of n is from **1** through **8000**. Max creates a maximum $+2^{(31)}-1$ bytes (2 GBytes).
Image	Use VARBINARY(max). See documentation.
Uniqueidentifier	16-byte Globally Unique Identifier (GUID). See documentation.
hierarchyid	See documentation.
Cursor	See documentation.
Table	See documentation.
XML	Use for storing XML data. See documentation.
Sql_variant	See documentation.

(a) continued - Common SQL Server 2014 Data Types

FIGURE 3-5   Continued

Numeric Data Types	Description
SMALLINT	Synonym for INTEGER, implemented as NUMBER(38,0).
INT	Synonym for INTEGER, implemented as NUMBER(38,0).
INTEGER	When specified as a data type, it is implemented as NUMBER(38,0).
NUMBER (p[,s])	1 to 22 bytes. Fixed precision (p) and scale (s) numbers. Range is from -10^{38} +1 to $10^{38} - 1$ with maximum precision (p) of 38. Precision ranges from 1 through 38, and default precision is 18. Scale (s) indicates the number of digits to the right of the decimal place. Default scale value is 0, and scale values range from –84 to 127, where s can be greater than p.
FLOAT (p)	1 to 22 bytes. Implemented as NUMBER(p). The value of p ranges from 1 to 126 bits.
BINARY_FLOAT	4-byte 32-bit floating point number.
BINARY_LONG	8-byte 64-bit floating point number.
RAW (n)	n-byte fixed-length raw binary data. Range of n is from 1 through 2000.
LONG RAW	Raw variable-length binary data. Maximum is 2 GBytes.
BLOB	Maximum [(4-GByte – 1)x(database block size)] binary large object.
BFILE	See documentation.
Date and Time Data Types	**Description**
DATE	7-bytes fixed. Default format is set explicitly with the NLS_DATE_FORMAT parameter. Range is from January 1, 4712 BC through December 31, 9999 AD. It contains the fields YEAR, MONTH, DAY, HOUR, MINUTE and SECOND (no fractional seconds). It does not include a time zone.
TIMESTAMP (p)	Includes fractional seconds base on a precision of p. Default of p is 6, and the range is 0 to 9. 7 to 11-bytes fixed, based on precision. Default format is set explicitly with the NLS_TIMESTAMP_FORMAT parameter. Range is from January 1, 4712 BC through December 31, 9999 AD. It contains the fields YEAR, MONTH, DAY, HOUR, MINUTE and SECOND. It contains fractional seconds. It does not include a time zone.
TIMESTAMP (p) WITH TIME ZONE	Includes fractional seconds base on a precision of p. Default of p is 6, and the range is 0 to 9. 13-bytes fixed. Default format is set explicitly with the NLS_TIMESTAMP_FORMAT parameter. Range is from January 1, 4712 BC through December 31, 9999 AD. It contains the fields YEAR, MONTH, DAY, TIMEZONE_HOUR, TIMEZONE_MINUTE and TIMEZONE_SECOND. It contains fractional seconds. It includes a time zone.
TIMESTAMP (p) WITH LOCAL TIME ZONE	Basically the same as TIMESTAMP WITH TIME ZONE, with the following modifications: (1) Data is stored with times based on the database time zone, and (2) Users view data in session time zone.

(b) Common Oracle Database Express Edition 11*g* Release 2 Data Types

(*continued*)

FIGURE 3-5 Continued

INTERVAL YEAR [p(year)] TO MONTH	See documentation.
INTERVAL DAY [p(day)] TO SECOND [p(seconds)]	See documentation.
String Data Types	**Description**
CHAR (n[BYTE | CHAR])	n-byte fixed-length string data (non-Unicode). Range of n is from 1 through **2000**. BYTE and CHAR refer to the semantic usage. See documentation.
VARCHAR2 (n[BYTE | CHAR])	n-byte variable-length string data (non-Unicode). Range of n is from 1 through **4000** BYTEs or CHARACTERs. BYTE and CHAR refer to the semantic usage. See documentation.
NCHAR (n)	(n x 2)-byte fixed-length **Unicode** string data. Up to (n x 3)-bytes for UTF8 encoding. Maximum size is from **2000** bytes.
NVARCHAR2 (n)	Variable-length **Unicode** string data. Up to (n x 3)-bytes for UTF8 encoding. Maximum size is from **4000** bytes.
LONG	Variable-length string data (non-Unicode) with maximum a maximum $2^{(31-1)}$ bytes (2 GBytes). See documentation.
CLOB	Maximum [(4-GByte – 1)x(database block size)] character large object (non-Unicode). Supports fixed-length and variable length character sets.
NCLOB	Maximum [(4-GByte – 1)x(database block size)] **Unicode** character large object. Supports fixed-length and variable length character sets.
Other Data Types	**Description**
ROWID	See documentation.
UROWID	See documentation.
HTTPURIType	See documentation.
XMLType	Use for storing XML data. See documentation.
SDO_GEOMETRY	See documentation.

(b) continued - Common Oracle Database Express Edition 11*g* Release 2 Data Types

NumericData Type	Description
BIT (M)	M = 1 to 64.
TINYINT	Range is from –128 to 127.
TINYINT UNSIGNED	Range is from 0 to 255.
BOOLEAN	0 = FALSE; 1 = TRUE.
SMALLINT	Range is from –32,768 to 32,767.
SMALLINT UNSIGNED	Range is from 0 to 65,535.
MEDIUMINT	Range is from –8,388,608 to 8,388,607.
MEDIUMINT UNSIGNED	Range is from 0 to 16,777,215.
INT or INTEGER	Range is from –2,147,483,648 to 2,147,483,647.

(c) Common MySQL 5.6 Data Types

FIGURE 3-5 Continued

NumericData Type	Description
INT UNSIGNED or INTEGER UNSIGNED	Range is from 0 to 4,294,967,295.
BIGINT	Range is from –9,223,372,036,854,775,808 to 9,223,372,036,854,775,807.
BIGINT UNSIGNED	Range is from 0 to 1,844,674,073,709,551,615.
FLOAT (P)	P = Precision; Range is from 0 to 24.
FLOAT (M, D)	Small (single-precision) floating-point number: M = Display width D = Number of significant digits
DOUBLE (M, P)	Normal (double-precision) floating-point number: M = Display width P = Precision; Range is from 25 to 53.
DEC (M[,D]) or DECIMAL (M[,D]) or FIXED (M[,D])	Fixed-point number: M = Total number of digits D = Number of decimals.
Date and Time Data Types	**Description**
DATE	YYYY-MM-DD : Range is from 1000-01-01 to 9999-12-31.
DATETIME	YYYY-MM-DD HH:MM:SS.
	Range is from 1000-01-01 00:00:00 to 9999-12-31 23:59:59.
TIMESTAMP	See documentation.
TIME	HH:MM:SS : Range is from 00:00:00 to 23:59:59.
YEAR (M)	M = 2 or 4 (default).
	IF M = 2, then range is from 1970 to 2069 (70 to 69).
	IF M = 4, then range is from 1901 to 2155.
String Data Types	**Description**
CHAR (M)	M = 0 to 255.
VARCHAR (M)	M = 1 to 255.
BLOB (M)	BLOB = Binary Large Object: maximum 65,535 characters.
TEXT (M)	Maximum 65,535 characters.
TINYBLOB MEDIUMBLOB LONGBLOB TINYTEXT MEDIUMTEXT LONGTEXT	See documentation.
ENUM ('value1', 'value2', . . .)	An enumeration. Only one value, but chosen from list. See documentation.
SET ('value1', 'value2', . . .)	A set. Zero or more values, all chosen from list. See documentation.

(c) continued - Common MySQL 5.6 Data Types

BTW

Even when Microsoft Access reads standard SQL, the results of running an SQL statement may be a bit different in Access. For example, Microsoft Access reads SQL statements containing both Char and VarChar data types, but converts both these data types to a fixed Text data type in the Access database.

Defining Primary Keys with Table Constraints

Although primary keys can be defined as shown in Figure 3-4, we prefer to define primary keys using a table constraint. Table constraints are identified by the **CONSTRAINT keyword** and can be used to implement various constraints. Consider the CREATE TABLE statements shown in Figure 3-6, with the ASSIGNMENT table now included, which shows how to define the primary key of a table by using a table constraint.

First, the columns of the table are defined as usual, except that the column that will be the primary key must be given the column constraint NOT NULL. After the table columns are defined, a table constraint, identified by the word CONSTRAINT, is used to create the primary key. Every table constraint has a name followed by the definition of the constraint. Note that in the DEPARTMENT table the DepartmentName column is now labeled as NOT NULL and a CONSTRAINT clause has been added at the end of the table definition. The constraint is named DEPARTMENT_PK, and it is defined by the keywords PRIMARY KEY(DepartmentName). The constraint name is selected by the developer, and the only naming restriction is that the constraint name must be unique in the database. Usually a standard naming convention is used. In this text, we name primary key constraints using the name of the table followed by an underscore and the letters:

```
CONSTRAINT  TABLENAME_PK    PRIMARY KEY({PrimaryKeyColumns})
```

FIGURE 3-6

Creating Primary Keys with Table Constraints

```
CREATE   TABLE DEPARTMENT(
        DepartmentName      Char(35)        NOT NULL,
        BudgetCode          Char(30)        NOT NULL,
        OfficeNumber        Char(15)        NOT NULL,
        Phone               Char(12)        NOT NULL,
        CONSTRAINT          DEPARTMENT_PK   PRIMARY KEY(DepartmentName)
        );

CREATE   TABLE EMPLOYEE(
        EmployeeNumber      Int             NOT NULL IDENTITY (1, 1),
        FirstName           Char(25)        NOT NULL,
        LastName            Char(25)        NOT NULL,
        Department          Char(35)        NOT NULL DEFAULT 'Human Resources',
        Phone               Char(12)        NULL,
        Email               VarChar(100)    NOT NULL UNIQUE,
        CONSTRAINT          EMPLOYEE_PK     PRIMARY KEY(EmployeeNumber),
        );

CREATE   TABLE PROJECT (
        ProjectID           Int             NOT NULL IDENTITY (1000, 100),
        ProjectName         Char(50)        NOT NULL,
        Department          Char(35)        NOT NULL,
        MaxHours            Numeric(8,2)    NOT NULL DEFAULT 100,
        StartDate           Date            NULL,
        EndDate             Date            NULL,
        CONSTRAINT          PROJECT_PK      PRIMARY KEY (ProjectID),
        );

CREATE   TABLE ASSIGNMENT (
        ProjectID           Int             NOT NULL,
        EmployeeNumber      Int             NOT NULL,
        HoursWorked         Numeric(6,2)    NULL,
        CONSTRAINT          ASSIGNMENT_PK   PRIMARY KEY (ProjectID, EmployeeNumber),
        );
```

Defining primary keys using table constraints offers three advantages. First, it is required for defining composite keys because the PRIMARY KEY column constraint cannot be used on more than one column. We previously excluded the ASSIGNMENT table from Figure 3-4 because it is not possible to declare the primary key of the ASSIGNMENT table using the technique in Figure 3-4, but Figure 3-6 now includes the ASSIGNMENT table and illustrates the declaration of the primary key ASSIGNMENT_PK as a composite key using the SQL phrase PRIMARY KEY(ProjectID, EmployeeNumber). The second advantage is that by using table constraints you can choose the name of the constraint that defines the primary key. Controlling the name of the constraint has advantages for administering the database, as you will see later when we discuss the SQL DROP statement.

Finally, using a table constraint to define the primary key allows us to easily define surrogate keys in some DBMS products. Notice that in Figure 3-6 the EmployeeNumber column definition in EMPLOYEE and the ProjectID column definition in PROJECT now include the **IDENTITY (M,N) property**. This illustrates how surrogate keys are defined in Microsoft SQL Server. The keyword IDENTITY indicates that this is a surrogate key that will start a value M for the first row created and increase by increment N as each additional row is created. Thus, EmployeeNumber will start with the number 1 and increase by an increment of 1 (that is, 1, 2, 3, 4, 5,...). ProjectID will start with the number 1000 and increase by 100 (that is, 1000, 1100, 1200,...). The exact techniques used to define surrogate key sequences vary extensively from DBMS to DBMS, so consult the documentation for your specific product.

Does Not Work with Microsoft Access ANSI-89 SQL

Although Microsoft Access does support an AutoNumber data type, it *always* starts at 1 and increments by 1. Further, AutoNumber *cannot* be used as an SQL data type.

Solution: Set the AutoNumber data type manually after the table is created. Any other numbering system must be supported manually or by application code.

Defining Foreign Keys with the Table Constraints

You may have noticed that none of the tables in Figure 3-4 or Figure 3-6 include any foreign key columns. You can also use table constraints to define foreign keys and their associated referential integrity constraints. Figure 3-7 shows the final SQL code for our tables, complete with the foreign key constraints.

EMPLOYEE has a table constraint named EMP_DEPART_FK that defines the foreign key relationship between the Department column in EMPLOYEE and the DepartmentName column in DEPARTMENT.

Notice the phrase ON UPDATE CASCADE. The **ON UPDATE phrase** shows what action should be taken if a value of the primary key DepartmentName in DEPARTMENT changes. The **CASCADE keyword** means that the same change should be made to the related Department column in EMPLOYEE. This means that if a department name *Marketing* is changed to *Sales and Marketing*, then the foreign key values should be updated to reflect this change. Because DepartmentName is not a surrogate key, the values could be changed, and setting ON UPDATE CASCADE is reasonable.

The PROJECT table has a similar foreign key relationship with DEPARTMENT, and the same logic applies, except that here there will be two types of project: completed and in-process. The business rules dealing with this situation are explored in the end-of-chapter exercises.

For the ASSIGNMENT table, there are two foreign key constraints: one to EMPLOYEE and one to PROJECT. The first one defines the constraint ASSIGN_PROJ_FK (the name is up to the developer, as long as it is unique) that specifies that ProjectID in ASSIGNMENT references the ProjectID column in PROJECT. Here the ON UPDATE phrase is set to **NO ACTION**. Recall that ProjectID is a surrogate key and thus will never change. In this situation, there is no need to cascade updates to the referenced primary key.

FIGURE 3-7

Creating Foreign Keys with Table Constraints

```
CREATE   TABLE DEPARTMENT(
        DepartmentName      Char(35)         NOT NULL,
        BudgetCode          Char(30)         NOT NULL,
        OfficeNumber        Char(15)         NOT NULL,
        Phone               Char(12)         NOT NULL,
        CONSTRAINT          DEPARTMENT_PK    PRIMARY KEY(DepartmentName)
        );

CREATE   TABLE EMPLOYEE(
        EmployeeNumber      Int              NOT NULL IDENTITY (1, 1),
        FirstName           Char(25)         NOT NULL,
        LastName            Char(25)         NOT NULL,
        Department          Char(35)         NOT NULL DEFAULT 'Human Resources',
        Phone               Char(12)         NULL,
        Email               VarChar(100)     NOT NULL UNIQUE,
        CONSTRAINT          EMPLOYEE_PK      PRIMARY KEY(EmployeeNumber),
        CONSTRAINT          EMP_DEPART_FK    FOREIGN KEY(Department)
                        REFERENCES DEPARTMENT(DepartmentName)
                            ON UPDATE CASCADE
        );

CREATE   TABLE PROJECT (
        ProjectID           Int              NOT NULL IDENTITY (1000, 100),
        ProjectName         Char(50)         NOT NULL,
        Department          Char(35)         NOT NULL,
        MaxHours            Numeric(8,2)     NOT NULL DEFAULT 100,
        StartDate           Date             NULL,
        EndDate             Date             NULL,
        CONSTRAINT          PROJECT_PK       PRIMARY KEY (ProjectID),
        CONSTRAINT          PROJ_DEPART_FK   FOREIGN KEY(Department)
                        REFERENCES DEPARTMENT(DepartmentName)
                            ON UPDATE CASCADE
        );

CREATE   TABLE ASSIGNMENT (
        ProjectID           Int              NOT NULL,
        EmployeeNumber      Int              NOT NULL,
        HoursWorked         Numeric(6,2)     NULL,
        CONSTRAINT          ASSIGNMENT_PK    PRIMARY KEY (ProjectID, EmployeeNumber),
        CONSTRAINT          ASSIGN_PROJ_FK   FOREIGN KEY (ProjectID)
                        REFERENCES PROJECT (ProjectID)
                            ON UPDATE NO ACTION
                            ON DELETE CASCADE,
        CONSTRAINT          ASSIGN_EMP_FK    FOREIGN KEY (EmployeeNumber)
                        REFERENCES EMPLOYEE (EmployeeNumber)
                            ON UPDATE NO ACTION
                            ON DELETE NO ACTION
        );
```

Notice that there is also an **ON DELETE phrase**, which shows what action should be taken if a row in PROJECT is deleted. Here the phrase ON DELETE CASCADE means that when a PROJECT row is deleted all rows in ASSIGNMENT that are connected to the deleted row in PROJECT also should be deleted. Thus, when a PROJECT row is deleted, all ASSIGNMENT rows for that PROJECT row will be deleted as well. This action implements the second business rule on page 124.

The second foreign key table constraint defines the foreign key constraint ASSIGN_ EMP_FK. This constraint indicates that the EmployeeNumber column references the EmployeeNumber column of EMPLOYEE. Again, the referenced primary key is a surrogate key, so ON UPDATE NO ACTION is appropriate for this constraint. The phrase ON DELETE NO ACTION indicates to the DBMS that no EMPLOYEE row deletion should be allowed if that row is connected to an ASSIGNMENT row. This declaration implements the first business rule on page 124.

Because ON DELETE NO ACTION is the default, you can omit the ON DELETE expression, and the declaration will default to no action. However, specifying it makes better documentation.[4]

Table constraints can be used for purposes other than creating primary and foreign keys. One of the most important purposes is to define constraints on data values, and we will explore defining CHECK constraints in the end-of-chapter exercises. As always, see the documentation for your DBMS for more information on this topic.

Does Not Work with Microsoft Access ANSI-89 SQL

Microsoft Access does not completely support foreign key CONSTRAINT phrases. Although the basic referential integrity constraint can be created using SQL, the ON UPDATE and ON DELETE clauses are not supported.

Solution: ON UPDATE and ON DELETE actions can be set manually after the relationship is created. See the discussion in this chapter's section of "The Access Workbench."

Submitting SQL to the DBMS

After you have developed a text file with SQL statements like those in Figures 3-4, 3-6, and 3-7, you can submit them to the DBMS. The means by which you do this varies from DBMS to DBMS. With SQL Server 2014, you can type them into a query window in the Microsoft SQL Server Management Studio, or you can enter them via Visual Studio.NET. Oracle Database Express Edition 11*g* Release 2 and MySQL 5.6 use similar techniques. How to do this in Microsoft Access is discussed in this chapter's section of "The Access Workbench."

Figure 3-8 shows the Microsoft SQL Server Management Studio window after the SQL statements in Figure 3-7 have been entered and processed in SQL Server Express Edition. The SQL code itself appears in a query window on the upper right, and the message "Command(s) completed successfully" in the Messages window on the lower right indicates that the SQL statements were processed correctly. The object icons representing the tables can be seen in the Object Explorer window on the left, where the name of each table is prefixed with *dbo*, which SQL Server uses for *database owner*.

Figure 3-9 shows the Oracle SQL Devleoper window after the SQL statements in Figure 3-7 (slightly modified to conform to Oracle Database syntax—see Appendix B) have been processed in Oracle Database 11*g* Release 2. The SQL code appears in a tabbed script window on the left, and object icons representing the newly created table can be seen in the tabbed Connections window on the right.

Figure 3-10 shows the MySQL Workbench window after the SQL statements in Figure 3-7 (slightly modified to conform to MySQL syntax—see Appendix C and note the

---

[4]You may be wondering why we don't use the ON DELETE phrase with the foreign key constraints between DEPARTMENT and EMPLOYEE and between DEPARTMENT and PROJECT. After all, there will probably be business rules defining what should be done with employees and projects if a department is deleted. However, enforcing those rules will be more complex than simply using an ON DELETE statement, and this topic is beyond the scope of this book. For a full discussion, see David M. Kroenke and David J. Auer, *Database Processing: Fundamentals, Design, and Implementation*, 13th edition (Upper Saddle River, NJ: Prentice Hall, 2014), Chapter 6.

FIGURE 3-8

Processing the CREATE TABLE Statements Using Microsoft SQL Server 2014

The SQL script in the tabbed script window

The objects representing the tables created by the script are shown in the expanded Tables folder—*dbo* stands for *database owner*

Messages are shown here—either that the commands were successful or appropriate error messages

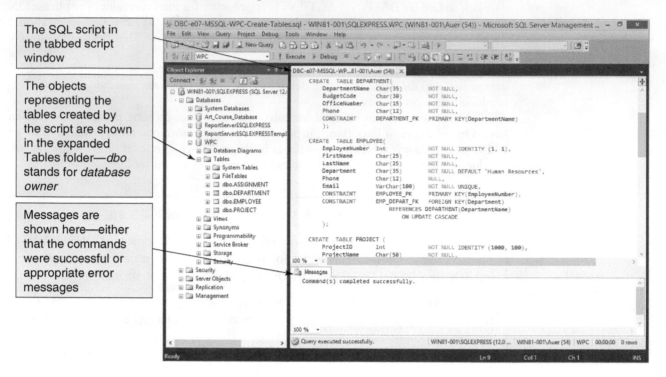

FIGURE 3-9

Processing the CREATE TABLE Statements Using Oracle Database Express Edition 11*g* Release 2

The SQL script in the tabbed **SQL Worksheet** window

The objects representing the tables created by the script are shown in the expanded Tables folder

Messages are shown here—either that the commands were successful or appropriate error messages

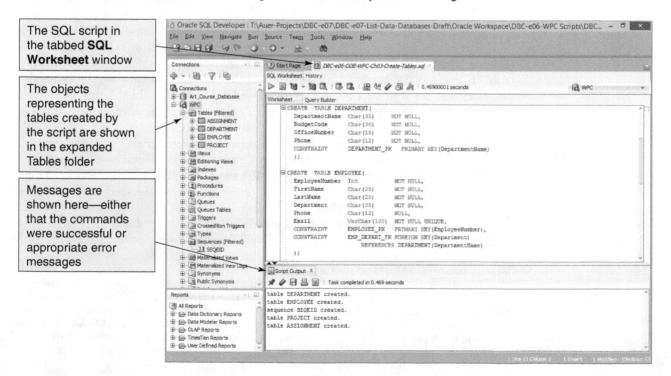

FIGURE 3-10

Processing the CREATE TABLE Statements Using MySQL 5.6

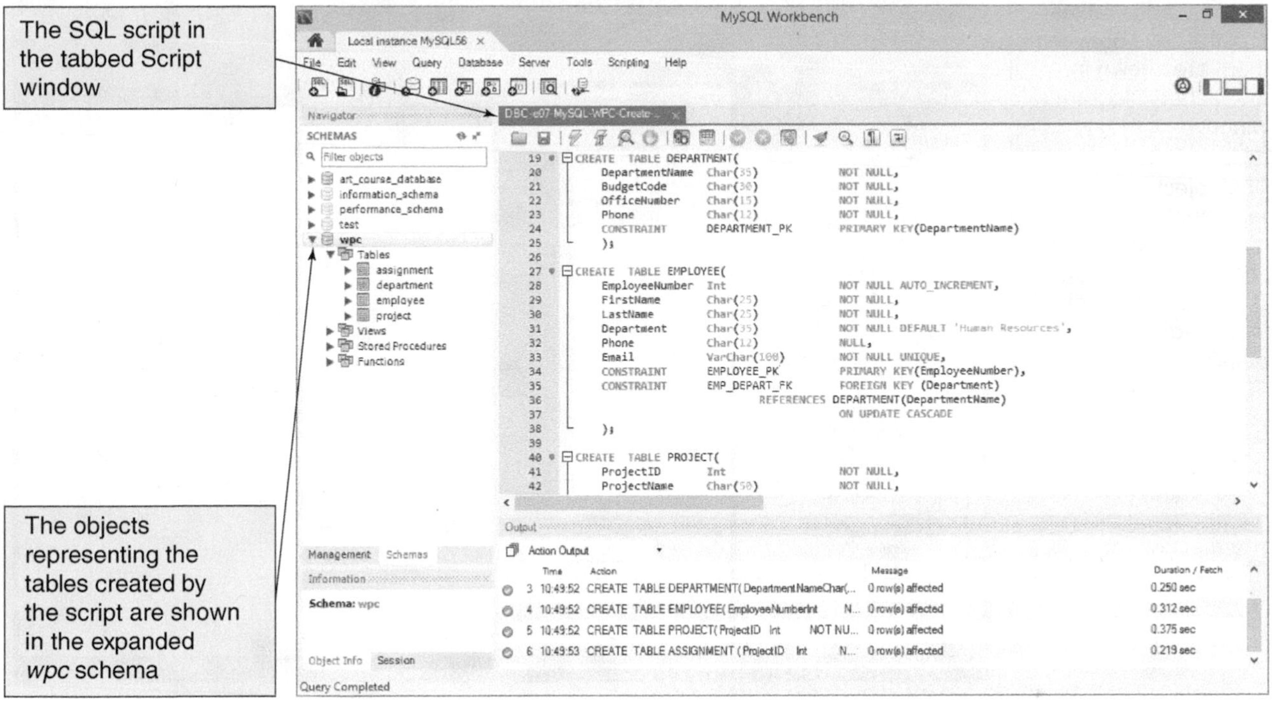

The SQL script in the tabbed Script window

The objects representing the tables created by the script are shown in the expanded *wpc* schema

AUTO_INCREMENT keyword instead of IDENTITY (1, 1)] have been processed in MySQL. The SQL code appears in a tabbed script window on the left, and the object icons representing the newly created tables can be seen in the Object Browser window on the left.

Does Not Work with Microsoft Access ANSI-89 SQL

Unlike SQL Server 2014, Oracle Database Express Edition 11*g* Release 2, and MySQL 5.6, Microsoft Access does not support SQL scripts.

Solution: You can still create tables by using the SQL CREATE command and inserting data by using the SQL INSERT command (discussed later in this chapter), but you must do so one command at a time. See the discussion in this chapter's section of "The Access Workbench."

Some DBMS products can create database diagrams that show the tables and relationships in a database. We've already used the Microsoft Access Relationships window (in Chapter 2's section of "The Access Workbench"). For SQL Server 2014, Figure 3-11 shows the WPC database structure in Microsoft SQL Server Management Studio.

SQL FOR DATA MANIPULATION (DML)—INSERTING DATA

The SQL DML is used to query databases and to modify data in the tables. In this section, we discuss how to use SQL to insert data into a database, how to query the data, and how to change and delete the data.

There are three possible data modification operations: insert, update, and delete. Because we need to populate our database tables, we discuss how to insert data at this time.

FIGURE 3-11

Database Diagram in the Microsoft SQL Server Management Studio

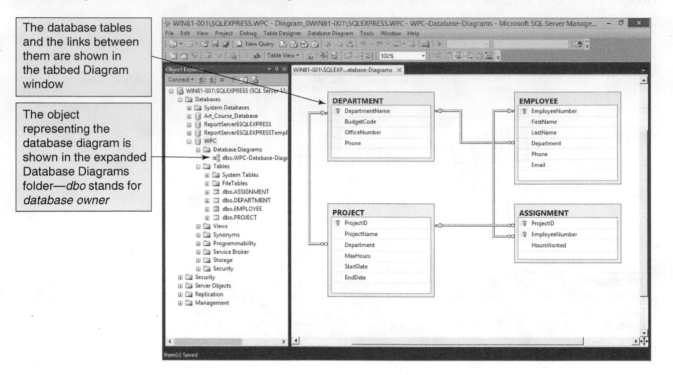

We will wait until later in the chapter, after we've discussed some other useful SQL syntax, to consider updating and deleting data.

Inserting Data

Data can be added to a relation by using the **SQL INSERT statement**. This statement has two forms, depending on whether data are supplied for all of the columns.

We'll put the data shown in Figure 3-2(a) into the DEPARTMENT table. If the data for all columns are supplied, such as for the administration department, then the following INSERT can be used:

```
INSERT INTO DEPARTMENT VALUES('Administration',
     'BC-100-10', 'BLDG01-300', '360-285-8100');
```

If the DBMS is providing a surrogate key, then the primary key value does not need to be specified.

SQL statements can also include an **SQL comment**, which is a block of text that is used to document the SQL statement but not executed as part of the SQL statement. SQL comments are enclosed in the symbols **/*** and ***/**, and any text between these symbols is ignored when the SQL statement is executed. For example, here is the previous SQL INSERT statement with an SQL comment added to document the statement by including a statement label:

```
/* *** SQL-INSERT-CH03-01 *** */
INSERT INTO DEPARTMENT VALUES('Administration',
     'BC-100-10', 'BLDG01-300', '360-285-8100');
```

Because the SQL comment is ignored when the SQL statement is executed, the result of running this statement will be identical to the result of running the statement without the comment. We will use similar comments to label the SQL statements in this chapter as an easy way to reference a specific SQL statement in the text.

The data shown in Figure 3-2(c) will be put in the PROJECT table. Because ProjectID is a surrogate key—specified as IDENTITY (1000, 100) in SQL Server—the same type of INSERT statement can be used when data are supplied for all other columns. For example, to insert the data for the 2014 Q3 Product Plan, the following INSERT can be used:

```
/* *** SQL-INSERT-CH03-02 *** */
INSERT INTO PROJECT VALUES('2014 Q3 Product Plan',
    'Marketing', 135.00, '10-MAY-14', '15-JUN-14');
```

Note that numbers such as Integer and Numeric values are not enclosed in single quotes, but Char, VarChar, and DateTime values are.

BTW

SQL is very fussy about single quotes. It wants the plain, nondirectional quotes found in basic text editors. The fancy directional quotes produced by many word processors will produce errors. For example, the data value '2014 Q3 Product Plan' is correctly stated, but '2014 Q3 Product Plan' is not. Do you see the difference?

If data for some columns are missing, then the names of the columns for which data are provided must be listed. For example, consider the 2014 Q4 Portfolio Analysis project, which does not have an EndDate value. The correct INSERT statement for this data is:

```
/* *** SQL-INSERT-CH03-03 *** */
INSERT INTO PROJECT
    (ProjectName, Department, MaxHours, StartDate)
    VALUES('2014 Q4 Portfolio Analysis', 'Finance',
    140.00, '05-OCT-14');
```

A NULL value will be inserted for EndDate.

Let's consider three points regarding the second version of the INSERT command. First, the order of the column names must match the order of the values. In the preceding example, the order of the column names is Name, Department, MaxHours, StartDate, so the order of the values must also be Name, Department, MaxHours, StartDate.

Second, although the order of the data must match the order of the column names, the order of the column names does not have to match the order of the columns in the table. For example, the following INSERT, where Department is placed at the beginning of the column list, would also work:

```
/* *** SQL-INSERT-CH03-04 *** */
INSERT INTO PROJECT
    (Department, ProjectName, MaxHours, StartDate)
    VALUES('Finance', '2014 Q4 Portfolio Analysis',
    140.00, '05-OCT-14');
```

Finally, for the INSERT to work, values for all NOT NULL columns must be provided. You can omit EndDate only because this column is defined as NULL.

Figure 3-12 shows the SQL INSERT statements needed to populate the WPC database tables created by the SQL CREATE TABLE statements in Figure 3-7. Note that the order in which the tables are populated does matter because of the foreign key referential integrity constraints.

FIGURE 3-12

SQL INSERT Statements

```
/*****   DEPARTMENT DATA   ****************************************************/

INSERT INTO DEPARTMENT VALUES(
      'Administration', 'BC-100-10', 'BLDG01-300', '360-285-8100');
INSERT INTO DEPARTMENT VALUES(
      'Legal', 'BC-200-10', 'BLDG01-200', '360-285-8200');
INSERT INTO DEPARTMENT VALUES(
      'Accounting', 'BC-300-10', 'BLDG01-100', '360-285-8300');
INSERT INTO DEPARTMENT VALUES(
      'Finance', 'BC-400-10', 'BLDG01-140', '360-285-8400');
INSERT INTO DEPARTMENT VALUES(
      'Human Resources', 'BC-500-10', 'BLDG01-180', '360-285-8500');
INSERT INTO DEPARTMENT VALUES(
      'Production', 'BC-600-10', 'BLDG02-100', '360-287-8600');
INSERT INTO DEPARTMENT VALUES(
      'Marketing', 'BC-700-10', 'BLDG02-200', '360-287-8700');
INSERT INTO DEPARTMENT VALUES(
      'InfoSystems', 'BC-800-10', 'BLDG02-270', '360-287-8800');


/*****   EMPLOYEE DATA   ******************************************************/

INSERT INTO EMPLOYEE VALUES(
      'Mary', 'Jacobs', 'Administration', '360-285-8110', 'Mary.Jacobs@WPC.com');
INSERT INTO EMPLOYEE VALUES(
      'Rosalie', 'Jackson', 'Administration', '360-285-8120',
      'Rosalie.Jackson@WPC.com');
INSERT INTO EMPLOYEE VALUES(
      'Richard', 'Bandalone', 'Legal', '360-285-8210',
      'Richard.Bandalone@WPC.com');
INSERT INTO EMPLOYEE VALUES(
      'Tom', 'Caruthers', 'Accounting', '360-285-8310',
'Tom.Caruthers@WPC.com');
INSERT INTO EMPLOYEE VALUES(
      'Heather', 'Jones', 'Accounting', '360-285-8320', 'Heather.Jones@WPC.com');
INSERT INTO EMPLOYEE VALUES(
      'Mary', 'Abernathy', 'Finance', '360-285-8410',
'Mary.Abernathy@WPC.com');
INSERT INTO EMPLOYEE VALUES(
      'George', 'Smith', 'Human Resources', '360-285-8510',
      'George.Smith@WPC.com');
INSERT INTO EMPLOYEE VALUES(
      'Tom', 'Jackson', 'Production', '360-287-8610', 'Tom.Jackson@WPC.com');
INSERT INTO EMPLOYEE VALUES(
      'George', 'Jones', 'Production', '360-287-8620',
      'George.Jones@WPC.com');
INSERT INTO EMPLOYEE VALUES(
      'Ken', 'Numoto', 'Marketing', '360-287-8710', 'Ken.Numoto@WPC.com');
INSERT INTO EMPLOYEE(FirstName, LastName, Department, Email)
      VALUES('James', 'Nestor', 'InfoSystems', 'James.Nestor@WPC.com');
INSERT INTO EMPLOYEE VALUES(
      'Rick', 'Brown', 'InfoSystems', '360-287-8820', 'Rick.Brown@WPC.com');
```

FIGURE 3-12 Continued

```
/*****    PROJECT DATA    ***********************************************************/

INSERT INTO PROJECT VALUES(
     '2014 Q3 Product Plan', 'Marketing', 135.00, '10-MAY-14', '15-JUN-14');
INSERT INTO PROJECT VALUES(
     '2014 Q3 Portfolio Analysis', 'Finance', 120.00, '05-JUL-14', '25-JUL-14');
INSERT INTO PROJECT VALUES(
     '2014 Q3 Tax Preparation', 'Accounting', 145.00, '10-AUG-14', '15-OCT-14');
INSERT INTO PROJECT VALUES(
     '2014 Q4 Product Plan', 'Marketing', 150.00, '10-AUG-14', '15-SEP-14');
INSERT INTO PROJECT (ProjectName, Department, MaxHours, StartDate)
     VALUES('2014 Q4 Portfolio Analysis', 'Finance', 140.00, '05-OCT-14');


/*****    ASSIGNMENT DATA    ********************************************************/

INSERT INTO ASSIGNMENT VALUES(1000, 1, 30.0);
INSERT INTO ASSIGNMENT VALUES(1000, 8, 75.0);
INSERT INTO ASSIGNMENT VALUES(1000, 10, 55.0);
INSERT INTO ASSIGNMENT VALUES(1100, 4, 40.0);
INSERT INTO ASSIGNMENT VALUES(1100, 6, 45.0);
INSERT INTO ASSIGNMENT VALUES(1200, 1, 25.0);
INSERT INTO ASSIGNMENT VALUES(1200, 2, 20.0);
INSERT INTO ASSIGNMENT VALUES(1200, 4, 45.0);
INSERT INTO ASSIGNMENT VALUES(1200, 5, 40.0);
INSERT INTO ASSIGNMENT VALUES(1300, 1, 35.0);
INSERT INTO ASSIGNMENT VALUES(1300, 8, 80.0);
INSERT INTO ASSIGNMENT VALUES(1300, 10, 50.0);
INSERT INTO ASSIGNMENT VALUES(1400, 4, 15.0);
INSERT INTO ASSIGNMENT VALUES(1400, 5, 10.0);
INSERT INTO ASSIGNMENT VALUES(1400, 6, 27.5);


/**********************************************************************************/
```

BTW

Oracle Database and MySQL handle surrogate keys in their own unique ways. Oracle Database uses sequences (see Appendix B and the Oracle Database Express Edition 11*g* Release 2 documentation), and MySQL treats the AUTO_INCREMENT value as a missing value so that you have to list all the other column names (see Appendix C and the MySQL 5.6 Community Server documentation).

SQL FOR DATA MANIPULATION (DML)—SINGLE TABLE QUERIES

After the tables have been defined and populated, you can use SQL DML to query data in many ways. You can also use it to change and delete data, but the SQL statements for these activities will be easier to learn if we begin with the query statements. In the following discussion, assume that the sample data shown in Figure 3-2 have been entered into the database.

The SQL SELECT/FROM/WHERE Framework

This section introduces the fundamental statement framework for SQL query statements. After we discuss this basic structure, you will learn how to submit SQL statements to Microsoft Access, SQL Server, Oracle Database, and MySQL. If you choose, you can then follow along with the text and process additional SQL statements as they are explained in the rest of this chapter. The basic form of SQL queries uses the **SQL SELECT/FROM/WHERE framework**. In this framework:

- The **SQL SELECT clause** specifies which *columns* are to be listed in the query results.
- The **SQL FROM clause** specifies which *tables* are to be used in the query.
- The **SQL WHERE clause** specifies which *rows* are to be listed in the query results.

We will use and expand this framework as we work through examples in the following sections. All the examples use the data in Figure 3-2 as the basis for the results of the queries.

Reading Specified Columns from a Single Table

The following SQL statement queries (reads) three of the six columns of the PROJECT table:

```
/* *** SQL-QUERY-CH03-01 *** */
SELECT      ProjectName, Department, MaxHours
FROM        PROJECT;
```

Notice that the names of the columns to be queried follow the keyword SELECT, and the name of the relation to use follows the keyword FROM. The result of this statement is:

	ProjectName	Department	MaxHours
1	2014 Q3 Product Plan	Marketing	135.00
2	2014 Q3 Portfolio Analysis	Finance	120.00
3	2014 Q3 Tax Preparation	Accounting	145.00
4	2014 Q4 Product Plan	Marketing	150.00
5	2014 Q4 Portfolio Analysis	Finance	140.00

To show you how the results look in actual DBMS management tools, Figure 3-13 shows the query as executed in Microsoft SQL Server 2014 using Microsoft SQL Server Management Studio, Figure 3-14 shows the query as executed in Oracle Database Express Edition 11*g* Release 2 using Oracle SQL Developer, and Figure 3-15 shows the query as executed in the MySQL 5.6 using MySQL Workbench.

The result of an SQL SELECT statement is a relation. This is always true for SELECT statements. They start with one or more relations, manipulate them in some way, and then produce a relation. Even if the result of the manipulation is a single number, that number is considered to be a relation with one row and one column.

The order of the column names after the keyword SELECT determines the order of the columns in the resulting table. Thus, if you change the order of columns in the previous SELECT statement to:

```
/* *** SQL-QUERY-CH03-02 *** */
SELECT      ProjectName, MaxHours, Department
FROM        PROJECT;
```

FIGURE 3-13

SQL Query Results in the Microsoft SQL Server Management Studio

The **New Query** button

The **Execute** button

The SQL statement in the tabbed query window

The query results

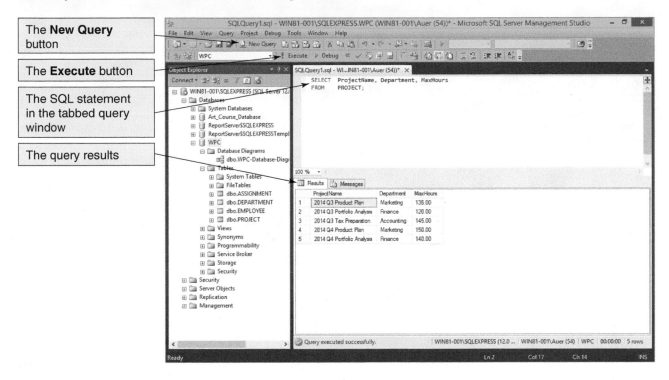

FIGURE 3-14

SQL Query Results in the Oracle SQL Developer

The **WPC** tabbed SQL Worksheet window

The **Run Statement** button

The SQL statement in the tabbed SQL Worksheet window

The query results in the tabbed **Query Result** window

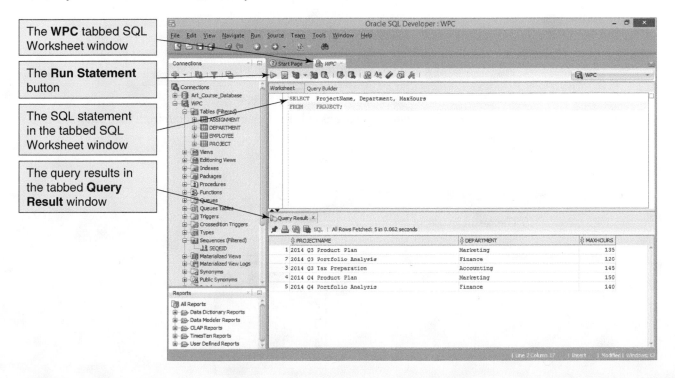

FIGURE 3-15

SQL Query Results in the MySQL Workbench

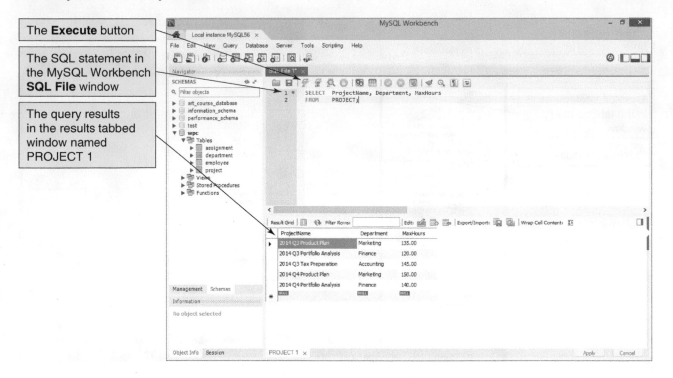

The result will be:

	Project Name	MaxHours	Department
1	2014 Q3 Product Plan	135.00	Marketing
2	2014 Q3 Portfolio Analysis	120.00	Finance
3	2014 Q3 Tax Preparation	145.00	Accounting
4	2014 Q4 Product Plan	150.00	Marketing
5	2014 Q4 Portfolio Analysis	140.00	Finance

The next SQL statement obtains only the Department column from the PROJECT table:

```
/* *** SQL-QUERY-CH03-03 *** */
SELECT     Department
FROM       PROJECT;
```

The result is:

	Department
1	Marketing
2	Finance
3	Accounting
4	Marketing
5	Finance

Notice that the first and fourth rows of this table are duplicates, as are the second and last rows. According to the definition of *relation* given in Chapter 2, such duplicate rows are prohibited. However, as also mentioned in Chapter 2, the process of checking for and eliminating duplicate rows is time-consuming. Therefore, by default, DBMS products do not check for duplication. Thus, in practice, duplicate rows can occur.

If you want the DBMS to check for and eliminate duplicate rows, you must use the **DISTINCT keyword**, as follows:

```
/* *** SQL-QUERY-CH03-04 *** */
SELECT      DISTINCT Department
FROM        PROJECT;
```

The result of this statement is:

	Department
1	Accounting
2	Finance
3	Marketing

The duplicate rows have been eliminated, as desired.

Reading Specified Rows from a Single Table

In the previous SQL statements, we selected certain columns for all rows of a table. SQL statements can also be used for the reverse; that is, they can be used to select all the columns for certain rows. The rows to be selected are specified by using the SQL WHERE clause. For example, the following SQL statement will obtain all the columns of the PROJECT table for projects sponsored by the finance department:

```
/* *** SQL-QUERY-CH03-05 *** */
SELECT      ProjectID, ProjectName, Department, MaxHours,
            StartDate, EndDate
FROM        PROJECT
WHERE       Department = 'Finance';
```

The result is:

	ProjectID	ProjectName	Department	MaxHours	StartDate	EndDate
1	1100	2014 Q3 Portfolio Analysis	Finance	120.00	2014-07-05	2014-07-25
2	1400	2014 Q4 Portfolio Analysis	Finance	140.00	2014-10-05	NULL

> ### BTW
>
> The specific treatment of date and time values varies widely among DBMS products. Note that we input the StartDate for ProjectID 1100 as 05-JUL-14 (DD-MMM-YY), but the output above shows it as 2014-07-05 (YYYY-MM-DD). As always, see the documentation for your DBMS product.

A second way to specify all the columns of a table is to use the **SQL asterisk (*) wild-card operator** after the keyword SELECT. The following SQL statement is equivalent to the previous one:

```
/* *** SQL-QUERY-CH03-06 *** */
SELECT      *
FROM        PROJECT
WHERE       Department = 'Finance';
```

The result is a table of all the columns of PROJECT for rows that have a Department value of Finance:

	ProjectID	ProjectName	Department	MaxHours	StartDate	EndDate
1	1100	2014 Q3 Portfolio Analysis	Finance	120.00	2014-07-05	2014-07-25
2	1400	2014 Q4 Portfolio Analysis	Finance	140.00	2014-10-05	NULL

As previously stated, the pattern SELECT/FROM/WHERE is the fundamental pattern of SQL SELECT statements. Many different conditions can be placed in a WHERE clause. For example, the query:

```
/* *** SQL-QUERY-CH03-07 *** */
SELECT      *
FROM        PROJECT
WHERE       MaxHours > 135;
```

selects all columns from PROJECT where the value of the MaxHours column is greater than 135. The result is:

	ProjectID	ProjectName	Department	MaxHours	StartDate	EndDate
1	1200	2014 Q3 Tax Preparation	Accounting	145.00	2014-08-10	2014-10-15
2	1300	2014 Q4 Product Plan	Marketing	150.00	2014-08-10	2014-09-15
3	1400	2014 Q4 Portfolio Analysis	Finance	140.00	2014-10-05	NULL

Notice that when the column data type is Char or VarChar, comparison values must be placed in single quotes. If the column is Integer or Numeric, no quotes are necessary. Thus, you use the notation Department = 'Finance' for a WHERE condition of the VarChar column Department, but you use the notation MaxHours = 100 for the Numeric column MaxHours.

Values placed in quotation marks may be case sensitive. For example, WHERE Department = 'Finance' and WHERE Department = 'FINANCE' may not be considered the same—check your DBMS documentation (or experiment with some data).

You can place more than one condition in a WHERE clause by using the AND keyword. If the **AND keyword** is used, only rows meeting *all* the conditions will be selected. For example, the following query determines which projects are sponsored by the finance department *and* are allocated a maximum number of hours greater than 135:

```
/* *** SQL-QUERY-CH03-08 *** */
SELECT      *
FROM        PROJECT
WHERE       Department = 'Finance'
    AND     MaxHours > 135;
```

The result of this query is:

	ProjectID	ProjectName	Department	MaxHours	StartDate	EndDate
1	1400	2014 Q4 Portfolio Analysis	Finance	140.00	2014-10-05	NULL

Reading Specified Columns and Specified Rows from a Single Table

You can combine the techniques just shown to select some columns and some rows from a table. For example, to obtain only the FirstName, LastName, Phone, and Department values of employees in the accounting department, you use:

```
/* *** SQL-QUERY-CH03-09 *** */
SELECT      FirstName, LastName, Phone, Department
FROM        EMPLOYEE
WHERE       Department = 'Accounting';
```

The result is:

	FirstName	LastName	Phone	Department
1	Tom	Caruthers	360-285-8310	Accounting
2	Heather	Jones	360-285-8320	Accounting

You can combine two or more conditions in the WHERE clause by using the AND keyword and the OR keyword. As stated previously, if the AND keyword is used, only rows meeting *all* the conditions will be selected. However, if the **OR keyword** is used, then rows that meet *any* of the conditions will be selected.

For example, the following query uses the AND keyword to ask for employees that work in accounting *and* have the phone number 360-285-8310:

```
/* *** SQL-QUERY-CH03-10 *** */
SELECT      FirstName, LastName, Phone, Department
FROM        EMPLOYEE
WHERE       Department = 'Accounting'
    AND     Phone = '360-285-8310';
```

The result is:

	FirstName	LastName	Phone	Department
1	Tom	Caruthers	360-285-8310	Accounting

However, the following query uses the OR keyword to ask for employees that work in accounting *or* have the phone number 360-285-8410:

```
/* *** SQL-QUERY-CH03-11 *** */
SELECT      FirstName, LastName, Phone, Department
FROM        EMPLOYEE
WHERE       Department = 'Accounting'
    OR      Phone = '360-285-8410';
```

The result is:

	First Name	Last Name	Phone	Department
1	Tom	Caruthers	360-285-8310	Accounting
2	Heather	Jones	360-285-8320	Accounting
3	Mary	Abernathy	360-285-8410	Finance

Another use of the WHERE clause is to specify that a column should have one of a set of values by using the **IN keyword**, as follows:

```
/* *** SQL-QUERY-CH03-12 *** */
SELECT      FirstName, LastName, Phone, Department
FROM        EMPLOYEE
WHERE       Department IN ('Accounting', 'Finance',
            'Marketing');
```

In this query, a row will be displayed if it has a Department value equal to Accounting, Finance, or Marketing. The result is:

	First Name	Last Name	Phone	Department
1	Tom	Caruthers	360-285-8310	Accounting
2	Heather	Jones	360-285-8320	Accounting
3	Mary	Abernathy	360-285-8410	Finance
4	Ken	Numoto	360-287-8710	Marketing

To select rows that do not have any of these Department values, you would use the **NOT keyword** in the **NOT IN phrase**, as follows:

```
/* *** SQL-QUERY-CH03-13 *** */
SELECT      FirstName, LastName, Phone, Department
FROM        EMPLOYEE
WHERE       Department NOT IN ('Accounting', 'Finance',
            'Marketing');
```

The result of this query is:

	First Name	Last Name	Phone	Department
1	Mary	Jacobs	360-285-8110	Administration
2	Rosalie	Jackson	360-285-8120	Administration
3	Richard	Bandalone	360-285-8210	Legal
4	George	Smith	360-285-8510	Human Resources
5	Tom	Jackson	360-287-8610	Production
6	George	Jones	360-287-8620	Production
7	James	Nestor	NULL	Info Systems
8	Rick	Brown	360-287-8820	Info Systems

Notice the essential difference between IN and NOT IN. When using IN, the column may equal *any* of the values in the list. When using NOT IN, the column must not be equal to *all* the values in the list.

Ranges, Wildcards, and Nulls in WHERE Clauses

WHERE clauses can refer to ranges of values and partial values. The BETWEEN keyword is used for ranges of values. For example, the statement:

```
/* *** SQL-QUERY-CH03-14 *** */
SELECT      FirstName, LastName, Phone, Department
FROM        EMPLOYEE
WHERE       EmployeeNumber BETWEEN 2 AND 5;
```

will produce the following result:

	First Name	Last Name	Phone	Department
1	Rosalie	Jackson	360-285-8120	Administration
2	Richard	Bandalone	360-285-8210	Legal
3	Tom	Caruthers	360-285-8310	Accounting
4	Heather	Jones	360-285-8320	Accounting

Note that the SQL keyword BETWEEN *includes* the end points, and thus SQL-QUERY-CH03-14 is equivalent to the following query, which uses the **SQL comparison operators** >= (greater than or equal to) and <= (less than or equal to):

```
/* *** SQL-QUERY-CH03-15 *** */
SELECT      FirstName, LastName, Phone, Department
FROM        EMPLOYEE
WHERE       EmployeeNumber >= 2
   AND      EmployeeNumber <= 5;
```

Thus, the end values of BETWEEN (here 2 and 5) are included in the selected range. The set of SQL comparison operators is shown in Figure 3-16. You can use any of them when creating WHERE clauses.

The **LIKE keyword** is used in SQL expressions to select partial values. It is used with **wildcard characters**, which represent unknown characters in a pattern. The SQL wildcard characters are the **underscore symbol** (_), which represents a single, unspecified character, and the **percent sign** (%), which is used to represent a series of one or more unspecified characters.

In the following query, LIKE is used with the underscore symbol to find values that fit a pattern:

```
/* *** SQL-QUERY-CH03-16 *** */
SELECT      *
FROM        PROJECT
WHERE       ProjectName LIKE '2014 Q_ Portfolio Analysis';
```

FIGURE 3-16

SQL Comparison Operators

Operator	Indicates
=	Equal to
>	Greater than
<	Less than
>=	Greater than or equal to
<=	Less than or equal to
<>	Not equal to

The underscore means that any character can occur in the spot occupied by the underscore. The result of this statement is:

	ProjectID	ProjectName	Department	MaxHours	StartDate	EndDate
1	1100	2014 Q3 Portfolio Analysis	Finance	120.00	2014-07-05	2014-07-25
2	1400	2014 Q4 Portfolio Analysis	Finance	140.00	2014-10-05	NULL

One underscore is used for each unknown character. To find all employees who have a Phone value that begins with 360-287-, you can use four underscores to represent any last four digits, as follows:

```
/* *** SQL-QUERY-CH03-17 *** */
SELECT      *
FROM        EMPLOYEE
WHERE       Phone LIKE '360-287-____';
```

The result is:

	EmployeeNumber	FirstName	LastName	Department	Phone	Email
1	8	Tom	Jackson	Production	360-287-8610	Tom.Jackson@WPC.com
2	9	George	Jones	Production	360-287-8620	George.Jones@WPC.com
3	10	Ken	Numoto	Marketing	360-287-8710	Ken.Numoto@WPC.com
4	12	Rick	Brown	Info Systems	360-287-8820	Rick.Brown@WPC.com

Because the percent sign represents one or more unknown characters, another way to write the query for employees who have a phone number that starts with 360-287- is:

```
/* *** SQL-QUERY-CH03-18 *** */
SELECT      *
FROM        EMPLOYEE
WHERE       Phone LIKE '360-287-%';
```

The result is the same as in the previous example:

	EmployeeNumber	FirstName	LastName	Department	Phone	Email
1	8	Tom	Jackson	Production	360-287-8610	Tom.Jackson@WPC.com
2	9	George	Jones	Production	360-287-8620	George.Jones@WPC.com
3	10	Ken	Numoto	Marketing	360-287-8710	Ken.Numoto@WPC.com
4	12	Rick	Brown	InfoSystems	360-287-8820	Rick.Brown@WPC.com

If you want to find all the employees who work in departments that end in *ing*, you can use the % character as follows:

```
/* *** SQL-QUERY-CH03-19 *** */
SELECT       *
FROM         EMPLOYEE
WHERE        Department LIKE '%ing';
```

The result is:

	EmployeeNumber	FirstName	LastName	Department	Phone	Email
1	4	Tom	Caruthers	Accounting	360-285-8310	Tom.Caruthers@WPC.com
2	5	Heather	Jones	Accounting	360-285-8320	Heather.Jones@WPC.com
3	10	Ken	Numoto	Marketing	360-287-8710	Ken.Numoto@WPC.com

BTW

The NOT keyword, which we used previously as part of the NOT IN phrase, can also be used with LIKE to form the **NOT LIKE phrase**. For example, if you want to find all the employees who work in departments that do *not* end in *ing*, you can use the following SQL query:

```
/* *** SQL-QUERY-CH03-20 *** */
SELECT       *
FROM         EMPLOYEE
WHERE        Department NOT LIKE '%ing';
```

Does Not Work with Microsoft Access ANSI-89 SQL

Microsoft Access ANSI-89 SQL uses wildcards but not the SQL-92 standard wildcards. Microsoft Access uses a **question mark (?)** instead of an underscore to represent single characters and an **asterisk (*)** instead of a percent sign to represent multiple characters. These symbols have their roots in the SQL-89 standard, where they are the correct standard.

(continued)

> Furthermore, Microsoft Access can sometimes be fussy about stored trailing spaces in a text field. You may have problems with a WHERE clause like this:
>
> ```
> WHERE    ProjectName LIKE '2014 Q? Portfolio Analysis';
> ```
>
> But the clause will work if you use a trailing asterisk (*), which allows for the trailing spaces:
>
> ```
> WHERE    ProjectName LIKE '2014 Q? Portfolio Analysis*';
> ```
>
> **Solution:** Use the appropriate Microsoft Access wildcard characters, and include a trailing asterisk (*), if needed.

Another useful SQL keyword is the **IS NULL keyword**, which can be used in a WHERE clause to search for null values. The following SQL will find the names and departments of all employees who have a null value for Phone:

```
/* *** SQL-QUERY-CH03-21 *** */
SELECT       FirstName, LastName, Phone, Department
FROM         EMPLOYEE
WHERE        Phone IS NULL;
```

The result of this query is:

	FirstName	LastName	Phone	Department
1	James	Nestor	NULL	InfoSystems

BTW

The NOT keyword can also be used with IS NULL to form the **IS NOT NULL phrase**. For example, if you want to find all the employees who do have phone numbers, you can use the following SQL query:

```
/* *** SQL-QUERY-CH03-22 *** */
SELECT       FirstName, LastName, Phone, Department
FROM         EMPLOYEE
WHERE        Phone IS NOT NULL;
```

Sorting the Results of a Query

The order of rows in the result of a SELECT statement is somewhat arbitrary. If this is undesirable, we can use the **ORDER BY clause** to sort the rows. For example, the following will display the names, phone numbers, and departments of all employees, sorted by Department:

```
/* *** SQL-QUERY-CH03-23 *** */
SELECT      FirstName, LastName, Phone, Department
FROM        EMPLOYEE
ORDER BY    Department;
```

The result is:

	First Name	Last Name	Phone	Department
1	Tom	Caruthers	360-285-8310	Accounting
2	Heather	Jones	360-285-8320	Accounting
3	Mary	Jacobs	360-285-8110	Administration
4	Rosalie	Jackson	360-285-8120	Administration
5	Mary	Abernathy	360-285-8410	Finance
6	George	Smith	360-285-8510	Human Resources
7	James	Nestor	NULL	InfoSystems
8	Rick	Brown	360-287-8820	InfoSystems
9	Richard	Bandalo...	360-285-8210	Legal
10	Ken	Numoto	360-287-8710	Marketing
11	Tom	Jackson	360-287-8610	Production
12	George	Jones	360-287-8620	Production

By default, SQL sorts in ascending order. The **ASC keyword** and **DESC keyword** can be used to specify ascending and descending order when necessary. Thus, to sort employees in descending order by Department, use:

```
/* *** SQL-QUERY-CH03-24 *** */
SELECT      FirstName, LastName, Phone, Department
FROM        EMPLOYEE
ORDER BY    Department DESC;
```

The result is:

	First Name	Last Name	Phone	Department
1	Tom	Jackson	360-287-8610	Production
2	George	Jones	360-287-8620	Production
3	Ken	Numoto	360-287-8710	Marketing
4	Richard	Bandalone	360-285-8210	Legal
5	James	Nestor	NULL	InfoSystems
6	Rick	Brown	360-287-8820	InfoSystems
7	George	Smith	360-285-8510	Human Resources
8	Mary	Abernathy	360-285-8410	Finance
9	Mary	Jacobs	360-285-8110	Administration
10	Rosalie	Jackson	360-285-8120	Administration
11	Tom	Caruthers	360-285-8310	Accounting
12	Heather	Jones	360-285-8320	Accounting

Two or more columns can be used for sorting purposes. To sort the employee names and departments first in descending value of Department and then within Department by ascending value of LastName, you specify:

```
/* *** SQL-QUERY-CH03-25 *** */
SELECT      FirstName, LastName, Phone, Department
FROM        EMPLOYEE
ORDER BY    Department DESC, LastName ASC;
```

The result is:

	First Name	Last Name	Phone	Department
1	Tom	Jackson	360-287-8610	Production
2	George	Jones	360-287-8620	Production
3	Ken	Numoto	360-287-8710	Marketing
4	Richard	Bandalone	360-285-8210	Legal
5	Rick	Brown	360-287-8820	InfoSystems
6	James	Nestor	NULL	InfoSystems
7	George	Smith	360-285-8510	Human Resources
8	Mary	Abernathy	360-285-8410	Finance
9	Rosalie	Jackson	360-285-8120	Administration
10	Mary	Jacobs	360-285-8110	Administration
11	Tom	Caruthers	360-285-8310	Accounting
12	Heather	Jones	360-285-8320	Accounting

SQL Built-in Functions and Calculations

SQL allows you to calculate values based on the data in the tables. You can use arithmetic formulas, and you can also use **SQL built-in functions**. SQL includes five built-in functions: **COUNT, SUM, AVG, MAX**, and **MIN**. These functions operate on the results of a SELECT statement. COUNT works regardless of column data type, but SUM, AVG, MAX, and MIN operate only on integer, numeric, and other number-oriented columns.

COUNT and SUM sound similar but are different. COUNT counts the number of rows in the result, whereas SUM totals the set of values of a numeric column. Thus, the following SQL statement counts the number of rows in the PROJECT table:

```
/* *** SQL-QUERY-CH03-26 *** */
SELECT      COUNT(*)
FROM        PROJECT;
```

The result of this statement is the following relation:

	(No column name)
1	5

As stated earlier, the result of an SQL SELECT statement is always a relation. If, as is the case here, the result is a single number, that number is considered to be a relation that has only a single row and a single column.

Note that the result shown above has no column name. You can assign a column name to the result by using the **AS keyword**:

```
/* *** SQL-QUERY-CH03-27 *** */
SELECT      COUNT(*) AS NumberOfProjects
FROM        PROJECT;
```

Now the resulting number is identified by the column title:

	NumberOfProjects
1	5

Consider the following two SELECT statements:

```
/* *** SQL-QUERY-CH03-28 *** */
SELECT      COUNT(Department) AS NumberOfDepartments
FROM        PROJECT;
```

and:

```
/* *** SQL-QUERY-CH03-29 *** */
SELECT      COUNT(DISTINCT Department) AS NumberOfDepartments
FROM        PROJECT;
```

The result of SQL-QUERY-CH03-28 is the relation:

	NumberOfDepartments
1	5

and the result of SQL-QUERY-CH03-29 is:

	NumberOfDepartments
1	3

The difference in answers occurs because duplicate rows were eliminated in the count of the departments in the second SELECT.

Does Not Work with Microsoft Access ANSI-89 SQL

Microsoft Access does not support the DISTINCT keyword as part of the COUNT expression, so while the SQL command with COUNT (Department) will work, the SQL command with COUNT (DISTINCT Department) will fail.

Solution: Use an SQL subquery structure (discussed later in this chapter) with the DISTINCT keyword in the subquery itself. The following SQL query works:

```
/* *** SQL-QUERY-CH03-29-Access *** */
SELECT       COUNT(*)  AS NumberOfDepartments
FROM         (SELECT   DISTINCT Department
             FROM      PROJECT) AS DEPT;
```

Note that this query is a bit different from the other queries using subqueries we show in this text because the subquery above is in the FROM clause instead of (as you'll see) the WHERE clause. Basically, this subquery builds a new temporary table named DEPT containing only distinct Department values, and the query counts the number of those values.

The following is another example of built-in functions:

```
/* *** SQL-QUERY-CH03-30 *** */
SELECT       MIN(MaxHours)  AS MinimumMaxHours,
             MAX(MaxHours)  AS MaximumMaxHours,
             SUM(MaxHours)  AS TotalMaxHours
FROM         PROJECT
WHERE        ProjectID <= 1200;
```

The result is:

	MinimumMaxHours	MaximumMaxHours	TotalMaxHours
1	120.00	145.00	400.00

Standard mathematical calculations can also be done in SQL. For example, suppose that all employees at Wedgewood Pacific Corporation are paid $18.50 per hour. Given that each project has a MaxHours value, you might want to calculate a *maximum project cost* value for each project that is equal to MaxHours multiplied by the hour wage rate. You can calculate the needed numbers by using the following query:

```
/* *** SQL-QUERY-CH03-31 *** */
SELECT       ProjectID, ProjectName, MaxHours,
             (18.50 * MaxHours) AS MaxProjectCost
FROM         PROJECT;
```

The result of the query, which now shows the maximum project cost for each project, is:

	ProjectID	ProjectName	MaxHours	MaxProjectCost
1	1000	2014 Q3 Product Plan	135.00	2497.5000
2	1100	2014 Q3 Portfolio Analysis	120.00	2220.0000
3	1200	2014 Q3 Tax Preparation	145.00	2682.5000
4	1300	2014 Q4 Product Plan	150.00	2775.0000
5	1400	2014 Q4 Portfolio Analysis	140.00	2590.0000

Note that the SQL standard does not allow column names to be mixed with built-in functions, except in certain uses of the SQL GROUP BY clause, as discussed in the next section. Thus, the following is not allowed:

```
/* *** SQL-QUERY-CH03-32 *** */
SELECT      MaxHours, SUM(MaxHours)
FROM        PROJECT
WHERE       ProjectID <= 1200;
```

SQL Server returns the following error message if you attempt to run this query:

```
Msg 8120, Level 16, State 1, Line 1
Column 'PROJECT.MaxHours' is invalid in the select list because
it is not contained in either an aggregate function or the GROUP
BY clause.
```

Also, DBMS products vary in the ways in which built-in functions can be used. Generally, built-in functions cannot be used in WHERE clauses. Thus, a WHERE clause such as the following is not normally allowed:

```
/* *** SQL-QUERY-CH03-33 *** */
SELECT      ProjectID, MaxHours
FROM        PROJECT
WHERE       MaxHours < AVG(MaxHours);
```

SQL Server returns the following error message if you attempt to run this query:

```
Msg 147, Level 15, State 1, Line 3
An aggregate may not appear in the WHERE clause unless it is
in a subquery contained in a HAVING clause or a select list,
and the column being aggregated is an outer reference.
```

Built-in Functions and Grouping

In SQL, you can use the **GROUP BY clause** to group rows by common values. This increases the utility of built-in functions because you can apply them to groups of rows. For example, the following statement counts the number of employees in each department:

```
/* *** SQL-QUERY-CH03-34 *** */
SELECT      Department, Count(*) AS NumberOfEmployees
FROM        EMPLOYEE
GROUP BY    Department;
```

The result is:

	Department	NumberOfEmployees
1	Accounting	2
2	Administration	2
3	Finance	1
4	Human Resources	1
5	InfoSystems	2
6	Legal	1
7	Marketing	1
8	Production	2

The GROUP BY keyword tells the DBMS to sort the table by the named column and then to apply the built-in function to groups of rows that have the same value for the named column. When GROUP BY is used, the name of the grouping column and built-in functions may appear in the SELECT clause. This is the *only* time that a column name and a built-in function can appear together.

We can further restrict the results by using the **HAVING clause** to apply conditions to the groups that are formed. For example, if you want to consider only groups with more than two members, you could specify:

```
/* *** SQL-QUERY-CH03-35 *** */
SELECT      Department, Count(*) AS NumberOfEmployees
FROM        EMPLOYEE
GROUP BY    Department
HAVING      COUNT(*) > 1;
```

The result of this SQL statement is:

	Department	NumberOfEmployees
1	Accounting	2
2	Administration	2
3	InfoSystems	2
4	Production	2

It is possible to add WHERE clauses when using GROUP BY. However, an ambiguity results when this is done. If the WHERE condition is applied before the groups are formed, we obtain one result. If, however, the WHERE condition is applied after the groups are formed, we get a different result. To resolve this ambiguity, the SQL standard specifies that when WHERE and GROUP BY occur together, the WHERE condition will be applied first. For example, consider the following query:

```
/* *** SQL-QUERY-CH03-36 *** */
SELECT      Department, Count(*) AS NumberOfEmployees
FROM        EMPLOYEE
WHERE       EmployeeNumber <= 6
GROUP BY    Department
HAVING      COUNT(*) > 1;
```

In this expression, first the WHERE clause is applied to select employees with an EmployeeNumber less than or equal to 6. Then the groups are formed. Finally, the HAVING condition is applied. The result is:

	Department	NumberOfEmployees
1	Accounting	2
2	Administration	2

SQL FOR DATA MANIPULATION (DML)—MULTIPLE TABLE QUERIES

The queries considered so far have involved data from a single table. However, at times, more than one table must be processed to obtain the desired information.

Querying Multiple Tables with Subqueries

For example, suppose we want to know the names of all employees who have worked more than 50 hours on any single assignment. The names of employees are stored in the EMPLOYEE table, but the hours they have worked are stored in the ASSIGNMENT table.

If we knew that employees with EmployeeNumber 8 and 10 have worked more than 50 hours on an assignment (which is true), we could obtain their names with the following expression:

```
/* *** SQL-QUERY-CH03-37 *** */
SELECT      FirstName, LastName
FROM        EMPLOYEE
WHERE       EmployeeNumber IN (8, 10);
```

The result is:

	FirstName	LastName
1	Tom	Jackson
2	Ken	Numoto

But, according to the problem description, we are not given the employee numbers. We can, however, obtain the appropriate employee numbers with the following query:

```
/* *** SQL-QUERY-CH03-38 *** */
SELECT      DISTINCT EmployeeNumber
FROM        ASSIGNMENT
WHERE       HoursWorked > 50;
```

The result is:

	EmployeeNumber
1	8
2	10

Now, we can combine these two SQL statements by using a **subquery**, as follows:

```
/* *** SQL-QUERY-CH03-39 *** */
SELECT      FirstName, LastName
FROM        EMPLOYEE
WHERE       EmployeeNumber IN
            (SELECT   DISTINCT EmployeeNumber
             FROM     ASSIGNMENT
             WHERE    HoursWorked > 50);
```

The result of this expression is:

	First Name	Last Name
1	Tom	Jackson
2	Ken	Numoto

These are indeed the names of the employees who have worked more than 50 hours on any single assignment.

Subqueries can be extended to include three, four, or even more levels. Suppose, for example, that you need to know the names of employees who have worked more than 40 hours on an assignment sponsored by the accounting department. You can obtain the project IDs of projects sponsored by accounting with:

```
/* *** SQL-QUERY-CH03-40 *** */
SELECT      ProjectID
FROM        PROJECT
WHERE       Department = 'Accounting';
```

The result is:

	Project ID
1	1200

You can obtain the employee numbers of employees working more than 40 hours on those projects with:

```
/* *** SQL-QUERY-CH03-41 *** */
SELECT      DISTINCT EmployeeNumber
FROM        ASSIGNMENT
WHERE       HoursWorked > 40
    AND     ProjectID IN
            (SELECT   ProjectID
             FROM     PROJECT
             WHERE    Department = 'Accounting');
```

The result is:

	Employee Number
1	4

Finally, you can obtain the names of the employees in the preceding SQL statement with:

```
/* *** SQL-QUERY-CH03-42 *** */
SELECT      FirstName, LastName
FROM        EMPLOYEE
WHERE       EmployeeNumber IN
            (SELECT   DISTINCT EmployeeNumber
             FROM     ASSIGNMENT
             WHERE    HoursWorked > 40
                 AND  ProjectID IN
                      (SELECT   ProjectID
                       FROM     PROJECT
                       WHERE    Department = 'Accounting'));
```

The final result is:

	First Name	Last Name
1	Tom	Caruthers

Querying Multiple Tables with Joins

Subqueries are effective for processing multiple tables, as long as the results come from a single table. If, however, we need to display data from two or more tables, subqueries do not work. We need to use an **SQL join operation** instead.

The basic idea of a join is to form a new relation by connecting the contents of two or more other relations. Consider the following example:

```
/* *** SQL-QUERY-CH03-43 *** */
SELECT      FirstName, LastName, HoursWorked
FROM        EMPLOYEE, ASSIGNMENT
WHERE       EMPLOYEE.EmployeeNumber =
               ASSIGNMENT.EmployeeNumber;
```

The function of this statement is to create a new table having the three columns LastName, FirstName, and HoursWorked. Those columns are to be taken from the EMPLOYEE and ASSIGNMENT tables, under the condition that EmployeeNumber in EMPLOYEE (written in the format *TABLENAME.ColumnName* as EMPLOYEE.EmployeeNumber) equals EmployeeNumber in ASSIGNMENT (written as ASSIGNMENT.EmployeeNumber). Whenever there is ambiguity about which table the column data are coming from, the column name is always preceded with the table name in the format *TABLENAME .ColumnName*.

> This ambiguity about which table the column data are coming from often happens (as in this case) because the primary key and foreign key column names are the same, but it can happen in other situations. For example, both EMPLOYEE and DEPARTMENT have a Phone column, but Phone is not a primary key or foreign key in either table. If we wanted to list employees with both their own phone number and their department phone number, we would have to qualify the field names as EMPLOYEE.Phone and DEPARTMENT.Phone.

You can think of the join operation working as follows. Start with the first row in EMPLOYEE. Using the value of EmployeeNumber in this first row (1 for the data in Figure 3-2(b)), examine the rows in ASSIGNMENT. When you find a row in ASSIGNMENT where EmployeeNumber is also equal to 1, join FirstName and LastName of the first row of EMPLOYEE with HoursWorked from the row you just found in ASSIGNMENT.

For the data in Figure 3-2(c), the first row of ASSIGNMENT has EmployeeNumber equal to 1, so you join FirstName and LastName from the first row of EMPLOYEE with HoursWorked from the first row in ASSIGNMENT to form the first row of the join. The result is:

	First Name	Last Name	Hours Worked
1	Mary	Jacobs	30.00

Now, still using the EmployeeNumber value of 1, look for a second row in ASSIGNMENT that has EmployeeNumber equal to 1. For our data, the sixth row of ASSIGNMENT has such a value. So, join FirstName and LastName from the first row of EMPLOYEE to HoursWorked in the sixth row of ASSIGNMENT to obtain the second row of the join, as follows:

	First Name	Last Name	Hours Worked
1	Mary	Jacobs	30.00
2	Mary	Jacobs	25.00

Continue in this way, looking for matches for the EmployeeNumber value of 1. There is one more in the 10th row, and you would add the data for that match to obtain the result:

	First Name	Last Name	Hours Worked
1	Mary	Jacobs	30.00
2	Mary	Jacobs	25.00
3	Mary	Jacobs	35.00

At this point, no more EmployeeNumber values of 1 appear in the sample data, so now you move to the second row of EMPLOYEE, obtain the new value of EmployeeNumber (2), and begin searching for matches for it in the rows of ASSIGNMENT. In this case, the seventh row has such a match, so you add FirstName, LastName, and HoursWorked to the result to obtain:

	FirstName	LastName	HoursWorked
1	Mary	Jacobs	30.00
2	Mary	Jacobs	25.00
3	Mary	Jacobs	35.00
4	Rosalie	Jackson	20.00

You continue until all rows of EMPLOYEE have been examined. The final result is:

	FirstName	LastName	HoursWorked
1	Mary	Jacobs	30.00
2	Mary	Jacobs	25.00
3	Mary	Jacobs	35.00
4	Rosalie	Jackson	20.00
5	Tom	Caruthers	45.00
6	Tom	Caruthers	40.00
7	Tom	Caruthers	15.00
8	Heather	Jones	10.00
9	Heather	Jones	40.00
10	Mary	Abernathy	45.00
11	Mary	Abernathy	27.50
12	Tom	Jackson	80.00
13	Tom	Jackson	75.00
14	Ken	Numoto	55.00
15	Ken	Numoto	50.00

Actually, that is the theoretical result. But remember that row order in an SQL query can be arbitrary. To ensure that you get the above result, you need to add an ORDER BY clause to the query:

```
/* *** SQL-QUERY-CH03-44 *** */
SELECT     FirstName, LastName, HoursWorked
FROM       EMPLOYEE, ASSIGNMENT
WHERE      EMPLOYEE.EmployeeNumber =
             ASSIGNMENT.EmployeeNumber
ORDER BY   EMPLOYEE.EmployeeNumber, ProjectID;
```

The actual result when the original query is run in SQL Server is:

	FirstName	LastName	HoursWorked
1	Mary	Jacobs	30.00
2	Tom	Jackson	75.00
3	Ken	Numoto	55.00
4	Tom	Caruthers	40.00
5	Mary	Abernathy	45.00
6	Mary	Jacobs	25.00
7	Rosalie	Jackson	20.00
8	Tom	Caruthers	45.00
9	Heather	Jones	40.00
10	Mary	Jacobs	35.00
11	Tom	Jackson	80.00
12	Ken	Numoto	50.00
13	Tom	Caruthers	15.00
14	Heather	Jones	10.00
15	Mary	Abernathy	27.50

The data results are the same, but the row order is definitely different!

A join is just another table, so all the earlier SQL SELECT commands are available for use. We could, for example, group the rows of the join by employee and sum the hours they worked. The following is the SQL for such a query:

```
/* *** SQL-QUERY-CH03-45 *** */
SELECT      FirstName, LastName,
            SUM(HoursWorked) AS TotalHoursWorked
FROM        EMPLOYEE AS E, ASSIGNMENT AS A
WHERE       E.EmployeeNumber = A.EmployeeNumber
GROUP BY    LastName, FirstName;
```

Note another use for the AS keyword, which is now used to assign aliases to table names so that we can use these aliases in the WHERE clause. This makes it much easier to write queries with long table names. The result of this query is:

	FirstName	LastName	TotalHoursWorked
1	Heather	Jones	50.00
2	Ken	Numoto	105.00
3	Mary	Abernathy	72.50
4	Mary	Jacobs	90.00
5	Rosalie	Jackson	20.00
6	Tom	Caruthers	100.00
7	Tom	Jackson	155.00

Or we could apply a WHERE clause during the process of creating the join as follows:

```
/* *** SQL-QUERY-CH03-46 *** */
SELECT      FirstName, LastName, HoursWorked
FROM        EMPLOYEE AS E, ASSIGNMENT AS A
WHERE       E.EmployeeNumber = A.EmployeeNumber
   AND      HoursWorked > 50;
```

The result of this join is:

	FirstName	LastName	HoursWorked
1	Tom	Jackson	75.00
2	Ken	Numoto	55.00
3	Tom	Jackson	80.00

Now, suppose we want to join PROJECT to EMPLOYEE and ASSIGNMENT to show the names of the projects that the employees worked on. We can use the same SQL statement structure as before, except for one complication—now you have to use two WHERE phrases combined by an AND to join the three tables:

```
/* *** SQL-QUERY-CH03-47 *** */
SELECT      ProjectName, FirstName, LastName, HoursWorked
FROM        EMPLOYEE AS E, PROJECT AS P, ASSIGNMENT AS A
WHERE       E.EmployeeNumber = A.EmployeeNumber
   AND      P.ProjectID = A.ProjectID
ORDER BY    P.ProjectID, A.EmployeeNumber;
```

The result of this query is:

	ProjectName	FirstName	LastName	HoursWorked
1	2014 Q3 Product Plan	Mary	Jacobs	30.00
2	2014 Q3 Product Plan	Tom	Jackson	75.00
3	2014 Q3 Product Plan	Ken	Numoto	55.00
4	2014 Q3 Portfolio Analysis	Tom	Caruthers	40.00
5	2014 Q3 Portfolio Analysis	Mary	Abernathy	45.00
6	2014 Q3 Tax Preparation	Mary	Jacobs	25.00
7	2014 Q3 Tax Preparation	Rosalie	Jackson	20.00
8	2014 Q3 Tax Preparation	Tom	Caruthers	45.00
9	2014 Q3 Tax Preparation	Heather	Jones	40.00
10	2014 Q4 Product Plan	Mary	Jacobs	35.00
11	2014 Q4 Product Plan	Tom	Jackson	80.00
12	2014 Q4 Product Plan	Ken	Numoto	50.00
13	2014 Q4 Portfolio Analysis	Tom	Caruthers	15.00
14	2014 Q4 Portfolio Analysis	Heather	Jones	10.00
15	2014 Q4 Portfolio Analysis	Mary	Abernathy	27.50

The SQL JOIN ON Syntax

Our SQL join examples so far have used the original, but older, form of the SQL join syntax. While it can still be used, today most SQL users prefer to use the **SQL JOIN ON syntax**. Consider our query example SQL-QUERY-CH03-43 as modified with an ORDER BY clause to become SQL-QUERY-CH03-44. This query uses a join in the WHERE clause:

```
/* *** SQL-QUERY-CH03-44 *** */
SELECT      FirstName, LastName, HoursWorked
FROM        EMPLOYEE, ASSIGNMENT
WHERE       EMPLOYEE.EmployeeNumber =
                ASSIGNMENT.EmployeeNumber
ORDER BY    EMPLOYEE.EmployeeNumber, ProjectID;
```

Using the JOIN ON syntax, SQL-QUERY-CH-44 would be modified as follows to become SQL-QUERY-CH03-48:

```
/* *** SQL-QUERY-CH03-48 *** */
SELECT      FirstName, LastName, HoursWorked
FROM        EMPLOYEE JOIN ASSIGNMENT
            ON    EMPLOYEE.EmployeeNumber =
                      ASSIGNMENT.EmployeeNumber
ORDER BY    EMPLOYEE.EmployeeNumber, ProjectID;
```

The result of the query, as you would expect, is:

	First Name	Last Name	Hours Worked
1	Mary	Jacobs	30.00
2	Mary	Jacobs	25.00
3	Mary	Jacobs	35.00
4	Rosalie	Jackson	20.00
5	Tom	Caruthers	40.00
6	Tom	Caruthers	45.00
7	Tom	Caruthers	15.00
8	Heather	Jones	40.00
9	Heather	Jones	10.00
10	Mary	Abernathy	45.00
11	Mary	Abernathy	27.50
12	Tom	Jackson	75.00
13	Tom	Jackson	80.00
14	Ken	Numoto	55.00
15	Ken	Numoto	50.00

Note that the SQL JOIN ON syntax links tables in the FROM clause with the **SQL JOIN keyword** instead of a comma, and then moves the join condition that was previous in the WHERE clause into the FROM clause by use of the **SQL ON keyword**. This creates easy to read lines of code that make semantic sense to the reader.

Our first example used only two tables, but we can also use the JOIN ON syntax for joins of more than two tables. Here is the previous query to combine data for EMPLOYEE, PROJECT, and ASSIGNMENT rewritten using the JOIN ON style:

```
/* *** SQL-QUERY-CH03-49 *** */
SELECT      ProjectName, FirstName, LastName, HoursWorked
FROM        EMPLOYEE AS E JOIN ASSIGNMENT AS A
            ON    E.EmployeeNumber = A.EmployeeNumber
                  JOIN PROJECT AS P
                        ON    A.ProjectID = P.ProjectID
ORDER BY    P.ProjectID, A.EmployeeNumber;
```

Note how the additional table is added into the query by the additional JOIN ON construction. For each new table added to the query, we simply add another JOIN ON phrase. For our earlier three-table example, the result, as you would expect, is the same as we obtained with the previous query:

	ProjectName	FirstName	LastName	HoursWorked
1	2014 Q3 Product Plan	Mary	Jacobs	30.00
2	2014 Q3 Product Plan	Tom	Jackson	75.00
3	2014 Q3 Product Plan	Ken	Numoto	55.00
4	2014 Q3 Portfolio Analysis	Tom	Caruthers	40.00
5	2014 Q3 Portfolio Analysis	Mary	Abernathy	45.00
6	2014 Q3 Tax Preparation	Mary	Jacobs	25.00
7	2014 Q3 Tax Preparation	Rosalie	Jackson	20.00
8	2014 Q3 Tax Preparation	Tom	Caruthers	45.00
9	2014 Q3 Tax Preparation	Heather	Jones	40.00
10	2014 Q4 Product Plan	Mary	Jacobs	35.00
11	2014 Q4 Product Plan	Tom	Jackson	80.00
12	2014 Q4 Product Plan	Ken	Numoto	50.00
13	2014 Q4 Portfolio Analysis	Tom	Caruthers	15.00
14	2014 Q4 Portfolio Analysis	Heather	Jones	10.00
15	2014 Q4 Portfolio Analysis	Mary	Abernathy	27.50

Does Not Work with Microsoft Access ANSI-89 SQL

Microsoft Access supports the JOIN ON syntax only with a keyword specifying a standard (INNER) or nonstandard (OUTER) JOIN. OUTER joins are discussed next in the text.

(continued)

Solution: The Microsoft Access JOIN ON queries run when written with the INNER keyword as:

```
/* *** SQL-QUERY-CH03-48-Access *** */
SELECT      FirstName, LastName, HoursWorked
FROM        EMPLOYEE INNER JOIN ASSIGNMENT
            ON   EMPLOYEE.EmployeeNumber =
                      ASSIGNMENT.EmployeeNumber
ORDER BY   EMPLOYEE.EmployeeNumber, ProjectID;
```

Further, Microsoft Access requires that the joins be grouped using parentheses when three or more tables are joined:

```
/* *** SQL-QUERY-CH03-40-Access *** */
SELECT      ProjectName, FirstName, LastName, HoursWorked
FROM        (EMPLOYEE AS E INNER JOIN ASSIGNMENT AS A
            ON   E.EmployeeNumber = A.EmployeeNumber)
                 INNER JOIN PROJECT AS P
                      ON   A.ProjectID = P.ProjectID
ORDER BY   P.ProjectID, A.EmployeeNumber;
```

Inner Joins and Outer Joins

Let's add a new project, the 2014 Q4 Tax Preparation project run by the accounting department, to the PROJECT table as follows:

```
/* *** SQL-INSERT-CH03-05 *** */
INSERT INTO PROJECT
    (ProjectName, Department, MaxHours, StartDate)
    VALUES('2014 Q4 Tax Preparation', 'Accounting',
    175.00, '10-DEC-14');
```

To see the updated PROJECT table, we use the query:

```
/* *** SQL-QUERY-CH03-50 *** */
SELECT * FROM PROJECT;
```

The results are:

	ProjectID	ProjectName	Department	MaxHours	StartDate	EndDate
1	1000	2014 Q3 Product Plan	Marketing	135.00	2014-05-10	2014-06-15
2	1100	2014 Q3 Portfolio Analysis	Finance	120.00	2014-07-05	2014-07-25
3	1200	2014 Q3 Tax Preparation	Accounting	145.00	2014-08-10	2014-10-15
4	1300	2014 Q4 Product Plan	Marketing	150.00	2014-08-10	2014-09-15
5	1400	2014 Q4 Portfolio Analysis	Finance	140.00	2014-10-05	NULL
6	1500	2014 Q4 Tax Preparation	Accounting	175.00	2014-12-12	NULL

Now, with the new project added to PROJECT, we'll rerun the previous query on EMPLOYEE, ASSIGNMENT, and PROJECT:

```
/* *** SQL-QUERY-CH03-51 *** */
SELECT      ProjectName, FirstName, LastName, HoursWorked
FROM        EMPLOYEE AS E JOIN ASSIGNMENT AS A
            ON   E.EmployeeNumber = A.EmployeeNumber
                 JOIN PROJECT AS P
                     ON   A.ProjectID = P.ProjectID
ORDER BY    P.ProjectID, A.EmployeeNumber;
```

The results are:

	ProjectName	FirstName	LastName	HoursWorked
1	2014 Q3 Product Plan	Mary	Jacobs	30.00
2	2014 Q3 Product Plan	Tom	Jackson	75.00
3	2014 Q3 Product Plan	Ken	Numoto	55.00
4	2014 Q3 Portfolio Analysis	Tom	Caruthers	40.00
5	2014 Q3 Portfolio Analysis	Mary	Abernathy	45.00
6	2014 Q3 Tax Preparation	Mary	Jacobs	25.00
7	2014 Q3 Tax Preparation	Rosalie	Jackson	20.00
8	2014 Q3 Tax Preparation	Tom	Caruthers	45.00
9	2014 Q3 Tax Preparation	Heather	Jones	40.00
10	2014 Q4 Product Plan	Mary	Jacobs	35.00
11	2014 Q4 Product Plan	Tom	Jackson	80.00
12	2014 Q4 Product Plan	Ken	Numoto	50.00
13	2014 Q4 Portfolio Analysis	Tom	Caruthers	15.00
14	2014 Q4 Portfolio Analysis	Heather	Jones	10.00
15	2014 Q4 Portfolio Analysis	Mary	Abernathy	27.50

The results shown here are correct, but a surprising result occurs. What happened to the new 2014 Q4 Tax Preparation project? The answer is that it does not appear in the join results because its ProjectID value of 1500 had no match in the ASSIGNMENT table. Nothing is wrong with this result; you just need to be aware that unmatched rows do not appear in the result of a join. The join operation discussed in the previous sections is sometimes referred to as an **SQL equijoin** or **SQL inner join**. An inner join only displays data from the rows that match based on join conditions, and as you saw in the last query in the previous section, data can be lost (or at least appear to be lost) when you perform an inner join. In particular, if a row has a value that does not match the WHERE clause condition, that row will not be included in the join result. The 2014 Q4 Tax Preparation project did not appear in the previous join because no row in ASSIGNMENT matched its ProjectID value. This kind of loss is not always desirable, so a special type of join, called an **SQL outer join**, was created to avoid it.

Consider the STUDENT and LOCKER tables in Figure 3-17(A), where we have drawn two tables to highlight the relationships between the rows in each table. The STUDENT table shows the StudentPK (student number) and StudentName of students at a university. The LOCKER table shows the LockerPK (locker number) and LockerType (full size or half

FIGURE 3-17

Types of JOINS

STUDENT

StudentPK	StudentName	LockerFK
1	Adams	NULL
2	Buchanan	NULL
3	Carter	10
4	Ford	20
5	Hoover	30
6	Kennedy	40
7	Roosevelt	50
8	Truman	60

LOCKER

LockerPK	LockerType
10	Full
20	Full
30	Half
40	Full
50	Full
60	Half
70	Full
80	Full
90	Half

(a) The STUDENT and LOCKER Tables Aligned to Show Row Relationships

Only the rows where LockerFK=LockerPK are shown—Note that some StudentPK and some LockerPK values are not in the results

StudentPK	StudentName	LockerFK	LockerPK	LockerType
3	Carter	10	10	Full
4	Ford	20	20	Full
5	Hoover	30	30	Half
6	Kennedy	40	40	Full
7	Roosevelt	50	50	Full
8	Truman	60	60	Half

(b) INNER JOIN of the STUDENT and LOCKER Tables

All rows from STUDENT are shown, even where there is no matching LockerFK=LockerPK value

StudentPK	StudentName	LockerFK	LockerPK	LockerType
1	Adams	NULL	NULL	NULL
2	Buchanan	NULL	NULL	NULL
3	Carter	10	10	Full
4	Ford	20	20	Full
5	Hoover	30	30	Half
6	Kennedy	40	40	Full
7	Roosevelt	50	50	Full
8	Truman	60	60	Half

(c) LEFT OUTER JOIN of the STUDENT and LOCKER Tables

All rows from LOCKER are shown, even where there is no matching LockerFK=LockerPK value

StudentPK	StudentName	LockerFK	LockerPK	LockerType
3	Carter	10	10	Full
4	Ford	20	20	Full
5	Hoover	30	30	Half
6	Kennedy	40	40	Full
7	Roosevelt	50	50	Full
8	Truman	60	60	Half
NULL	NULL	NULL	70	Full
NULL	NULL	NULL	80	Full
NULL	NULL	NULL	90	Half

(d) RIGHT OUTER JOIN of the STUDENT and LOCKER Tables

size) of lockers at the recreation center on campus. If we run a join between these two tables as shown in SQL-QUERY-CH03-52, we get a table of students who have lockers assigned to them together with their assigned locker. This result is shown in Figure 3-17(B).

```
* *** EXAMPLE CODE - DO NOT RUN *** */
/* *** SQL-Query-CH03-52 *** */
SELECT     StudentPK, StudentName, LockerFK,
           LockerPK, LockerType
FROM       STUDENT INNER JOIN LOCKER
           ON  STUDENT.LockerFK = LOCKER.LockerPK
ORDER BY   StudentPK;
```

The type of SQL join shown in SQL QUERY-CH03-52 is an SQL inner join using an SQL JOIN ON syntax that uses the **SQL INNER JOIN syntax**.

Now, suppose we want to show all the rows already in the join, but also want to show any rows (students) in the STUDENT table that are not included in the inner join. This means that we want to see all students, including those who have not been assigned a locker. To do this, we use the SQL outer join, which is designed for this very purpose. And because the table we want is listed first in the query and is thus on the left side of the table listing, we specifically use an **SQL left outer join**, which uses the **SQL LEFT JOIN syntax**. This is shown in SQL QUERY-CH03-53, which produces the results shown in Figure 3-17(C).

```
/* *** EXAMPLE CODE - DO NOT RUN *** */
/* *** SQL-Query-CH03-53 *** */
SELECT     StudentPK, StudentName, LockerFK,
           LockerPK, LockerType
FROM       STUDENT LEFT OUTER JOIN LOCKER
           ON  STUDENT.LockerFK = LOCKER.LockerPK
ORDER BY   StudentPK;
```

In the results shown in Figure 3-17(C), note that all the rows from the STUDENT table are now included and that rows that have no match in the LOCKER table are shown with NULL values. Looking at the output, we can see that the students Adams and Buchanan have no linked rows in the LOCKER table. This means that Adams and Buchanan have not been assigned a locker in the recreation center.

If we want to show all the rows already in the join, but now also any rows in the LOCKER table that are not included in the inner join, we specifically use an **SQL right outer join**, which uses the **SQL RIGHT JOIN syntax** because the table we want is listed second in the query and is thus on the right side of the table listing. This means that we want to see all lockers, including those that have not been assigned to a student. This is shown in SQL QUERY-CH03-54, which produces the results shown in Figure 3-17(D).

```
/* *** EXAMPLE CODE - DO NOT RUN *** */
/* *** SQL-Query-CH03-54 *** */
SELECT     StudentPK, StudentName, LockerFK,
           LockerPK, LockerType
FROM       STUDENT RIGHT OUTER JOIN LOCKER
           ON  STUDENT.LockerFK = LOCKER.LockerPK
ORDER BY   LockerPK;
```

In the results shown in Figure 3-17(D), note that all the rows from the LOCKER table are now included and that rows that have no match in the STUDENT table are shown with NULL values. Looking at the output, we can see that the lockers numbered 70, 80, and 90 have no linked rows in the STUDENT table. This means that these lockers are currently unassigned to a student and are available for use. DBMS products today support outer joins, but the specific SQL syntax for the outer join varies by DBMS product. Be sure to consult the documentation for the DBMS product you are using.

Returning to our WPC database example, consider the following SQL statement and notice the use of the JOIN ON syntax—the **LEFT keyword** is simply added to the SQL query:

```
/* *** SQL-QUERY-CH03-55 *** */
SELECT      ProjectName, EmployeeNumber, HoursWorked
FROM        PROJECT LEFT JOIN ASSIGNMENT
            ON PROJECT.ProjectID = ASSIGNMENT.ProjectID;
```

The purpose of this join is to append rows of PROJECT to those of ASSIGNMENT, as described previously, except that if any row in the table on the *left side* of the FROM clause (in this case, PROJECT) has no match, it is included in the results anyway. The result of this query is:

	ProjectName	EmployeeNumber	HoursWorked
1	2014 Q3 Product Plan	1	30.00
2	2014 Q3 Product Plan	8	75.00
3	2014 Q3 Product Plan	10	55.00
4	2014 Q3 Portfolio Analysis	4	40.00
5	2014 Q3 Portfolio Analysis	6	45.00
6	2014 Q3 Tax Preparation	1	25.00
7	2014 Q3 Tax Preparation	2	20.00
8	2014 Q3 Tax Preparation	4	45.00
9	2014 Q3 Tax Preparation	5	40.00
10	2014 Q4 Product Plan	1	35.00
11	2014 Q4 Product Plan	8	80.00
12	2014 Q4 Product Plan	10	50.00
13	2014 Q4 Portfolio Analysis	4	15.00
14	2014 Q4 Portfolio Analysis	5	10.00
15	2014 Q4 Portfolio Analysis	6	27.50
16	2014 Q4 Tax Preparation	NULL	NULL

Notice that the last row of this table appends a null value to the 2014 Q4 Tax Preparation project.

Right outer joins operate similarly, except that the **RIGHT keyword** is used, and rows in the table on the right-hand side of the FROM clause are included. For example, you could join all three tables together with the following right outer join:

```
/* *** SQL-QUERY-CH03-56 *** */
SELECT      ProjectName, HoursWorked, FirstName, LastName
FROM        (PROJECT AS P JOIN ASSIGNMENT AS A
            ON P.ProjectID = A.ProjectID)
                RIGHT JOIN EMPLOYEE AS E
                    ON A.EmployeeNumber = E.EmployeeNumber
ORDER BY    P.ProjectID, A.EmployeeNumber;
```

The result of this join, which now shows not only the employees assigned to projects but also those employees who are *not* assigned to any projects, is:

	ProjectName	HoursWorked	FirstName	LastName
1	NULL	NULL	Richard	Bandalone
2	NULL	NULL	George	Smith
3	NULL	NULL	George	Jones
4	NULL	NULL	James	Nestor
5	NULL	NULL	Rick	Brown
6	2014 Q3 Product Plan	30.00	Mary	Jacobs
7	2014 Q3 Product Plan	75.00	Tom	Jackson
8	2014 Q3 Product Plan	55.00	Ken	Numoto
9	2014 Q3 Portfolio Analysis	40.00	Tom	Caruthers
10	2014 Q3 Portfolio Analysis	45.00	Mary	Abernathy
11	2014 Q3 Tax Preparation	25.00	Mary	Jacobs
12	2014 Q3 Tax Preparation	20.00	Rosalie	Jackson
13	2014 Q3 Tax Preparation	45.00	Tom	Caruthers
14	2014 Q3 Tax Preparation	40.00	Heather	Jones
15	2014 Q4 Product Plan	35.00	Mary	Jacobs
16	2014 Q4 Product Plan	80.00	Tom	Jackson
17	2014 Q4 Product Plan	50.00	Ken	Numoto
18	2014 Q4 Portfolio Analysis	15.00	Tom	Caruthers
19	2014 Q4 Portfolio Analysis	10.00	Heather	Jones
20	2014 Q4 Portfolio Analysis	27.50	Mary	Abernathy

Does Not Work with Microsoft Access ANSI-89 SQL

Even with the following syntax, which is what worked before in Microsoft Access, the error message *Join expression not supported* is returned when the query is run.

```
/* *** SQL-QUERY-CH03-56-Access *** */
SELECT     ProjectName, HoursWorked, FirstName, LastName
FROM       (PROJECT AS P INNER JOIN ASSIGNMENT AS A
           ON P.ProjectID = A.ProjectID)
               RIGHT JOIN EMPLOYEE AS E
                   ON A.EmployeeNumber =
                       E.EmployeeNumber
ORDER BY   P.ProjectID, A.EmployeeNumber;
```

Solution: Build an equivalent query or set of queries using the Microsoft Access Query by Example (QBE). Query by Example (QBE) is discussed in this chapter's section of "The Access Workbench."

SQL FOR DATA MANIPULATION (DML)—DATA MODIFICATION AND DELETION

The SQL DML contains commands for the three possible data modification operations: insert, modify, and delete. We have already discussed inserting data, and now we consider modifying and deleting data.

Modifying Data

You can modify the values of existing data by using the **SQL UPDATE...SET statement**. However, this is a powerful command that needs to be used with care. Consider the EMPLOYEE table. We can see the current data in the table by using the command:

```
/* *** SQL-QUERY-CH03-57 *** */
SELECT * FROM EMPLOYEE;
```

The current data in the EMPLOYEE table look like this:

	EmployeeNumber	FirstName	LastName	Department	Phone	Email
1	1	Mary	Jacobs	Administration	360-285-8110	Mary.Jacobs@WPC.com
2	2	Rosalie	Jackson	Administration	360-285-8120	Rosalie.Jackson@WPC.com
3	3	Richard	Bandalone	Legal	360-285-8210	Richard.Bandalone@WPC.com
4	4	Tom	Caruthers	Accounting	360-285-8310	Tom.Caruthers@WPC.com
5	5	Heather	Jones	Accounting	360-285-8320	Heather.Jones@WPC.com
6	6	Mary	Abernathy	Finance	360-285-8410	Mary.Abernathy@WPC.com
7	7	George	Smith	Human Resources	360-285-8510	George.Smith@WPC.com
8	8	Tom	Jackson	Production	360-287-8610	Tom.Jackson@WPC.com
9	9	George	Jones	Production	360-287-8620	George.Jones@WPC.com
10	10	Ken	Numoto	Marketing	360-287-8710	Ken.Numoto@WPC.com
11	11	James	Nestor	InfoSystems	NULL	James.Nestor@WPC.com
12	12	Rick	Brown	InfoSystems	360-287-8820	Rick.Brown@WPC.com

Note that James Nestor (EmployeeNumber = 11) has a NULL value for his phone number. Suppose that he has just gotten a phone with phone number 360-287-8810. We can change the value of the Phone column for his data row by using the SQL UPDATE...SET statement, as shown in the following SQL command:

```
/* *** SQL-UPDATE-CH03-01 *** */
UPDATE      EMPLOYEE
SET         Phone = '360-287-8810'
WHERE       EmployeeNumber = 11;
```

To see the result, we repeat the command:

```
/* *** SQL-QUERY-CH03-58 *** */
SELECT * FROM EMPLOYEE;
```

The revised data in the EMPLOYEE table with the new phone number now look like this:

	EmployeeNumber	FirstName	LastName	Department	Phone	Email
1	1	Mary	Jacobs	Administration	360-285-8110	Mary.Jacobs@WPC.com
2	2	Rosalie	Jackson	Administration	360-285-8120	Rosalie.Jackson@WPC.com
3	3	Richard	Bandalone	Legal	360-285-8210	Richard.Bandalone@WPC.com
4	4	Tom	Caruthers	Accounting	360-285-8310	Tom.Caruthers@WPC.com
5	5	Heather	Jones	Accounting	360-285-8320	Heather.Jones@WPC.com
6	6	Mary	Abernathy	Finance	360-285-8410	Mary.Abernathy@WPC.com
7	7	George	Smith	Human Res...	360-285-8510	George.Smith@WPC.com
8	8	Tom	Jackson	Production	360-287-8610	Tom.Jackson@WPC.com
9	9	George	Jones	Production	360-287-8620	George.Jones@WPC.com
10	10	Ken	Numoto	Marketing	360 287 8710	Ken.Numoto@WPC.com
11	11	James	Nestor	InfoSystems	360-287-8810	James.Nestor@WPC.com
12	12	Rick	Brown	InfoSystems	360-287-8820	Rick.Brown@WPC.com

Now consider why this command is dangerous. Suppose that while intending to make this update, we make an error and forget to include the WHERE clause. Thus, we submit the following to the DBMS:

```
/* *** EXAMPLE CODE - DO NOT RUN *** */
/* *** SQL-UPDATE-CH03-02 *** */
UPDATE       EMPLOYEE
SET          Phone = '360-287-8810';
```

After this command has executed, we would again use a SELECT command to display the contents of the EMPLOYEE relation:

```
/* *** SQL-QUERY-CH03-59 *** */
SELECT * FROM EMPLOYEE;
```

The EMPLOYEE relation will appear as follows:

	EmployeeNumber	FirstName	LastName	Department	Phone	Email
1	1	Mary	Jacobs	Administration	360-287-8810	Mary.Jacobs@WPC.com
2	2	Rosalie	Jackson	Administration	360-287-8810	Rosalie.Jackson@WPC.com
3	3	Richard	Bandalone	Legal	360-287-8810	Richard.Bandalone@WPC.com
4	4	Tom	Caruthers	Accounting	360-287-8810	Tom.Caruthers@WPC.com
5	5	Heather	Jones	Accounting	360-287-8810	Heather.Jones@WPC.com
6	6	Mary	Abernathy	Finance	360-287-8810	Mary.Abernathy@WPC.com
7	7	George	Smith	Human Resources	360-287-8810	George.Smith@WPC.com
8	8	Tom	Jackson	Production	360-287-8810	Tom.Jackson@WPC.com
9	9	George	Jones	Production	360-287-8810	George.Jones@WPC.com
10	10	Ken	Numoto	Marketing	360-287-8810	Ken.Numoto@WPC.com
11	11	James	Nestor	InfoSystems	360-287-8810	James.Nestor@WPC.com
12	12	Rick	Brown	InfoSystems	360-287-8810	Rick.Brown@WPC.com

This is clearly not what we intended to do. If you did this at a new job where there are 10,000 rows in the EMPLOYEE table, you would experience a sinking feeling in the pit of your stomach and make plans to update your résumé. The message here: The SQL UPDATE...SET statement is powerful and easy to use, but it is also capable of causing disasters.

The SQL UPDATE...SET statement can modify more than one column value at a time, as shown in the following statement. For example, if Heather Jones (EmployeeNumber = 5) is transferred to the finance department from accounting and given a new finance phone number, you can use the following command to update her data:

```
/* *** SQL-UPDATE-CH03-03 *** */
UPDATE       EMPLOYEE
SET          Department = 'Finance', Phone = '360-285-8420'
WHERE        EmployeeNumber = 5;
```

This command changes the values of Phone and Department for the indicated employee. You can use a SELECT command to see the results:

```
/* *** SQL-QUERY-CH03-60 *** */
SELECT       *
FROM         EMPLOYEE
WHERE        EmployeeNumber = 5;
```

The results are as follows:

	EmployeeNumber	FirstName	LastName	Department	Phone	Email
1	5	Heather	Jones	Finance	360-285-8420	Heather.Jones@WPC.com

SQL:2003 introduced the **SQL MERGE statement**, which essentially combines the INSERT and UPDATE statements into one statement that can either insert or update data depending upon whether some condition is met. Thus, the MERGE statement requires some rather complex SQL code, and you should concentrate on thoroughly understanding both the INSERT and UPDATE statements at this point. Later, when you are ready, consult the documentation for your specific DBMS product to see how it implements the MERGE statement.

Deleting Data

You can eliminate rows with the **SQL DELETE statement**. However, the same warnings pertain to DELETE as to UPDATE. DELETE is deceptively simple to use and easy to apply in unintended ways. The following, for example, deletes all projects sponsored by the marketing department:

```
/* *** EXAMPLE CODE - DO NOT RUN *** */
/* *** SQL-DELETE-CH03-01 *** */
DELETE
FROM         PROJECT
WHERE        Department = 'Marketing';
```

Given that we created an ON DELETE CASCADE referential integrity constraint, this DELETE operation not only removes PROJECT rows, it also removes any related ASSIGNMENT rows. For the WPC data in Figure 3-2, this DELETE operation removes the projects with ProjectID 1000 (2014 Q3 Product Plan) and 1300 (2014 Q3 Product Plan) and six rows (rows 1, 2, and 3 for ProjectID 1000 and rows 10, 11, and 12 for ProjectID 1300) of the ASSIGNMENT table.

As with the SQL UPDATE…SET statement, if you forget to include the WHERE clause, disaster ensues. For example, the SQL code:

```
/* *** EXAMPLE CODE - DO NOT RUN *** */
/* *** SQL-DELETE-CH03-02 *** */
DELETE
FROM        PROJECT;
```

deletes *all* the rows in PROJECT (and because of the ON DELETE CASCADE constraint, *all* the ASSIGNMENT rows as well). This truly would be a disaster!

Observe how the referential integrity constraint differs with the EMPLOYEE table. Here, if we try to process the command:

```
/* *** EXAMPLE CODE - DO NOT RUN *** */
/* *** SQL-DELETE-CH03-03 *** */
DELETE
FROM        EMPLOYEE
WHERE       EmployeeNumber = 1;
```

the DELETE operation fails because rows in ASSIGNMENT depend on the EmployeeNumber value of 1 in EMPLOYEE. If you want to delete the row for this employee, you must first reassign or delete his or her rows in ASSIGNMENT.

SQL FOR DATA DEFINITION (DDL)—TABLE AND CONSTRAINT MODIFICATION AND DELETION

There are many data definition SQL statements that we have not yet described. Two of the most useful are the SQL DROP TABLE and SQL ALTER TABLE statements.

The SQL DROP TABLE Statement

The **SQL DROP TABLE statement** is also one of the most dangerous SQL statements because it drops the table's structure along with all of the table's data. For example, to drop the ASSIGNMENT table and all its data, you use the following SQL statement:

```
/* *** EXAMPLE CODE - DO NOT RUN *** */
/* *** SQL-DROP-TABLE-CH03-01 *** */
DROP TABLE ASSIGNMENT;
```

The SQL DROP TABLE statement does not work if the table contains or could contain values needed to fulfill referential integrity constraints. EMPLOYEE, for example, contains values of EmployeeNumber needed by the foreign key constraint ASSIGN_EMP_FK. In this case, an attempt to issue the statement DROP TABLE EMPLOYEE fails, and an error message is generated.

The SQL ALTER TABLE Statement

To drop the EMPLOYEE table, you must first drop the ASSIGNMENT table or at least delete the foreign key constraint ASSIGN_EMP_FK. This is one place where the ALTER TABLE command is useful. You use the **SQL ALTER TABLE statement** to add, modify, and drop columns and constraints. For example, you can use it to drop the ASSIGN_EMP_FK constraint with the statement:

```
/* *** EXAMPLE CODE - DO NOT RUN *** */
/* *** SQL-ALTER-TABLE-CH03-01 *** */
ALTER TABLE ASSIGNMENT DROP CONSTRAINT ASSIGN_EMP_FK;
```

After either dropping the ASSIGNMENT table or the ASSIGN_EMP_FK foreign key constraint, you can then successfully drop the EMPLOYEE table.

> ## BTW
>
> Now you know why it is an advantage to control constraint names by using the CONSTRAINT syntax. Because we created the foreign key constraint name ASSIGN_EMP_FK ourselves, we know what it is. This makes it easy to use when we need it.

The SQL TRUNCATE TABLE Statement

The **SQL TRUNCATE TABLE statement** was added in the SQL:2008 standard, so it is one of the latest additions to SQL. Like the SQL DELETE statement, it is used to remove all data from a table while leaving the table structure itself in the database. However, unlike the SQL DELETE statement, the SQL TRUNCATE TABLE statement also *resets any surrogate primary key values* back to the starting point. The SQL TRUNCATE TABLE statement does not use an SQL WHERE clause to specify conditions for the data deletion—*all* the data in the table are *always* removed when the TRUNCATE TABLE statement is used.

The following statement could be used to remove all the data in the PROJECT table:

```
/* *** EXAMPLE CODE - DO NOT RUN *** */
/* *** SQL-ALTER-TABLE-CH03-01 *** */
TRUNCATE TABLE PROJECT;
```

The TRUNCATE TABLE statement *cannot* be used with a table that is referenced by a foreign key constraint because this could create foreign key values that have no corresponding primary key value. Thus, while we can use TRUNCATE TABLE with the PROJECT table, we cannot use it with the DEPARTMENT table.

The CHECK Constraint

We can also use the SQL ALTER TABLE statement to add a constraint. For example, consider the PROJECT table, which has the columns StartDate and EndDate. Obviously, the StartDate must be earlier than the EndDate, but there is currently nothing in the table definition to enforce this. This is a perfect place to use a CHECK constraint. CHECK constraints are similar to WHERE clauses in SQL queries. They can contain the keywords IN, NOT IN, and LIKE (for the specification of decimal places), and they can use less than (<) and greater than (>) signs for range checks.

Does Not Work with Microsoft Access ANSI-89 SQL

As discussed earlier, Microsoft Access does not support the CHECK column constraints.

Solution: An equivalent constraint can be set in the table Design view. See the discussion in this chapter's section of "The Access Workbench."

To modify the PROJECT table with the needed constraint, we use the following SQL statement:

```
/* *** SQL-ALTER-TABLE-CH03-21 *** */
ALTER TABLE PROJECT
     ADD CONSTRAINT PROJECT_Check_Dates
          CHECK (StartDate < EndDate);
```

The ALTER TABLE statement is handy when you need to add or drop columns. For example, suppose that you want to add a column to PROJECT to track how many hours have actually been worked on a project. If the name of this column is CurrentTotalHours, you can add it to the table with the SQL statement (note that the keyword COLUMN is *not* used in this command):

```
/* *** EXAMPLE CODE - DO NOT RUN *** */
/* *** SQL-ALTER-TABLE-CH03-03 *** */
ALTER TABLE PROJECT
     ADD CurrentTotalHours Numeric(8,2) NULL;
```

Note that because you are adding a column to an existing table that contains data, you cannot add a NOT NULL column; the constraint would immediately be violated because there would be missing data in each row. If you want a column to be NOT NULL, you must create it as NULL, insert the needed data, and then modify the column to NOT NULL. For example, after putting the necessary data into CurrentTotalHours for the existing rows, you could convert it to NOT NULL (and supply a DEFAULT value at the same time) by using the SQL statement:

```
/* *** EXAMPLE CODE - DO NOT RUN *** */
/* *** SQL-ALTER-TABLE-CH03-04 *** */
ALTER TABLE PROJECT
     ALTER COLUMN CurrentTotalHours Numeric(8,2) NOT NULL
          DEFAULT 1;
```

If you decided that this column was not needed, you could drop it from the PROJECT table by using the SQL statement:

```
/* *** EXAMPLE CODE - DO NOT RUN *** */
/* *** SQL-ALTER-TABLE-CH03-04 *** */
ALTER TABLE PROJECT
     DROP COLUMN CurrentTotalHours;
```

We can also use the SQL ALTER TABLE statement to modify data types, but you have to be careful because this can result in a loss of data. Check your DBMS documentation carefully before attempting to modify data types.[5]

SQL VIEWS

SQL contains a powerful tool known as an SQL view. An **SQL view** is a virtual table created by a DBMS-stored SELECT statement and thus can combine access to data in multiple tables and even in other views. SQL views are discussed in online Appendix E, "SQL Views," where we show how to create and use SQL views and discuss several specific applications of SQL views in database applications. This is important material that you will find very useful when building databases and database applications, and we will use SQL views in our discussion of Online Analytical Processing (OLAP) reporting systems in Chapter 8.

THE ACCESS WORKBENCH

Section 3

Working with Queries in Microsoft Access

In the previous sections of "The Access Workbench," you learned to create Microsoft Access databases, tables, forms, and reports in multiple-table databases. In this section, you'll:

- Learn how to use Access SQL.
- Learn how to run queries in single and multiple tables, using both SQL and Query by Example (QBE).
- Learn how to manually set table and relationship properties that Access SQL does not support.

In this section, we will continue to use the WMCRM database you've been using. At this point, we've created and populated (that is, inserted the data into) the CUSTOMER and CONTACT tables and set the referential integrity constraint between them.

Working with Microsoft Access SQL

You work with Microsoft Access SQL in the SQL view of a query window. The following simple query shows how this works:

```
/* *** SQL-QUERY-AW03-01 *** */
SELECT    *
FROM      CUSTOMER;
```

Opening an Access Query Window in Design View

1. Start Microsoft Access 2013.
2. Click the **File** command tab to display the File menu and then click the **WMCRM.accdb** database filename in the quick access list to open the database.

---

[5]Also see David M. Kroenke and David J. Auer, *Database Processing: Fundamentals, Design, and Implementation*, 13th edition (Upper Saddle River, NJ: Prentice Hall, 2014), Chapter 8.

FIGURE AW-3-1

The CREATE Command Tab

The **CREATE** command tab

The **Query Design** button

3. Click the **Create** command tab to display the Create command groups, as shown in Figure AW-3-1.
4. Click the **Query Design** button.
5. The Query1 tabbed document window is displayed in Design view, along with the Show Table dialog box, as shown in Figure AW-3-2.
6. Click the **Close** button on the Show Table dialog box. The Query1 document window now looks as shown in Figure AW-3-3. This window is used for creating and editing Access queries in Design view and is used with Access QBE, as discussed later in this section.

Note that in Figure AW-3-3 the Select button is selected in the Query Type group on the Design tab. You can tell this is so because active or selected buttons are always shown in color on the Ribbon. This indicates that we are creating a query that is the equivalent of an SQL SELECT statement.

Also note that in Figure AW-3-3 the View gallery is available in the Results group of the Design tab. We can use this gallery to switch between Design view and SQL view. However, we can also just use the displayed SQL View button to switch to SQL view, which is being displayed because Access considers that to be the view you would most likely choose in the gallery if you used it. Access always presents a "most likely needed" view choice as a button above the View gallery.

Opening an Access SQL Query Window and Running an Access SQL Query

1. Click the **SQL View** button in the Results group on the Design tab. The Query1 window switches to the SQL view, as shown in Figure AW-3-4. Note the basic SQL command **SELECT;** that's shown in the window. This is an incomplete command, and running it will not produce any results.

(Continued)

FIGURE AW-3-2

The Show Table Dialog Box

The **Query1** tabbed document window

The **Show Table** dialog box

Click the **Close** button

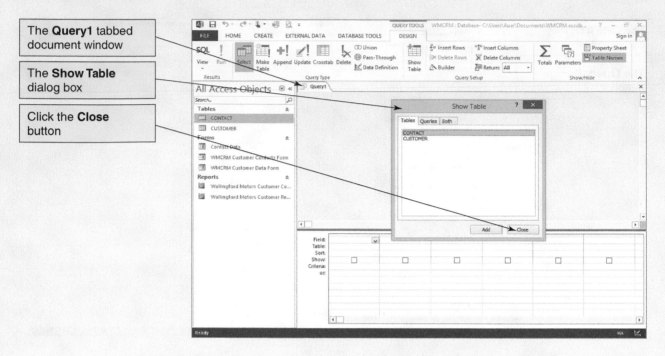

FIGURE AW-3-3

The Query Tools Contextual Command Tab

The **QUERY TOOLS** command tab

The **SQL View** button

The **View gallery** drop-down arrow button

The **Select** Query Type button

The **Query Type** command group

The **Query1** tabbed document window in Design view

The **DESIGN** command tab

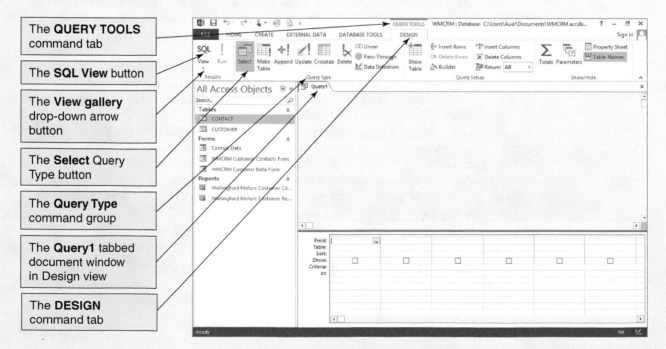

FIGURE AW-3-4

The Query1 Window in SQL View

The **Query1** window in SQL view

The SQL **SELECT;** statement—this is an incomplete statement and will not run as written—it is intended as the start of an SQL query

2. Edit the SQL SELECT command to read

```
SELECT  *
FROM    CUSTOMER;
```

as shown in Figure AW-3-5.

3. Click the **Run** button on the Design tab.
4. Click the **Shutter Bar Open/Close** button to minimize the Navigation Pane and then click the **Query1** document tab to select the Query1 window. The query results appear, as shown in Figure AW-3-6.

   Just as we can save Access objects such as tables, forms, and reports, we can save Access queries for future use.

FIGURE AW-3-5

The SQL Query

The **Run** button

The complete SQL query statement— **SELECT * FROM CUSTOMER;**

(Continued)

The SQL Query Results

The query results

Saving an Access SQL Query

1. To save the query, click the **Save** button on the Quick Access Toolbar. The Save As dialog box appears, as shown in Figure AW-3-7.
2. Type in the query name **SQL-Query-AW03-01** and then click the **OK** button. The query is saved, and the window is renamed with the query name, as shown in Figure AW-3-8.
3. Click the **Shutter Bar Open/Close** button to expand the Navigation Pane. As shown in Figure AW-3-8, the query document window is now named SQL-Query-AW03-01, and a newly created SQL-Query-AW03-01 query object appears in a Queries section of the Navigation Pane.
4. Close the Query-AW-03-01 window by clicking the document window's **Close** button.
5. If Access displays a dialog box asking whether you want to save changes to the design of the query SQL-Query-AW03-01, click the **Yes** button.

The Save As Dialog Box

*The **Save** button*

*The **Save As** dialog box*

*The **OK** button*

FIGURE AW-3-8

The Named and Saved Query

The query window is now named **SQL-Query-AW03-01**

The **Queries** section of the Navigation Pane

The **SQL-Query-AW03-01** query object

Working with Microsoft Access QBE

By default, Microsoft Access does not use the SQL interface. Instead, it uses a version of Query by Example (QBE), which uses the Access GUI to build queries. To understand how this works, we'll use QBE to recreate the SQL query we just created using QBE.

Creating and Running an Access QBE Query

1. Click the **Create** command tab to display the Create command groups.
2. Click the **Query Design** button.
3. The Query1 tabbed document window is displayed in Design view, along with the Show Table dialog box, as shown in Figure AW-3-2.
4. Click **CUSTOMER** to select the CUSTOMER table. Click the **Add** button to add the CUSTOMER table to the query.
5. Click the **Close** button to close the Show Table dialog box.
6. Rearrange and resize the query window objects in the Query1 query document window, using standard Windows drag-and-drop techniques. Rearrange the window elements until they look as shown in Figure AW-3-9.
7. Note the elements of the Query1 window shown in FigureAW-3-9: Tables and their associated set of columns—called a *field list*—that are included in the query are shown in the upper pane, and the columns (fields) actually included in the query are shown in the lower pane. For each included column (field), you can set whether this column's data appear in the results, how the data are sorted, and the criteria for selecting which rows of data will be shown. Note that the first entry in the table's field list is the asterisk (*), which has its standard SQL meaning of "all columns in the table."
8. Include columns in the query by dragging them from the table's field list to a field column in the lower pane. Click and drag the * in CUSTOMER to the first field column, as shown in Figure AW-3-10. Note that the column is entered as **CUSTOMER.*** from the table CUSTOMER.
9. To save the QBE query, click the **Save** button on the Quick Access Toolbar to display the Save As dialog box. Type in the query name **QBE-Query-AW03-02**, and then click the **OK** button. The query is saved, the window is renamed QBEQuery-AW-03-02, and a newly created QBEQuery-AW-03-02 query object appears in a Queries section of the Navigation Pane.

(Continued)

FIGURE AW-3-9

The QBE Query1 Query Window

This query is a Select query

Tables in the query appear in the top pane, together with a list of their columns (the *field list*) and an asterisk (*), meaning "all columns"

Columns in the query are called fields and appear in the bottom pane, together with related property values

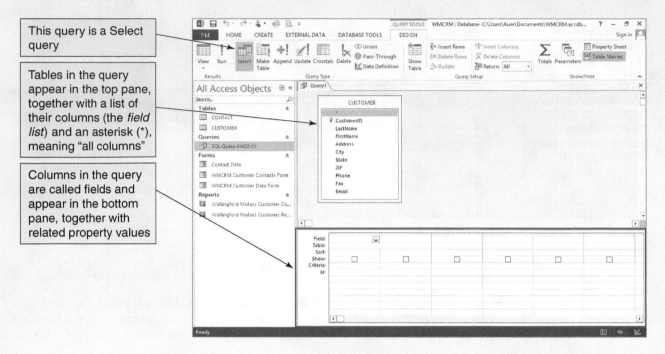

FIGURE AW-3-10

Adding Columns to the QBE Query

To add a column to the query, click the column name and drag it to a cell in the Field: row in the lower pane

The asterisk (*) symbol was dragged and dropped here to add the **CUSTOMER.*** field to the query

The table name is automatically added to the query to specify the source of the column—this is important if there is more than one table in the query with the same column name

FIGURE AW-3-11

The QBE Query Results

As expected, the query results are identical to those shown in Figure AW-3-6

The results are sorted by CustomerID

10. Click the **Run** button on the Query Design toolbar.
11. Click the **Shutter Bar Open/Close** button to minimize the Navigation Pane. You may need to resize column widths to see all the data. The query results appear, as shown in Figure AW-3-11. Note that these results are identical to the results shown in Figure AW-3-6.
12. Click the **Shutter Bar Open/Close** button to expand the Navigation Pane and then click the query document tab to select it.
13. Close the QBE-Query-AW03-02 query.
14. If Access displays a dialog box asking whether you want to save changes to the layout of the query QBE-Query-AW03-02, click the **Yes** button.

This query is about as simple as they get, but we can use QBE for more complicated queries. For example, consider a query that uses only some of the columns in the table, includes the SQL WHERE clause, and also sorts data using the SQL ORDER BY clause:

```
/* *** SQL-Version of QBE-QUERY-AW03-03 *** */
SELECT      CustomerID, LastName, FirstName
FROM        CUSTOMER
WHERE       CustomerID > 2
ORDER BY    LastName DESC;
```

This QBE query, named QBE-Query-AW03-03, is shown in Figure AW-3-12. Note that now we've included the specific columns that we want used in the query instead of the asterisk, we've used the Sort property for CustomerID, and we've included row selection conditions in the Criteria property for LastName.

(Continued)

FIGURE AW-3-12

The QBEQuery-AW03-03 Query Window

The **CustomerID, LastName,** and **FirstName** fields are in the query

The results will be sorted by LastName in descending order (Z–A)

The results will show only customers with a CustomerID greater than 2

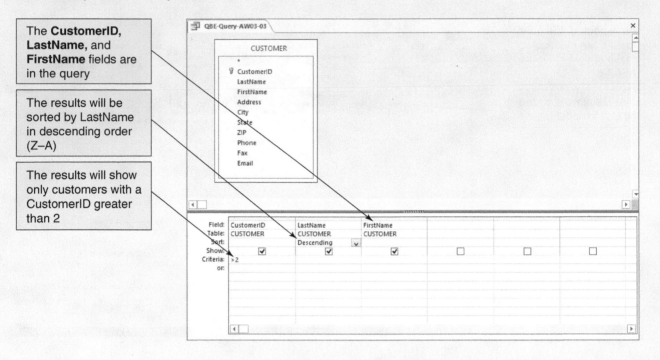

Creating and Running QBEQuery-AW03-03

1. Using the previous instructions for QBEQuery-AW-03-02, create, run, and save QBEQuery-AW-03-03. The query results are shown in Figure AW-3-13.

   Of course, we can use more than one table in a QBE query. Next, we'll create the QBE version of this SQL query:

```
/* *** SQL-Version-of-QBE-QUERY-AW-CH03-04 *** */
SELECT      LastName, FirstName,
            ContactDate, ContactType, Remarks
FROM        CUSTOMER, CONTACT
WHERE       CUSTOMER.CustomerID = CONTACT.CustomerID
            AND CustomerID = 3
ORDER BY    Date;
```

FIGURE AW-3-13

The QBEQuery-AW03-03 Query Results

The results show only customers with a CustomerID greater than 2, sorted by LastName in descending order (Z–A)

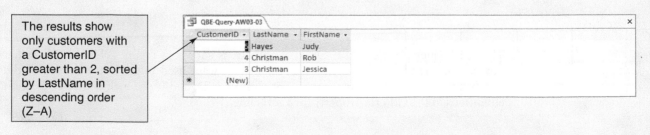

Creating and Running an Access QBE Query with Multiple Tables

1. Click the **Create** command tab.
2. Click the **Query Design** button.
3. The Query1 tabbed document window is displayed in Design view, along with the Show Table dialog box.
4. Click **CUSTOMER** to select the CUSTOMER table. Click the **Add** button to add the CUSTOMER table to the query.
5. Click **CONTACT** to select the CONTACT table. Click the **Add** button to add the CUSTOMER table to the query.
6. Click the **Close** button to close the Show Table dialog box.
7. Rearrange and resize the query window objects in the Query1 query document window by using standard Windows drag-and-drop techniques. Rearrange the window elements until they look as shown in Figure AW-3-14. Note that the relationship between the two tables is already included in the diagram. This implements the SQL clause:

```
WHERE CUSTOMER.CustomerID = CONTACT.CustomerID
```

8. From the CUSTOMER table, click and drag the **CustomerID, LastName,** and **FirstName** column names to the first three field columns in the lower pane.
9. From the CONTACT table, click and drag the **Date, Type,** and **Remarks** column names to the next three field columns in the lower pane.
10. In the field column for CustomerID, uncheck the **Show** check box so that the data from this column is not included in the results display.
11. In the field column for CustomerID, type the number **3** in the Criteria row.
12. In the field column for Date, set the Sort setting to **Ascending**. The completed QBE query appears, as shown in Figure AW-3-15.

FIGURE AW-3-14

The Query Window with Two Tables

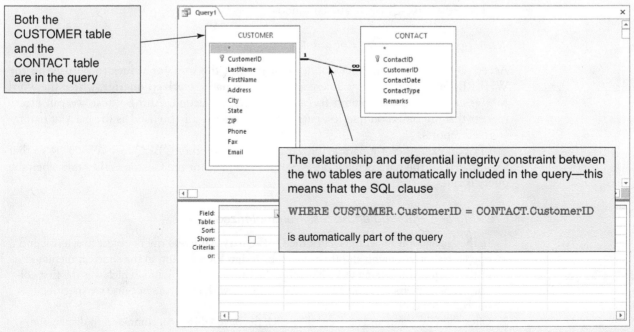

Both the CUSTOMER table and the CONTACT table are in the query

The relationship and referential integrity constraint between the two tables are automatically included in the query—this means that the SQL clause

```
WHERE CUSTOMER.CustomerID = CONTACT.CustomerID
```

is automatically part of the query

(Continued)

The Completed Two-Table Query

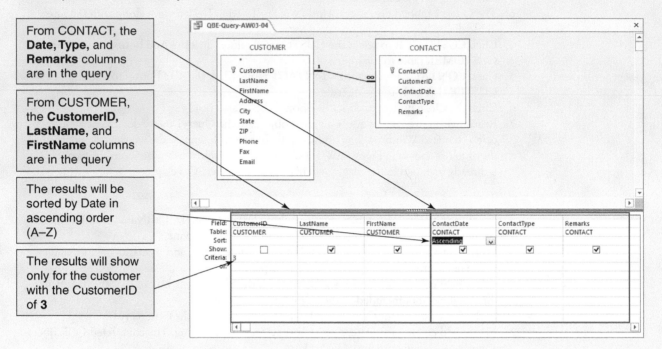

From CONTACT, the **Date, Type,** and **Remarks** columns are in the query

From CUSTOMER, the **CustomerID, LastName,** and **FirstName** columns are in the query

The results will be sorted by Date in ascending order (A–Z)

The results will show only for the customer with the CustomerID of **3**

13. Click the **Run** button. The query results appear, as shown in Figure AW-3-16.
14. To save the query, click the **Save** button on the Quick Access Toolbar to display the Save As dialog box. Type in the query name **QBE-Query-AW03-04**, and then click the **OK** button. The query is saved, the document window is renamed with the new query name, and the QBE-Query-AW03-04 object is added to the Queries section of the Navigation Pane.
15. Close the QBE-Query-AW03-04 window.

Working with Microsoft Access Parameter Queries

Access allows us to construct queries that prompt the user for values to be used in the WHERE clause of the query. These are known as **parameterized queries**, where the word *parameter* refers to the column for which a value is needed. And because we can create reports that are based on queries, parameterized queries can be used as the basis of parameterized reports.

For an example of a parameterized query, we'll modify QBEQuery-AW-03-04 so that CustomerID is the parameter and the user is prompted for the CustomerID value when the query is run.

Creating and Running an Access Parameterized Query

1. In the Navigation Pane, right-click the **QBE-Query-AW03-04** query object to select it and open the shortcut menu and then click the **Design View** button in the shortcut menu to open the query in Design view. Note that the CustomerID column, which was the first column, now appears as the *last column* in Design view. This occurs because we specified that the column would *not* be displayed.
2. Click the **File** command tab, and then click the **Save Object As** command to display the Save As dialog box, as shown in Figure AW-3-17.

FIGURE AW-3-16

The Two-Table Query Results

The results are shown for the customer with the CustomerID of 3, which is Jessica Christman

The results are sorted by Date in ascending order (earliest date to latest date)

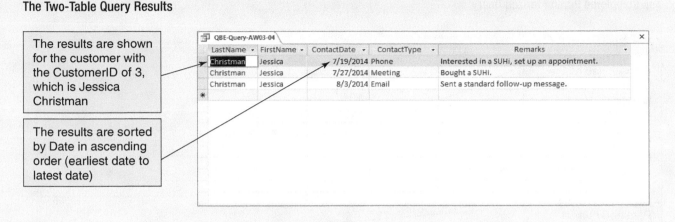

3. In the Save 'QBE-Query-AW03-04' to: text box of the Save As dialog box, edit the query name to read **QBE-Query-AW03-05**.
4. Click the **OK** button to save the query.
5. Click the **Design** command tab to return to Design view of query, which is now renamed QBE-Query-AW03-05.
6. Click the **Shutter Bar Open/Close** button to minimize the Navigation Pane.
7. In the Criteria row of the CustomerID column, delete the number value (which is 3), and enter the text **[Enter the CustomerID Number:]** in its place. You will need to expand the CustomerID column width for all the text to be visible at the same time. The QBE-Query-AW03-05 window now looks as shown in Figure AW-3-18.

FIGURE AW-3-17

The Paste As Dialog Box

The **FILE** command tab

Right-click the query object **QBE-Query-AW03-04** to display a shortcut menu, and then click the **Copy** command

The **Paste As** dialog box

Type the new query name **QBE-Query-AW03-05** in this text box

The **OK** button

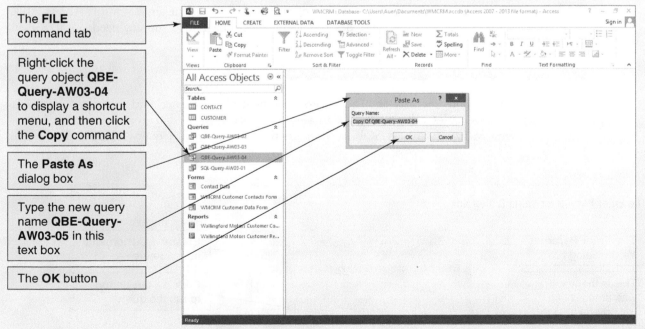

(Continued)

FIGURE AW-3-18

The Completed Parameterized Query

The CustomerID column has been repositioned as the last column because it is not displayed in the query results

Criteria for the CustomerID column now contains the text for a prompt to be displayed in the Enter Parameter Value dialog box that will be displayed to get a parameter value from the user

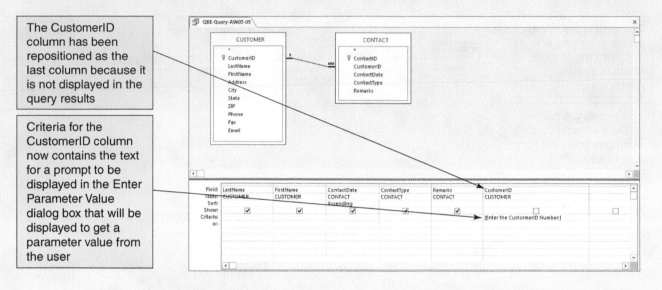

8. Click the **Save** button on the Quick Access Toolbar to save the changes to the query design.
9. Click the **Run** button. The **Enter Parameter Value** dialog box appears, as shown in Figure AW-3-19. Note that the text we entered in the Criteria row now appears as a prompt in the dialog box.
10. Enter the CustomerID number **3** as a parameter value and then click the **OK** button. The query results appear. They are identical to those shown in Figure AW-3-16.
11. Click the **Save** button to save the changes to the design of the query and then close the query.
12. Click the **Shutter Bar Open/Close** button to expand the Navigation Pane.

This completes our discussion of SQL and QBE queries in Microsoft Access 2013. With the query tools we've described, you should be able to run any needed query in an Access database.

Creating Tables with Microsoft Access SQL

In previous sections of "The Access Workbench," we created and populated Microsoft Access tables using table Design view. Now we'll create and populate a table by using Microsoft Access SQL, as done in the SQL view of a query window. So far, the

FIGURE AW-3-19

The Enter Parameter Value Dialog Box

The **Enter Parameter Value** dialog box

This is the text that was entered into the criteria field for CustomerID

Enter the CustomerID number here

Click the **OK** button to run the query

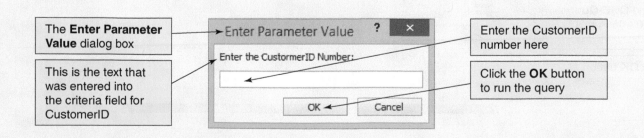

FIGURE AW-3-20

Database Column Characteristics for the SALESPERSON Table

Column Name	Type	Key	Required	Remarks
NickName	Text (35)	Primary Key	Yes	
LastName	Text (25)	No	Yes	
FirstName	Text (25)	No	Yes	
HireDate	Date/Time	No	Yes	Medium Date
WageRate	Number	No	Yes	Double, Currency, Default value = $12.50
CommissionRate	Number	No	Yes	Double, Percent, 3 Decimal places
Phone	Text (12)	No	Yes	
Email	Text (100)	No	Yes	Unique

Wallingford Motors CRM has been for use by only a single salesperson. Now we'll add a SALESPERSON table. Each salesperson at Wallingford Motors is identified by a nickname. The nickname may be the person's actual first name or a true nickname, but it must be unique. We can assume that one salesperson is assigned to each customer and that only that salesperson makes contact with the customer.

The full set of tables in the WMCRM database will now look like this:

SALESPERSON (NickName, LastName, FirstName, HireDate, WageRate, CommissionRate, Phone, Email)

CUSTOMER (CustomerID, LastName, FirstName, Address, City, State, ZIP, Phone, Fax, Email, *NickName*)

CONTACT (ContactID, *CustomerID*, Date, Type, Remarks)

The referential integrity constraints are:

NickName in CUSTOMER must exist in NickName in SALESPERSON

CustomerID in CONTACT must exist in CustomerID in CUSTOMER

The database column characteristics for SALESPERSON are shown in Figure AW-3-20, and SALESPERSON data are shown in Figure AW-3-21.

FIGURE AW-3-21

Data for the SALESPERSON Table

Nick Name	Last Name	First Name	Hire Date	Wage Rate	Commission Rate	Phone	Email
Tina	Smith	Tina	10-AUG-08	$ 15.50	12.500%	206-287-7010	Tina@WM.com
Big Bill	Jones	William	25-SEP-08	$ 15.50	12.500%	206-287-7020	BigBill@WM.com
Billy	Jones	Bill	17-MAY-09	$ 12.50	12.000%	206-287-7030	Billy@WM.com

(Continued)

Note that adding the SALESPERSON table will require alterations to the existing CUSTOMER table. We need a new column for the foreign key NickName, a referential integrity constraint between CUSTOMER and SALESPERSON, and new data for the column.

First, we'll build the SALESPERSON table. The correct SQL statement is:

```
/* *** SQL-CREATE-TABLE-AW03-01 *** */
CREATE TABLE SALESPERSON(
     NickName           Char(35)              NOT NULL,
     LastName           Char(25)              NOT NULL,
     FirstName          Char(25)              NOT NULL,
     HireDate           DateTime              NOT NULL,
     WageRate           Numeric(5,2)          NOT NULL
                                                  DEFAULT(12.50),
     CommissionRate     Numeric(5,3)          NOT NULL,
     Phone              Char(12)              NOT NULL,
     Email              Varchar(100)          NOT NULL UNIQUE,
     CONSTRAINT         SALESPERSON_PK        PRIMARY KEY
                                                  (NickName)

     );
```

This statement uses standard SQL data types (specifically SQL Server data types), but this is not a problem because Access will correctly read them and translate them into Access data types. However, from the SQL discussion in this chapter, we know that Access does not support the numeric data type with the (*m,n*) syntax (where *m* = total number of digits and *n* = number of digits to the right of the decimal). Further, Access does not support the UNIQUE constraint or the DEFAULT keyword. Therefore, we have to create an SQL statement without these items and then use the Access GUI to fine-tune the table after it is created.

The SQL that will run in Access is:

```
/* *** SQL-CREATE-TABLE-AW03-02 *** */
CREATE TABLE SALESPERSON(
     NickName           Char(35)              NOT NULL,
     LastName           Char(25)              NOT NULL,
     FirstName          Char(25)              NOT NULL,
     HireDate           DateTime              NOT NULL,
     WageRate           Numeric               NOT NULL,
     CommissionRate     Numeric               NOT NULL,
     Phone              Char(12)              NOT NULL,
     Email              Varchar(100)          NOT NULL,
     CONSTRAINT         SALESPERSON_PK        PRIMARY KEY
                                                  (NickName)

     );
```

Creating the SALESPERSON Table by Using Access SQL

1. As described earlier in this chapter's section of "The Access Workbench," open an Access query window in SQL view.
2. Type the SQL code into the query window. The query window now looks as shown in Figure AW-3-22.

FIGURE AW-3-22

The SQL CREATE TABLE SALESPERSON Statement

The complete SQL CREATE TABLE SALESPERSON statement

```
CREATE TABLE SALESPERSON(
    NickName        Char(35)         NOT NULL,
    LastName        Char(25)         NOT NULL,
    FirstName       Char(25)         NOT NULL,
    HireDate        Date             NOT NULL,
    WageRate        Numeric          NOT NULL,
    CommissionRate  Numeric          NOT NULL,
    Phone           Char(12)         NOT NULL,
    Email           Varchar(100)     NOT NULL,
    CONSTRAINT      SALESPERSON_PK   PRIMARY KEY(NickName)
);
```

3. Click the **Run** button. The statement runs, but because this statement creates a table the only immediately visible results are that the SALESPERSON table object is added to the Tables section of the Navigation Pane.
4. Save the query as **Create-Table-SALESPERSON**.
5. Close the query window. The Create-Table-SALESPERSON query object now appears in the Queries section of the Navigation Pane, as shown in Figure AW-3-23.

Modifying Access Tables to Add Data Requirements Not Supported by Access SQL

To modify the SALESPERSON table to add the table requirements not supported by Access SQL, we use the Access table Design view.[6]

FIGURE AW-3-23

The SALESPERSON Objects in the Navigation Pane

The **SALESPERSON** table

The **Create-Table-SALESPERSON** query—note the Design icon that identifies this as a data definition query

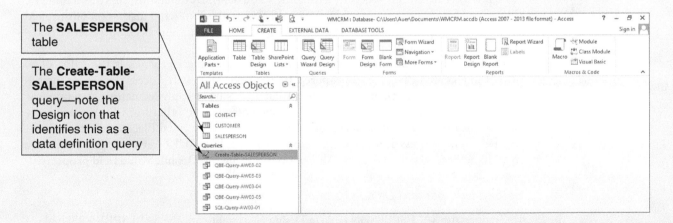

[6]Although we do not fully discuss the matter in this book, it's important to mention that Access SQL confounds the treatment of the SQL NOT NULL column constraint. When you use NOT NULL in defining a column, Access properly sets the column's Required field property to Yes. (We discussed how to do this manually in Chapter 1's section of "The Access Workbench" when we created the CUSTOMER table.) However, Access adds a second field property, the **Allow Zero Length field property**, which it sets to Yes. To truly match NOT NULL, this value should be set to *No*. For a full discussion of setting the Allow Zero Length field property, see the Microsoft Access help system.

(Continued)

FIGURE AW-3-24

The SALESPERSON Table in Design View

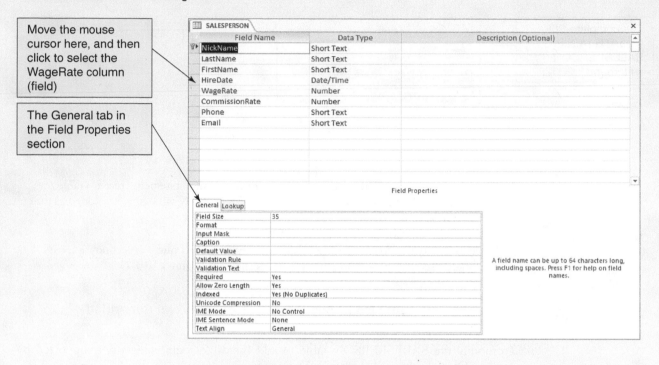

Move the mouse cursor here, and then click to select the WageRate column (field)

The General tab in the Field Properties section

First, recall that Access SQL does not support the numeric (m,n) syntax, where m is the number of digits stored and n is the number of digits to the right of the decimal place. We can set the number of digits to some extent by setting the **Field Size field property** (which is as close as Access gets to setting the value of m). By default, Access sets a numeric value Field Size property to double. We could change this, but a full discussion of this field property is beyond the scope of this book—see the Microsoft Access help system discussion of the Field Size property for more information.

We can, however, easily set the number of decimal places (which is the value of n) using the **Decimal Places field property**. In addition, Microsoft Access does have the advantage of having a **Format field property** that allows us to apply formatting to a numeric value so that the data appear as currency, a percentage, or in other formats. We will leave the default Field Size setting and change the Format and Decimal Places property values.

Recall that Access SQL does not support the SQL DEFAULT keyword, so we will have to add any needed default values. We can do this using the **Default Value field property**.

Setting Number and Default Value Field Properties

1. To open the SALESPERSON table in Design view, right-click the **SALESPERSON** table object to select it and open the shortcut menu and then click the **Design View** button in the shortcut menu. The SALESPERSON table appears in Design view, as shown in Figure AW-3-24.
2. Select the **WageRate** field. The WageRate field properties are displayed in the General tab, as shown in Figure AW-3-25.
3. Click the **Format** text field. A drop-down list arrow appears on the right end of the text field, as shown in Figure AW-3-26. Click the drop-down list arrow to display the list and select **Currency**.

FIGURE AW-3-25

The WageRate Field Properties

The WageRate column is selected

The **Format** text box

The **Decimal Places** text box

The **Default Value** text box

- **NOTE:** When you do this, a small icon appears to the left of the text field. This is the Property Update Options drop-down list. Simply ignore it, and it will disappear when you take the next action. Then it will reappear for that action! In general, ignore it and keep working.

4. Click the **Decimal Places** text field (which is currently set to Auto). Again, a drop-down list arrow appears. Use the drop-down list to select **2** decimal places.
5. Click the **Default Value** text box. The Expression Builder icon appears, as shown in Figure AW-3-27. We do not need to use the Expression Builder at this point. Type **12.50** into the Default Value text box. We have finished setting the field property values for WageRate. The final values are shown in Figure AW-3-28.
   - **NOTE:** Access actually stores this number as 12.5, which is the same value without the trailing zero. Don't be alarmed if you look at these property values again and notice the missing zero!
6. Click the **Save** button to save the completed changes to the SALESPERSON table.
7. Select the **CommissionRate** field. The CommissionRate field properties are displayed in the General tab.
8. Set the **Format** value to **Percentage**.
9. Set the **Decimal Places** value to **3**.
10. Select the **HireDate** field. The HireDate field properties are displayed in the General tab.
11. Set the **Format** value to **Medium Date**.
12. Click the **Save** button to save the completed changes to the SALESPERSON table.
13. Leave the SALESPERSON table open in Design view for the next set of steps.

The UNIQUE constraint is another SQL constraint that Access SQL does not support. To set a UNIQUE constraint in Access, we set the value of the **Indexed field property**.

(Continued)

FIGURE AW-3-26

The Format Text Box

Click in the **Format** text box to select it

Click the **Format** text box drop-down arrow to display the drop-down list

Select **Currency**

	SALESPERSON			×
	Field Name	Data Type	Description (Optional)	
▼	NickName	Short Text		
	LastName	Short Text		
	FirstName	Short Text		
	HireDate	Date/Time		
	WageRate	Number		
	CommissionRate	Number		
	Phone	Short Text		
	Email	Short Text		

Field Properties

General | Lookup

Field Size	Double
Format	
Decimal Places	General Number $456.789
Input Mask	Currency	$3,456.79
Caption	Euro	€3,456.79
Default Value	Fixed	3456.79
Validation Rule	Standard	3,456.79
Validation Text	Percent	123.00%
Required	Scientific	3.46E+03
Indexed	No
Text Align	General

The display layout for the field. Select a pre-defined format or enter a custom format. Press F1 for help on formats.

FIGURE AW-3-27

The Default Value Text Box

	SALESPERSON			×
	Field Name	Data Type	Description (Optional)	
▼	NickName	Short Text		
	LastName	Short Text		
	FirstName	Short Text		
	HireDate	Date/Time		
	WageRate	Number		
	CommissionRate	Number		
	Phone	Short Text		
	Email	Short Text		

The **Property Update Options** icon—you can simply ignore it

Click in the **Default Value** text box to select it

The **Expression Builder** button, which we will not use at this time

Field Properties

General | Lookup

Field Size	Double
Format	Currency
Decimal Places	2
Input Mask	
Caption	
Default Value	
Validation Rule	
Validation Text	
Required	Yes
Indexed	No
Text Align	General

A value that is automatically entered in this field for new items

FIGURE AW-3-28

The Completed WageRate Field Properties

Data format is set to **Currency**

Number of decimal places is set to **2**

The default value is set to **12.50**

Access initially sets this value to No, which means that no index (a tool for making queries more efficient) is built for this column. The two other possible values of this property are **Yes (Duplicates OK)** and **Yes (No Duplicates)**. We enforce the UNIQUE constraint by setting the property value to **Yes (No Duplicates)**.

Setting Indexed Field Properties

1. The **SALESPERSON** table should already be open in Design view. If it isn't, open the table in Design view.
2. Select the **Email** field.
3. Click the **Indexed** text field. A drop-down list arrow button appears on the right end of the text field, as shown in Figure AW-3-29. Click the **Indexed** drop-down list arrow button to display the list and select **Yes (No Duplicates)**.
4. Click the **Save** button to save the completed changes to the SALESPERSON table.
5. Close the SALESPERSON table.

Finally, we'll implement the SQL CHECK constraint. When we created the CONTACT table, the only allowed data types for the Type column were Phone, Fax, Email, and Meeting. The correct SQL statement to add this constraint to the CONTACT table would be:

```
/* *** SQL-ALTER-TABLE-AW03-01 *** */
ALTER TABLE CONTACT
   ADD CONSTRAINT CONTACT_Check_ContactType
      CHECK
            (ContactType IN ('Phone', 'Fax', 'Email',
            'Meeting'));
```

(Continued)

FIGURE AW-3-29

The Email Field Properties

To implement the CHECK constraint in Access, we set the value of the **Validation Rule field property** for the Type column.

Creating the CHECK Constraint for the CONTACT Table

1. Open the **CONTACT** table in Design view.
2. Select the **ContactType** column.
3. Click the Validation Rule text box and then type in the text **Phone or Fax or Email or Meeting**, as shown in Figure AW-3-30.
   - **NOTE:** Do *not* enclose the allowed terms in quotation marks. Access will add quotation marks to each term when it saves the changes to the table design. If you add your own set of quotation marks, you'll end up with each word enclosed in two sets of quotes, and Access will not consider this a match to the existing data in the table when it runs the data integrity check discussed in step 4.
4. Click the **Save** button on the Quick Access Toolbar to save the CONTACT table. As shown in Figure AW-3-31, Access displays a dialog box warning that existing data may not match the data integrity rule we have just established by setting a validation rule.
5. Click the **Yes** button on the dialog box
6. Close the CONTACT table.

Inserting Data with Microsoft Access SQL

We can use Access SQL to enter the data shown in Figure AW-3-20 into the SALESPERSON table. The only problem here is that Access will not handle multiple SQL commands in one query, so each row of data must be input individually. The SQL commands to enter the data are:

FIGURE AW-3-30

Specifying a Validation Rule

The **ContactType** row is selected

Enter the possible values for the column in the **Validation Rule** text box separated by the word *or*

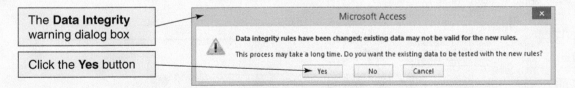

FIGURE AW-3-31

The Data Integrity Warning Dialog Box

The **Data Integrity** warning dialog box

Click the **Yes** button

```
/* *** SQL-INSERT-AW03-01 *** */
INSERT INTO SALESPERSON
     VALUES('Tina', 'Smith', 'Tina', '10-AUG-08',
     '15.50', '.125', '206-287-7010', 'Tina@WM.com');
/* *** SQL-INSERT-AW03-02 *** */
INSERT INTO SALESPERSON
     VALUES('Big Bill', 'Jones', 'William', '25-SEP-08',
     '15.50', '.125', '206-287-7020', 'BigBill@WM.com');
/* *** SQL-INSERT-AW03-03 *** */
INSERT INTO SALESPERSON
     VALUES('Billy', 'Jones', 'Bill', '17-MAY-09',
     '12.50', '.120', '206-287-7030', 'Billy@WM.com');
```

(Continued)

Inserting Data into the SALESPERSON Table by Using Access SQL

1. As described previously, open an Access query window in SQL view.
2. Type the SQL code for the first SQL INSERT statement into the query window.
3. Click the **Run** button. As shown in Figure AW-3-32, the query changes to Append Query, and a dialog box appears, asking you to confirm that you want to insert the data.
4. Click the **Yes** button in the dialog box. The data are inserted into the table.
5. Repeat steps 2, 3, and 4 for the rest of the SQL INSERT statements for the SALESPERSON data.
6. Close the Query1 window. A dialog box appears, asking if you want to save the query. Click the **No** button—there is no need to save this SQL statement.
7. Open the **SALESPERSON** table in Datasheet view.
8. Click the **Shutter Bar Open/Close** button to minimize the Navigation Pane and then arrange the columns so that all column names and data are displayed correctly.
9. The table looks as shown in Figure AW-3-33. Note that the rows are sorted alphabetically, in ascending order, on the primary key (NickName) value—they do not appear in the order in which they were input.
   - **NOTE:** This is *not* typical of an SQL DBMS. Normally, if you run a SELECT * FROM SALESPERSON query on the table, the data appear in the order in which they were input, unless you added an ORDER BY clause.
10. Click the **Shutter Bar Open/Close** button to expand the Navigation Pane.
11. Click the **Save** button on the Quick Access Toolbar to save the change to the table layout.
12. Close the SALESPERSON table.

At this point, the SALESPERSON table has been created and populated. At Wallingford Motors each customer is assigned to one and only one salesperson, so

FIGURE AW-3-32

Inserting Data into the SALESPERSON Table

| The SQL **INSERT** command |
| The dialog box confirming the INSERT |
| Click the **Yes** button to complete the INSERT |

```
Query1
INSERT INTO SALESPERSON
  VALUES('Tina', 'Smith', 'Tina', '10-AUG-08',
  '15.50', '.125', '206-287-7010', 'Tina@WM.com');
```

Microsoft Access

You are about to append 1 row(s).

Once you click Yes, you can't use the Undo command to reverse the changes. Are you sure you want to append the selected rows?

[Yes]   [No]

FIGURE AW-3-33

The Data in the SALESPERSON Table

| The data is stored by NickName (the primary key value), in ascending order |

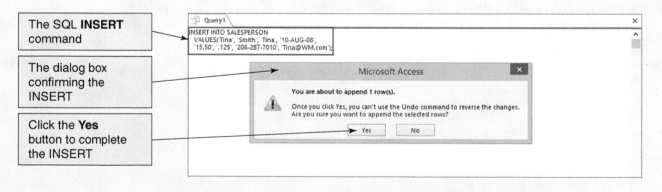

NickName	LastName	FirstName	HireDate	WageRate	CommissionRate	Phone	Email
Big Bill	Jones	William	9/25/2008	$15.50	0.125	206-287-7020	BigBill@WM.com
Billy	Jones	Bill	5/17/2009	$12.50	0.12	206-287-7030	Billy@WM.com
Tina	Smith	Tina	8/10/2008	$15.50	0.125	206-287-7010	Tina@WM.com
*				$12.50			

FIGURE AW-3-34

Database Column Characteristics for the NickName Column

Column Name	Type	Key	Required	Remarks
NickName	Text (35)	Foreign Key	Yes	

FIGURE AW-3-35

CUSTOMER NickName Data

CustomerID	LastName	FirstName	...	NickName
1	Griffey	Ben	...	Big Bill
3	Christman	Jessica	...	Billy
4	Christman	Rob	...	Tina
5	Hayes	Judy	...	Tina

now we need to create the relationship between SALESPERSON and CUSTOMER. This will require a foreign key in CUSTOMER to provide the needed link to SALESPERSON.

The problem is that the column needed for the foreign key—NickName—does not exist in CUSTOMER. Therefore, before creating the foreign key constraint, we must modify the CUSTOMER table by adding the NickName column and the appropriate data values.

Figure AW-3-34 shows the column characteristics for the NickName column in the CUSTOMER table, and Figure AW-3-35 shows the data for the column.

As shown in Figure AW-3-34, NickName is constrained as NOT NULL. As discussed in this chapter, however, adding a populated NOT NULL column requires multiple steps. First, the column must be added as a NULL column. Next, the column values must be added. Finally, the column must be altered to NOT NULL. We could do this by using Access's GUI interface, but because we are working with Access SQL in this section, we will do these steps in SQL. The needed SQL statements are:

```
/* *** SQL-ALTER-TABLE-AW03-02 *** */
ALTER TABLE CUSTOMER
     ADD NickName Char(35) NULL;
/* *** SQL-UPDATE-AW03-01 *** */
UPDATE CUSTOMER
SET       NickName = 'Big Bill'
WHERE     CustomerID = 1;
/* *** SQL-UPDATE-AW03-02 *** */
UPDATE CUSTOMER
SET       NickName = 'Billy'
WHERE     CustomerID = 3;
```

(Continued)

```
/* *** SQL-UPDATE-TAW-CH03-03 *** */
UPDATE CUSTOMER
SET        NickName = 'Tina'
WHERE      CustomerID = 4;
/* *** SQL-UPDATE-AW03-04 *** */
UPDATE CUSTOMER
SET        NickName = 'Tina'
WHERE      CustomerID = 5;
/* *** SQL-ALTER-TABLE-AW03-03 *** */
ALTER TABLE CUSTOMER
     ALTER COLUMN NickName Char(35) NOT NULL;
```

Creating and Populating the NickName Column in the CUSTOMER Table by Using Access SQL

1. As described previously, open an Access query window in SQL view.
2. Type the SQL code for the first SQL ALTER TABLE statement into the query window.
3. Click the **Run** button.
   - **NOTE:** The only indication that the command has run successfully is the fact that *no* error message is displayed.
4. Type the SQL code for the first SQL UPDATE statement into the query window.
5. Click the **Run** button. When the dialog box appears, asking you to confirm that you want to insert the data, click the **Yes** button in the dialog box. The data are inserted into the table.
6. Repeat steps 4 and 5 for the rest of the SQL UPDATE statements for the CUSTOMER data.
7. Type the SQL code for the second SQL ALTER TABLE statement into the query window.
8. Click the **Run** button.
   - **NOTE:** Again, the only indication that the command has run successfully is the fact that *no* error message is displayed.
9. Close the Query1 window. A dialog box appears, asking if you want to save the query. Click the **No** button—there is no need to save this SQL statement.
10. Open the **CUSTOMER** table.
11. Click the **Shutter Bar Open/Close** button to minimize the Navigation Pane and then scroll to the right so that the added NickName column and the data in it are displayed. The table looks as shown in Figure AW-3-36.

FIGURE AW-3-36

The CUSTOMER Table with NickName Data

FIGURE AW-3-37

The Altered CUSTOMER Table

The added **NickName** column

Data in the column are required, which is the Access equivalent of NOT NULL

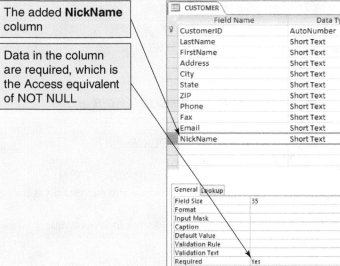

12. Click the **Shutter Bar Open/Close** button to expand the Navigation Pane and then click the Design View button to switch the **CUSTOMER** table into Design view.
13. Click the **NickName** field name to select it.
14. The table with the added NickName column looks as shown in Figure AW-3-37. Note that the data are required in the column—this is Access equivalent of NOT NULL.
15. Close the CUSTOMER table.

Adding Referential Integrity Constraints by Using Access SQL

Now that the NickName column has been added and populated in the CUSTOMER table, we can create the needed referential integrity constraint by adding a foreign key constraint between SALESPERSON and CUSTOMER. Because NickName is not a surrogate key, we will want any changed values of NickName in SALESPERSON to be updated in CUSTOMER. However, if a row is deleted from SALESPERSON, we do *not* want that deletion to cause the deletion of CUSTOMER data. Therefore, the needed constraint, written as an SQL ALTER TABLE statement, is:

```
/* *** SQL-ALTER-TABLE-AW03-04 *** */
ALTER TABLE CUSTOMER
     ADD CONSTRAINT CUSTOMER_SP_FK FOREIGN KEY(NickName)
         REFERENCES SALESPERSON(NickName)
             ON UPDATE CASCADE;
```

(Continued)

Unfortunately, as discussed in this chapter, Access SQL does not support ON UPDATE and ON DELETE clauses. Therefore, we have to set ON UPDATE CASCADE manually after creating the basic constraint with the SQL statement:

```
/* *** SQL-ALTER-TABLE-AW03-05 *** */
ALTER TABLE CUSTOMER
        ADD CONSTRAINT CUSTOMER_SP_FK FOREIGN KEY(NickName)
                REFERENCES SALESPERSON(NickName);
```

Creating the Referential Integrity Constraint Between CUSTOMER and SALESPERSON by Using Access SQL

1. As described previously, open an Access query window in SQL view.
2. Type the SQL code for the SQL ALTER TABLE statement into the query window.
3. Click the **Run** button.
   - **NOTE:** As before, the only indication that the command has run successfully is the fact that *no* error message is displayed.
4. Close the Query1 window. A dialog box appears, asking if you want to save the query. Click the **No** button; there is no need to save this SQL statement.

Modifying Access Databases to Add Constraints Not Supported by Access SQL

We'll set the ON UPDATE CASCADE constraint by using the Relationships window and the Edit Relationships dialog box, as discussed in Chapter 2's section of "The Access Workbench."

Creating a Referential Integrity Constraint Between CUSTOMER and SALESPERSON by Using Access SQL

1. Click the **Database Tools** command tab and then click the **Relationships** button in the Show/Hide group. The Relationships window appears, as shown in Figure AW-3-38.
2. Click the **Show Table** button in the Relationships group of the Design ribbon. The Show Table dialog box appears, as shown in Figure AW-3-39.
3. In the Show Table dialog box, click **SALESPERSON** to select it and then click the **Add** button to add SALESPERSON to the Relationships window.

FIGURE AW-3-38

The Relationships Window with the Current Relationship Diagram

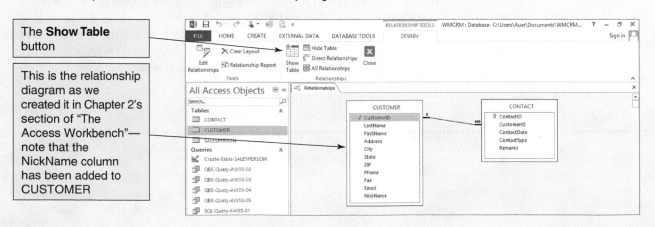

The **Show Table** button

This is the relationship diagram as we created it in Chapter 2's section of "The Access Workbench"—note that the NickName column has been added to CUSTOMER

FIGURE AW-3-39

Adding the SALESPERSON Table to the Relationship Diagram

The **Show Table** dialog box—click a table name to select it, and then click the **Add** button to add the table to the relationship diagram

The **Add** button

When you have added all the tables needed, click the **Close** button

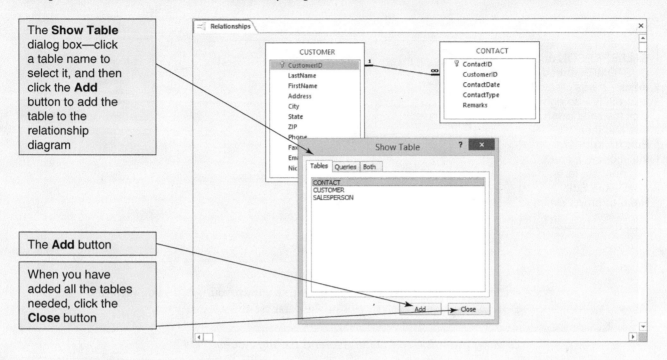

4. Click the **Close** button to close the Show Table dialog box.
5. Rearrange and resize the table objects in the Relationships window by using standard Windows drag-and-drop techniques. Rearrange the SALESPERSON, CUSTOMER, and CONTACT table objects until they look as shown in Figure AW-3-40. Note that the relationship between SALESPERSON and CUSTOMER that we created using SQL is already shown in the diagram.
6. Right-click the **relationship line** between SALESPERSON and CUSTOMER, and then click **Edit Relationship** in the shortcut menu that appears. The **Edit Relationships** dialog box appears. Note that the **Enforce Referential Integrity** check box is already checked—this was set by the SQL ALTER TABLE statement that created the relationship between the two tables.
7. Set ON UPDATE CASCADE by clicking the **Cascade Update Related Fields** check box. The Edit Relationships dialog box now looks as shown in Figure AW-3-41.
8. Click the **OK** button. An Access dialog box appears, asking whether you want to save changes to the layout of "Relationships." Click the **Yes** button to save the changes and close the window.

Closing the Database and Exiting Access

Now we're done adding the SALESPERSON table to the database. We created the SALESPERSON table, added data, altered the CUSTOMER data with a new column and foreign key values, and created the referential integrity constraint between the two tables. In the process, we saw where Access SQL does not support the standard SQL language and learned how to use the Access GUI to compensate for the lacking SQL language features.

That completes the work we'll do in this chapter's section of "The Access Workbench." If you have taken a class in Microsoft Access, you probably did many of the tasks we covered in a different way. In Microsoft Access, SQL DDL is usually quite hidden, but in this

(Continued)

FIGURE AW-3-40

The Updated Relationship Diagram

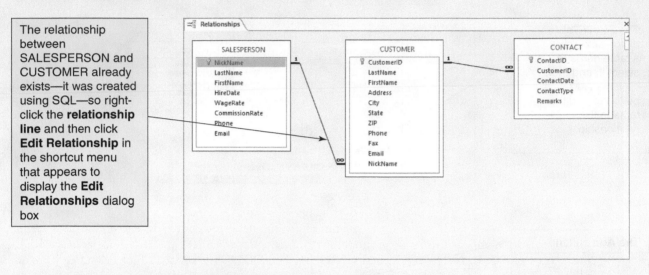

The relationship between SALESPERSON and CUSTOMER already exists—it was created using SQL—so right-click the **relationship line** and then click **Edit Relationship** in the shortcut menu that appears to display the **Edit Relationships** dialog box

section of "The Access Workbench," we've shown you how to complete the tasks using SQL. As usual, we finish by closing the database and Access.

Closing the WMCRM Database and Exiting Access

1. Close the WMCRM database and exit Access by clicking the **Close** button in the upper-right corner of the Microsoft Access window.

FIGURE AW-3-41

The Completed Edit Relationships Dialog Box

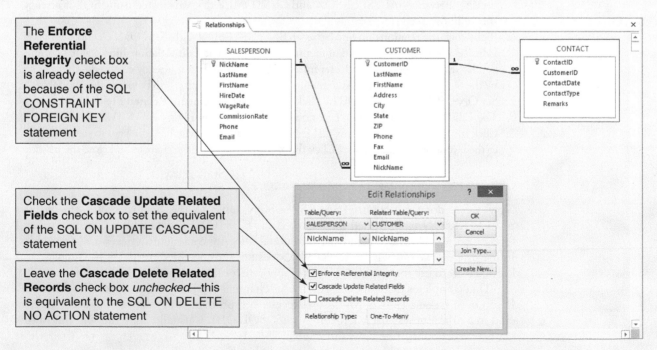

The **Enforce Referential Integrity** check box is already selected because of the SQL CONSTRAINT FOREIGN KEY statement

Check the **Cascade Update Related Fields** check box to set the equivalent of the SQL ON UPDATE CASCADE statement

Leave the **Cascade Delete Related Records** check box *unchecked*—this is equivalent to the SQL ON DELETE NO ACTION statement

SUMMARY

Structured Query Language (SQL) is a data sublanguage that has constructs for defining and processing a database. SQL has several components, two of which are discussed in this chapter: a data definition language (DDL), which is used for creating database tables and other structures, and a data manipulation language (DML), which is used to query and modify database data. SQL can be embedded into scripting languages, such as VBScript, or programming languages, such as Java and C#. In addition, SQL statements can be processed from a command window. SQL was developed by IBM and has been endorsed as a national standard by the American National Standards Institute (ANSI). There have been several versions of SQL. Our discussion is based on SQL-92, but later versions exist that have added, in particular, support for Extensible Markup Language (XML). Modern DBMS products provide graphic facilities for accomplishing many of the tasks that SQL does. Use of SQL is mandatory for programmatically creating SQL statements.

Microsoft Access 2013 uses a variant of SQL known as ANSI-89 SQL, or Microsoft Jet SQL, which differs significantly from SQL-92. Not all SQL statements written in SQL-92 and later versions run in Access ANSI-89 SQL.

The SQL CREATE TABLE statement is used to create relations. Each column is described in three parts: the column name, the data type, and optional column constraints. Column constraints considered in this chapter are PRIMARY KEY, FOREIGN KEY, NULL, NOT NULL, and UNIQUE. The DEFAULT keyword (not considered a constraint) is also considered. If no column constraint is specified, the column is set to NULL.

Standard data types are Char, VarChar, Integer, Numeric, and DateTime. These types have been supplemented by DBMS vendors. Figure 3-4 shows some of the additional data types for SQL Server, Oracle Database, and MySQL.

If a primary key has only one column, you can define it by using the primary key constraint. Another way to define a primary key is to use the table constraint. You can use such constraints to define single-column and multicolumn primary keys, and you can also implement referential integrity constraints by defining foreign keys. Foreign key definitions can specify that updates and deletions should cascade.

After the tables and constraints are created, you can add data by using The SQL INSERT statement and you can query data by using The SQL SELECT statement. The basic format of the SQL SELECT statement is SELECT (column names or the asterisk symbol [*]), FROM (table names, separated by commas if there is more than one), WHERE (conditions). You can use SELECT to obtain specific columns, specific rows, or both.

Conditions after WHERE require single quotes around values for Char and VarChar columns. However, single quotes are not used for Integer and Numeric columns. You can specify compound conditions with AND and OR. You can use sets of values with IN (match any in the set) and NOT IN (not match any in the set). You can use the wildcard symbols _ and % (? and * in Microsoft Access) with LIKE to specify a single unknown character or multiple unknown characters, respectively. You can use IS NULL to test for null values.

You can sort results by using the ORDER BY command. The five SQL built-in functions are COUNT, SUM, MAX, MIN, and AVG. SQL can also perform mathematical calculations. You can create groups by using GROUP BY, and you can limit groups by using HAVING. If the keywords WHERE and HAVING both occur in an SQL statement, WHERE is applied before HAVING.

You can query multiple tables by using either subqueries or joins. If all the result data come from a single table, then subqueries can be used. If results come from two or more tables, then joins must be used. The JOIN...ON syntax can be used for joins. Rows that do not match the join conditions do not appear in the results. Outer joins can be used to ensure that all rows from a table appear in the results.

You can modify data by using The SQL UPDATE...SET statement and delete data by using The SQL DELETE statement. The SQL UPDATE and SQL DELETE statements can easily cause disasters, so the commands must be used with great care.

You can remove tables (and their data) from a database by using the SQL DROP TABLE statement. You can remove constraints by using the SQL ALTER TABLE DROP CONSTRAINT command. You can modify tables and constraints by using The SQL ALTER TABLE statement. Finally, you can use the CHECK constraint to validate data values.

KEY TERMS

/* and */ (SQL comment symbols)
American National Standards
  Institute (ANSI)
AND keyword
AS keyword
ASC keyword
asterisk (*)
AVG
business rule
CASCADE keyword
CHECK constraint
comparison operators
CONSTRAINT keyword
COUNT
data control language (DCL)
data definition language (DDL)
data manipulation language (DML)
data sublanguage
DEFAULT keyword
DESC keyword
DISTINCT keyword
Extensible Markup Language (XML)
FOREIGN KEY constraint
graphical user interface (GUI)
GROUP BY clause
HAVING clause
IDENTITY (M,N) property
IN keyword
International Organization for
  Standardization (ISO)

IS NOT NULL phrase
IS NULL keyword
LEFT keyword
LIKE keyword
MAX
MIN
NO ACTION keyword
NOT IN phrase
NOT keyword
NOT LIKE phrase
NOT NULL constraint
NULL constraint
ON DELETE phrase
ON UPDATE phrase
OR keyword
ORDER BY clause
percent sign (%)
PRIMARY KEY constraint
Query by Example (QBE)
question mark (?)
RIGHT keyword
SQL ALTER TABLE statement
SQL asterisk (*) wildcard operator
SQL built-in functions
SQL comment
SQL CREATE TABLE statement
SQL DELETE statement
SQL DROP TABLE statement
SQL equijoin
SQL FROM clause

SQL inner join
SQL INNER JOIN syntax
SQL INSERT statement
SQL JOIN keyword
SQL join operation
SQL JOIN ON syntax
SQL left outer join
SQL LEFT JOIN syntax
SQL MERGE statement
SQL ON keyword
SQL outer join
SQL right outer join
SQL RIGHT JOIN syntax
SQL SELECT clause
SQL SELECT/FROM/WHERE
  framework
SQL TRUNCATE TABLE
  statement
SQL UPDATE...SET statement
SQL view
SQL WHERE clause
SQL/Persistent stored modules
  (SQL/PSM)
Structured Query Language (SQL)
subquery
SUM
transaction control language (TCL)
underscore symbol (_)
UNIQUE constraint
wildcard characters

REVIEW QUESTIONS

3.1   What does *SQL* stand for?

3.2   What is a data sublanguage?

3.3   Explain the importance of SQL-92.

3.4   Why is it important to learn SQL?

3.5   Describe in your own words the purpose of the two business rules listed on page 124.

3.6   Why do some standard SQL-92 statements fail to run successfully in Microsoft Access?

Use the following tables for your answers to questions 3.7 through 3.51:

      PET_OWNER (OwnerID, OwnerLastName, OwnerFirstName,
          OwnerPhone, OwnerEmail)

      PET (PetID, PetName, PetType, PetBreed, PetDOB, *OwnerID*)

Sample data for these tables are shown in Figures 3-18 and 3-19. For each SQL statement you write, show the results based on these data.

FIGURE 3-18

PET_OWNER Data

OwnerID	OwnerLastName	OwnerFirstName	OwnerPhone	OwnerEmail
1	Downs	Marsha	555-537-8765	Marsha.Downs@somewhere.com
2	James	Richard	555-537-7654	Richard.James@somewhere.com
3	Frier	Liz	555-537-6543	Liz.Frier@somewhere.com
4	Trent	Miles		Miles.Trent@somewhere.com

If possible, run the statements you write for the questions that follow in an actual DBMS, as appropriate, to obtain results. Use data types that are consistent with the DBMS you are using. If you are not using an actual DBMS, consistently represent data types by using either the SQL Server, Oracle Database, or MySQL data types shown in Figure 3-5.

3.7 Write an SQL CREATE TABLE statement to create the PET_OWNER table, with OwnerID as a surrogate key. Justify your choices of column properties.

3.8 Write an SQL CREATE TABLE statement to create the PET table *without* a referential integrity constraint on OwnerID in PET. Justify your choices of column properties. Why not make every column NOT NULL?

3.9 Create a referential integrity constraint on OwnerID in PET. Assume that deletions should not cascade.

3.10 Create a referential integrity constraint on OwnerID in PET. Assume that deletions should cascade.

The following table schema for the PET_2 table is an alternate version of the PET table—use it to answer review questions 3.11 and 3.12:

PET_2 (PetName, PetType, PetBreed, PetDOB, OwnerID)

3.11 Write the required SQL statements to create the PET_2 table.

3.12 Is PET or PET_2 a better design? Explain your rationale.

3.13 Write the SQL statements necessary to remove the PET_OWNER table from the database. Assume that the referential integrity constraint is to be removed. *Do not run these commands in an actual database!*

FIGURE 3-19

PET Data

PetID	PetName	PetType	PetBreed	PetDOB	OwnerID
1	King	Dog	Std. Poodle	27-Feb-11	1
2	Teddy	Cat	Cashmere	01-Feb-12	2
3	Fido	Dog	Std. Poodle	17-Jul-10	1
4	AJ	Dog	Collie Mix	05-May-11	3
5	Cedro	Cat	Unknown	06-Jun-09	2
6	Wooley	Cat	Unknown		2
7	Buster	Dog	Border Collie	11-Dec-08	4

3.14 Write the SQL statements necessary to remove the PET_OWNER table from the database. Assume that the PET table is to be removed. *Do not run these commands in an actual database!*

3.15 Write an SQL statement to display all columns of all rows of PET. Do not use the asterisk (*) notation.

3.16 Write an SQL statement to display all columns of all rows of PET. Use the asterisk (*) notation.

3.17 Write an SQL statement to display the breed and type of all pets.

3.18 Write an SQL statement to display the breed, type, and DOB of all pets having the type Dog.

3.19 Write an SQL statement to display the PetBreed column of PET.

3.20 Write an SQL statement to display the PetBreed column of PET. Do not show duplicates.

3.21 Write an SQL statement to display the breed, type, and DOB for all pets having the type Dog and the breed Std. Poodle.

3.22 Write an SQL statement to display the name, breed, and type for all pets that are not of type Cat, Dog, or Fish.

3.23 Write an SQL statement to display the pet ID, breed, and type for all pets having a four-character name starting with *K*.

3.24 Write an SQL statement to display the last name, first name, and email of all owners who have an email address ending with *somewhere.com*. Assume that email account names can be any number of characters.

3.25 Write an SQL statement to display the last name, first name, and email of any owner who has a NULL value for OwnerPhone.

3.26 Write an SQL statement to display the name and breed of all pets, sorted by PetName.

3.27 Write an SQL statement to display the name and breed of all pets, sorted by PetBreed in ascending order and by PetName in descending order within PetBreed.

3.28 Write an SQL statement to count the number of pets.

3.29 Write an SQL statement to count the number of distinct breeds.

The following table schema for the PET_3 table is another alternate version of the PET table:

PET_3 (PetID, PetName, PetType, PetBreed, PetDOB, PetWeight, *OwnerID*)

Data for PET_3 are shown in Figure 3-20. Except as specifically noted in the question itself, use the PET_3 table for your answers to all the remaining review questions.

3.30 Write the required SQL statements to create the PET_3 table. Assume that PetWeight is Numeric(4,1).

3.31 Write an SQL statement to display the minimum, maximum, and average weight of dogs.

3.32 Write an SQL statement to group the data by PetBreed and display the average weight per breed.

3.33 Answer question 3.32 but consider only breeds for which two or more pets are included in the database.

3.34 Answer question 3.33 but do not consider any pet having the breed of Unknown.

3.35 Write an SQL statement to display the last name, first name, and email of any owners of cats. Use a subquery.

3.36 Write an SQL statement to display the last name, first name, and email of any owners of cats with the name Teddy. Use a subquery.

FIGURE 3-20

PET_3 Data

PetID	PetName	PetType	PetBreed	PetDOB	PetWeight	OwnerID
1	King	Dog	Std. Poodle	27-Feb-11	25.5	1
2	Teddy	Cat	Cashmere	01-Feb-12	10.5	2
3	Fido	Dog	Std. Poodle	17-Jul-10	28.5	1
4	AJ	Dog	Collie Mix	05-May-11	20.0	3
5	Cedro	Cat	Unknown	06-Jun-09	9.5	2
6	Wooley	Cat	Unknown		9.5	2
7	Buster	Dog	Border Collie	11-Dec-08	25.0	4

The following table schema for the BREED table shows a new table to be added to the pet database:

BREED (BreedName, MinWeight, MaxWeight, AverageLifeExpectancy)

Assume that Breed in PET_3 is a foreign key that matches the primary key BreedName in BREED and that BreedName in BREED is now a foreign key linking the two tables with the referential integrity constraint:

BreedName in PET_3 must exist in BreedName in BREED

If needed, you may also assume that a similar referential integrity constraint exists between PET and BREED and between PET_2 and BREED. The BREED table data are shown in Figure 3-21.

3.37 Write SQL statements to (1) create the BREED table, (2) insert the data in Figure 3-21 into the BREED table, (3) alter the PET_3 table so that PetBreed is a foreign key referencing BreedName in BREED, and (4) with the BREED table added to the pet database, write an SQL statement to display the last name, first name, and email of any owner of a pet that has an AverageLifeExpectancy value greater than 15. Use a subquery.

3.38 Answer question 3.35 but use a join using JOIN ON syntax.

3.39 Answer question 3.36 but use a join using JOIN ON syntax.

3.40 Answer part (4) of question 3.37 but use joins using JOIN ON syntax.

3.41 Write an SQL statement to display the OwnerLastName, OwnerFirstName, PetName, PetType, PetBreed, and AverageLifeExpectancy for pets with a known PetBreed.

FIGURE 3-21

BREED Data

BreedName	MinWeight	MaxWeight	AverageLifeExpectancy
Border Collie	15.0	22.5	20
Cashmere	10.0	15.0	12
Collie Mix	17.5	25.0	18
Std. Poodle	22.5	30.0	18
Unknown			

FIGURE 3-22

Additional PET_OWNER Data

OwnerID	OwnerLastName	OwnerFirstName	OwnerPhone	OwnerEmail
5	Rogers	Jim	555-232-3456	Jim.Rogers@somewhere.com
6	Keenan	Mary	555-232-4567	Mary.Keenan@somewhere.com
7	Melnik	Nigel	555-232-5678	Nigel.Melnik@somewhere.com
8	Mayberry	Jenny	555-454-1243	
9	Roberts	Ken	555-454-2354	
10	Taylor	Sam	555-454-3465	

3.42   Write an SQL statement to add three new rows to the PET_OWNER table. Assume that OwnerID is a surrogate key and that the DBMS will provide a value for it. Use the first three lines of data provided in Figure 3-22.

3.43   Write an SQL statement to add three new rows to the PET_OWNER table. Assume that OwnerID is a surrogate key and that the DBMS will provide a value for it. Assume, however, that you have only OwnerLastName, OwnerFirstName, and OwnerPhone and that therefore OwnerEmail is NULL. Use the last three lines of data provided in Figure 3-22.

3.44   Write an SQL statement to change the value of Std. Poodle in BreedName of PET_3 to Poodle, Std.

3.45   Explain what will happen if you leave the WHERE clause off your answer to question 3.44.

3.46   Write an SQL statement to delete all rows of pets of type Anteater. What will happen if you forget to code the WHERE clause in this statement?

3.47   Write an SQL statement to add a PetWeight column like the one in PET_3 to the PET table, given that this column is NULL. Again, assume that PetWeight is Numeric(4,1).

3.48   Write SQL statements to insert data into the PetWeight column you created in question 3.47. Use the PetWeight data from the PET_3 table as shown in Figure 3-20.

3.49   Write SQL statements to add a PetWeight column like the one in PET_3 to the PET table, given that this column is NOT NULL. Again, assume that PetWeight is Numeric(4,1). Use the PetWeight data from the PET_3 table as shown in Figure 3-20.

3.50   Write an SQL statement to add a CHECK constraint to the PET table so that the weight data recorded in the PetWeight column you added to the table in either question 3.47 or 3.49 is less than 250.

3.51   Write an SQL statement to drop the PetWeight column you added to the PET table in either question 3.47 or 3.49.

EXERCISES

The following is a set of tables for the Art Course database shown in Figure 1-10. For the data for these tables, use the data shown in Figure 1-10.

CUSTOMER (CustomerNumber, CustomerLastName, CustomerFirstName, Phone)
COURSE (CourseNumber, Course, CourseDate, Fee)
ENROLLMENT (*CustomerNumber*, *CourseNumber*, AmountPaid)

where:

CustomerNumber and CourseNumber are surrogate keys. Therefore, these numbers will never be modified, and there is no need for cascading updates. No customer data are ever deleted, so there is no need to cascade deletions. Courses can be deleted. If there are enrollment entries for a deleted class, they should also be deleted.

These tables, referential integrity constraints, and data are used as the basis for the SQL statements you will create in the exercises that follow. If possible, run these statements in an actual DBMS, as appropriate, to obtain results. Name your database ART_COURSE_DATABASE. For each SQL statement you write, show the results based on these data. Use data types consistent with the DBMS you are using. If you are not using an actual DBMS, consistently represent data types using either the SQL Server, Oracle Database, or MySQL data types shown in Figure 3-5.

3.52 Write and run the SQL statements necessary to create the tables and their referential integrity constraints.

3.53 Populate the tables with data.

3.54 Write and run an SQL query to list all occurrences of Adv. Pastels. Include all associated data for each occurrence of the class.

3.55 Write and run an SQL query to list all students and courses they are registered for. Include, in this order, CustomerNumber, CustomerLastName, CustomerFirstName, Phone, CourseNumber, and AmountPaid.

3.56 Write and run an SQL query to list all students registered in Adv. Pastels starting on October 1, 2015. Include, in this order, Course, CourseDate, Fee, CustomerLastName, CustomerFirstName, and Phone.

3.57 Write and run an SQL query to list all students registered in Adv. Pastels starting on October 1, 2015. Include in this order, Course, CourseDate, CustomerLastName, CustomerFirstName, Phone, Fee, and AmountPaid. Use a join.

3.58 Modify your query to include all students, regardless of whether they registered in the Adv. Pastels, starting October 1, 2015. Include, in this order, CustomerLastName, CustomerFirstName, Phone, Course, CourseDate, Fee, and AmountPaid.

3.59 Write a set of SQL statements (*hint:* Use the SQL ALTER TABLE command) to add a FullFeePaid column to ENROLLMENT and populate the column, assuming that the column is NULL. The only possible values for this column are Yes and No. (Compare COURSE.Fee to ENROLLMENT.AmountPaid to determine data values.)

3.60 Write a set of SQL statements (*hint:* Use the SQL ALTER TABLE command) to add a FullFeePaid column to ENROLLMENT and populate the column, assuming that the column is NOT NULL. The only possible values for this column are Yes and No. (Compare COURSE.Fee to ENROLLMENT.AmountPaid to determine data values.) What is the difference between your answer to this question and your answer to question 3.59?

3.61 Write an ALTER TABLE statement to add a CHECK constraint to the ENROLLMENT table to ensure that the value of FullFeePaid is either Yes or No.

The following exercises are intended for use with a DBMS other than Microsoft Access. If you are using Microsoft Access, see the equivalent questions in the "Access Workbench Exercises" that follow.

3.62 If you haven't done so, create the WPC database, tables, and relationships described in this chapter, using the SQL DBMS of your choice. Be sure to populate the tables with the data shown in Figure 3-2.

3.63 Using the SQL DBMS of your choice, create and run queries to answer the questions in exercise AW.3.1.

3.64 Using the SQL DBMS of your choice, complete steps A through E in exercise AW.3.3, but *exclude step F.*

ACCESS WORKBENCH KEY TERMS

Allow Zero Length field property	parameterized query
Decimal Places field property	Validation Rule field property
Default Value field property	Yes (Duplicates OK)
Field Size field property	Yes (No Duplicates)
Format field property	
Indexed field property	

ACCESS WORKBENCH EXERCISES

In the "Access Workbench Exercises" in Chapters 1 and 2, you created a database for the Wedgewood Pacific Corporation (WPC) of Seattle, Washington. In this set of exercises, you'll:

- Create and run queries against the database by using Access SQL.
- Create and run queries against the database by using Access QBE.
- Create tables and relationships by using Access SQL.
- Populate tables by using Access SQL.

AW.3.1 Using Access SQL, create and run queries to answer the questions that follow. Save each query using the query name format SQLQuery-AWE-3-1-## where the ## sign is replaced by the letter designator of the question. For example, the first query will be saved as SQLQuery-AWE-3-1-A.

A. What projects are in the PROJECT table? Show all information for each project.

B. What are the ProjectID, ProjectName, StartDate, and EndDate values of projects in the PROJECT table?

C. What projects in the PROJECT table started before August 1, 2014? Show all the information for each project.

D. What projects in the PROJECT table have not been completed? Show all the information for each project.

E. Who are the employees assigned to each project? Show ProjectID, EmployeeNumber, LastName, FirstName, and Phone.

F. Who are the employees assigned to each project? Show ProjectID, ProjectName, and Department. Show EmployeeNumber, LastName, FirstName, and Phone.

G. Who are the employees assigned to each project? Show ProjectID, ProjectName, Department, and Department Phone. Show EmployeeNumber, LastName, FirstName, and Employee Phone. Sort by ProjectID, in ascending order.

H. Who are the employees assigned to projects run by the marketing department? Show ProjectID, ProjectName, Department, and Department Phone. Show

EmployeeNumber, LastName, FirstName, and Employee Phone. Sort by ProjectID, in ascending order.

I. How many projects are being run by the marketing department? Be sure to assign an appropriate column name to the computed results.

J. What is the total MaxHours of projects being run by the marketing department? Be sure to assign an appropriate column name to the computed results.

K. What is the average MaxHours of projects being run by the marketing department? Be sure to assign an appropriate column name to the computed results.

L. How many projects are being run by each department? Be sure to display each DepartmentName and to assign an appropriate column name to the computed results.

AW.3.2   Using Access QBE, create and run new queries to answer the questions in exercise AW.3.1. Save each query using the query name format QBEQuery-AWE-3-1-## where the ## sign is replaced by the letter designator of the question. For example, the first query will be saved as QBEQuery-AWE-3-1-A.

AW.3.3   WPC has decided to keep track of computers used by the employees. In order to do this, two new tables will be added to the database. The schema for these tables, as related to the existing EMPLOYEE table, is:

EMPLOYEE (EmployeeNumber, FirstName, LastName, *Department*, Phone, Email)

COMPUTER (SerialNumber, Make, Model, ProcessorType, ProcessorSpeed, MainMemory, DiskSize)

COMPUTER_ASSIGNMENT (*SerialNumber*, *EmployeeNumber*, DateAssigned, DateReassigned)

The referential integrity constraints are:

Serial Number in COMPUTER_ASSIGNMENT must exist in SerialNumber in COMPUTER

EmployeeNumber in COMPUTER_ASSIGNMENT must exist in EmployeeNumber in EMPLOYEE

EmployeeNumber is a surrogate key and never changes. Employee records are never deleted from the database. SerialNumber is not a surrogate key because it is not generated by the database. However, a computer's SerialNumber never changes, and, therefore, there is no need to cascade updates. When a computer is at its end of life, the record in COMPUTER for that computer and all associated records in COMPUTER_ASSIGNMENT are deleted from the database.

A. Figure 3-23 shows the column characteristics for the WPC COMPUTER table. Using the column characteristics, use Access SQL to create the COMPUTER table and its associated constraints in the WPC.accdb database. Are there any table characteristics that cannot be created in SQL? If so, what are they? Use the Access GUI to finish setting table characteristics, if necessary.

B. The data for the COMPUTER table are in Figure 3-24. Use Access SQL to enter these data into your COMPUTER table.

(Continued)

FIGURE 3-23

Database Column Characteristics for the COMPUTER Table

Column Name	Type	Key	Required	Remarks
SerialNumber	Number	Primary Key	Yes	Long Integer
Make	Text (12)	No	Yes	Must be "Dell" or "Gateway" or "HP" or "Other"
Model	Text (24)	No	Yes	
ProcessorType	Text (24)	No	No	
ProcessorSpeed	Number	No	Yes	Double [3,2], Between 1.0 and 4.0
MainMemory	Text (15)	No	Yes	
DiskSize	Text (15)	No	Yes	

C. Figure 3-25 shows the column characteristics for the WPC COMPUTER_ASSIGNMENT table. Using the column characteristics, use Access SQL to create the COMPUTER_ASSIGNMENT table and the associated constraints in the WPC.accdb database. Are there any table or relationship settings or characteristics that cannot be created in SQL? If so, what are they? Use the Access GUI to finish setting table characteristics and relationship settings, if necessary.

D. The data for the COMPUTER_ASSIGNMENT table are in Figure 3-26. Use Access SQL to enter these data into your COMPUTER_ASSIGNMENT table.

FIGURE 3-24

WPC COMPUTER Data

Serial Number	Make	Model	Processor Type	Processor Speed	Main Memory	Disk Size
9871234	HP	Pavilion 500-210qe	Intel i5-4530	3.00	6.0 Gbytes	1.0 Tbytes
9871245	HP	Pavilion 500-210qe	Intel i5-4530	3.00	6.0 Gbytes	1.0 Tbytes
9871256	HP	Pavilion 500-210qe	Intel i5-4530	3.00	6.0 Gbytes	1.0 Tbytes
9871267	HP	Pavilion 500-210qe	Intel i5-4530	3.00	6.0 Gbytes	1.0 Tbytes
9871278	HP	Pavilion 500-210qe	Intel i5-4530	3.00	6.0 Gbytes	1.0 Tbytes
9871289	HP	Pavilion 500-210qe	Intel i5-4530	3.00	6.0 Gbytes	1.0 Tbytes
6541001	Dell	OptiPlex 9020	Intel i7-4770	3.40	8.0 GBytes	1.0 Tbytes
6541002	Dell	OptiPlex 9020	Intel i7-4770	3.40	8.0 GBytes	1.0 Tbytes
6541003	Dell	OptiPlex 9020	Intel i7-4770	3.40	8.0 GBytes	1.0 Tbytes
6541004	Dell	OptiPlex 9020	Intel i7-4770	3.40	8.0 GBytes	1.0 Tbytes
6541005	Dell	OptiPlex 9020	Intel i7-4770	3.40	8.0 GBytes	1.0 Tbytes
6541006	Dell	OptiPlex 9020	Intel i7-4770	3.40	8.0 GBytes	1.0 Tbytes

FIGURE 3-25

Database Column Characteristics for the COMPUTER_ASSIGNMENT Table

Column Name	Type	Key	Required	Remarks
SerialNumber	Number	Primary Key, Foreign Key	Yes	Long Integer
EmployeeNumber	Number	Primary Key, Foreign Key	Yes	Long Integer
DateAssigned	Date/Time	Primary Key	Yes	Medium Date
DateReassigned	Date/Time	No	No	Medium Date

E. Who is currently using which computer at WPC? Create an appropriate SQL query to answer this question. Show SerialNumber, Make, and Model. Show EmployeeID, LastName, FirstName, Department, and Employee Phone. Sort first by Department and then by employee LastName. Save this query using the query naming rules in exercise AW.3.1.

F. Who is currently using which computer at WPC? Create an appropriate QBE query to answer this question. Show SerialNumber, Make, Model, ProcessorType, and ProcessorSpeed. Show the EmployeeID, LastName, FirstName, Department, and Employee Phone. Sort first by Department and then by employee LastName. Save this query using the query naming rules in exercise AW.3.2.

FIGURE 3-26

WPC COMPUTER_ASSIGNMENT Data

SerialNumber	EmployeeNumber	DateAssigned	DateReassigned
9871234	11	15-Sep-2014	21-Oct-2014
9871245	12	15-Sep-2014	21-Oct-2014
9871256	4	15-Sep-2014	
9871267	5	15-Sep-2014	
9871278	8	15-Sep-2014	
9871289	9	15-Sep-2014	
6541001	11	21-Oct-2014	
6541002	12	21-Oct-2014	
6541003	1	21-Oct-2014	
6541004	2	21-Oct-2014	
6541005	3	21-Oct-2014	
6541006	6	21-Oct-2014	
9871234	7	21-Oct-2014	
9871245	10	21-Oct-2014	

HEATHER SWEENEY DESIGNS **CASE QUESTIONS**

Heather Sweeney is an interior designer who specializes in home kitchen design. She offers a variety of seminars at home shows, kitchen and appliance stores, and other public locations. The seminars are free; she offers them as a way of building her customer base. She earns revenue by selling books and videos that instruct people on kitchen design. She also offers custom-design consulting services.

After someone attends a seminar, Heather wants to leave no stone unturned in attempting to sell that person one of her products or services. She would therefore like to develop a database to keep track of customers, the seminars they have attended, the contacts she has made with them, and the purchases they have made. She wants to use this database to continue to contact her customers and offer them products and services, including via a Web application that allows customers to create an account and purchase items online.

We use the task of designing a database for Heather Sweeney Designs (HSD) as an example for our discussion of developing first the HSD data model in Chapter 4 (pages 262–270) and then the HSD database design in Chapter 5 (pages 310–317). Although you will study the HSD database development in detail in these chapters, *you do not need to know that material to answer the following questions.* Here we will take that final database design and actually implement it in a database using the SQL techniques that you learned in this chapter.

BTW

Some instructors and professors will follow the chapter order as we present it in this book, whereas others prefer to cover Chapters 4 and 5 before teaching the SQL techniques in this chapter. It is really a matter of personal preference (although you may hear some strong arguments in favor of one approach or the other), and these case questions are designed to be independent of the order in which you learn SQL, data modeling, and database design.

For reference, the SQL statements shown here are built from the HSD database design in Figure 5-27, the column specifications in Figure 5-26, and the referential integrity constraint specifications detailed in Figure 5-28.

Figure 3-27 shows the tables in the Heather Sweeney Designs database as they appear in the Microsoft Access 2013 Relationships view. This is similar to the view of the WPC database tables shown in Figure 3-1, and illustrates the tables in the HSD database and the relationships between them.

The SQL statements to create the Heather Sweeney Designs (HSD) database are shown in Figure 3-28 in SQL Server syntax. The SQL statements to populate the HSD database are shown in Figure 3-29, again in SQL Server syntax.

Write SQL statements and answer questions for this database as follows:

A. Create a database named HSD in your DBMS.

B. Write an SQL script based on Figure 3-28 to create the tables and relationships for the HSD database. Save this script, and then execute the script to create the HSD tables.

C. Write an SQL script based on Figure 3-29 to insert the data for the HSD database. Save this script, and then execute the script to populate the HSD tables.
  - **NOTE:** For your answers to parts D through O, you should create an SQL script to save and store your SQL statements. You can use one script to contain all the necessary statements. You can also include your answer to part P, but be sure to put it in

FIGURE 3-27

The Heather Sweeney Designs Database Tables in Microsoft Access 2013

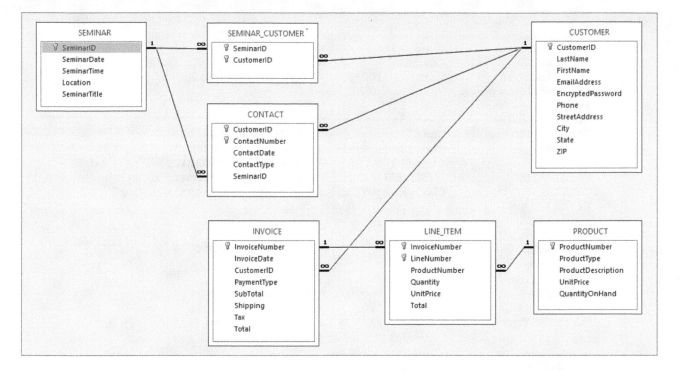

comment marks so that it is interpreted as a comment by the DBMS and cannot actually be run!

D. Write SQL statements to list all columns for all tables.

E. Write an SQL statement to list LastName, FirstName, and Phone for all customers that live in Dallas.

F. Write an SQL statement to list LastName, FirstName, and Phone for all customers that live in Dallas and have a LastName that begins with the letter *T*.

G. Write an SQL statement to list the INVOICE.InvoiceNumber for sales that include the *Heather Sweeney Seminar Live in Dallas on 25-OCT-13* video. Use a subquery. (*Hint:* The correct solution uses three tables in the query because the question asks for INVOICE.InvoiceNumber. Otherwise, there is a possible solution with only two tables in the query.)

H. Answer part G but use a join in JOIN ON syntax. (*Hint:* The correct solution uses three tables in the query because the question asks for INVOICE.InvoiceNumber. Otherwise, there is a possible solution with only two tables in the query.)

I. Write an SQL statement to list the FirstName, LastName and Phone of customers (list each name only once) who have attended the *Kitchen on a Big D Budget* seminar.

J. Write an SQL statement to list the FirstName, LastName, Phone, ProductNumber, and Description names for customers (list each combination of name and product only

FIGURE 3-28

SQL Statements to Create the HSD Database

```
CREATE   TABLE CUSTOMER(
        CustomerID          Int              NOT NULL IDENTITY (1, 1),
        LastName            Char(25)         NOT NULL,
        FirstName           Char(25)         NOT NULL,
        EmailAddress        VarChar(100)     NOT NULL,
        EncryptedPassword   VarChar(50)      NULL,
        Phone               Char(12)         NOT NULL,
        StreetAddress       Char(35)         NULL,
        City                Char(35)         NULL DEFAULT 'Dallas',
        [State]             Char(2)          NULL DEFAULT 'TX',
        ZIP                 Char(10)         NULL DEFAULT '75201',
        CONSTRAINT          CUSTOMER_PK      PRIMARY KEY(CustomerID),
        CONSTRAINT          CUSTOMER_EMAIL   UNIQUE(EmailAddress)
        );

CREATE   TABLE SEMINAR(
        SeminarID           Int              NOT NULL IDENTITY (1, 1),
        SeminarDate         Date             NOT NULL,
        SeminarTime         Time             NOT NULL,
        Location            VarChar(100)     NOT NULL,
        SeminarTitle        VarChar(100)     NOT NULL,
        CONSTRAINT          SEMINAR_PK       PRIMARY KEY(SeminarID)
        );

CREATE   TABLE SEMINAR_CUSTOMER(
        SeminarID           Int              NOT NULL,
        CustomerID          Int              NOT NULL,
        CONSTRAINT          S_C_PK           PRIMARY KEY(SeminarID, CustomerID),
        CONSTRAINT          S_C_SEMINAR_FK   FOREIGN KEY(SeminarID)
                            REFERENCES SEMINAR(SeminarID)
                                ON UPDATE NO ACTION
                                ON DELETE NO ACTION,
        CONSTRAINT          S_C_CUSTOMER_FK FOREIGN KEY(CustomerID)
                            REFERENCES CUSTOMER(CustomerID)
                                ON UPDATE NO ACTION
                                ON DELETE NO ACTION
        );

CREATE   TABLE CONTACT(
        CustomerID          Int              NOT NULL,
        ContactNumber       Int              NOT NULL,
        ContactDate         Date             NOT NULL,
        ContactType         VarChar(30)      NOT NULL,
        SeminarID           Int              NULL,
        CONSTRAINT          CONTACT_PK       PRIMARY KEY(CustomerID, ContactNumber),
        CONSTRAINT          CONTACT_ContactType
                            CHECK (ContactType IN ('Seminar',
                                'WebAccountCreation', 'WebPurchase',
                                'EmailAccountMessage', 'EmailSeminarMessage',
                                'EmailPurchaseMessage',
                                'EmailMessageExchange','FormLetterSeminar',
                                'PhoneConversation')),
        CONSTRAINT          CONTACT_SEMINAR_FK FOREIGN KEY(SeminarID)
                            REFERENCES SEMINAR(SeminarID)
                                ON UPDATE NO ACTION
                                ON DELETE NO ACTION,
```

FIGURE 3-28   Continued

```
        CONSTRAINT              CONTACT_CUSTOMER_FK FOREIGN KEY(CustomerID)
                                    REFERENCES CUSTOMER(CustomerID)
                                        ON UPDATE NO ACTION
                                        ON DELETE NO ACTION
        );

CREATE   TABLE PRODUCT(
        ProductNumber           Char(35)           NOT NULL,
        ProductType             Char(24)           NOT NULL,
        ProductDescription VarChar(100)            NOT NULL,
        UnitPrice               Numeric(9,2)       NOT NULL,
        QuantityOnHand          Int                NOT,
        CONSTRAINT              PRODUCT_PK          PRIMARY KEY(ProductNumber),
        CONSTRAINT              PRODUCT_ProductType
                                    CHECK (ProductType IN ('Video',
                                            'Video Companion', 'Book'))
        );

CREATE   TABLE INVOICE(
        InvoiceNumber           Int                NOT NULL IDENTITY (35000, 1),
        InvoiceDate             Date               NOT NULL,
        CustomerID              Int                NOT NULL,
        PaymentType             Char(25)           NOT NULL DEFAULT 'Cash',
        SubTotal                Numeric(9,2)       NULL,
        Shipping                Numeric(9,2)       NULL,
        Tax                     Numeric(9,2)       NULL,
        Total                   Numeric(9,2)       NULL,
        CONSTRAINT              INVOICE_PK         PRIMARY KEY (InvoiceNumber),
        CONSTRAINT              INVOICE_PaymentType
                                    CHECK (PaymentType IN ('VISA',
                                            'MasterCard', 'American Express',
                                            'PayPal', 'Check', 'Cash')),
        CONSTRAINT              INVOICE_CUSTOMER_FK FOREIGN KEY(CustomerID)
                                    REFERENCES CUSTOMER(CustomerID)
                                        ON UPDATE NO ACTION
                                        ON DELETE NO ACTION
        );

CREATE   TABLE LINE_ITEM(
        InvoiceNumber           Int                NOT NULL,
        LineNumber              Int                NOT NULL,
        ProductNumber           Char(35)           NOT NULL,
        Quantity                Int                NOT NULL,
        UnitPrice               Numeric(9,2)       NULL,
        Total                   Numeric(9,2)       NULL,
        CONSTRAINT              LINE_ITEM_PK       PRIMARY KEY (InvoiceNumber, LineNumber),
        CONSTRAINT              L_I_INVOICE_FK  FOREIGN KEY(InvoiceNumber)
                                    REFERENCES INVOICE(InvoiceNumber)
                                        ON UPDATE NO ACTION
                                        ON DELETE CASCADE,
        CONSTRAINT              L_I_PRODUCT_FK  FOREIGN KEY(ProductNumber)
                                    REFERENCES PRODUCT (ProductNumber)
                                        ON UPDATE CASCADE
                                        ON DELETE NO ACTION
        );
```

FIGURE 3-29

SQL Statements to Populate the HSD Database

```
/*****    CUSTOMER DATA    *******************************************************/
INSERT INTO CUSTOMER VALUES(
     'Jacobs', 'Nancy', 'Nancy.Jacobs@somewhere.com', 'nf46tG9E',
     '817-871-8123', '1440 West Palm Drive', 'Fort Worth', 'TX', '76110');
INSERT INTO CUSTOMER VALUES(
     'Jacobs', 'Chantel', 'Chantel.Jacobs@somewhere.com', 'b65TG03f',
     '817-871-8234',    '1550 East Palm Drive', 'Fort Worth', 'TX', '76112');
INSERT INTO CUSTOMER VALUES(
     'Able', 'Ralph', 'Ralph.Able@somewhere.com', 'm56fGH08',
     '210-281-7987', '123 Elm Street', 'San Antonio', 'TX', '78214');
INSERT INTO CUSTOMER VALUES(
     'Baker', 'Susan', 'Susan.Baker@elsewhere.com', 'PC93fEk9',
     '210-281-7876', '456 Oak Street', 'San Antonio', 'TX', '78216');
INSERT INTO CUSTOMER VALUES(
     'Eagleton', 'Sam', 'Sam.Eagleton@elsewhere.com', 'bnvR44W8',
     '210-281-7765', '789 Pine Street', 'San Antonio', 'TX', '78218');
INSERT INTO CUSTOMER VALUES(
     'Foxtrot', 'Kathy', 'Kathy.Foxtrot@somewhere.com', 'aa8tY4GL',
     '972-233-6234', '11023 Elm Street', 'Dallas', 'TX', '75220');
INSERT INTO CUSTOMER VALUES(
     'George', 'Sally', 'Sally.George@somewhere.com', 'LK8G2tyF',
     '972-233-6345', '12034 San Jacinto', 'Dallas', 'TX', '75223');
INSERT INTO CUSTOMER VALUES(
     'Hullett', 'Shawn', 'Shawn.Hullett@elsewhere.com', 'bu78WW3t',
     '972-233-6456', '13045 Flora', 'Dallas', 'TX', '75224');
INSERT INTO CUSTOMER VALUES(
     'Pearson', 'Bobbi', 'Bobbi.Pearson@elsewhere.com', 'kq6N2O0p',
     '512-974-3344', '43 West 23rd Street', 'Auston', 'TX', '78710');
INSERT INTO CUSTOMER VALUES(
     'Ranger', 'Terry', 'Terry.Ranger@somewhere.com', 'bv3F9Qc4',
     '512-974-4455', '56 East 18th Street', 'Auston', 'TX', '78712');
INSERT INTO CUSTOMER VALUES(
     'Tyler', 'Jenny', 'Jenny.Tyler@somewhere.com', 'Yu4be77Z',
     '972-233-6567', '14056 South Ervay Street', 'Dallas', 'TX', '75225');
INSERT INTO CUSTOMER VALUES(
     'Wayne', 'Joan', 'Joan.Wayne@elsewhere.com', 'JW4TX6g',
     '817-871-8245', '1660 South Aspen Drive', 'Fort Worth', 'TX', '76115');


/*****    SEMINAR    ************************************************************/
INSERT INTO SEMINAR VALUES(
     '12-OCT-2013', '11:00 AM', 'San Antonio Convention Center',
     'Kitchen on a Budget');
INSERT INTO SEMINAR VALUES(
     '26-OCT-2013', '04:00 PM', 'Dallas Convention Center',
     'Kitchen on a Big D Budget');
INSERT INTO SEMINAR VALUES(
     '02-NOV-2013', '08:30 AM', 'Austin Convention Center',
     'Kitchen on a Budget');
INSERT INTO SEMINAR VALUES(
     '22-MAR-2014', '11:00 AM', 'Dallas Convention Center',
     'Kitchen on a Big D Budget');
INSERT INTO SEMINAR VALUES(
     '23-MAR-2014', '11:00 AM', 'Dallas Convention Center',
     'Kitchen on a Big D Budget');
INSERT INTO SEMINAR VALUES(
     '05-APR-2014', '08:30 AM', 'Austin Convention Center',
     'Kitchen on a Budget');
```

FIGURE 3-29 Continued

```
/*****   SEMINAR_CUSTOMER DATA   **********************************************/

INSERT INTO SEMINAR_CUSTOMER VALUES(1, 1);
INSERT INTO SEMINAR_CUSTOMER VALUES(1, 2);
INSERT INTO SEMINAR_CUSTOMER VALUES(1, 3);
INSERT INTO SEMINAR_CUSTOMER VALUES(1, 4);
INSERT INTO SEMINAR_CUSTOMER VALUES(1, 5);
INSERT INTO SEMINAR_CUSTOMER VALUES(2, 6);
INSERT INTO SEMINAR_CUSTOMER VALUES(2, 7);
INSERT INTO SEMINAR_CUSTOMER VALUES(2, 8);
INSERT INTO SEMINAR_CUSTOMER VALUES(3, 9);
INSERT INTO SEMINAR_CUSTOMER VALUES(3, 10);
INSERT INTO SEMINAR_CUSTOMER VALUES(4, 6);
INSERT INTO SEMINAR_CUSTOMER VALUES(4, 7);
INSERT INTO SEMINAR_CUSTOMER VALUES(4, 11);
INSERT INTO SEMINAR_CUSTOMER VALUES(4, 12);


/*****   CONTACT DATA   ********************************************************/

INSERT INTO CONTACT VALUES(1, 1, '12-OCT-2013', 'Seminar', 1);
INSERT INTO CONTACT VALUES(2, 1, '12-OCT-2013', 'Seminar', 1);
INSERT INTO CONTACT VALUES(3, 1, '12-OCT-2013', 'Seminar', 1);
INSERT INTO CONTACT VALUES(4, 1, '12-OCT-2013', 'Seminar', 1);
INSERT INTO CONTACT VALUES(5, 1, '12-OCT-2013', 'Seminar', 1);

INSERT INTO CONTACT (CustomerID, ContactNumber, ContactDate,  ContactType)
     VALUES(1, 2, '15-OCT-2013', 'EmailSeminarMessage');
INSERT INTO CONTACT (CustomerID, ContactNumber, ContactDate,  ContactType)
     VALUES(2, 2, '15-OCT-2013', 'EmailSeminarMessage');
INSERT INTO CONTACT (CustomerID, ContactNumber, ContactDate,  ContactType)
     VALUES(3, 2, '15-OCT-2013', 'EmailSeminarMessage');
INSERT INTO CONTACT (CustomerID, ContactNumber, ContactDate,  ContactType)
     VALUES(4, 2, '15-OCT-2013', 'EmailSeminarMessage');
INSERT INTO CONTACT (CustomerID, ContactNumber, ContactDate,  ContactType)
     VALUES(5, 2, '15-OCT-2013', 'EmailSeminarMessage');

INSERT INTO CONTACT (CustomerID, ContactNumber, ContactDate,  ContactType)
     VALUES(1, 3, '15-OCT-2013', 'FormLetterSeminar');
INSERT INTO CONTACT (CustomerID, ContactNumber, ContactDate,  ContactType)
     VALUES(2, 3, '15-OCT-2013', 'FormLetterSeminar');
INSERT INTO CONTACT (CustomerID, ContactNumber, ContactDate,  ContactType)
     VALUES(3, 3, '15-OCT-2013', 'FormLetterSeminar');
INSERT INTO CONTACT (CustomerID, ContactNumber, ContactDate,  ContactType)
     VALUES(4, 3, '15-OCT-2013', 'FormLetterSeminar');
INSERT INTO CONTACT (CustomerID, ContactNumber, ContactDate,  ContactType)
     VALUES(5, 3, '15-OCT-2013', 'FormLetterSeminar');

INSERT INTO CONTACT VALUES(6, 1, '26-OCT-2013', 'Seminar', 2);
INSERT INTO CONTACT VALUES(7, 1, '26-OCT-2013', 'Seminar', 2);
INSERT INTO CONTACT VALUES(8, 1, '26-OCT-2013', 'Seminar', 2);
```

(continued)

FIGURE 3-29 **Continued**

```
INSERT INTO CONTACT (CustomerID, ContactNumber, ContactDate,  ContactType)
       VALUES(6, 2, '30-OCT-2013', 'EmailSeminarMessage');
INSERT INTO CONTACT (CustomerID, ContactNumber, ContactDate,  ContactType)
       VALUES(7, 2, '30-OCT-2013', 'EmailSeminarMessage');
INSERT INTO CONTACT (CustomerID, ContactNumber, ContactDate,  ContactType)
       VALUES(8, 2, '30-OCT-2013', 'EmailSeminarMessage');

INSERT INTO CONTACT (CustomerID, ContactNumber, ContactDate,  ContactType)
       VALUES(6, 3, '30-OCT-2013', 'FormLetterSeminar');
INSERT INTO CONTACT (CustomerID, ContactNumber, ContactDate,  ContactType)
       VALUES(7, 3, '30-OCT-2013', 'FormLetterSeminar');
INSERT INTO CONTACT (CustomerID, ContactNumber, ContactDate,  ContactType)
       VALUES(8, 3, '30-OCT-2013', 'FormLetterSeminar');

INSERT INTO CONTACT VALUES(9, 1, '02-NOV-2013', 'Seminar', 3);
INSERT INTO CONTACT VALUES(10, 1, '02-NOV-2013', 'Seminar', 3);

INSERT INTO CONTACT (CustomerID, ContactNumber, ContactDate,  ContactType)
       VALUES(9, 2, '06-NOV-2013', 'EmailSeminarMessage');
INSERT INTO CONTACT (CustomerID, ContactNumber, ContactDate,  ContactType)
       VALUES(10, 2, '06-NOV-2013', 'EmailSeminarMessage');

INSERT INTO CONTACT (CustomerID, ContactNumber, ContactDate,  ContactType)
       VALUES(9, 3, '06-NOV-2013', 'FormLetterSeminar');
INSERT INTO CONTACT (CustomerID, ContactNumber, ContactDate,  ContactType)
       VALUES(10, 3, '06-NOV-2013', 'FormLetterSeminar');

INSERT INTO CONTACT (CustomerID, ContactNumber, ContactDate,  ContactType)
       VALUES(3, 4, '20-FEB-2014', 'WebAccountCreation');
INSERT INTO CONTACT (CustomerID, ContactNumber, ContactDate,  ContactType)
       VALUES(3, 5, '20-FEB-2014', 'EmailAccountMessage');
INSERT INTO CONTACT (CustomerID, ContactNumber, ContactDate,  ContactType)
       VALUES(6, 4, '22-FEB-2014', 'WebAccountCreation');
INSERT INTO CONTACT (CustomerID, ContactNumber, ContactDate,  ContactType)
       VALUES(6, 5, '22-FEB-2014', 'EmailAccountMessage');
INSERT INTO CONTACT (CustomerID, ContactNumber, ContactDate,  ContactType)
       VALUES(7, 4, '25-FEB-2014', 'WebAccountCreation');
INSERT INTO CONTACT (CustomerID, ContactNumber, ContactDate,  ContactType)
       VALUES(7, 5, '25-FEB-2014', 'EmailAccountMessage');
INSERT INTO CONTACT (CustomerID, ContactNumber, ContactDate,  ContactType)
       VALUES(8, 4, '07-MAR-2014', 'WebAccountCreation');
INSERT INTO CONTACT (CustomerID, ContactNumber, ContactDate,  ContactType)
       VALUES(8, 5, '07-MAR-2014', 'EmailAccountMessage');


INSERT INTO CONTACT VALUES(6, 6, '22-MAR-2014', 'Seminar', 4);
INSERT INTO CONTACT VALUES(7, 6, '22-MAR-2014', 'Seminar', 4);
INSERT INTO CONTACT VALUES(11, 1, '22-MAR-2014', 'Seminar', 4);
INSERT INTO CONTACT VALUES(12, 1, '22-MAR-2014', 'Seminar', 4);

/*****    PRODUCT DATA    ************************************************************/

INSERT INTO PRODUCT VALUES(
       'VK001', 'Video', 'Kitchen Remodeling Basics',14.95, 50);
INSERT INTO PRODUCT VALUES(
       'VK002', 'Video', 'Advanced Kitchen Remodeling', 14.95, 35);
INSERT INTO PRODUCT VALUES(
       'VK003', 'Video', 'Kitchen Remodeling Dallas Style', 19.95, 25);
```

FIGURE 3-29   Continued

```
INSERT INTO PRODUCT VALUES(
      'VK004', 'Video', 'Heather Sweeney Seminar Live in Dallas on 25-OCT-13',
      24.95, 20);
INSERT INTO PRODUCT VALUES(
      'VB001', 'Video Companion', 'Kitchen Remodeling Basics', 7.99, 50);
INSERT INTO PRODUCT VALUES(
      'VB002', 'Video Companion', 'Advanced Kitchen Remodeling I',7.99, 35);
INSERT INTO PRODUCT VALUES(
      'VB003', 'Video Companion', 'Kitchen Remodeling Dallas Style', 9.99, 25);
INSERT INTO PRODUCT VALUES(
      'BK001', 'Book', 'Kitchen Remodeling Basics For Everyone', 24.95, 75);
INSERT INTO PRODUCT VALUES(
      'BK002', 'Book', 'Advanced Kitchen Remodeling For Everyone', 24.95, 75);
INSERT INTO PRODUCT VALUES(
      'BK003', 'Book', 'Kitchen Remodeling Dallas Style For Everyone',
      24.95, 75);


/*****    INVOICE DATA    ****************************************************/

/*****    Invoice 35000   ****************************************************/
INSERT INTO INVOICE VALUES(
      '15-Oct-13', 3, 'VISA', 22.94, 5.95, 1.31, 30.20);
INSERT INTO LINE_ITEM VALUES(35000, 1, 'VK001', 1, 14.95, 14.95);
INSERT INTO LINE_ITEM VALUES(35000, 2, 'VB001', 1, 7.99, 7.99);


/*****    Invoice 35001   ****************************************************/
INSERT INTO INVOICE VALUES(
      '25-Oct-13', 4, 'MasterCard', 47.89, 5.95, 2.73, 56.57);
INSERT INTO LINE_ITEM VALUES(35001, 1, 'VK001', 1, 14.95, 14.95);
INSERT INTO LINE_ITEM VALUES(35001, 2, 'VB001', 1, 7.99, 7.99);
INSERT INTO LINE_ITEM VALUES(35001, 3, 'BK001', 1, 24.95, 24.95);


/*****    Invoice 35002   ****************************************************/
INSERT INTO INVOICE VALUES(
      '20-Dec-13', 7, 'VISA', 24.95, 5.95, 1.42, 32.32);
INSERT INTO LINE_ITEM VALUES(35002, 1, 'VK004', 1, 24.95, 24.95);


/*****    Invoice 35003   ****************************************************/
INSERT INTO INVOICE VALUES(
      '25-Mar-14', 4, 'MasterCard', 64.85, 5.95, 3.70, 74.50);
INSERT INTO LINE_ITEM VALUES(35003, 1, 'VK002', 1, 14.95, 14.95);
INSERT INTO LINE_ITEM VALUES(35003, 2, 'BK002', 1, 24.95, 24.95);
INSERT INTO LINE_ITEM VALUES(35003, 3, 'VK004', 1, 24.95, 24.95);


/*****    Invoice 35004   ****************************************************/
INSERT INTO INVOICE VALUES(
      '27-Mar-14', 6, 'MasterCard', 94.79, 5.95, 5.40, 106.14);
INSERT INTO LINE_ITEM VALUES(35004, 1, 'VK002', 1, 14.95, 14.95);
INSERT INTO LINE_ITEM VALUES(35004, 2, 'BK002', 1, 24.95, 24.95);
INSERT INTO LINE_ITEM VALUES(35004, 3, 'VK003', 1, 19.95, 19.95);
INSERT INTO LINE_ITEM VALUES(35004, 4, 'VB003', 1, 9.99, 9.99);
INSERT INTO LINE_ITEM VALUES(35004, 5, 'VK004', 1, 24.95, 24.95);
```

(continued)

FIGURE 3-29 **Continued**

```
/*****   Invoice 35005    ***************************************************/
INSERT INTO INVOICE VALUES(
     '27-Mar-14', 7, 'MasterCard', 94.80, 5.95, 5.40, 106.15);
INSERT INTO LINE_ITEM VALUES(35005, 1, 'BK001', 1, 24.95, 24.95);
INSERT INTO LINE_ITEM VALUES(35005, 2, 'BK002', 1, 24.95, 24.95);
INSERT INTO LINE_ITEM VALUES(35005, 3, 'VK003', 1, 19.95, 19.95);
INSERT INTO LINE_ITEM VALUES(35005, 4, 'VK004', 1, 24.95, 24.95);

/*****   Invoice 35006    ***************************************************/
INSERT INTO INVOICE VALUES(
     '31-Mar-14', 9, 'VISA', 47.89, 5.95, 2.73, 56.57);
INSERT INTO LINE_ITEM VALUES(35006, 1, 'BK001', 1, 24.95, 24.95);
INSERT INTO LINE_ITEM VALUES(35006, 2, 'VK001', 1, 14.95, 14.95);
INSERT INTO LINE_ITEM VALUES(35006, 3, 'VB001', 1, 7.99, 7.99);


/*****   Invoice 35007    ***************************************************/
INSERT INTO INVOICE VALUES(
     '03-Apr-14', 11, 'MasterCard', 109.78, 5.95, 6.26, 121.99);
INSERT INTO LINE_ITEM VALUES(35007, 1, 'VK003', 2, 19.95, 39.90);
INSERT INTO LINE_ITEM VALUES(35007, 2, 'VB003', 2, 9.99, 19.98);
INSERT INTO LINE_ITEM VALUES(35007, 3, 'VK004', 2, 24.95, 49.90);

/*****   Invoice 35008    ***************************************************/
INSERT INTO INVOICE VALUES(
     '08-Apr-14', 5, 'MasterCard', 47.89, 5.95, 2.73, 56.57);
INSERT INTO LINE_ITEM VALUES(35008, 1, 'BK001', 1, 24.95, 24.95);
INSERT INTO LINE_ITEM VALUES(35008, 2, 'VK001', 1, 14.95, 14.95);
INSERT INTO LINE_ITEM VALUES(35008, 3, 'VB001', 1, 7.99, 7.99);

/*****   Invoice 35009    ***************************************************/
INSERT INTO INVOICE VALUES(
     '08-Apr-14', 1, 'VISA', 47.89, 5.95, 2.73, 56.57);
INSERT INTO LINE_ITEM VALUES(35009, 1, 'BK001', 1, 24.95, 24.95);
INSERT INTO LINE_ITEM VALUES(35009, 2, 'VK001', 1, 14.95, 14.95);
INSERT INTO LINE_ITEM VALUES(35009, 3, 'VB001', 1, 7.99, 7.99);

/*****   Invoice 35010    ***************************************************/
INSERT INTO INVOICE VALUES(
     '23-Apr-14', 3, 'VISA', 24.95, 5.95, 1.42, 32.32);
INSERT INTO LINE_ITEM VALUES(35010, 1, 'BK001', 1, 24.95, 24.95);

/*****   Invoice 35011    ***************************************************/
INSERT INTO INVOICE VALUES(
     '07-May-14', 9, 'VISA', 22.94, 5.95, 1.31, 30.20);
INSERT INTO LINE_ITEM VALUES(35011, 1, 'VK002', 1, 14.95, 14.95);
INSERT INTO LINE_ITEM VALUES(35011, 2, 'VB002', 1, 7.99, 7.99);

/*****   Invoice 35012    ***************************************************/
INSERT INTO INVOICE VALUES(
     '21-May-14', 8, 'MasterCard', 54.89, 5.95, 3.13, 63.97);
INSERT INTO LINE_ITEM VALUES(35012, 1, 'VK003', 1, 19.95, 19.95);
INSERT INTO LINE_ITEM VALUES(35012, 2, 'VB003', 1, 9.99, 9.99);
INSERT INTO LINE_ITEM VALUES(35012, 3, 'VK004', 1, 24.95, 24.95);
```

FIGURE 3-29 **Continued**

```
/*****    Invoice 35013    ****************************************************/
INSERT INTO INVOICE VALUES(
     '05-Jun-14', 3, 'VISA', 47.89, 5.95, 2.73, 56.57);
INSERT INTO LINE_ITEM VALUES(35013, 1, 'VK002', 1, 14.95, 14.95);
INSERT INTO LINE_ITEM VALUES(35013, 2, 'VB002', 1, 7.99, 7.99);
INSERT INTO LINE_ITEM VALUES(35013, 3, 'BK002', 1, 24.95, 24.95);

/*****    Invoice 35014    ****************************************************/
INSERT INTO INVOICE VALUES(
     '05-Jun-14', 11, 'MasterCard', 45.88, 5.95, 2.62, 54.45);
INSERT INTO LINE_ITEM VALUES(35014, 1, 'VK002', 2, 14.95, 29.90);
INSERT INTO LINE_ITEM VALUES(35014, 2, 'VB002', 2, 7.99, 15.98);

/*****    Invoice 35015    ****************************************************/
INSERT INTO INVOICE VALUES(
     '05-Jun-14', 12, 'MasterCard', 94.79, 5.95, 5.40, 106.14);
INSERT INTO LINE_ITEM VALUES(35015, 1, 'VK002', 1, 14.95, 14.95);
INSERT INTO LINE_ITEM VALUES(35015, 2, 'BK002', 1, 24.95, 24.95);
INSERT INTO LINE_ITEM VALUES(35015, 3, 'VK003', 1, 19.95, 19.95);
INSERT INTO LINE_ITEM VALUES(35015, 4, 'VB003', 1, 9.99, 9.99);
INSERT INTO LINE_ITEM VALUES(35015, 5, 'VK004', 1, 24.95, 24.95);

/*****    Invoice 35016    ****************************************************/
INSERT INTO INVOICE VALUES(
     '05-Jun-14', 3, 'VISA', 45.88, 5.95, 2.62, 54.45);
INSERT INTO LINE_ITEM VALUES(35016, 1, 'VK001', 1, 14.95, 14.95);
INSERT INTO LINE_ITEM VALUES(35016, 2, 'VB001', 1, 7.99, 7.99);
INSERT INTO LINE_ITEM VALUES(35016, 3, 'VK002', 1, 14.95, 14.95);
INSERT INTO LINE_ITEM VALUES(35016, 4, 'VB002', 1, 7.99, 7.99);

/************************************************************************************/
```

once) who have purchased a video product. Sort the results by LastName in descending order, then by FirstName in descending order, and then by ProductNumber in descending order. (*Hint:* Video products have a ProductNumber that starts with *VK*.)

K. Write an SQL statement to show all Heather Sweeney Designs seminars and the customers that attended them. The output from this statement should include any seminars that do not have any customers shown as attending them. The SQL statement output should list SeminarID, SeminarDate, Location, SeminarTitle, CustomerID, LastName, and FirstName. (*Hint:* Use JOIN ON syntax.)

L. Write an SQL statement to show all customers and the products that they have purchased. The output from this statement should include any products that have not been purchased by any customer. The SQL statement output should list CustomerID, LastName, FirstName, InvoiceNumber, ProductNumber, ProductType, and ProductDescription. (*Hint:* Use JOIN ON syntax.)

M. Write an SQL statement to show the sum of Subtotal (this is the money earned by HSD on products sold exclusive of shipping costs and taxes) for INVOICE as SumOfSubTotal.

N. Write an SQL statement to show the average of Subtotal (this is the money earned by HSD on products sold exclusive of shipping costs and taxes) for INVOICE as AverageOfSubTotal.

O. Write an SQL statement to show both the sum and the average of Subtotal (this is the money earned by HSD on products sold exclusive of shipping costs and taxes) for INVOICE as SumOfSubTotal and AverageOfSubTotal respectively.

P. Write an SQL statement to modify PRODUCT UnitPrice for ProductNumber VK004 to $34.95 instead of the current UnitPrice of $24.95.

Q. Write an SQL statement to undo the UnitPrice modification in part P.

R. *Do not run your answer to the following question in your actual database!* Write the fewest number of DELETE statements possible to remove all the data in your database but leave the table structures intact.

✳ GARDEN GLORY PROJECT QUESTIONS

Assume that Garden Glory designs a database with the following tables:

OWNER (OwnerID, OwnerName, OwnerEmail, OwnerType)

OWNED_PROPERTY (PropertyID, PropertyName, PropertyType, Street, City, State, Zip, *OwnerID*)

GG_SERVICE (ServiceID, ServiceDescription, CostPerHour);

EMPLOYEE (EmployeeID, LastName, FirstName, CellPhone, ExperienceLevel)

PROPERTY_SERVICE (PropertyServiceID, *PropertyID*, *ServiceID*, ServiceDate, *EmployeeID*, HoursWorked)

The referential integrity constraints are:

OwnerID in OWNED_PROPERTY must exist in OwnerID in OWNER

PropertyID in PROPERTY_SERVICE must exist in PropertyID in OWNED_PROPERTY

ServiceID in PROPERTY_SERVICE must exist in ServiceID in GG_SERVICE

EmployeeID in PROPERTY_SERVICE must exist in EmployeeID in EMPLOYEE

Assume that OwnerID in OWNER, PropertyID in PROPERTY, and EmployeeID in EMPLOYEE are surrogate keys with values as follows:

OwnerID	Start at 1	Increment by 1
PropertyID	Start at 1	Increment by 1
ServiceID	Start at 1	Increment by 1
EmployeeID	Start at 1	Increment by 1
PropertyServiceID	Start at 1	Increment by 1

Sample data are shown in Figures 3-30, 3-31, 3-32, 3-33, and 3-34. OwnerType is either Individual or Corporation, PropertyType is Office, Apartments, or Private Residence, and ExperienceLevel is one of Junior, Senior, or Master. These tables, referential integrity constraints, and data are used as the basis for the SQL statements you will create in the exercises that follow. If possible, run these statements in an actual DBMS, as appropriate, to obtain your results. Name your database GARDEN_GLORY.

Use data types consistent with the DBMS you are using. If you are not using an actual DBMS, consistently represent data types using either the SQL Server, Oracle Database,

FIGURE 3-30

Sample Data for the Garden Glory OWNER Table

OwnerID	OwnerName	OwnerEmail	OwnerType
1	Mary Jones	Mary.Jones@somewhere.com	Individual
2	DT Enterprises	DTE@dte.com	Corporation
3	Sam Douglas	Sam.Douglas@somewhere.com	Individual
4	UNY Enterprises	UNYE@unye.com	Corporation
5	Doug Samuels	Doug.Samuels@somewhere.com	Individual

FIGURE 3-31

Sample Data for the Garden Glory OWNED_PROPERTY Table

PropertyID	PropertyName	PropertyType	Street	City	State	ZIP	OwnerID
1	Eastlake Building	Office	123 Eastlake	Seattle	WA	98119	2
2	Elm St Apts	Apartments	4 East Elm	Lynwood	WA	98223	1
3	Jefferson Hill	Office	42 West 7th St	Bellevue	WA	98007	2
4	Lake View Apts	Apartments	1265 32nd Avenue	Redmond	WA	98052	3
5	Kodak Heights Apts	Apartments	65 32nd Avenue	Redmond	WA	98052	4
6	Jones House	Private Residence	1456 48th St	Bellevue	WA	98007	1
7	Douglas House	Private Residence	1567 51st St	Bellevue	WA	98007	3
8	Samuels House	Private Residence	567 151st St	Redmond	WA	98052	5

or MySQL data types shown in Figure 3-5. For each SQL statement you write, show the results based on your data.

Write SQL statements and answer questions for this database as follows:

A. Write CREATE TABLE statements for each of these tables.

B. Write foreign key constraints for the relationships in each of these tables. Make your own assumptions regarding cascading updates and deletions and justify those assumptions. (*Hint:* You can combine the SQL for your answers to questions A and B.)

FIGURE 3-32

Sample Data for the Garden Glory EMPLOYEE Table

EmployeeID	LastName	FirstName	CellPhone	ExperienceLevel
1	Smith	Sam	206-254-1234	Master
2	Evanston	John	206-254-2345	Senior
3	Murray	Dale	206-254-3456	Junior
4	Murphy	Jerry	585-545-8765	Master
5	Fontaine	Joan	206-254-4567	Senior

FIGURE 3-33

Sample Data for the Garden Glory GG_SERVICE Table

ServiceID	ServiceDescription	CostPerHour
1	Mow Lawn	25.00
2	Plant Annuals	25.00
3	Weed Garden	30.00
4	Trim Hedge	45.00
5	Prune Small Tree	60.00
6	Trim Medium Tree	100.00
7	Trim Large Tree	125.00

FIGURE 3-34

Sample Data for the Garden Glory PROPERTY_SERVICE Table

PropertyServiceID	PropertyID	ServiceID	ServiceDate	EmployeeID	HoursWorked
1	1	2	2014-05-05	1	4.50
2	3	2	2014-05-08	3	4.50
3	2	1	2014-05-08	2	2.75
4	6	1	2014-05-10	5	2.50
5	5	4	2014-05-12	4	7.50
6	8	1	2014-05-15	4	2.75
7	4	4	2014-05-19	1	1.00
8	7	1	2014-05-21	2	2.50
9	6	3	2014-06-03	5	2.50
10	5	7	2014-06-08	4	10.50
11	8	3	2014-06-12	4	2.75
12	4	5	2014-06-15	1	5.00
13	7	3	2014-06-19	2	4.00

C. Write SQL statements to insert the data into each of the five Garden Glory database tables. Assume that any surrogate key value will be supplied by the DBMS. Use the data in Figures 3-30, 3-31, 3-32, 3-33, and 3-34.

D. Write SQL statements to list all columns for all tables.

E. Write an SQL statement to list LastName, FirstName, and CellPhone for all employees having an experience level of Master.

F. Write an SQL statement to list Name and CellPhone for all employees having an experience level of Master and Name that begins with the letter *J*.

G. Write an SQL statement to list the names of employees who have worked on a property in Seattle. Use a subquery.

H. Answer question G but use a join using JOIN ON syntax.

I. Write an SQL statement to list the names of employees who have worked on a property owned by a corporation. Use a subquery.

J. Answer question I but use a join using JOIN ON syntax.

K. Write an SQL statement to show the name and sum of hours worked for each employee.

L. Write an SQL statement to show the sum of hours worked for each ExperienceLevel of EMPLOYEE. Sort the results by ExperienceLevel, in descending order.

M. Write an SQL statement to show the sum of HoursWorked for each type of OWNER but exclude services of employees who have ExperienceLevel of Junior.

N. Write an SQL statement to show all properties and the services performed at those properties. The output from this statement should include any *properties* that have not had any service performed at them. The SQL statement output should list PropertyID, PropertyName, PropertyType, PropertyServiceID, ServiceID, ServiceDate, and ServiceDescription. (*Hint:* Use JOIN ON syntax.)

O. Write an SQL statement to show all properties and the services performed at those properties. The output from this statement should include any *Garden Glory services* that have not been performed at any property. The SQL statement output should list PropertyID, PropertyName, PropertyType, PropertyServiceID, ServiceID, ServiceDate, and ServiceDescription. (*Hint:* Use JOIN ON syntax.)

P. Write an SQL statement to modify all EMPLOYEE rows with ExperienceLevel of Master to SuperMaster.

Q. Write an SQL statement to switch the values of ExperienceLevel so that all rows currently having the value Junior will have the value Senior and all rows currently having the value Senior will have the value Junior.

R. Given your assumptions about cascading deletions in your answer to question B, write the fewest number of DELETE statements possible to remove all the data in your database but leave the table structures intact. Do *not* run these statements if you are using an actual database!

JAMES RIVER JEWELRY PROJECT QUESTIONS

The James River Jewelry project questions are available in online Appendix D, which can be download from the textbook's Web site: **www.pearsonhighered.com/kroenke**.

THE QUEEN ANNE CURIOSITY SHOP PROJECT QUESTIONS

Assume that The Queen Anne Curiosity Shop designs a database with the following tables:

CUSTOMER (<u>CustomerID</u>, LastName, FirstName, Address, City, State, ZIP, Phone, Email)

EMPLOYEE (<u>EmployeeID</u>, LastName, FirstName, Phone, Email)

VENDOR (<u>VendorID</u>, CompanyName, ContactLastName, ContactFirstName, Address, City, State, ZIP, Phone, Fax, Email)

ITEM (<u>ItemID</u>, ItemDescription, PurchaseDate, ItemCost, ItemPrice, *VendorID*)

SALE (<u>SaleID</u>, *CustomerID*, *EmployeeID*, SaleDate, SubTotal, Tax, Total)

SALE_ITEM (<u>*SaleID*</u>, <u>SaleItemID</u>, *ItemID*, ItemPrice)

The referential integrity constraints are:

VendorID in ITEM must exist in VendorID in VENDOR

CustomerID in SALE must exist in CustomerID in CUSTOMER

EmployeeID in SALE must exist in EmployeeID in EMPLOYEE

SaleID in SALE_ITEM must exist in SaleID in SALE

ItemID in SALE_ITEM must exist in ItemID in ITEM

Assume that CustomerID of CUSTOMER, EmployeeID of EMPLOYEE, ItemID of ITEM, SaleID of SALE, and SaleItemID of SALE_ITEM are all surrogate keys with values as follows:

CustomerID	Start at 1	Increment by 1
EmployeeID	Start at 1	Increment by 1
VendorID	Start at 1	Increment by 1
ItemID	Start at 1	Increment by 1
SaleID	Start at 1	Increment by 1

A vendor may be an individual or a company. If the vendor is an individual, the CompanyName field is left blank, while the ContactLastName and ContactFirstName fields must have data values. If the vendor is a company, the company name is recorded in the CompanyName field, and the name of the primary contact at the company is recorded in the ContactLastName and ContactFirstName fields.

Sample data are shown in Figures 3-35, 3-36, 3-37, 3-38, 3-39, and 3-40. These tables, referential integrity constraints, and data are used as the basis for the SQL statements you will create in the exercises that follow. If possible, run these statements in an actual DBMS, as appropriate, to obtain your results. Name your database QACS.

Use data types consistent with the DBMS you are using. If you are not using an actual DBMS, consistently represent data types using either the SQL Server, Oracle Database, or MySQL data types shown in Figure 3-5. For each SQL statement you write, show the results based on your data.

Write SQL statements and answer questions for this database as follows:

A.   Write SQL CREATE TABLE statements for each of these tables.

B.   Write foreign key constraints for the relationships in each of these tables. Make your own assumptions regarding cascading deletions and justify those assumptions. (*Hint:* You can combine the SQL for your answers to parts A and B.)

FIGURE 3-35

Sample Data for the QACS CUSTOMER Table

CustomerID	LastName	FirstName	Address	City	State	ZIP	Phone	Email
1	Shire	Robert	6225 Evanston Ave N	Seattle	WA	98103	206-524-2433	Robert.Shire@somewhere.com
2	Goodyear	Katherine	7335 11th Ave NE	Seattle	WA	98105	206-524-3544	Katherine.Goodyear@somewhere.com
3	Bancroft	Chris	12605 NE 6th Street	Bellevue	WA	98005	425-635-9788	Chris.Bancroft@somewhere.com
4	Griffith	John	335 Aloha Street	Seattle	WA	98109	206-524-4655	John.Griffith@somewhere.com
5	Tiemey	Doris	14510 NE 4th Street	Bellevue	WA	98005	425-635-8677	Doris.Tiemey@somewhere.com
6	Anderson	Donna	1410 Hillcrest Parkway	Mt. Vemon	WA	98273	360-538-7566	Donna.Anderson@elsewhere.com
7	Svane	Jack	3211 42nd Street	Seattle	WA	98115	206-524-5766	Jack.Svane@somewhere.com
8	Walsh	Denesha	6712 24th Avenue NE	Redmond	WA	98053	425-635-7566	Denesha.Walsh@somewhere.com
9	Enquist	Craig	534 15th Street	Bellingham	WA	98225	360-538-6455	Craig.Enquist@elsewhere.com
10	Anderson	Rose	6823 17th Ave NE	Seattle	WA	98105	206-524-6877	Rose.Anderson@elsewhere.com

FIGURE 3-36

Sample Data for the QACS EMPLOYEE Table

EmployeeID	LastName	FirstName	Phone	Email
1	Stuart	Anne	206-527-0010	Anne.Stuart@QACS.com
2	Stuart	George	206-527-0011	George.Stuart@QACS.com
3	Stuart	Mary	206-527-0012	Mary.Stuart@QACS.com
4	Orange	William	206-527-0013	William.Orange@QACS.com
5	Griffith	John	206-527-0014	John.Griffith@QACS.com

C. Write SQL statements to insert the data into each of these tables. Assume that all surrogate key column values will be supplied by the DBMS. Use the data in Figures 3-35, 3-36, 3-37, 3-38, 3-39, and 3-40.

D. Write SQL statements to list all columns for all tables.

E. Write an SQL statement to list ItemID and ItemDescription for all items that cost $1000 or more.

F. Write an SQL statement to list ItemNumber and Description for all items that cost $1000 or more and were purchased from a vendor whose CompanyName starts with the letters *New*.

G. Write an SQL statement to list LastName, FirstName, and Phone of the customer who made the purchase with SaleID 1. Use a subquery.

H. Answer part G but use a join using JOIN ON syntax.

I. Write an SQL statement to list LastName, FirstName, and Phone of the customers who made the purchase with SaleIDs 1, 2, and 3. Use a subquery.

J. Answer part I but use a join using JOIN ON syntax.

K. Write an SQL statement to list LastName, FirstName, and Phone of customers who have made at least one purchase with SubTotal greater than $500. Use a subquery.

L. Answer part K but use a join using JOIN ON syntax.

M. Write an SQL statement to list LastName, FirstName, and Phone of customers who have purchased an item that has an ItemPrice of $500 or more. Use a subquery.

N. Answer part M but use a join using JOIN ON syntax.

O. Write an SQL statement to list LastName, FirstName, and Phone of customers who have purchased an item that was supplied by a vendor with a CompanyName that begins with the letter *L*. Use a subquery.

P. Write an SQL statement to show all customers and the items these customers have purchased. The output from this statement should include any *items* (if any) that have not been purchased by a customer. The SQL statement output should list CustomerID, LastName, FirstName, SaleID, SaleItemID, and ItemDescription. (*Hint:* Use JOIN ON syntax.)

FIGURE 3-37

Sample Data for the QACS VENDOR Table

VendorID	CompanyName	ContactLastName	ContactFirstName	Address	City	State	ZIP	Phone	Fax	Email
1	Linens and Things	Huntington	Anne	1515 NW Market Street	Seattle	WA	98107	206-325-6755	206-329-9675	LAT@business.com
2	European Specialties	Tadema	Ken	6123 15th Avenue NW	Seattle	WA	98107	206-325-7866	206-329-9786	ES@business.com
3	Lamps and Lighting	Swanson	Sally	506 Prospect Street	Seattle	WA	98109	206-325-8977	206-329-9897	LAL@business.com
4	NULL	Lee	Andrew	1102 3rd Street	Kirkland	WA	98033	425-746-5433	NULL	Andrew.Lee@somewhere.com
5	NULL	Hamison	Denise	533 10th Avenue	Kirkland	WA	98033	425-746-4322	NULL	Denise.Hamison@somewhere.com
6	New York Brokerage	Smith	Mark	621 Roy Street	Seattle	WA	98109	206-325-9088	206-329-9908	NYB@business.com
7	NULL	Walsh	Denesha	6712 24th Avenue NE	Redmond	WA	98053	425-635-7566	NULL	Denesha.Walsh@somewhere.com
8	NULL	Bancroft	Chris	12605 NE 6th Street	Bellevue	WA	98005	425-635-9788	425-639-9978	Chris.Bancroft@somewhere.com
9	Specialty Antiques	Nelson	Fred	2512 Lucky Street	San Francisco	CA	94110	415-422-2121	415-423-5212	SA@business.com
10	General Antiques	Gamer	Patty	2515 Lucky Street	San Francisco	CA	94110	415-422-3232	415-429-9323	GA@business.com

FIGURE 3-38

Sample Data for the QACS ITEM Table

ItemID	ItemDescription	PurchaseDate	ItemCost	ItemPrice	VendorID
1	Antique Desk	2013-11-07	$1,800.00	$3,000.00	2
2	Antique Desk Chair	2013-11-10	$300.00	$500.00	4
3	Dining Table Linens	2013-11-14	$600.00	$1,000.00	1
4	Candles	2013-11-14	$30.00	$50.00	1
5	Candles	2013-11-14	$27.00	$45.00	1
6	Desk Lamp	2013-11-14	$150.00	$250.00	3
7	Dining Table Linens	2013-11-14	$450.00	$750.00	1
8	Book Shelf	2013-11-21	$150.00	$250.00	5
9	Antique Chair	2013-11-21	$750.00	$1,250.00	6
10	Antique Chair	2013-11-21	$1,050.00	$1,750.00	6
11	Antique Candle Holders	2013-11-28	$210.00	$350.00	2
12	Antique Desk	2014-01-05	$1,920.00	$3,200.00	2
13	Antique Desk	2014-01-05	$2,100.00	$3,500.00	2
14	Antique Desk Chair	2014-01-06	$285.00	$475.00	9
15	Antique Desk Chair	2014-01-06	$339.00	$565.00	9
16	Desk Lamp	2014-01-06	$150.00	$250.00	10
17	Desk Lamp	2014-01-06	$150.00	$250.00	10
18	Desk Lamp	2014-01-06	$144.00	$240.00	3
19	Antique Dining Table	2014-01-10	$3,000.00	$5,000.00	7
20	Antique Sideboard	2014-01-11	$2,700.00	$4,500.00	8
21	Dining Table Chairs	2014-01-11	$5,100.00	$8,500.00	9
22	Dining Table Linens	2014-01-12	$450.00	$750.00	1
23	Dining Table Linens	2014-01-12	$480.00	$800.00	1
24	Candles	2014-01-17	$30.00	$50.00	1
25	Candles	2014-01-17	$36.00	$60.00	1

Q. Write an SQL statement to show all customers and the items these customers have purchased. The output from this statement should include any *customers* (if any) that have not purchased any item. The SQL statement output should list CustomerID, LastName, FirstName, SaleID, SaleItemID, and ItemDescription. (*Hint:* Use JOIN ON syntax.)

R. Answer part O but use a join using JOIN ON syntax.

S. Write an SQL statement to show the sum of SubTotal for each customer. List CustomerID, LastName, FirstName, Phone, and the calculated result. Name the sum of SubTotal as SumOfSubTotal and sort the results by CustomerID, in descending order.

FIGURE 3-39

Sample Data for the QACS SALE Table

	SaleID	CustomerID	EmployeeID	SaleDate	SubTotal	Tax	Total
1	1	1	1	2013-12-14	$3,500.00	$290.50	$3,790.50
2	2	2	1	2013-12-15	$1,000.00	$83.00	$1,083.00
3	3	3	1	2013-12-15	$50.00	$4.15	$54.15
4	4	4	3	2013-12-23	$45.00	$3.74	$48.74
5	5	1	5	2014-01-05	$250.00	$20.75	$270.75
6	6	5	5	2014-01-10	$750.00	$62.25	$812.25
7	7	6	4	2014-01-12	$250.00	$20.75	$270.75
8	8	2	1	2014-01-15	$3,000.00	$249.00	$3,249.00
9	9	5	5	2014-01-25	$350.00	$29.05	$379.05
10	10	7	1	2014-02-04	$14,250.00	$1,182.75	$15,432.75
11	11	8	5	2014-02-04	$250.00	$20.75	$270.75
12	12	5	4	2014-02-07	$50.00	$4.15	$54.15
13	13	9	2	2014-02-07	$4,500.00	$373.50	$4,873.50
14	14	10	3	2014-02-11	$3,675.00	$305.03	$3,980.03
15	15	2	2	2014-02-11	$800.00	$66.40	$866.40

T. Write an SQL statement to modify the vendor with CompanyName of *Linens and Things* to *Linens and Other Stuff.*

U. Write SQL statements to switch the values of vendor CompanyName so that all rows currently having the value *Linens and Things* will have the value *Lamps and Lighting* and all rows currently having the value *Lamps and Lighting* will have the value *Linens and Things.*

V. Given your assumptions about cascading deletions in your answer to part B, write the fewest number of DELETE statements possible to remove all the data in your database but leave the table structures intact. Do *not* run these statements if you are using an actual database!

FIGURE 3-40

Sample Data for the QACS SALE_ITEM Table

SaleID	SaleItemID	ItemID	ItemPrice
1	1	1	$3,000.00
1	2	2	$500.00
2	1	3	$1,000.00
3	1	4	$50.00
4	1	5	$45.00
5	1	6	$250.00
6	1	7	$750.00
7	1	8	$250.00
8	1	9	$1,250.00
8	2	10	$1,750.00
9	1	11	$350.00
10	1	19	$5,000.00
10	2	21	$8,500.00
10	3	22	$750.00
11	1	17	$250.00
12	1	24	$50.00
13	1	20	$4,500.00
14	1	12	$3,200.00
14	2	14	$475.00
15	1	23	$800.00

PART 2 Database Design

I n Part I, you were introduced to the fundamental concepts and techniques of relational database management. In Chapter 1, you learned that databases consist of related tables, and you learned the major components of a database system. Chapter 2 introduced you to the relational model, and you learned the basic ideas of functional dependencies and normalization. In Chapter 3, you learned how to use SQL statements to create and process a database.

All the material you have learned so far gives you a background for understanding the nature of database management and the required basic tools and techniques. However, you do not yet know how to apply all this technology to solve a business problem. Imagine, for example, that you walk into a small business—for example, a bookshop—and are asked to build a database to support a frequent buyer program. How would you proceed? So far, we have assumed that the database design already exists. How would you go about creating the design of the database?

The next two chapters address this important topic. We begin Chapter 4 with an overview of the database design process and then we describe data modeling: a technique for representing database requirements. In Chapter 5, you will learn how to transform a data model into a relational database design. After that database design is complete, it will be implemented in a DBMS using the SQL statements we previously discussed in Chapter 3. You will learn about managing and using the implemented database in Part III.

Note the dual use of the term *database design*. We speak of database design as a process—the *database design process*—that results in a final product—the *database design*—that is the plan for actually building the database in a DBMS. The overall topic of Part 2 is database design as a process, and the topic of Chapter 5 is the database design as the final plan for the database.

CHAPTER 4

Data Modeling and the Entity-Relationship Model

CHAPTER OBJECTIVES

- Learn the basic stages of database development

- Understand the purpose and role of a data model

- Know the principal components of the E-R data model

- Understand how to interpret traditional E-R diagrams

- Understand how to interpret the Information Engineering (IE) model's Crow's Foot E-R diagrams

- Learn to construct E-R diagrams

- Know how to represent 1:1, 1:N, N:M, and binary relationships with the E-R model

- Understand two types of weak entities and know how to use them

- Understand nonidentifying and identifying relationships and know how to use them

- Know how to represent subtype entities with the E-R model

- Know how to represent recursive relationships with the E-R model

- Learn how to create an E-R diagram from source documents

The **database development process**, as we describe it here, is a subset of the **systems development life cycle (SDLC)** process. The SDLC is described in detail in online Appendix D, "Getting Started in Systems Analysis and Design," and if you want more information about how the database development process fits into the creation of the information systems used in businesses today, you should refer to Appendix D. It is important to understand and remember that database development is usually done as a part of an information system or application development process and that the database itself is only one component of the information system or application. Users use the entire information system or application—they do not just use the database by itself!

For our purposes, the database development process consists of three major stages: requirements analysis, component design, and implementation. During the **requirements analysis stage** (also referred to as the requirements stage), system users are interviewed and sample forms, reports, queries, and descriptions of update activities are obtained. These system requirements are used to create a **data model** as part of the requirements analysis stage. A data model is a representation of the content, relationships, and constraints of the data needed to support the system requirements. Often, prototypes, or working demonstrations of selected portions of the future system, are created during the requirements phase. Such prototypes are used to obtain feedback from the system users.

During the **component design stage** (also referred to as the **system design stage** and the **design stage**), the data model is transformed into a **database design**. Such a design consists of tables, relationships, and constraints. The design includes the table names and the names of all table columns. The design also includes the data types and properties of the columns, as well as a description of primary and foreign keys. Data constraints consist of limits on data values (for example, part numbers are seven-digit numbers starting with the number 3), referential integrity constraints, and business rules. An example of a business rule for a manufacturing company is that every purchased part will have a quotation from at least two suppliers.

The last stage of database development is the **implementation stage**. During this stage, the database is constructed in the DBMS and populated with data; queries, forms, and reports are created; application programs are written; and all these are tested. Finally, during this stage users are trained, documentation is written, and the new system is put into use.

In this chapter, we will briefly discuss the requirements analysis stage and then focus on the data modeling component of requirements analysis. In Chapter 5, we will see how a data model is converted to a database design in the component design stage. The database itself would be built and populated with data in a DBMS during the implementation step of the SDLC, and this would be done using SQL as we previously described in Chapter 3.

REQUIREMENTS ANALYSIS

The first step in the database development process is user requirements analysis. Sources of user requirements are listed in Figure 4-1. As described in online Appendix D, and as you will learn in your systems development class, the general practice is to identify the users of the new information system and to interview them. During the interviews, examples of existing forms, reports, and queries are obtained. In addition, the users are asked about the need for changes to existing forms, reports, and queries and also about the need for new forms, reports, and queries.

Use cases are descriptions of the ways users will employ the features and functions of the new information system. A use case consists of a description of the roles users will play when utilizing the new system, together with descriptions of activities' scenarios. Inputs provided to the system and outputs generated by the system are defined. Sometimes dozens of such use cases are necessary. Use cases provide sources of requirements and also can be used to validate the data model, the database design, and the actual database implementation.

In addition to these requirements, you need to document characteristics of data items. For each data item in a form, report, or query, the team needs to determine its data type, properties, and limits on values.

Finally, during the process of establishing requirements system developers need to document business rules that constrain actions on database activity. Generally, such rules

FIGURE 4-1

Sources of
Requirements for a
Database Application

User interviews
Forms
Reports
Queries
Use cases
Business rules

arise from business policy and practice. For example, the following business rules could pertain to an academic database:

- Students must declare a major before enrolling in any class.
- Graduate classes can be taken by juniors or seniors with a grade point average of 3.70 or greater.
- No adviser may have more than 25 advisees.
- Students may declare one or two majors but no more.

THE ENTITY-RELATIONSHIP DATA MODEL

The system requirements described in the preceding section, although necessary and important as a first step, are not sufficient for designing a database. In order to be useful as the basis for a database design, these requirements must be transformed into a *data model*. When you write application programs, program logic must first be documented in flowcharts or object diagrams—when you create a database, data requirements must first be documented in a data model.

> ### BTW
>
> Books on systems analysis and design often identify three design stages:
>
> - Conceptual design (conceptual schema)
> - Logical design (logical schema)
> - Physical design (physical schema)
>
> The *data model* we are discussing is equivalent to the *conceptual design* as defined in these books.

A number of different techniques can be used to create data models. By far the most popular is the **entity-relationship model**, first published by Peter Chen[1] in 1976. Chen's basic model has since been extended to create the **extended entity-relationship (E-R) model**. Today, when we say *E-R model*, we mean the extended E-R model, and we use it in this text.

Several versions of the E-R model are in use today. We begin with the traditional E-R model. Later in the chapter, after the basic principles of E-R models have been examined, we will look at and use another version of the E-R model.

The most important elements of the E-R model are entities, attributes, identifiers, and relationships. We now consider each of these in turn.

Entities

An **entity** is something that users want to track. Examples of entities are CUSTOMER John Doe, PURCHASE 12345, PRODUCT A4200, SALES_ORDER 1000, SALESPERSON John Smith, and SHIPMENT 123400. Entities of a given type are grouped into an **entity class**. Thus, the EMPLOYEE entity class is the collection of all EMPLOYEE entities. In this text, entity classes are shown in capital letters.

---

[1]Peter P. Chen, "The Entity-Relationship Model—Towards a Unified View of Data," *ACM Transactions on Database Systems* (January 1976): 9–36. For information on Peter Chen, see **http://en.wikipedia.org/wiki/Peter_Chen**, and for a copy of the article, see **http://csc.lsu.edu/news/erd.pdf**.

FIGURE 4-2

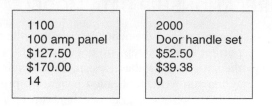

Entity Class

1100	2000
100 amp panel	Door handle set
$127.50	$52.50
$170.00	$39.38
14	0

Two Entity Instances

An **entity instance** of an entity class is the occurrence of a particular entity, such as CUSTOMER 12345. It is important to understand the differences between an entity class and an entity instance. An entity class is a collection of entities and is described by the structure of the entities in that class. There are usually many instances of an entity in an entity class. For example, the class CUSTOMER has many instances—one for each customer represented in the database. The ITEM entity class and two of its instances are shown in Figure 4-2.

When developing a data model, the developers analyze the forms, reports, queries, and other system requirements. Entities are usually the subject of one or more forms or reports, or they are a major section in one or more forms or reports. For example, a form named Product Data Entry Form indicates the likelihood of an entity class called PRODUCT. Similarly, a report named Customer Purchase Summary indicates that most likely the business has CUSTOMER and PURCHASE entities.

Attributes

Entities have **attributes**, which describe the entity's characteristics. Examples of attributes include EmployeeName, DateOfHire, and JobSkillCode. In this text, attributes are printed in a combination of uppercase and lowercase letters. The E-R model assumes that all instances of a given entity class have the same attributes. For example, in Figure 4-2 the ITEM entity has the attributes ItemNumber, Description, Cost, ListPrice, and QuantityOnHand.

An attribute has a data type (character, numeric, date, currency, and the like) and properties that are determined from the requirements. Properties specify whether the attribute is required, whether it has a default value, whether its value has limits, and any other constraint.

Identifiers

Entity instances have **identifiers**, which are attributes that name, or identify, entity instances. For example, the ITEM entity in Figure 4-2 uses ItemNumber as an identifier. Similarly, EMPLOYEE instances could be identified by SocialSecurityNumber, by EmployeeNumber, or by EmployeeName. EMPLOYEE instances are not likely to be identified by attributes such as Salary or DateOfHire because these attributes normally are not used in a naming role. CUSTOMER instances could be identified by CustomerNumber or CustomerName, and SALES_ORDER instances could be identified by OrderNumber.

The identifier of an entity instance consists of one or more of the entity's attributes. Identifiers that consist of two or more attributes are called **composite identifiers**. Examples are (AreaCode, LocalNumber), (ProjectName, TaskName), and (FirstName, LastName, PhoneExtension).

An identifier may be either unique or nonunique. The value of a **unique identifier** identifies one, and only one, entity instance. In contrast, the value of a **nonunique identifier** identifies a set of instances. EmployeeNumber is normally a unique identifier, but EmployeeName is most likely a nonunique identifier (for example, more than one John Smith might be employed by the company).

BTW

As you can tell from these definitions, identifiers are similar to keys in the relational model, but with two important differences. First, an identifier is a logical concept: It is one or more attributes that users think of as indicating an occurrence (instance) of the entity. Such identifiers might or might not be represented as keys in the database design. Second, primary and candidate keys must be unique, whereas identifiers might or might not be unique.

As shown in Figure 4-3, entities are portrayed in three levels of detail in a data model. Sometimes an entity and all its attributes are displayed. In such cases, the identifier of the attribute is shown at the top of the entity and a horizontal line is drawn after the identifier, as shown in Figure 4-3(a). In a large data model, so much detail can make the data model diagrams unwieldy. In those cases, the entity diagram is abbreviated by showing just the identifier, as in Figure 4-3(b), or by showing just the name of the entity in a rectangle, as shown in Figure 4-3(c).

Relationships

Entities can be associated with one another in **relationships**. The E-R model contains relationship classes and relationship instances. **Relationship classes** are associations among entity classes, and **relationship instances** are associations among entity instances. In the original specification of the E-R model, relationships could have attributes. In modern practice, that feature is not used, and only entities have attributes.

A relationship class can involve many entity classes. The number of entity classes in the relationship is known as the **degree** of the relationship. In Figure 4-4(a), the SUPPLIER-QUOTATION relationship is of degree two because it involves two entity classes: SUPPLIER and QUOTATION. The PARENT relationship in Figure 4-4(b) is of degree three because it involves three entity classes: MOTHER, FATHER, and CHILD.

FIGURE 4-3

Levels of Entity Attribute Display

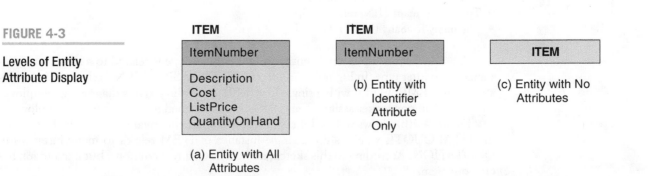

(a) Entity with All Attributes

(b) Entity with Identifier Attribute Only

(c) Entity with No Attributes

FIGURE 4-4

Example Relationships

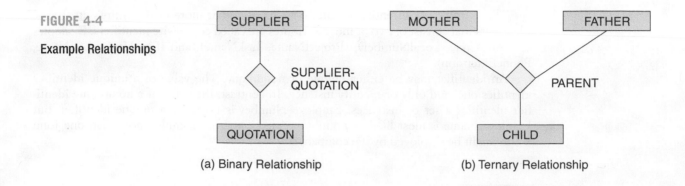

(a) Binary Relationship   (b) Ternary Relationship

Relationships of degree two, which are the most common, are called **binary relationships**. Similarly, relationships of degree three are called **ternary relationships**.

BTW

You may be wondering what the difference is between an *entity* and a *table*. They may seem like different terms for the same thing. *The principal difference between an entity and a table is that you can express a relationship between entities without using foreign keys.* In the E-R model, you can specify a relationship just by drawing a line connecting two entities. Because you are doing *logical data modeling* and not physical database design, you need not worry about primary and foreign keys, referential integrity constraints, and the like.

This characteristic makes entities easier to work with than tables, especially early in a project when entities and relationships are fluid and uncertain. You can show relationships between entities before you even know what the identifiers are. For example, you can say that a DEPARTMENT relates to many EMPLOYEEs before you know any of the attributes of either EMPLOYEE or DEPARTMENT. This characteristic allows you to work from the general to the specific. When you are creating a data model, you first identify the entities, then you think about the relationships, and finally you determine the attributes.

Three Types of Binary Relationships   Figure 4-5 shows the three types of binary relationships:

- The one-to-one (1:1) relationship
- The one-to-many (1:N) relationship
- The many-to-many (N:M) relationship

In a 1:1 relationship, a single entity instance of one type is related to a single entity instance of another type. In Figure 4-5(a), the LOCKER-ASSIGNMENT relationship associates a single EMPLOYEE with a single LOCKER. According to this diagram, no employee has more than one locker assigned, and no locker is assigned to more than one employee.

Figure 4-5(b) shows a 1:N binary relationship. In this relationship, which is called the ITEM-QUOTE relationship, a single instance of ITEM relates to many instances of QUOTATION. According to this sketch, an item has many quotations, but a quotation has only one item.

FIGURE 4-5

Three Types of Binary Relationships

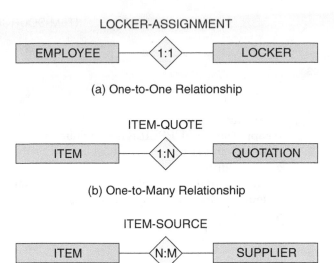

(a) One-to-One Relationship

(b) One-to-Many Relationship

(c) Many-to-Many Relationship

Think of the diamond as representing the relationship. The position of the 1 indicates that the relationship has one ITEM; the position of the N indicates that it also has many QUOTATION entities. Thus, each instance of the relationship consists of one ITEM and many QUOTATIONS. Notice that if the 1 and the N were reversed and the relationship were written N:1, each instance of the relationship would have many ITEMs and one QUOTATION.

When discussing 1:N relationships, the terms *parent* and *child* are sometimes used. The **parent entity** is the entity on the one side of the relationship and the **child entity** is the entity on the many side of the relationship. Thus, in the 1:N relationship between ITEM and QUOTATION, ITEM is the parent and QUOTATION is the child.

Figure 4-5(c) shows an N:M binary relationship. This relationship is named ITEM-SOURCE, and it relates instances of ITEM to instances of SUPPLIER. In this case, an item can be supplied by many suppliers, and a supplier can supply many items.

Maximum Cardinality   The three types of binary relationships are named and classified by their **cardinality**, which is a word that means *count*. In each of the relationships in Figure 4-5, the numbers inside the relationship diamond show the *maximum* number of entity instances that can occur on each side of the relationship. These numbers are called the relationship's **maximum cardinality**, which is the maximum number of entity instances that can participate in a relationship instance.

The ITEM-QUOTATION relationship in Figure 4-5(b), for example, is said to have a maximum cardinality of 1:N. However, the cardinalities are not restricted to the values shown here. It is possible, for example, for the maximum cardinality to be other than 1 and N. The relationship between BASKETBALL-TEAM and PLAYER, for example, could be 1:5, indicating that a basketball team has at most five players.

Minimum Cardinality   Relationships also have a **minimum cardinality**, which is the minimum number of entity instances that *must* participate in a relationship instance. Minimum cardinality can be shown in several different ways. One way, illustrated in Figure 4-6, is to place a *hash mark* across the relationship line to indicate that an entity must exist in the relationship and to place an *oval* across the relationship line to indicate that an entity might or might not be in the relationship.

Accordingly, Figure 4-6 shows that an ITEM must have a relationship with at least one SUPPLIER but that a SUPPLIER is not required to have a relationship with an ITEM. The complete relationship restrictions are that an ITEM has a minimum cardinality of zero and

FIGURE 4-6

A Relationship with
Minimum Cardinalities

ITEM-SOURCE

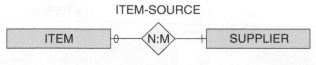

a maximum cardinality of many—a SUPPLIER can supply *many* items, but does *not* have to supply any. A SUPPLIER has a minimum cardinality of one and a maximum cardinality of many—an ITEM may be available from *many* suppliers, and *must* be associated with at least one supplier.

If the minimum cardinality is zero, the entity's participation in the relationship is **optional**. If the minimum cardinality is one, the entity's participation in the relationship is **mandatory**.

> ## BTW
>
> Interpreting minimum cardinalities in diagrams such as Figure 4-6 is often one of the most difficult parts of E-R models. It is very easy to become confused about which entity is optional and which is required (mandatory). An easy way to clarify this situation is to imagine that you are standing in the diamond, on the relationship line, and looking toward one of the entities. If you see an oval in that direction, then that entity is optional (has a minimum cardinality of zero). If you see a hash mark, then that entity is required (has a minimum cardinality of one). Thus, in Figure 4-6, if you stand on the diamond and look toward SUPPLIER, you see a hash mark. This means that SUPPLIER is required in the relationship.

ENTITY-RELATIONSHIP DIAGRAMS

The sketches in Figures 4-5 and 4-6 are called **entity-relationship (E-R) diagrams**. Such diagrams are standardized, but only loosely. According to this standard, entity classes are shown using rectangles, relationships are shown using diamonds, the maximum cardinality of the relationship is shown inside the diamond, and the minimum cardinality is shown by the oval or hash mark next to the entity. The name of the entity is shown inside the rectangle, and the name of the relationship is shown near the diamond. You will see examples of such E-R diagrams, and it is important for you to be able to interpret them.

> ## BTW
>
> Relationships like those in Figures 4-5 and 4-6 are sometimes called **HAS-A relationships**. This term is used because each entity instance has a relationship to a second entity instance. An employee has a badge, and a badge has an employee. If the maximum cardinality is greater than one, then each entity has a set of other entities. An employee has a set of skills, for example, and a skill has a set of employees who have that skill.

Variations of the E-R Model

This original notation is seldom used today. Instead, a number of different versions of the E-R model are in use, and they use different symbols.

At least three different versions of the E-R model are currently in use. One of them, called **Information Engineering (IE)**, was developed by James Martin in 1990. This model uses "crow's feet" to show the many side of a relationship, and it is sometimes called the **IE Crow's Foot model**. It is easy to understand, and we will use it in this text.

Other significant variations include the IDEF1X version and the Unified Modeling Language (UML) version of the E-R model.[2] In 1993, the National Institute of Standards and Technology announced that the **Integrated Definition 1, Extended (IDEF1X)**[3] version of the E-R model would be a national standard. This standard incorporates the basic ideas of the E-R model but uses different graphical symbols that, unfortunately, make it difficult to understand and use. Still, it is a national standard used in government work, and therefore it may be important to you. To add further complication, an object-oriented development methodology called the **Unified Modeling Language (UML)** adopted the E-R model but introduced its own symbols while putting an object-oriented programming spin on it. UML has begun to be widely used among object-oriented programming (OOP) practitioners, and you may encounter UML notation in systems development courses.

In addition to differences due to different versions of the E-R model, differences also arise due to software products. For example, two products that both implement the IE Crow's Foot model may do so in different ways. Thus, when creating a data model diagram, you need to know not just the version of the E-R model you are using, but also the idiosyncrasies of the data modeling product you use.

The IE Crow's Foot E-R Model

Figure 4-7 shows the same N:M optional-to-mandatory relationship in two different models. Figure 4-7(a) shows the original E-R model version. Figure 4-7(b) shows the IE Crow's Foot model using common IE Crow's Foot symbols. Notice that the line representing the relationship is drawn as a dashed line. (The reason for this is explained later in this chapter.) Notice the **crow's foot symbol** used to show the many side of the relationship. The IE Crow's Foot model uses the notation shown in Figure 4-8 to indicate relationship cardinality.

In the IE Crow's Foot model, the symbol closest to the entity shows the maximum cardinality, and the other symbol shows the minimum cardinality. A hash mark indicates one (and therefore also mandatory), a circle indicates zero (and thus optional), and the crow's foot indicates many. Thus, the diagram in Figure 4-7(b) shows that a DEPARTMENT has

FIGURE 4-7

Two Versions of a 1:N Relationship

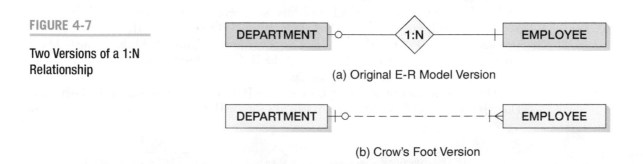

(a) Original E-R Model Version

(b) Crow's Foot Version

---

[2]For more information on these models, see David M. Kroenke and David J. Auer, *Database Processing: Fundamentals, Design, and Implementation*, 13th edition (Upper Saddle River, NJ: Prentice Hall, 2014), Appendix B (IDEF1X) and Appendix C (UML).

[3]National Institute of Standards and Technology, *Integrated Definition for Information Modeling (DEF1X)*. Federal Information Processing Standards Publication 184, 1993.

FIGURE 4-8

Crow's Foot Notation

Symbol	Meaning	Numeric Meaning
	Mandatory—One	Exactly one
	Mandatory—Many	One or more
	Optional—One	Zero or one
	Optional—Many	Zero or more

one or more EMPLOYEEs (the symbol shows many and mandatory), and an EMPLOYEE belongs to zero or one DEPARTMENT (the symbol shows one and optional).

A 1:1 relationship would be drawn in a similar manner, but the line connecting to each entity would be similar to the connection shown for the one side of the 1:N relationship in Figure 4-7(b).

Figure 4-9 shows the same N:M optional-to-mandatory relationship in two different models. According to the original E-R model diagram shown in Figure 4-9(a), an EMPLOYEE must have a SKILL and may have several. At the same time, although a particular SKILL may or may not be held by any EMPLOYEE, a SKILL may also be held by several EMPLOYEES. The IE Crow's Foot version in Figure 4-9(b) shows the N:M cardinalities using the notation in Figure 4-8. The IE Crow's Foot symbols again indicate the minimum cardinalities for the relationship.

Throughout the rest of this text, we use the IE Crow's Foot model for E-R diagrams. There is no completely standard set of symbols for the IE Crow's Foot notation, but we use

FIGURE 4-9

Two Versions of an N:M
Relationship

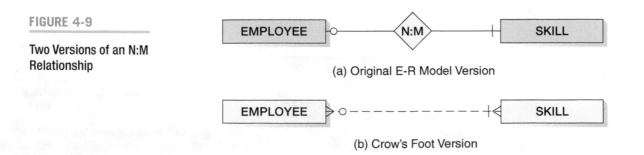

(a) Original E-R Model Version

(b) Crow's Foot Version

the symbols and notation described in this chapter. You can obtain various modeling products that will produce IE Crow's Foot models, and they are easily understood and related to the original E-R model. However, those products may use the oval, hash mark, crow's foot, and other symbols in slightly differently ways.

BTW

You can try a number of modeling products, each with its own idiosyncrasies. First, Computer Associates produces CA ERwin Data Modeler, a commercial data modeling product (available in several editions) that handles both data modeling and database design tasks. You can download the CA ERwin Data Modeler Community Edition, a free, basic version from the Computer Associates Web site. You can use ERwin to produce either IE Crow's Foot or IDEF1X diagrams. Second, Microsoft Visio Professional 2013 is also a possibility. A trial version is available from the Microsoft Web site (**http://www.microsoftstore.com/store/msusa/en_US/list/Visio/categoryID.62687700**). For more information on working with Microsoft Visio 2013, see online Appendix E, "Getting Started with Microsoft Visio 2013." Finally, Oracle is continuing development of the MySQL Workbench, which is both the GUI utility for the MySQL database and a database design tool. The MySQL Workbench is downloadable at the MySQL Web site (**http://dev.mysql.com/downloads/tools/workbench/**). (*Note:* If you are using a Windows operating system, you should install the MySQL Workbench using the MySQL Installer for Windows available at **http://dev.mysql.com/downloads/windows/installer/**). Although MySQL Workbench is better for database designs than data models, it is a very useful tool, and the database designs it produces can be used with any DBMS, not just MySQL. For more information on working with the MySQL Workbench, see online Appendix C, "Getting Started with MySQL 5.6 Community Server Edition." These are just a few of the many data modeling products available.

Weak Entities

The E-R model defines a special type of entity called a weak entity. A **weak entity** is an entity that cannot exist in a database unless another type of entity also exists in that database. An entity that is *not* weak is called a **strong entity**.

ID-Dependent Entities

The E-R model includes a special type of weak entity called an **ID-dependent entity**. With this type of entity, the identifier of the entity includes the identifier of another entity. Consider the entities BUILDING and APARTMENT, shown in Figure 4-10(a).

As you would expect, the identifier of BUILDING is a single attribute, in this case BuildingName. The identifier of APARTMENT, however, is *not* the single attribute ApartmentNumber, but rather the composite identifier (BuildingName, ApartmentNumber). This happens because logically and physically an APARTMENT simply cannot exist unless a BUILDING exists for that APARTMENT to be part of. Whenever this type of situation occurs, an ID-dependent entity exists. In this case,

FIGURE 4-10

Example ID-Dependent Entities

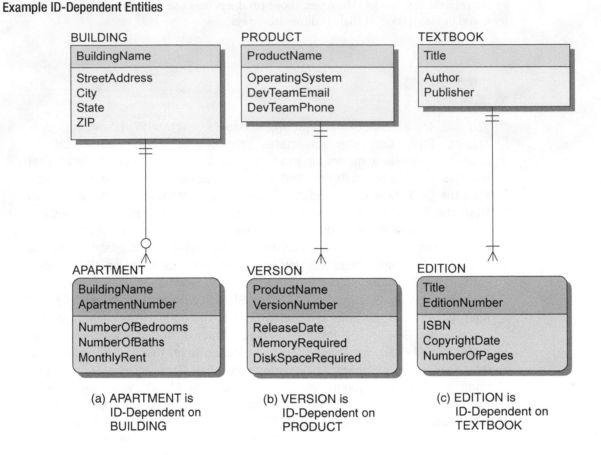

(a) APARTMENT is
ID-Dependent on
BUILDING

(b) VERSION is
ID-Dependent on
PRODUCT

(c) EDITION is
ID-Dependent on
TEXTBOOK

APARTMENT is ID-dependent on BUILDING. The identifier of an ID-dependent entity is always a composite that includes the identifier of the entity that the ID-dependent entity depends on for its existence.

As shown in Figure 4-10, in our E-R models we use an entity with rounded corners to represent the ID-dependent entity. We also use a solid line to represent the relationship between the ID-dependent entity and its parent. This type of a relationship is called an **identifying relationship**. A relationship drawn with a dashed line (refer to Figure 4-7) is used between strong entities and is called a **nonidentifying relationship** because there are no ID-dependent entities in the relationship.

ID-dependent entities are common. Another example is shown in Figure 4-10(b), where the entity VERSION is ID-dependent on the entity PRODUCT. Here PRODUCT is a software product, and VERSION is a release of that software product. The identifier of PRODUCT is ProductName, and the identifier of VERSION is (ProductName, VersionNumber). A third example is shown in Figure 4-10(c), where EDITION is ID-dependent on TEXTBOOK. The identifier of TEXTBOOK is Title, and the identifier of EDITION is (Title, EditionNumber). In each of these cases, the ID-dependent entity cannot exist unless the parent (the entity on which it depends) also exists. Thus, the minimum cardinality from the ID-dependent entity to the parent is always one.

However, whether the parent is required to have an ID-dependent entity depends on business requirements. In Figure 4-10(a), the database can contain a BUILDING, such as a store or warehouse, so APARTMENT is optional. In Figure 4-10(b), every PRODUCT made by this company has versions (including version 1.0), so VERSION is mandatory. Similarly, in Figure 4-10(c), every TEXTBOOK has an EDITION number (including the first edition), which makes EDITION mandatory. Those restrictions arise from the nature of each business and its applications and not from any logical requirement.

Finally, notice that you cannot add an ID-dependent entity instance until the parent entity instance is created, and when you delete the parent entity instance you must delete all the ID-dependent entity instances as well.

Non–ID-Dependent Weak Entities

All ID-dependent entities are weak entities. However, there are other entities that are weak but not ID-dependent. To understand weak entities, consider the relationship between the AUTO_MODEL and VEHICLE entity classes in the database of a car manufacturer, such as Ford or Honda, as shown in Figure 4-11.

In Figure 4-11(a), each VEHICLE is assigned a sequential number as it is manufactured. So, for the "Super SUV" AUTO_MODEL, the first VEHICLE manufactured gets a ManufacturingSeqNumber of 1, the next gets a ManufacturingSeqNumber of 2, and so on. This is clearly an ID-dependent relationship because ManufacturingSeqNumber is based on the Manufacturer and Model.

Now let us assign VEHICLE an identifier that is independent of the Manufacturer and Model. We will use a VIN (vehicle identification number), as shown in Figure 4-11(b). Now the VEHICLE has a unique identifier of its own and does not need to be identified by its relation to AUTO_MODEL.

This is an interesting situation. VEHICLE has an identity of its own and therefore is not ID-dependent, yet the VEHICLE is an AUTO_MODEL, and if that particular AUTO_MODEL did not exist the VEHICLE itself would never have existed. Therefore, VEHICLE is now a *weak but non–ID-dependent entity.*

Consider *your* car—let us say it is a Ford Mustang just for the sake of this discussion. Your individual Mustang is a VEHICLE, and it exists as a physical object and is

FIGURE 4-11

Weak Entity Examples

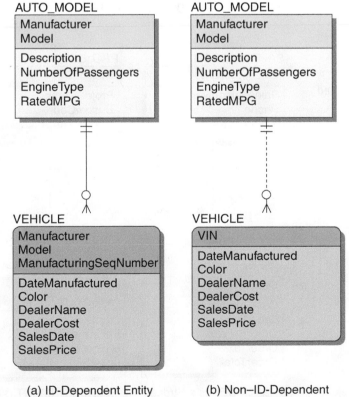

(a) ID-Dependent Entity

(b) Non–ID-Dependent Weak Entity

identified by the VIN that is required for each licensed automobile. It is *not* ID-dependent on AUTO_MODEL, which in this case is Ford Mustang, for its identity. However, if the Ford Mustang had never been created as an AUTO_MODEL—a logical concept that was first designed on paper—your car would never have been built because *no* Ford Mustangs would ever have been built! Therefore, your physical individual VEHICLE would not exist without a logical AUTO_MODEL of Ford Mustang, and in a data model (which *is* what we're talking about) a VEHICLE cannot exist without a related AUTO_MODEL. This makes VEHICLE a weak but non–ID-dependent entity.

Unfortunately, an ambiguity is hidden in the definition of *weak entity*, and this ambiguity is interpreted differently by different database designers (as well as different textbook authors). The ambiguity is that, in a strict sense, if a weak entity is defined as any entity whose presence in the database depends on another entity, then any entity that participates in a relationship having a minimum cardinality of one to a second entity is a weak entity. Thus, in an academic database, if a STUDENT must have an ADVISER, then STUDENT is a weak entity because a STUDENT entity cannot be stored without an ADVISER.

This interpretation seems too broad to some people. A STUDENT is not physically dependent on an ADVISER (unlike an APARTMENT to a BUILDING), and a STUDENT is not logically dependent on an ADVISER (despite how it might appear to either the student or the adviser). Therefore, STUDENT should be considered a strong entity.

To avoid such situations, some people interpret the definition of weak entity more narrowly. They say that to be a weak entity an entity must logically depend on another entity. According to this definition, APARTMENT is a weak entity, but STUDENT is not. An APARTMENT cannot exist without a BUILDING in which it is located. However, a STUDENT can logically exist without an ADVISER, even if a business rule requires it.

To illustrate this interpretation, consider the examples shown in Figure 4-12. Suppose that a data model includes the relationship between an ORDER and a SALESPERSON shown in Figure 4-12(a). Although you might state that an ORDER must have a SALESPERSON, it does not necessarily require one for its existence. (The ORDER could be a cash sale in which the salesperson is not recorded.) Hence, the minimum cardinality of one arises from a business rule, not from logical necessity. Thus,

FIGURE 4-12

Examples of Required Entities

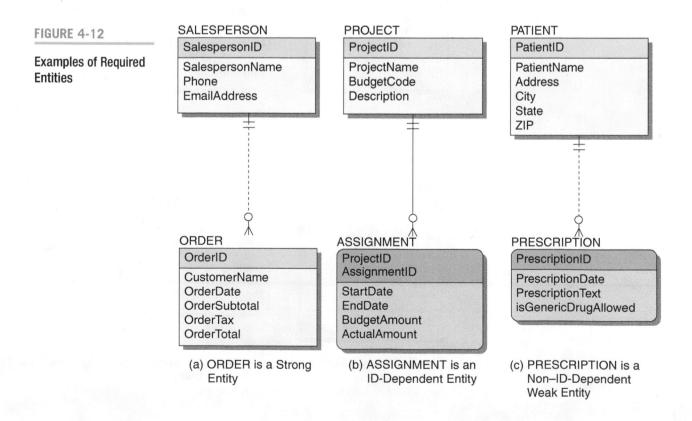

(a) ORDER is a Strong Entity

(b) ASSIGNMENT is an ID-Dependent Entity

(c) PRESCRIPTION is a Non–ID-Dependent Weak Entity

ORDER requires a SALESPERSON but is not existence-dependent on it. Therefore, ORDER is a strong entity.

Now, consider ASSIGNMENT in Figure 4-12(b), which is ID-dependent on PROJECT, and the identifier of ASSIGNMENT contains the identifier of PROJECT. Here, not only does ASSIGNMENT have a minimum cardinality of one and not only is ASSIGNMENT existence-dependent on PROJECT, but ASSIGNMENT is also ID-dependent on PROJECT because its identifier requires the key of the parent entity. Thus, ASSIGNMENT is a weak entity that is ID-dependent.

Finally, consider the relationship of PATIENT and PRESCRIPTION in Figure 4-12(c). Here a PRESCRIPTION cannot logically exist without a PATIENT. Hence, not only is the minimum cardinality one, but the PRESCRIPTION is also existence-dependent on PATIENT. Thus, PRESCRIPTION is a weak entity.

In this text, we define a weak entity as an entity that logically depends on another entity. Hence, not all entities that have a minimum cardinality of one in relation to another entity are weak. Only those that are logically dependent are weak. This definition implies that all ID-dependent entities are weak. In addition, every weak entity has a minimum cardinality of one on the entity on which it depends, but every entity that has a minimum cardinality of one is not necessarily weak.

As illustrated in Figures 4-11 and 4-12, in our E-R models we again use an entity with rounded corners to represent the non–ID-dependent entity, but we also use a dashed line to represent the nonidentifying relationship between the non–ID-dependent entity and its parent.

Associative Entities

Let's take another look that the Wedgewood Pacific Corporation (WPC) database that we used in our discussion of SQL in Chapter 3. At WPC, employees are assigned to projects. If all we are interested in knowing is (1) which employees are assigned a single project and (2) which projects a single employee has been assigned to, we have a simple N:M relationship between EMPLOYEE and PROJECT. This is illustrated in Figure 4-13(a).

FIGURE 4-13

The Associative Entity

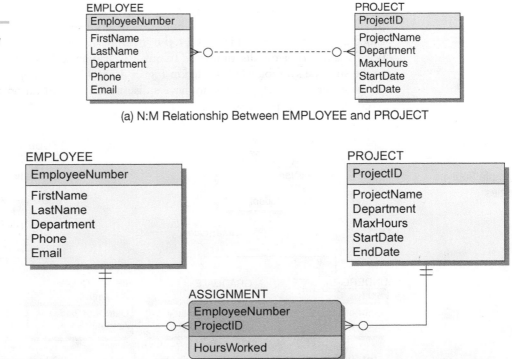

(a) N:M Relationship Between EMPLOYEE and PROJECT

(b) EMPLOYEE and PROJECT 1:N Relationships with the Associative Entity ASSIGNMENT

However, WPC also wants to record the number of hours each employee works on each project in an attribute named HoursWorked. Where should we put this attribute? If we add it to EMPLOYEE, it will total the number of hours that employee has worked on all assigned projects, not the number of hours worked per project. Similarly, if we add it to PROJECT, it will record the total number of hours worked on that project by all assigned employees. Neither of these solutions will record the data that WPC needs.

One way of thinking about this situation is that HoursWorked is an attribute of the assignment relationship between EMPLOYEE and PROJECT. But we can't put an attribute in a relationship, so what can we do?

The answer is to create a new entity between EMPLOYEE and PROJECT named ASSIGNMENT to record both (1) the actual assignments of employees to projects and (2) the hours each employee works on each project in the HoursWorked attribute. This type of entity is called an **associative entity** (or **association entity**) and is used whenever a pure N:M relationship cannot properly hold attributes that are describing aspects of the relationship between two entities. This is illustrated in Figure 4-13(b), and if you look back at Figure 3-1, you will see that the WPC has always had such a structure.

Subtype Entities

The extended E-R model introduced the concept of subtypes. A **subtype entity** is a special case of another entity called the **supertype entity**. Students, for example, may be classified as undergraduate or graduate students. In this case, STUDENT is the supertype, and UNDERGRADUATE and GRADUATE are subtypes. Figure 4-14 shows these subtypes for a student database. Note that the identifier of the supertype is also the identifier of the subtypes.

Alternatively, a student could be classified as a freshman, sophomore, junior, or senior. In that case, STUDENT would be the supertype, and FRESHMAN, SOPHOMORE, JUNIOR, and SENIOR would be the subtypes.

As illustrated in Figure 4-14, in our E-R models we use a circle with a line under it as a subtype symbol to indicate a supertype/subtype relationship. Think of this as a symbol for an optional (the circle) 1:1 (the line) relationship. In addition, we use a solid line to represent an ID-dependent subtype entity because each subtype is ID-dependent on the supertype. Also note that none of the line end symbols shown in Figure 4-8 are used on the connecting lines.

In some cases, an attribute of the supertype indicates which of the subtypes is appropriate for a given instance. An attribute that determines which subtype is appropriate is called a **discriminator**. In Figure 4-14, the attribute isGradStudent (which has only the values Yes and No) is the discriminator. In our E-R diagrams, the discriminator is shown next to the subtype symbol, as illustrated in Figure 4-14(a). Not all supertypes have a discriminator. Where a supertype does not have a discriminator, application code must be written to create the appropriate subtype.

FIGURE 4-14

Example Subtype Entities

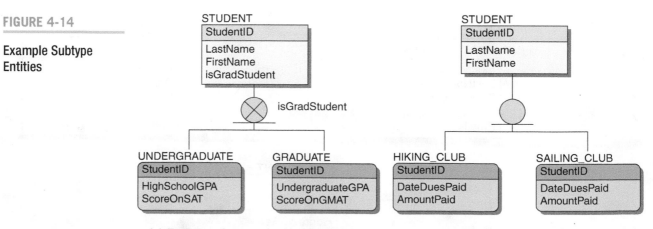

(a) Exclusive Subtypes with Discriminator   (b) Inclusive Subtypes

Subtypes can be exclusive or inclusive. With **exclusive subtypes**, a supertype instance is related to at most one subtype. With **inclusive subtypes**, a supertype instance can relate to one or more subtypes. In Figure 4-14(a), the *X* in the circle means that the UNDERGRADUATE and GRADUATE subtypes are exclusive. Thus, a STUDENT can be either an UNDERGRADUATE or a GRADUATE, but not both.

Figure 4-14(b) shows that a STUDENT can join either the HIKING_CLUB or the SAILING_CLUB or both or neither. These subtypes are inclusive (note that there is no *X* in the circle). Because a supertype may relate to more than one subtype, inclusive subtypes do not have a discriminator.

Subtypes are used in a data model to avoid inappropriate NULL values. Undergraduate students take the SAT exam and report that score, whereas graduate students take the GMAT and report their score on that exam. Thus, the SAT score would be NULL in all STUDENT entities for graduates, whereas the GMAT score would be NULL for all undergraduates. Such NULL values can be avoided by creating subtypes.

BTW

The relationships that connect supertypes and subtypes are called **IS-A relationships** because a subtype is the same entity as the supertype. Because this is so, the identifier of a supertype and all its subtypes must be the same; they all represent different aspects of the same entity. Contrast this with HAS-A relationships, in which an entity has a relationship to another entity but the identifiers of the two entities are different.

Recursive Relationships

It is possible for an entity to have a relationship to itself. Figure 4-15 shows a CUSTOMER entity in which one customer can refer to many other customers. This is called a **recursive relationship** (and because it has only one entity, it is also known as a **unary relationship**). As with binary relationships, recursive relationships can be 1:1, 1:N (shown in Figure 4-15), and N:M. We discuss each of these three types further in Chapter 5.

FIGURE 4-15

Example Recursive Relationship

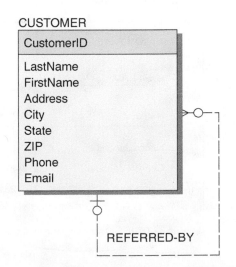

DEVELOPING AN EXAMPLE E-R DIAGRAM

The best way to gain proficiency with data modeling is to do it. In this section, we examine a set of documents used by a small business and create a data model from those documents. After you have read this section, you should practice creating data models with one or more of the projects at the end of the chapter.

Heather Sweeney Designs

Heather Sweeney is an interior designer who specializes in home kitchen design. She offers a variety of seminars at home shows, kitchen and appliance stores, and other public locations. The seminars are free; she offers them as a way of building her customer base. She earns revenue by selling books and videos that instruct people on kitchen design. She also offers custom-design consulting services.

After someone attends a seminar, Heather wants to leave no stone unturned in attempting to sell that person one of her products or services. She would therefore like to develop a database to keep track of customers, the seminars they have attended, the contacts she has made with them, and the purchases they have made. She wants to use this database to continue to contact her customers and offer them products and services.

The Seminar Customer List

Figure 4-16 shows the seminar customer list form that Heather or her assistant fills out at seminars. This form includes basic data about the seminar as well as the name, phone, and email address of each seminar attendee. If we examine this list in terms of a data model, you see two potential entities: SEMINAR and CUSTOMER. From the form in Figure 4-16, we can conclude that a SEMINAR relates to many CUSTOMERs, and we can make the initial E-R diagram shown in Figure 4-17(a).

However, from this single document we *cannot* determine a number of other facts. For example, we are not sure about cardinalities. Currently, we show a 1:N relationship, with both entities required in the relationship, but we are not certain about this. Neither do we know what to use for the identifier of each entity.

FIGURE 4-16

Example Seminar Customer List

Heather Sweeney Designs
Seminar Customer List

Date:	October 11, 2014	Location:	San Antonio Convention Center
Time:	11 AM	Title:	Kitchen on a Budget

Name	Phone	Email Address
Nancy Jacobs	817–871–8123	NJ@somewhere.com
Chantel Jacobs	817–871–8234	CJ@somewhere.com
Ralph Able	210–281–7687	RA@somewhere.com
Etc.		

27 names in all

FIGURE 4-17

Initial E-R Diagram for Heather Sweeney Designs

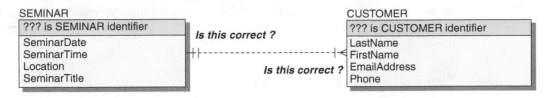

(a) First Version of the SEMINAR and CUSTOMER E-R Diagram

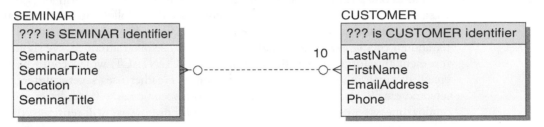

(b) Second Version of the SEMINAR and CUSTOMER E-R Diagram

(c) Third Version of the SEMINAR and CUSTOMER E-R Diagram

Having missing facts is typical during the data modeling process. We examine documents and conduct user interviews, and then we create a data model with the data we have. We also note where data are missing and supply those data later as we learn more. Thus, there is no need to stop data modeling when something is unknown; we just note that it is unknown and keep going, with the goal of supplying missing information at some later point.

Suppose we talk with Heather and determine that customers can attend as many seminars as they would like, but she would like to be able to record customers even if they have not been to a seminar. ("Frankly, I'll take a customer wherever I can find one!" was her actual response.) Also, she never offers a seminar to fewer than 10 attendees. Given this information, you can fill out more of the E-R diagram, as shown in Figure 4-17(b).

Before continuing, consider the minimum cardinality of the relationship from SEMINAR to CUSTOMER in Figure 4-17(b). The notation says that a seminar must have at least 10 customers, which is what we were told. However, this means that we cannot add a new SEMINAR to the database unless it already has 10 customers. This is incorrect. When Heather first schedules a seminar, it probably has no customers at all, but she would still like to record it in the database. Therefore, even though she has a business policy of requiring at least 10 customers at a seminar, we cannot place this limit as a constraint in the data model.

In Figure 4-17(b), neither of the entities has an identifier. For SEMINAR, the composites (SeminarDate, SeminarTime, Location) and (SeminarDate, SeminarTime, SeminarTitle) are probably unique, and either could be the identifier. However, identifiers will become table keys during database design, and these will be large character keys. A surrogate key is probably a better idea here, so we should create an equivalent unique identifier (SeminarID) for this entity. For CUSTOMER, looking at the data and thinking about the nature of email addresses, we can reasonably suppose that EmailAddress can be the identifier of CUSTOMER. However, some couples share an email address, and it may not be completely unique. Therefore, we will use CustomerID as our unique identifier. All these decisions are shown for the E-R diagram in Figure 4-17(c).

The Customer Form Letter

Heather records every customer contact she makes. She considers customer attendance at a seminar as one type of customer contact, and Figure 4-18 shows a form letter that Sweeney Designs uses as another type of customer contact and as a follow-up to seminar attendance.

Heather also sends messages like this via email. In fact, she sends both a written letter and an email message as a follow-up with every seminar attendee. We should therefore represent this form letter with an entity called CONTACT, which could be a letter, an email, or some other form of customer contact. Heather uses several different form letters and emails, and she refers to each one by a specific name (form letter seminar, email seminar message, email purchase message, etc.). For now, we will represent the attributes

FIGURE 4-18

Heather Sweeney
Designs Customer
Form Letter

Heather Sweeney Designs
122450 Rockaway Road
Dallas, Texas 75227
972-233-6165

Ms. Nancy Jacobs
1400 West Palm Drive
Fort Worth, Texas 76110

Dear Ms. Jacobs:

Thank you for attending my seminar "Kitchen on a Budget" at the San Antonio Convention Center. I hope that you found the seminar topic interesting and helpful for your design projects.

As a seminar attendee, you are entitled to a 15 percent discount on all of my video and book products. I am enclosing a product catalog and I would also like to invite you to visit our Web site at www.Sweeney.com.

Also, as I mentioned at the seminar, I do provide customized design services to help you create that just-perfect kitchen. In fact, I have a number of clients in the Fort Worth area. Just give me a call at my personal phone number of 555-122-4873 if you'd like to schedule an appointment.

Thanks again and I look forward to hearing from you!

Best regards,

Heather Sweeney

of CONTACT as ContactNumber, ContactDate and ContactType, where ContactType can be Seminar, FormLetterSeminar, EmailSeminarMessage, EmailPurchaseMessage, or some other type.

Reading the form letter, we see that it refers to both a seminar and a customer. Therefore, we can add it to the E-R diagram with relationships to both of those entities, as shown in Figure 4-19.

As shown in the design in Figure 4-19(a), a seminar can result in many contacts and a customer may receive many contacts, so the maximum cardinality of these relationships is N. However, neither a customer nor a seminar need generate a contact, so the minimum cardinality of these relationships is zero.

Working from CONTACT back to SEMINAR and CUSTOMER, we can determine that the contact is for a single CUSTOMER and refers to a single SEMINAR, so the maximum cardinality in that direction is one. Also, some of the messages to customers refer to seminars and some do not, so the minimum cardinality back to SEMINAR is zero. However, a contact must have a customer, so the minimum cardinality of that relationship is one. These cardinalities are shown in Figure 4-19(a).

Now, however, consider the identifier of CONTACT, which is shown as unknown in Figure 4-19(a). What could be the identifier? None of the attributes by themselves suffice because many contacts will have the same values for ContactNumber, ContactDate, or ContactType. Reflect on this for a minute, and you will begin to realize that some attribute of CUSTOMER has to be part of CONTACT. That realization is a signal that something is wrong. In a data model, the same attribute should not logically need to be part of two different entities.

Could it be that CONTACT is a weak entity? Can a CONTACT logically exist without a SEMINAR? Yes, because not all CONTACTs refer to a SEMINAR. Can a CONTACT logically exist without a CUSTOMER? The answer to that question has to be no. Who would we be contacting without a CUSTOMER? Aha! That is it: CONTACT is a weak entity, depending on CUSTOMER. In fact, it is an ID-dependent entity because the identifier of CONTACT includes the identifier of CUSTOMER.

Figure 4-19(b) shows the data model with CONTACT as an ID-dependent entity on CUSTOMER. After further interviews with Heather, we determine that she often contacts a customer more than once on the same day (both the form letter and email message thanking the customer for seminar attendance are always sent on the same day), so (CustomerID, Date) cannot be the identifier of CONTACT. We will choose to use the ContactNumber attribute, which is a simple sequence number, as the second part of the composite identifier (CustomerID, ContactNumber) for CONTACT.

This E-R diagram has a couple of other problems, because Heather has some other data requirements. First, the contact letter has the customer's address, but the CUSTOMER entity has no address attributes. Consequently, they need to be added. Second, Heather allows customers to create a login account on her Web site so that they can purchase items online securely. She uses the customer EmailAddress as their login name, and has them create a password. For security, we need to allow for encryption of this password and storage of it in the CUSTOMER entity. The additional attributes for these requirements are added to the CUSTOMER entity, as shown in Figure 4-19(c). This adjustment is typical; as more forms and reports are obtained new attributes and other changes will need to be made to the data model.

The Sales Invoice

The sales invoice that Heather uses to sell books and videos is shown in Figure 4-20. The sales invoice itself needs to be an entity, and because the sales invoice has customer data it has a relationship back to CUSTOMER. (Note that we do not duplicate the customer data because we can obtain data items via the relationship; if data items are missing, we add them to CUSTOMER.) Because Heather runs her computer with minimal security, she decided that she did not want to record credit card numbers in her computer database. Instead, she

FIGURE 4-19

Heather Sweeney Designs Data Model with CONTACT

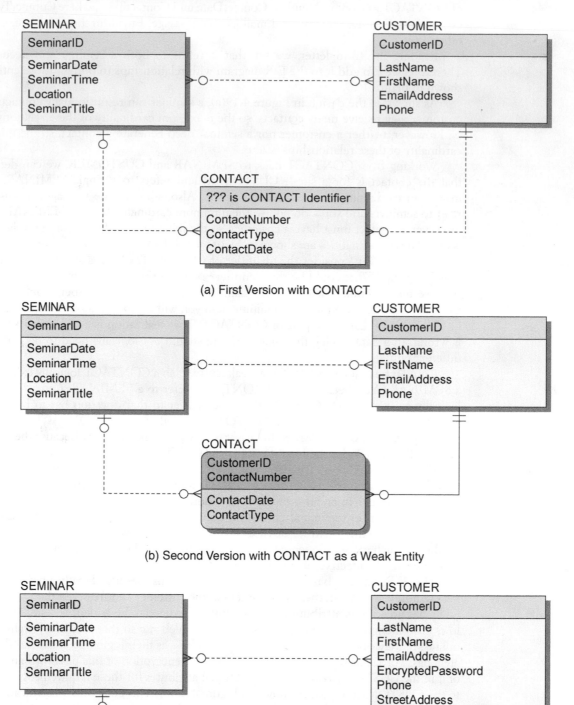

(a) First Version with CONTACT

(b) Second Version with CONTACT as a Weak Entity

(c) Third Version with Modified CUSTOMER

FIGURE 4-20

Heather Sweeney Designs Sales Invoice

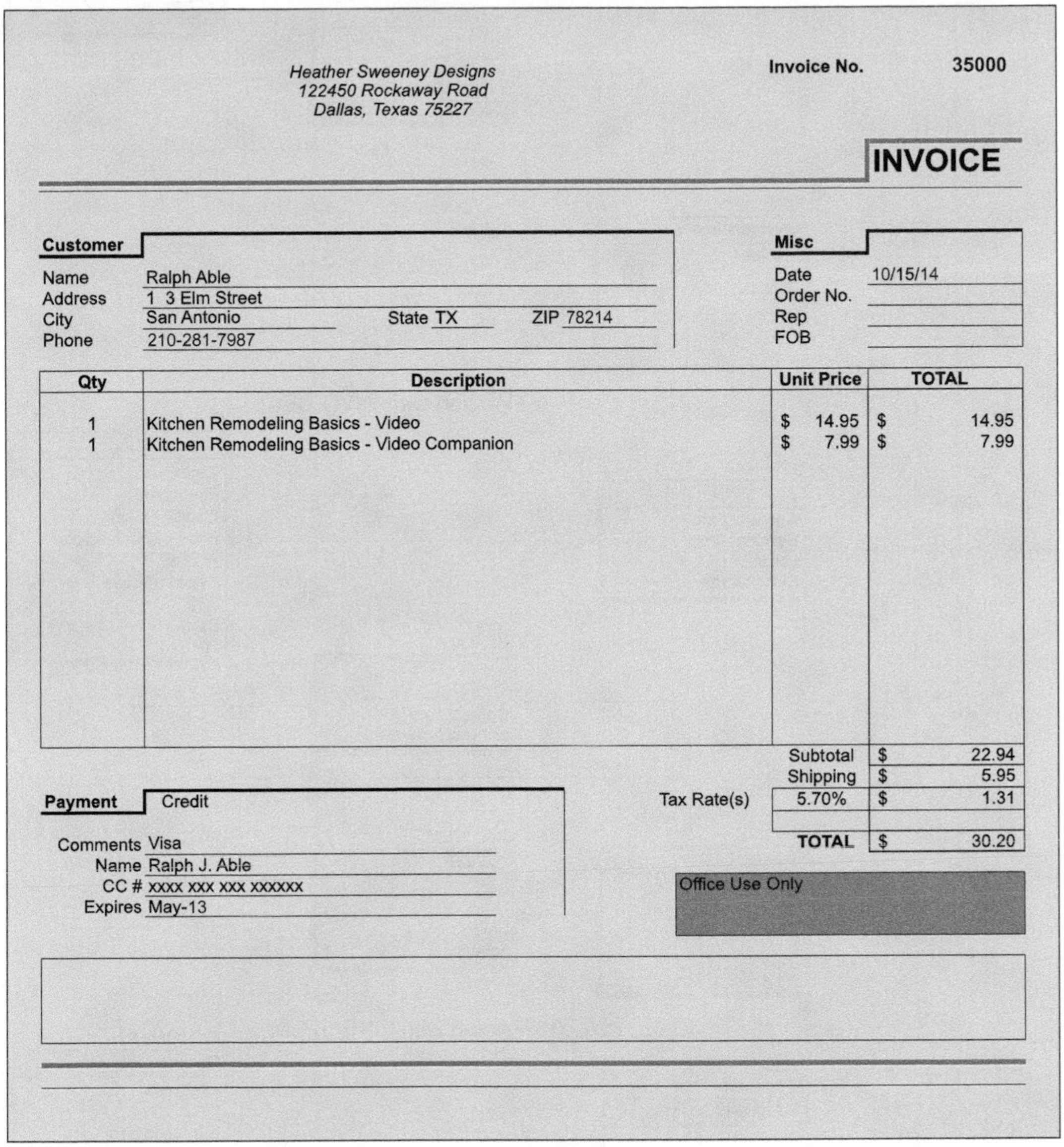
Heather Sweeney Designs
122450 Rockaway Road
Dallas, Texas 75227

Invoice No. 35000

INVOICE

Customer

Name Ralph Able
Address 1 3 Elm Street
City San Antonio State TX ZIP 78214
Phone 210-281-7987

Misc

Date 10/15/14
Order No.
Rep
FOB

Qty	Description	Unit Price	TOTAL
1	Kitchen Remodeling Basics - Video	$ 14.95	$ 14.95
1	Kitchen Remodeling Basics - Video Companion	$ 7.99	$ 7.99
		Subtotal	$ 22.94
		Shipping	$ 5.95
	Tax Rate(s)	5.70%	$ 1.31
		TOTAL	$ 30.20

Payment Credit

Comments Visa
Name Ralph J. Able
CC # xxxx xxx xxx xxxxxx
Expires May-13

Office Use Only

records only the PaymentType value in the database and files the credit card receipts in a (locked) physical file with a notation that relates them back to an invoice number.

Figure 4-21 shows the completion of the Heather Sweeney Designs data model. Figure 4-21(a) shows a first attempt at the data model with INVOICE. This diagram is missing data about the line items on the order. Because there are multiple line items, the line item data cannot be stored in INVOICE. Instead, an ID-dependent entity, LINE_ITEM, must be defined. The need for an ID-dependent entity is typical for documents that contain a group of repeating data. If the repeating group is not logically independent, then it must be made into an ID-dependent weak entity. Figure 4-21(b) shows the adjusted design.

Because LINE_ITEM belongs to an identifying relationship from INVOICE, it needs an attribute that can be used to identify a particular LINE_ITEM within an INVOICE. The identifier we will use for LINE_ITEM will be the composite (InvoiceNumber,

FIGURE 4-21

The Final Data Model for Heather Sweeney Designs

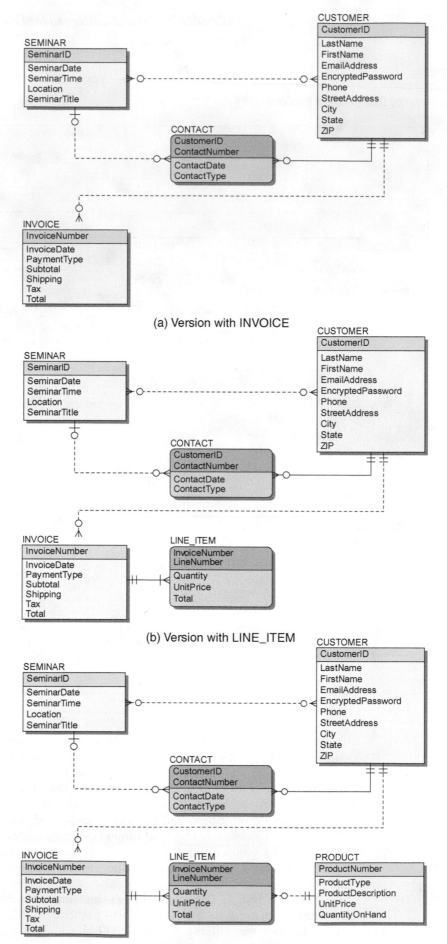

(a) Version with INVOICE

(b) Version with LINE_ITEM

(c) The Finished Data Model

LineNumber), where InvoiceNumber is the identifier of INVOICE and the LineNumber attribute identifies the line within the INVOICE on which an item appears.

We need to make one more correction to this data model. Heather sells standard products—that is, her books and videos have standardized names and prices. She does not want the person who fills out an order to be able to use nonstandard names or prices. We therefore need to add a PRODUCT entity and relate it to LINE_ITEM, as shown in Figure 4-21(c).

Observe that UnitPrice is an attribute of both PRODUCT and LINE_ITEM. This was done so that Heather can update UnitPrice without affecting the recorded orders. At the time a sale is made, UnitPrice in LINE_ITEM is set equal to UnitPrice in PRODUCT. The LINE_ITEM UnitPrice never changes. However, as time passes and Heather changes prices for her products she can update UnitPrice in PRODUCT. If UnitPrice were not copied into LINE_ITEM, when the PRODUCT price changes, the price in already stored LINE_ITEMs would change as well, and Heather does not want this to occur. Therefore, although two attributes are named UnitPrice, they are different attributes used for different purposes.

Note in Figure 4-21(c) that based on interviews with Heather we have added ProductNumber and QuantityOnHand to PRODUCT. These attributes do not appear in any of the documents, but they are known by Heather and are important to her.

Attribute Specifications

The data model in Figure 4-21(c) shows entities, attributes, and entity relationships, but it does not document details about attributes. These details are normally dealt with as column specifications during the creation of the database design from the data model as described in Chapter 5. However, during the requirements analysis, you may learn of some desired or required attribute specifications (such as default values). These should be documented for use in creating the database design column specifications.

Business Rules

When creating a data model, we need to be on the lookout for business rules that constrain data values and the processing of the database. We encountered such a business rule with regard to CONTACT, when Heather Sweeney stated that no more than one form letter or email per day is to be sent to a customer.

In more complicated data models, many such business rules would exist. These rules are generally too specific or too complicated to be enforced by the DBMS. Rather, application programs or other forms of procedural logic need to be developed to enforce such rules.

Validating the Data Model

After a data model has been completed, it needs to be validated. The most common way to do this is to show it to the users and obtain their feedback. However, a large, complicated data model is off-putting to many users, so often the data model needs to be broken into sections and validated piece by piece or expressed in some other terms that are more understandable.

As mentioned earlier in this chapter, prototypes are sometimes constructed for users to review. Prototypes are easier for users to understand and evaluate than data models. We can develop prototypes that show the consequences of data model design decisions without requiring the users to learn E-R modeling. For example, showing a form with room for only one customer is a way of indicating that the maximum cardinality of a relationship is one. If the users respond to such a form with the question "But where do I put the second customer?" you know that the maximum cardinality is greater than one.

It is relatively easy to create mock-ups of forms and reports by using Microsoft Access wizards. We can even develop such mock-ups in situations where Microsoft Access is not going to be used as the operational DBMS because they are still useful for demonstrating the consequences of data modeling decisions.

Finally, a data model needs to be evaluated against all use cases. For each use case, we need to verify that all the data and relationships necessary to support the use case are present and accurately represented in the data model.

Data model validation is exceedingly important. It is far easier and less expensive to correct errors at this stage than it is to correct them after the database has been designed and implemented. Changing the cardinality in a data model is a simple adjustment to a document, but changing the cardinality later might require the construction of new tables, new relationships, new queries, new forms, new reports, and so forth. So every minute spent validating a data model will pay great dividends down the line.

THE ACCESS WORKBENCH

Section 4

Prototyping Using Microsoft Access

In this chapter, when discussing data modeling concepts and techniques we talked about building a **prototype database** for users to review as a model-validation technique. Prototypes are easier for users to understand and evaluate than data models. In addition, they can be used to show the consequences of data-model design decisions.

Because it is relatively easy to create mock-ups of forms and reports by using Microsoft Access wizards, mock-ups are often developed even in situations in which Microsoft Access is not going to be used as the operational DBMS. The mock-ups can be used as a prototyping tool to demonstrate the consequences of data modeling decisions. In this section, you will use Microsoft Access as a prototyping tool. We will continue to use the WMCRM database. At this point, we have created and populated the CONTACT, CUSTOMER, and SALESPERSON tables. In the preceding sections of "The Access Workbench," you also learned how to create forms, reports, and queries. And if you studied Appendix E's section of "The Access Workbench" together with Chapter 3, you have learned how to create and use view-equivalent queries.

Let us start by considering what the WMCRM database looks like from a data modeling point of view. Figure AW-4-1 shows the WMCRM database as an IE Crow's Foot E-R model.

This model is based on the business rule that each CUSTOMER works with one and only one SALESPERSON. Therefore, we have a 1:N relationship between SALESPERSON and CUSTOMER, which shows that each SALESPERSON can work with many CUSTOMERs but each CUSTOMER is attended to by only one SALESPERSON. Further, because there is no doubt about which SALESPERSON is

FIGURE AW-4-1

The WMCRM Database as a Data Model

SALESPERSON	CUSTOMER	CONTACT
NickName	CustomerID	ContactID
LastName	LastName	ContactDate
FirstName	FirstName	ContactType
HireDate	Address	Remarks
WageRate	City	
CommissionRate	State	
Phone	ZIP	
Email	Phone	
	Fax	
	Email	

The Modified WMCRM Data Model

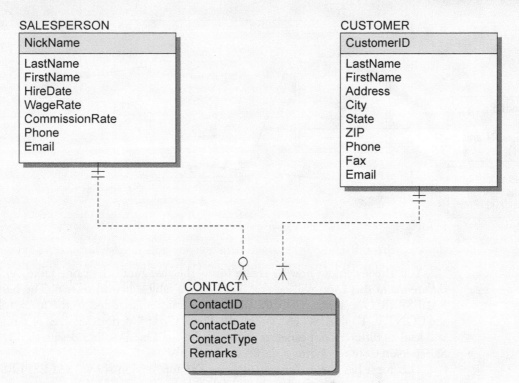

involved in each CONTACT with a CUSTOMER, the connection to CONTACT is a 1:N relationship to CUSTOMER.

But all this would change if the business rule were that any CUSTOMER could work with more than one SALESPERSON. This would allow any SALESPERSON to contact the CUSTOMER as needed rather than relying on just one SALESPERSON to be available whenever needed for work with a particular CUSTOMER. Each CONTACT would now need to be linked to the CUSTOMER contacted and the SALEPERSON making the CONTACT. This results in a data model like the one shown in Figure AW-4-2.

Here we have a 1:N relationship between SALESPERSON and CONTACT instead of between SALESPERSON and CUSTOMER, while the 1:N relationship between CUSTOMER and CONTACT remains the same. CONTACTs for one CUSTOMER can now be linked to various SALESPERSONs.

Imagine that you have been hired as a consultant to create the WMCRM database. You now have two alternative data models that you need to show to managers at Wallingford Motors so that they can make a decision about which model to use. But they do not understand E-R data modeling.

How can you illustrate the differences between the two data models? One way is to generate some mock-up prototype forms and reports in Microsoft Access. Users can more easily understand forms and reports than they can understand your abstract E-R model.

Creating a Prototype Form for the Original Data Model

We will start by creating a sample form in the current version of the WMCRM database, which we are treating here as a prototype we created to illustrate the first data model. (This includes populating the database with sample data.) The database structure for this database is shown in the Relationships window in Figure AW-4-3.

(Continued)

FIGURE AW-4-3

The Original WMCRM Database

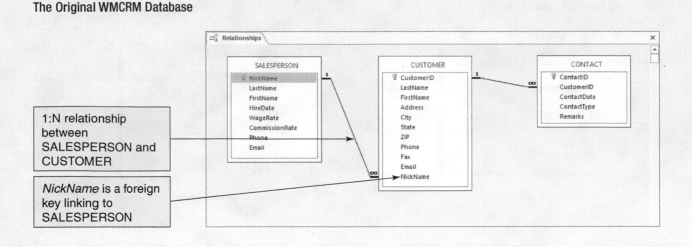

You already know how to create forms that use more than one table, and the only difference in this form will be that it uses three tables instead of two. The basic table is SALESPERSON, with CUSTOMER as the second table added to the form, followed by the CONTACT table. When you use the Form Wizard, various choices of design options will lead to different appearances of the final form. One possible design of the WMCRM Salesperson Contacts Form is shown in Figure AW-4-4.

This form has three distinct sections: The top section shows SALESPERSON data, the middle section shows selectable CUSTOMER data, and the bottom section shows the CONTACT data for the current CUSTOMER. It should be fairly easy to explain this form to the Wallingford Motors management and users.

FIGURE AW-4-4

The WMCRM Salesperson Contacts Form

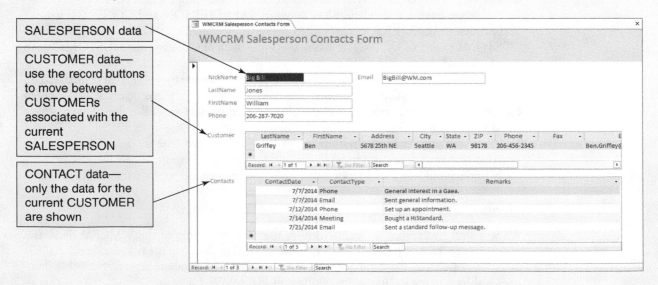

Creating a Prototype Form for the Modified Data Model

Before we can create the equivalent WMCRM Salesperson Contacts Form for the second data model, we must prototype the resulting database in Microsoft Access. Fortunately, we do not need to create a new database from scratch—we can simply make a copy of the existing Microsoft Access database. One of the nice features of Microsoft Access is that each database is stored in one *.accdb file. For example, recall from Chapter 1's section of "The Access Workbench" that the original database was named WMCRM.accdb and stored in the Documents library. We can make renamed copies of this file as the basis for prototyping other data models.

Copying the WMCRM.accdb Database

1. Select **Start | Documents** to open the My Documents library.
2. Right-click the **WMCRM.accdb** file object to display the shortcut menu, and then click **Copy**.
3. Right-click anywhere in the empty area of the Documents library window to display the shortcut menu and then click **Paste**. A file object named **WMCRM - Copy.accdb** appears in the Documents library window.
4. Right-click the **WMCRM - Copy.accdb** file object to display the shortcut menu, and then click **Rename**.
5. Edit the file name to read **WMCRM-AW04-v02.accdb**, and then press the **Enter** key.

Now we need to modify this database file. The goal is the set of database relationships shown in Figure AW-4-5.

FIGURE AW-4-5

The Modified WMCRM Database

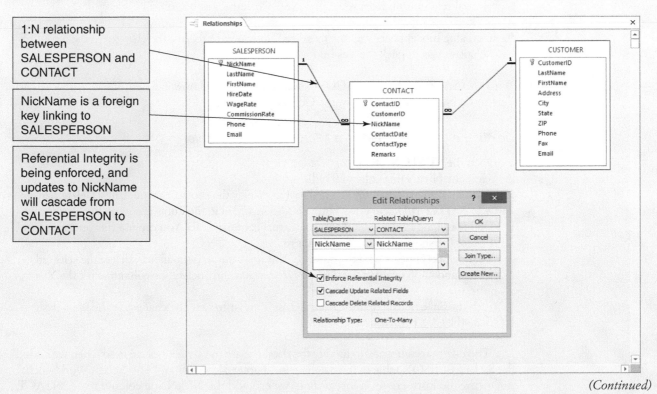

The modifications are straightforward, and we have done most of the steps in previous sections. We need to:

- Remove the relationship between SALESPERSON and CUSTOMER (this is new).
- Delete the NickName field in CUSTOMER (this is new).
- Add the NickName field to CONTACT as NULL.
- Populate the NickName field in CONTACT.
- Modify the NickName field in CONTACT to NOT NULL.
- Create the relationship between SALESPERSON and CONTACT.

The only new steps are deleting a relationship and deleting a field from a table.

Deleting the SALESPERSON-to-CUSTOMER Relationship

1. Start Microsoft Access 2014.
2. If the File command tab is not selected, click the **File** command tab to display the Backstage view, and then click the **Open** button. The Open dialog box appears. Browse to the **WMCRM-AW04-v02.accdb** file, click the file name to highlight it, and then click the **Open** button.
3. The **Security Warning** bar appears with the database. Click the Security Warning bar's **Enable Content** button.
4. Click the **Database Tools** command tab.
5. Click the **Relationships** button in the Relationships command group. The Relationships tabbed document window appears. Note that along with the Relationships window a contextual tab named Relationship Tools is displayed and that this tab adds a new command tab named Design to the set of command tabs displayed.
6. Right-click the **relationship line** between SALESPERSON and CUSTOMER to display the shortcut menu, and then click **Delete**.
7. A dialog box appears with the message "Are you sure you want to permanently delete the selected relationship from your database?" Click the **Yes** button.
8. Click the Relationships window's **Close** button to close the window.
9. If a dialog box appears with the message "Do you want to save the changes to the layout of 'Relationships'?" click the **Yes** button.

With the SALESPERSON-to-CUSTOMER relationship now deleted, we can proceed to delete the NickName field from the CUSTOMER table.

Deleting a Column (Field) in a Microsoft Access Table

1. Open the **CUSTOMER** table in Design view.
2. Select the **NickName** column (field).
3. Right-click anywhere in the selected row to display the shortcut menu. Click **Delete Rows**.
   - **NOTE:** A Delete Rows button is also included in the Tools group on the Design command tab of the Table Tools contextual command tab. You can use this button instead of the shortcut menu if you want to.
4. A dialog box appears with the message "Do you want to permanently delete the selected field(s) and all the data in the field(s)?" To permanently delete the column, click the **Yes** button.
5. Click the **Save** button on the Quick Access Toolbar to save the changes to the table design.
6. Close the **CUSTOMER** table.

The other steps needed to modify the database are the same ones we used when we added the SALESPERSON table to the database in Chapter 3's section of "The Access Workbench." Following the instructions in that section, we can add the NickName column to CONTACT,

FIGURE AW-4-6

The NickName Column in CONTACT

populate it, and create the relationship between SALESPERSON and CONTACT. In Chapter 3's section of "The Access Workbench," we used Microsoft Access SQL to accomplish these tasks. In this section, we will walk through similar steps with Microsoft Access QBE. Note that Figure AW-4-5 shows NickName inserted as the third column (field) in the table—it could just as easily be added as the last column in the table. In a relational table, the column order does not matter: We use the one that makes it easier for database developers to read!

Figure AW-4-6 shows the NickName column as it is initially added to the CONTACT table. Note that the data type is Short Text(35), but currently the column is *not* required. This is the Microsoft Access equivalent of the SQL NULL constraint.

Figure AW-4-7 shows the NickName column data added to the CONTACT table. Now each CONTACT record contains the name of the salesperson making the contact.

FIGURE AW-4-7

The NickName Data in CONTACT

(Continued)

FIGURE AW-4-8

The Required NickName Column in CONTACT

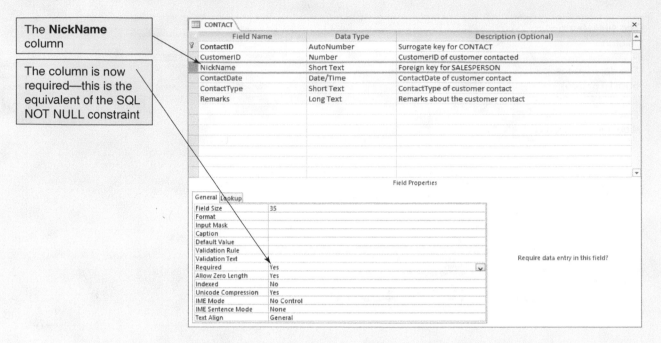

The **NickName** column

The column is now required—this is the equivalent of the SQL NOT NULL constraint

After the NickName column data have been added to the CONTACT table, we need to set the NickName column's Required field property to Yes, as shown in Figure AW-4-8. This is the equivalent of the SQL NOT NULL constraint, and because NickName is a foreign key linking to SALESPERSON the NickName column in CONTACT must be NOT NULL.

With the CONTACT table modifications done, we need to build the new relationship between the SALESPERSON and CONTACT tables. This relationship is shown in Figure AW-4-5, with the Edit Relationships dialog box showing that referential integrity is being enforced for the relationship, and Cascade Update Related Fields is also checked. Close the Relationships window.

With these modifications done, we now create another version of the WMCRM Salesperson Contacts Form. This version is shown in Figure AW-4-9.

This form has two distinct sections: The top section shows SALESPERSON data, and the bottom section shows that the data for each CUSTOMER are combined with the CONTACT data for each customer contact. This form is distinctively different from the form based on the first data model, but, again, it should be fairly easy to explain this form to Wallingford Motors' management and users. Based on the two forms, management and users will be able to decide how they want the data presented, and this decision will then determine which data model should be used.

The Microsoft Access Banded Form and Report Editors

The form in Figure AW-4-9 has extensively rearranged labels and data text boxes in the Customer Contact section of the form. Microsoft Access uses **banded form editors** and **banded report editors**, where each element of the form or report is displayed in its own band (for example, Header, Detail, or Footer), which makes such rearranging very easy to do. The form shown in Figure AW-4-9 is shown in Design view in Figure AW-4-10.

FIGURE AW-4-9

The WMCRM Salesperson Contacts Form for the Modified Database

SALESPERSON data

The Customer Contact data area now includes CUSTOMER data as well as the CONTACT data—each contact record shows which customer was contacted

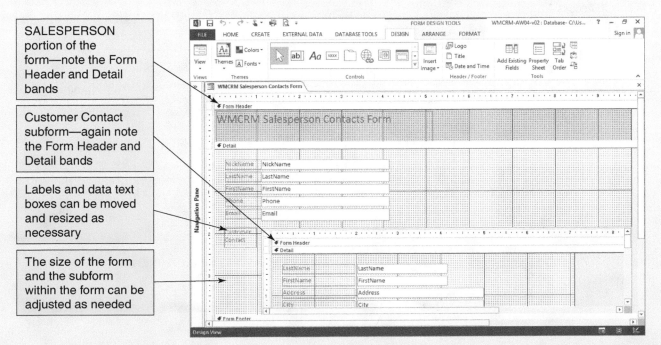

Note that the form and the CONTACT subform each have their own Form Header, Detail, and Form Footer sections. You can resize these as necessary, and you can resize the entire form itself and change the size and position of the subform area within the form. You can move or resize the labels and text boxes that display the data by using standard Windows drag-and-drop actions. You can edit label text, and you can add additional labels

FIGURE AW-4-10

The Microsoft Access 2014 Banded Form Editor

SALESPERSON portion of the form—note the Form Header and Detail bands

Customer Contact subform—again note the Form Header and Detail bands

Labels and data text boxes can be moved and resized as necessary

The size of the form and the subform within the form can be adjusted as needed

(Continued)

or other text. Although Figure AW-4-10 shows a form, report formats can be edited exactly the same way.

Working with Microsoft Access Switchboards

Most users would find working with Microsoft Access 2014 database applications at the level of detail that we have been using to be intimidating. Users want a simple way to access forms (so that they can input data) and reports (so that they can view and print them). They really don't want all the complexity of tables, views, and relationships. This is particularly true when prototyping applications—users want to see what the application can do, not how it does it! In Microsoft Access 2014, we can build a **switchboard** that will provide this functionality. A switchboard is simply a specialized Microsoft Access form that provides a way for the user to easily navigate the application with a button-based menu system. An example for our WMCRM database is shown in Figure AW-4-11. A full discussion of Microsoft Access switchboards and how to create them can be found in online Appendix H, "The Access Workbench," Section H, "Microsoft Access Switchboards."

Closing the Database and Exiting Microsoft Access

This completes the work we will do in this chapter's "The Access Workbench." As usual, we finish by closing the database and Microsoft Access.

Closing the WMCRM-AW04-v02 Database

1. To close the WMCRM-AW04-v02 database and exit Microsoft Access, click the **Close** button in the upper-right corner of the Microsoft Access window.

FIGURE AW-4-11

A Microsoft Access 2013 Switchboard

SUMMARY

The process of developing a database system consists of three stages: requirements analysis, component design, and implementation. During the requirements analysis stage, you interview users, document systems requirements, and construct a data model. Oftentimes, you will create prototypes of selected portions of the future system. During the component design stage, you transform the data model into a relational database design. During the implementation stage, you construct the database, fill it with data, and create queries, forms, reports, and application programs.

In addition to creating a data model, you must also determine data-item data types, properties, and limits on data values. You also need to document business rules that constrain database activity.

The entity-relationship (E-R) model is the most popular tool used to develop a data model. With the E-R model, entities, which are identifiable things of importance to the users, are defined. All the entities of a given type form an entity class. A particular entity is called an instance. Attributes describe the characteristics of entities, and one or more attributes identify an entity. Identifiers can be unique or nonunique.

Relationships are associations among entities. The E-R model explicitly defines relationships. Each relationship has a name, and there are relationship classes as well as relationship instances. According to the original specification of the E-R model, relationships may have attributes; however, this is not common in contemporary data models.

The degree of a relationship is the number of entities participating in the relationship. Most relationships are binary. The three types of binary relationships are 1:1, 1:N, and N:M. A recursive relationship occurs when an entity has a relationship to itself.

In traditional E-R diagrams, such as the traditional E-R model, entities are shown in rectangles and relationships are shown in diamonds. The maximum cardinality of a relationship is shown inside the diamond. The minimum cardinality is indicated by a hash mark or an oval.

A weak entity is one whose existence depends on another entity; an entity that is not weak is called a strong entity. In this text, we further define a weak entity as an entity that logically depends on another entity. An entity can have a minimum cardinality of one in a relationship with another entity and not necessarily be a weak entity. ID-dependent entities must include the identifier of the entity on which the ID-dependent entity depends as part of the identifier of the ID-dependent entity.

When a data model has one or more attributes that seem to be associated with a relationship between two entities rather than with either of the entities themselves, an associative entity (also called an association entity) must be added to the data model. Each of the original entities will have a 1:N relationship with the associative entity, which will have a composite primary key consisting of the two primary keys of the original entities. The associative entity will be ID-dependent on both of the original entities.

The extended E-R model introduced the concept of subtypes. A subtype entity is a special case of another entity known as its supertype. In some cases, an attribute of the supertype, called a discriminator, indicates which of the subtypes is appropriate for a given instance. Subtypes can be exclusive (the supertype relates to at most one subtype) or inclusive (the supertype can relate to one or more subtypes). The identifier of the subtype is the identifier of the supertype.

This text's E-R diagrams use the Information Engineering Crow's Foot E-R model. You should be familiar with diagrams of that style, but you should also realize that when creating a database design no fundamental difference exists between the traditional style and this style. When creating a data model, it is important to document business rules that constrain database activity.

After E-R models are completed, they must be evaluated. You can show the data model, or portions of the data model, directly to the users for evaluation. This requires the users to learn how to interpret an E-R diagram. Sometimes, instead of showing users a data model you may create prototypes that demonstrate the consequences of the data model. Such prototypes are easier for users to understand.

KEY TERMS

association entity
associative entity
attribute
binary relationship
cardinality
child entity
component design stage
composite identifier
crow's foot symbol
data model
database design
database development process
degree
design stage
discriminator
entity
entity class
entity instance
entity-relationship (E-R) diagram
entity-relationship model

exclusive subtype
extended entity-relationship (E-R)
    model
HAS-A relationship
ID-dependent entity
identifier
identifying relationship
IE Crow's Foot model
implementation stage
inclusive subtype
Information Engineering (IE)
    model
Integrated Definition 1, Extended
    (IDEF1X)
IS-A relationship
mandatory
maximum cardinality
minimum cardinality
nonidentifying relationship
nonunique identifier

optional
parent entity
recursive relationship
relationship
relationship class
relationship instance
requirements analysis stage
strong entity
subtype entity
supertype entity
system design stage
systems development life cycle
    (SDLC)
ternary relationship
unary relationship
Unified Modeling Language
    (UML)
unique identifier
use case
weak entity

REVIEW QUESTIONS

4.1   Name the three stages in the process of developing database systems. Summarize the tasks in each.

4.2   What is a data model, and what is its purpose?

4.3   What is a prototype, and what is its purpose?

4.4   What is a use case, and what is its purpose?

4.5   Give an example of a data constraint.

4.6   Give an example of a business rule that would need to be documented in a database development project.

4.7   Define the term *entity* and give an example other than those used in this book.

4.8   Explain the difference between an entity class and an entity instance.

4.9   Define the term *attribute* and give examples for the entity you described in question 4.7.

4.10   Define the term *identifier* and indicate which attribute defined in your answer to question 4.9 identifies the entity.

4.11   Define the term *composite identifier* and give an example other than those used in this book.

4.12   Define the term *relationship* and give an example other than those used in this book.

4.13   Explain the difference between a relationship class and a relationship instance.

4.14   Define the term *degree of relationship*. Give an example, other than one used in this text, of a relationship greater than degree two.

4.15   List and give an example of the three types of binary relationships other than the ones used in this book. Draw both a traditional E-R diagram and an IE Crow's Foot E-R diagram for each.

4.16   Define the terms *maximum cardinality* and *minimum cardinality*.

4.17 Draw an IE Crow's Foot E-R diagram for the entities DEPARTMENT and EMPLOYEE and the 1:N relationship between them. Assume that a DEPARTMENT does not need to have an EMPLOYEE but that every EMPLOYEE is assigned to a DEPARTMENT. Include appropriate identifiers and attributes for each entity.

4.18 Define the term *ID-dependent entity* and give an example other than one used in this text. Draw an IE Crow's Foot E-R diagram for your example.

4.19 Define the term *weak entity* and give an example other than one used in this text. Draw an IE Crow's Foot E-R diagram for your example.

4.20 Explain the ambiguity in the definition of the term *weak entity*. Explain how this book interprets this term.

4.21 Define the term *associative entity*, and give an example other than one used in this text. Your example should start with a N:M relationship between two strong entities and then be modified by an additional data requirement. Draw IE Crow's Foot E-R diagrams for both your N:M relationship and for the relationships among the three entities that include the associative entity.

4.22 Define the terms *supertype*, *subtype*, and *discriminator*.

4.23 What is an exclusive subtype relationship? Give an example other than one shown in this book. Draw an IE Crow's Foot E-R diagram for your example.

4.24 What is an inclusive subtype relationship? Give an example other than one shown in this chapter. Draw an IE Crow's Foot E-R diagram for your example.

4.25 Give an example of a recursive relationship other than the one shown in this chapter. Draw an IE Crow's Foot E-R diagram for your example.

4.26 Give an example of a business rule for your work for question 4.17.

4.27 Describe why it is important to evaluate a data model.

4.28 Summarize one technique for evaluating a data model and explain how that technique could be used to evaluate the data model in Figure 4-21(c).

EXERCISES

4.29 Suppose that Heather Sweeney wants to include records of her consulting services in her database. Extend the data model in Figure 4-21(c) to include CONSULTING_PROJECT and DAILY_PROJECT_HOURS entities. CONSULTING_PROJECT contains data about a particular project for one of Heather's customers, and DAILY_PROJECT_HOURS contains data about the hours spent and a description of the work accomplished on a particular day for a particular project. Use strong and/or weak entities, as appropriate. Specify minimum and maximum cardinalities. Use the IE Crow's Foot E-R model for your E-R diagrams.

4.30 Extend your work for question 4.29 to include supplies that Heather uses on a project. Assume that she wants to track the description, price, and amount used of each supply. Supplies are used on multiple days of a project. Use the IE Crow's Foot E-R model for your E-R diagrams.

4.31 Using recursive relationships, as appropriate, develop a data model of the boxcars on a railway train. Use the IE Crow's Foot E-R model for your E-R diagrams.

4.32 Develop a data model of a genealogical diagram. Model only biological parents; do not model stepparents. Use the IE Crow's Foot E-R model for your E-R diagrams.

4.33 Develop a data model of a genealogical diagram. Model all parents, including stepparents. Use the IE Crow's Foot E-R model for your E-R diagrams.

ACCESS WORKBENCH KEY TERMS

banded form editor   prototype database
banded report editor   switchboard

ACCESS WORKBENCH EXERCISES

"The Access Workbench" section in this chapter describes how to create two prototype databases and sample forms. That section details some steps that are new, but you have done most of the needed steps before. In the following set of exercises, you will:

- Create prototype forms.
- Create prototype reports.

AW.4.1   You have built an extensive database for the Wedgewood Pacific Corporation (WPC.accdb). You will now use it to build some prototype forms and reports so that the users at WPC can evaluate the proposed database. In this case, there is no need to restructure the database.

A.   Create a form that allows users to view and edit employee data. The form should show information about the employee, the department that he or she works for, and which projects the employee is assigned to.

B.   Create a report that displays the employee information shown on the form you created in part A. The report should show this information for all users, sorted alphabetically in ascending order by LastName.

C.   Create a form that allows users to view and edit project data. The form should show information about the project and the department that is responsible for the project, and it should list all employees who are assigned to work on that project.

D.   Create a report that displays the project information shown on the form you created in part C. The report should show this information for all projects, sorted in ascending order by ProjectID.

HIGHLINE UNIVERSITY MENTOR PROGRAM CASE QUESTIONS

Highline University is a 4-year undergraduate school located in the Puget Sound region of Washington State.[4] Highline University, like many colleges and universities in the Pacific Northwest, is accredited by the Northwest Commission on Colleges and Universities (NWCCU—see **www.nwccu.org**). Like all the colleges and universities accredited by the NWCCU, Highline University must be reaccredited at approximately 5-year intervals. Additionally, the NWCCU requires annual status-update reports. Highline University is made up of five colleges: the College of Business, the College of Social Sciences and Humanities, the College of Performing Arts, the College of Sciences and Technology, and the College of Environmental Sciences. Jan Smathers is the president of Highline

---

[4]Highline University is a *fictional* university and should not be confused with Highline Community College located in Des Moines, Washington. Any resemblance between Highline University and Highline Community College is unintentional and purely coincidental.

University, and Dennis Endersby is the provost (a provost is a vice president of academics; the deans of the colleges report to the provost).

A discussion of the design of a college information system for Highline University is used in Appendix D, "Getting Started with Systems and Analysis and Design," as an example of creating data models (discussed in this chapter) and database designs (discussed in Chapter 5). In this set of case questions, we will consider a different information system for Highline University, one that will be used by Highline University's Mentor Program. The Highline University Mentor Program recruits business professionals as mentors for Highline University students. The mentors are unpaid volunteers who work together with the students' advisers to ensure that the students in the mentoring program learn needed and relevant management skills. In this case study, you will develop a data model for the Mentor Program Information System.

A. Draw an E-R data model for the Highline University Mentor Program Information System (MPIS). Use the IE Crow's Foot E-R model for your E-R diagrams. Justify the decisions you make regarding minimum and maximum cardinality.

Your model should track students, advisers, and mentors. Additionally, Highline University needs to track alumni because the program administrators view alumni as potential mentors.

1. Create separate entities for students, alumni, faculty advisers, and mentors.

   - At Highline University, all students are required to live on campus and are assigned Highline University ID numbers and email accounts in the format *FirstName.LastName@students.hu.edu*. The student entity should track student last name, student first name, student University ID number, student email address, dorm name, dorm room number, and dorm phone number.

   - At Highline University, all faculty advisers have on-campus offices and are assigned Highline University ID numbers and email accounts in the format *FirstName.LastName@.hu.edu*. The faculty entity should track faculty last name, faculty first name, faculty University ID number, faculty email address, department, office building name, office building room number, and office phone number.

   - Highline University alumni live off campus and were previously assigned Highline University ID numbers. Alumni have private email accounts in the format *FirstName.LastName@somewhere.com*. The alumni entity should track alumnus last name, alumnus first name, alumnus former-student number, email address, home address, home city, home state, home ZIP code, and phone number.

   - Highline University mentors work for companies and use their company address, phone, and email address for contact information. They do not have Highline University ID numbers as mentors. Email addresses are in the format *FirstName.LastName@companyname.com*. The mentor entity should track mentor last name, mentor first name, mentor email address, company name, company address, company city, company state, company ZIP code, and company phone number.

2. Create relationships between entities based on the following facts:

   - Each student is assigned one and only one faculty adviser and must have an adviser. One faculty member may advise several students, but faculty members are not required to advise students. Only the fact of this assignment is to be recorded in the data model—not possible related data (such as the date the adviser was assigned to the student).

   - Each student may be assigned one and only one mentor, but students are not required to have a mentor. One mentor may mentor several students, and a person may be listed as a mentor before he or she is actually assigned students to mentor. Only the fact of this assignment is to be recorded in the data model—not possible related data (such as the date the mentor was assigned to the student).

- Each mentor is assigned to work and coordinate with one and only one faculty member, and each mentor must work with a faculty member. One faculty member may work with several mentors, but faculty members are not required to work with mentors. Only the fact of this assignment is to be recorded in the data model—not possible related data (such as the date the faculty member was assigned to the mentor).

- Each mentor may be an alumnus, but mentors are not required to be alumni. Alumni cannot, of course, be required to become mentors.

B. Revise the E-R data model you created in part A to create a new E-R data model based on the fact that students, faculty, alumni, and mentors are all a PERSON. Use the IE Crow's Foot E-R model for your E-R diagrams. Justify the decisions you make regarding minimum and maximum cardinality. Note that:

- A person may be a current student, an alumnus, or both because Highline University does have alumni return for further study.

- A person may be a faculty member or a mentor, but not both.

- A person may be a faculty member and an alumnus.

- A person may be a mentor and an alumnus.

- A current student cannot be a mentor.

- Each mentor may be an alumnus, but mentors are not required to be alumni. Alumni cannot, of course, be required to become mentors.

C. Extend and modify the E-R data model you created in part B to allow more data to be recorded in the MPIS system. Use the IE Crow's Foot E-R model for your E-R diagrams. Justify the decisions you make regarding minimum and maximum cardinality. The MPIS needs to record:

- The date a student enrolled at Highline University, the date the student graduated, and the degree the student received

- The date an adviser was assigned to a student and the date the assignment ended

- The date an adviser was assigned to work with a mentor and the date the assignment ended

- The date a mentor was assigned to a student and the date the assignment ended

D. Write a short discussion of the difference between the three data models you have created. How does data model B differ from data model A, and how does data model C differ from data model B? What additional features of the E-R data model were introduced when you created data models B and C?

WASHINGTON STATE PATROL CASE QUESTIONS

Consider the Washington State Patrol traffic citation shown in Figure 4-22. The rounded corners on this form provide visual hints about the boundaries of the entities represented.

A. Draw an E-R data model based on the traffic citation form. Use five entities, create identifiers (watch out for any composite identifiers that may be needed, and you can use surrogate identifiers if appropriate) and use the data items on the form to specify attributes for the entities. Use the IE Crow's Foot E-R model for your E-R diagram.

B. Specify relationships among the entities. Name the relationships, and specify the relationship types and cardinalities. Justify the decisions you make regarding minimum and maximum cardinalities, indicating which cardinalities can be inferred from the data on the form and which need to be checked out with the system users.

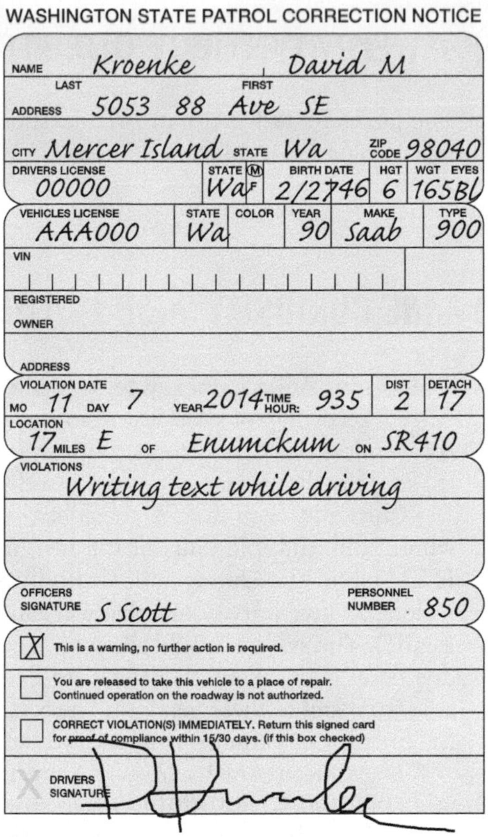
WASHINGTON STATE PATROL CORRECTION NOTICE

NAME Kroenke (LAST), David M (FIRST)

ADDRESS 5053 88 Ave SE

CITY Mercer Island STATE Wa ZIP CODE 98040

DRIVERS LICENSE	STATE	M/F	BIRTH DATE	HGT	WGT	EYES
00000	Wa	M	2/27/46	6	165	Bl

VEHICLES LICENSE	STATE	COLOR	YEAR	MAKE	TYPE
AAA000	Wa		90	Saab	900

VIN

REGISTERED OWNER

ADDRESS

VIOLATION DATE MO 11 DAY 7 YEAR 2014 TIME HOUR: 935 DIST 2 DETACH 17

LOCATION 17 MILES E OF Enumckum ON SR410

VIOLATIONS Writing text while driving

OFFICERS SIGNATURE S Scott PERSONNEL NUMBER 850

[X] This is a warning, no further action is required.

[ ] You are released to take this vehicle to a place of repair. Continued operation on the roadway is not authorized.

[ ] CORRECT VIOLATION(S) IMMEDIATELY. Return this signed card for proof of compliance within 15/30 days. (if this box checked)

X DRIVERS SIGNATURE

FIGURE 4-22

WSP Traffic Citation

GARDEN GLORY PROJECT QUESTIONS

Garden Glory wants to expand its database applications beyond the recording of property services. The company still wants to maintain data on owners, properties, employees, services and the service work done at the properties, but it wants to include other data as well. Specifically, Garden Glory wants to track equipment, how it is used during services, and equipment repairs. In addition, employees need to be trained before they use certain equipment, and management wants to be able to determine who has obtained training on which equipment.

With regard to properties, Garden Glory has determined that most of the properties it services are too large and complex to be described in one record. The company wants the database to allow for many subproperty descriptions of a property. Thus, a particular property might have subproperty descriptions such as Front Garden, Back Garden, Second-Level Courtyard, and so on. For better accounting to the customers, services are to be related to the subproperties rather than to the overall property.

A. Draw an E-R data model for the Garden Glory database schema shown in Chapter 3's "Garden Glory Project Questions." Use the IE Crow's Foot E-R model for your E-R diagrams. Justify the decisions you make regarding minimum and maximum cardinality.

B. Extend and modify the E-R data model to meet Garden Glory's new requirements. Use the IE Crow's Foot E-R model for your E-R diagrams. Create appropriate identifiers and attributes for each entity. Justify the decisions you make regarding minimum and maximum cardinality.

C. Describe how you would go about validating the model in part B.

JAMES RIVER JEWELRY PROJECT QUESTIONS

The James River Jewelry project questions are available in online Appendix D, which can be downloaded from the textbook's Web site: **www.pearsonhighered.com/kroenke**.

THE QUEEN ANNE CURIOSITY SHOP PROJECT QUESTIONS

The Queen Anne Curiosity Shop wants to expand its database applications beyond the current recording of sales. The company still wants to maintain data on customers, employees, vendors, sales, and items, but it wants to (a) modify the way it handles inventory and (b) simplify the storage of customer and employee data.

Currently, each item is considered unique, which means the item must be sold as a whole, and multiple units of the item in stock must be treated as separate items in the ITEM table. The Queen Anne Curiosity Shop management wants the database modified to include an inventory system that will allow multiple units of an item to be stored under one ItemID. The system should allow for a quantity on hand, a quantity on order, and an order due date. If the identical item is stocked by multiple vendors, the item should be orderable from any of these vendors. The SALE_ITEM table should then include Quantity and ExtendedPrice columns to allow for sales of multiple units of an item.

The Queen Anne Curiosity Shop management has noticed that some of the fields in CUSTOMER and EMPLOYEE store similar data. Under the current system, when an employee buys something at the store, his or her data has to be reentered into the CUSTOMER table. The managers would like to have the CUSTOMER and EMPLOYEE tables redesigned using subtypes.

A. Draw an E-R data model for The Queen Anne Curiosity Shop database schema shown in Chapter 3's "The Queen Anne Curiosity Shop Project Questions." Use the IE Crow's Foot E-R model for your E-R diagrams. Justify the decisions you make regarding minimum and maximum cardinality.

B. Extend and modify the E-R data model by adding *only* The Queen Anne Curiosity Shop's inventory system requirements. Use the IE Crow's Foot E-R model for your E-R diagrams. Create appropriate identifiers and attributes for each entity. Justify the decisions you make regarding minimum and maximum cardinality.

C. Extend and modify the E-R data model by adding *only* The Queen Anne Curiosity Shop's need for more efficient storage of CUSTOMER and EMPLOYEE data. Use the IE Crow's Foot E-R model for your E-R diagrams. Create appropriate identifiers and attributes for each entity. Justify the decisions you make regarding minimum and maximum cardinality.

D. Combine the E-R data models from parts B and C to meet all of The Queen Anne Curiosity Shop's new requirements, making additional modifications, as needed. Use the IE Crow's Foot E-R model for your E-R diagrams.

E. Describe how you would go about validating your data model in part D.

CHAPTER 5 Database Design

CHAPTER OBJECTIVES

- Learn how to transform E-R data models into relational designs

- Practice applying the normalization process

- Understand the need for denormalization

- Learn how to represent weak entities with the relational model

- Know how to represent 1:1, 1:N, and N:M binary relationships

- Know how to represent 1:1, 1:N, and N:M recursive relationships

- Learn SQL statements for creating joins over binary and recursive relationships

In Chapter 4, we defined the database development process as consisting of three major stages: requirements analysis, component design, and implementation and then discussed the requirements analysis stage and how to create a **data model** in entity-relationship (E-R) notation. This chapter describes a process for converting an E-R data model into a relational *database design*. We begin by explaining how data model entities are expressed as relations (or tables) in a relational database design. We then apply the normalization process that you learned in Chapter 2. Next, we show how to represent relationships using foreign keys, including how to use these techniques for representing recursive relationships. Finally, we apply all these techniques to design a database for the data model of Heather Sweeney Designs that we developed in Chapter 4.

Database design occurs in the **component design** step of the **systems development life cycle (SDLC)**. For an introduction to systems analysis and design, and to the SDLC, see Appendix D.

THE PURPOSE OF A DATABASE DESIGN

A **database design** is a set of database specifications that can actually be implemented as a database in a DBMS. The *data model* we discussed in Chapter 4 is a *generalized, non-DBMS specific* design. A database design, on the other hand, is a *DBMS specific* design intended to be implemented in a DBMS product such as Microsoft SQL Server 2014 or MySQL 5.6. Since each DBMS product has its own way of doing things, even if based on the same relational database model and the same SQL standards, each database design must be created for a particular DBMS product. The same data model will result in slightly different database designs depending upon the intended DBMS product.

BTW

Books on systems analysis and design often identify three design stages:

- Conceptual design (conceptual schema)
- Logical design (logical schema)
- Physical design (physical schema)

The *database design* we are discussing is basically equivalent to the *logical design*, which is defined in these books as the conceptual design as modified to be implemented in a specific DBMS product. The *physical design* deals with aspects of the database encountered when it is actually implemented in the DBMS, such as physical record and file structure and organization, indexing, and query optimization. However, our discussion of database design *will* include data type specifications, which is often considered a physical design issue in systems analysis and design.

TRANSFORMING A DATA MODEL INTO A DATABASE DESIGN

The steps for transforming a data model into a **database design** are shown in Figure 5-1. First, we create a table for each entity in the data model, including creating a primary key and specifying column properties. Then we make sure that each of the tables is properly normalized. Finally, we create the relationships between the tables.[1]

BTW

As you learned in Chapter 2, the technically correct term for the representation of an entity in a relational model is **relation**. However, the use of the synonym **table** is common, and we use it in this chapter. Just remember that the two terms mean the same thing when used to discuss databases.

---

[1]The transformation is actually a bit more complex than this when you consider the need to enforce minimum cardinalities. Although the referential integrity constraints (with ON UPDATE and ON DELETE) handle some parts of this, application logic is required to handle other parts, and that is beyond the scope of this book. See David M. Kroenke and David J. Auer, *Database Processing: Fundamentals, Design, and Implementation*, 13th edition (Upper Saddle River, NJ: Prentice Hall, 2014), Chapter 6.

FIGURE 5-1

The Steps for Transforming a Data Model into a Database Design

1. Create a table for each entity:

    – Specify primary key (consider surrogate keys as appropriate)

    – Specify properties for each column:

    - Data type

    - Null status

    - Default value (if any)

    - Specify data constraints (if any)

    – Verify normalization

2. Create relationships by placing foreign keys:

    – Strong entity relationships (1:1, 1:N, N:M)

    – ID-dependent and non–ID-dependent weak entity relationships

    – Subtypes

    – Recursive (1:1, 1:N, N:M)

FIGURE 5-1

The Steps for Transforming a Data Model into a Database Design

REPRESENTING ENTITIES WITH THE RELATIONAL MODEL

The representation of entities using the relational model is direct and straightforward. First, you define a table for each entity and give that table the same name as the entity. You make the primary key of the relation the identifier of the entity. Then you create a column in the relation for each attribute in the entity. Finally, you apply the normalization process described in Chapter 2 to remove any normalization problems. To understand this process, we will consider three examples.

Representing the ITEM Entity

Consider the ITEM entity shown in Figure 5-2(a), which contains the attributes ItemNumber, Description, Cost, ListPrice, and QuantityOnHand. To represent this entity with a table, we define a table named ITEM and place the attributes in it as columns in the relation. ItemNumber is the identifier of the entity and becomes the primary key of the table. The result is shown in Figure 5-2(b), where a key symbol identifies the primary key. The ITEM table can also be written as:

ITEM (<u>ItemNumber</u>, Description, Cost, ListPrice, QuantityOnHand)

Note that in this notation the primary key of the table is underlined.

FIGURE 5-2

The ITEM Entity and Table

ITEM	
ItemNumber	
Description	
Cost	
ListPrice	
QuantityOnHand	

(a) The ITEM Entity

ITEM	
🔑 ItemNumber	
Description	
Cost	
ListPrice	
QuantityOnHand	

(b) The ITEM Table

Surrogate Keys The ideal primary key is short, numeric, and nonchanging. ItemNumber meets these criteria. However, if the primary key does not meet these criteria, a DBMS-generated **surrogate key** should be used. Surrogate key values are numeric, are unique within a table, and never change. These keys are assigned when a row is created and removed when the row is deleted—the numbers are never reused. Surrogate keys would be ideal primary keys except for a couple of considerations.

First, the numbers generated have no intrinsic meaning. For example, if surrogate key values are used as the values of ItemNumber in the ITEM table, you cannot interpret them in a meaningful way. Second, although the surrogate key values may not be duplicated within a table, they may not be unique between two databases. Consider two databases, each of which has an ITEM table with the surrogate ID of ItemNumber. If the data from these databases are ever shared, this may present a problem. Nonetheless, surrogate keys are very useful and are commonly used as ID numbers in tables.

Column Properties Note that each attribute in the ITEM entity has become a column in the ITEM table. You need to specify certain **column properties** for each column, as mentioned in the discussion of attributes at the end of Chapter 4. These include data types, null status, default values, and any constraints on the values.

Data Types Each DBMS supports certain **data types**. (Data types for SQL Server 2014, MySQL 5.6, and Oracle Database Express Edition 11*g* Release 2 were discussed in Chapter 3, and data types for Microsoft Access 2013 were discussed in Chapter 1.) For each column, you indicate exactly what type of data will be stored in that column. Data types are usually set when the table is actually created in the database, as discussed in Chapter 3.

NULL Status Next, you need to decide which column must have data values entered when a new row is created in the table. If a column *must* have a data value entered, then this column will be designated NOT NULL. If the value can be left empty, then the column will be designated NULL. The **NULL status**—NULL or NOT NULL—of the column is usually set when the table is actually created in the database, as discussed in Chapter 3.

You have to be careful here: If you specify columns as NOT NULL when you do not know the data value at the time the row is being created, you will not be able to create the row. For this reason, some columns that may appear to you as needing to be NOT NULL must actually be specified as NULL. This data will be entered, but not at the exact moment the row is created in the table.

For the ITEM table, you set only ListPrice as NULL. This is a number that may not have been determined by management at the time data on an ITEM are entered into the database. All other columns should have known values at the time a row is created and are NOT NULL.

Default Values A **default value** is a value that the DBMS automatically supplies when a new row is created. The default value may be a static value (one that remains the same) or one calculated by application logic. In this book, we deal with only static values. Default values are usually set when the table is actually created in the database, as discussed in Chapter 3. In the ITEM table, you should specify a default of 0 for QuantityOnHand. This will indicate that the ITEM is out of stock until this value is updated.

Data Constraints The data values in some columns may be subject to restrictions on the values that can exist in those columns. Such limitations are called **data constraints**. An example we have already seen is the referential integrity constraint, which states that the only values allowed in a foreign key column are values already existing in the corresponding primary key column in the related table. Data constraints are usually set when the table is actually created in the database, as discussed in Chapter 3. In the ITEM table, one needed data constraint is (ListPrice > Cost), which ensures that you do not inadvertently sell an ITEM for less than you paid for it.

Verifying Normalization Finally, you need to verify that the ITEM table is properly normalized because the table results from converting an entity sometimes have

FIGURE 5-3

The Final ITEM Table

ITEM

🔑 ItemNumber: int IDENTITY(10000,1)
Description: varchar(100) NOT NULL
Cost: numeric(9,2) NOT NULL
ListPrice: numeric(9,2) NULL
QuantityOnHand: int NOT NULL

normalization problems. Therefore, the next step is to apply the normalization process from Chapter 2 and we strongly suggest that at this point you review the normalization definitions and processes discussed in that chapter so that you are familiar with them before proceeding with our discussion of normalization.

In the case of ITEM, the only candidate key is the primary key, which is ItemNumber, and no other functional dependencies exist. Therefore, the ITEM table is normalized to **Boyce-Codd Normal Form (BCNF)**. The final ITEM table, with column types, surrogate key indicator, and NULL/NOT NULL constraints indicated, is shown in Figure 5-3. Generally, we do not show this much detail in the illustrations of the tables in this chapter, but note that these types of details are available in commercial database design programs and can usually be displayed as needed.

Representing the CUSTOMER Entity

To understand an entity that gives rise to normalization problems, consider the CUSTOMER entity in Figure 5-4(a). If you transform the entity as just described, you obtain the table shown in Figure 5-4(b):

CUSTOMER (<u>CustomerNumber</u>, CustomerName, StreetAddress, City, State, ZIP, ContactName, Phone)

CustomerNumber is the key of the relation, and you can assume that you have done all the necessary work on column definition.

According to the normalization process (see page 79), you need to check for functional dependencies besides those involving the primary key. At least one exists:[2]

ZIP → (City, State)

FIGURE 5-4

The CUSTOMER Entity and Table

CUSTOMER

CustomerNumber
CustomerName
StreetAddress
City
State
ZIP
ContactName
Phone

CUSTOMER

🔑 CustomerNumber
CustomerName
StreetAddress
City
State
ZIP
ContactName
Phone

(a) The CUSTOMER Entity   (b) The CUSTOMER Table

---

[2]While the example of ZIP determining City and State is a commonly used and very understandable example, a five-digit ZIP code (as commonly used instead of a nine-digit number) does not, in fact, determine City and State! There are cases of one ZIP code determining more than one city and state. For example, both Sparta, IL, and Eden, IL, have the ZIP code 62286.

The only candidate key in CUSTOMER is CustomerNumber. ZIP is *not* a candidate key for this relation; therefore, this relation is not normalized. Furthermore, another possible functional dependency involves Phone. Is Phone the phone number of the CUSTOMER, or is it the phone number of the contact? If PhoneNumber is the phone number of the CUSTOMER, then:

CustomerNumber → Phone

and no additional normalization problem exists. However, if the PhoneNumber is that of the contact, then:

ContactName → Phone

and because ContactName is not a candidate key, there are normalization problems here as well.

You can determine whose phone number it is by asking the users. Assume that you do that, and the users say that it is indeed the phone number of the contact. Thus:

ContactName → Phone

Given these facts, you can proceed to normalize the CUSTOMER table. According to the normalization process, you pull the attributes of the functional dependencies out of the tables while leaving a copy of their determinants in the original relation as foreign keys. The result is the three relations shown in Figure 5-5:

CUSTOMER (<u>CustomerNumber</u>, CustomerName, StreetAddress, *ZIP*, *ContactName*)
ZIP (<u>ZIP</u>, City, State)
CONTACT (<u>ContactName</u>, Phone)

with the referential integrity constraints:

ZIP in CUSTOMER must exist in ZIP in ZIP
ContactName in CUSTOMER must exist in ContactName in CONTACT

FIGURE 5-5

The Normalized CUSTOMER and Associated Tables

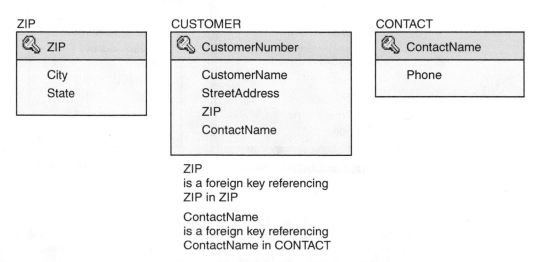

These three relations are now normalized, and you can continue with the design process. However, let us first consider another perspective on normalization.

Denormalization

It is possible to take normalization too far. Most practitioners would consider the construction of a separate ZIP table to be going too far. People are accustomed to writing their city, state, and ZIP as a group, and breaking City and State away from ZIP will make the design difficult to use. It will also mean that the DBMS has to read two separate tables just to get the customer's address. Therefore, even though it results in normalization problems, a better overall design would result by leaving ZIP, City, and State in the CUSTOMER relation. This is an example of **denormalization**.

What are the consequences of this decision to denormalize? Consider the three basic operations: insert, update, and delete. If you leave ZIP, City, and State in CUSTOMER, then you will not be able to insert data for a new ZIP code until a customer has that ZIP code. However, you will never want to do that. You only care about ZIP code data when one of the customers has that ZIP code. Therefore, leaving the ZIP data in CUSTOMER does not pose problems when inserting.

What about modifications? If a city changes its ZIP code, then you might have to change multiple rows in CUSTOMER. How frequently do cities change their ZIP codes, though? Because the answer is almost never, updates in the denormalized relation are not a problem. Finally, what about deletes? If only one customer has the ZIP data (80210, Denver, Colorado), then if you delete that customer you will lose the fact that 80210 is in Denver. This does not really matter because when another customer with this ZIP code is inserted that customer also will provide the city and state.

Therefore, denormalizing CUSTOMER by leaving the attributes ZIP, City, and State in the relation will make the design easier to use and not cause modification problems. The denormalized design is better, and it is shown in Figure 5-6:

CUSTOMER (CustomerNumber, CustomerName, StreetAddress, City, State, ZIP, ContactName)
CONTACT (ContactName, Phone)

with the referential integrity constraints:

ContactName in CUSTOMER must exist in ContactName in CONTACT

FIGURE 5-6

The Denormalized CUSTOMER and Associated CONTACT Tables

CUSTOMER

🔑 CustomerNumber
CustomerName
StreetAddress
City
State
ZIP
ContactName

CONTACT

🔑 ContactName
Phone

ContactName
is a foreign key referencing
ContactName in CONTACT

The need for denormalization can also arise for reasons such as security and performance. If the cost of modification problems is low (as for ZIP codes) and if other factors cause denormalized relations to be preferred, then denormalizing is a good idea.

A Relational Design for the SALES_COMMISSION Entity

To summarize the discussion so far, when representing an entity with the relational model the first step is to construct a table that has all the entity's attributes as columns. The identifier of the entity becomes the primary key of the table, and we define the column constraints. Then the table is normalized. A reason might exist for leaving parts of a table denormalized.

By proceeding in this way, we always consider the normalized design. If we make a decision to denormalize, we then do so from a position of knowledge and not from ignorance.

To reinforce these ideas, let us consider a third example: the SALES_COMMISSION entity in Figure 5-7(a). First, you create a relation that has all the attributes as columns, as shown in Figure 5-7(b):

SALES_COMMISSION (SalespersonNumber, SalespersonLastName, SalespersonFirstName, Phone, CheckNumber, CheckDate, CommissionPeriod, TotalCommissionSales, CommissionAmount, BudgetCategory)

As shown, the primary key of the table is CheckNumber, the identifier of the entity. The attributes of the relation have three additional functional dependencies:

SalespersonNumber →
    (SalespersonLastName, SalespersonFirstName, Phone, BudgetCategory)

CheckNumber → CheckDate

(SalespersonNumber, CommissionPeriod) →
    (TotalCommissionSales, CommissionAmount, CheckNumber, CheckDate)

According to the normalization process, you extract the attributes of these functional dependencies from the original table and make the determinants the primary keys of the new tables. You also leave a copy of the determinants in the original table as foreign keys. The only complication in this case is that the name of the original table

FIGURE 5-7

The SALES_
COMMISSION Entity
and Table

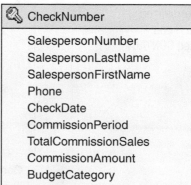

SALES_COMMISSION	SALES_COMMISSION
CheckNumber	CheckNumber
SalespersonNumber	SalespersonNumber
SalespersonLastName	SalespersonLastName
SalespersonFirstName	SalespersonFirstName
Phone	Phone
CheckDate	CheckDate
CommissionPeriod	CommissionPeriod
TotalCommissionSales	TotalCommissionSales
CommissionAmount	CommissionAmount
BudgetCategory	BudgetCategory

(a) The SALES_COMMISSION Entity   (b) The SALES_COMMISSION Table

actually makes more sense when used for one of the new tables that has been created! The original table, given the primary key CheckNumber, should actually be called COMMISSION_CHECK, and it has been renamed as such in the normalization results shown in Figure 5-8:

SALESPERSON (<u>SalespersonNumber</u>, SalespersonLastName,
   SalespersonFirstName, Phone, BudgetCategory)

SALES_COMMISSION (<u>*SalespersonNumber*</u>, <u>CommissionPeriod</u>,
   TotalCommissionSales, CommissionAmount, *CheckNumber*)
   COMMISSION_CHECK (<u>CheckNumber</u>, CheckDate)

with the referential integrity constraints:

SalespersonNumber in SALES_COMMISSION must exist in
   SalespersonNumber in SALESPERSON

CheckNumber in SALES_COMMISSION must exist in CheckNumber
   in COMMISSION_CHECK

Now consider denormalization. Is there any reason not to create these new relations? Is the design better if you leave them in the COMMISSION_CHECK relation (the renamed SALES_COMMISSION relation)? In this case, there is no reason to denormalize, so you leave the normalized relations alone.

Representing Weak Entities

The process described so far works for all entity types, but weak entities sometimes require special treatment. Recall that a weak entity logically depends on another entity. In Figure 5-8, SALES_COMMISSION is an ID-dependent weak entity that depends on SALESPERSON for its existence. In this model, there cannot be a SALES_COMMISSION without a SALESPERSON. Also note that in Figure 5-8 we consider COMMISSION_CHECK to be a strong entity because once the check is written it has a separate, physical existence of its own, just like a SALESPERSON (an alternate conceptualization would require an additional CHECKING_ACCOUNT entity as the strong entity with CHECK as an ID-dependent weak entity, in which case the composite primary key of CHECK would be used as the foreign key in SALES_COMMISSION).

FIGURE 5-8

The Normalized SALES_COMMISSION and Associated Tables

SALESPERSON	SALES_COMMISSION	COMMISSION_CHECK
🔑 SalespersonNumber	🔑 SalespersonNumber 🔑 CommissionPeriod	🔑 CheckNumber
SalespersonLastName SalespersonFirstName Phone BudgetCategory	TotalCommissionSales CommissionAmount CheckNumber	CheckDate

SalespersonNumber is a foreign key referencing
SalespersonNumber in SALESPERSON

SALES_COMMISSION is ID-dependent on SALESPERSON

CheckNumber is a foreign key referencing CheckNumber
in COMMISSION_CHECK

If a weak entity is not ID-dependent, it can be represented as a table, using the techniques just described. The dependency needs to be recorded in the relational design so that no application will create a weak entity without its proper parent (the entity on which the weak entity depends). Finally, a business rule will need to be implemented so that when the parent is deleted the weak entity is also deleted. These rules are part of the relational design and, in this case, take the form of an ON DELETE CASCADE constraint on the weak, non–ID-dependent table.

The situation is slightly different if a weak entity is also ID-dependent. This is the case in the dependence of SALES_COMMISSION on SALESPERSON because each SALES_COMMISSION is identified by the SALESPERSON who made the sale. When creating a table for an ID-dependent entity, we must ensure that the identifier of the parent and the identifier of the ID-dependent weak entity itself appear in the table. For example, consider what would happen if you established the table for SALES_COMMISSION without including the key of SALESPERSON. What would be the key of this table? It would be just CommissionPeriod, but because SALES_COMMISSION is ID-dependent this is not a complete key. In fact, without the needed reference to SALESPERSON included, CommissionPeriod by itself cannot be the primary key because this table would likely have duplicate rows. (This would happen if two occurrences of a specific CommissionPeriod had the same TotalCommissionSales in the same BudgetCategory, which could happen because this table records data for more than one SALESPERSON.) Thus, for an ID-dependent weak entity it is necessary to add the primary key of the parent entity to the weak entity's table, and this added attribute becomes part of that table's key. In Figure 5-8, note that SALES_COMMISSION has the correct composite primary key (SalespersonNumber, CommissionPeriod).

As another example, consider Figure 5-9(a), where LINE_ITEM is an ID-dependent weak entity. It is weak because its logical existence depends on INVOICE, and it is ID-dependent because its identifier contains the identifier of INVOICE. Again, consider what would happen if you established a relation for LINE_ITEM without including the key of INVOICE. What would be the key of this relation? It would be just LineNumber, but because LINE_ITEM is ID-dependent that cannot be a complete key. Without the needed reference to ITEM included, LINE_ITEM, like SALESPERSON_SALES in the previous example, would likely have duplicate rows. (This would happen if two invoices had the same quantity of the same item on the same line.) Figure 5-9(b) shows LINE_ITEM with the correct composite primary key (InvoiceNumber, LineNumber). Note that the tables in Figure 5-9(b) are intentionally shown without a relationship—we will discuss adding relationships in the next section.

FIGURE 5-9

Relational Representation of a Weak Entity

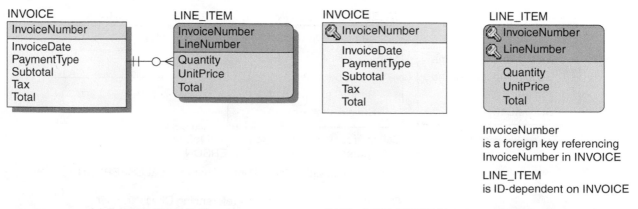

(a) Example Weak Entity   (b) The LINE_ITEM Table with the Correct Primary Key

REPRESENTING RELATIONSHIPS

So far, you have learned how to create a relational design for the entities in an E-R model. However, to convert a data model to a relational design we must also represent the relationships.

The techniques used to represent E-R relationships depend on the maximum cardinality of the relationships. As you saw in Chapter 4, three relationship possibilities exist: one-to-one (1:1), one-to-many (1:N), and many-to-many (M:N). A fourth possibility, many-to-one (N:1), is represented in the same way as 1:N, so we need not consider it as a separate case. In general, we create relationships by placing foreign keys in tables. The following sections consider various types of relationships.

Relationships Between Strong Entities

The easiest relationships to work with are relationships between strong entities. We will start with these and then consider other types of relationships.

Representing 1:1 Strong Entity Relationships

The simplest form of binary relationship is a 1:1 relationship, in which an entity of one type is related to at most one entity of another type. In Figure 5-10(a), the same 1:1 relationship that was used in Figure 4-5(a) between EMPLOYEE and LOCKER is shown in IE Crow's Foot notation. According to this diagram, an employee is assigned at most one locker, and a locker is assigned to at most one employee.

Representing a 1:1 relationship with the relational model is straightforward. First, each entity is represented with a table as just described, and then the key of one of the tables is placed in the other as a foreign key. In Figure 5-10(b), the key of LOCKER is stored in EMPLOYEE as a foreign key, and you create the referential integrity constraint:

LockerNumber in EMPLOYEE must exist in LockerNumber in LOCKER

FIGURE 5-10

1:1 Strong Entity Relationships

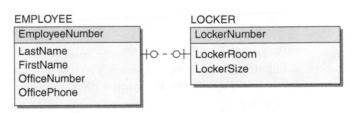

(a) 1:1 Strong Entity Relationship Example

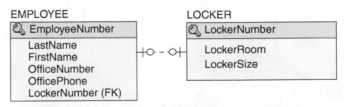

(b) Placing the Primary Key of LOCKER into EMPLOYEE

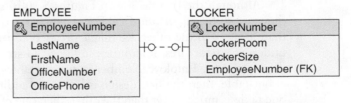

(c) Placing the Primary Key of EMPLOYEE into LOCKER

In Figure 5-10(c), the key of EMPLOYEE is stored in LOCKER as a foreign key, and you create the referential integrity constraint:

EmployeeNumber in LOCKER must exist in EmployeeNumber in EMPLOYEE

In general, for a 1:1 relationship the key of either table can be placed as a foreign key in the other table. To verify that this is so, consider both cases in Figure 5-10. Suppose that for the design in Figure 5-10(b) you have an employee and want the locker assigned to that employee. To get the employee data, you use EmployeeNumber to obtain the employee's row in EMPLOYEE. From this row, you obtain the LockerNumber of the locker assigned to that employee. You then use that number to look up the locker data in LOCKER.

Now consider the other direction. Assume that you have a locker and want to know which employee is assigned to that locker. Using the design in Figure 5-10(b), you access the EMPLOYEE table and look up the row that has the given LockerNumber. The data of the employee who has been assigned that locker appears in that row.

You take similar actions to travel in either direction for the alternative design in which the foreign key of EmployeeNumber is placed in LOCKER, as shown in Figure 5-10(c). Using this design, to go from EMPLOYEE to LOCKER you go directly to the LOCKER table and look up the row in LOCKER that has the given employee's number as its value of EmployeeNumber. To travel from LOCKER to EMPLOYEE, you look up the row in LOCKER that has a given LockerNumber. From this row, you extract the EmployeeNumber and use it to access the employee data in EMPLOYEE.

In this situation, we are using the term *look up* to mean "to find a row given a value of one of its columns." Another way to view this is in terms of joins. For the relations in Figure 5-10(b), you can form the following join:

```
/* *** EXAMPLE CODE-DO NOT RUN *** */
/* *** SQL-QUERY-CH05-01 *** */
SELECT       *
FROM         EMPLOYEE, LOCKER
WHERE        EMPLOYEE.LockerNumber=LOCKER.LockerNumber;
```

Because the relationship is 1:1, the result of this join will have a single row for a given combination of employee and locker. The row will have all columns from both tables.

For the relations in Figure 5-10(c), you can join the two tables on EmployeeNumber as follows:

```
/* *** EXAMPLE CODE - DO NOT RUN *** */
/* *** SQL-QUERY-CH05-02 *** */
SELECT       *
FROM         EMPLOYEE, LOCKER
WHERE        EMPLOYEE.EmployeeNumber=LOCKER.EmployeeNumber;
```

Again, one row will be found for each combination of employee and locker. In both of these joins, neither unassigned employees nor unassigned lockers will appear.

Although the two designs in Figures 5-10(b) and 5-10(c) are equivalent in concept, they may differ in performance. For instance, if a query in one direction is more common than a query in the other, we might prefer one design to the other. Also, depending on underlying structures, if an index (a metadata structure that makes searches for specific data faster) for EmployeeNumber is in both tables but no index on LockerNumber is in either table, then the first design is better. In addition, considering the join operation, if one table is much larger than the other, then one of these joins might be faster to perform than the other.

Another example of a 1:1 strong entity relationship is the relationship between the CUSTOMER and CONTACT tables shown in Figure 5-6. For each CUSTOMER, there is one and only one CONTACT, and based on the normalization we did we have used the primary key of CONTACT as the foreign key in CUSTOMER. The resulting relationship is shown in Figure 5-11.

To actually implement a 1:1 relationship in a database, we must constrain the values of the designated foreign key as UNIQUE. This can be done in the SQL CREATE TABLE statement that is used to build the table containing the foreign key, or it can be done by altering the table structure after the table is created using the SQL ALTER TABLE statement. Consider the EMPLOYEE-to-LOCKER relationships. If, for example, we decide that to place the foreign key EmployeeNumber in the LOCKER table to create the relationship, we will need to constrain EmployeeNumber in LOCKER as UNIQUE. To do this we will use the SQL statement:

```
/* *** EXAMPLE CODE - DO NOT RUN *** */
/* *** SQL-CONSTRAINT-CH05-01 *** */
CONSTRAINT UniqueEmployeeNumber UNIQUE(EmployeeNumber)
```

as a line of SQL code either in the original CREATE TABLE LOCKER command or in the following ALTER TABLE LOCKER command (which assumes that any data already in LOCKER will not violate the UNIQUE constraint),

```
/* *** EXAMPLE CODE - DO NOT RUN *** */
/* *** SQL-ALTER-TABLE-CH05-01 *** */
ALTER TABLE LOCKER
    ADD CONSTRAINT UniqueEmployeeNumber
            UNIQUE (EmployeeNumber);
```

Representing 1:N Strong Entity Relationships The second type of binary relationship, known as 1:N, is a relationship in which an entity of one type can be related to many entities of another type. In Figure 5-12(a), the 1:N relationship that was used in Figure 4-5(b) between ITEM and QUOTATION is shown in IE Crow's Foot notation. According to this diagram, we have received from zero to several quotations for each item in the database.

The terms **parent** and **child** are sometimes applied to relations in 1:N relationships. The parent relation is on the one side of the relationship, and the child relation is on the many side. In Figure 5-12(a), ITEM is the parent entity and QUOTATION is the child entity.

Representing 1:N relationships is simple and straightforward. First, each entity is represented by a table, as described, and then the key of the table representing the *parent entity* is placed in the table representing the *child entity* as a foreign key. Thus, to

FIGURE 5-11

1:1 Strong Entity Relationship Between CUSTOMER and CONTACT

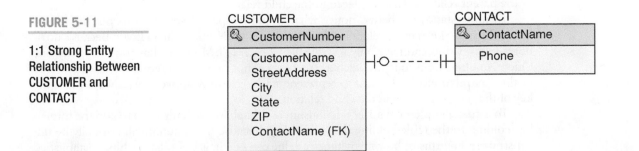

FIGURE 5-12

1:N Strong Entity Relationships

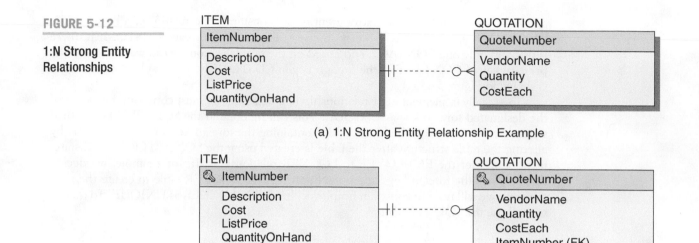

(a) 1:N Strong Entity Relationship Example

(b) Placing the Primary Key of ITEM into QUOTATION

represent the relationship in Figure 5-12(a) you place the primary key of ITEM, which is ItemNumber, into the QUOTATION table, as shown in Figure 5-12(b), and you create the referential integrity constraint:

ItemNumber in QUOTATION must exist in ItemNumber in ITEM

Notice that with ItemNumber stored as a foreign key in QUOTATION you can process the relationship in both directions. Given a QuoteNumber, you can look up the appropriate row in QUOTATION and get the ItemNumber of the item from the row data. To obtain the rest of the ITEM data, you use the ItemNumber obtained from QUOTATION to look up the appropriate row in ITEM. To determine all the quotes associated with a particular item, you look up all rows in QUOTATION that have the item's ItemNumber as a value for ItemNumber. Quotation data are then taken from those rows.

In terms of joins, you can obtain the item and quote data in one table with the following:

```
/* *** EXAMPLE CODE - DO NOT RUN *** */
/* *** SQL-QUERY-CH05-03 *** */
SELECT    *
FROM      ITEM, QUOTATION
WHERE     ITEM.ItemNumber = QUOTATION.ItemNumber;
```

Contrast this 1:N relationship design strategy with that for 1:1 relationships. In both cases, we store the key of one relation as a foreign key in the second relation. In a 1:1 relationship, we can place the key of either relation in the other. In a 1:N relationship, however, the key of the parent relation *must* be placed in the child relation.

To understand this better, notice what would happen if you tried to put the key of the child into the parent relation (that is, put QuoteNumber in ITEM). Because attributes in a relation can have only a single value, each ITEM record has room for only one QuoteNumber. Consequently, such a structure cannot be used to represent the many side of the 1:N relationship. Hence, to represent a 1:N relationship we must always place the key of the parent relation in the child relation.

To actually implement a 1:N relationship in a database, we only need to add the foreign key column to the table holding the foreign key. Because this column will normally be unconstrained in terms of how many times a value can occur, a 1:N relationship is established by default. In fact, this is the reason that we must use a column constraint to create a 1:1 relationship, as discussed early in this chapter. We will illustrate this point in this chapter's section of "The Access Workbench."

Representing N:M Strong Entity Relationships

The third and final type of binary relationship is N:M, in which an entity of one type corresponds to many entities of the second type and an entity of the second type corresponds to many entities of the first type.

Figure 5-13(a) shows an E-R diagram of the N:M relationship between students and classes. A STUDENT entity can correspond to many CLASS entities, and a CLASS entity can correspond to many STUDENT entities. Notice that both participants in the relationship are optional: A student does not need to be enrolled in a class, and a class is not required to have any students. Figure 5-13(b) gives sample data.

N:M relationships cannot be represented directly by relations in the same way that 1:1 and 1:N relationships are represented. To understand why this is so, try using the same strategy as for 1:1 and 1:N relationships—placing the key of one relation as a foreign key into the other relation. First, define a relation for each of the entities; call them STUDENT and CLASS. Then try to put the primary key of STUDENT, which is SID, into CLASS. Because multiple values are not allowed in the cells of a relation, you have room for only one StudentNumber, so you have no place to record the StudentNumber of the second and subsequent students.

A similar problem occurs if you try to put the primary key of CLASS, which is ClassNumber, into STUDENT. You can readily store the identifier of the first class in which a student is enrolled, but you have no place to store the identifier of additional classes.

Figure 5-14 shows another (but incorrect) strategy. In this case, a row is stored in the CLASS relation for each STUDENT enrolled in one class, so you have two records for Class 10 and two for Class 30. The problem with this scheme is that it duplicates the class data and creates modification anomalies. Many rows will need to be changed if, for example, the schedule for Class 10 is modified. Also, consider the insertion and deletion anomalies: How can you schedule a new class until a student has enrolled? In addition, what will happen if Student 300 drops out of Class 40? This strategy is unworkable.

The solution to this problem is to create a third table, called an **intersection table**, that represents the relationship itself. The intersection table is a *child* table that is connected to

FIGURE 5-13

N:M Strong Entity Relationships

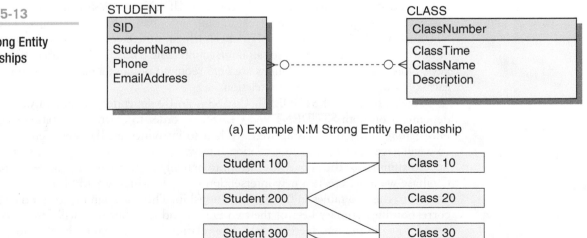

(a) Example N:M Strong Entity Relationship

(b) Sample Data for the STUDENT-to-CLASS Relationship

SID	Other STUDENT Data
100	...
200	...
300	...

STUDENT

ClassNumber	ClassTime	Other CLASS Data	SID
10	10:00 MWF	...	100
10	10:00 MWF	...	200
30	3:00 TH	...	200
30	3:00 TH	...	300
40	8:00 MWF	...	300

CLASS

two *parent* tables by *two* 1:N relationships which replace the *single* N:M relationship in the data model. Thus, we define a table named STUDENT_CLASS, as shown in Figure 5-15(a):

STUDENT (SID, StudentName, Phone, EmailAddress)
CLASS (ClassNumber, ClassTime, ClassName, Description)
STUDENT_CLASS (*SID*, *ClassNumber*)

with the referential integrity constraints:

SID in STUDENT_CLASS must exist in SID in STUDENT
ClassNumber in STUDENT_CLASS must exist in ClassNumber in CLASS

Some instances of this relation are shown in Figure 5-15(b). Such relations are called *intersection tables* because each row documents the intersection of a particular student with a particular class. Notice in Figure 5-15(b) that the intersection relation has one row for each line between STUDENT and CLASS, as in Figure 5-13(b).

In Figure 5-15(a), notice that the relationship from STUDENT to STUDENT_CLASS is 1:N and the relationship from CLASS to STUDENT_CLASS is also 1:N. In essence, we have decomposed the M:N relationship into two 1:N relationships. The key of STUDENT_CLASS is (SID, ClassNumber), which is the combination of the primary keys of both of its parents. The key for an intersection table is *always* the combination of parent keys. Note that the parent relations are *both* required because a parent must now exist for each key value in the intersection relation.

Finally, notice that STUDENT_CLASS is an ID-dependent weak entity, which is ID-dependent on both STUDENT and CLASS. In order to create a database design for an N:M *strong entity* relationship we have had to introduce an ID-dependent *weak entity*! (We will have more to say about relationships with weak entities in the next section.)

To summarize the above discussion, to actually implement an N:M relationship in a database we must create a new intersection table, to which we add foreign key columns linking to the two tables in the N:M relationship. These foreign key columns will be the corresponding primary keys of the two tables, and together they will form a composite primary key in the intersection table. The relationship between each table and the intersection table will be a 1:N relationship, and thus we implement an N:M relation by creating two 1:N relationships. And because each primary key in the original tables appears as in the primary key of the intersection table, the intersection table is ID-dependent on both original tables.

FIGURE 5-15

Representing an N:M Strong Entity Relationship

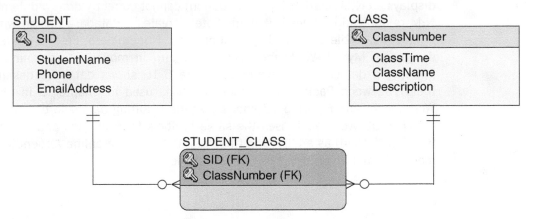

(a) The STUDENT_CLASS Intersection Table

(b) Sample Data for the STUDENT-to-CLASS Relationship

You can obtain data about students and classes by using the following SQL statement:

```
/* *** EXAMPLE CODE - DO NOT RUN *** */
/* *** SQL-Query-CH05-04 *** */
SELECT     *
FROM       STUDENT, CLASS, STUDENT_CLASS
WHERE      STUDENT.SID = STUDENT_CLASS.SID
    AND    STUDENT_CLASS.ClassNumber = CLASS.ClassNumber;
```

The result of this SQL statement is a table with all columns for a student and the classes the student takes. The student data will be repeated in the table for as many classes as the student takes, and the class data will be repeated in the relation for as many students as are taking the class.

BTW

Now that you know that an N:M relationship in a data model is transformed into two 1:N relationships in a database design let us revisit the topic of data modeling and database design software products discussed in Chapter 4. Some products, such as Computer Associates' ERwin Data Modeler, can create true data models with correctly drawn N:M relationships. These products

(continued)

are also capable of correctly transforming the data models into database designs with intersection tables. Oracle's MySQL Workbench (even though it displays an N:M relationship as an option) cannot correctly draw a data model N:M relationship. Instead, it immediately creates a database design with an intersection table and two 1:N relationships. Nonetheless, creating database designs in MySQL Workbench can be helpful in modeling, designing, and building a database. For example, Figure 5-16 shows database design for the Wedgewood Pacific Corporation database used in Chapter 3 in MySQL Workbench, and Figure 5-17 shows just the resulting database design. Note that MySQL Workbench uses the same symbols for line ends and line types (solid or dashed) as are used in Chapters 4 and 5. See online Appendix C for more information on using MySQL Workbench.

Relationships Using Weak Entities

Because weak entities exist, they are bound to end up as tables in relationships! We have just seen one place where this occurs: In the case of the STUDENT and CLASS entities in Figure 5-15, a new ID-dependent entity is created and becomes the table that represents an N:M relationship. Note that the intersection table that is formed in this case has only the columns that make up its composite primary key. In the STUDENT_CLASS table, this key is (SID, ClassNumber).

FIGURE 5-16

The Database Design Tools in MySQL Workbench

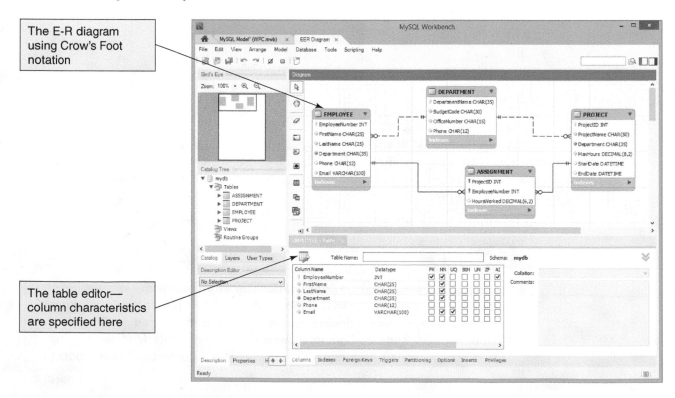

FIGURE 5-17

The WPC Database Design in MySQL Workbench

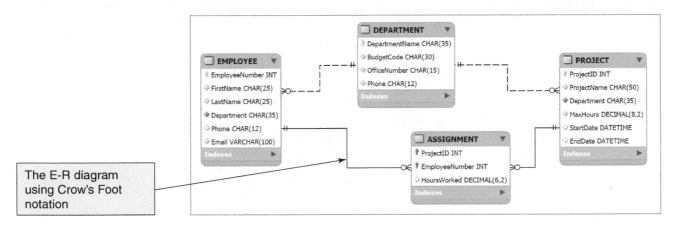

The E-R diagram using Crow's Foot notation

Another ID-dependent weak entity occurs when we take an intersection table and add entity attributes (table columns) beyond those in the composite primary key. For example, Figure 5-18 shows the table and relationship structure of Figure 5-15(a) but with one new attribute (column)—Grade—added to STUDENT_CLASS.

STUDENT_CLASS is an example of the **associative entity** that we discussed in Chapter 4, and this entity has been converted into the new STUDENT_CLASS table. Note that although STUDENT_CLASS still connects STUDENT and CLASS (and is still ID-dependent on both of these tables), it now has data that are uniquely its own. This pattern is called an **association relationship**.

Finally, let us take another look at the tables shown in Figure 5-8, where you normalized SALES_COMMISSION into three related tables. Figure 5-19 shows these tables with their correct relationships.

Note the 1:N identifying relationship between SALESPERSON and the ID-dependent table SALES_COMMISSION, which correctly uses the primary key of SALESPERSON as part of the composite primary key of SALES_COMMISSION. Also note the 1:1 relationship between SALES_COMMISSION and COMMISSION_CHECK. Because

FIGURE 5-18

The Association Relationship

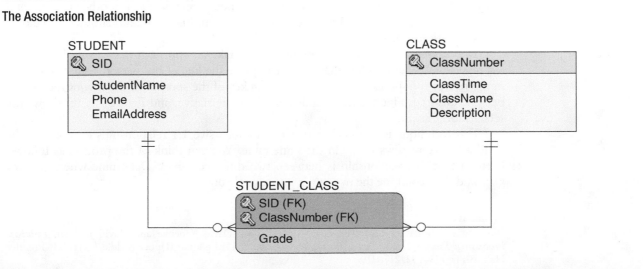

FIGURE 5-19

**Mixed Entity
Relationship Example**

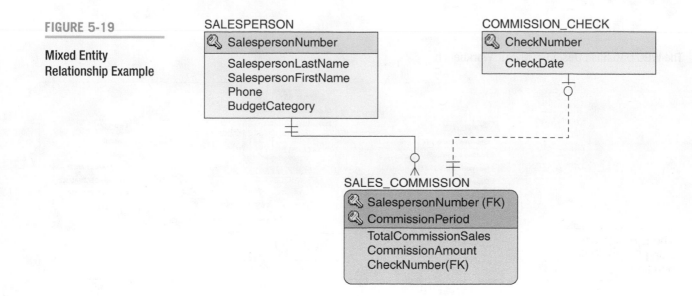

COMMISSION_CHECK is a strong entity and has its own unique primary key, this is a non-identifying relationship. This set of tables and relationships illustrates a **mixed entity pattern**.[3]

Relationships with Subtypes

Because the identifier of a subtype entity is the identifier of the associated supertype entity, creating relationships between the SALES_COMMISSION and COMMISSION_CHECK tables is simple. The identifier of the subtype becomes the primary key of the subtype *and* the foreign key linking the subtype to the supertype. Figure 5-20(a) shows the E-R model in Figure 4-13(a), and Figure 5-20(b) shows the equivalent database design.

Representing Recursive Relationships

A recursive relationship is a relationship among entities of the same class. Recursive relationships are not fundamentally different from other relationships and can be represented using the same techniques. As with nonrecursive relationships, three types of recursive relationships are possible: 1:1, 1:N, and N:M. Figure 5-21 shows an example of each of these three types.

Let us start by considering the 1:1 recursive SPONSORED_BY relationship in Figure 5-21(a). As with a regular 1:1 relationship, one person can sponsor another person, and each person is sponsored by no more than one person. Figure 5-22(a) shows sample data for this relationship.

To represent 1:1 recursive relationships, we take an approach nearly identical to that for regular 1:1 relationships; that is, we can place the key of the person being sponsored in the row of the sponsor, or we can place the key of the sponsor in the row of the person being sponsored. Figure 5-22(b) shows the first alternative, and Figure 5-22(c) shows the second. Both work.

This technique is identical to that for nonrecursive 1:1 relationships except that the child and parent rows reside in the same table. You can think of the process as follows: Pretend that the relationship is between two different tables. Determine where the key goes and then combine the two tables into a single one.

---

[3]For more information on mixed entity patterns, see David Kroenke and David J. Auer, *Database Processing: Fundamentals, Design, and Implementation*, 13th edition (Upper Saddle River, NJ: Prentice Hall, 2014): 179–182, 217–219.

FIGURE 5-20

Representing Subtypes

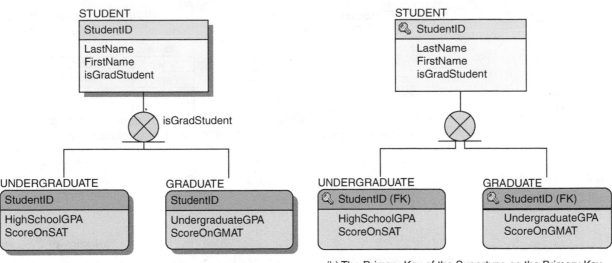

(a) Example Subtype-Supertype Relationship

(b) The Primary Key of the Supertype as the Primary Key and Foreign Key of the Subtype

FIGURE 5-21

Example Recursive Relationships

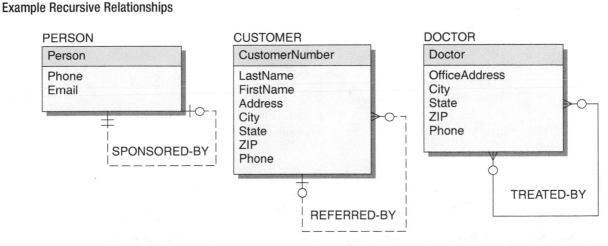

(a) 1:1 Recursive Relationship

(b) 1:N Recursive Relationship

(c) N:M Recursive Relationship

We also can use SQL joins to process recursive relationships; to do so, however, we need to introduce additional SQL syntax. In the FROM clause, it is possible to assign a synonym for a table name. For example, the expression FROM CUSTOMER A assigns the synonym A to the table CUSTOMER. Using this syntax, you can create a join on a recursive relationship for the design in Figure 5-22(b) as follows:

```
/* *** EXAMPLE CODE - DO NOT RUN *** */
/* *** SQL-Query-CH05-05 *** */
SELECT      *
FROM        PERSON1 A, PERSON1 B
WHERE       A.Person = B.PersonSponsored;
```

FIGURE 5-22

Example 1:1 Recursive Relationships

Person
Jones
Smith
Parks
Myrtle
Pines

PERSON1 Relation

Person	PersonSponsored
Jones	Smith
Smith	Parks
Parks	null
Myrtle	Pines
Pines	null

Referential integrity constraint:
PersonSponsored in PERSON1
must exist in Person in PERSON1

PERSON2 Relation

Person	PersonSponsoredBy
Jones	null
Smith	Jones
Parks	Smith
Myrtle	null
Pines	Myrtle

Referential integrity constraint:
PersonSponsoredBy in PERSON2
must exist in Person in PERSON2

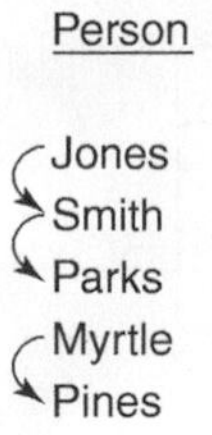

(a) Sample Data for a 1:1
Recursive Relationship

(b) First Alternative for Representing a
1:1 Recursive Relationship

(c) Second Alternative for Representing a
1:1 Recursive Relationship

The result is a table with one row for each person that has all the columns of the person and also of the person that he or she sponsors.

Similarly, to create a join of the recursive relationship shown in Figure 5-22(c), you would use:

```
/* *** EXAMPLE CODE - DO NOT RUN *** */
/* *** SQL-Query-CH05-06 *** */
SELECT     *
FROM       PERSON2 A, PERSON2 B
WHERE      A.Person = B.PersonSponsoredBy;
```

The result is a table with a row for each person that has all the columns of the person and also of the sponsoring person.

Now consider the 1:N recursive relationship REFERRED-BY in Figure 5-21(b). This is a 1:N relationship, as shown in the sample data in Figure 5-23(a).

FIGURE 5-23

Example 1:N Recursive Relationship

Customer Number	Referred These Customers
100	200, 400
300	500
400	600, 700

CUSTOMER Relation

CustomerNumber	CustomerData	ReferredBy
100	...	null
200	...	100
300	...	null
400	...	100
500	...	300
600	...	400
700	...	400

Referential integrity constraint:
ReferredBy in CUSTOMER must exist in
CustomerNumber in CUSTOMER

(a) Sample Data for a 1:N Recursive Relationship

(b) Representing a 1:N Recursive Relationship
Within a Table

When these data are placed in a table, one row represents the referrer, and the other rows represent those who have been referred. The referrer row takes the role of the parent, and the referred rows take the role of the child. As with all 1:N relationships, you place the key of the parent in the child. In Figure 5-21(b), you place the CustomerNumber of the referrer in all the rows for people who have been referred.

You can join the 1:N recursive relationship with:

```
/* *** EXAMPLE CODE - DO NOT RUN *** */
/* *** SQL-Query-CH05-07 *** */
SELECT     *
FROM       CUSTOMER A, CUSTOMER B
WHERE      A.CustomerNumber = B.ReferredBy;
```

The result is a row for each customer that is joined to the data for the customer who referred the person.

Finally, let us consider N:M recursive relationships. The TREATED-BY relationship in Figure 5-21(c) represents a situation in which doctors give treatments to each other. Sample data are shown in Figure 5-24(a).

As with other N:M relationships, you must create an intersection table that shows pairs of related rows. The name of the doctor in the first column is the one who provided the treatment, and the name of the doctor in the second column is the one who

FIGURE 5-24

Example of an N:M Recursive Relationship

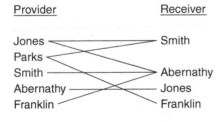

Provider	Receiver
Jones	Smith
Parks	Abernathy
Smith	Jones
Abernathy	Franklin
Franklin	

DOCTOR Relation

Name	Other Attributes
Jones	...
Parks	...
Smith	...
Abernathy	...
O'Leary	...
Franklin	...

TREATMENT-INTERSECTION Relation

Physician	Patient
Jones	Smith
Parks	Smith
Smith	Abernathy
Abernathy	Jones
Parks	Franklin
Franklin	Abernathy
Jones	Abernathy

Referential integrity constraints:
Physician in TREATMENT-INTERSECTION must exist in Name in DOCTOR

Patient in TREATMENT-INTERSECTION must exist in Name in DOCTOR

(a) Sample Data for an N:M Recursive Relationship

(b) Representing an N:M Recursive Relationship Using Tables

received the treatment. This structure is shown in Figure 5-24(b). You can join the N:M relationship with:

```
/* *** EXAMPLE CODE - DO NOT RUN *** */
/* *** SQL-Query-CH05-08 *** */
SELECT      *
FROM        DOCTOR A, TREATMENT-INTERSECTION, DOCTOR B
WHERE       A.Name = TREATMENT-INTERSECTION.Physician
    AND     TREATMENT-INTERSECTION.Patient = B.Name;
```

The result of this is a table that has rows of doctor (as treatment provider) joined to doctor (as patient). The doctor data will be repeated once for every patient treated and once for every time the doctor was treated.

Recursive relationships are thus represented in the same way as are other relationships; however, the rows of the tables can take two different roles. Some are parent rows, and others are child rows. If a key is supposed to be a parent key and the row has no parent, its value is NULL. If a key is supposed to be a child key and the row has no child, its value is NULL.

DATABASE DESIGN AT HEATHER SWEENEY DESIGNS

Figure 5-25 shows the final E-R diagram for Heather Sweeney Designs, the database example discussed in Chapter 4. To transform this E-R diagram into a relational design, we follow the process described in the preceding sections. First, represent each entity with a relation of its own, and specify a primary key for each relation:

SEMINAR (SeminarID, SeminarDate, SeminarTime, Location, SeminarTitle)

CUSTOMER (CustomerID, LastName, FirstName, EmailAddress, EncryptedPassword, Phone, StreetAddress, City, State, ZIP)

CONTACT (*CustomerID*, ContactNumber, ContactDate, ContactType)

PRODUCT (ProductNumber, ProductType, ProductDescription, UnitPrice, QuantityOnHand)

INVOICE (InvoiceNumber, InvoiceDate, PaymentType, SubTotal, Shipping, Tax, Total)

LINE_ITEM (*InvoiceNumber*, LineNumber, Quantity, UnitPrice, Total)

Weak Entities

This model has two weak entities, and they are both ID-dependent. CONTACT is a weak entity, and its identifier depends, in part, on the identifier of CUSTOMER. Thus, we have placed the key of CUSTOMER, which is CustomerID, into CONTACT. Similarly, LINE_ITEM is a weak entity, and its identifier depends on the identifier of INVOICE. Consequently, we have placed the key of INVOICE in LINE_ITEM. Note that in the preceding schema text both CONTACT.CustomerID and LINE_ITEM.InvoiceNumber are underlined and italicized because they are part of a primary key and also a foreign key.

Verifying Normalization

Next, apply the normalization process to each of these tables. Do any of them have a functional dependency that does not involve the primary key? From what we know so far, the only such functional dependency to consider moving to a separate table is:

ZIP $\rightarrow$ (City, State)

FIGURE 5-25

The Final Data Model for Heather Sweeney Designs

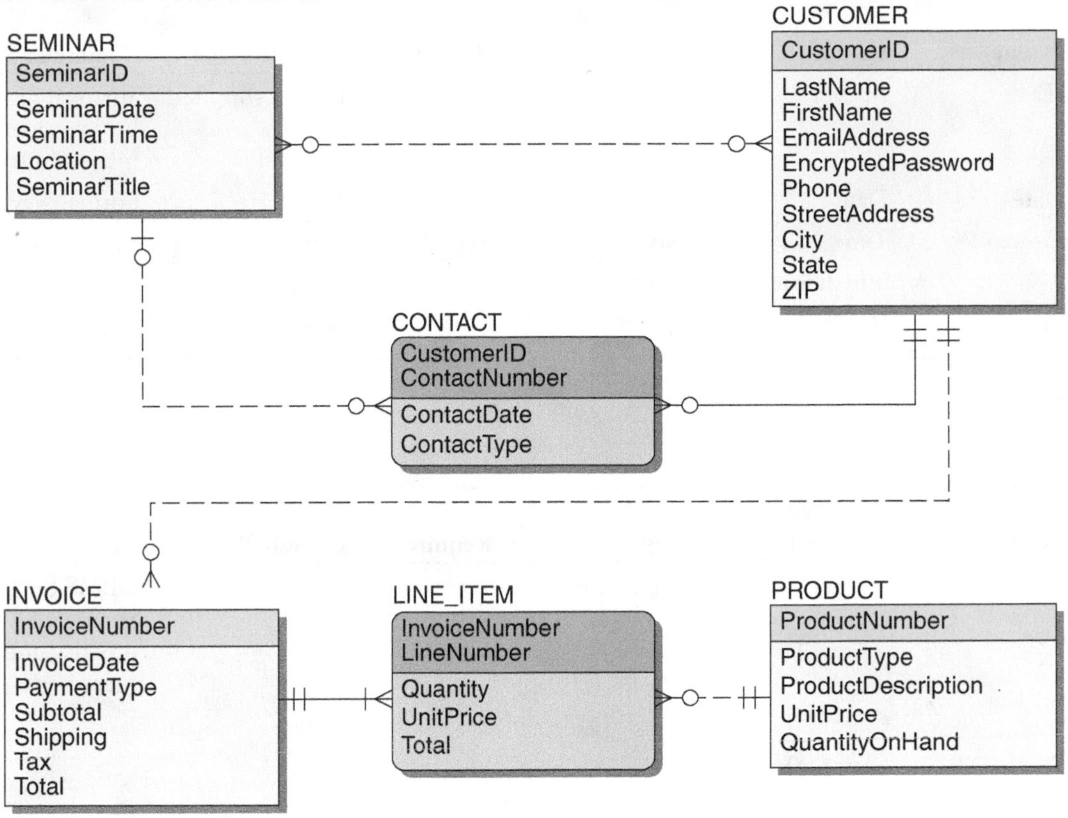

However, for the reasons explained earlier, we choose not to place ZIP in its own table.

One possible functional dependency concerns locations, dates, times, or titles. If, for example, Heather offers seminars only at certain times in some locations or if she only gives certain seminar titles in some locations, then a functional dependency would exist with Location as its determinant. It would be important for the design team to check this out, but for now assume that no such dependency exists.

Specifying Column Properties

The data model in Figure 5-25 shows entities, attributes, and entity relationships, but it does not document details about attributes. We do this as part of creating the database design columns. Figure 5-26 documents the data type, null status, default values, data constraints, and other properties of the columns in each table *before the addition of foreign keys other than those already in the data model because of ID-dependent entities.*

Relationships

Now, considering the relationships in this diagram, 1:N relationships exist between SEMINAR and CONTACT, between CUSTOMER and INVOICE, and between PRODUCT and LINE_ITEM. For each of these, we place the key of the parent in the child as a foreign key. Thus, we place the key of SEMINAR in CONTACT, the key of

FIGURE 5-26

Heather Sweeney Designs Column Specifications

Column Name	Data Type (Length)	Key	Required	Default Value	Remarks
SeminarID	Integer	Primary Key	Yes	DBMS supplied	Surrogate Key: Initial value=1 Increment=1
SeminarDate	Date	No	Yes	None	Format: yyyy-mm-dd
SeminarTime	Time	No	Yes	None	Format: 00:00:00.000
Location	VarChar (100)	No	Yes	None	
SeminarTitle	VarChar (100)	No	Yes	None	

(a) SEMINAR

Column Name	Data Type (Length)	Key	Required	Default Value	Remarks
CustomerID	Integer	Primary Key	Yes		DBMS Supplied Surrogate Key: Initial Value=1 Increment=1
LastName	Char (25)	No	Yes	None	
FirstName	Char (25)	No	Yes	None	
EmailAddress	VarChar (100)	Primary Key	Yes	None	
EncryptedPassword	VarChar(50)	No	No	None	
Phone	Char (12)	No	Yes	None	Format: ###-###-####
City	Char (35)	No	No	Dallas	
State	Char (2)	No	No	TX	Format: AA
ZIP	Char (10)	No	No	75201	Format: #####-####

(b) CUSTOMER

Column Name	Data Type (Length)	Key	Required	Default Value	Remarks
CustomerID	Integer	Primary Key, Foreign Key	Yes	None	REF: CUSTOMER
ContactNumber	Integer	No	Yes	None	Format: yyyy-mm-dd
ContactDate	Date	Primary Key	Yes	None	
ContactType	Char (15)	No	Yes	None	

(c) CONTACT

FIGURE 5-26 Continued

Column Name	Data Type (Length)	Key	Required	Default Value	Remarks
InvoiceNumber	Integer	Primary Key	Yes	DBMS supplied	Surrogate Key: Initial value=35000 Increment=1
InvoiceDate	Date	No	Yes	None	Format: yyyy-mm-dd
PaymentType	Char (25)	No	Yes	Cash	
Subtotal	Numeric (9,2)	No	No	None	
Shipping	Numeric (9,2)	No	No	None	
Tax	Numeric (9,2)	No	No	None	
Total	Numeric (9,2)	No	No	None	

(d) INVOICE

Column Name	Data Type (Length)	Key	Required	Default Value	Remarks
InvoiceNumber	Integer	Primary Key, Foreign Key	Yes	None	REF: INVOICE
LineNumber	Integer	Primary Key	Yes	None	This is not quite a Surrogate Key—for *each* InvoiceNumber: Increment=1 Application logic will be needed to supply the correct value
Quantity	Integer	No	No	None	
UnitPrice	Numeric (9,2)	No	No	None	
Total	Numeric (9,2)	No	No	None	

(e) LINE_ITEM

Column Name	Data Type (Length)	Key	Required	Default Value	Remarks
ProductNumber	Integer	Primary Key	Yes	DBMS supplied	Surrogate Key: Initial value=100 Increment=1
ProductType	Char(24)	No	Yes	None	
ProductDescription	VarChar (100)	No	Yes	None	
UnitPrice	Numeric (9, 2)	No	Yes	None	
QuantityOnHand	Integer	No	Yes	0	

(f) PRODUCT

CUSTOMER in INVOICE, and the key of PRODUCT in LINE_ITEM. The relations are now as follows:

SEMINAR (<u>SeminarID</u>, SeminarDate, SeminarTime, Location, SeminarTitle)

CUSTOMER (<u>CustomerID</u>, LastName, FirstName, EmailAddress, EncryptedPassword, Phone, StreetAddress, City, State, ZIP)

CONTACT (*<u>CustomerID</u>*, <u>ContactNumber</u>, ContactDate, ContactType, *SeminarID*)

PRODUCT (<u>ProductNumber</u>, ProductType, ProductDescription, UnitPrice, QuantityOnHand)

INVOICE (<u>InvoiceNumber</u>, InvoiceDate, *CustomerID*, PaymentType, SubTotal, Tax, Total)

LINE_ITEM (*<u>InvoiceNumber</u>*, <u>LineNumber</u>, *ProductNumber*, Quantity, UnitPrice, Total)

Finally, one N:M relationship exists between SEMINAR and CUSTOMER. To represent it, we create an intersection table, which we name SEMINAR_CUSTOMER. As with all intersection tables, its columns are the keys of the two tables involved in the N:M relationship. The final set of tables is:

SEMINAR (<u>SeminarID</u>, SeminarDate, SeminarTime, Location, SeminarTitle)

CUSTOMER (<u>CustomerID</u>, LastName, FirstName, EmailAddress, EncryptedPassword, Phone, StreetAddress, City, State, ZIP)

SEMINAR_CUSTOMER (*<u>SeminarID</u>*, *<u>CustomerID</u>*)

CONTACT (*<u>CustomerID</u>*, <u>ContactDate</u>, ContactDate, ContactType, *SeminarID*)

PRODUCT (<u>ProductNumber</u>, ProductType, ProductDescription, UnitPrice, QuantityOnHand)

INVOICE (<u>InvoiceNumber</u>, InvoiceDate, *CustomerID*, PaymentType, SubTotal, Tax, Total)

LINE_ITEM (*<u>InvoiceNumber</u>*, <u>LineNumber</u>, *ProductNumber*, Quantity, UnitPrice, Total)

The set of referential integrity constraints will be discussed in the next section.

Now, to express the minimum cardinalities of children back to their parents, we need to decide whether foreign keys are required. In Figure 5-25, we see that an INVOICE is required to have a CUSTOMER and that LINE_ITEM is required to have a PRODUCT. Thus, we will make INVOICE.EmailAddress and LINE_ITEM.ProductNumber required. CONTACT.SeminarID will not be required because a contact is not required to refer to a seminar. The final design is shown in the data structure diagram in Figure 5-27 and the revised table column specification for those tables affected by the addition of foreign keys is shown in Figure 5-28.

Enforcing Referential Integrity

Figure 5-29 summarizes the relationship enforcement for Heather Sweeney Designs. SeminarID is a surrogate key, so no cascading update behavior will be necessary for any of the relationships that it carries. Similarly, CustomerID in CUSTOMER and InvoiceNumber in INVOICE are unchanging values, so these relationships do not need cascading updates. However, updates of ProductNumber do need to cascade through their relationships.

With regard to cascading deletions, rows in the intersection table require a SEMINAR and a CUSTOMER parent. Therefore, when a user attempts to cancel a seminar or to

FIGURE 5-27

Database Design for Heather Sweeney Designs

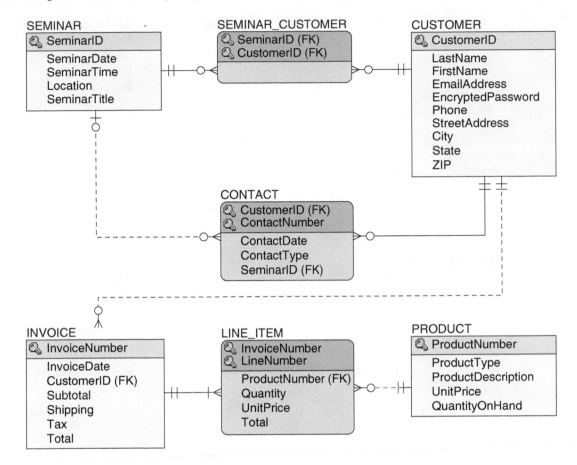

remove a customer record the deletion must either cascade or be prohibited. We must discuss this issue with Heather and her employees and determine whether users should be able to remove seminars that have customers enrolled or to remove customers who have enrolled in a seminar. We decide that neither seminars nor customers are *ever* deleted from the database (Heather *never* cancels a seminar, even if no customers show up, and once

FIGURE 5-28

Modified Column Specifications for HSD Tables with Added Foreign Keys

Column Name	Data Type (Length)	Key	Required	Default Value	Remarks
SeminarID	Integer	Primary Key, Foreign Key	Yes	None	
CustomerID	Integer	Primary Key, Foreign Key	Yes	None	

(a) SEMINAR_CUSTOMER

(continued)

FIGURE 5-28 Continued

Column Name	Data Type (Length)	Key	Required	Default Value	Remarks
CustomerID	Integer	Primary Key, Foreign Key	Yes	None	REF: CUSTOMER
ContactNumber	Integer	Primary Key	Yes	None	This is not quite a Surrogate Key—for *each* ContactNumber: Start=1 Increment=1 Application logic will be needed to supply the correct value
ContactDate	Date	No	Yes	None	Format: yyyy-mm-dd
ContactType	Char (15)	No	Yes	None	
SeminarID	**Integer**	**Foreign Key**	**No**	**None**	**REF: SEMINAR**

(b) CONTACT

Column Name	Data Type (Length)	Key	Required	Default Value	Remarks
InvoiceNumber	Integer	Primary Key	Yes	DBMS supplied	Surrogate Key: Initial value=35000 Increment=1
InvoiceDate	Date	No	Yes	None	Format: yyyy-mm-dd
CustomerID	**Integer**	**Foreign Key**	**Yes**	**None**	**REF: CUSTOMER**
PaymentType	Char (25)	No	Yes	Cash	
Subtotal	Numeric (9,2)	No	No	None	
Shipping	Numeric (9,2)	No	No	None	
Tax	Numeric (9,2)	No	No	None	
Total	Numeric (9,2)	No	No	None	

(c) INVOICE

Column Name	Data Type (Length)	Key	Required	Default Value	Remarks
InvoiceNumber	Integer	Primary Key, Foreign Key	Yes	None	REF: INVOICE
LineNumber	Integer	Primary Key	Yes	None	This is not quite a Surrogate Key—for *each* InvoiceNumber: Start=1 Increment=1 Application logic will be needed to supply the correct value
ProductNumber	**Integer**	**Foreign Key**	**Yes**	**None**	**REF: PRODUCT**
Quantity	Integer	No	No	None	
UnitPrice	Numeric (9,2)	No	No	None	
Total	Numeric (9,2)	No	No	None	

(d) LINE_ITEM

FIGURE 5-29

Referential Integrity Constraint Enforcement for Heather Sweeney Designs

Relationship		Referential Integrity Constraint	Cascading Behavior	
Parent	**Child**		**On Update**	**On Delete**
SEMINAR	SEMINAR_CUSTOMER	SeminarID in SEMINAR_CUSTOMER must exist in SeminarID in SEMINAR	No	No
CUSTOMER	SEMINAR_CUSTOMER	CustomerID in SEMINAR_CUSTOMER must exist in CustomerID in CUSTOMER	No	No
SEMINAR	CONTACT	SeminarID in CONTACT must exist in SeminarID in SEMINAR	No	No
CUSTOMER	CONTACT	CustomerID in CONTACT must exist in CustomerID in CUSTOMER	No	No
CUSTOMER	INVOICE	CustomerID in INVOICE must exist in CustomerID in CUSTOMER	No	No
INVOICE	LINE_ITEM	InvoiceNumber in LINE_ITEM must exist inInvoiceNumber in INVOICE	No	Yes
PRODUCT	LINE_ITEM	ProductNumber in LINE_ITEM must exist in ProductNumber in PRODUCT	Yes	No

Heather has a customer record she *never* lets go of it!). Hence, as shown in Figure 5-29, neither of these relationships has cascading deletions.

Figure 5-29 shows other decisions reached in the example. Because of the need to keep historic information about seminar attendance and contacts, we cannot delete a customer record. Doing so would distort seminar attendance data and data about contacts such as email messages and regular mail letters, which need to be accounted for. Foreign key constraints thus prohibit deleting the primary key record in CUSTOMER.

As shown in Figure 5-29, the deletion of an INVOICE will cause the deletion of related LINE_ITEMs. Finally, an attempt to delete a PRODUCT that is related to one or more LINE_ITEMs will fail; cascading the deletion here would cause LINE_ITEMs to disappear out of ORDERs, a situation that cannot be allowed.

The database design for the Heather Sweeney Designs database is now complete enough to create tables, columns, relationships, and referential integrity constraints using a DBMS. Before going on, we would need to document any additional business rules to be enforced by application programs or other DBMS techniques. After this, the database can be created, using the SQL statements discussed in Chapter 3. The full set of the SQL statements needed to create and populate the database in SQL Server 2014 are located in the Chapter 3 Heather Sweeney Designs Case Questions on pages 222–232. These SQL statements will need to be slightly modified for use with Oracle Database Express Edition 11*g* Release 2 or MySQL 5.6.

THE ACCESS WORKBENCH

Section 5

Relationships in Microsoft Access

At this point, we have created and populated the CONTACT, CUSTOMER, and SALESPERSON tables in the Wallingford Motors CRM database. You learned how to create forms, reports, and queries in the preceding sections of "The Access Workbench." If you have worked through Chapter 3's section of "The Access Workbench," you know how to create and use view equivalent queries.

All the tables you have used so far have had 1:N relationships. But how are 1:1 and N:M relationships managed in Microsoft Access? In this section, you will:

- Understand 1:1 relationships in Microsoft Access.
- Understand N:M relationships in Microsoft Access.

N:M Relationships in Microsoft Access

We will start by discussing N:M relationships. This is actually a nonissue because pure N:M relationships only occur in data modeling. Remember that when a data model is transformed into a database design an N:M relationship is broken down into two 1:N relationships. Each 1:N relationship is between a table resulting from one of the original entities in the N:M relationship and a new intersection table. If this does not make sense to you, then review the chapter section "Representing N:M Strong Entity Relationships" and see Figures 5-13 and 5-15 for an illustration of how N:M relationships are converted to two 1:N relationships.

Because databases are built in DBMSs, such as Microsoft Access, from the database design, Microsoft Access only deals with the resulting 1:N relationships. As far as Microsoft Access is concerned, there are no N:M relationships!

1:1 Relationships in Microsoft Access

Unlike N:M relationships, 1:1 relationships definitely exist in Microsoft Access. At this point the WMCRM database does not contain a 1:1 relationship, and here we will add one. We will let each SALESPERSON use one and only one car from the Wallingford Motors inventory as a demo vehicle. The database design with this addition is shown in Figure AW-5-1.

Note that both SALESPERSON and VEHICLE are optional in this relationship. First, a VEHICLE does not have to be assigned to a SALESPERSON, which makes sense because there will be a lot of cars in inventory and only a few SALESPERSONs. Second, a SALESPERSON does not have to take a demo car and may choose not to (yeah, right!). Also note that we have chosen to put the foreign key in SALESPERSON. In this case, there is an advantage to putting the foreign key in one table or the other because if we put it in VEHICLE the foreign key column (which would have been NickName) would be NULL for every car except the few used as demo vehicles. Finally, note that we are using this table just to illustrate a 1:1 relationship—a functional VEHICLE table would have a lot more columns.

The column characteristics for the VEHICLE table are shown in Figure AW-5-2, and the data for the table are shown in Figure AW-5-3.

Let us open the WMCRM.accdb database and add the VEHICLE table to it.

Opening the WMCRM.accdb Database

1. Start Microsoft Access.
2. If necessary, click the **File** command tab, and then click the **WMCRM.accdb** file name in the quick access list of recently opened databases to open the database.

FIGURE AW-5-1

The WMCRM Database Design with VEHICLE

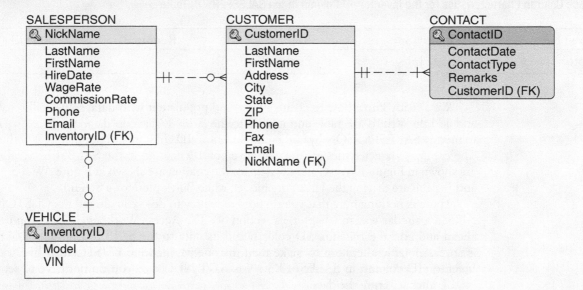

FIGURE AW-5-2

Database Column Characteristics for the VEHICLE Table

Column Name	Type	Key	Required	Remarks
InventoryID	AutoNumber	Primary Key	Yes	Surrogate Key
Model	Text(25)	No	Yes	
VIN	Text(35)	No	Yes	

FIGURE AW-5-3

Wallingford Motors VEHICLE Data

InventoryID	Model	VIN
[AutoNumber]	HiStandard	G15HS123400001
[AutoNumber]	HiStandard	G15HS123400002
[AutoNumber]	HiStandard	G15HS123400003
[AutoNumber]	HiLuxury	G15HL234500001
[AutoNumber]	HiLuxury	G15HL234500002
[AutoNumber]	HiLuxury	G15HL234500003
[AutoNumber]	SUHi	G15HU345600001
[AutoNumber]	SUHi	G15HU345600002
[AutoNumber]	SUHi	G15HU345600003
[AutoNumber]	HiElectra	G15HE456700001

(Continued)

Database Column Characteristics for the InventoryID Column in the SALESPERSON Table

Column Name	Type	Key	Required	Remarks
InventoryID	Long Integer	Foreign Key	No	

We already know how to create a table and populate it with data, so we will go ahead and add the VEHICLE table and its data to the WMCRM.accdb database. Next, we need to modify SALESPERSON by adding the InventoryID column and populating it with data. The column characteristics for the new InventoryID column in the SALESPERSON table are shown in Figure AW-5-4, and the data for the column are shown in Figure AW-5-5. (Tina and Big Bill are driving the HiLuxury model, while Billy opted for a SUHi.)

There is nothing here that you do not know how to do—you altered the CUSTOMER table in a similar way in Chapter 3's section of "The Access Workbench"—so you can go ahead and add the InventoryID column and its data to the SALESPERSON table. This is an easier table alteration to make than the one we made to CUSTOMER because the InventoryID column in SALESPERSON is NOT NULL, so you do not have to set it to NULL after entering the data.

Now, we are ready to establish the relationship between the two tables.

Creating the Relationship Between SALESPERSON and VEHICLE

1. If you have any tables open, close them, and the click the **Database Tools** command tab.
2. Click the **Shutter Bar Open/Close** button to minimize the Navigation Pane.
3. Click the **Relationships** button in the Relationships group. The Relationships tabbed document window appears.
   - ■ **NOTE: Warning!** The next steps lead to a peculiarity of Microsoft Access, not the final outcome that we want. Remember that we want a 1:1 relationship. See if you can figure out what is happening as we go along.
4. Click the **Show Table** button in the Relationships group of the Design ribbon.
5. In the Show Table dialog box, click **VEHICLE** to select it, and then click the **Add** button to add VEHICLE to the Relationships window.
6. In the Show Table dialog box, click the **Close** button to close the dialog box.
7. Rearrange and resize the table objects in the Relationships window by using standard Windows drag-and-drop techniques. Rearrange the SALESPERSON, CUSTOMER, CONTACT, and VEHICLE table objects until they look as shown in Figure AW-5-6.
   - ■ **NOTE:** Remember that we create a relationship between two tables in the Relationships window by dragging a *primary key* column and dropping it on top of the *corresponding foreign key* column.

SALESPERSON InventoryID Data

NickName	LastName	FirstName	...	InventoryID
Tina	Smith	Tina	...	4
Big Bill	Jones	William	...	5
Billy	Jones	Bill	...	7

FIGURE AW-5-6

The Relationships Window with the Current Relationship Diagram

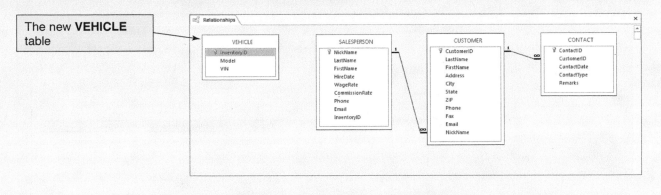

The new **VEHICLE** table

8. Click and hold the column name **InventoryID** in the VEHICLE table object, then drag it over the column name **InventoryID** in the **SALESPERSON** table, and then release the mouse button. The Edit Relationships dialog box appears.
9. Click the **Enforce Referential Integrity** check box.
10. Click the **Create** button to create the relationship between VEHICLE and SALESPERSON.
11. Right-click the **relationship line** between VEHICLE and SALESPERSON, and then click **Edit Relationship** in the shortcut menu that appears. The **Edit Relationships** dialog box appears.
12. The relationship between the tables now appears in the Relationships window, as shown in Figure AW-5-7.

But now we have a serious problem: The relationship that was created is a 1:N relationship, not the 1:1 relationship that we wanted. It seems like there should be a way to fix the relationship somewhere on the Edit Relationships dialog box. Unfortunately, there is not. Go ahead and try everything you can think of, but it will not work. This is the peculiarity of Microsoft Access that was mentioned earlier.

FIGURE AW-5-7

The Completed VEHICLE-to-SALESPERSON Relationship

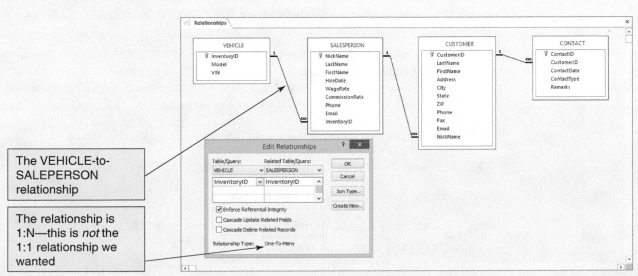

The VEHICLE-to-SALEPERSON relationship

The relationship is 1:N—this is *not* the 1:1 relationship we wanted

(Continued)

FIGURE AW-5-8

Setting the Indexed Property Value in the SALESPERSON Table

So what is the trick to creating a 1:1 relationship in Microsoft Access? As discussed in this chapter, the trick is to create a UNIQUE constraint on the foreign key column. To do this in Microsoft Access, we set the **Indexed field property** of the foreign key column (InventoryID in SALESPERSON in this case) to **Yes (No Duplicates)**, as shown in Figure AW-5-8. As long as the same value can occur more than once in the foreign key column Microsoft Access will create a 1:N relationship instead of the desired 1:1 relationship.

To create the 1:1 relationship, we need to delete the existing relationship, modify the InventoryID property in SALESPERSON, and create a new relationship between the tables. First, we will delete the existing 1:N relationship.

Deleting the Incorrect Relationship Between SALESPERSON and VEHICLE

1. Click the **OK** button on the Edit Relationships dialog box.
2. Right-click the **relationship line** between VEHICLE and SALESPERSON to display the shortcut menu, and then click **Delete**.
3. A dialog box appears asking whether you are sure you want to permanently delete the selected relationship from your database. Click the **Yes** button.
4. Close the Relationships window.
5. A dialog box appears asking whether you want to save the changes to the layout of Relationships. Click the **Yes** button.
6. Click the **Shutter Bar Open/Close** button to expand the Navigation Pane.

Next, we will modify the SALESPSERSON table.

Setting the Indexed Property of the InventoryID Column in SALESPERSON

1. Open the **SALESPERSON** table in Design view.
2. Select the **InventoryID** field. The InventoryID field properties are displayed in the General tab.

3. Click the **Indexed** text field. A drop-down list arrow appears on the right end of the text field. Click the drop-down list arrow to display the list and select **Yes (No Duplicates)**. The result appears as shown in Figure AW-5-8.
4. Click the **Save** button to save the completed changes to the SALESPERSON table.
5. Close the SALESPERSON table.

Finally, we create the 1:1 relationship that we want between the SALESPERSON and VEHICLE tables.

Creating the Correct 1:1 Relationship Between SALESPERSON and VEHICLE

1. Click the **Database Tools** command tab.
2. Click the **Shutter Bar Open/Close** button to minimize the Navigation Pane.
3. Click the **Relationships** button in the Relationships group. The Relationships tabbed document window appears.
4. Click and hold the column name **InventoryID** in the **VEHICLE** table object, then drag it over the column name **InventoryID** in the **SALESPERSON** table, and then release the mouse button. The Edit Relationships dialog box appears.
5. Click the **Enforce Referential Integrity** check box.
6. Click the **Create** button to create the relationship between VEHICLE and SALESPERSON.
7. To verify that you now have the correct 1:1 relationship, right-click the **relationship line** between SALESPERSON and VEHICLE, and then click **Edit Relationship** in the short-cut menu that appears. The **Edit Relationships** dialog box appears.
8. Note that the correct one-to-one relationship between the tables now appears in the Relationships window, as shown in Figure AW-5-9.
9. Click the **Cancel** button on the Edit Relationships dialog box.
10. Close the Relationships window.

FIGURE AW-5-9

The Correct 1:1 VEHICLE-to-SALESPERSON Relationship

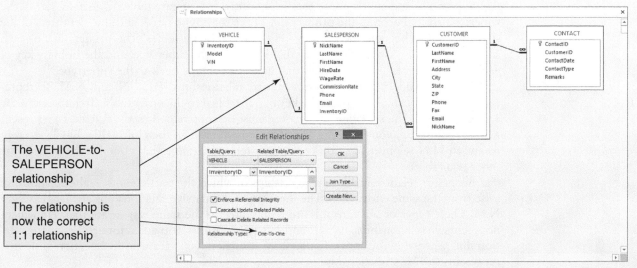

The VEHICLE-to-SALEPERSON relationship

The relationship is now the correct 1:1 relationship

(Continued)

11. If a dialog box appears asking whether you want to save the changes to the layout of Relationships window, click the **Yes** button.
12. Click the **Shutter Bar Open/Close** button to expand the Navigation Pane.

We have successfully created the 1:1 relationship that we wanted. We just had to learn the Microsoft Access way of doing it.

Closing the Database and Exiting Microsoft Access

That completes the work we will do in this chapter's section of "The Access Workbench." As usual, we finish by closing the database and Microsoft Access.

Closing the WMCRM Database and Exiting Microsoft Access

1. To close the WMCRM database and exit Microsoft Access, click the Microsoft Access **Close** button in the upper-right corner of the Microsoft Access window.

SUMMARY

To transform an E-R data model into a relational database design, you create a table for each entity. The attributes of the entity become the columns of the table, and the identifier of the entity becomes the primary key of the table. For each column, you must define data types, null status, any default values, and any data constraints. You then apply the normalization process to each table and create additional tables, if necessary. In some cases, you need to denormalize a table. When you do, the table will have insertion, update, and deletion problems.

Denormalization makes sense if the benefit of not normalizing outweighs the possible problems that could be caused by such modifications.

Weak entities are represented by a table. ID-dependent entities must include the key columns of the tables on which they depend, as well as of the identifiers of the entities themselves. Non–ID-dependent entities must have their existence dependence recorded as business rules.

Supertypes and subtypes are each represented by separate tables. The identifier of the supertype entity becomes the primary key of the supertype table, and the identifiers of the subtype entities become the primary keys of the subtype tables. The primary key of each subtype is also the same primary key that is used for the supertype, and the primary key of each subtype serves as a foreign key that links the subtype back to the supertype.

The E-R model has three types of binary relationships: 1:1, 1:N, and N:M. To represent a 1:1 relationship, you place the key of one table into the other table. To implement the 1:1 relationship, the specified foreign key must be constrained as UNIQUE. To represent a 1:N relationship, you place the key of the parent table in the child table. Finally, to represent an M:N relationship, you create an intersection table that contains the keys of the other two tables.

Recursive relationships are relationships in which the participants in the relationship arise from the same entity class. The three types of recursive relationships are 1:1, 1:N, and N:M. These types of relationships are represented in the same way as are their equivalent nonrecursive relationships. For 1:1 and 1:N relationships, you add a foreign key to the relation that represents the entity. For an N:M recursion, you create an intersection table that represents the M:N relationship.

KEY TERMS

association entity
associative entity
association relationship
Boyce-Codd Normal Form
   (BCNF)
child
column property
component design

data constraint
data model
data type
database design
default value
denormalization
intersection table
mixed entity pattern

multivalued dependency
NULL status
parent
relation
surrogate key
systems development life cycle
   (SDLC)
table

REVIEW QUESTIONS

5.1   Explain how entities are transformed into tables.

5.2   Explain how attributes are transformed into columns. What column properties do you take into account when making the transformations?

5.3   Why is it necessary to apply the normalization process to the tables created according to your answer to question 5.1?

5.4   What is denormalization?

5.5   When is denormalization justified?

5.6   Explain the problems that unnormalized tables have for insert, update, and delete actions.

5.7   Explain how the representation of weak entities differs from the representation of strong entities.

5.8   Explain how supertype and subtype entities are transformed into tables.

5.9   List the three types of binary relationships and give an example of each. Do not use the examples given in this text.

5.10   Define the term *foreign key* and give an example.

5.11   Show two different ways to represent the 1:1 relationship in your answer to question 5.9. Use IE Crow's Foot E-R diagrams.

5.12   For your answers to question 5.11, describe a method for obtaining data about one of the entities, given the key of the other. Describe a method for obtaining data about the second entity, given the key of the first. Describe methods for both of your alternatives in question 5.11.

5.13   Code SQL statements to create a join that has all data about both tables from your work for question 5.11.

5.14   Define the terms *parent* and *child* as they apply to tables in a database design and give an example of each.

5.15   Show how to represent the 1:N relationship in your answer to question 5.9. Use an IE Crow's Foot E-R diagram.

5.16   For your answer to question 5.15, describe a method for obtaining data for all the children, given the key of the parent. Describe a method for obtaining data for the parent, given a key of the child.

5.17   For your answer to question 5.15, code an SQL statement that creates a table that has all data from both tables.

5.18   For a 1:N relationship, explain why you must place the key of the parent table in the child table rather than place the key of the child table in the parent table.

5.19 Give examples of binary 1:N relationships, other than those in this text, for (a) an optional-to-optional relationship, (b) an optional-to-mandatory relationship, (c) a mandatory-to-optional relationship, and (d) a mandatory-to-mandatory relationship. Illustrate your answer by using IE Crow's Foot E-R diagrams.

5.20 Show how to represent the N:M relationship in your answer to question 5.9. Use an IE Crow's Foot E-R diagram.

5.21 Explain the meaning of the term *intersection table*.

5.22 Explain how the terms *parent table* and *child table* relate to the tables in your answer to question 5.20.

5.23 For your answers to questions 5.20, 5.21, and 5.22, describe a method for obtaining the children for one of the entities in the original data model, given the primary key of the table based on the second entity. Also, describe a method for obtaining the children for the second entity, given the primary key of the table based on the first entity.

5.24 For your answer to question 5.20, code an SQL statement that creates a relation that has all data from all tables.

5.25 Why is it not possible to represent N:M relationships with the same strategy used to represent 1:N relationships?

5.26 What is an *associative entity* (also called an *association entity*)? What is an *association relationship*? Give an example of an association relationship other than one shown in this text. Illustrate your answer using an IE Crow's Foot E-R diagram.

5.27 Give an example of a 1:N relationship with an ID-dependent weak entity, other than one shown in this text. Illustrate your answer using an IE Crow's Foot E-R diagram.

5.28 Give an example of a supertype–subtype relationship, other than one shown in this text. Illustrate your answer using an IE Crow's Foot E-R diagram.

5.29 Define the three types of recursive binary relationships and give an example of each, other than the ones shown in this text.

5.30 Show how to represent the 1:1 recursive relationship in your answer to question 5.29. How does this differ from the representation of 1:1 nonrecursive relationships?

5.31 Code an SQL statement that creates a table with all columns from the parent and child tables in your answer to question 5.30.

5.32 Show how to represent a 1:N recursive relationship in your answer to question 5.29. How does this differ from the representation of 1:N nonrecursive relationships?

5.33 Code an SQL statement that creates a table with all columns from the parent and child tables in your answer to question 5.32.

5.34 Show how to represent the M:N recursive relationship in your answer to question 5.29. How does this differ from the representation of M:N nonrecursive relationships?

5.35 Code an SQL statement that creates a table with all columns from the parent and child tables in your answer to question 5.34. Code an SQL statement using a left outer join that creates a table with all columns from the parent and child tables. Explain the difference between these two SQL statements.

EXERCISES

5.36 Consider the following table, which holds data about employee project assignments:

ASSIGNMENT (<u>EmployeeNumber</u>, <u>ProjectNumber</u>, ProjectName, HoursWorked)

Assume that ProjectNumber determines ProjectName and explain why this relation is not normalized. Demonstrate an insertion anomaly, a modification anomaly, and a deletion anomaly. Apply the normalization process to this relation. State the referential integrity constraint.

5.37 Consider the following relation that holds data about employee assignments:

ASSIGNMENT (<u>EmployeeNumber</u>, ProjectNumber, ProjectName, HoursWorked)

Assume that ProjectNumber determines ProjectName and explain why this relation is not normalized. Demonstrate an insertion anomaly, a modification anomaly, and a deletion anomaly. Apply the normalization process to this relation. State the referential integrity constraint.

5.38 Explain the difference between the two ASSIGNMENT tables in questions 5.36 and 5.37. Under what circumstances is the table in question 5.36 more correct? Under what circumstances is the table in question 5.37 more correct?

5.39 Create a relational database design for the data model you developed for question 4.30.

5.40 Create a relational database design for the data model you developed for question 4.31.

5.41 Create a relational database design for the data model you developed for question 4.32.

5.42 Create a relational database design for the data model you developed for question 4.33.

ACCESS WORKBENCH KEY TERM

Indexed field property

ACCESS WORKBENCH EXERCISES

AW.5.1   Using an IE Crow's Foot E-R diagram, draw a database design for the Wedgewood Pacific Corporation (WPC) database completed at the end of Chapter 3's section of "The Access Workbench."

AW.5.2   This chapter's section of "The Access Workbench" describes how to create 1:1 relationships in Microsoft Access. In particular, we added the business rule that each salesperson at Wallingford Motors can have one and only one vehicle as a demo car. Suppose that the rule has been changed so that each salesperson can have one or more cars as demo vehicles.

A.   Using an IE Crow's Foot E-R diagram, redraw the database design in Figure AW-5-1 to show the new relationship between VEHICLE and SALESPERSON. Which table(s) is (are) the parent(s) in the relationship? Which table(s) is (are) the child(ren)? In which table(s) do you place a foreign key?

(Continued)

B. Start with the Wallingford Motors database that you have created so far (**WMCRM.accdb**) as it exists after working through all the steps in this chapter's section of "The Access Workbench." (If you have not completed those actions, do so now.) Copy the **WMCRM.accdb** database and rename the copy **WMCRM-AW05-v02.accdb**. Modify the WMCRM-AW05-v02.accdb database to implement the new relationship between VEHICLE and SALESPERSON. (*Note:* Copying a Microsoft Access database is discussed in Chapter 4's section of "The Access Workbench.")

AW.5.3 This chapter's section of "The Access Workbench" describes how to create 1:1 relationships in Microsoft Access. In particular, we added the business rule that each salesperson at Wallingford Motors can have one and only one vehicle as a demo car. Suppose that the rule has been changed so that (1) each salesperson can have one or more cars as demo vehicles and (2) each demo vehicle can be shared by two or more salespersons.

A. Using an IE Crow's Foot E-R diagram, redraw the database design in Figure AW-5-1 to show the new relationship between VEHICLE and SALESPERSON. Which table(s) is (are) the parent(s) in the relationship? Which table(s) is (are) the child(ren)? In which table(s) do you place a foreign key?

B. Start with the Wallingford Motors database that you have created so far (**WMCRM.accdb**) as it exists after working through all the steps in this chapter's section of "The Access Workbench." (If you have not completed those actions, do so now.) Copy the **WMCRM.accdb** database and rename the copy **WMCRM-AW05-v03.accdb**. Modify the WMCRM-AW05-v03.accdb database to implement the new relationship between VEHICLE and SALESPERSON. (*Note:* Copying a Microsoft Access database is discussed in Chapter 4's section of "The Access Workbench.")

SAN JUAN SAILBOAT CHARTERS CASE QUESTIONS

San Juan Sailboat Charters (SJSBC) is an agency that leases (charters) sailboats. SJSBC does not own the boats. Instead, SJSBC leases boats on behalf of boat owners who want to earn income from their boats when they are not using them, and SJSBC charges the owners a fee for this service. SJSBC specializes in boats that can be used for multiday or weekly charters. The smallest sailboat available is 28 feet in length and the largest is 51 feet in length.

Each sailboat is fully equipped at the time it is leased. Most of the equipment is provided at the time of the charter. Most of the equipment is provided by the owners, but some is provided by SJSBC. The owner-provided equipment includes equipment that is attached to the boat, such as radios, compasses, depth indicators and other instrumentation, stoves, and refrigerators. Other owner-provided equipment, such as sails, lines, anchors, dinghies, life preservers, and equipment in the cabin (dishes, silverware, cooking utensils, bedding, and so on), is not physically attached to the boat. SJSBC provides consumable supplies, such as charts, navigation books, tide and current tables, soap, dish towels, toilet paper, and similar items. The consumable supplies are treated as equipment by SJSBC for tracking and accounting purposes.

Keeping track of equipment is an important part of SJSBC's responsibilities. Much of the equipment is expensive, and those items not physically attached to the boat can be easily damaged, lost, or stolen. SJSBC holds the customer responsible for all of the boat's equipment during the period of the charter.

SJSBC likes to keep accurate records of its customers and charters, and customers are required to keep a log during each charter. Some itineraries and weather conditions are more dangerous than others, and the data from these logs provide information about the customer experience. This information is useful for marketing purposes, as well as for evaluating a customer's ability to handle a particular boat and itinerary.

Sailboats need maintenance. Note that two definitions of *boat* are (1) "break out another thousand" and (2) "a hole in the water into which one pours money." SJSBC is required by its contracts with the boat owners to keep accurate records of all maintenance activities and costs.

A data model of a proposed database to support an information system for SJSBC is shown in Figure 5-30. Note that because the OWNER entity allows for owners to be companies as well as individuals SJSBC can be included as an equipment owner (note that the cardinalities in the diagram allow SJSBC to own equipment while *not* owning any boats). Also note that this model relates EQUIPMENT to CHARTER rather than BOAT even when the equipment is physically attached to the boat. This is only one possible way to handle EQUIPMENT, but it is satisfactory to the managers of SJSBC.

A. Convert this data model to a database design. Specify tables, primary keys, and foreign keys. Using Figures 5-26 and 5-28 as guides, specify column properties.

FIGURE 5-30

Data Model for San Juan Sailboat Charters

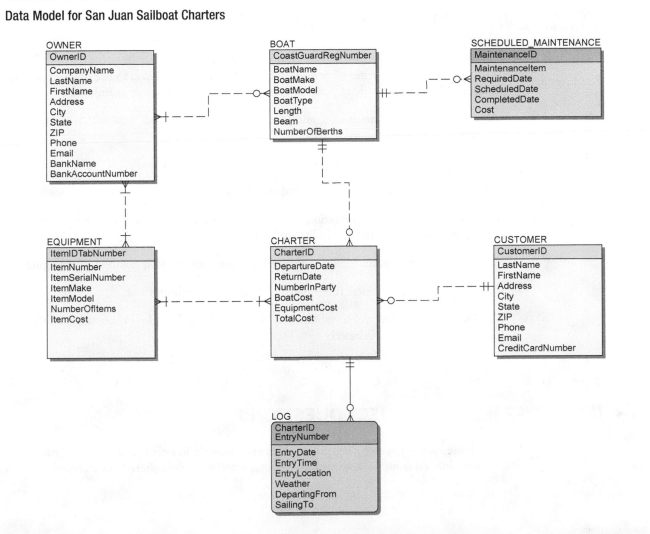

B. Describe how you have represented weak entities, if any exist.

C. Describe how you have represented supertype and subtype entities, if any exist.

D. Create a visual representation of your database design as an IE Crow's Foot E-R diagram similar to the one in Figure 5-27.

E. Document referential integrity constraint enforcement, using Figure 5-29 as a guide.

WASHINGTON STATE PATROL CASE QUESTIONS

Answer the Washington State Patrol Case Questions in Chapter 4 if you have note already done so. Design a database for your data model from Chapter 4. Your design should include a specification of tables and (using Figures 2-26 and 5-28 as guides) column properties, as well as primary, candidate, and foreign keys. Create visual representation of your database design as an IE Crow's Foot E-R diagram similar to the one in Figure 5-27. Document your referential integrity constraint enforcement in the format shown in Figure 5-29.

GARDEN GLORY PROJECT QUESTIONS

Convert the data model you constructed for Garden Glory in part B at the end of Chapter 4 (or an equivalent data model that your instructor provides for you to use) into a relational database design for Garden Glory. Document your database design as follows.

A. Specify tables, primary keys, and foreign keys. Using Figures 5-26 and 5-28 as guides, specify column properties.

B. Describe how you have represented weak entities, if any exist.

C. Describe how you have represented supertype and subtype entities, if any exist.

D. Create a visual representation of your database design as an IE Crow's Foot E-R diagram similar to the one in Figure 5-27.

E. Document referential integrity constraint enforcement, using Figure 5-29 as a guide.

F. Document any business rules that you think might be important.

G. Describe how you would validate that your design is a good representation of the data model on which it is based.

JAMES RIVER JEWELRY PROJECT QUESTIONS

The James River Jewelry project questions are available in online Appendix D, which can be downloaded from the textbook's Web site: **www.pearsonhighered.com/kroenke**.

THE QUEEN ANNE CURIOSITY SHOP PROJECT QUESTIONS

Convert the data model you constructed for The Queen Anne Curiosity Shop in part D at the end of Chapter 4 (or an equivalent data model that your instructor provides for you to use) into a relational database design for The Queen Anne Curiosity Shop. Document your database design as follows.

A. Specify tables, primary keys, and foreign keys. Using Figures 5-26 and 5-28 as guides, specify column properties.

B. Describe how you have represented weak entities, if any exist.

C. Describe how you have represented supertype and subtype entities, if any exist.

D. Create a visual representation of your database design as an IE Crow's Foot E-R diagram similar to the one in Figure 5-27.

E. Document referential integrity constraint enforcement, using Figure 5-29 as a guide.

F. Document any business rules that you think might be important.

G. Describe how you would validate that your design is a good representation of the data model on which it is based.

PART 3 — Database Management

So far, you have been introduced to the fundamental concepts and techniques of relational database management and database design. In Chapter 1, you learned about databases and the major components of a database system. Chapter 2 introduced you to the relational model, functional dependencies, and normalization. In Chapter 3, you learned how to use SQL statements to create and process a database. Chapter 4 gave you an overview of the database design process and a detailed introduction to data modeling. In Chapter 5, you learned how to transform a data model into a relational database design. Now that you know how to design, create, and query databases, it is time to learn how to manage databases and use them to solve business problems.

In Chapter 6, you will learn about database management and some of the problems that occur when a database is processed concurrently by more than one user. In Chapter 7, you will learn how to create Web database applications, which use databases to support Web sites. Finally, in Chapter 8 you will learn how databases support data warehouses and modern business intelligence (BI) systems and about Big Data, the NoSQL movement, and cloud computing. After completing these chapters, you will have surveyed all the basics of database technology.

CHAPTER 6 Database Administration

This chapter describes the major tasks of an important business function called *database administration*. This function involves managing a database in order to maximize its value to an organization. Usually, database administration involves balancing the conflicting goals of protecting the database and maximizing its availability and benefit to users. Both the terms *data administration* and *database administration* are used in the industry. In some cases, the terms are considered to be synonymous; in other cases, they have different meanings. Most commonly, the term **data administration** refers to a function that applies to an entire organization; it is a management-oriented function that concerns corporate data privacy and security issues. The term **database administration** refers to a more technical function that is specific to a particular database, including the applications that process that database. This chapter addresses database administration.

Databases vary considerably in size and scope, from single-user personal databases to large interorganizational databases, such as airline reservation systems. All databases have a need for database administration, although the tasks to be accomplished vary in complexity. When using a personal database, for example, individuals follow simple procedures for backing up their data, and they keep minimal records for documentation. In this case, the person who uses the database also performs the DBA functions, even though he or she is probably unaware of it.

For multiuser database applications, database administration becomes both more important and more difficult. Consequently, it generally has formal recognition. For some applications, one or two people are given this function on a part-time basis. For large Internet or intranet databases, database administration responsibilities are often too time-consuming and too varied to be handled even by a single full-time person. Supporting a database with dozens or hundreds of users requires considerable time as well as both technical knowledge and diplomatic skill, and it is usually handled by an office of database administration. The manager of the office is often known as the **database administrator**. In this case, **DBA** refers to either the office or the manager.

The overall responsibility of a DBA is to facilitate the development and use of a database. Usually, this means balancing the conflicting goals of protecting the database and maximizing its availability and benefit to users. The DBA is responsible for the development, operation, and maintenance of the database and its applications.

In this chapter, we examine three important database administration functions: concurrency control, security, and backup and recovery. Then we discuss the need for configuration change management. But before you learn about any of this, we will create the Heather Sweeney Designs database discussed in the previous chapters; you'll use it as an example database for the discussion in this chapter and in Chapters 7 and 8.

THE HEATHER SWEENEY DESIGNS DATABASE

The SQL statements to create the Heather Sweeney Designs (HSD) database are shown in Figure 3-28. These SQL statements are in Microsoft SQL Server 2014 syntax and will need to be appropriately modified to implement the HSD database in Oracle Database or MySQL. The SQL statements are built from the HSD database design in Figure 5-27, and the column constraints follow the attribute specifications in Figures 5-26 and 5-28, and the referential integrity constraint specifications outlined in Figure 5-29.

The SQL statements to populate the HSD database are shown in Figure 3-29. Again, these SQL statements are shown in SQL Server syntax and will need to be appropriately modified for use in Oracle Database or MySQL. The completed HSD database is shown in the Microsoft SQL Server Management Studio in Figure 6-1.

THE NEED FOR CONTROL, SECURITY, AND RELIABILITY

Databases come in a variety of sizes and scopes, from single-user databases to huge, interorganizational databases, such as inventory management systems. As shown in Figure 6-2, databases also vary in the way they are processed.

We will define and discuss the various pieces of the environment shown in Figure 6-2 in detail in Chapter 7 when we discuss database processing applications. For now, just realize that it is possible for every one of the application elements in Figure 6-2 to be operating at the same time. Queries, forms, and reports can be generated while Web pages [using Active Server Pages (ASP) and Java Server Pages (JSP)] access the database, possibly invoking stored procedures. Traditional application programs running in Visual Basic, C#, Java, and other programming languages can be processing transactions on the database. All this activity can cause pieces of programming code stored in the DBMS—which are known as **SQL/Persistent Stored Modules (SQL/PSM)**, which include **user-defined functions**,

FIGURE 6-1

The HSD Database in Microsoft SQL Server 2014

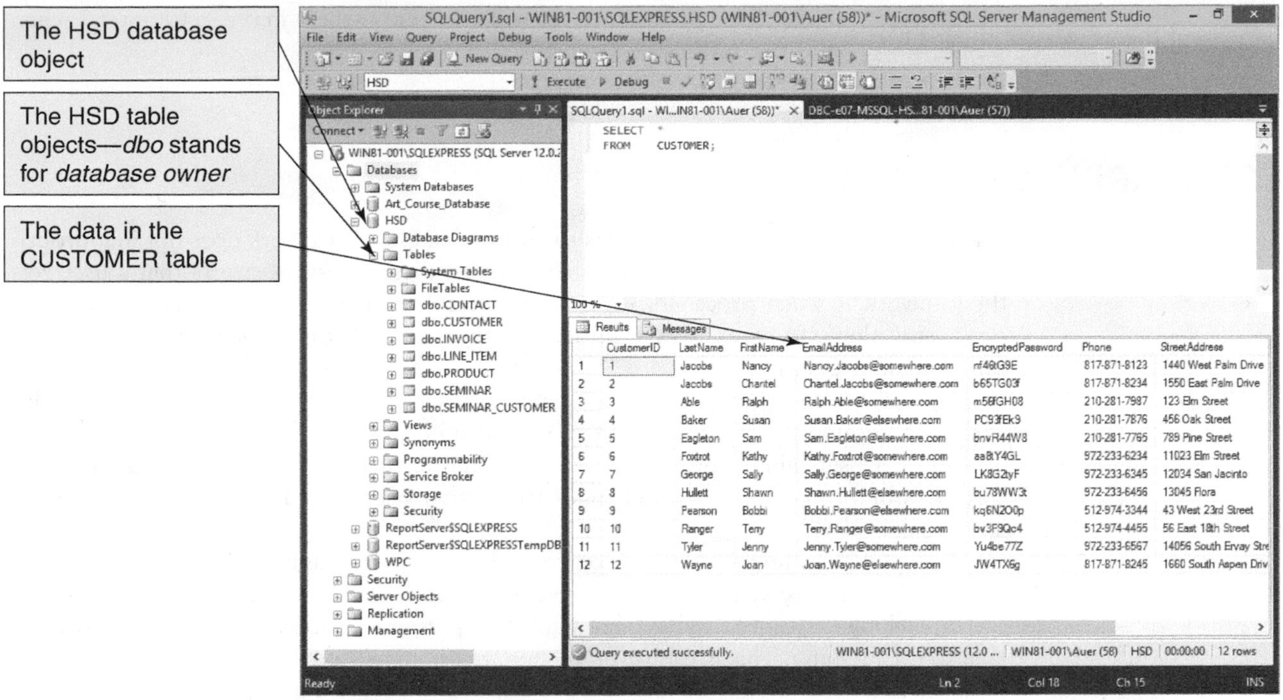

> The HSD database object

> The HSD table objects—*dbo* stands for *database owner*

> The data in the CUSTOMER table

FIGURE 6-2

The Database Processing Environment

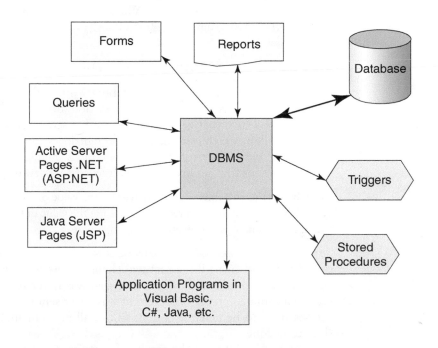

triggers and stored procedures, and which are discussed in Appendix E—to be invoked. While all this is occurring, constraints, such as those on referential integrity, must be enforced. Finally, hundreds, or even thousands, of people might be using the system, and they might want to process the database 24 hours a day, 7 days a week.

Three database administration functions are necessary to bring order to this potential chaos. First, the actions of concurrent users must be controlled to ensure that results are consistent with what is expected. Second, security measures must be in place and enforced so that only authorized users can take authorized actions at appropriate times. Finally, backup and recovery techniques and procedures must be operating to protect the database in case of failure and to recover it as quickly and accurately as possible when necessary. We will consider each of these, in turn, and we will see some of them in use in Chapter 7 when we use Web applications to access databases.

CONCURRENCY CONTROL

The purpose of concurrency control is to ensure that one user's work does not inappropriately influence another user's work. In some cases, these measures ensure that a user gets the same result when processing with other users as that person would have received if processing alone. In other cases, it means that the user's work is influenced by other users but in an anticipated way.

For example, in an order-entry system, a user should be able to enter an order and get the same result, whether there are no other users or hundreds of other users. However, a user who is printing a report of the most current inventory status might want to obtain in-process data changes from other users, even if those changes might later be canceled.

Unfortunately, no concurrency control technique or mechanism is ideal for all circumstances; they all involve trade-offs. For example, a user can obtain strict concurrency control by locking the entire database, but while that person is processing no other user will be able to do anything. This is robust protection, but it comes at a high cost. As you will see, other measures are available that are more difficult to program and enforce but that allow more throughput. Still other measures are available that maximize throughput but for a low level of concurrency control. When designing multiuser database applications, developers need to choose among these trade-offs.

The Need for Atomic Transactions

In most database applications, users submit work in the form of **transactions**, also known as **logical units of work (LUWs)**. A transaction (or LUW) is a series of actions to be taken on a database such that all of them are performed successfully or none of them are performed at all, in which case the database remains unchanged. Such a transaction is sometimes called *atomic* because it is performed as a unit. Consider the following sequence of database actions that could occur when recording a new order:

1. Change the customer record, increasing the value of Amount Owed.
2. Change the salesperson record, increasing the value of Commission Due.
3. Insert the new-order record into the database.

Suppose the last step fails, perhaps because of insufficient file space. Imagine the confusion that would ensue if the first two changes were made but the third one was not. The customer would be billed for an order that was never received, and a salesperson would receive a commission on an order that was never sent to the customer. Clearly, these three actions need to be taken as a unit: Either all of them should be done or none of them should be done.

Figure 6-3 compares the results of performing these activities as a series of independent steps [Figure 6-3(a)] and as an atomic transaction [Figure 6-3(b)].

Notice that when the steps are carried out atomically and one fails no changes are made in the database. Also note that the application program must issue the commands equivalent to Start Transaction, Commit Transaction, and Rollback Transaction to mark the boundaries of the transaction logic. The particular form of these commands varies from one DBMS product to another.

Comparison of the
Results of Applying
Serial Actions Versus
a Multiple-Step
Transaction

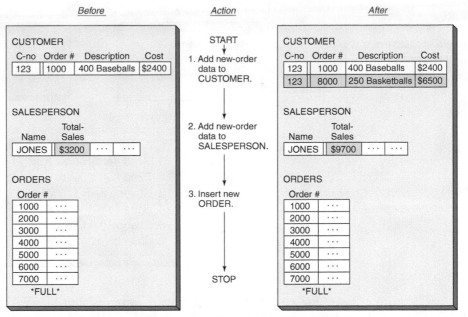

(a) Two of Three Activities Successfully Completed, Resulting in Database Anomalies

(b) No Change Made Because Entire Transaction Not Successful

Concurrent Transaction Processing

When two transactions are being processed against a database at the same time, they are termed **concurrent transactions**. Although it might appear to the users that concurrent transactions are being processed simultaneously, this cannot be true because the central processing unit (CPU) of the machine processing the database can execute only one instruction at a time. Usually transactions are interleaved, which means the operating system switches CPU services among tasks so that some portion of each of them is carried out in a given interval. This switching among tasks is done so quickly that two people seated at browsers side by side, processing against the same database, might believe that their two transactions are completed simultaneously. However, in reality, the two transactions are interleaved.

FIGURE 6-4

Example of Concurrent Processing of Two Users' Tasks

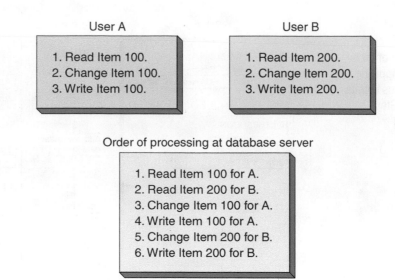

User A

1. Read Item 100.
2. Change Item 100.
3. Write Item 100.

User B

1. Read Item 200.
2. Change Item 200.
3. Write Item 200.

Order of processing at database server

1. Read Item 100 for A.
2. Read Item 200 for B.
3. Change Item 100 for A.
4. Write Item 100 for A.
5. Change Item 200 for B.
6. Write Item 200 for B.

Figure 6-4 shows two concurrent transactions. User A's transaction reads Item 100, changes it, and rewrites it in the database. User B's transaction takes the same actions but on Item 200. The CPU processes User A's transaction until the CPU must wait for a read or write operation to complete or for some other action to finish. The operating system then shifts control to User B. The CPU processes User B's transaction until a similar interruption in the transaction processing occurs, at which point the operating system passes control back to User A. Again, to the users, the processing appears to be simultaneous, but in reality it is interleaved, or concurrent.

The Lost Update Problem

The concurrent processing illustrated in Figure 6-4 poses no problems because the users are processing different data. Now suppose both users want to process Item 100. For example, User A wants to order 5 units of Item 100, and User B wants to order 3 units of Item 100. Figure 6-5 illustrates this problem.

User A reads Item 100's record, which is transferred into a user work area. According to the record, 10 items are in inventory. Then User B reads Item 100's record, and it goes

FIGURE 6-5

Example of the Lost Update Problem

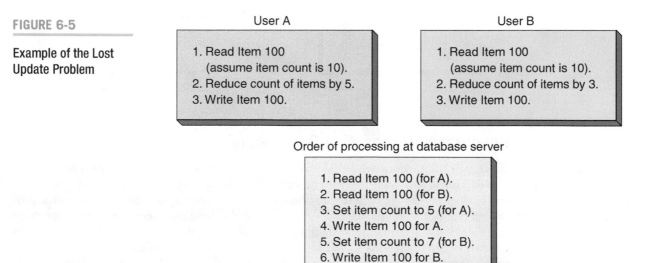

User A

1. Read Item 100
   (assume item count is 10).
2. Reduce count of items by 5.
3. Write Item 100.

User B

1. Read Item 100
   (assume item count is 10).
2. Reduce count of items by 3.
3. Write Item 100.

Order of processing at database server

1. Read Item 100 (for A).
2. Read Item 100 (for B).
3. Set item count to 5 (for A).
4. Write Item 100 for A.
5. Set item count to 7 (for B).
6. Write Item 100 for B.

Note: The change and write in steps 3 and 4 are lost.

into another user work area. Again, according to the record, 10 items are in inventory. Now, User A takes 5 of them, decrements the count of items in its user work area to 5, and rewrites the record for Item 100. Then User B takes 3, decrements the count in its user work area to 7, and rewrites the record for Item 100. The database now shows, incorrectly, that 7 units of Item 100 remain in inventory. To review, the inventory started at 10, then User A took 5, User B took 3, and the database wound up showing that 7 were left in inventory. Clearly, this is a problem.

Both users obtained data that were correct at the time they obtained the data. However, when User B read the record, User A already had a copy that it was about to update. This situation is called the **lost update problem**, or the **concurrent update problem**. Another similar problem is called the **inconsistent read problem**. In this situation, User A reads data that have been processed by only a portion of a transaction from User B. As a result, User A reads incorrect data.

Resource Locking

One remedy for the inconsistencies caused by concurrent processing is to prevent multiple applications from obtaining copies of the same rows or tables when those rows or tables are about to be changed. This remedy, called **resource locking**, prevents concurrent processing problems by disallowing sharing by locking data that are retrieved for update. Figure 6-6 shows the order of processing using a lock command.

Because of the lock, User B's transaction must wait until User A is finished with the Item 100 data. Using this strategy, User B can read Item 100's record only after User A has completed the modification. In this case, the final item count stored in the database is 2, which is what it should be. (It started with 10, then A took 5 and B took 3, leaving 2.)

Locks can be placed automatically by the DBMS or by a command issued to the DBMS from the application program or query user. Locks placed by the DBMS are called **implicit locks**; those placed by command are called **explicit locks**.

In the preceding example, the locks were applied to rows of data; however, not all locks are applied at this level. Some DBMS products lock at the page level, some at the

FIGURE 6-6

Example of Concurrent Processing with Explicit Locks

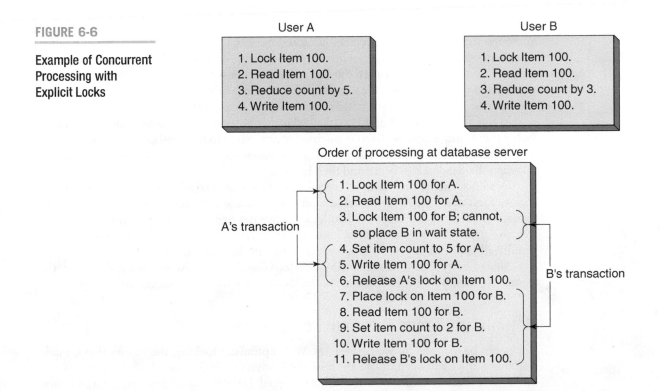

User A

1. Lock Item 100.
2. Read Item 100.
3. Reduce count by 5.
4. Write Item 100.

User B

1. Lock Item 100.
2. Read Item 100.
3. Reduce count by 3.
4. Write Item 100.

Order of processing at database server

A's transaction
1. Lock Item 100 for A.
2. Read Item 100 for A.
3. Lock Item 100 for B; cannot, so place B in wait state.
4. Set item count to 5 for A.
5. Write Item 100 for A.
6. Release A's lock on Item 100.
7. Place lock on Item 100 for B.
8. Read Item 100 for B.
9. Set item count to 2 for B.
10. Write Item 100 for B.
11. Release B's lock on Item 100.

B's transaction

table level, and some at the database level. The size of a lock is referred to as the **lock granularity**. Locks with large granularity are easy for the DBMS to administer but frequently cause conflicts. Locks with small granularity are difficult to administer (the DBMS has many more details to keep track of and check), but conflicts are less common.

Locks also vary by type. An **exclusive lock** locks an item from access of any type. No other transaction can read or change the data. A **shared lock** locks an item from being changed but not from being read; that is, other transactions can read the item as long as they do not attempt to alter it.

Serializable Transactions

When two or more transactions are processed concurrently, the results in the database should be logically consistent with the results that would have been achieved had the transactions been processed in an arbitrary serial fashion. A scheme for processing concurrent transactions in this way is said to be **serializable**.

Serializability can be achieved through a number of different means. One way is to process the transaction by using **two-phase locking**. With this strategy, transactions are allowed to obtain locks as necessary, but when the first lock is released, no other lock can be obtained. Transactions have a growing phase in which the locks are obtained and a shrinking phase in which the locks are released.

A special case of two-phase locking is used with a number of DBMS products. With it, locks are obtained throughout the transaction, but no lock is released until the COMMIT or ROLLBACK command is issued. This strategy is more restrictive than two-phase locking requires, but it is easier to implement.

Consider an order-entry transaction that involves processing data in the CUSTOMER, SALESPERSON, and ORDER tables. To make sure the database will suffer no anomalies due to concurrency, the order-entry transaction issues locks on CUSTOMER, SALESPERSON, and ORDER, as needed; makes all the database changes; and then releases all its locks.

Deadlock

Although locking solves one problem, it causes another. Consider what might happen when two users want to order two items from inventory. Suppose User A wants to order some paper, and, if she can get the paper, she also wants to order some pencils. In addition, suppose that User B wants to order some pencils, and, if he can get the pencils, he also wants to order some paper. An example of the possible order of processing is shown in Figure 6-7.

In this figure, Users A and B are locked in a condition known as **deadlock**, sometimes called the **deadly embrace**. Each is waiting for a resource that the other person has locked. Two common ways of solving this problem are preventing the deadlock from occurring and allowing the deadlock to occur and then breaking it.

Deadlock can be prevented in several ways. One way is to allow users to issue only one lock request at a time; in essence, users must lock all the resources they want at once. For example, if User A in Figure 6-7 had locked both the paper and the pencil records at the beginning, the deadlock would not have occurred. A second way to prevent deadlock is to require all application programs to lock resources in the same order.

Almost every DBMS has algorithms for detecting deadlock. When deadlock occurs, the normal solution is to roll back one of the transactions to remove its changes from the database.

Optimistic Versus Pessimistic Locking

Locks can be invoked in two basic styles. With **optimistic locking**, the assumption is made that no conflict will occur. Data are read, the transaction is processed, updates are issued, and then a check is made to see if conflict occurred. If there was no conflict, the transaction

FIGURE 6-7

Example of Deadlock

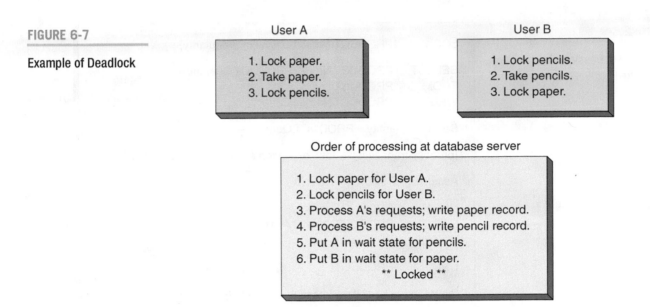

finishes. If there was conflict, the transaction is repeated until it processes with no conflict. With **pessimistic locking**, the assumption is made that conflict will occur. Locks are issued, the transaction is processed, and then the locks are freed.

Figures 6-8 and 6-9 show examples of both styles of locking for a transaction that is reducing the quantity of the pencil row in the PRODUCT table by 5. Figure 6-8 shows optimistic locking. First, the data are read and the current value of Quantity of pencils is saved in the variable OldQuantity. The transaction is then processed, and, if everything is okay, a lock is obtained on PRODUCT. The lock might be only for the pencil row, or it might be at a larger level of granularity. In any case, an SQL statement is issued to update the pencil row with a WHERE condition that the current value of Quantity equals OldQuantity. If no

FIGURE 6-8

Example of Optimistic Locking

```
SELECT     PRODUCT.Name, PRODUCT.Quantity
FROM       PRODUCT
WHERE      PRODUCT.Name = 'Pencil'

OldQuantity = PRODUCT.Quantity

Set NewQuantity = PRODUCT.Quantity – 5

{process transaction – take exception action if NewQuantity < 0, etc.

Assuming all is OK: }

LOCK PRODUCT {at some level of granularity}

UPDATE     PRODUCT
SET        PRODUCT.Quantity = NewQuantity
WHERE      PRODUCT.Name = 'Pencil'
    AND    PRODUCT.Quantity = OldQuantity

UNLOCK   PRODUCT

{check to see if update was successful;
if not, repeat transaction}
```

FIGURE 6-9

Example of Pessimistic Locking

```
LOCK        PRODUCT {at some level of granularity}

SELECT      PRODUCT.Name, PRODUCT.Quantity
FROM        PRODUCT
WHERE       PRODUCT.Name = 'Pencil'

Set NewQuantity = PRODUCT.Quantity – 5

{process transaction – take exception action if NewQuantity < 0, etc.

Assuming all is OK: }

UPDATE      PRODUCT
SET         PRODUCT.Quantity = NewQuantity
WHERE       PRODUCT.Name = 'Pencil'

UNLOCK      PRODUCT

{no need to check if update was successful}
```

other transaction has changed the Quantity of the pencil row, then this UPDATE will be successful. If another transaction has changed the Quantity of the pencil row, the UPDATE will fail, and the transaction will need to be repeated.

Figure 6-9 shows the logic for the same transaction using pessimistic locking. In this case, a lock is obtained on PRODUCT (at some level of granularity) before any work is begun. Then values are read, the transaction is processed, the UPDATE occurs, and PRODUCT is unlocked.

The advantage of optimistic locking is that the lock is obtained only after the transaction has been processed. Thus, the lock is held for less time than with pessimistic locking. If the transaction is complicated or if the client is slow (due to transmission delays or to the user doing other work, getting a cup of coffee, or shutting down without exiting the application), the lock will be held for considerably less time. This advantage is especially important if the lock granularity is large (for example, the entire PRODUCT table).

The disadvantage of optimistic locking is that if a lot of activity occurs on the pencil row the transaction might have to be repeated many times. Thus, transactions that involve a lot of activity on a given row (purchasing a popular stock, for example) are poorly suited for optimistic locking.

SQL TRANSACTION CONTROL LANGUAGE AND DECLARING LOCK CHARACTERISTICS

Concurrency control is a complicated subject; some of the decisions about lock types and strategy have to be made on the basis of trial and error. For this and other reasons, database application programs generally do not explicitly issue locks, as shown in Figures 6-8 and 6-9. Instead, the programs mark transaction boundaries using **SQL Transaction Control Language (TCL)** and then declare the type of locking behavior they want the DBMS to use. In this way, the DBMS can place and remove locks and even change the level and type of locks dynamically.

Figure 6-10 shows the pencil transaction with transaction boundaries marked with the SQL standard commands for controlling transactions:

* The **SQL BEGIN TRANSACTION statement**,
* The **SQL COMMIT TRANSACTION statement**, and
* The **SQL ROLLBACK TRANSACTION statement**.

FIGURE 6-10

**Example of Marking
Transaction Boundaries**

```
BEGIN TRANSACTION:

SELECT        PRODUCT.Name, PRODUCT.Quantity
FROM          PRODUCT
WHERE         PRODUCT.Name = 'Pencil'

Old Quantity = PRODUCT.Quantity

Set NewQuantity = PRODUCT.Quantity – 5

{process part of transaction – take exception action if NewQuantity < 0, etc.}

UPDATE        PRODUCT
SET           PRODUCT.Quantity = NewQuantity
WHERE         PRODUCT.Name = 'Pencil'

{continue processing transaction} . . .


IF transaction has completed normally        THEN

        COMMIT TRANSACTION

ELSE

        ROLLBACK TRANSACTION

END IF

Continue processing other actions not part of this transaction . . .
```

The SQL BEGIN TRANSACTION statement explicitly marks the start of a new transaction, while the SQL COMMIT TRANSACTION statement makes any database changes made by the transaction permanent and marks the end of the transaction. If there is a need to undo the changes made during the transaction due to an error in the process, the SQL ROLLBACK TRANSACTION statement is used to undo all transaction changes and return the database to the state it was in before the transaction was attempted. Thus, the SQL ROLLBACK TRANSACTION statement also marks the end of the transaction, but with a very different outcome.

These boundaries are the essential information that the DBMS needs to enforce the different locking strategies. If the developer now declares via a system parameter that he or she wants optimistic locking, the DBMS will implicitly set locks for that locking style. If, however, the developer declares pessimistic locking, the DBMS will set the locks differently.

BTW

As usual, each DBMS product implements these SQL statements in a slightly different way. SQL Server does not require the SQL keyword TRANSACTION, allows the abbreviation TRANS, and also allows the use of the SQL WORK keyword with COMMIT and ROLLBACK. Oracle Database uses SET TRANSACTION with COMMIT and ROLLBACK. MySQL does not use the SQL keyword TRANSACTION, while it allows (but does not require) use of the SQL WORK keyword in its place.

Consistent Transactions

Sometimes the acronym *ACID* is applied to transactions. An **ACID transaction** is one that is *atomic, consistent, isolated,* and *durable.* Atomic and durable are easy to define. As mentioned earlier in this chapter, an **atomic** transaction is one in which all the database actions occur or none of them do. A **durable** transaction is one in which all committed changes are permanent. The DBMS will not remove such changes, even in the case of failure. If the transaction is durable, the DBMS will provide facilities to recover the changes of all committed actions when necessary.

The terms *consistent* and *isolated* are not as definitive as the terms *atomic* and *durable.* Consider the following SQL UPDATE command:

```
/* *** EXAMPLE CODE - DO NOT RUN *** */
/* *** SQL-UPDATE-CH06-01 *** */
UPDATE    CUSTOMER
  SET     AreaCode = '425'
  WHERE   ZIPCode = '98050';
```

Suppose the CUSTOMER table has 500,000 rows, and 500 of them have a ZIPCode value equal to 98050. It will take some time for the DBMS to find all 500 rows. During that time, will other transactions be allowed to update the AreaCode or ZIPCode fields of CUSTOMER? If the SQL statement is **consistent**, such updates will be disallowed. The update will apply to the set of rows as they existed at the time the SQL statement started. Such consistency is called **statement-level consistency**.

Now consider a transaction that contains two SQL UPDATE statements:

```
/* *** EXAMPLE CODE - DO NOT RUN *** */
/* *** SQL-TRANSACTION-CH06-01 *** */
BEGIN TRANSACTION
/* *** SQL-UPDATE-CH06-01 *** */
UPDATE    CUSTOMER
  SET     AreaCode = '425'
  WHERE   ZIPCode = '98050';
. . .
{other transaction work}
. . .
/* *** SQL-UPDATE-CH06-02 *** */
UPDATE    CUSTOMER
  SET     Discount = 0.05
  WHERE   AreaCode = '425';
. . .
{other transaction work}
. . .
COMMIT TRANSACTION
```

In this context, what does *consistent* mean? Statement-level consistency means that each statement independently processes consistent rows, but changes from other users to those rows might be allowed during the interval between the two SQL statements. **Transaction-level consistency** means that all rows affected by either of the SQL statements are protected from changes during the entire transaction.

However, for some implementations of transaction-level consistency, a transaction will not see its own changes. In this example, the second SQL statement might not see rows changed by the first SQL statement.

Thus, when you hear the term *consistent* look further to determine which type of consistency is intended. Be aware as well of the potential trap of transaction-level consistency. The situation is even more complicated for the term *isolated*, which we consider next.

Transaction Isolation Level

The term *isolated* has several different meanings. To understand those meanings, we need first to define several terms that describe various problems that can occur when we read data from a database, and which are summarized in Figure 6-11.

- A **dirty read** occurs when one transaction reads a changed record that has not been committed to the database. This can occur, for example, if one transaction reads a row changed by a second transaction and the second transaction later cancels its changes.
- A **nonrepeatable read** occurs when a transaction rereads data it has previously read and finds modifications or deletions caused by another transaction.
- A **phantom read** occurs when a transaction rereads data and finds new rows that were inserted by a different transaction after the prior read.

In order to deal with these potential data read problems, the SQL standard defines four **transaction isolation levels** or **isolation levels** that specify which of the concurrency control problems are allowed to occur. These isolation levels are summarized in Figure 6-12.

FIGURE 6-11

Summary of Data Read Problems

Data Read Problem Type	Definition
Dirty Read	The transaction reads a row that has been changed, but the change has *not* been committed. If the change is rolled back, the transaction has incorrect data.
Nonrepeatable Read	The transaction rereads data that has been changed, and finds changes due to committed transactions.
Phantom Read	The transaction rereads data and finds new rows inserted by a committed transaction.

FIGURE 6-12

Summary of Isolation Levels

		Isolation Level			
		Read Uncommitted	Read Committed	Repeatable Read	Serializable
Problem Type	Dirty Read	Possible	Not possible	Not possible	Not possible
	Nonrepeatable Read	Possible	Possible	Not possible	Not possible
	Phantom Read	Possible	Possible	Possible	Not possible

The goal of having four isolation levels is to allow the application programmer to declare the type of isolation level desired and then to have the DBMS manage locks to achieve that level of isolation. The transaction isolation levels shown in Figure 6-12 can be defined as:

- The **read uncommitted isolation level** allows dirty reads, nonrepeatable reads, and phantom reads to occur.
- The **read committed isolation level** allows nonrepeatable reads and phantom reads, but disallows dirty reads.
- The **repeatable reads isolation level** allows phantom reads, but disallows both dirty reads and nonrepeatable reads.
- The **serializable isolation level** does not allow any of these three data read problems to occur.

Generally, the more restrictive the isolation level, the less throughput, although much depends on the workload and how the application programs were written. Moreover, not all DBMS products support all these levels. Products also vary in the manner in which they are supported and in the burden they place on the application programmer.

CURSOR TYPES

A cursor is a pointer into a set of rows that are the result set from an SQL SELECT statement, and cursors are usually defined using SELECT statements. For example, the following statement defines a cursor named TransCursor that operates over the set of rows indicated by this SELECT statement:

```
/* *** EXAMPLE CODE - DO NOT RUN *** */
/* *** SQL-DECLARE-CURSOR-CH06-01 *** */
DECLARE CURSOR TransCursor AS
     SELECT     *
     FROM       [TRANSACTION]
     WHERE      PurchasePrice > '10000';
```

After an application program opens a cursor, it can place the cursor somewhere in the result set. Most commonly, the cursor is placed on the first or last row, but other possibilities exist.

A transaction can open several cursors—either sequentially or simultaneously. In addition, two or more cursors may be open on the same table, either directly on the table or through an SQL view on that table. Because cursors require considerable memory, having many cursors open at the same time (for example, for a thousand concurrent transactions) consumes considerable memory. One way to reduce cursor burden is to define reduced-capability cursors and use them when a full-capability cursor is not needed.

Figure 6-13 lists three cursor types supported by SQL Server 2014. In SQL Server 2014, cursors may be either forward-only cursors or scrollable cursors. With a **forward-only cursor**, the application can only move forward through the records, and changes made by other cursors in this transaction and other transactions will be visible only if they occur to the rows ahead of the cursor. With a **scrollable cursor**, the application can scroll forward and backward through the records.

There are three types of cursors, each of which can be implemented as either a forward-only or scrollable cursor. A **static cursor** takes a snapshot of a relation and processes that snapshot. Changes made using this cursor are visible; changes from other sources are not visible.

FIGURE 6-13

Summary of Cursor
Types

Cursor Type	Description	Comments
Static	Application sees the data as they were at the time the cursor was opened.	Changes made by this cursor are visible. Changes from other sources are not visible. Backward and forward scrolling are allowed.
Keyset	When the cursor is opened, a primary key value is saved for each row in the recordset. When the application accesses a row, the key is used to fetch the current values for the row.	Updates from any source are visible. Inserts from sources outside this cursor are not visible (there is no key for them in the keyset). Inserts from this cursor appear at the bottom of the recordset. Deletions from any source are visible. Changes in row order are not visible. If the isolation level is dirty read, then committed updates and deletions are visible; otherwise, only committed updates and deletions are visible.
Dynamic	Changes of any type and from any source are visible.	All inserts, updates, deletions, and changes in recordset order are visible. If the isolation level is dirty read, then uncommitted changes are visible. Otherwise, only committed changes are visible.

A **dynamic cursor** is a fully featured cursor. All inserts, updates, deletions, and changes in row order are visible to a dynamic cursor. Unless the isolation level of the transaction is a dirty read, only committed changes are visible.

Keyset cursors combine some features of static cursors with some features of dynamic cursors. When the cursor is opened, a primary key value is saved for each row. When the application positions the cursor on a row, the DBMS uses the key value to read the current value of the row. Inserts of new rows by other cursors (in this transaction or in other transactions) are not visible. If the application issues an update on a row that has been deleted by a different cursor, the DBMS creates a new row with the old key value and places the updated values in the new row (assuming that all required fields are present). As with dynamic cursors, unless the isolation level of the transaction is a dirty read, only committed updates and deletions are visible to the cursor.

Cursor types for DBMSs besides SQL Server 2014 are similar, except that the forward-only cursor is sometimes implemented as a fourth cursor type. In this case, the static, keyset, and dynamic cursors will be strictly scrollable cursors.

The amount of overhead and processing required to support a cursor is different for each type. In general, the cost goes up as you move down the cursor types shown in Figure 6-13. In order to improve DBMS performance, therefore, an application developer should create cursors that are just powerful enough to do the job. It is also very important to understand how a particular DBMS implements cursors and whether cursors are located on the server or on the client. In some cases, it might be better to place a dynamic cursor on the client than to have a static cursor on the server. No general rule can be stated because performance depends on the implementation used by the DBMS product and the application requirements.

> ## BTW
>
> A word of caution: If you do *not* specify the isolation level of a transaction or do not specify the type of cursors you open, the DBMS will use a default level and types. These defaults may be perfect for your application, but they also may be terrible. Thus, even though you can ignore these issues, you cannot avoid their consequences. You must learn the capabilities of your DBMS product.

DATABASE SECURITY

The goal of database security is to ensure that only authorized users can perform authorized activities at authorized times. This goal is usually broken into two parts: **authentication**, which makes sure the user has the basic right to use the system in the first place, and **authorization**, which assigns the authenticated user specific rights or **permissions** to do specific activities on the system. As shown in Figure 6-14, user authentication is achieved by requiring the user to log in to the system with a password (or other means of positive identification, such as a biometric scan of a fingerprint), whereas user authorization is achieved by granting DBMS-specific permissions.

Note that authentication (when the user logs in to the system) by itself is not sufficient for use of the database—unless the user has been granted permissions, he or she cannot access the database or take any actions that use it.

Permissions can be managed using **SQL Data Control Language (DCL)** statements:

- The **SQL GRANT statement** is used to assign permissions to users and groups, so that the users or groups can perform various operations on the data in the database.
- The **SQL REVOKE statement** is used to take existing permissions away from users and groups.

While these statements can be used in SQL scripts and with SQL command line utilities, we will find it much easier to use the GUI DBMS administration utilities provided for use with each of the major DBMS products to manage user permissions.

The goal of database security is difficult to achieve, and to make any progress at all the database development team must determine (1) which users should be able to use the database (authentication) and (2) the processing rights and responsibilities of each user. These security requirements can then be enforced using the security features of the DBMS, as well as additions to those features that are written into the application programs.

FIGURE 6-14

Database Security Authentication and Authorization

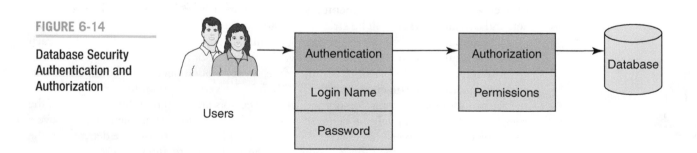

FIGURE 6-15

Creating the Database Server Login

The user's DMBS login name

The user's DBMS password

The HSD database

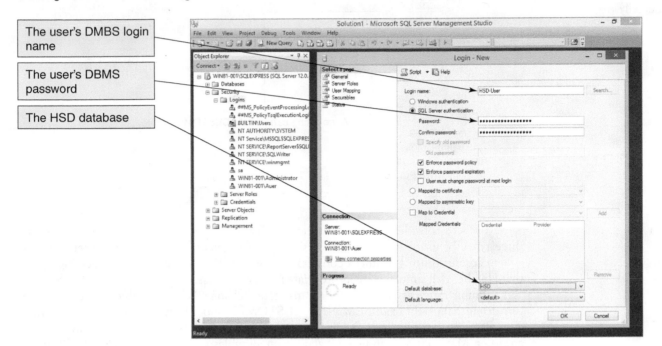

User Accounts

Consider, for example, the database security needs of Heather Sweeney Designs. There must be some means of controlling which employees can have access to the database. There is: You can create a **user account** for each employee. Figure 6-15 shows the creation of the user login HSD-User at the DBMS security level in SQL Server.

This step creates the initial user account in the DBMS—*not* a specific database. The password being assigned is *HSD-User+password*, which we will also need for the HSD Web pages in Chapter 7. Note that in the Windows environment there are two choices for controlling authentication: We can use the Windows operating system to control authentication, or we can create an SQL Server internal user account with its own login name and password. For other DBMS products that are not as operating system specific as SQL Server, only the second option of internal user accounts can be used.

User accounts and passwords need to be managed carefully. The exact terminology, features, and functions of DBMS account and password security depend on the DBMS product used.

User Processing Rights and Responsibilities

All major DBMS products provide security tools that limit certain actions on certain objects to certain users. A general model of DBMS security is shown in Figure 6-16.

According to Figure 6-16, a user can be assigned to one or more roles (groups), and a role can have one or more users. Users, roles, and objects (used in a generic sense) have many permissions. Each permission is assigned to one user or role and one object. Once a user is authenticated by the DBMS, the DBMS limits the person's actions to the defined permissions for that user and to the permissions for roles to which that user has been assigned.

FIGURE 6-16

A Model of DBMS Security

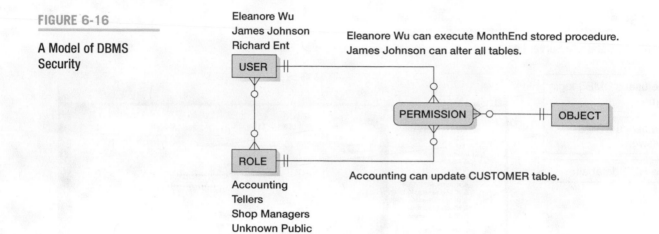

Now, let's consider user authorization at Heather Sweeney Designs. The company has three types of users: administrative assistants, management (Heather and others), and a system administrator (Heather's consultant). Figure 6-17 summarizes the processing rights that Heather determined were appropriate for her business.

Administrative assistants can read, insert, and change data in all tables. However, they can delete data only from SEMINAR_CUSTOMER and LINE_ITEM. This means that administrative assistants can disenroll customers from seminars and can remove items from an order. Management can take all actions on all tables except delete CUSTOMER data. Heather believes that for as hard as she works to get a customer, she does not want to ever run the risk of accidentally deleting one.

Finally, the system administrator can modify the database structure and grant rights (assign permissions) to other users but can take no action on data. The system administrator is not a user and so should not be allowed access to user data. This limitation

FIGURE 6-17

Processing Rights at Heather Sweeney Designs

DATABASE RIGHTS GRANTED

Table	Administrative Assistants	Management	System Administrator
SEMINAR	Read, Insert, Change	Read, Insert, Change, Delete	Grant Rights, Modify Structure
CUSTOMER	Read, Insert, Change	Read, Insert, Change	Grant Rights, Modify Structure
SEMINAR_ CUSTOMER	Read, Insert, Change, Delete	Read, Insert, Change, Delete	Grant Rights, Modify Structure
CONTACT	Read, Insert, Change	Read, Insert, Change, Delete	Grant Rights, Modify Structure
INVOICE	Read, Insert, Change	Read, Insert, Change, Delete	Grant Rights, Modify Structure
LINE_ITEM	Read, Insert, Change, Delete	Read, Insert, Change, Delete	Grant Rights, Modify Structure
PRODUCT	Read, Insert, Change	Read, Insert, Change, Delete	Grant Rights, Modify Structure

might seem weak. After all, if the system administrator can assign permissions, he or she can get around the security system by changing the permissions to take whatever action is desired, make the data changes, and then change the permissions back. This is true, but it would leave an audit trail in the DBMS logs. That, coupled with the need to make the security system changes, will dissuade the administrator from unauthorized activity. It is certainly better than allowing the administrator to have user data access permissions with no effort.

A very important principle of database security administration (and of network administration) is that the types of permissions shown in Figure 6-17 are given to user *groups* (also known as user *roles*) and *not* to individual users unless absolutely necessary. There may be some cases in which specific users need to be assigned permissions within the database, but we want to avoid this whenever possible. Note that because groups or roles are used, it is necessary to have a means for assigning users to groups or roles. When Heather Sweeney signs onto the computer, some means must be available to determine which group or groups she belongs to.

Now, we need to make role and permission assignments in the HSD database. HSD-User is one of Heather's administrative assistants and, therefore, needs the ability to read, insert, and change data in all tables. First, we need to grant HSD-User permission to use the HSD database within the DBMS. Figure 6-18 shows the creation of the *database-level user* named *HSD-Database-User* at the HSD database security level in SQL Server. Note that this user is being created specifically for the HSD database but is based on the already created DBMS login name. Also note that in SQL Server no password is assigned at the database security level, only at the DBMS security level.

Figure 6-19 shows the fixed database roles in SQL Server and their associated permissions. Because HSD-Database-User needs to be able to read, insert, and change data in all tables in the HSD database, we should assign HSD-Database-User to the roles db_datareader and db_datawriter. Figure 6-20 shows HSD Database User being added to the db_datareader role. (We cover this further in the next section.)

FIGURE 6-18

Creating the Database User Name

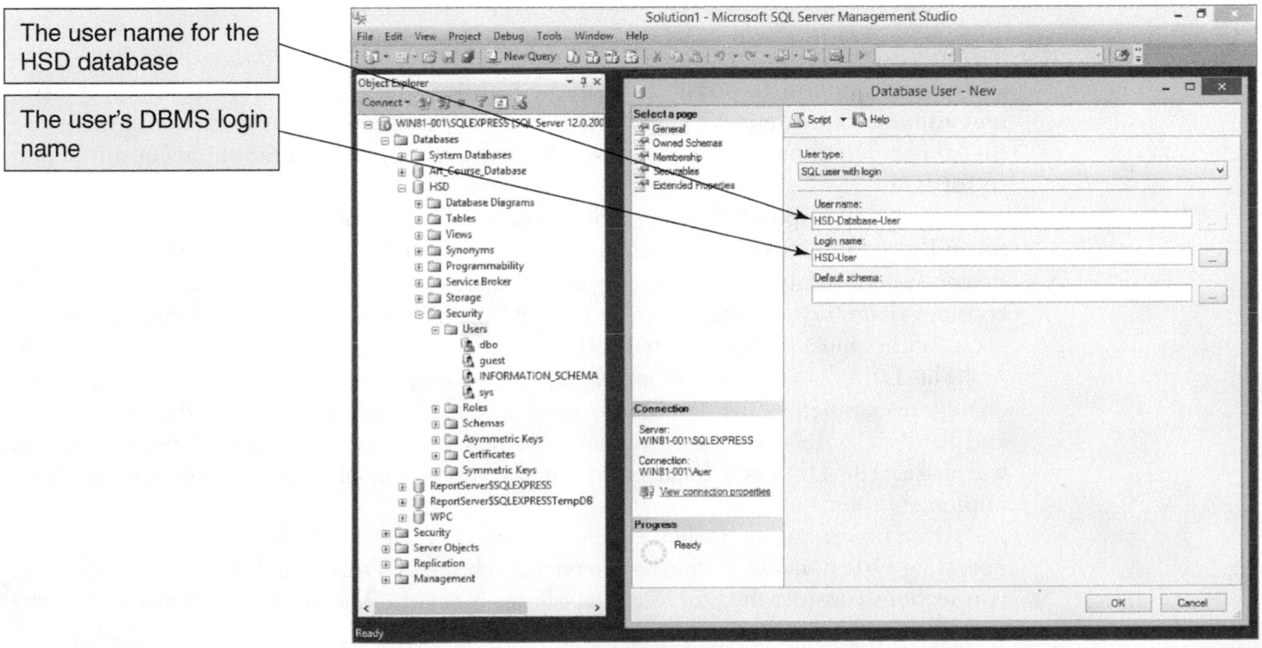

The user name for the HSD database

The user's DBMS login name

FIGURE 6-19

SQL Server Fixed Database Roles

Fixed Database Role	Database-Specific Permissions	DBMS Server Permissions
db_accessadmin	Permissions granted: ALTER ANY USER, CREATE SCHEMA Permissions granted with GRANT option: CONNECT	Permissions granted: VIEW ANY DATABASE
db_backupoperator	Permissions granted: BACKUP DATABASE, BACKUP LOG, CHECKPOINT	Permissions granted: VIEW ANY DATABASE
db_datareader	Permissions granted: SELECT	Permissions granted: VIEW ANY DATABASE
db_datawriter	Permissions granted: DELETE, INSERT, UPDATE	Permissions granted: VIEW ANY DATABASE
db_ddladmin	Permissions granted: *See SQL Server documentation*	Permissions granted: VIEW ANY DATABASE
db_denydatareader	Permissions *denied*: SELECT	Permissions granted: VIEW ANY DATABASE
db_denydatawriter	Permissions *denied*: DELETE, INSERT, UPDATE	Permissions granted: VIEW ANY DATABASE
db_owner	Permissions granted with GRANT option: CONTROL	Permissions granted: VIEW ANY DATABASE
db_securityadmin	Permissions granted: ALTER ANY APPLICATION ROLE, ALTER ANY ROLE, CREATE SCHEMA, VIEW DEFINITION	Permissions granted: VIEW ANY DATABASE

Note: For the definitions of each of the SQL Server permissions shown in the table, consult the SQL Server documentation.

In this discussion, we have used the phrase *processing rights and responsibilities*. As this phrase implies, responsibilities go with processing rights. If, for example, the system administrator deletes CUSTOMER data, it is that person's responsibility to ensure that those deletions do not adversely affect the company's operation, accounting, and so forth.

Processing responsibilities cannot be enforced by the DBMS or the database applications. Responsibilities are, instead, encoded in manual procedures and explained to users during systems training. These are topics for a systems development book, and we do not consider them further here except to reiterate that responsibilities go with rights. Such responsibilities must be documented and enforced.

The DBA has the task of managing processing rights and responsibilities, which change over time. As the database is used and as changes are made to the applications and to the DBMS's structure, the need for new or different rights and responsibilities will arise. The DBA is a focal point for the discussion of such changes and for their implementation.

After processing rights have been defined, they can be implemented at many levels: operating system, network directory service, Web server, DBMS, and application. The next two sections consider the DBMS and application aspects. The other aspects are beyond the scope of this book.

FIGURE 6-20

Assigning HSD-Database-User to the db_datareader Role

The **Database Role Properties – db_datareader** dialog box

The HSD database user name HSD-Database-User

The Database Role db_datawriter

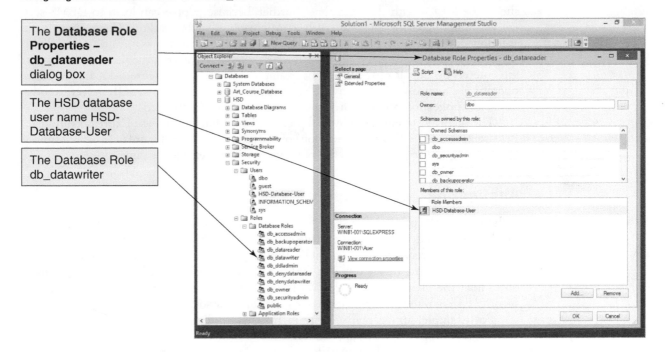

DBMS-Level Security

Security guidelines for a DBMS are shown in Figure 6-21. First, the DBMS should be run behind a firewall. In most cases, no communication with the DBMS or database applications should be allowed to be initiated from outside the organization's network. For example, the company's Web site should be hosted on a separate, dedicated Web server. The Web server will have to communicate through the firewall, and the DBMS server should be protected behind it.

Second, service packs and fixes for the operating system and the DBMS must be applied as soon as possible. In spring 2003, the slammer worm exploited a security hole in SQL Server, bringing major organizational database applications to their knees. Microsoft had published a patch that eliminated the hole prior to the release of the slammer worm, so any organization that had applied that patch was not affected by the worm.

A third protection is to limit the capabilities of the DBMS to only those features and functions that the applications need. For example, Oracle Database can support many different communications protocols. To improve security, any Oracle-supported protocol that is not used should be removed or disabled. Similarly, every DBMS ships with hundreds of system-stored procedures. Any procedure that is not used should be removed from operational databases.

FIGURE 6-21

DBMS Security
Guidelines

- Run the DBMS behind a firewall
- Apply the latest operating system and DBMS service packs and fixes
- Limit DBMS functionality to needed features
- Protect the computer that runs the DBMS
- Manage accounts and passwords
- Encryption of sensitive data transmitted across the network
- Encryption of sensitive data stored in databases

Another important security measure is to protect the computer that runs the DBMS. No users should be allowed to work on the DBMS computer, and that computer should reside in a separate facility, behind locked doors. Visits to the room housing the DBMS should be logged with date and time. Further, because people can login to DBMS servers via remote-control software (such as Microsoft Remote Desktop Connection in the Windows environment), who has (and who can grant) remote access must be controlled.

A user can enter a name and password; in some applications, the name and password are entered on behalf of the user. For example, as we saw in Figure 6-15, the Windows operating system user name and password can be passed directly to SQL Server. In other cases, an application program provides the user name and password.

The security systems used by SQL Server 2014, Oracle Database Express Edition 11*g* Release 2, and MySQL 5.6 are variations of the model shown in Figure 6-13. The terminology used might vary, but the essence of their security systems is the same.

Application-Level Security

Although DBMS products, such as SQL Server 2014, Oracle Database Express Edition 11*g* Release 2, and MySQL 5.6, provide substantial database security capabilities, they are generic by their very nature. If an application requires specific security measures—such as disallowing users to view a row of a table or a join of a table that has an employee name other than the user's own—the DBMS facilities will not be adequate. In these cases, the security system must be augmented by features in the associated application programming.

For example, application security in Internet applications is often provided on the Web server computer. When application security is executed on this server, sensitive security data do not need to be transmitted over the network. To understand this better, suppose an application is written such that when users click a particular button on a browser page the following query is sent to the Web server and then to the DBMS:

```
/* *** EXAMPLE CODE - DO NOT RUN *** */
/* *** SQL-QUERY-CH06-01 *** */
SELECT     *
FROM       EMPLOYEE;
```

This statement returns all EMPLOYEE rows. If the application security allows employees to access only their own data, then a Web server could add the following WHERE clause to this query:

```
/* *** EXAMPLE CODE - DO NOT RUN *** */
/* *** SQL-QUERY-CH06-02 *** */
SELECT     *
FROM       EMPLOYEE
WHERE      EMPLOYEE.Name = '<%SESSION("EmployeeName")%>';
```

An expression like this causes the Web server to fill in the employee's name for the WHERE clause. For a user signed on under the name Benjamin Franklin, the following statement results from this expression:

```
/* *** EXAMPLE CODE - DO NOT RUN *** */
/* *** SQL-QUERY-CH06-03 *** */
SELECT     *
FROM       EMPLOYEE
WHERE      EMPLOYEE.Name = 'Benjamin Franklin';
```

Because the name is inserted by a program on the Web server, the browser user does not know it is occurring and cannot interfere with it. Such security processing can be done as shown here on a Web server, and it can also be done within the application programs themselves or written as code stored within the DBMS to be executed by the DBMS at the appropriate times.

You can also store additional data in a security database that is accessed by the Web server as well as by stored DBMS code. That security database could contain, for example, the identities of users paired with additional values of WHERE clauses. For example, suppose the users in the personnel department can access more than just their own data. The predicates for appropriate WHERE clauses could be stored in the security database, read by the application program, and appended to SQL SELECT statements, as necessary.

Many other possibilities exist for extending DBMS security with application processing. In general, you should use the DBMS security features first. Only if they are inadequate for the requirements should you add to them with application code. The closer the security enforcement is to the data, the lower the chance for infiltration. Also, using the DBMS security features is faster, less expensive, and likely to produce higher-quality results than if you develop your own.

DATABASE BACKUP AND RECOVERY

Computer systems fail. Hardware breaks. Programs have bugs. Procedures written by humans contain errors. People make mistakes. All these failures can and do occur in database applications. Because a database is shared by many people and because it often is a key element of an organization's operations, it is important to recover it as soon as possible.

Several problems must be addressed. First, from a business standpoint, business functions must continue. For example, customer orders, financial transactions, and packing lists must be completed manually. Later, when the database application is operational again, the new data can be entered. Second, computer operations personnel must restore the system to a usable state as quickly as possible and as close as possible to what it was when the system crashed. Third, users must know what to do when the system becomes available again. Some work might need to be reentered, and users must know how far back they need to go.

When failures occur, it is impossible simply to fix the problem and resume processing. Even if no data are lost during a failure (which assumes that all types of memory are non-volatile—an unrealistic assumption), the timing and scheduling of computer processing are too complex to be accurately recreated. Enormous amounts of overhead data and processing would be required for the operating system to be able to restart processing precisely where it was interrupted. It is simply not possible to roll back the clock and put all the electrons in the same configuration they were in at the time of the failure. However, two other approaches are possible: **recovery via reprocessing** and **recovery via rollback/rollforward**.

Recovery via Reprocessing

Because processing cannot be resumed at a precise point, the next-best alternative is to go back to a known point and reprocess the workload from there. The simplest form of this type of recovery involves periodically making a copy of the database (called a *database save*) and keeping a record of all transactions processed since the save. Then, when failure occurs, the operations staff can restore the database from the save and reprocess all the transactions.

Unfortunately, this simple strategy normally is not feasible. First, reprocessing transactions takes the same amount of time as processing them in the first place. If the computer is heavily scheduled, the system might never catch up. Second, when transactions are processed concurrently, events are asynchronous. Slight variations in human activity, such as a user reading an email message before responding to an application prompt, could change the order of the execution of concurrent transactions. Therefore, whereas Customer A got the last seat on a flight during the original processing, Customer B might get the last seat during reprocessing. For these reasons, reprocessing is normally not a viable form of recovery from failure in multiuser systems.

Recovery via Rollback and Rollforward

A second approach to database recovery involves periodically making a copy of the database (the database save) and keeping a log of the changes made by transactions against the database since the save. Then, when a failure occurs, one of two methods can be used. With the first method, called **rollforward**, the database is restored using the saved data and all valid transactions since the save are reapplied. Note that we are not reprocessing the transactions because the application programs are not involved in the rollforward. Instead, the processed changes, as recorded in the log, are reapplied.

With the second method, **rollback**, we correct mistakes caused by erroneous or partially processed transactions by undoing the changes they made in the database. Then the valid transactions that were in process at the time of the failure are restarted.

As stated, both of these methods require that a **log** of the transaction results be kept. This log contains records of the data changes in chronological order. Note that transactions must be written to the log before they are applied to the database. That way, if the system crashes between the time a transaction is logged and the time it is applied, at worst, there is a record of an unapplied transaction. If transactions were applied before being logged, it would be possible (and undesirable) to change the database without having a record of the change. If this happens, an unwary user might reenter an already completed transaction.

In the event of a failure, we use the log to undo and redo transactions, as shown in Figure 6-22. To undo a transaction as shown in Figure 6-22(a), the log must contain a copy of every database record before it was changed. Such records are called **before-images**. A transaction is undone by applying before-images of all its changes to the database.

To redo a transaction as shown in Figure 6-22(b), the log must contain a copy of every database record (or page) after it was changed. These records are called **after-images**. A transaction is redone by applying after-images of all its changes to the database. Possible data items of a transaction log are shown in Figure 6-23.

For this example transaction log, each transaction has a unique name for identification purposes. Furthermore, all images for a given transaction are linked together with pointers. One pointer points to the previous change made by this transaction (the reverse pointer),

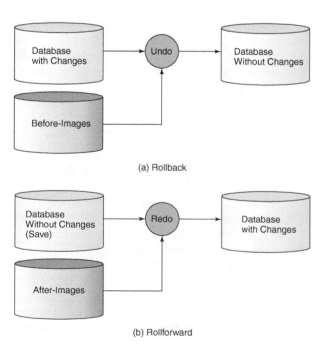

FIGURE 6-22

Undo and Redo Transactions

(a) Rollback

(b) Rollforward

FIGURE 6-23

Transaction Log
Example

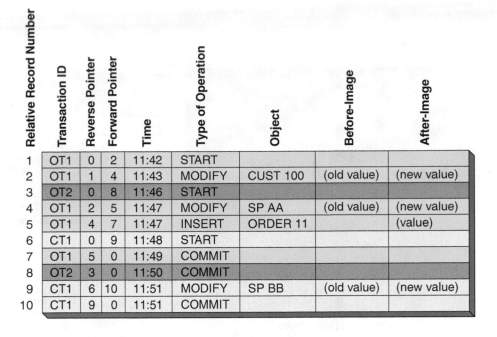

Relative Record Number	Transaction ID	Reverse Pointer	Forward Pointer	Time	Type of Operation	Object	Before-Image	After-Image
1	OT1	0	2	11:42	START			
2	OT1	1	4	11:43	MODIFY	CUST 100	(old value)	(new value)
3	OT2	0	8	11:46	START			
4	OT1	2	5	11:47	MODIFY	SP AA	(old value)	(new value)
5	OT1	4	7	11:47	INSERT	ORDER 11		(value)
6	CT1	0	9	11:48	START			
7	OT1	5	0	11:49	COMMIT			
8	OT2	3	0	11:50	COMMIT			
9	CT1	6	10	11:51	MODIFY	SP BB	(old value)	(new value)
10	CT1	9	0	11:51	COMMIT			

and the other points to the next change made by this transaction (the forward pointer). A zero in the pointer field means that this is the end of the list. The DBMS recovery subsystem uses these pointers to locate all records for a particular transaction. Figure 6-23 shows an example of the linking of log records.

Other data items in the log are:

- The time of the action
- The type of operation (START marks the beginning of a transaction, and COMMIT terminates a transaction, releasing all locks that were in place)
- The object acted upon, such as record type and identifier
- The before-images and after-images.

Given a log with before-images and after-images, the undo and redo actions are straightforward. Figure 6-24 shows how recovery for a system crash is accomplished.

To undo the transaction in Figure 6-24(a), the recovery processor simply replaces each changed record with its before-image, as shown in Figure 6-24(b). When all before-images have been restored, the transaction is undone. To redo a transaction, the recovery processor starts with the version of the database at the time the transaction started and applies all after-images. This action assumes that an earlier version of the database is available from a database save.

Restoring a database to its most recent save and reapplying all transactions might require considerable processing. To reduce the delay, DBMS products sometimes use checkpoints. A **checkpoint** is a point of synchronization between the database and the transaction log. To perform a checkpoint, the DBMS refuses new requests, finishes processing outstanding requests, and writes its buffers to disk. The DBMS then waits until the operating system notifies it that all outstanding write requests to the database and to the log have been completed successfully. At this point, the log and the database are synchronized. A checkpoint record is then written to the log. Later, the database can be recovered from the checkpoint, and only after-images for transactions that started after the checkpoint need to be applied.

Checkpoints are inexpensive operations, and it is feasible to make three or four (or more) per hour. This way, no more than 15 or 20 minutes of processing needs to be recovered. Most DBMS products perform automatic checkpoints, making human intervention unnecessary.

You will need to learn more about backup and recovery if you work in database administration using products such as SQL Server 2014, Oracle Database Express Edition 11g Release 2, or MySQL 5.6. For now, you just need to understand the basic ideas and to

FIGURE 6-24

Recovery Example

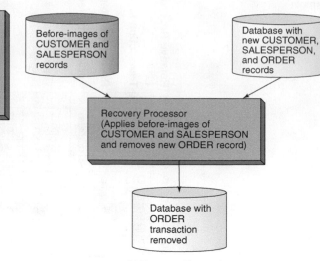

Accept order data from browser.
Read CUSTOMER and SALESPERSON records.
Change CUSTOMER and SALESPERSON records.
Rewrite CUSTOMER record.
Rewrite SALESPERSON record. } (Log records written here)
Insert new ORDER record.

****CRASH****

Before-images of
CUSTOMER and
SALESPERSON
records

Database with
new CUSTOMER,
SALESPERSON,
and ORDER
records

Recovery Processor
(Applies before-images of
CUSTOMER and SALESPERSON
and removes new ORDER record)

Database with
ORDER
transaction
removed

(a) Processing with a Problem   (b) Recovery Processing

realize that it is the responsibility of the DBA to ensure that adequate backup and recovery plans have been developed and that database saves and logs are generated as required. You should also understand that many DBMS GUI utilities allow the DBA to easily make database backups as needed, even without a backup plan and backup schedule. Figure 6-25 shows the Microsoft SQL Server Management Studio being used to make a simple recovery model full database backup of the HSD database.

FIGURE 6-25

Backing Up the HSD Database

The **Back Up Database – HSD** dialog box	
The **HSD** database	
The **SIMPLE** recovery model	
The **Full** backup type	
The database itself is being backed up	

Solution1 - Microsoft SQL Server Management Studio

File Edit View Project Debug Tools Window Help

Back Up Database - HSD

Select a page
General
Media Options
Backup Options

Script ▾ Help

Source

Database: HSD

Recovery model: SIMPLE

Backup type: Full

☐ Copy-only backup

Backup component:

⦿ Database

◯ Files and filegroups

Destination

Back up to: Disk

C:\Program Files\Microsoft SQL Server\MSSQL12.SQLEXPRESS\MSSQL\Backup\HSD.bak

Add...
Remove
Contents

Connection

Server:
WIN81-001\SQLEXPRESS

Connection:
WIN81-001\Auer

View connection properties

Progress

Ready

OK   Cancel

Ready

ADDITIONAL DBA RESPONSIBILITIES

Concurrency control, security, and reliability are the three major concerns of database administration. However, other administrative and managerial DBA functions are also important.

For one, a DBA needs to ensure that a system exists to gather and record user-reported errors and other problems. A means needs to be devised to prioritize those errors and problems and to ensure that they are corrected accordingly. In this regard, the DBA works with the development team not only to resolve these problems but also to evaluate features and functions of new releases of the DBMS.

As the database is used and as new requirements develop and are implemented, requests for changes to the structure of the database will occur. Changes to an operational database need to be made with great care and thoughtful planning. Because databases are shared resources, a change to the structure of a database to implement features desired by one user or group can be detrimental to the needs of other users or groups.

Therefore, a DBA needs to create and manage a process for controlling the database configuration. Such a process includes procedures for recording change requests, conducting user and developer reviews of such requests, and creating projects and tasks for implementing changes that are approved. All these activities need to be conducted with a community-wide view.

Finally, a DBA is responsible for ensuring that appropriate documentation is maintained about database structure, concurrency control, security, backup and recovery, applications use, and a myriad of other details that concern the management and use of the database. Some vendors provide tools for recording such documentation. At a minimum, a DBMS will have its own metadata that it uses to process the database. Some products augment these metadata with facilities for storing and reporting application metadata, as well as operational procedures.

A DBA has significant responsibilities in the management and administration of a database. These responsibilities vary with the database type and size, the number of users, and the complexity of the applications. However, the responsibilities are important for all databases. You should know about the need for DBA services and consider the material in this chapter even for small, personal databases.

THE ACCESS WORKBENCH

Section 6

Database Administration in Microsoft Access

At this point, we have created and populated the CONTACT, CUSTOMER, SALESPERSON, and VEHICLE tables in the Wallingford Motors' CRM database. We have learned how to create forms, reports, and queries in the preceding sections of "The Access Workbench" and how to create and use view-equivalent queries in Appendix E. We have also studied how 1:1. 1:N, and N:M relationships are created and managed in Microsoft Access.

This chapter deals with database administration topics, and in this section of "The Access Workbench" we will look at database security in Microsoft Access. In this section, you will:

- Understand database security in Microsoft Access 2013.

Database Security in Microsoft Access

Until Microsoft Access 2007, Microsoft Access had a user-level security system that allowed a DBA to grant specific database permissions to individual users or groups of users on a basis similar to that discussed in this chapter. Starting with Microsoft Access 2007, however, a very

(Continued)

different security model has been implemented. This model is based on whether the entire database itself is trustworthy, and it seems like Microsoft is saying that Microsoft Access really is for personal (or small workgroup) databases and that if you need user-level security you should be using SQL Server 2014 (especially because the SQL Server 2014 Express edition is a free download). At the same time, Microsoft Access 2013 (and the earlier Microsoft Access 2007 and 2010) will still work with the earlier user-level security system for Microsoft Access databases in the Microsoft Access 2003 (and earlier) *.mdb file format. In this section of "The Access Workbench," we will focus on the current Microsoft Access 2013 security system.

First, however, we need to make a copy of our WMCRM.accdb database file. This is necessary because we have already enabled all features of that database. In earlier sections of "The Access Workbench," we learned how to make copies of Microsoft Access 2013 databases—we simply make a copy the **WMCRM.accdb** database file in the My Documents folder in the Documents library and rename this new file **WMCRM-AW06-01.accdb**.

Database Security in Microsoft Access 2013

You can secure Microsoft Access 2013 files in three basic ways:

- By creating trusted locations for Microsoft Access database storage
- By password encrypting and decrypting Microsoft Access databases
- By deploying databases packaged with digital signatures

Let us look at each of these, in turn.

Trusted Locations

Up until now, whenever we have opened a Microsoft Access database for the first time during our work in "The Access Workbench" the **Security Warning message bar** has been displayed, as shown in Figure AW-6-1 where we have just opened the WMCRM-AW06-01 .accdb database for the first time.

Thus far, we have always clicked the **Enable Content** button to enable the disabled content. Note that we only need to do this once for each database—the first time we open the database after it has been created. We have done this so we could use Microsoft Access features that are otherwise disabled and unavailable to us, including:

- Microsoft Access database queries (either SQL or QBE) that add, update, or delete data
- Data definition language (DDL) (either SQL or QBE) actions that create or alter database objects, such as tables

FIGURE AW-6-1

The Security Warning Message Bar

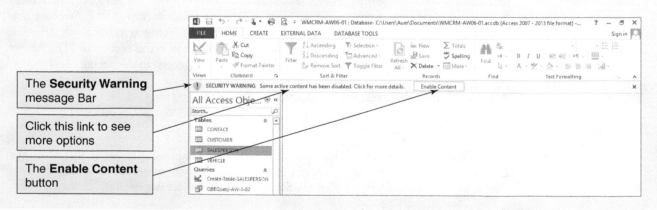

The **Security Warning** message Bar

Click this link to see more options

The **Enable Content** button

- SQL commands being sent from a Microsoft Access application to a database server, such as Microsoft SQL Server 2014, that support the Open Database Connectivity (ODBC) standard
- ActiveX controls

We obviously need the first of these features if we are going to build Microsoft Access 2013 databases. The third feature is important if we are using a Microsoft Access 2013 database as an application front end (containing the application forms, queries, and reports) for data stored in an SQL Server 2014 database. (This use of Microsoft Access and the ODBC standard is discussed in Chapter 7.) Finally, **ActiveX controls** are software code written to Microsoft's **ActiveX specification**, and they are often used as Web browser plug-ins. The problem here is that Microsoft Access 2013 databases can be targeted by code written in ActiveX-compliant programming languages that can manipulate the databases just as Microsoft Access itself would.

Although we can simply click the **Enable Content** button to activate these features, note that Microsoft Access 2013 also provides other options for dealing with this security problem. If we click the link labeled *Some active content has been disabled. Click for more details* shown in Figure AW-6-1, we are switched to the Info page in the Backstage view and specifically to the Security Warning section of that page, as shown in Figure AW-6-2.

Clicking the **Enable Content** button displays two options, as shown in Figure AW-6-3—*Enable All Content* and *Advanced Options*. Clicking the **Enable All Content** button produces the same results as clicking the Enable Content button on the Security Warning toolbar, and all features of the database will always be available to us. Clicking the **Advanced Options** button displays the Microsoft Office Security Options dialog box, as shown in Figure AW-6-4.

FIGURE AW-6-2

The Security Warning Section of the File | Info Page

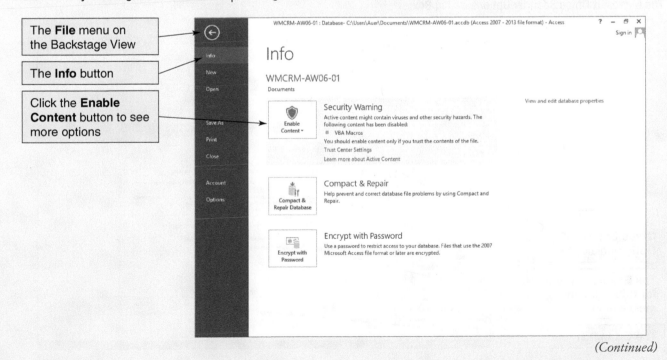

The Enable Content Options

Clicking **Enable All Content** is the same as clicking the *Enable Content* button on the Security Warning toolbar

Click **Advanced Options** to display the *Microsoft Office Security Options* dialog box

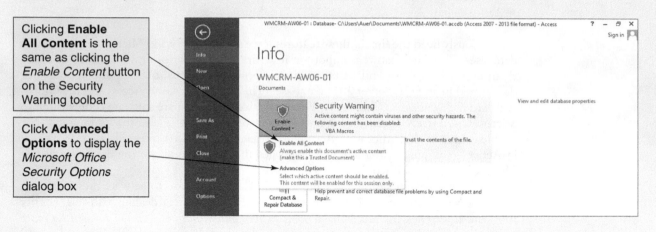

The Microsoft Office Security Options dialog box provides the final two options. The first option is to allow Microsoft Access to continue to disable the possible security risks. Thus the *Help protect me from unknown content (recommended)* radio button is selected as the default. This option is the same as simply closing the Security Warning toolbar when it is first displayed. The second option is to enable the content in the database for *only* this use ("session") of the database by checking the *Enable content for this session* radio button. This is the first new choice we have really been given, and we will open the database using this option. Note that this means that the

The Microsoft Office Security Options Dialog Box

The **Microsoft Office Security Options** dialog box

The **Enable content for this session** radio button

The **OK** button

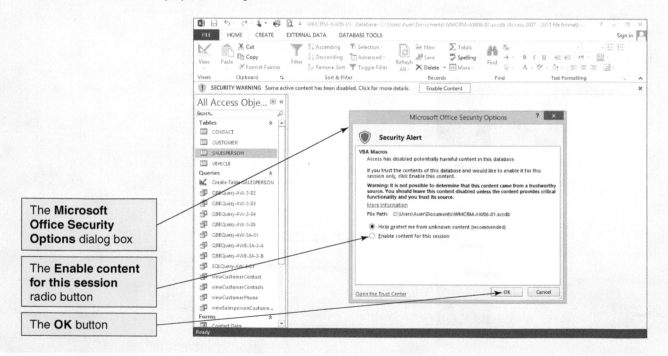

Security Warning message bar will be displayed again the next time this database file is opened!

However, we (nearly) always need these Microsoft Access features enabled. Is there a way to permanently enable them so that we do not have to deal with the Security Warning bar every time we open a new Microsoft Access database? Yes, there is.

The word Microsoft uses to describe our situation is *trust*: Do we *trust the content* of our database? If so, we can create a **trusted location** in which to store our trusted databases. And databases we use from the trusted location are opened *without* the security warning but *with* all features enabled.

Creating a Trusted Location

1. Start Microsoft Access.
2. If necessary, click the **File** command tab to display the Backstage view.
3. Click the **Options** command on the Backstage view. The Microsoft Access Options dialog box appears.
4. Click the **Trust Center** button to display the Trust Center page, as shown in Figure AW-6-5.
5. Click the **Trust Center Settings** button to display the Trust Center dialog box, as shown in Figure AW-6-6. Note that the Message Bar Settings for all Office Applications page is currently displayed and that the setting that enables the display of the Security Options message bar is currently selected.

FIGURE AW-6-5

The Access Options Trust Center Page

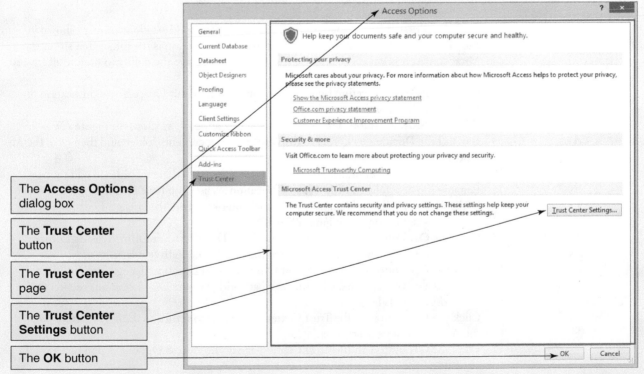

(Continued)

FIGURE AW-6-6

The Trust Center Dialog Box

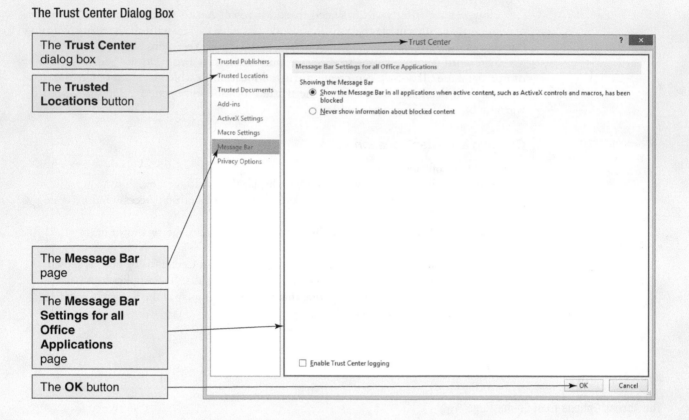

The **Trust Center** dialog box

The **Trusted Locations** button

The **Message Bar** page

The **Message Bar Settings for all Office Applications** page

The **OK** button

6. Click the **Trusted Locations** button to display the Trusted Locations page, as shown in Figure AW-6-7. Note that the only currently trusted location is the folder that stores the Microsoft Access wizard databases. Also note that we have the ability to disable all trusted locations if we choose to do so.

7. Click the **Add new location** button to display the Microsoft Office Trusted Location dialog box, as shown in Figure AW-6-8.

8. Click the **Browse** button. The Browse dialog box appears, as shown in Figure AW-6-9.

9. Expand the **Documents** library to display the My Documents folder, and then click the **My Documents** folder to select it.

10. Click the **New Folder** button to create a new folder named New Folder in edit mode.

11. Rename the new folder as **My-Trusted-Location**. When you have finished typing in the folder name *My-Trusted-Location*, press the **Enter** key. The My-Trusted-Location folder now appears, as shown in Figure AW-6-10.

12. Click the **OK** button on the Browse dialog box. The Microsoft Office Trusted Location dialog box appears, with the new trusted location in the Path text box.

13. Click the **OK** button on the Microsoft Office Trusted Location dialog box. The Trust Center dialog box appears, with the new path added to the User Locations section of the Trusted Locations list.

14. Click the **OK** button on the Trust Center dialog box to return to the Trust Center page of the Access Options dialog box.

15. Click the **OK** button on the Trust Center page of the Access Options dialog box to close it.

16. Close Microsoft Access.

FIGURE AW-6-7

The Trusted Locations Page

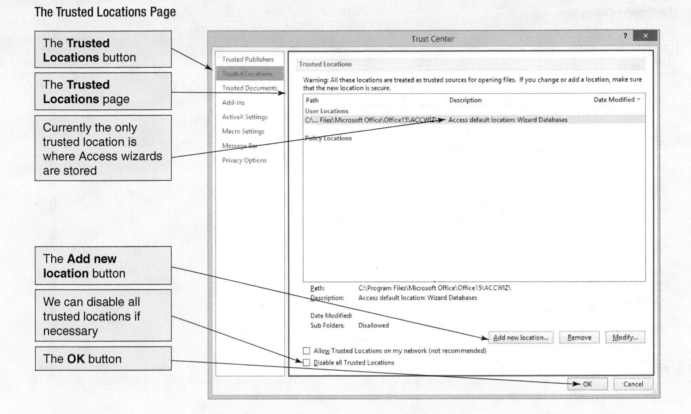

The **Trusted Locations** button

The **Trusted Locations** page

Currently the only trusted location is where Access wizards are stored

The **Add new location** button

We can disable all trusted locations if necessary

The **OK** button

Earlier in this section of "The Access Workbench" we created a copy of the WMCRM .accdb database file as the new file WMCRM-AW06-01.accdb. We used this file in our discussion of the Security Warning message bar and its associated options. At this point, we will still see the Security Warning message bar whenever we open WMCRM-AW06-01 .accdb database file in its current location in the Documents library.

Now we make a copy of the **WMCRM-AW06-01.accdb** file in the Document library and rename it as **WMCRM-AW06-02.accdb**. After making the WMCRM-AW06-02 .accdb file, we move it to the My-Trusted-Documents folder. Now we can try opening the WMCRM-AW06-02.accdb file from a Microsoft Access 2013 trusted location.

FIGURE AW-6-8

The Microsoft Office Trusted Location Dialog Box

The **Microsoft Office Trusted Location** dialog box

The **Browse** button

We can enable trust of all subfolders of the trusted location

The **OK** button

(Continued)

FIGURE AW-6-9

The Browse Dialog Box

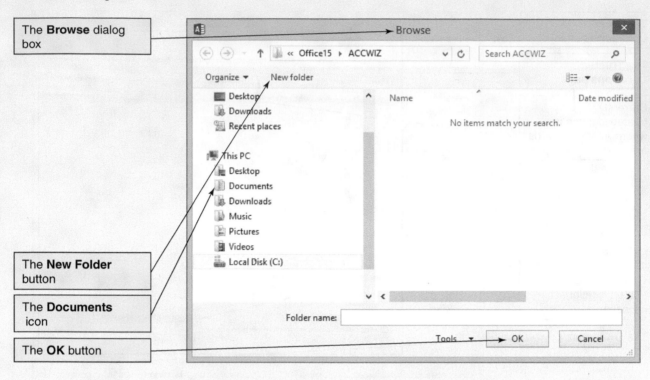

The **Browse** dialog box

The **New Folder** button

The **Documents** icon

The **OK** button

FIGURE AW-6-10

The My-Trusted-Location Folder

The **Browse** dialog box

The **My-Trusted-Location** folder— there are currently *no* files in this folder

The **OK** button

Opening a Microsoft Access Database from a Trusted Location

1. Start Microsoft Access.
2. If necessary, click the **File** command tab to display the Backstage view.
3. Click the **Open** button. The Microsoft Access Open dialog box is displayed.
4. Browse to the **WMCRM-AW06-02.accdb** file in the My-Trusted-Location folder, as shown in Figure AW-6-11.
5. Click the file name to highlight it and then click the **Open** button.
6. The Microsoft Access 2013 application window appears, with the WMCRM-AW06-02 database open in it. Note that the Security Warning bar does *not* appear when the database is opened.
7. Close Microsoft Access 2013 and the WMCRM-AW06-02 database.

Database Encryption with Passwords

Next, let us look at database encryption. In this case, Microsoft Access will encrypt the database, which will convert it into a secure, unreadable file format. To be able to use the encrypted database, a Microsoft Access user must enter a password to prove that he or she has the right to use the database. After the password is entered, Microsoft Access will decrypt the database and allow the user to work with it.

Each password should be a **strong password**—a password that includes lowercase letters, uppercase letters, numbers, and special characters (symbols) and that is at least 15 characters in length. Be sure to remember or record your password in a safe place—lost or forgotten passwords cannot be recovered!

For this example, we want to use a new copy of the **WMCRM.accdb** database file so that our encryption actions apply only to that file. Specifically, make a copy of **WMCRM-AW06-02.accdb** in the My-Trusted-Documents folder and name this new file **WMCRM-AW06-03.accdb**.

FIGURE AW-6-11

The WMCRM-AW06-02 File in the Open Dialog Box

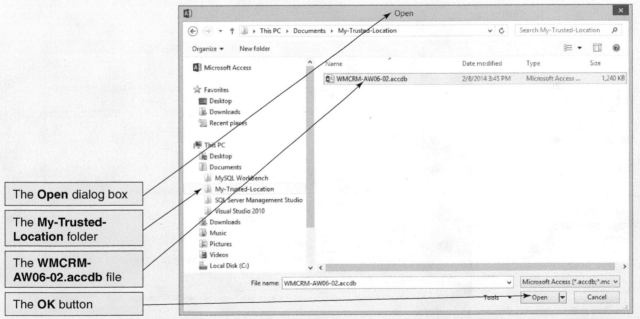

The **Open** dialog box

The **My-Trusted-Location** folder

The **WMCRM-AW06-02.accdb** file

The **OK** button

(Continued)

In order to encrypt a Microsoft Access database file, the file must be opened in **Exclusive mode**. This gives us exclusive use of the database and prevents any other users who have rights to use the database from opening it or using it. We start by opening WMCRM-AW06-03.accdb for our exclusive use.

Opening a Microsoft Access Database in Exclusive Mode

1. Start Microsoft Access.
2. If necessary, click the **File** command tab to display the Backstage view.
3. Click the **Open** button. The Microsoft Access Open dialog box appears.
4. Browse to the **WMCRM-AW06-03.accdb** file in the My-Trusted-Location folder. Click the file object *once* to select it, but *not* twice, which would open the file in Microsoft Access.
5. Click the **Open** button drop-down list arrow, as shown in Figure AW-6-12. The Open button drop-down list appears.
6. Click the **Open Exclusive** button in the Open button drop-down list to open the WMCRM-AW06-03 database in Microsoft Access 2013.
   - **NOTE:** The Security Warning bar does *not* appear when the database is opened because you are opening it from a trusted location.
   - **NOTE:** The Open button mode options shown in Figure AW-6-12 are always available when you open a Microsoft Access database. Normally, you use just Open mode because you want complete read and write permission in the database. Open Read-Only mode prevents the user from making changes to the database. Exclusive mode, as you have seen, stops other users from using the database while you are using it. Exclusive Read-Only mode, as the name implies, combines Exclusive and Read-Only modes.

Now that the database is open in Exclusive mode, we can encrypt the database and set the database password.

FIGURE AW-6-12

The Open Exclusive Button

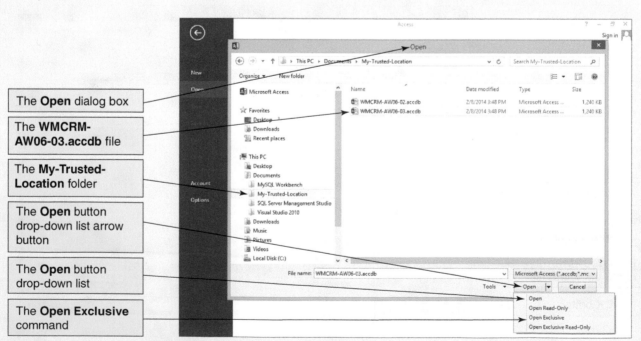

The **Open** dialog box

The **WMCRM-AW06-03.accdb** file

The **My-Trusted-Location** folder

The **Open** button drop-down list arrow button

The **Open** button drop-down list

The **Open Exclusive** command

Encrypting a Microsoft Access Database

1. Click the **File** command tab to display the Backstage view.
2. The Info page should be displayed. If it is not, click the **Info** button to display the Info page, as shown in Figure AW-6-13.
3. In the Encrypt with Password section of the Info page, click the **Encrypt with Password** button. The **Set Database Password** dialog box appears, as shown in Figure AW-6-14.
4. In the **Password** text box of the Set Database Password dialog box, type in the password **AW06+password**.
5. In the **Verify** text box of the Set Database Password dialog box, again type in the password **AW06+password**.
6. Click the **OK** button of the Set Database Password dialog box to set the database password and encrypt the database file.
7. Microsoft Access displays the warning dialog box shown in Figure AW-6-15 regarding the effect of encrypting on row level locking. Click the **OK** button to clear the warning.

FIGURE AW-6-13

The File | Info Page

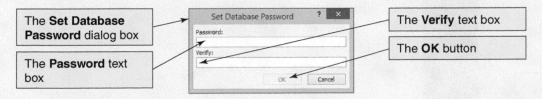

The **File** Backstage view

The **Info** button

The **Encrypt with Password** button

FIGURE AW-6-14

The Set Database Password Dialog Box

The **Set Database Password** dialog box

The **Password** text box

The **Verify** text box

The **OK** button

(Continued)

FIGURE AW-6-15

The Row Level Locking Warning Dialog Box

The **Row Level Locking Warning** dialog box

The **OK** button

8. You can check that the encryption action has been accomplished by clicking the **File** command tab and the **Info** button. After the database is encrypted, the Encrypt with Password button changes to a Decrypt Database button, as shown in Figure AW-6-16.

   - **NOTE:** As the Decrypt Database button name implies, if we wanted to change the database file back to its original unencrypted form we can do so using that button.

9. Click the **File** command tab and then click the **Close Database** button to close the WMCRM-AW06-03 database while leaving Microsoft Access 2013 open.

   Now we can open the now-encrypted WMCRM-AW06-03.accdb database file.

FIGURE AW-6-16

The Decrypt Database Button

The **File** backstage view

The **Info** button

The **Decrypt Database** button

Opening an Encrypted Microsoft Access Database

1. Microsoft Access should still be open. If it is not, start Microsoft Access.
2. If necessary, click the **File** command tab to display the Backstage view.
3. Click the **WMCRM-AW06-03.accdb** file name in the quick access list of recent databases. As shown in Figure AW-6-17, the **Password Required** dialog box appears.
4. In the **Enter database password** text box, type in the password **AW06+password**, and then click the **OK** button. The Microsoft Access 2013 application window appears, with the WMCRM-AW06-03 database open in it.
   - ■ **NOTE:** The Security Warning bar does *not* appear when the database is opened because you are opening it from a trusted location.
5. Close the WMCRM-AW06-03 database and exit Microsoft Access 2013.

Packaging and Signing a Microsoft Access Database

Microsoft has included some tools in Microsoft Access 2013 to help us distribute secured copies of Microsoft Access databases to users. Let us look at how to use them.

Compiling Microsoft Visual Basic for Applications (VBA) Code

Microsoft **Visual Basic for Applications (VBA)** is included in Microsoft Access. VBA is a version of the Microsoft Visual Basic programming language that is intended to help users add specific programmed actions to Microsoft Access applications. How to use VBA is beyond the scope of this section of "The Access Workbench," but we need to know how to secure VBA code if it is included in a Microsoft Access database.

Microsoft Access 2013 includes a **Make ACCDE command** to compile and hide VBA code so that although the VBA programming still functions correctly, the user can no longer see or modify the VBA code. When we use this tool, Microsoft Access creates a version of the database file with an ***.accde file extension**.

In the next set of steps, we well use another copy of the **WMCRM.accdb** database file so that our actions apply only to that file. Specifically, make a copy of **WMCRM-AW06-02 .accdb** in the My-Trusted-Documents folder and name this new file **WMCRM-AW06-04 .accdb**. We start by opening the WMCRM-AW06-04.accdb database file.

Creating a Microsoft Access *.accde Database

1. Open Microsoft Access.
2. If necessary, click the **File** command tab to display the Backstage view.
3. Click the **Open** button. The Microsoft Access Open dialog box appears.
4. Browse to the **WMCRM-AW06-04.accdb** file in the My-Trusted-Location folder. Double-click the file object to open it.
   - ■ **NOTE:** The Security Warning bar does *not* appear when the database is opened because you are opening it from a trusted location.

FIGURE AW-6-17

The Unset Database Password Dialog Box

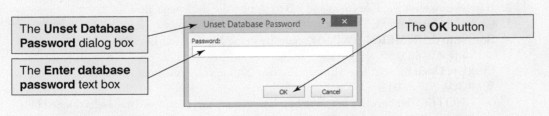

(Continued)

FIGURE AW-6-18

The File | Save As Page—Make ACCDE Command

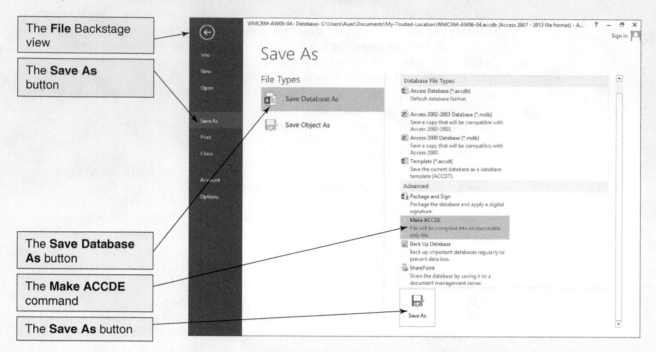

The **File** Backstage view

The **Save As** button

The **Save Database As** button

The **Make ACCDE** command

The **Save As** button

5. Click the **File** command tab to display the Backstage view.
6. Click the **Save As** button to display the Save As page, as shown in Figure AW-6-18.
7. Click the **Make ACCDE** button in the Advanced group in the Save Database As section, and then click the **Save As** button. The Save As dialog box appears, as shown in Figure AW-6-19.
8. Click the **Save** button in the Save As dialog box. The WMCRM-AW06-04.accde file is created.
   - **NOTE:** The displayed database name does *not* change. The only sign that this action has been completed is that the WMCRM-AW06-04.accde object will now be displayed in the list of Microsoft Access files in the Open dialog box (and other file system tools, such as Windows Explorer).
9. Close the WMCRM-AW06-04 database and exit Microsoft Access.

To see the new database, we open it as we would any other Microsoft Access database.

Opening a Microsoft Access *.accde Database

1. Start Microsoft Access.
2. If necessary, click the **File** command tab to display the Backstage view.
3. Click the **Open** button. The Microsoft Access Open dialog box appears.
4. Browse to the **WMCRM-AW06-04.accde** file in the My-Trusted-Location folder, as shown in Figure AW-6-20.
5. Click the **Open** button. The Microsoft Access 2013 application window appears, with the WMCRM-AW06-04.accde database open in it.
   - **NOTE:** The Security Warning bar does *not* appear when the database is opened because you are opening it from a trusted location.

FIGURE AW-6-19

The Save As Dialog Box

The **Save As** dialog box

The **My-Trusted-Location** folder

The file extension is **accde**

The **Save** button

FIGURE AW-6-20

The WMCRM-AW06-04.accde File

The **WMCRM-AW06-04.accdb** file

The **WMCRM-AW06-04.accde** file

The **Open** button

(Continued)

- **NOTE:** Although any previously existing VBA modules have been compiled and all editable source code for them has been removed, the functionality of this code is still in the database. Further note that VBA itself is still functional in the database—it has *not* been disabled.

6. Close the WMCRM-AW06-04 database and exit Microsoft Access.

Creating a Signed Package in Microsoft Access

A **digital signature scheme** is a type of **public-key cryptography** (also known as **asymmetric cryptography**), which uses two encryption keys (a **private key** and a **public key**) to encode documents and files to protect them. Although fascinating and important topics in their own right, cryptography in general and public-key cryptography in particular are beyond the scope of this section of "The Access Workbench."[1] For our purposes, a **digital signature** is a means of guaranteeing another user of a database that the database is, indeed, from us and that it is safe to use.

To use a digital signature, of course, we have to have one, so the first thing we have to do is to create one. This is not done in Microsoft Access, but rather with the Digital Certificate for VBA Projects utility provided with Microsoft Office 2013.

Creating a Digital Signature

1. Switch to the Windows Start screen, and search for **Digital Certificate for VBA Projects**. When the app appears in the Apps search results, click on the app icon to open the Create Digital Certificate dialog box, as shown in Figure AW-6-21.
2. In the **Your certificate's name** text box, type the text **Digital-Certificate-AW06-001** and then click the **OK** button. The certificate is created, and the SelfCert Success dialog box appears, as shown in Figure AW-6-22.
3. Click the **OK** button in the SelfCert Success dialog box.

Now that we have a digital certificate, we can use it to package and sign our database.

Creating a Microsoft Access Signed Package

1. Start Microsoft Access.
2. Open the **WMCRM-AW06-04.accde** database file.
   - **NOTE:** The Security Warning bar does *not* appear when the database is opened because you are opening it from a trusted location.

The **Create Digital Certificate** dialog box

The **Your certificate's name** text box

The **OK** button

Create Digital Certificate

This program creates a self-signed digital certificate that bears the name you type below. This type of certificate does not verify your identity.

Since a self-signed digital certificate might be a forgery, users will receive a security warning when they open a file that contains a macro project with a self-signed signature.

Office will only allow you to trust a self-signed certificate on the machine on which it was created.

A self-signed certificate is only for personal use. If you need an authenticated code signing certificate for signing commercial or broadly distributed macros, you will need to contact a certification authority.

Click here for a list of commercial certificate authorities

Your certificate's name:

OK   Cancel

---

[1]For more information, see the following Wikipedia articles: **Public-Key Cryptography**, **Digital Signature**, and **Public Key Certificate**.

FIGURE AW-6-22

The SelfCert Success
Dialog Box

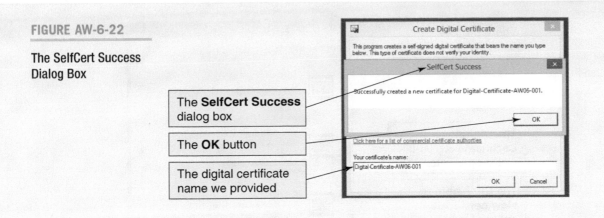

The **SelfCert Success**
dialog box

The **OK** button

The digital certificate
name we provided

3. Click the **File** command tab to display the Backstage view.
4. Click the **Save As** button to display the Save As page, as shown in Figure AW-6-23.
5. Click the **Package and Sign** button to select the Package and Sign option, and then click the **Save As** button. The Windows Security Confirm Certificate dialog box appears, as shown in Figure AW-6-24.
6. Only one certificate is shown, and although the full name is not visible, it is the one we created and want to use. However, to verify this, click the **Click here to view certificate properties** link. The Certificate Details dialog box appears, as shown in Figure AW-6-25, and our certificate name is clearly visible in the dialog box.
7. Click the **OK** button in the Certificate Details dialog box to close the dialog box.

FIGURE AW-6-23

The File | Save As—Package and Sign Command

The **File** backstage
view

The **Save As** button

WMCRM-AW06-04 : Database- C:\Users\Auer\Documents\My-Trusted-Documents\WMCRM-AW06-04.accde (Access 2007 - 2013... ? — □ ✕
David Auer ▾

Save As

Info

New

Open

File Types

Save As

Save Database As

Print

Save Object As

Close

Account

Options

The **Package and
Sign** command

The **Save As** button

Save Database As

Database File Types

Access Database (*.accdb)
Default database format.

Access 2002-2003 Database (*.mdb)
Save a copy that will be compatible with
Access 2002-2003.

Access 2000 Database (*.mdb)
Save a copy that will be compatible with
Access 2000.

Template (*.accdt)
Save the current database as a database
template (ACCDT).

Advanced

Package and Sign
Package the database and apply a digital
signature.

Back Up Database
Back up important databases regularly to
prevent data loss.

SharePoint
Share the database by saving it to a
document management server.

Save As

(Continued)

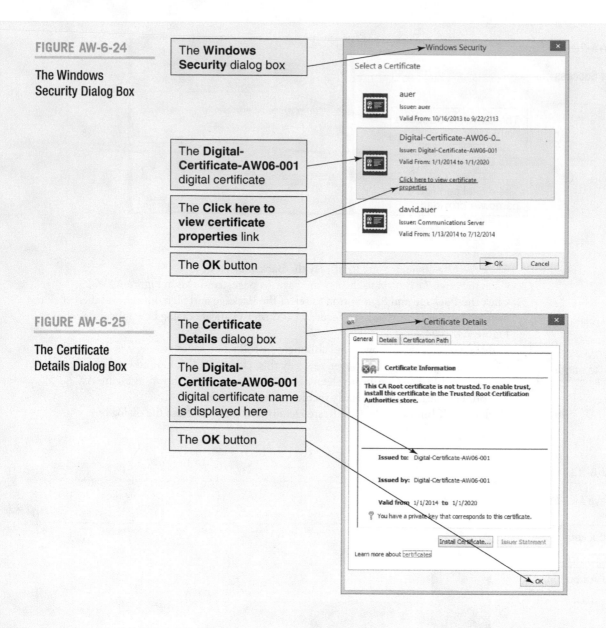

FIGURE AW-6-24

The Windows Security Dialog Box

The **Windows Security** dialog box

The **Digital-Certificate-AW06-001** digital certificate

The **Click here to view certificate properties** link

The **OK** button

FIGURE AW-6-25

The Certificate Details Dialog Box

The **Certificate Details** dialog box

The **Digital-Certificate-AW06-001** digital certificate name is displayed here

The **OK** button

8. Click the **OK** button in the Microsoft Security Confirm Certificate dialog box to close the dialog box. The Create Microsoft Office Access Signed Package dialog box appears, as shown in Figure AW-6-26.
9. Click the **Create** button to create the signed package.
10. Close the WMCRM-AW06-04 database and Microsoft Access 2013.

We now have a signed package, which uses the ***.accdc file extension**, ready to distribute to other users. To simulate this, in the My Documents folder of the Documents library create a new folder named **My-Distributed-Databases** and then copy the WMCRM-AW06-04.accdc file into it. Now we can open the signed package from this location.

Opening a Microsoft Access *.accdc Database

1. Start Microsoft Access.
2. If necessary, click the File command tab to display the Backstage view.

FIGURE AW-6-26

The Create Microsoft Office Access Signed Package Dialog Box

The **Create Microsoft Office Access Signed Package** dialog box

The **WMCRM-AW06-04.accdc** file name

The **Create** button

3. Click the **Open** button. The Open dialog box appears.
4. Browse to the **WMCRM-AW06-04.accdc** file in the My-Distributed-Databases folder, as shown in Figure AW-6-27. Note that you must change file type in order to see any of the *.accdc files.
5. Click the **WMCRM-AW06-04.accdc** file to select it and then click the **Open** button. The Microsoft Access Security Notice dialog box appears, as shown in Figure AW-6-28.

FIGURE AW-6-27

The WMCRM-AW06-04.accdc File

The **Open** dialog box

The **My-Distributed-Access-Databases** folder

You must select the ***.accdc** file type in order to see the file

(Continued)

FIGURE AW-6-28

The Microsoft Access
Security Notice
Dialog Box

The **Microsoft
Access Security
Notice** dialog box

The **Open** button

6. Click the **Trust all from publisher** button. The **Extract Database To** dialog box appears. This dialog box is essentially the same as a Save To dialog box, so browse to the My-Distributed-Databases folder and then click the **OK** button.

7. Another **Microsoft Access Security Notice** dialog box similar to the one shown in Figure AW-6-28 appears. Click the **Open** button.

8. The **WMCRM-AW06-04.accde** database is opened in Microsoft Access.
   - **NOTE:** The Security Warning bar does *not* appear when the database is opened because you have chosen to trust the source of the database as documented in the digital certificate rather than open it from a trusted location.

9. Close the WMCRM-AW06-04 database and Microsoft Access 2013.

Using Windows Explorer, look at the contents of the Libraries\Documents\My Documents\My-Distributed-Databases folder. Notice that the WMCRM-AW06-04.accde file has been extracted from the WMCRM-AW06-04.accdc package and is now available for use. This is the database file that the user will open when he or she uses the database. Also note that when users open the database they will see the Microsoft Access Security Notice dialog box just discussed. But we chose *Trust all from publisher* in step 6, so why is this happening? The reason has to do with the *location* where the digital certificate has been stored on the workstation. This is a technical matter beyond the scope of this discussion, but we can at least see exactly what the problem is by following the next set of steps.

Viewing the Certification Path in the Certificate Dialog Box

1. Start Microsoft Access 2013.

2. Open the **WMCRM-AW06-04.accde** file in the My-Distributed-Databases folder.

3. When the Microsoft Access Security Notice dialog box appears, click the **Open** button.

4. Click the **File** command tab.

5. Click the **Options** command. The Access Options dialog box appears.

6. Click the **Trust Center** button to display the Trust Center page.

7. Click the **Trust Center Settings** button to display the Trust Center dialog box.

8. Click the **Trusted Publishers** button to display the Trusted Publishers page.

9. Click the trusted publisher name **Digital-Certificate-AW06-001** to select it and then click the **View** button. The Certificate dialog box appears.

10. Click the **Certification Path** tab in the Certificate dialog box. The Certification Path page appears, as shown in Figure AW-6-29.

11. Note the **Certificate status** area, which reads "This CA Root certificate is not trusted because it is not in the Trusted Root Certification Authorities store." This is the problem that needs to be resolved before the database will open without the Microsoft Access Security Notice dialog box being displayed every time the database is opened.

12. Click the **OK** button to close the Certificate dialog box.

FIGURE AW-6-29

The Certification Path Page

The **Certificate** dialog box

The **Certificate Path** page

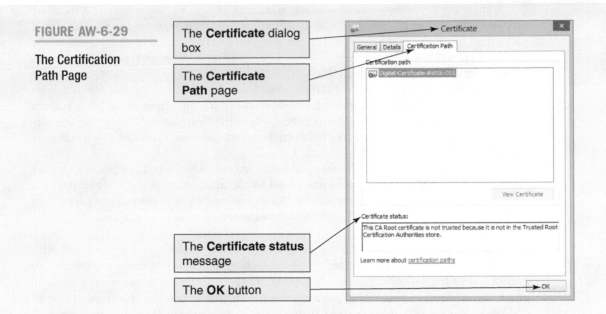

The **Certificate status** message

The **OK** button

13. Click the **OK** button to close the Trust Center dialog box.
14. Click the **OK** button to close the Access Options dialog box.
15. Close the WMCRM-AW06-04 database and exit Microsoft Access.

This completes our discussion of how Microsoft Access 2013 handles database security for Microsoft Access 2013 *.accdb files. Note that Microsoft Access 2013 can also open and work with older Microsoft Access 2003 *.mdb database files, which have a built-in user-level database security system that is very different from the Microsoft Access 2013 database security we have discussed. If you need to work with one of these older *.mdb files, consult the Microsoft Access documentation.

SUMMARY

Database administration is a business function that involves managing a database in order to maximize its value to an organization. The conflicting goals of protecting the database and maximizing its availability and benefit to users must be balanced using good administration.

All databases need database administration. The database administration for small, personal databases is informal; database administration for large, multiuser databases can involve an office and many people. DBA can stand for *database administration* or *database administrator*. Three basic database administration functions are necessary: concurrency control, security, and backup and recovery.

The goal of concurrency control is to ensure that one user's work does not inappropriately influence another user's work. No single concurrency control technique is ideal for all circumstances. Trade-offs need to be made between the level of protection and data throughput.

A transaction, or logical unit of work, is a series of actions taken against a database that occur as an atomic unit; either all of them occur or none of them do. The activity of concurrent transactions is interleaved on the database server. In some cases, updates can be lost if concurrent transactions are not controlled. Another concurrency problem concerns inconsistent reads.

A dirty read occurs when one transaction reads a changed record that has not been committed to the database. A nonrepeatable read occurs when one transaction rereads data it has previously read and finds modifications or deletions caused by another transaction. A phantom read occurs when a transaction rereads data and finds new rows that were inserted by a different transaction.

To avoid concurrency problems, database elements are locked. Implicit locks are placed by the DBMS; explicit locks are issued by the application program. The size of a locked resource is called lock granularity. An exclusive lock prohibits other users from reading the locked resource; a shared lock allows other users to read the locked resource but not to update it.

Two transactions that run concurrently and generate results that are consistent with the results that would have occurred if the transactions had run separately are referred to as serializable transactions. Two-phase locking, in which locks are acquired in a growing phase and released in a shrinking phase, is one scheme for serializability. A special case of two-phase locking is to acquire locks throughout the transaction but not to free any lock until the transaction is finished.

Deadlock, or the deadly embrace, occurs when two transactions are each waiting on a resource that the other transaction holds. Deadlock can be prevented by requiring transactions to acquire all locks at the same time. When deadlock occurs, the only way to cure it is to abort one of the transactions and back out of partially completed work.

Optimistic locking assumes that no transaction conflict will occur and then deals with the consequences if it does. Pessimistic locking assumes that conflict will occur and so prevents it ahead of time with locks. In general, optimistic locking is preferred for the Internet and for many intranet applications.

Most application programs do not explicitly declare locks. Instead, they mark transaction boundaries with SQL transaction control statements—such as BEGIN, COMMIT, and ROLLBACK statements—and declare the concurrent behavior they want. The DBMS then places locks for the application that will result in the desired behavior. An ACID transaction is one that is atomic, consistent, isolated, and durable. Durable means that database changes are permanent. Consistency can refer to either statement-level or transaction-level consistency. With transaction-level consistency, a transaction may not see its own changes.

The three types of data read problems that can occur are dirty read, nonrepeatable read, and phantom read. These problems are summarized in Figure 6-11. The 1992 SQL standard defines four transaction isolation levels: read uncommitted, read committed, repeatable read, and serializable. The characteristics of each are summarized in Figure 6-12.

A cursor is a pointer into a set of records. Four cursor types are prevalent: forward only, static, keyset, and dynamic. Developers should select isolation levels and cursor types that are appropriate for their application workload and for the DBMS product in use.

The goal of database security is to ensure that only authorized users can perform authorized activities at authorized times. To develop effective database security, the processing rights and responsibilities of all users must be determined.

DBMS products provide security facilities. Most involve the declaration of users, groups, objects to be protected, and permissions or privileges on those objects. Almost all DBMS products use some form of user name and password security. DBMS security can be augmented by application security.

In the event of system failure, the database must be restored to a usable state as soon as possible. Transactions in process at the time of the failure must be reapplied or restarted. Although in some cases recovery can be done by reprocessing, the use of logs and before-images and after-images with rollback and rollforward is almost always preferred. Checkpoints can be made to reduce the amount of work that needs to be done after a failure.

In addition to concurrency control, security, and backup and recovery, a DBA needs to ensure that a system exists to gather and record errors and problems. The DBA works with the development team to resolve such problems on a prioritized basis and also to evaluate features and functions of new releases of the DBMS. In addition, the DBA needs to create and manage a process for controlling the database configuration so that changes to the database structure are made with a community-wide view. Finally, the DBA is responsible for ensuring that appropriate documentation is maintained about database structure, concurrency control, security, backup and recovery, and other details that concern the management and use of the database.

KEY TERMS

ACID transaction
after-image
atomic
authentication
authorization
before-image
checkpoint
concurrent transaction
concurrent update problem
consistent
data administration
database administration
database administrator
DBA
deadlock
deadly embrace
dirty read
durable
dynamic cursor
exclusive lock
explicit lock
forward-only cursor
implicit lock
inconsistent read problem

isolation level
keyset cursor
lock granularity
log
logical unit of work (LUW)
lost update problem
nonrepeatable read
optimistic locking
permissions
pessimistic locking
phantom read
read committed isolation level
read uncommitted isolation level
recovery via reprocessing
recovery via rollback/
  rollforward
repeatable read isolation level
resource locking
rollback
rollforward
scrollable cursor
serializable
serializable isolation level
shared lock

SQL BEGIN TRANSACTION
  statement
SQL COMMITT TRANSACTION
  statement
SQL Data Control Language
  (DCL)
SQL GRANT statement
SQL/Persistent Stored Modules
  (SQL/PSM)
SQL REVOKE statement
SQL ROLLBACK
  TRANSACTION statement
SQL Transaction Control Language
  (TCL)
statement-level consistency
static cursor
stored procedure
transaction
transaction isolation level
transaction-level consistency
trigger
two-phase locking
user account
user-defined function

REVIEW QUESTIONS

6.1 What is the purpose of database administration?

6.2 Explain how database administration tasks vary with the size and complexity of the database.

6.3 What are two interpretations of the abbreviation *DBA*?

6.4 What is the purpose of concurrency control?

6.5 What is the goal of a database security system?

6.6 Explain the meaning of the word *inappropriately* in the phrase "one user's work does not inappropriately influence another user's work."

6.7 Explain the trade-off that exists in concurrency control.

6.8 Describe what an atomic transaction is and explain why atomicity is important.

6.9 Explain the difference between concurrent transactions and simultaneous transactions. How many CPUs are required for simultaneous transactions?

6.10 Give an example, other than the one in this text, of the lost update problem.

6.11 Define the terms *dirty read*, *nonrepeatable read*, and *phantom read*.

6.12 Explain the difference between an explicit lock and an implicit lock.

6.13 What is lock granularity?

6.14 Explain the difference between an exclusive lock and a shared lock.

6.15 Explain two-phase locking.

6.16 How does releasing all locks at the end of a transaction relate to two-phase locking?

6.17 What is deadlock? How can it be avoided? How can it be resolved when it occurs?

6.18 Explain the difference between optimistic and pessimistic locking.

6.19 Explain the benefits of marking transaction boundaries, declaring lock characteristics, and letting a DBMS place locks.

6.20 Explain the use of the SQL transaction control language (TCL) statements BEGIN TRANSACTION, COMMIT TRANSACTION, and ROLLBACK TRANSACTION.

6.21 Explain the meaning of the expression *ACID transaction*.

6.22 Describe statement-level consistency.

6.23 Describe transaction-level consistency. What disadvantage can exist with it?

6.24 What is the purpose of transaction isolation levels?

6.25 Explain what read uncommitted isolation level is. Give an example of its use.

6.26 Explain what read committed isolation level is. Give an example of its use.

6.27 Explain what repeatable read isolation level is. Give an example of its use.

6.28 Explain what serializable isolation level is. Give an example of its use.

6.29 Explain the term *cursor*.

6.30 Explain why a transaction may have many cursors. Also, how is it possible that a transaction may have more than one cursor on a given table?

6.31 What is the advantage of using different types of cursors?

6.32 Explain forward-only cursors. Give an example of their use.

6.33 Explain static cursors. Give an example of their use.

6.34 Explain keyset cursors. Give an example of their use.

6.35 Explain dynamic cursors. Give an example of their use.

6.36 What happens if you do not declare transaction isolation level and cursor type to a DBMS? Is not declaring the isolation level and cursor type good or bad?

6.37 Explain the necessity of defining processing rights and responsibilities. How are such responsibilities enforced? What is SQL data control language (DCL), and what SQL statements are used in DCL?

6.38 Explain the relationships of users, groups, permission, and objects for a generic database security system.

6.39   Describe the advantages and disadvantages of DBMS-provided security.

6.40   Describe the advantages and disadvantages of application-provided security.

6.41   Explain how a database could be recovered via reprocessing. Why is this generally not feasible?

6.42   Define the terms *rollback* and *rollforward.*

6.43   Why is it important to write to a log before changing the database values?

6.44   Describe the rollback process. Under what conditions should rollback be used?

6.45   Describe the rollforward process. Under what conditions should rollforward be used?

6.46   What is the advantage of making frequent checkpoints of a database?

6.47   Summarize a DBA's responsibilities for managing database user problems.

6.48   Summarize a DBA's responsibilities for configuration control.

6.49   Summarize a DBA's responsibilities for documentation.

EXERCISES

6.50   If you have access to SQL Server, search its help system to answer the following questions.

A. Does SQL Server support both optimistic and pessimistic locking?

B. What levels of transaction isolation are available?

C. What types of cursors, if any, does SQL Server use?

D. How does the security model for SQL Server differ from that shown in Figure 6-16?

E. Summarize the types of SQL Server backup.

F. Summarize the SQL Server recovery models.

6.51   If you have access to Oracle Database Express Edition 11*g* Release 2 search its help system to answer the following questions.

A. How does Oracle Database Express Edition 11*g* Release 2 use read locks and write locks?

B. What, if any, levels of transaction isolation are available in Oracle Database Express Edition 11*g* Release 2?

C. How does the security model for Oracle Database Express Edition 11*g* Release 2 differ from that shown in Figure 6-16?

D. Summarize the backup capabilities of Oracle Database Express Edition 11*g* Release 2.

E. Summarize the recovery capabilities of Oracle Database Express Edition 11*g* Release 2.

6.52   If you have access to MySQL 5.6, search its help system to answer the following questions.

    A. How does MySQL 5.6 use read locks and write locks?

    B. What, if any, levels of transaction isolation are available in MySQL 5.6?

    C. What types of cursors, if any, does MySQL 5.6 use?

    D. How does the security model for MySQL 5.6 differ from that shown in Figure 6-16?

    E. Summarize the backup capabilities of MySQL 5.6.

    F. Summarize the recovery capabilities of MySQL 5.6.

ACCESS WORKBENCH KEY TERMS

*.accdc file extension	Make ACCDE command
*.accde file extension	private key
ActiveX control	public key
ActiveX specification	public-key cryptography
asymmetric cryptography	Security Warning message bar
digital signature	strong password
digital signature scheme	trusted location
Exclusive mode	Visual Basic for Applications (VBA)

ACCESS WORKBENCH EXERCISES

AW.6.1   Use the Wedgewood Pacific Corporation (WPC) database developed in previous sections of "The Access Workbench" to answer the following questions.

    A.   Analyze the data in the WPC database tables (particularly DEPARTMENT and EMPLOYEE) and create a database security plan, using Figure 6-16 as an example.

    B.   If you have not already created a My-Trusted-Location folder, follow the steps in this chapter's section of "The Access Workbench" to do so now.

    C.   Make a copy of the WPC.accdb file in the My-Trusted-Location folder and name it *WPC-AW06-01.accdb*. Open the WPC-AW06-01.accdb database to confirm that it opens without displaying the Security Warning bar, and then close the database.

    D.   Make a copy of the WPC.accdb file in the My-Trusted-Location folder and name it *WPC-AW06-02.accdb*. Encrypt the WPC-AW06-02.accdb database with the password *AW06EX+password*. Close the WPC-AW06-02.accdb database and then reopen it to confirm that it opens properly using the password. Close the WPC-AW06-02.accdb database.

    E. If you have not already created the Digital-Certificate-AW06-001 digital certificate, follow the steps in this chapter's section of "The Access Workbench" to do so now.

    F. Make a copy of the WPC.accdb file in the My-Trusted-Location folder and name it *WPC-AW06-03.accdb*. Create an AACDE version of the WPC-AW06-03.accdb database. Create a signed package using the WPC-AW06-03.accde database and the Digital-Certificate-AW06-001 digital certificate.

    G. If you have not already created a My-Distributed-Databases folder, follow the steps in this chapter's section of "The Access Workbench" to do so now.

    H. Make a copy of the WPC-AW06-03.accdc file in the My-Distributed-Databases folder. Extract the WPC-AW06-03.accde file into the folder and then open it to confirm that the database opens properly. Close the database.

MARCIA'S DRY CLEANING CASE QUESTIONS

Ms. Marcia Wilson owns and operates Marcia's Dry Cleaning, which is an upscale dry cleaner in a well-to-do suburban neighborhood. Marcia makes her business stand out from the competition by providing superior customer service. She wants to keep track of each of her customers and their orders. Ultimately, she wants to notify them that their clothes are ready via email.

Assume that Marcia has hired you as a database consultant to develop an operational database having the following four tables:

CUSTOMER (<u>CustomerID</u>, FirstName, LastName, Phone, Email)

INVOICE (<u>InvoiceNumber</u>, *CustomerID*, DateIn, DateOut, Subtotal, Tax, TotalAmount)

INVOICE_ITEM (*<u>InvoiceNumber</u>*, <u>ItemNumber</u>, *ServiceID*, Quantity, UnitPrice, ExtendedPrice)

SERVICE (<u>ServiceID</u>, ServiceDescription, UnitPrice)

    A. Assume that Marcia's has the following personnel: two owners, a shift manager, a part-time seamstress, and two salesclerks. Prepare a two-to-three-page memo that addresses the following points:

        1. The need for database administration.

        2. Your recommendation as to who should serve as database administrator. Assume that Marcia's is not sufficiently large to need or afford a full-time database administrator.

        3. Using the main topics in this chapter as a guide, describe the nature of database administration activities at Marcia's. As an aggressive consultant, keep in mind that you can recommend yourself for performing some of the DBA functions.

    B. For the employees described in part A, define users, groups, and permissions on data in these four tables. Use the security scheme shown in Figure 6-16 as an example. Create a table like that in Figure 6-17. Don't forget to include yourself.

C. Suppose that you are writing a part of an application to create new records in SERVICE for new services that Marcia's will perform. Suppose that you know that while your procedure is running another part of the same application that records new or modifies existing customer orders and order line items can also be running. Additionally, suppose that a third part of the application that records new customer data also can be running.

1. Give an example of a dirty read, a nonrepeatable read, and a phantom read among this group of stored procedures.

2. What concurrency control measures are appropriate for the part of the application that you are creating?

3. What concurrency control measures are appropriate for the two other parts of the application?

GARDEN GLORY PROJECT QUESTIONS

The following Garden Glory database design is used in Chapter 3:

OWNER (OwnerID, OwnerName, OwnerEmail, OwnerType)
OWNED_PROPERTY (PropertyID, PropertyName, Street, City, State, ZIP, OwnerID)
GG_SERVICE (ServiceID, ServiceDescription, CostPerHour)
EMPLOYEE (EmployeeID, LastName, FirstName, CellPhone, ExperienceLevel)
PROPERTY_SERVICE (PropertyID, ServiceID, ServiceDate, EmployeeID, HoursWorked)

The referential integrity constraints are:

OwnerID in OWNED_PROPERTY must exist in OwnerID in OWNER
PropertyID in PROPERTY_SERVICE must exist in PropertyID in OWNED_PROPERTY
ServiceID in PROPERTY_SERVICE must exist in ServiceID in GG_SERVICE
EmployeeID in PROPERTY_SERVICE must exist in EmployeeID in EMPLOYEE

Garden Glory has modified the EMPLOYEE table by adding a TotalHoursWorked column:

EMPLOYEE (EmployeeID, LastName, FirstName, CellPhone, ExperienceLevel, TotalHoursWorked)

The office personnel at Garden Glory use a database application to record services and related data changes in this database. For a new service, the service-recording application reads a row from the OWNED_PROPERTY table to get the PropertyID. It then creates a new row in GG_SERVICE and updates TotalHoursWorked in EMPLOYEE by adding the HoursWorked value in the new GG_SERVICE record to TotalHoursWorked. This operation is referred to as a Service Update Transaction.

In some cases, the employee record does not exist before the service is recorded. In such a case, a new EMPLOYEE row is created, and then the service is recorded. This is called a Service Update for New Employee Transaction.

A. Explain why it is important for the changes made by the Service Update Transaction to be atomic.

B. Describe a scenario in which an update of TotalHoursWorked could be lost during a Service Update Transaction.

C. Assume that many Service Update Transactions and many Service Update for New Employee Transactions are processed concurrently. Describe a scenario for a nonrepeatable read and a scenario for a phantom read.

D. Explain how locking could be used to prevent the lost update in your answer to part B.

E. Is it possible for deadlock to occur between two Service Update Transactions? Why or why not? Is it possible for deadlock to occur between a Service Update Transaction and a Service Update for New Employee Transaction? Why or why not?

F. Do you think optimistic or pessimistic locking would be better for the Service Update Transactions?

G. Suppose Garden Glory identifies three groups of users: managers, administrative personnel, and system administrators. Suppose further that the only job of administrative personnel is to make Service Update Transactions. Managers can make Service Update Transactions and Service Updates for New Employee Transactions. System administrators have unrestricted access to the tables. Describe processing rights that you think would be appropriate for this situation. Use Figure 6-17 as an example. What problems might this security system have?

H. Garden Glory has developed the following procedure for backup and recovery. The company backs up the database from the server to a second computer on its network each night. Once a month, it copies the database to a CD and stores it at a manager's house. It keeps paper records of all services provided for an entire year. If it ever loses its database, it plans to restore it from a backup and reprocess all service requests. Do you think this backup and recovery program is sufficient for Garden Glory? What problems might occur? What alternatives exist? Describe any changes you think the company should make to this system.

JAMES RIVER JEWELRY PROJECT QUESTIONS

The James River Jewelry project questions are in online Appendix D, which can be downloaded for the textbook's Web site: **www.pearsonhighereducation.com/kroenke**.

THE QUEEN ANNE CURIOSITY SHOP PROJECT QUESTIONS

The Queen Anne Curiosity Shop database design used in Chapter 3 was:

CUSTOMER (<u>CustomerID</u>, LastName, FirstName, Address, City, State, ZIP, Phone, Email)

EMPLOYEE (<u>EmployeeID</u>, LastName, FirstName, Phone, Email)

VENDOR (<u>VendorID</u>, CompanyName, ContactLastName, ContactFirstName, Address, City, State, ZIP, Phone, Fax, Email)

ITEM (<u>ItemID</u>, ItemDescription, PurchaseDate, ItemCost, ItemPrice, VendorID)

SALE (<u>SaleID</u>, *CustomerID*, *EmployeeID*, SaleDate, SubTotal, Tax, Total)

SALE_ITEM (<u>*SaleID*</u>, <u>SaleItemID</u>, *ItemID*, ItemPrice)

The referential integrity constraints are:

VendorID in ITEM must exist in VendorID in VENDOR

CustomerID in SALE must exist in CustomerID in CUSTOMER

EmployeeID in SALE must exist in EmployeeID in EMPLOYEE

SaleID in SALE_ITEM must exist in SaleID in SALE

ItemID in SALE_ITEM must exist in ItemID in ITEM

The Queen Anne Curiosity Shop has modified the ITEM and SALE_ITEM tables as follows:

ITEM (<u>ItemID</u>, ItemDescription, UnitCost, UnitPrice, QuantityOnHand, *VendorID*)

SALE_ITEM (<u>*SaleID*</u>, <u>SaleItemID</u>, *ItemID*, Quantity, ItemPrice, Extended Price)

These changes allow the sales system to handle nonunique items that can be bought and sold in quantity. When new items from vendors arrive at The Queen Anne Curiosity Shop, the office personnel unpack the items, put them in the stockroom, and run an Item Quantity Received Transaction that adds the quantity received to QuantityOnHand. At the same time, another transaction, called an Item Price Adjustment Transaction is run, if necessary, to adjust UnitCost and UnitPrice. Sales may occur at any time, and when a sale occurs the Sale Transaction is run. Every time a SALE_ITEM line is entered, the input Quantity is subtracted from QuantityOnHand in ITEM, and the ItemPrice is set to the UnitPrice.

A. Explain why it is important for the changes made by each of these transactions to be atomic.

B. Describe a scenario in which an update of QuantityOnHand could be lost.

C. Describe a scenario for a nonrepeatable read and a scenario for a phantom read.

D. Explain how locking could be used to prevent the lost update in your answer to part B.

E. Is it possible for deadlock to occur between two Sale Transactions? Why or why not? Is it possible for deadlock to occur between a Sale Transaction and an Item Quantity Received Transaction? Why or why not?

F. For each of the three types of transaction, describe whether you think optimistic or pessimistic locking would be better. Explain the reasons for your answer.

G. Suppose that The Queen Anne Curiosity Shop identifies four groups of users: sales personnel, managers, administrative personnel, and system administrators. Suppose further that managers and administrative personnel can perform Item Quantity Received Transactions, but only managers can perform Item Price Adjustment Transactions. Describe processing rights that you think would be appropriate for this situation. Use Figure 6-17 as an example.

H. The Queen Anne Curiosity Shop has developed the following procedure for backup and recovery. The company backs up the entire database from the server to tape every Saturday night. The tapes are taken to a safety deposit box at a local bank on the following Thursday. Printed paper records of all sales are kept for 5 years. If the database is ever lost, the plan is to restore the database from the last full backup and reprocess all the sales records. Do you think this backup and recovery program is sufficient for the Queen Anne Curiosity Shop? What problems might occur? What alternatives exist? Describe any changes you think the company should make to this system.

CHAPTER 7 Database Processing Applications

CHAPTER OBJECTIVES

- Understand and be able to set up Web database processing

- Learn the basic concepts of Extensible Markup Language (XML)

T his chapter introduces topics that build on the fundamentals you have learned in the first six chapters of this book. Now that you have designed and built a database, you are ready to put it to work. In this chapter, we will look at some of the various applications that use database processing, with a primary focus on Web-based database processing. We will also look at Extensible Markup Language (XML), which is rapidly expanding what can be done with Web-based applications.

In this chapter, we will continue to use the Heather Sweeney Designs (HSD) database that we modeled in Chapter 4, designed in Chapter 5, and created in Chapter 6. The name of the database is HSD, and an SQL Server database diagram for the HSD database is shown in Figure 7-1.

FIGURE 7-1

The HSD Database
Diagram

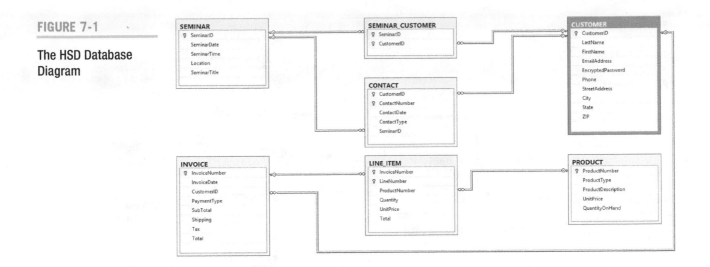

THE DATABASE PROCESSING ENVIRONMENT

Databases exist to be used in applications for users—they do *not* exist in isolation. As shown in Figure 7-2, which repeats Figure 1-15, databases are created in and controlled by DBMS programs for the purpose of managing data for applications needed by users.

Databases vary considerably in size and scope, from single-user databases to large, interorganizational databases, such as airline reservation systems. As shown in Figure 7-3, which repeats Figure 6-2, they also vary in the way they are processed.

Some databases are used with only a few forms and reports. Others are processed by **World Wide Web (WWW)** (commonly just called **Web**[1] applications using Internet technology such as *Active Server Pages .NET (ASP.NET)* and *Java Server Pages (JSP)*. Still others are processed by application programs coded in Visual Basic .NET, Java, C#, or another language. Each of these applications may use SQL/Persistent Stored Modules (SQL/PSM) user-defined functions, stored procedures, and triggers that are stored in the database itself to facilitate data processing.

We will consider each of these types of database processing in this chapter. Because of the overwhelming importance of Web database applications, we will discuss those at length—in fact, that discussion will be the main topic of this chapter.

Queries, Forms, and Reports

This book has focused on the use of a DBMS to build and process databases. For example, it has covered the need to specify rules, such as cascading updates or deletions. Applications, however, are built to use the databases managed by a DBMS. Queries, forms, and reports

FIGURE 7-2

Components of a
Database System

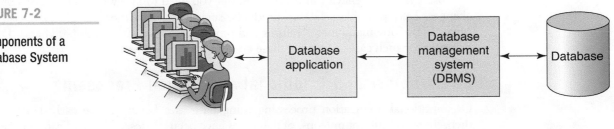

Users

---

[1]In 2014, the World Wide Web celebrated its twenty-fifth anniversary. It was created in 1989 by Tim Berners-Lee while he was working at CERN (the European Organization for Nuclear Research, which celebrated its sixtieth anniversary in 2014). For more information, see the Web 25th Anniversary Web site.

FIGURE 7-3

The Database
Processing
Environment

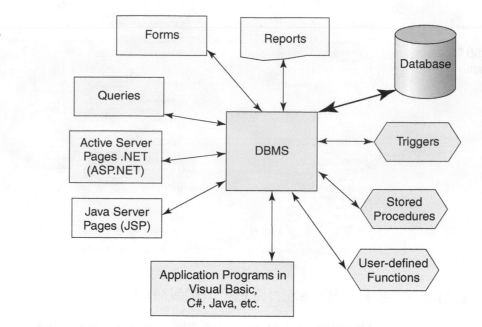

are the basis of applications. Query, form, and report generators can be built into a database product, such as Microsoft Access, or they can be run as separate products.[2]

Now, let us think about some of the tasks that the DBMS—for example, Microsoft Access—needs to do in the background to implement the database processing commands. Suppose, for example, that you create a delete query on a table that has a 1:N relationship to a second table that has On Delete Cascade. Suppose further that the second table has a 1:N relationship to a third table, which has Enforce Referential Integrity but not On Delete Cascade. When running your delete query, Microsoft Access needs to delete rows from the first and second tables consistent with these relationship properties.

The situation is even more complicated if a second user is creating a report on these three tables as your delete query is operating. What should Microsoft Access do? Should it show the report with whatever data remain as your query runs? Or should Microsoft Access protect the report from your deletions and not make any of them until the report is finished? Should it deny your query or do something else completely?

As a simpler example, suppose you create a form that has data from one table in the main section and data from a second table in a subform. Now, suppose a user makes changes in five rows in the subform, makes changes to some of the data in the first form, and then presses the Escape key. Which of these changes will actually be made to the database? None? Changes to the subform data only? Or some other option?

Even in the case of simple queries, forms, and reports, management of the background functions is complex. You can change properties in your database to govern some of Microsoft Access' behavior in these cases, but you need to know the implications of such changes. Enterprise-class DBMS products, such as SQL Server, Oracle Database, and MySQL, provide many more features and functions that let the developer change DBMS behavior for such cases. (Many of these are discussed in Chapter 6.)

Client/Server and Traditional Application Processing

Organizational application processing using databases began in the early 1970s. Since then, thousands, if not millions, of databases have been processed by application programs

---

[2]Until Microsoft Access 2013, it was possible to easily use Microsoft Access for its query, form, and report features while connecting to a database in another DBMS, such as SQL Server. In this way, the Microsoft Access "database" actually ran as an application that used an attached, but distinct, database. Unfortunately, this capability was removed from Microsoft Access 2013.

written in such programming languages as Visual Basic, C, C++, C#, and
languages embed SQL statements or their equivalent into programs writte
dard languages.

For example, to process an online order for Heather Sweeney Designs,
needs to perform the following functions:

1. Communicate with a user to obtain the customer identifier.
2. Read CUSTOMER data.
3. Present an order-entry form to a user.
4. Obtain PRODUCT and quantity data from the customer.
5. Verify stock levels for PRODUCTs.
6. Remove PRODUCTs from inventory.
7. Schedule back orders as necessary.
8. Schedule inventory picking and shipping.
9. Update CUSTOMER, INVOICE, and LINE_ITEM data (and if a sale is considered a
   type of customer contact, then update CONTACT).

The application will be written to respond to exceptions, such as data not present, data in
error, communication failure, and dozens of other potential problems.

In addition, an order-processing application program will be written so that it can be
used by many users concurrently—it is possible that 50 to 100 users might be trying to run
such an application at the same time.

SQL/PSM: User-Defined Functions, Stored Procedures, and Triggers

Enterprise-class DBMS products such as SQL Server, Oracle Database, MySQL, and DB2
include features that enable developers to create modules of logic and database actions.
These features are know as **SQL/Persistent Stored Modules (SQL/PSM)** and include
user-defined functions, stored procedures, and *triggers*. SQL/PSM, user-defined functions,
stored procedures, and triggers are discussed in detail in Appendix E, "SQL Views," and
here we will provide only a brief description of this functionality.

User-defined functions, stored procedures, and triggers are typically[3] written in languages provided by the DBMS.[4] For example, SQL Server has a language called Transact-
SQL (T-SQL), and Oracle has developed a language called PL/SQL. Programmers can
embed SQL statements into these programming languages.

A **user-defined function** is similar to a computer program function and provides a re-
usable, single-purpose shortcut to completing some task. Stored in the database that uses it,
the function receives input values, and it returns a calculated or otherwise processed result.
A mathematical example is a function to compute the square root of a number. An example
for the HSD database would be a function similar to the one described in Appendix E to
concatenate a customer name in a last-name-first order (e.g., *John* and *Smith* would become
Smith, John). User-defined functions can be used in SQL queries, SQL views, and stored
procedures.

A **stored procedure** is similar to a computer program subroutine, but it is stored within
the database that performs database activity. An example for the HSD database would be
a stored procedure to update the columns of INVOICE for a particular InvoiceNumber as
LINE_ITEMs are added to the INVOICE. Application programs, Web applications, and
interactive query users can invoke the stored procedure, pass parameters to it, and receive
results.

---

[3]Some recent versions of DBMS systems allow SQL/PSM components to be written in standard programming language. For example, Microsoft SQL Server 2014 allows them to be written in C++.

[4]For more information on triggers, stored procedures, and their uses, see David M. Kroenke and David J.
Auer, *Database Processing: Fundamentals, Design, and Implementation*, 13th edition (Upper Saddle River,
NJ: Prentice Hall, 2014): Chapters 7, 10A, 10B, and 10C.

A **trigger** is a program attached to a specific table or view within a database and executed ("fired") by the DBMS when specific events occur using that table or view. The events are typically SQL commands that use the INSERT, UPDATE, or DELETE statements. These events are then handled with BEFORE, AFTER, or INSTEAD OF trigger logic. Thus, you find such trigger combinations as BEFORE DELETE, INSTEAD OF UPDATE, and AFTER INSERT. (Note that these are only some examples—see Appendix E for a full discussion of the nine possible combinations of trigger logic and SQL statements.)

Different DBMS products support different sets of triggers. For example, Oracle Database Express Edition 11*g* Release 2 supports BEFORE, AFTER, and INSTEAD OF triggers. MySQL 5.6 supports only BEFORE and AFTER triggers, while SQL Server 2014 supports AFTER and INSTEAD OF triggers.

WEB APPLICATION DATABASE PROCESSING

Today, Web applications based on database processing are the rule, not the exception. For example, *Amazon.com*, *Facebook*, and *Twitter* (and thousands of other Web applications) could not function without a well organized and efficient database processing environment to support them. Therefore, it is important that you thoroughly understand the Web application database processing environment.

The environment in which today's Internet technology database applications reside is rich and complicated. As shown in Figure 7-4, a typical Web server needs to publish applications that involve data of many different data types. In this text, we have considered only relational databases, but there are many other data types as well.

Several standard interfaces have been developed for accessing database servers. Every DBMS product has an **Application Programming Interface (API)**. An API is a collection of objects, methods, and properties for executing DBMS functions from program code. Unfortunately, each DBMS has its own API, and APIs vary from one DBMS product

FIGURE 7-4

The Web Application Database Processing Environment

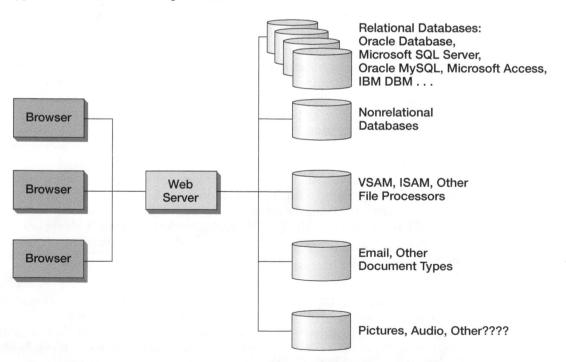

to another. To save programmers from having to learn to use many different interfaces, the computer industry has developed standards for database access.

The **Open Database Connectivity (ODBC)** standard was developed in the early 1990s to provide a DBMS-independent means for processing relational database data. It is a well-established standard and is seeing new prominence as the preferred tool to connect applications and relational databases to the "NoSQL" nonrelational data structures introduced in Chapter 8 and discussed in detail in Appendix K, "Big Data." Because it is a widely known and implemented standard, we will use it in this chapter.

In the mid-1990s, Microsoft announced **OLE DB**, which is an object-oriented interface that encapsulates data-server functionality. OLE DB was designed not just for access to relational databases, but also for accessing many other types of data. OLE DB is readily accessible to programmers, using such programming languages as C, C#, and Java. However, OLE DB is not as accessible to users of Visual Basic (VB) and scripting languages. Therefore, Microsoft developed **Active Data Objects (ADO)**, which is a set of objects for utilizing OLE DB that is designed for use by any language, including Visual Basic (VB), VBScript, and JScript. ADO has now been followed by **ADO.NET** (pronounced "A-D-O-dot-NET"), which is an improved version of ADO developed as part of Microsoft's **.NET** (pronounced "dot-NET") initiative.

ASP.NET, the follow up to Microsoft **Active Server Pages** is used in Web pages to create Web-based database applications. Shown in Figure 7-3 as part of the database processing environment, ASP.NET uses Hypertext Markup Language (HTML) and the Microsoft .NET languages to create Web pages that can read and write database data and transmit it over public and private networks, using Internet protocols. ASP.NET runs on Microsoft's Web server product, Internet Information Services (IIS). ASP.NET is part of the Microsoft .NET Framework and relies upon ADO.NET. The use of ADO.NET is illustrated in Figure 7-5.[5]

Also shown in Figure 7-3 is **Java Server Pages (JSP)** technology. JSP is a combination of HTML and Java that accomplishes the same function as ASP by compiling pages into Java servlets. JSPs are often used on the open-source **Apache** Web server. Another favorite combination of Web developers is the Apache Web server with the MySQL database and either the Pearl or PHP language. This combination is called **AMP** (Apache–MySQL–PHP/Pearl). When running on the Linux operating system, it is referred to as **LAMP**; when running on the Windows operating system, it is referred to as **WAMP**.[6]

In a Web-based database processing environment, if the Web server and the DBMS can run on the same computer, the system has **two-tier architecture**. (One tier is for the browsers, and one is for the Web server/DBMS computer.) Alternatively, the Web server and DBMS can run on different computers, in which case the system has **three-tier architecture**.

FIGURE 7-5

The Role of ADO.NET

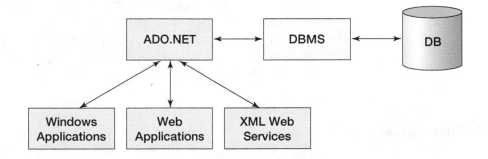

---

[5]For more information on the Microsoft .NET framework and ADO.NET, see David M. Kroenke and David J. Auer, *Database Processing: Fundamentals, Design, and Implementation*, 13th edition (Upper Saddle River, NJ: Prentice Hall, 2014): Chapter 11.

[6]For information on JSP, JDBC, and related technology and tools, see David M. Kroenke and David J. Auer, *Database Processing: Fundamentals, Design, and Implementation*, 13th edition (Upper Saddle River, NJ: Prentice Hall, 2014): Chapter 11.

High-performance applications might use many Web server computers, and in some systems several computers can run the DBMS as well. In the latter case, if the DBMS computers are processing the same databases, the system is referred to as a *distributed database*. (Distributed databases are discussed in Chapter 8.)

ODBC

Now that we have discussed various Web application database processing connectivity, we will examine it in depth and learn how to use it to create a Web application for Heather Sweeney Designs that connects to and uses the HSD database.

The ODBC standard allows programmers to code instructions to various DBMS products using ODBC standard statements. These instructions are passed to an ODBC driver, which translates them into the API of the particular DBMS in use. The driver receives results back from the DBMS and translates those results into a form that is part of the ODBC standard.

ODBC Architecture The basic **ODBC architecture** in a three-tier Web server environment—*in a configuration without OLE DB and ADO*—is shown in Figure 7-6. The application program, the **ODBC driver manager**, and the **ODBC DBMS driver** (a multiple-tier driver in this case) all reside on the Web server. The DBMS driver sends requests to data sources, which reside on the database server. According to the ODBC standard, a **data source** is the database and its associated DBMS, operating system, and network platform.

The application issues requests to create a connection with a data source; to issue SQL statements and receive results; to process errors; and to start, commit, and roll back transactions. ODBC provides a standard means for each of these requests, and it defines a standard set of error codes and messages.

The driver manager serves as an intermediary between the application and the DBMS drivers. When the application requests a connection, the driver determines the type of DBMS that processes a given ODBC data source and loads that driver in memory (if it is not already loaded).

A **driver** processes ODBC requests and submits specific SQL statements to a given type of data source. There is a different driver for each data source type. It is the responsibility of the driver to ensure that standard ODBC commands execute correctly. The driver also converts data source error codes and messages into the ODBC standard codes and messages.

ODBC identifies two types of drivers: single tier and multiple tier. A **single-tier driver** processes both ODBC calls and SQL statements. A **multiple-tier driver** processes ODBC calls but passes the SQL requests directly to the database server. Although it may reformat an SQL request to conform to the dialect of a particular data source, it does not process the SQL.

Establishing an ODBC Data Source Name A data source is an ODBC data structure that identifies a database and the DBMS that processes it. The three types of data sources are file, system, and user. A **file data source** is a file that can be shared among database users. The only requirement is that the users have the same DBMS driver and privilege to access the database. A **system data source** is local to a single computer. The

FIGURE 7-6

ODBC Three-Tier Web Server Architecture

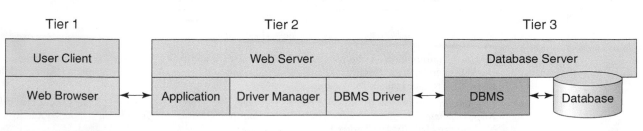

SQL Commands

operating system and any user on that system (with proper permissions) can use a system data source. A **user data source** is available only to the user who created it. Each created data source is given a **data source name (DSN)** that is used to reference the data source.

In general, the best choice for Internet applications is to create a *system data source* on the *Web server*. Browser users then access the Web server, which, in turn, uses a system data source to set up a connection with the DBMS and the database.

We need a system data source for the Heather Sweeney Designs HSD database so that we can use it in a Web database processing application. We created the HSD database in SQL Server 2014, and the system data source will have to provide a connection to the SQL Server 2014 DBMS. To create a system data source in the Windows operating system, you use the **ODBC Data Source Administrator**.

In Windows 7, you open the ODBC Data Source Administrator[7] as follows:

1. Open the Windows Control Panel by clicking the **Start** button and then clicking **Control Panel**.
2. In the Control Panel window, click **System and Security**.
3. In the System and Security window, click **Administrative Tools**.
4. In the Administrative Tools window, double-click the **Data Sources (ODBC)** shortcut icon.

Here is how you create a system data source named HSD for use with the Heather Sweeney Designs HSD database on a Microsoft SQL Server 2014 DBMS:

1. In the ODBC Data Source Administrator, click the **System DSN** tab and then click the **Add** button.
2. In the Create New Data Source dialog box, we need to connect to SQL Server 2014, so we select the **ODBC Driver 11 for SQL Server**, as shown in Windows 7 in Figure 7-7.
3. Click the **Finish** button. The Create New Data Source to SQL Server dialog box appears, as shown in Figure 7-8(a)
4. In the Create New Data Source to SQL Server dialog box, enter the information for the HSD database shown in Figure 7-8(a) (note that the database server is selected from the Server drop-down list), and then click the **Next** button.
   - **NOTE:** If the SQL server does not appear in the Server drop-down list, enter it manually as **ComputerName\SQLServerInstanceName**.

FIGURE 7-7

The Create New Data Source Dialog Box

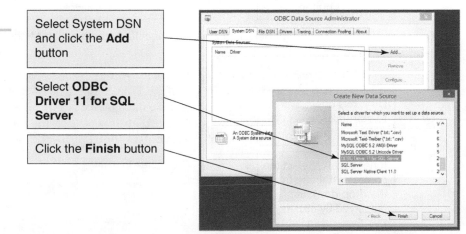

Select System DSN and click the **Add** button

Select **ODBC Driver 11 for SQL Server**

Click the **Finish** button

---

[7]*Warning:* There are actually *multiple versions* of the ODBC Data Source Administrator in the 64-bit versions of Windows 8.1, Windows 8, and Windows 7. You must use the correct version depending on whether the DBMS you are using is a 32-bit or 64-bit version. To make matters worse, all the versions use the same file name of *odbcad32.exe*! The instructions on this page open the 32-bit version, which works with 32-bit programs. If you are using ODBC to connect to a 64-bit version of Microsoft Access 2013, Microsoft SQL Server 2014, Oracle Database Express Edition 11*g* Release 2, or MySQL 5.6, then you must use the version of the ODBC Data Source Administrator located at **C:\Windows\SysWOW64\odbcad32.exe**.

FIGURE 7-8

The Create New Data Source to SQL Server Dialog Box

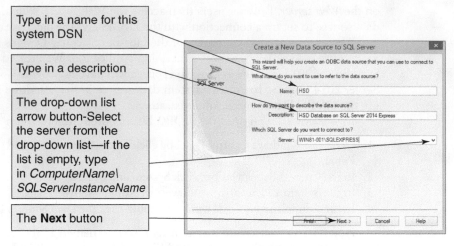

Type in a name for this system DSN

Type in a description

The drop-down list arrow button-Select the server from the drop-down list—if the list is empty, type in *ComputerName\ SQLServerInstanceName*

The **Next** button

(a) Naming the ODBC Data Source

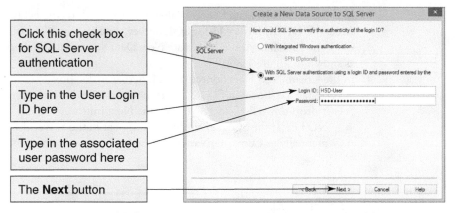

Click this check box for SQL Server authentication

Type in the User Login ID here

Type in the associated user password here

The **Next** button

(b) Selecting the User Login ID Authentication Method

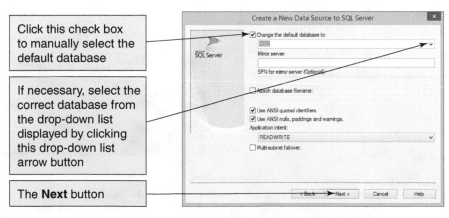

Click this check box to manually select the default database

If necessary, select the correct database from the drop-down list displayed by clicking this drop-down list arrow button

The **Next** button

(c) Selecting the Default Database

FIGURE 7-8   **Continued**

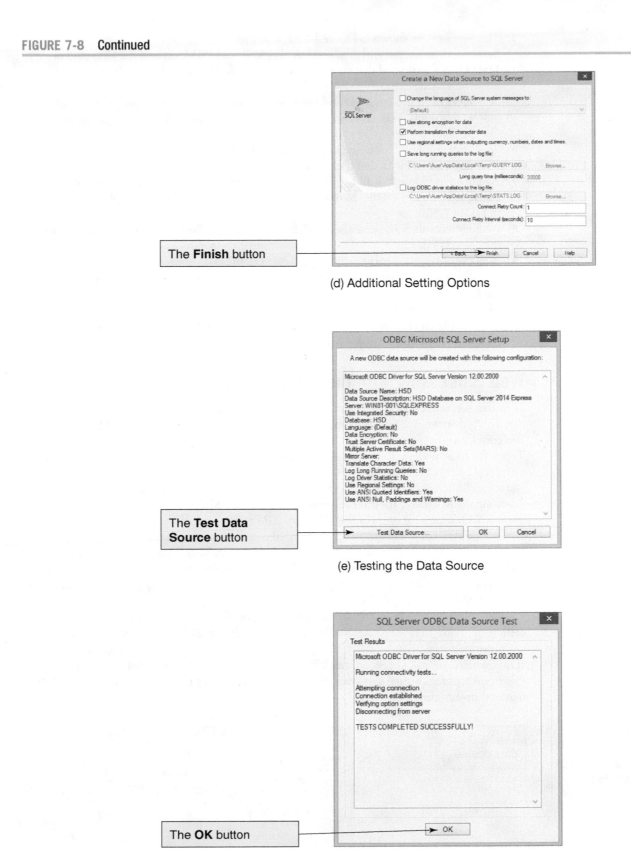

The **Finish** button

(d) Additional Setting Options

The **Test Data Source** button

(e) Testing the Data Source

The **OK** button

(f) The Successfully Tested Data Source

5. The next step, as shown in Figure 7-8(b), is to click the radio button that selects **SQL Server authentication** and then enter the Login ID of **HSD-User** and the Password of **HSD-User + password** that we created in Chapter 6. After this data has been entered, click then **Next** button.

   ■ **NOTE:** If the Login ID and Password are not correct, an error message is displayed at this point. Make sure you have correctly created the SQL Server login, as discussed in Chapter 6, and that you have entered the correct data here.

6. As shown in Figure 7-8(c), click the check box to change the default database, set the default database to **HSD**, and then click the **Next** button.

7. As shown in Figure 7-8(d), we do not need to set any options on the next page, so click the **Finish** button. The ODBC Microsoft SQL Server Setup dialog box is displayed, as shown in Figure 7-8(e).

8. In the Microsoft SQL Server Setup dialog box, click the **Test Data Source** button to test the connection.

9. If all the settings are correct, the **SQL Server ODBC Data Source Test** dialog box appears, as shown in Figure 7-8(f), showing that the tests were successfully completed. Click the **OK** button.

10. Click the **OK** button in the ODBC Microsoft SQL Server Setup dialog box.

11. The completed HSD system data source is shown in Figure 7-9. Click the **OK** button to close the ODBC Data Source Administrator.

Web Processing with the Microsoft IIS

Now that we have created our ODBC data source, let us take a look at Web database processing. To do this, we will need a Web server to store the Web pages that we will build and use. We could use the Apache HTTP Server (available from the Apache Software Foundation). This is the most widely used Web server, and there is a version that will run on just about every operating system in existence. However, because we have been using the Windows operating system and Microsoft Access 2013 in "The Access Workbench" sections, we will build a Web site using the Microsoft **Internet Information Services (IIS)** Web server. One advantage of using this Web server for users of the Windows XP Professional, Windows Vista, and Windows 7 operating systems is that IIS is included with the operating system: IIS version 5.1 is included with Windows XP, IIS version 7.0 is included with Windows Vista, and IIS version 7.5 is included with Windows 7. IIS is not installed by default, but it can be easily installed at any time. This means that any user can practice creating and using Web pages on his or her own Windows workstation.

Complete instructions for setting up IIS 7.5 on Windows 7, including installing and setting up both PHP and the NetBeans IDE (which are discussed later in this chapter), are presented in Appendix E, "Getting Started with Web Servers, PHP, and the NetBeans IDE," which you can access online. We strongly recommend that you read that appendix at this point and make sure that your computer is correctly set up before continuing with the material in this chapter.

FIGURE 7-9

The Completed HSD System Data Source

The **HSD** system data source

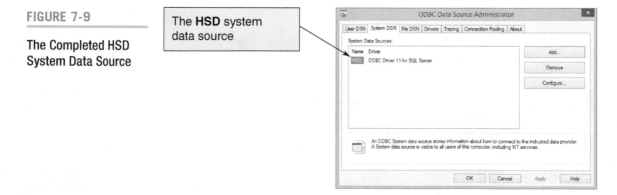

BTW

This discussion of Web database processing has been written to be as widely applicable as possible. With minor adjustments to the following steps, you should be able to use the Apache Web server if you have it available. Whenever possible, we have chosen to use products and technologies that are available for many operating systems.

When IIS is installed, it creates an **inetpub folder** on the C: drive as C:\inetpub. Within the inetpub folder is the **wwwroot folder**, which is where IIS stores the most basic Web pages used by the Web server. Figure 7-10 shows this directory structure after IIS has been installed, with the files in the wwwroot folder displayed in the file pane. Note that the wwwroot folder security properties need to be set correctly to allow users access to this folder. As discussed in detail in the online Appendix I, we need to give the Windows Users group *Modify* and *Write* permissions to the wwwroot folder.

IIS is managed using a program called **Internet Information Services Manager** in Windows 8.1, Window 8, and Windows 7. To open either program, open **Control Panel** and then select **Administrative Tools**. The shortcut icon for Internet Information Services/ Internet Information Services Manager is located in Administrative Tools. Figure 7-11 shows the Internet Information Services Manager window.

Note that the files shown in the **Default Web Site folder** in Figure 7-11 are the same files that are in the wwwroot folder in Figure 7-10—they are the default files created by IIS when it is installed. The file **iisstart.htm** generates the Web page that Internet Explorer (or any other Web browser contacting this Web server over the Internet) will see displayed.

FIGURE 7-10

The IIS wwwroot Folder

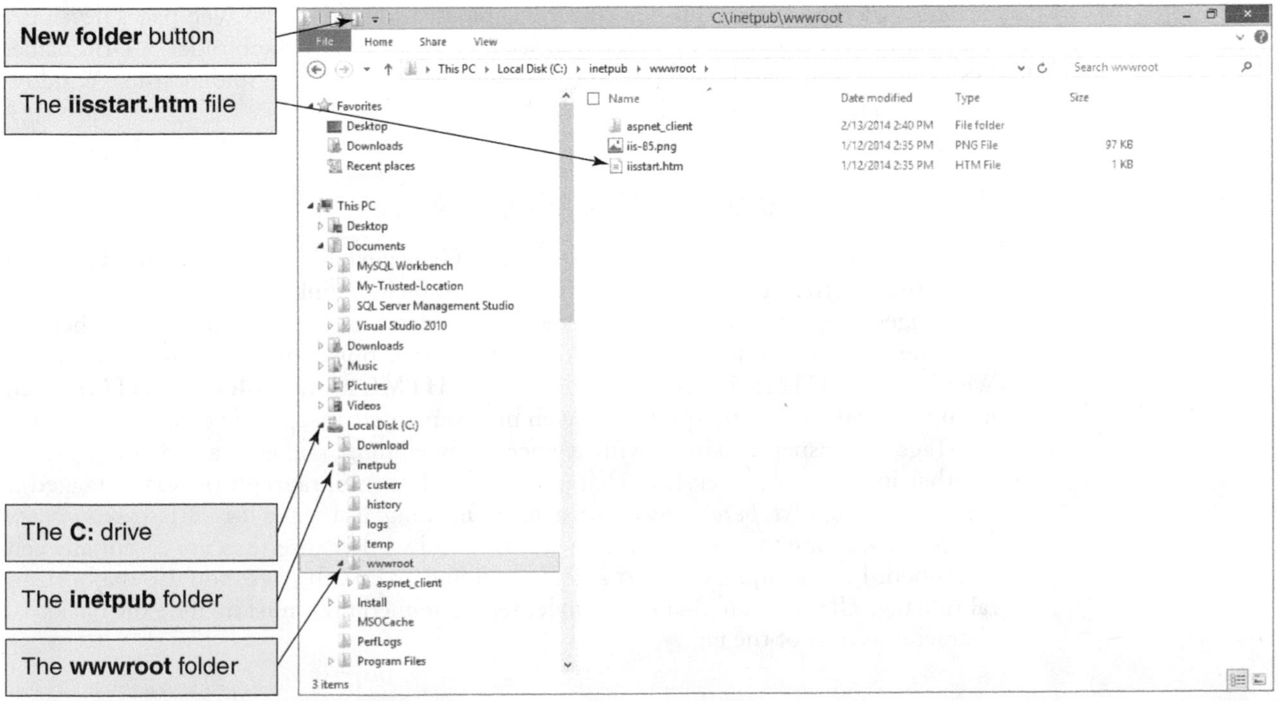

FIGURE 7-11

Managing IIS

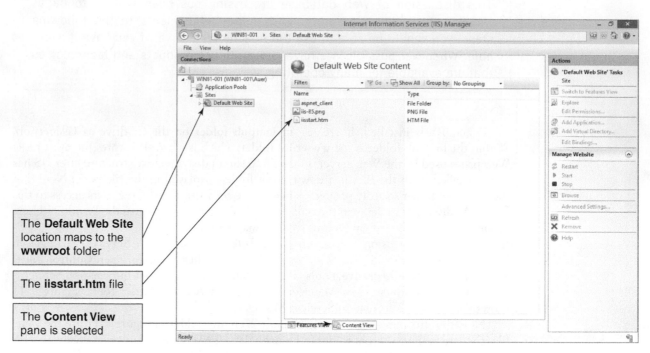

The **Default Web Site** location maps to the **wwwroot** folder

The **iisstart.htm** file

The **Content View** pane is selected

To test the Web server installation, open your Web browser, type in the URL **http://localhost**, and press the **Enter** key. For Windows 8.1, the Web page shown in Figure 7-12 appears. If the appropriate Web page is not displayed in your Web browser, your Web server is not installed properly.

Now, let us set up a small Web site that can be used for Web database processing of the HSD database. First, we will create a new folder named DBC (database concepts) under the wwwroot folder. This new folder will be used to hold all the Web pages developed in discussions and exercises in this book. Second, we will create a subfolder of DBC named HSD. This folder will hold the HSD Web site. You create these folders using Windows Explorer, which is shown in Figure 7-10.

Getting Started with HTML Web Pages

The most basic Web pages are created using **Hypertext Markup Language (HTML)**. The term *hypertext* refers to the fact that you can include links to other objects, such as Web pages, maps, pictures, and even audio and video files in a Web page, and when you click the link you are immediately taken to that other object and it is displayed in your Web browser. HTML itself is a standard set of **HTML syntax rules** and **HTML document tags** that can be interpreted by Web browsers to create specific onscreen displays.

Tags are usually paired, with a specific beginning tag and a matching ending tag that includes the backslash character (/). Thus, a paragraph of text is tagged as <p>{*paragraph text here*}</p>, and a main heading is tagged as <h1>{*heading text here*}</h1>. Some tags do not need a separate end tag because they are essentially self-contained. For example, to insert a horizontal line on a Web page, you use the horizontal rule tag, <hr />. Note that such single, self-contained tags must include the backslash character as part of the tag.

FIGURE 7-12

The Default IIS Web Page

This Web page is
generated by the
iisstart.htm file

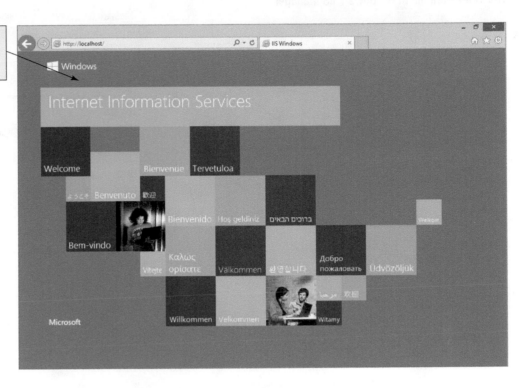

The rules of HTML are defined as standards by the **World Wide Web Consortium (W3C)**, and the details of current and proposed standards can be found on their Web site (this site also has several excellent tutorials on HTML[8]). The W3C Web site has current standards for HTML; **Extensible Markup Language (XML)**, which we will discuss later in this chapter; and a mixture of the two called **XHTML**. A full discussion of these standards is beyond the scope of this text—this chapter uses the new **HTML5** standard.

In this chapter, we will create a simple HTML home page for the Heather Sweeney Designs Web site and place it in the HSD folder. We will discuss some of the numerous available Web page editors shortly, but all you really need to create Web pages is a simple text editor. For this first Web page, we will use the Microsoft Notepad ASCII text editor, which has the advantage of being supplied with every version of the Windows operating system.

The index.html Web Page

The name for the file we are going to create is **index.html**. We need to use the name index .html because it is a special name as far as Web servers are concerned. The file name index .html is one of only a few file names that *most* Web servers automatically display when a URL request is made without a specific file reference, and thus it will become the new default display page for our Web database application. However, note the phrase "*most*

---

[8]To learn more about HTML, go to the W3C Web site. For good HTML tutorials, see the following tutorials by David Raggett: "Getting Started with HTML" "More Advanced Features" and "Adding a Touch of Style".

FIGURE 7-13

The index.html file in Windows 7 IIS Manager

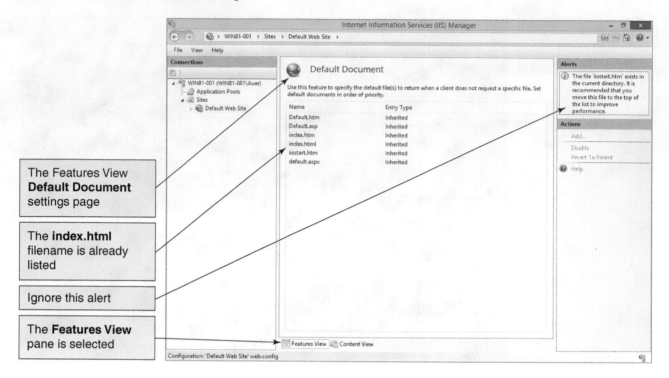

The Features View **Default Document** settings page

The **index.html** filename is already listed

Ignore this alert

The **Features View** pane is selected

Web servers" in the last sentence. Apache, IIS 7.0, IIS 7.5, IIS 8.0 and IIS 8.5 (as shown in Figure 7-13) are configured to recognize index.html; however, IIS 5.1 is not.[9]

Creating the index.html Web Page

Now we can create the index.html Web page, which consists of the basic HTML statements shown in Figure 7-14. Figure 7-15 shows the HTML code in Notepad.

BTW

In the HTML code for index.html, the HTML code segment:

```
<!DOCTYPE html>
```

is an HTML/XML **document type declaration (DTD)**, which is used to check and validate the contents of the code that you write. DTDs are discussed later in this chapter. For right now, just include the code as it is written.

---

[9]If you are using Windows XP and IIS 5.1, you need to add index.html to the list of recognized files. You do this by using Internet Information Services. In the Internet Information Services window, you right-click the **Web Sites** object to display the shortcut menu and then click **Properties** to display the Web Sites Properties dialog box. You then click the **Documents** tab and the **Add** button to display the Add Default Document dialog box. Then enter the document name (file name) **index.html** and click the **OK** button. Finally, we close the Web Sites Properties dialog box.

FIGURE 7-14

The HTML Code for the index.html File in the *HSD* Folder

```html
<!DOCTYPE html>
<html>
    <head>
        <title>Heather Sweeney Designs Demonstration Pages Home Page</title>
        <meta charset="UTF-8">
        <meta name="viewport" content="width=device-width, initial-scale=1.0">
    </head>
    <body>
        <h1 style="text-align: center; color: blue">
            Database Concepts (7th Edition)
        </h1>
        <p style="text-align: center; font-weight: bold">
            David M. Kroenke
        </p>
        <p style="text-align: center; font-weight: bold">
            David J. Auer
        </p>
        <hr />
        <h2 style="text-align: center; color: blue">
            Welcome to the Heather Sweeney Designs Home Page
        </h2>
        <hr />
        <p>Chapter 7 Demonstration Pages From Figures in the Text:</p>
        <p>Example 1:   
            <a href="ReadSeminar.php">
                Display the SEMINAR Table (No surrogate key)
            </a>
        </p>
        <hr />
    </body>
</html>
```

If we now use the URL **http://localhost/DBC/HSD**, we get the Web page shown in Figure 7-16.

Web Database Processing Using PHP

Now that we have our basic Web site set up, we will expand its capabilities with a Web development environment that allows us to connect Web pages to our database. Several technologies allow us to do this. Developers using Microsoft products usually work with the .NET framework and use ASP.NET technology. Developers who use the Apache Web server may prefer creating JSP files in the JavaScript scripting language or using the Java programming language in the Java Enterprise Edition (Java EE) environment.

The PHP Scripting Language   In this chapter, we will use the scripting language **PHP**. PHP, which is an abbreviation for **PHP: Hypertext Processor** (and which was previously known as the *Personal Hypertext Processor*), is a scripting language that can be embedded in Web pages. PHP is extremely popular. In the January of 2013, more than 2 million Internet domains had servers running PHP,[10] and the May 2014 TIOBE

---

[10]See the PHP Web site.

FIGURE 7-15

The HTML Code for the index.html File in Notepad

The **index.html** HTML code—note how indentation is used to keep the code organized and readable

```
index.html - Notepad
File  Edit  Format  View  Help
<!DOCTYPE html>
<html>
    <head>
        <title>Heather Sweeney Designs Demonstration Pages Home Page</title>
        <meta charset="UTF-8">
        <meta name="viewport" content="width=device-width, initial-scale=1.0">
    </head>
    <body>
        <h1 style="text-align: center; color: blue">
                    Database Concepts (7th Edition)
            </h1>
            <p style="text-align: center; font-weight: bold">
                    David M. Kroenke
            </p>
            <p style="text-align: center; font-weight: bold">
                    David J. Auer
            </p>
            <hr />
            <h2 style="text-align: center; color: blue">
                    Welcome to the Heather Sweeney Designs Home Page
            </h2>
            <hr />
            <p>Chapter 7 Demonstration Pages From Figures in the Text:</p>
            <p>Example 1:   
                    <a href="ReadSeminar.php">
                            Display the SEMINAR Table (No surrogate key)
                    </a>
            </p>
            <!-- New Code Added Here -->
            <hr />
        </body>
</html>
```

FIGURE 7-16

The index.html Web Page in HSD

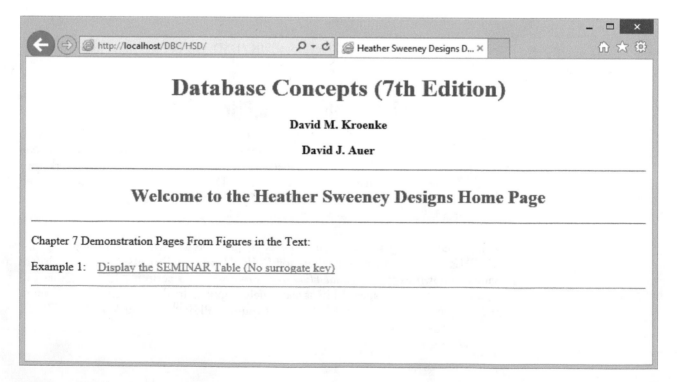

Programming Community Index ranked PHP as the seventh most popular programming language (following, in order, C, Java, Objective-C, C++, Visual Basic, and C#).[11] In May of 2013, PHP had ranked sixth (leading Visual Basic), while in 2010 PHP held down third place for a while. PHP appears to be maintaining popularity among programmers and Web page designers. PHP is easy to learn and can be used in most Web server environments and with most databases. It is also an open-source product that is freely downloadable from the PHP Web site.

The NetBeans Integrated Development Environment (IDE)   Although a simple text editor such as Notepad is fine for simple Web pages, as we start creating more complex pages we will move to an **Integrated Development Environment (IDE)**. An IDE gives you the most robust and user-friendly means of creating and maintaining your Web pages. If you are working with Microsoft products, you will likely use Visual Studio (or the freely downloadable Visual Studio 2013 Express Edition, available at **www.microsoft.com/express/**), or the WebMatrix3 (downloadable from **www.microsoft.com/web/webmatrix/**). If you are working with JavaScript or Java, you might prefer the Eclipse IDE.

For this chapter, we will again turn to the open-source development community and use the **NetBeans IDE**. NetBeans provides a framework that can be modified by add-in plugin modules for many purposes. For PHP, we can use Netbeans as modified for the **PHP plugin**, which is specifically intended to provide a PHP development environment in NetBeans.

For more information on installing and using PHP and NetBeans, see Appendix I, "Getting Started with Web Servers, PHP and the NetBeans IDE." Figure 7-17 shows the

FIGURE 7-17

The HTML Code for the index.html File in the NetBeans IDE

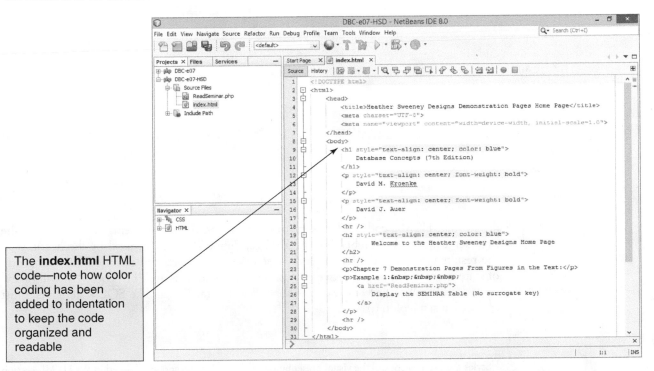

The **index.html** HTML code—note how color coding has been added to indentation to keep the code organized and readable

---

[11]See the Tiobe Software Web site.

index.html file as created in a NetBeans project named DBC-e07-HSD in the NetBeans IDE. Compare this version with the Notepad version in Figure 7-16.

Now that we have our basic Web site set up, we will start to integrate PHP into the Web pages. First, we will create a page to read data from a database table and display the results in a Web page. Specifically, we will create a Web page in the HSD folder named ReadSeminar.php to run the SQL query:

```
/* *** SQL-UPDATE-CH07-01 *** */
SELECT * FROM SEMINAR;
```

This page displays the result of the query, without the table's surrogate key of SeminarID, in a Web page. The HTML and PHP code for ReadSeminar.php is shown in Figure 7-18, and the same code is shown in the NetBeans IDE in Figure 7-19.

If you use the URL **http://localhost/DBC/HSD** in your Web browser and then click the **Example 1: Display the SEMINAR Table (No surrogate key)** link on that page, the Web page shown in Figure 7-20 is displayed.

The ReadSeminar.php code blends HTML (executed on the user's workstation) and PHP statements (executed on the Web server). In Figure 7-18, the statements included between **<?php** and **?>** is program code that is to be executed on the Web server computer. All the rest of the code is HTML that is generated and sent to the browser client. In Figure 7-18, the statements:

```
<!DOCTYPE html>
<html>
    <head>
        <meta charset=UTF-8">
        <title>ReadSeminar PHP Page</title>
        <style type="text/css">
            h1 {text-align: center; color: blue}
            h2 {font-family: Ariel, sans-serif;
                text-align: left; color: blue}
            p.footer {text-align: center}
            table.output {font-family: Ariel, sans-serif}
        </style>
    </head>
    <body>
```

are normal HTML code. When sent to the browser, these statements set the title of the browser window to ReadSeminar PHP Page; define styles to be used by the headings,[12] the results table, and the footer; and cause other HTML-related actions. The next group of statements are included between <?php and ?> and thus are PHP code that will be executed on the Web server. Also note that all PHP statements, like SQL statements, must end with a semicolon (;).

---

[12]Styles are used to control the visual presentation of the Web page and are defined in the HTML section between the <style> and </style> tags. For more information about styles, see David Raggett's tutorial "Adding a Touch of Style".

FIGURE 7-18

The HTML and PHP Code for ReadSeminar.php

```
<!DOCTYPE html>
<html>
    <head>
        <meta charset=UTF-8">
        <title>ReadSeminar PHP Page</title>
        <style type="text/css">
            h1 {text-align: center; color: blue}
            h2 {font-family: Ariel, sans-serif; text-align: left; color: blue}
            p.footer {text-align: center}
            table.output {font-family: Ariel, sans-serif}
        </style>
    </head>
    <body>
<?php
        // Get connection
        $Conn = odbc_connect('HSD', 'HSD-User','HSD-User+password');

        // Test connection
        if (!Conn)
            {
            exit ("ODBC Connection Failed: " . $Conn);
            }
        // Create SQL statement
        $SQL = "SELECT * FROM SEMINAR";

        // Execute SQL statement
        $RecordSet = odbc_exec($Conn,$SQL);

        // Test existence of recordset
        if (!$RecordSet)
            {
            exit ("SQL Statement Error: " . $SQL);
            }
?>
        <!-- Page Headers -->
        <h1>
            The Heather Sweeney Designs SEMINAR Table
        </h1>
        <hr />
        <h2>
            SEMINAR
        </h2>
<?php

        // Table headers
        echo "<table class='output' border='1'>
            <tr>
                <th>SeminarDate</th>
                <th>SeminarTime</th>
                <th>Location</th>
                <th>SeminarTitle</th>
            </tr>";
```

(continued)

FIGURE 7-18   Continued

```php
        // Table data
        while($RecordSetRow = odbc_fetch_array($RecordSet))
            {
            echo "<tr>";
            echo "<td>" . $RecordSetRow['SeminarDate'] . "</td>";
            echo "<td>" . $RecordSetRow['SeminarTime'] . "</td>";
            echo "<td>" . $RecordSetRow['Location'] . "</td>";
            echo "<td>" . $RecordSetRow['SemniarTitle'] . "</td>";
            echo "</tr>";
            }
        echo "</table>";

        // Close connection
        odbc_close($Conn);
    ?>
        <br />
        <hr />
        <p class="footer">
            <a href="../HSD/index.html">
                Return to Heather Sweeney Designs Home Page
            </a>
        </p>
        <hr />
    </body>
</html>
```

FIGURE 7-19

The HTML and PHP Code for ReadSeminar.php in the NetBeans IDE

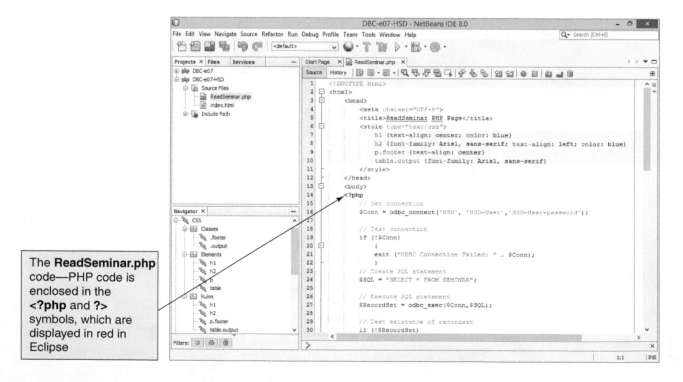

The **ReadSeminar.php** code—PHP code is enclosed in the **<?php** and **?>** symbols, which are displayed in red in Eclipse

FIGURE 7-20

The Results of ReadSeminar.php

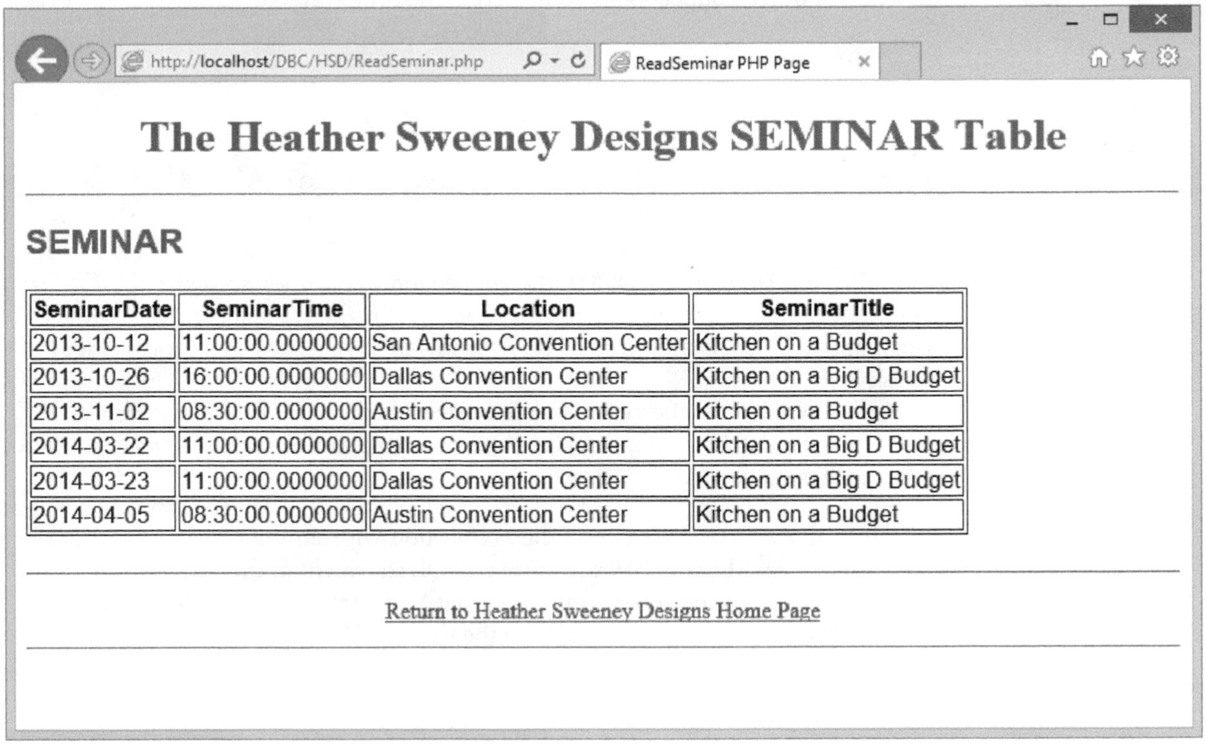

The browser window shows:

The Heather Sweeney Designs SEMINAR Table

SEMINAR

SeminarDate	SeminarTime	Location	SeminarTitle
2013-10-12	11:00:00.0000000	San Antonio Convention Center	Kitchen on a Budget
2013-10-26	16:00:00.0000000	Dallas Convention Center	Kitchen on a Big D Budget
2013-11-02	08:30:00.0000000	Austin Convention Center	Kitchen on a Budget
2014-03-22	11:00:00.0000000	Dallas Convention Center	Kitchen on a Big D Budget
2014-03-23	11:00:00.0000000	Dallas Convention Center	Kitchen on a Big D Budget
2014-04-05	08:30:00.0000000	Austin Convention Center	Kitchen on a Budget

Return to Heather Sweeney Designs Home Page

Creating a Connection to the Database   In the HTML and PHP code in Figure 7-18, the following PHP code is embedded in the HTML code to create and test a connection to the database:

```php
<?php
    // Get connection
    $Conn = odbc_connect('HSD', 'HSD-User', 'HSD-User+password');
    // Test connection
    if (!$Conn)
    {
        exit ("ODBC Connection Failed: " . $Conn);
    }
```

After it runs, the variable $Conn can be used to connect to the ODBC data source HSD. Note that all PHP variables start with the dollar sign symbol ($).

BTW

Be sure to use comments to document your Web pages. PHP code segments with two forward slashes (//) in front of them are comments. This symbol is used to define single-line comments. In PHP, comments can also be inserted in blocks between the symbols /* and */, whereas in HTML comments *must* be inserted between the symbols <!-- and -->.

The connection is used to open the HSD ODBC data source. Here the user ID of HSD-User and the password of HSD-User+password that we created in Chapter 6 are being used to authenticate the DBMS.

The test of the connection is contained in the code segment:

```
// Test connection
if (!$Conn)
{
    exit ("ODBC Connection Failed: " . $Conn);
}
```

In English, this statement says, "IF the connection Conn does not exist, THEN print the error message 'ODBC Connection Failed' followed by the contents of the variable $Conn." Note that the code (!Conn) means NOT Conn—in PHP the exclamation point symbol (!) means NOT.

At this point, a connection has been established to the DBMS via the ODBC data source, and the database is open. The $Conn variable can be used whenever a connection to the database is needed.

Creating a Recordset   Given the connection with an open database, the following code segment from Figure 7-18 will store an SQL statement in the variable $SQL and then use the PHP odbc_exec command to run that SQL statement against the database to retrieve the query results and store them in the variable $RecordSet:

```
// Create SQL statement
$SQL = "SELECT * FROM SEMINAR";
// Execute SQL statement
$RecordSet = odbc_exec($Conn, $SQL);
// Test existence of recordset
if (!$objRecordSet)
{
    exit ("SQL Statement Error: " . $SQL);
}
?>
```

Note that again you need to test the results to be sure the PHP command executed correctly.

Displaying the Results   Now that the recordset has been created and populated, we can process the recordset collection with the following code:

```
<!-- Page Headers -->
<h1>
    The Heather Sweeney Designs SEMINAR Table
</h1>
<hr />
<h2>
    SEMINAR
</h2>
<?php
```

```
       // Table headers
       echo "<table class='output' border='1'>
            <tr>
                 <th>SeminarDate</th>
                 <th>SeminarTime</th>
                 <th>Location</th>
                 <th>SeminarTitle</th>
            </tr>";
       // Table data
       while($RecordSetRow = odbc_fetch_array($RecordSet))
            {
            echo "<tr>";
            echo "<td>" . $RecordSetRow['SeminarDate'] . "</td>";
            echo "<td>" . $RecordSetRow['SeminarTime'] . "</td>";
            echo "<td>" . $RecordSetRow['Location'] . "</td>";
            echo "<td>" . $RecordSetRow['SeminarTitle'] . "</td>";
            echo "</tr>";
            }
       echo "</table>";
```

The HTML section defines the page headers, and the PHP section defines how to display the SQL results in a table format. Note the use of the PHP command echo to allow PHP to use HTML syntax within the PHP code section. Also note that a loop is executed to iterate through the rows of the recordset using the PHP variable $RecordSetRow.

Disconnecting from the Database   Now that we have finished running the SQL statement and displaying the results, we can end our ODBC connection to the database with the code:

```
       // Close connection
       odbc_close($Conn);
?>
```

The basic page we have created here illustrates the basic concepts of using ODBC and PHP to connect to a database and process data from that database in a Web database processing application. You can build on this foundation by studying PHP command syntax and incorporating additional PHP features into your Web pages. For more information on PHP, see the PHP documentation.

Updating a Table with PHP

The previous example of a PHP Web page just read data. The next example shows how to update table data by adding a row to a table with PHP. Figure 7-21 shows a modification we need to make to the HSD index.html file in order to link to the new pages we are going to create—modify your index.html file before creating the new pages. Figure 7-22 shows the modified HSD home page in the Web browser.

Figure 7-23 shows a Web page data entry form that will capture new seminar data and create a new row in the HSD SEMINAR table. This form has four data entry fields: the Seminar Date and Seminar Time fields are text boxes where the user types in the date and time of the new seminar, whereas the Location and Seminar Title have been

FIGURE 7-21

The HTML Code to Modify index.html File in the *HSD* Folder

```
        <p>Example 1:   
            <a href="ReadSeminar.php">
                Display the SEMINAR Table (No surrogate key)
            </a>
        </p>
        <!-- New Code Added Here -->
        <p>Example 2:   
            <a href="NewSeminarForm.html">
                Add a New Seminar to the SEMINAR Table
            </a>
        </p>
        <!-- New Code Added to Here -->
        <hr />
    </body>
</html>
```

FIGURE 7-22

The Modified HSD Web Home Page

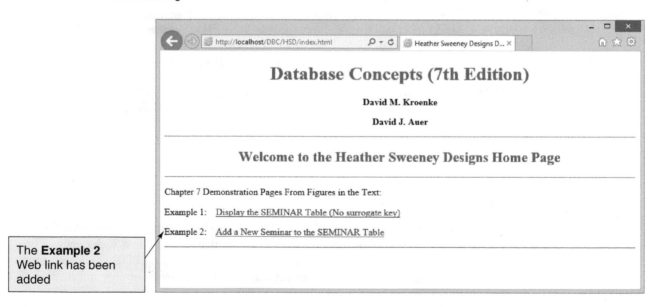

The **Example 2** Web link has been added

implemented as drop-down lists to control the possible values and to make sure they are spelled correctly. Figure 7-24 shows data entered in the form and illustrates the use of the Select Seminar Location drop-down box to select the Location value from a list (Houston Convention Center in this case).

When the user clicks the Add New Seminar button, the seminar is added to the database. If the results are successful, the acknowledgment Web page in Figure 7-25, which also displays the SEMINAR table with the new row added, will be displayed. We have tested these pages by adding a session of Heather's *Kitchen on a Budget* seminar to be held on June 23, 2014, starting at 2:00 pm at the Houston Convention Center.

FIGURE 7-23

The NewSeminarForm Web Page

Text box to enter data

Drop-down list arrow button to select data from set values

FIGURE 7-24

Entering Data Values in the NewSeminarForm Web Page

Data entered in the text box

Selecting a data value from the drop-down list

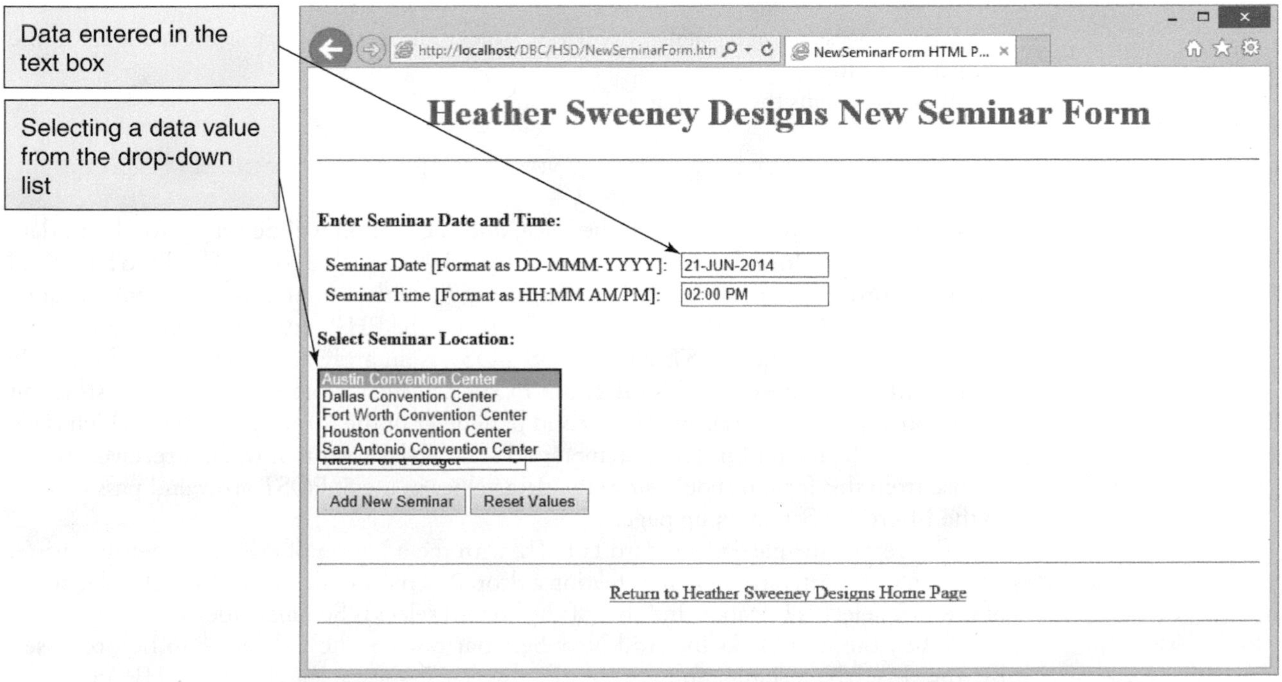

FIGURE 7-25

The New Seminar Data in the SEMINAR Table

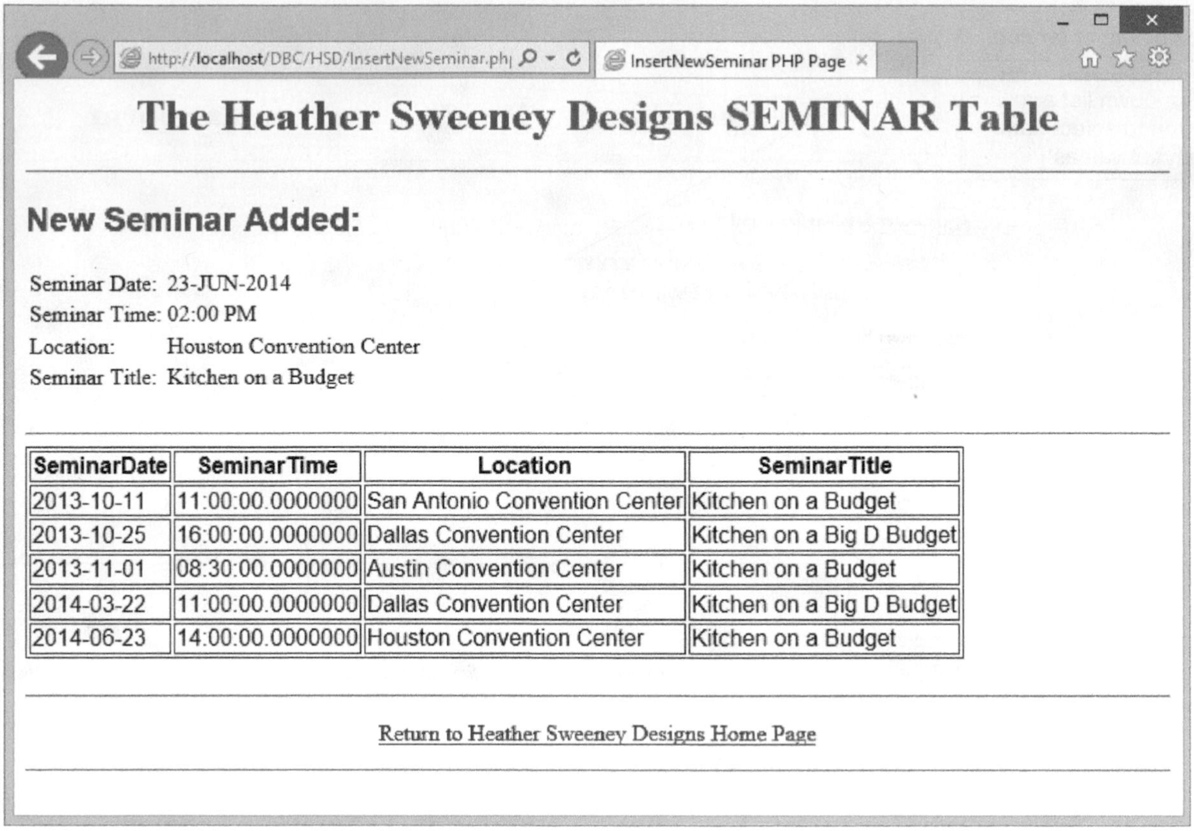

This processing necessitates two PHP pages. The first, shown in Figure 7-26, is the data entry form.

It also contains the form tag:

```
<form action="InsertNewSeminar.php" method="POST">
```

This tag defines a form section on the page, and the section will be set up to obtain data entry values. This form has only one data entry value: the table name. The **POST method** refers to a process that causes the data in the form (here the seminar date, the seminar time, the location, and the seminar title) to be delivered to the PHP server so it can be used in an array variable named $_POST. Note that $_POST is an array and thus can have multiple values. An alternative method is GET, but POST can carry more data, and this distinction is not too important to us here. The second parameter of the form tag is *action,* which is set to InsertNewSeminar.php. This parameter tells the Web server that when it receives the response from this form it should store the data values in the $_POST array and pass control to the InsertNewSeminar.php page.

The rest of the page is standard HTML, with the addition of the <select><option>...</option></select> structure for creating a drop-down list in the form. Note that the name of the first select is Location and that of the second select is SeminarTitle.

When the user clicks the Add New Seminar button, these data are to be processed by the InsertNewSeminar.php page. Figure 7-27 shows the HTML/PHP code for

FIGURE 7-26

The HTML Code for NewSeminarForm.html File

```
!DOCTYPE html>
<html>
   <head>
      <title>NewSeminarForm HTML Page</title>
      <meta charset="UTF-8">
      <meta name="viewport" content="width=device-width, initial-scale=1.0">
      <style type="text/css">
         h1 {text-align: center; color: blue}
         h2 {font-family: Ariel, sans-serif; text-align: left; color: blue}
         p.footer {text-align: center}
         table.output {font-family: Ariel, sans-serif}
      </style>
   </head>
   <body>
      <form action="InsertNewSeminar.php" method="POST">
         <!-- Page Headers -->
         <h1>
            Heather Sweeney Designs New Seminar Form
         </h1>
         <hr />
         <br />
         <p>
            <b>Enter Seminar Date and Time:</b>
         </p>
         <table>
            <tr>
               <td> Seminar Date [Format as DD-MMM-YYYY]:  </td>
               <td>
                  <input type="text" name="SeminarDate" size="16" />
               </td>
            </tr>
            <tr>
               <td> Seminar Time [Format as HH:MM AM/PM]:  </td>
               <td>
                  <input type="text" name="SeminarTime" size="16" />
               </td>
            </tr>
         </table>
         <p>
            <b>Select Seminar Location:</b>
         </p>
         <select name="Location">
            <option value="Austin Convention Center">Austin Convention Center</option>
            <option value="Dallas Convention Center">Dallas Convention Center</option>
            <option value="Fort Worth Convention Center">Fort Worth Convention
Center</option>
            <option value="Houston Convention Center">Houston Convention Center</option>
            <option value="San Antonio Convention Center">San Antonio Convention
Center</option>
         </select>
         <br />
         <p>
            <b>Select Seminar Title:</b>
         </p>
```

(continued)

FIGURE 7-26 **Continued**

```
<select name="SeminarTitle">
    <option value="Kitchen on a Budget">Kitchen on a Budget</option>
    <option value="Kitchen on a Big D Budget">Kitchen on a Big D Budget</option>
</select>
<br /><p>
    <input type="submit" value="Add New Seminar" />
    <input type="reset" value="Reset Values" />
</p>
</form>
<br />
<hr />
<p class="footer">
    <a href="../HSD/index.html">
        Return to Heather Sweeney Designs Home Page
    </a>
</p>
<hr />
</body>
</html>
```

InsertNewSeminar.php, the page that will be invoked when the response is received from the form. Note that the variable values for the INSERT statement are obtained from the $_POST[] array. First, we create short variable names for the $_POST version of the name, and then we use these short variable names to create the SQL INSERT statement. Thus:

```
// Create short variable names
$SeminarDate = $_POST["SeminarDate"];
$SeminarTime = $_POST["SeminarTime"];
$Location = $_POST["Location"];
$SeminarTitle = $_POST["SeminarTitle"];
// Create SQL statement to INSERT new data
$SQLINSERT = "INSERT INTO SEMINAR ";
$SQLINSERT .= "VALUES('$SeminarDate', '$SeminarTime',
    '$Location', '$SeminarTitle')";
```

Note the use of the **PHP concatenation operator (.=)** (a combination of a period and an equals sign) to combine the two sections of the SQL INSERT statement. As another example, to create a variable named $AllOfUs with the value *me, myself, and I* we would use:

```
$AllOfUs = "me, ";
$AllOfUs .= "myself, ";
$AllOfUs .= "and I";
```

Most of the code is self-explanatory, but make sure you understand how it works.

Challenges for Web Database Processing

Web database application processing is complicated by an important characteristic of HTTP. Specifically, HTTP is stateless; it has no provision for maintaining sessions between requests. Using HTTP, a client at a browser makes a request of a Web server.

FIGURE 7-27

The HTML/PHP Code to for the InsertNewSeminar.php File

```
<!DOCTYPE html>
<html>
    <head>
        <meta charset=UTF-8">
        <title>InsertNewSeminar PHP Page</title>
        <style type="text/css">
            h1 {text-align: center; color: blue}
            h2 {font-family: Ariel, sans-serif; text-align: left; color: blue}
            p.footer {text-align: center}
            table.output {font-family: Ariel, sans-serif}
        </style>
    </head>
    <body>
    <?php
        // Get connection
        $DSN = "HSD";
        $User = "HSD-User";
        $Password = "HSD-User+password";

        $Conn = odbc_connect($DSN, $User, $Password);

        // Test connection
        if (!$Conn)
            {
                exit ("ODBC Connection Failed: " . $Conn);
            }
        // Create short variable names
        $SeminarDate = $_POST["SeminarDate"];
        $SeminarTime = $_POST["SeminarTime"];
        $Location = $_POST["Location"];
        $SeminarTitle = $_POST["SeminarTitle"];

        // Create SQL statement to INSERT new data
        $SQLINSERT = "INSERT INTO SEMINAR ";
        $SQLINSERT .= "VALUES('$SeminarDate', '$SeminarTime', '$Location',
'$SeminarTitle')";

        // Execute SQL statement
        $Result = odbc_exec($Conn, $SQLINSERT);

        // Test existence of result
        echo "<h1>
            The Heather Sweeney Designs SEMINAR Table
            </h1>
            <hr />";
        if ($Result){
            echo "<h2>
                New Seminar Added:
            </h2>
            <table>
                <tr>";
                echo "<td>Seminar Date:</td>";
                echo "<td>" . $SeminarDate . "</td>";
                echo "</tr>";
                echo "<tr>";
                echo "<td>Seminar Time:</td>";
                echo "<td>" . $SeminarTime . "</td>";
```

(continued)

FIGURE 7-27   Continued

```php
            echo "</tr>";
            echo "<tr>";
            echo "<td>Location:</td>";
            echo "<td>" . $Location . "</td>";
            echo "</tr>";
            echo "<td>Seminar Title:</td>";
            echo "<td>" . $SeminarTitle . "</td>";
            echo "</tr>";
         echo "</table><br /><hr />";
         }
         else {
            exit ("SQL Statement Error: " . $SQL);
         }

    // Create SQL statement to read SEMINAR table data
    $SQL = "SELECT * FROM SEMINAR";

    // Execute SQL statement
    $RecordSet = odbc_exec($Conn,$SQL);

    // Test existence of recordset
    if (!$RecordSet)
        {
            exit ("SQL Statement Error: " . $SQL);
        }
    // Table headers
     echo "<table class='output' border='1'>
            <tr>
                <th>SeminarDate</th>
                <th>SeminarTime</th>
                <th>Location</th>
                <th>SeminarTitle</th>
            </tr>";

     // Table data
     while($RecordSetRow = odbc_fetch_array($RecordSet))
        {
        echo "<tr>";
        echo "<td>" . $RecordSetRow['SeminarDate'] . "</td>";
        echo "<td>" . $RecordSetRow['SeminarTime'] . "</td>";
        echo "<td>" . $RecordSetRow['Location'] . "</td>";
        echo "<td>" . $RecordSetRow['SeminarTitle'] . "</td>";
        echo "</tr>";
        }
     echo "</table>";

    // Close connection
    odbc_close($Conn);
  ?>
    <br />
    <hr />
    <p class="footer">
        <a href="../HSD/index.html">
            Return to Heather Sweeney Designs Home Page
        </a>
    </p>
    <hr />
 </body>
</html>
```

The server services the client request, sends results back to the browser, and forgets about the interaction with that client. A second request from that same client is treated as a new request from a new client. No data are kept to maintain a session or connection with the client.

This characteristic poses no problem for serving content, either static Web pages or responses to queries of a database. However, it is not acceptable for applications that require multiple database actions in an atomic transaction. Recall from Chapter 6 that in some cases a group of database actions needs to be grouped into a transaction, with all of them committed to the database or none of them committed to the database. In this case, the Web server or other program must augment the base capabilities of HTTP.

For example, IIS provides features and functions for maintaining data about sessions between multiple HTTP requests and responses. Using these features and functions, the application program on the Web server can save data to and from the browser. A particular session will be associated with a particular set of data. In this way, the application program can start a transaction, conduct multiple interactions with the user at the browser, make intermediate changes to the database, and commit or roll back all changes when ending the transaction. Other means are used to provide for sessions and session data with Apache.

In some cases, the application programs must create their own methods for tracking session data. PHP does include support for sessions—see the PHP documentation for more information.

The particulars of session management are beyond the scope of this chapter. However, you should be aware that HTTP is stateless, and, regardless of the Web server, additional code must be added to database applications to enable transaction processing.

SQL Injection Attacks

Our example of a Web page for a Web database application was a read-only example. To make a Web database application truly useful, we would have to have Web pages that allow us to input data as well as read it.

When we do this, however, we must use care in creating input Web pages, or we may create a vulnerability that allows an **SQL injection attack**. An SQL injection attack is similar to the application-level security example we discussed in Chapter 6 and attempts to issue SQL commands to the DBMS. For example, suppose that a Web page is used to update a user's phone number and thus requires the user to input the new phone number. The Web application would then use PHP code to create and run an SQL statement such as:

```
// Create SQL statement
$varSQL = "UPDATE CUSTOMER SET PHONE = '$NewPhone' ";
$varSQL .= "WHERE CustomerID = '$CustomerID'";
// Execute SQL statement
    $RecordSet = odbc_exec($Conn, $varSQL);
```

If the input value of NewPhone is not carefully checked, it may be possible for an attacker to use an input value such as:

```
678-345-1234; DELETE FROM CUSTOMER;
```

If this input value is accepted and the SQL statement is run, we may lose all data in the CUSTOMER table if the Web application has DELETE permissions on the CUSTOMER table. Therefore, Web database applications must be very carefully constructed to provide for data checking and to ensure that only necessary database permissions are granted.

DATABASE PROCESSING AND XML

XML is a standard means for defining the structure of documents and for transmitting documents from one computer to another. XML is important for database processing because it provides a standardized means of submitting data to a database and for receiving results back from the database. XML is a large, complicated subject that requires several books to explain fully. Here we touch on the fundamentals and further explain why XML is important for database processing.

The Importance of XML

Database processing and document processing need each other. Database processing needs document processing for transmitting database views, and document processing needs database processing for storing and manipulating data. In the early 1990s, the Web development and database communities began to meet, and the result of their work became XML.

XML provides a standardized yet customizable way to describe the content of documents. It can therefore be used to describe any database view but in a standardized way. Database data can automatically be extracted from XML documents. And there are standardized ways of defining how document components are mapped to database schema components and vice versa. Today, XML is used for many purposes. One of the most important is its use as a standardized means to define and communicate documents for processing over the Internet.

XML as a Markup Language

As a markup language, XML is significantly better than HTML in several ways. First, XML provides a clean separation between document structure, content, and materialization. XML has facilities for dealing with each, and they cannot be confounded, as they can with HTML.

Second, XML is standardized, but, as its name implies, the standards allow for extension by developers. With XML, you are not limited to a fixed set of elements with tags such as <h1>...</h1> and <p>...</p>. Instead, you can create your own tags.

Third, XML forces consistent tag use. HTML tags can be used for different purposes. For example, consider the following HTML:

```
<h2>HSD Seminar Data</h2>
```

Although the <h2> tag can be used to structurally mark a level-two heading in a Web page, it can be used for other purposes, too, such as causing "HSD Seminar Data" to be displayed in a particular font size, weight, and color. Because an HTML tag has potentially many purposes, you cannot rely on HTML tags to describe the structure of an HTML page.

In contrast, the structure of an XML document is formally defined. Tags are defined in relationship to one another. If you find the XML tag <city>...</city>, you know exactly what data you have, where that data belong in the document, and how that tag relates to other tags.

XML and Database Processing

What does XML have to do with database processing? How are the XML documents to be generated in the first place? In addition, after a company has received and validated an XML document, how does it place the data from that document into its database?

The answer is to use database applications. Such applications can be written to accept XML documents and extract the data for storage in the database. One way is to extend SQL to cause the results from an SQL statement to be produced in XML format. For example, Figure 7-32 shows the following SQL statement, which uses the **SQL FOR XML clause**, run on SQL Server:

```
/* *** SQL-QUERY-CH07-01 * ***/
SELECT  *
FROM    SEMINAR
        FOR XML AUTO, ELEMENTS;
```

Note that in Figure 7-28, the output (which is all in one cell in this format) in the Messages window is a hyperlink. Clicking the hyperlink produces the XML output shown in Figure 7-29.

XML Web Services

The use of XML for the transmission of database data is especially important because of the development of a new standard called XML Web Services. **XML Web Services** (or just **Web Services**) involves several standards, including XML. XML is used for its ability to create data tags, and XML Web Services is a means for sharing elements of program functionality over the Web.

For example, suppose you have created a database application that converts currencies. Your program will receive the amount of money stated in one currency and convert it to a second currency. You can convert U.S. dollars into Mexican pesos, Japanese yen into euros, and so on. Using XML Web Services, you can publish your database application over the Web in such a way that other programs can consume your program as if it were on their own machine. It will appear to them as if they are using a local program, even though your program might be on the other side of the world.

FIGURE 7-28

An SQL FOR XML Query

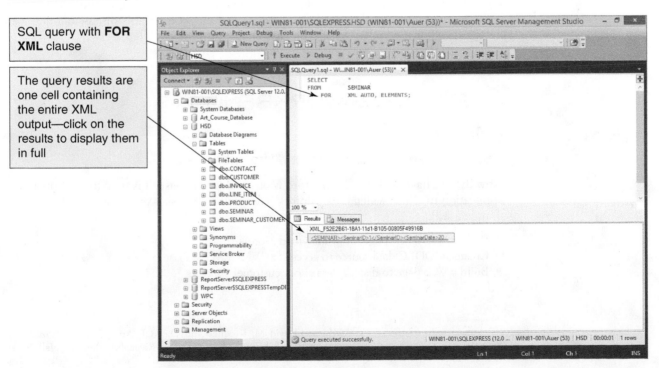

FIGURE 7-29

Results of the SQL FOR XML Query

The query results are now displayed in full—note the XML tags and data content

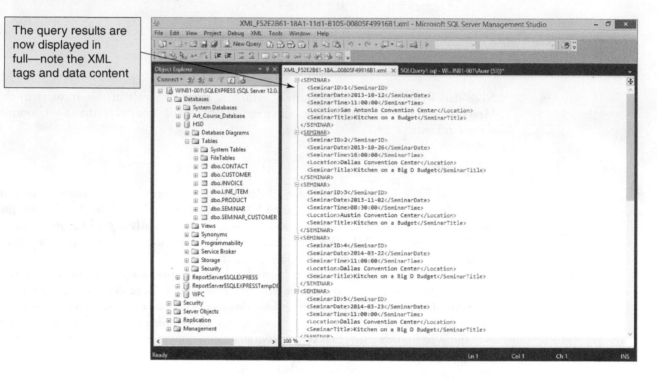

Perhaps you have heard the statement "The Internet is the computer." That statement becomes a reality when different computers, connected via Internet plumbing, can share programs as if they were all on the same machine. When database applications are written as XML Web Services, any computer in the world can access the database applications using standard interfaces, and it appears as if the applications are local to the machine that uses those applications. The particulars are beyond the scope of this discussion, but Web Services are now pervasive in the Web environment.[13]

THE ACCESS WORKBENCH

Section 7

Web Database Processing Using Microsoft Access

Now that we have built the Wallingford Motors CRM database, it is time to develop a Web application to allow Wallingford Motors' sales staff to access it over the Web. In this section, you will:

- Build a Web home page for Wallingford Motors.
- Create an ODBC data source to access the WMCRM database.
- Build a Web page to display data about customer contacts.

---

[13]For more information about XML, see David M. Kroenke and David J. Auer, *Database Processing: Fundamentals, Design and Implementation*, 13th Edition (Upper Saddle River, NJ: Prentice Hall 2014): Chapter 11.

Creating the Customer Contacts View

We want to display a list of customer contacts in a Web page. The list will contain a combination of data from the CONTACT and CUSTOMER tables. To simplify the process, we will define a view named viewCustomerContacts. SQL views are discussed in Appendix E; if you have not studied that material, take a few minutes to read it and work through the Appendix's section of "The Access Workbench." As discussed there, in Microsoft Access a view is simply a saved query. Figure AW-7-1 shows the details of the viewCustomerContacts query.

There is nothing new here. You know how to create Microsoft Access QBE queries, so go ahead and create and save the viewCustomerContacts query. When you are done, close both the WMCRM database and Microsoft Access.

A Web Home Page for Wallingford Motors

The actions we need to take to create a Web page for Wallingford Motors (WM) are the same actions discussed for Heather Sweeney Designs in this chapter. We will create a folder to hold the Web site files and build a home page named index.html in that folder. The HTML code for the WM index.html page is shown in Figure AW-7-2.[14]

The code in Figure AW-7-2 can be used in any text editor or Web page editor, but the simplest editor to use for our purposes is the Microsoft Notepad ASCII text editor. Notepad is not fancy, but it does the job, produces clean HTML (what you type in and only what you type in), and comes with Windows. The following steps describe how to create the file using Notepad, but if you have learned how to use the NetBeans IDE described in the chapter, you can use it instead.

FIGURE AW-7-1

The viewCustomerContacts Query

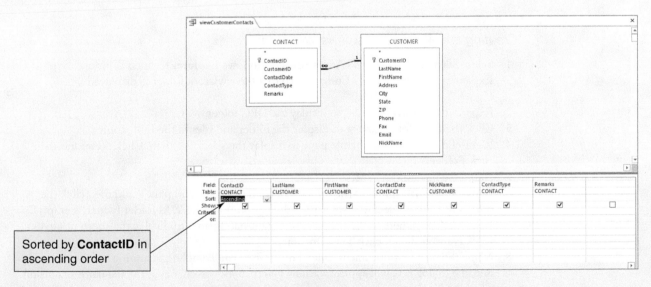

Sorted by **ContactID** in ascending order

---

[14]If you are using IIS 5.1 on Windows XP and you haven't already added index.html to the list of default documents for the Web server, follow the steps in footnote 7 on page 399 to do so now.

(Continued)

FIGURE AW-7-2

The HTML Code for the index.html File in the WM Folder

```html
<!DOCTYPE html>
<html>
    <head>
        <meta charset="UTF-8">
        <meta name="viewport" content="width=device-width, initial-scale=1.0">
        <title>Wallingford Motors CRM Demonstration Pages Home Page</title>
    </head>
    <body>
        <h1 style="text-align: center; color: blue">
            Database Concepts (7th Edition)
        </h1>
        <h2 style="font-family: Ariel, sans-serif; text-align: center">
            The Access Workbench
        </h2>
        <hr />
        <h2 style="text-align: center; color: blue">
            Welcome to the Wallingford Motors Home Page
        </h2>
        <hr />
        <p>The Access Workbench Section 7 Web Pages:</p>
        <p>Report 1:     
            <a href="CustomerContacts.php">
                Display the Customer Contacts List (viewCustomerContacts)
            </a>
        </p>
        <hr />
    </body>
</html>
```

Creating the Wallingford Motors Web Site

1. Select **Start | All Programs | Accessories | Windows Explorer** to open Windows Explorer. Expand the **C:** drive in **My Computer** so that the wwwroot folder is displayed. See Figure 7-10 for this display.
2. Expand the **wwwroot** folder to display the DBC folder.
3. Click the **DBC** folder object to display the folder and files in the DBC folder.
4. Right-click anywhere in the file pane to display the shortcut menu. Click **New**, and then click **Folder**.
5. Name the new folder **WM**.
6. Expand the DBC folder in the folder tree pane (the left-hand pane), and then click the new **WM folder** object to display the folder and files in the WM folder (which is empty).
7. Right-click anywhere in the file pane (the right-hand pane) to display the shortcut menu. Click **New**, and then click **Text Document**.
8. Name the new text document **index.html.** When you complete renaming the file, a Rename dialog box will appear warning you that you are changing the file name extension. Click the **Yes** button in the Rename dialog box.
9. Right-click the **index.html** file to display the shortcut menu. Click **Open With**, and then click **Notepad**.
10. In Notepad, enter the text shown in Figure AW-7-2 into the open index.html file. Figure AW-7-3 shows the HTML code in Notepad.

FIGURE AW-7-3

The index.html File in Notepad

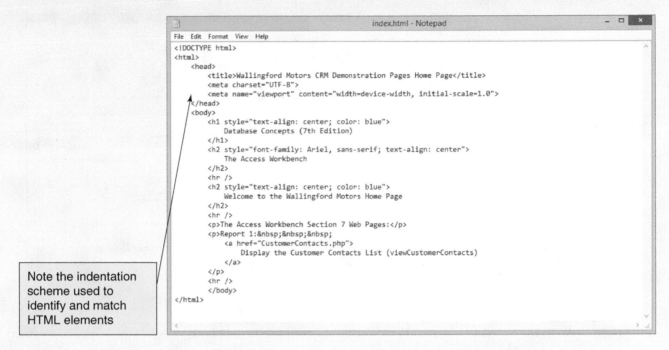

Note the indentation scheme used to identify and match HTML elements

11. Use the Notepad **File | Save** menu command to save the index.html file.
12. Close Notepad.

Notepad is a good, basic text editor that is available on every workstation running the Windows operating system. Dedicated Web page editors, however, do a superior job of working with HTML and PHP text. Figure AW-7-4 shows the index.html file being edited in a NetBeans project named DBC-e07-WM in the NetBeans IDE.

Viewing the Wallingford Motors Web Site

1. Open Windows Internet Explorer or whatever Web browser you use.
2. Type the URL **http://localhost/DBC/WM** into the Address text box and press the **Enter** key. The WM home page appears in the Web browser, as shown in Figure AW-7-5.
3. Close the Web browser.

Selecting the Database File

You will be working with the Wallingford Motors CRM database, so put a copy of the **WMCRM.accdb** file from your My Documents folder—which already contains the view-CustomerContacts query—in the WM Web site folder.

Creating an ODBC Data Source

We now have the basic Wallingford Motors Web site set up. Now, we need to create an ODBC data source. Again, we follow steps similar to those outlined in the chapter.

(Continued)

FIGURE AW-7-4

FIGURE AW-7-4

The index.html File in the NetBeans IDE

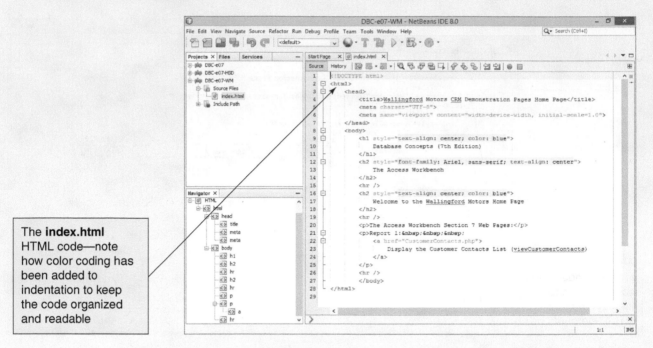

The **index.html** HTML code—note how color coding has been added to indentation to keep the code organized and readable

Creating the WM System Data Source

1. Open the Windows Control Panel by clicking the **Start** button, and then clicking **Control Panel** [if you have added the Data Sources (ODBC) icon to the Windows Start menu as described in Appendix E, then click the **Data sources (ODBC)** icon and go directly to step 4].
2. In the Control Panel window, click **System and Security** to display the System and Security window, and then click **Administrative Tools** to display the Administrative Tools window.

FIGURE AW-7-5

The Wallingford Motors Home Page

Type the URL text here and then press the **Enter** key

http://localhost/DBC/WM/

Wallingford Motors CRM D... ×

Database Concepts (7th Edition)

The Access Workbench

Welcome to the Wallingford Motors Home Page

The Access Workbench Section 7 Web Pages:

Report 1: Display the Customer Contacts List (viewCustomerContacts)

FIGURE AW-7-6

Selecting the Microsoft Access Driver

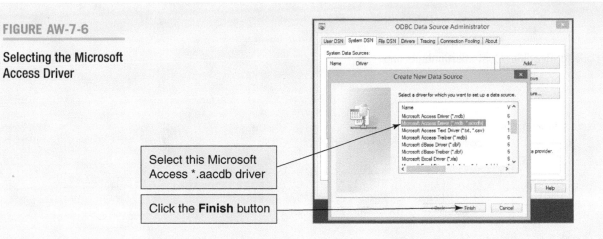

Select this Microsoft Access *.aacdb driver

Click the **Finish** button

3. In the Administrative Tools window, click the **Data Sources (ODBC)** shortcut icon.
4. In the ODBC Data Source Administrator, click the **System DSN** tab, and then click the **Add** button.
5. In the Create New Data Source dialog box, select **Microsoft Access Driver**, as shown in Figure AW-7-6, and then click the **Finish** button.
6. The ODBC Microsoft Access Setup dialog box appears. In the Data Source Name text box, type **WM**. In the Description text box, type **Wallingford Motors CRM on Microsoft Access 2013**.
7. Click the **Database: Select** button, and then browse to the **WMCRM.accdb** database in the Select Database dialog box, as shown in Figure AW-7-7.
8. Click the **OK** button to close the Select Database dialog box.
9. Click the **OK** button to close the ODBC Microsoft Access Setup dialog box.
10. Click the **OK** button to close the ODBC Data Source Administrator.

Creating the PHP Page

Now we need to create a PHP that we will name ReadViewCustomerContacts.php. This is the Web page that will query the database and display the returned data. The code for the ReadViewCustomerContacts.php is shown in Figure AW-7-8.

FIGURE AW-7-7

Selecting the WMCRM.accdb Database

Browse to the **c:\Inetpub\wwwroot\ DBC\WM** folder (directory)

Select the **WMCRM.accdb** database

(Continued)

The PHP Code for ReadViewCustomerContacts.php

```
<!DOCTYPE html>
<html>
    <head>
            <meta charset=UTF-8">
            <title>CustomerContacts PHP Page</title>
            <style type="text/css">
                    h1 {text-align: center; color: blue}
                    h2 {font-family: Ariel, sans-serif; text-align: left; color: blue}
                    p.footer {text-align: center}
                    table.output {font-family: Ariel, sans-serif}
            </style>
    </head>
    <body>
    <?php
            // Get connection
            $Conn = odbc_connect('WM', '', '');

            // Test connection
            if (!Conn)
                    {
                    exit ("ODBC Connection Failed: " . $Conn);
                    }
            // Create SQL statement
            $SQL = "SELECT * FROM viewCustomerContacts";

            // Execute SQL statement
            $RecordSet v odbc_exec($Conn,$SQL

            // Test existence of recordset
            if (!$RecordSet)
                    {
                    exit ("SQL Statement Error: " . $SQL);
                    }
    ?>
            <!-- Page Headers -->
            <h1>
                    The Wallingford Motors CRM Customer Contacts List
            </h1>
            <hr />
            <h2>
                    viewCustomerContacts
            </h2>
    <?php
            // Table headers
            echo "<table class='output' border='1'>
                    <tr>
                            <th>ContactID</th>
                            <th>LastName</th>
                            <th>FirstName</th>
                            <th>ContactDate</th>
                            <th>NickName</th>
                            <th>Type</th>
                            <th>Remarks</th>
                    </tr>";

            // Table data
            while($RecordSetRow = odbc_fetch_array($RecordSet))
```

FIGURE AW-7-8 Continued

```
            {
            echo "<tr>";
            echo "<td>" . $RecordSetRow['ContactID'] . "</td>";
            echo "<td>" . $RecordSetRow['LastName'] . "</td>";
            echo "<td>" . $RecordSetRow['FirstName'] . "</td>";
            echo "<td>" . $RecordSetRow['ContactDate'] . "</td>";
            echo "<td>" . $RecordSetRow['NickName'] . "</td>";
            echo "<td>" . $RecordSetRow['Type'] . "</td>";
            echo "<td>" . $RecordSetRow['Remarks'] . "</td>";
            echo "</tr>";
            }
echo "</table>";

        // Close connection
        odbc_close($Conn);
?>
        <br />
        <hr />
        <p class="footer">
            <a href="../WM/index.html">Return to Wallingford Motors Home Page</a>
        </p>
        <hr />
</body>
</html>
```

We will create the ReadViewCustomerContact.php file in the NetBeans IDE, but you could instead do this using another IDE or a text editor such as Microsoft Notepad. We'll store the file in the WM folder. Figure AW-7-9 shows the ReadViewCustomerContacts.php file being edited in the NetBeans IDE.

Running the PHP Page

Now you can try out the CustomerContacts.php file.

Using the ReadViewCustomerContacts.php File

1. Open Internet Explorer or another Web browser.
2. Type the URL **http://localhost/DBC/WM** into the Address text box and press the **Enter** key. The WM home page appears in the Web browser.
3. Click the **Display the Customer Contacts List (viewCustomerContacts)** hyperlink. The Web page appears, as shown in Figure Figure AW-7-10.
4. Close the Web browser.

In Closing

Neither the WMCRM database nor Microsoft Access 2013 is open, so you do not have to close them. You now know how to connect to a Microsoft Access database from a Web page.

(Continued)

FIGURE AW-7-9

The ReadViewCustomerContacts.php File in the NetBeans IDE

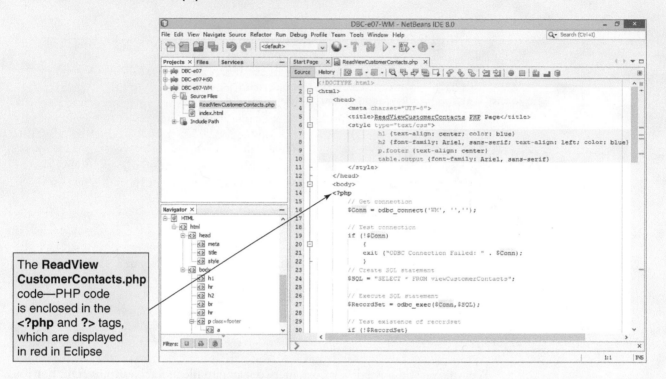

The **ReadView CustomerContacts.php** code—PHP code is enclosed in the **<?php** and **?>** tags, which are displayed in red in Eclipse

FIGURE AW-7-10

Results for ReadViewCustomerContacts.php

Sorted by ContactID in ascending order

The Wallingford Motors CRM Customer Contacts List

viewCustomerContacts

ContactID	LastName	FirstName	ContactDate	NickName	ContactType	Remarks
1	Griffey	Ben	2014-07-07 00:00:00	Big Bill	Phone	General interest in a Gaea.
2	Griffey	Ben	2014-07-07 00:00:00	Big Bill	Email	Sent general information.
3	Griffey	Ben	2014-07-12 00:00:00	Big Bill	Phone	Set up an appointment.
4	Griffey	Ben	2014-07-14 00:00:00	Big Bill	Meeting	Bought a HiStandard.
5	Christman	Jessica	2014-07-19 00:00:00	Billy	Phone	Interested in a SUHi, set up an appointment.
6	Griffey	Ben	2014-07-21 00:00:00	Big Bill	Email	Sent a standard follow-up message.
7	Christman	Rob	2014-07-27 00:00:00	Tina	Phone	Interested in a HiStandard, set up an appointment.
8	Christman	Jessica	2014-07-27 00:00:00	Billy	Meeting	Bought a SUHi.
9	Christman	Rob	2014-08-02 00:00:00	Tina	Meeting	Talked up to a HiLuxury. Customer bought one.
10	Christman	Jessica	2014-08-03 00:00:00	Billy	Email	Sent a standard follow-up message.
11	Christman	Rob	2014-08-10 00:00:00	Tina	Email	Sent a standard follow-up message.
12	Hayes	Judy	2014-08-15 00:00:00	Tina	Phone	General interest in a Gaea.

Return to Wallingford Motors Home Page

SUMMARY

This chapter introduced Web database processing and Extensible Markup Language (XML).

Databases vary not only in size, scope, and the number of users, but also in the way they are processed. Some databases are processed just by queries, forms, and reports; some are processed by ASP and JSP, which use Internet technology to publish database applications; some are processed by traditional application programs; and some are processed by stored procedures and triggers. Other databases are processed by all these types of applications, with hundreds or thousands of concurrent users.

Web database processing systems consist of users who use browsers that connect via HTTP to a Web server that processes communications and database applications. The database applications process the database via the DBMS. In a two-tiered system, the Web server and the DBMS reside on the same computer, but this is not a good configuration for performance and security reasons. Better is a three-tiered system, where the Web server and DBMS reside on different computers. Higher-capacity systems use more than one Web server and may use multiple database servers in clusters.

If the Web server host runs Windows, the Web server software is usually IIS. IIS processes HTTP and ASP. ASP is a blend of HTML and scripting code. Database application logic is often processed using such scripts. If the Web server host runs Linux or Unix, the Web server software is normally Apache.

Every DBMS has its own API. The Open Database Connectivity (ODBC) standard provides an interface by which database applications can access and process relational data sources in a DBMS-independent manner. ODBC involves an applications program, a driver manager, a DBMS driver, and data source components. Single-tier and multiple-tier drivers are defined. The three types of data source names are file, system, and user. System data sources are recommended for Web servers. The process of defining a system data source name involves specifying the type of driver and the identity of the database to be processed.

Microsoft's latest Web server offering is ASP.NET. With it, object-oriented programming languages such as Visual Basic .NET, C#, and C++ can be used. ASP.NET pages are compiled but not interpreted.

Web database processing is complicated by the fact that HTTP is stateless. When processing atomic transactions, application programs must include logic to provide for session state. The means by which this is done depends on the Web server and language in use.

PHP (PHP: Hypertext Processor) is a scripting language that can be embedded in Web pages. PHP is extremely popular and easy to learn, and it can be used in most Web server environments and with most databases.

For creating complex pages, you need an Integrated Development Environment (IDE). An IDE gives you the most robust and user-friendly means of creating and maintaining Web pages. Microsoft Visual Studio, NetBeans for Java users, and the open-source Eclipse IDE are all good IDEs. Microsoft Visual Studio, NetBeans, and Eclipse all provide a framework that can be modified by add-in modules.

Using XML is becoming the standard means for defining documents and transmitting them from one computer to another. Increasingly, it is being used to transmit data to and from database applications. XML tags are not fixed but can be extended by document designers.

Although XML can be used to materialize Web pages, more important is its use for describing, representing, and materializing database views. XML is a better markup language than HTML primarily because XML provides a clear separation between document structure, content, and materialization. Also, XML tags are not ambiguous.

SQL Server, Oracle Database, and MySQL can produce XML documents from database data. SQL Server supports an add-on expression to the SQL SELECT statement, the FOR XML expression. XML is important because it facilitates the sharing of XML documents (and hence database data) among organizations.

KEY TERMS

.NET
?>
<?php
Active Data Objects (ADO)
Active Server Pages
ASP.NET
ADO.NET
AMP
Apache
Application Programming
  Interface (API)
data source
data source name (DSN)
Default Web Site folder
document type definitions (DTD)
driver
Extensible Markup Language (XML)
file data source
HTML document tags
HTML syntax rules
HTML5
http://localhost
Hypertext Markup Language
  (HTML)

iisstart.htm
index.html
inetpub folder
Integrated Development
  Environment (IDE)
Internet Information
  Services (IIS)
Internet Information Services
  Manager
Java Server Pages (JSP)
LAMP
multiple-tier driver
NetBeans IDE
ODBC architecture
ODBC Data Source
  Administrator
ODBC DBMS driver
ODBC driver manager
OLE DB
Open Database Connectivity
  (ODBC)
PHP
PHP: Hypertext Processor
POST method

PHP concatenation operator (.=)
PHP plugin
single-tier driver
SQL FOR XML clause
SQL injection attack
SQL/Persistent stored modules
  (SQL/PSM)
stored procedure
system data source
three-tier architecture
trigger
two-tier architecture
user data source
user defined function
WAMP
Web Services
Web
World Wide Web
World Wide Web Consortium
  (W3C)
wwwroot folder
XHTML
XML Web Services

REVIEW QUESTIONS

7.1   Describe five different ways databases can be processed (use Figure 7-3).

7.2   Summarize the issues involved in processing a form, as described in this chapter.

7.3   Describe, in your own words, the nature of traditional database processing applications.

7.4   What is a trigger, and how is it used?

7.5   Name three types of triggers.

7.6   What is a stored procedure, and how is it used?

7.7   Describe why the data environment is complicated.

7.8   Name the three major components of a Web database application.

7.9   As explained in this chapter, what are the two major functions of a Web server?

7.10 Explain the difference between two-tier and three-tier architecture.

7.11 What is IIS, and what functions does it serve?

7.12 What do the abbreviations ASP and JSP stand for?

7.13 What is ASP.NET?

7.14 What is Apache, and what function does it serve?

7.15 What are AMP, LAMP, and WAMP?

7.16   Explain the relationship among ODBC, OLE DB, and ADO.

7.17   Name the components of the ODBC standard.

7.18   What role does the driver manager serve?

7.19   What role does the DBMS driver serve?

7.20   What is a single-tier driver?

7.21   What is a multiple-tier driver?

7.22   Explain the differences between the three types of ODBC data sources.

7.23   Which ODBC data source type is recommended for Web servers?

7.24   What is an API, and what function does it serve?

7.25   What is Hypertext Markup Language (HTML), and what function does it serve?

7.26   What are HTML document tags, and how are they used?

7.27   What is the World Wide Web Consortium (W3C)?

7.28   Why is index.html a significant file name?

7.29   What is PHP, and what function does it serve?

7.30   How is PHP code designated in a Web page?

7.31   How are comments designated in PHP code?

7.32   How are comments designated in HTML code?

7.33   What is an Integrated Development Environment (IDE), and how is it used?

7.34   What Microsoft IDE is generally used in a Windows environment?

7.35   What is the NetBeans IDE?

7.36   Show a snippet of PHP code for creating a connection to a database. Explain the meaning of the code.

7.37   Show a snippet of PHP code for creating a recordset. Explain the meaning of the code.

7.38   Show a snippet of PHP code for displaying the contents of a recordset. Explain the meaning of the code.

7.39   Show a snippet of PHP code for disconnecting from the database. Explain the meaning of the code.

7.40   With respect to HTTP, what does *stateless* mean?

7.41   Under what circumstances does statelessness pose a problem for database processing?

7.42   In general terms, how are sessions managed by database applications when using HTTP?

7.43   What are the problems in interpreting tags such as <h1>...</h1> in HTML?

7.44   What does *XML* stand for?

7.45   How does XML differ from HTML?

7.46   Explain why XML is extensible.

7.47   In general terms, explain why XML is important for database processing.

7.48   What is the purpose of the FOR XML expression in an SQL statement?

7.49   What is the purpose of XML Web Services?

EXERCISES

7.50 In this exercise, you will create a Web page in the DBC folder and link it to the HSD Web page in the HSD folder.

A. Figure 7-30 shows the HTML code for a Web page for the DBC folder. Note that the page is called index.html, the same name as the Web page in the HSD folder. This is not a problem because the files are in different folders. Create the index.html Web page in the DBC folder.

FIGURE 7-30

The HTML Code for the index.html File in the DBC Folder

```
<!DOCTYPE html>
<html>
    <head>
        <title>DBC-e07 Home Page</title>
        <meta charset="UTF-8">
        <meta name="viewport" content="width=device-width, initial-scale=1.0">
    </head>
    <body>
        <h1 style="text-align: center; color: blue">
            Database Concepts (7th Edition) Home Page
        </h1>
        <hr />
        <h3 style="text-align: center">
            Use this page to access Web-based materials from Chapter 7 of:
        </h3>
        <h2 style="text-align: center; color: blue">
            Database Concepts (7th Edition)
        </h2>
        <p style="text-align: center; font-weight: bold">
            David M. Kroenke
        </p>
        <p style="text-align: center; font-weight: bold">
            David J. Auer
        </p>
        <hr />
        <h3>Chapter 7 Demonstration Pages From Figures in the Text:</h3>
        <p>
            <a href="HSD/index.html">
                Heather Sweeney Designs Demonstration Pages
            </a>
        </p>
        <p>
            <a href="WM/index.html">
                Wallingford Motors CRM Demonstration Pages
            </a>
        </p>
        <hr />
    </body>
</html>
```

FIGURE 7-31

The HTML Modifications for the index.html File in the DBC Folder

```
            <p>Chapter 7 Demonstration Pages From Figures in the Text:</p>
            <p>Example 1:   
                <a href="ReadSeminar.php">
                        Display the SEMINAR Table (No surrogate key)
                </a>
            </p>
            <hr />
    <!-- NEW CODE STARTS HERE -->
            <p style="text-align: center">
                <a href="../index.html">
                        Return to the Database Concepts Home Page
                </a>
            </p>
            <hr />
    <!-- NEW CODE ENDS HERE -->
            </body>
    </html>
```

B. Figure 7-31 shows some additional HTML to be added near the end of the code for the HSD Web page in the file index.html in the HSD folder. Update the HSD index.html file with the code.

C. Try out the pages. Type **http://localhost/DBC** into your Web browser to display the DBC home page. From there, you should be able to move back and forth between the two pages by using the hyperlinks on each page. *Note:* You may need to click the Refresh button on your Web browser when using the HSD home page to get the hyperlink back to the DBC home page to work properly.

7.51 Create a Web page for Heather Sweeney Designs to display all the data in the CUSTOMER table. Add a hyperlink to the HSD home page to access the page.

7.52 Create a Web page for Heather Sweeney Designs to display the EmailAddress, LastName, FirstName, and Phone of customers in the CUSTOMER table. Add a hyperlink to the HSD home page to access the page.

7.53 Create a Web page for Heather Sweeney Designs to display the data in the SEMINAR_CUSTOMER table. Add a hyperlink to the HSD home page to access the page.

7.54 Create a Web page for Heather Sweeney Designs to display the data in the SEMINAR_CUSTOMER table for the SEMINAR with SeminarID = 3. Add a hyperlink to the HSD home page to access the page.

7.55 Create a Web page for Heather Sweeney Designs to display data in the SEMINAR, SEMINAR_CUSTOMER, and CUSTOMER tables to list the SEMINAR data and the EmailAddress, LastName, FirstName, and Phone of any CUSTOMER who attended the SEMINAR with SeminarID = 3. Add a hyperlink to the HSD home page to access the page.

7.56 Code two HTML/PHP pages to add a new CUSTOMER to the HSD database. Create data for two new CUSTOMERs and add them to the database to demonstrate that your pages work.

ACCESS WORKBENCH EXERCISES

AW.7.1   If you haven't completed exercise 7.50, do it now.

AW.7.2   Link the WM Web page to the DBC Web page.

AW.7.3   Using the WMCRM database, code a PHP Web page to display the data in SALESPERSON. Add a hyperlink on the WM Web page to access the page. Using your database, demonstrate that your page works.

AW.7.4   Using the WMCRM database, code a PHP Web page to display the data in VEHICLE. Add a hyperlink on the WM Web page to access the page. Using your database, demonstrate that your page works.

AW.7.5   Using the WMCRM database, create a view named viewSalespersonVehicle and include in it all the columns in both the SALESPERSON and VEHICLE tables. Code a PHP Web page to display viewSalespersonVehicle. Add a hyperlink on the WM Web page to access the page. Using your database, demonstrate that your page works.

AW.7.6   Using the WMCRM database, code two HTML/PHP pages to add a new CUSTOMER to the WMCRM database. Create data for two new CUSTOMERs and add them to the database to demonstrate that your pages work.

MARCIA'S DRY CLEANING CASE QUESTIONS

Ms. Marcia Wilson owns and operates Marcia's Dry Cleaning, which is an upscale dry cleaner in a well-to-do suburban neighborhood. Marcia makes her business stand out from the competition by providing superior customer service. She wants to keep track of each of her customers and their orders. Ultimately, she wants to notify them that their clothes are ready via email.

Assume that Marcia has hired you as a database consultant to develop an operational database named MDC that has the following four tables:

CUSTOMER (<u>CustomerID</u>, FirstName, LastName, Phone, Email)

INVOICE (<u>InvoiceNumber</u>, *CustomerID*, DateIn, DateOut, Subtotal, Tax, TotalAmount)

INVOICE_ITEM (<u>*InvoiceNumber*</u>, <u>ItemNumber</u>, *ServiceID*, Quantity, UnitPrice, ExtendedPrice)

SERVICE (<u>ServiceID</u>, ServiceDescription, UnitPrice)

A Microsoft Access 2013 version of the MDC database and SQL scripts to create and populate the MDC database are available for Microsoft SQL Server 2013, Oracle Database Express Edition 11*g* Release 2, and MySQL 5.6 Community Server at the Database Concepts Web site at **www.pearsonhighered.com/kroenke**. Sample data for the CUSTOMER table are shown in Figure 7-32, for the SERVICE table in Figure 7-33, for the INVOICE table in Figure 7-34, and for the INVOICE_ITEM table in Figure 7-35.

A. Create a database in your DBMS named MDC, and use the MDC SQL scripts for your DBMS to create and populate the database tables. Create a user named MDC-User with the password MDC-User+password. Assign this user to database roles so that the user can read, insert, delete, and modify data.

B. If you haven't completed exercise 7.50, do it now.

C. Add a new folder to the DBC Web site named MDC. Create a Web page for Marcia's Dry Cleaning in this folder—using the file name index.html. Link this page.

D. Create an appropriate ODBC data source for your database.

FIGURE 7-32

Sample Data for the MDC CUSTOMER Table

CustomerID	FirstName	LastName	Phone	Email
100	Nikki	Kaccaton	723-543-1233	Nikki.Kaccaton@somewhere.com
105	Brenda	Catnazaro	723-543-2344	Brenda.Catnazaro@somewhere.com
110	Bruce	LeCat	723-543-3455	Bruce.LeCat@somewhere.com
115	Betsy	Miller	723-654-3211	Betsy.Miller@somewhere.com
120	George	Miller	723-654-4322	George.Miller@somewhere.com
125	Kathy	Miller	723-514-9877	Kathy.Miller@somewhere.com
130	Betsy	Miller	723-514-8766	Betsy.Miller@elsewhere.com

FIGURE 7-33

Sample Data for the
MDC SERVICE Table

ServiceID	ServiceDescription	UnitPrice
10	Men's Shirt	$1.50
11	Dress Shirt	$2.50
15	Women's Shirt	$1.50
16	Blouse	$3.50
20	Slacks— Men's	$5.00
25	Slacks—Women's	$6.00
30	Skirt	$5.00
31	Dress Skirt	$6.00
40	Suit – Men's	$9.00
45	Suit – Women's	$8.50
50	Tuxedo	$10.00
60	Formal Gown	$10.00

E. Add a new column, Status, to INVOICE. Assume that Status can have the values ['Waiting', 'In-process', 'Finished', 'Pending'].

F. Create a view called CustomerInvoiceView that has the columns LastName, FirstName, Phone, InvoiceNumber, DateIn, DateOut, Total, and Status.

G. Code a PHP page to display CustomerInvoiceView. Using your sample database, demonstrate that your page works.

H. Code two HTML/PHP pages to receive a date value AsOfDate and to display rows of CustomerInvoiceView for orders having DateIn greater than or equal to AsOfDate. Using your sample database, demonstrate that your pages work.

I. Code two HTML/PHP pages to receive customer Phone, LastName, and FirstName and to display rows for customers having that Phone, LastName, and FirstName. Using your sample database, demonstrate that your pages work.

FIGURE 7-34

Sample Data for the MDC INVOICE Table

InvoiceNumber	CustomerID	DateIn	DateOut	SubTotal	Tax	TotalAmount
2014001	100	04-Oct-14	06-Oct-14	$158.50	$12.52	$171.02
2014002	105	04-Oct-14	06-Oct-14	$25.00	$1.98	$26.98
2014003	100	06-Oct-14	08-Oct-14	$49.00	$3.87	$52.87
2014004	115	06-Oct-14	08-Oct-14	$17.50	$1.38	$18.88
2014005	125	07-Oct-14	11-Oct-14	$12.00	$0.95	$12.95
2014006	110	11-Oct-14	13-Oct-14	$152.50	$12.05	$164.55
2014007	110	11-Oct-14	13-Oct-14	$7.00	$0.55	$7.55
2014008	130	12-Oct-14	14-Oct-14	$140.50	$11.10	$151.60
2014009	120	12-Oct-14	14-Oct-14	$27.00	$2.13	$29.13

 GARDEN GLORY PROJECT QUESTIONS

If you have not already implemented the Garden Glory database shown in Chapter 3 in a DBMS product, create and populate the Garden Glory database now in the DBMS of your choice (or as assigned by your instructor).

A. Create a user named GG-User with the password GG-User+password. Assign this user to database roles so that the user can read, insert, delete, and modify data.

B. If you haven't completed exercise 7.50, do it now.

C. Add a new folder to the DBC Web site named GG. Create a Web page for Garden Glory in this folder—using the file name index.html. Link this page to the DBC Web page.

D. Create an appropriate ODBC data source for your database.

E. Code a Web page using PHP to display the data in OWNED_PROPERTY. Add a hyperlink on the GG Web page to access the page. Using your database, demonstrate that your page works.

F. Code a Web page using PHP to display the data in PROPERTY_SERVICE. Add a hyperlink on the GG Web page to access the page. Using your database, demonstrate that your page works.

G. Create a view named Property_Service_View that displays OWNED_PROPERTY .PropertyID, PropertyName, PROPERY_SERVICE.EmployeeID, ServiceDate, and HoursWorked. Code a Web page using PHP to display the data in Property Service_ View. Add a hyperlink to the GG Web page to access the page. Using your database, demonstrate that your page works.

FIGURE 7-35

Sample Data for the MDC INVOICE_ITEM Table

InvoiceNumber	ItemNumber	ServiceID	Quantity	UnitPrice	ExtendedPrice
2014001	1	16	2	$3.50	$7.00
2014001	2	11	5	$2.50	$12.50
2014001	3	50	2	$10.00	$20.00
2014001	4	20	10	$5.00	$50.00
2014001	5	25	10	$6.00	$60.00
2014001	6	40	1	$9.00	$9.00
2014002	1	11	10	$2.50	$25.00
2014003	1	20	5	$5.00	$25.00
2014003	2	25	4	$6.00	$24.00
2014004	1	11	7	$2.50	$17.50
2014005	1	16	2	$3.50	$7.00
2014005	2	11	2	$2.50	$5.00
2014006	1	16	5	$3.50	$17.50
2014006	2	11	10	$2.50	$25.00
2014006	3	20	10	$5.00	$50.00
2014006	4	25	10	$6.00	$60.00
2014007	1	16	2	$3.50	$7.00
2014008	1	16	3	$3.50	$10.50
2014008	2	11	12	$2.50	$30.00
2014008	3	20	8	$5.00	$40.00
2014008	4	25	10	$6.00	$60.00
2014009	1	40	3	$9.00	$27.00

H. Code two HTML/PHP pages to add a new OWNER to the GG database. Create data for two new OWNERs and add them to the database to demonstrate that your pages work.

JAMES RIVER JEWELRY PROJECT QUESTIONS

The James River Jewelry project questions are available in online Appendix D, which can be downloaded from the textbook's Web site: **www.pearsonhighered.com/kroenke**.

THE QUEEN ANNE CURIOSITY SHOP PROJECT QUESTIONS

If you have not already implemented The Queen Anne Curiosity Shop database shown in Chapter 3 in a DBMS product, create and populate the QACS database now in the DBMS of your choice (or as assigned by your instructor).

A. Create a user named QACS-User with the password QACS-User+password. Assign this user to database roles so that the user can read, insert, delete, and modify data.

B. If you haven't completed exercise 7.50, do it now.

C. Add a new folder to the DBC Web site named QACS. Create a Web page for The Queen Anne Curiosity Shop in this folder—use the file name index.html. Link this page to the DBC Web page.

D. Create an appropriate ODBC data source for your database.

E. Code a Web page using PHP to display the data in SALE. Add a hyperlink on the QACS Web page to access the page. Using your database, demonstrate that your page works.

F. Code a Web page using PHP to display the data in ITEM. Add a hyperlink on the QACS Web page to access the page. Using your database, demonstrate that your page works.

G. Create a view named Sale_Item_Item_View that displays SALE.SaleID, SALE_ITEM .SaleItemID, SALE.SaleDate, ITEM.ItemDescription, and SALE_ITEM.ItemPrice. Code a Web page using PHP to display the data in Sale_Item_Item_View. Add a hyperlink to the QACS Web page to access the page. Using your database, demonstrate that your page works.

H. Code two HTML/PHP pages to add a new CUSTOMER to the QACS database. Create data for two new CUSTOMERs and add them to the database to demonstrate that your pages work.

CHAPTER 8 Big Data, Data Warehouses, and Business Intelligence Systems

CHAPTER OBJECTIVES

- Learn the basic concepts of Big Data, structured storage, and the MapReduce process

- Learn the basic concepts of data warehouses and data marts

- Learn the basic concepts of dimensional databases

- Learn the basic concepts of business intelligence (BI) systems

- Learn the basic concepts of Online Analytical Processing (OLAP)

This chapter introduces topics that build on the fundamentals you have learned in the first seven chapters of this book. Now that we have designed and built a database, we are ready to put it to work. In Chapter 7, we built a Web database application. This chapter looks at the problems associated with the rapidly expanding amount of data that is being stored and used in enterprise information systems and some of the technology that is being used to address those problems. These problems are generally included in the need to deal with **Big Data**, which is the current term for the enormous datasets generated by Web applications such as search tools (for example, Google and Bing) and Web 2.0 social networks (for example, Facebook, LinkedIn, and Twitter). Although these new and very visible Web applications are highlighting the problems of dealing with large datasets, these problems were already present in other areas, such as scientific research and business operations.[1]

Just how big is Big Data? Figure 8-1 defines some commonly used terms for data storage capacity. Note that computer storage is calculated based on binary numbers (base 2), not the usual decimal (base 10) numbers we are more familiar with. Therefore, a kilobyte is 1,024 bytes instead of the 1,000 bytes we would otherwise expect.

If we consider the desktop and notebook computers generally in use as this book is being written (early 2014), a quick check online of available computers shows notebooks

---

[1]For more information, see the Wikipedia article on **Big Data**.

FIGURE 8-1

Storage Capacity
Terms

Name	Symbol	Approximate Value for Reference	Actual Value
Byte			8 bits [Store one character]
Kilobyte	KB	About 10^3	2^{10} = 1,024 bytes
Megabyte	MB	About 10^6	2^{20} = 1,024 KB
Gigabyte	GB	About 10^9	2^{30} = 1,024 MB
Terabyte	TB	About 10^{12}	2^{40} = 1,024 GB
Petabyte	PB	About 10^{15}	2^{50} = 1,024 TB
Exabyte	EB	About 10^{18}	2^{60} = 1,024 PB
Zettabyte	ZB	About 10^{21}	2^{70} = 1,024 EB
Yottabyte	YB	About 10^{24}	2^{80} = 1,024 ZB

being sold with hard drives up to 1 TB in capacity, whereas some desktops are available with 2 TB. That is just for one computer. Facebook is reported to handle more than 40 billion photos in its database.[2] If a typical digital photo is about 2 MB in size, that would require about 9.3 PB of storage!

As another measure of Big Data, Amazon.com reported that on November 29, 2010, orders for 13.7 million products were placed. This is an average of 158 product orders per second.[3] Amazon.com also reported that on the peak day of the 2010 holiday season its worldwide fulfillment network shipped more than 9 million items to 178 countries. This volume of both primary business transactions (item sales) and supporting transactions (shipping, tracking, and financial transactions) truly requires Amazon.com to handle Big Data.

The need to deal with larger and larger datasets has grown over time. We will look at some of the components of this growth. We will start with the need for business analysts to have large datasets available for analysis by business intelligence (BI) applications and briefly look at BI systems, particularly Online Analytical Processing (OLAP), and the data warehouse structures that were designed for their use. We will then look at distributed databases, clustered servers, and finally the evolving NoSQL systems.

In this chapter, we will continue to use the Heather Sweeney Designs database that we modeled in Chapter 4, designed in Chapter 5, created in Chapter 6, and built a Web database application for in Chapter 7. The name of the database is HSD, and a SQL Server database diagram for the HSD database is shown in Figure 8-2.

---

[2]Wikipedia article on **Big Data** (accessed April 2014).

3Amazon.com, "Third-Generation Kindle Now the Bestselling Product of All Time on Amazon Worldwide," News release, December 27, 2010 (accessed Janaury 2012).

FIGURE 8-2

The HSD Database Diagram

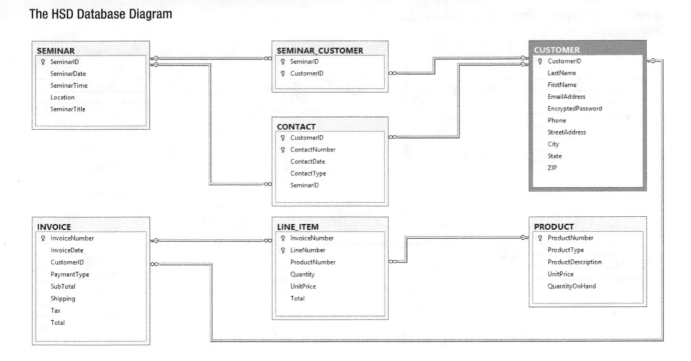

BUSINESS INTELLIGENCE SYSTEMS

Business intelligence (BI) systems are information systems that assist managers and other professionals in the analysis of current and past activities and in the prediction of future events. Unlike transaction processing systems, they do not support operational activities, such as the recording and processing of orders. Instead, BI systems are used to support management assessment, analysis, planning, control, and, ultimately, decision making.

THE RELATIONSHIP BETWEEN OPERATIONAL AND BI SYSTEMS

Figure 8-3 summarizes the relationship between operational and business intelligence systems. **Operational systems**, such as sales, purchasing, and inventory-control systems, support primary business activities. They use a DBMS to both read data from and store data in the operational database. They are also known as **transactional systems** or **online transaction processing (OLTP) systems** because they record the ongoing stream of business transactions.

Instead of supporting the primary business activities, BI systems support management's analysis and decision-making activities. BI systems obtain data from three possible sources. First, they read and process data existing in the operational database—they use the operational DBMS to obtain such data, but they do not insert, modify, or delete operational data. Second, BI systems process data that are extracted from operational databases. In this situation, they manage the extracted database using a BI DBMS, which may be the same as or different from the operational DBMS. Finally, BI systems read data purchased from data vendors.

We will look at BI systems in detail in online Appendix G, but for now we will summarize the basic elements of a BI system.

FIGURE 8-3

The Relationship Between Operational and BI Applications

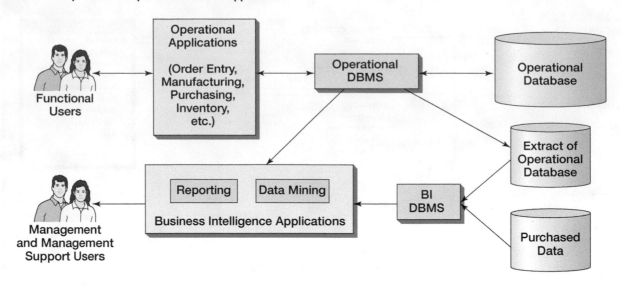

REPORTING SYSTEMS AND DATA MINING APPLICATIONS

BI systems fall into two broad categories: reporting systems and data mining applications. **Reporting systems** sort, filter, group, and make elementary calculations on operational data. **Data mining applications**, in contrast, perform sophisticated analyses on data, analyses that usually involve complex statistical and mathematical processing. The characteristics of BI applications are summarized in Figure 8-4.

Reporting Systems

Reporting systems filter, sort, group, and make simple calculations. All reporting analyses can be performed using standard SQL, although extensions to SQL, such as those used for **Online Analytical Processing (OLAP)**, are sometimes used to ease the task of report production.

FIGURE 8-4

Characteristics of
Business Intelligence
Applications

- Reporting
    - Filter, sort, group, and make simple calculations
    - Summarize current status
    - Compare current status to past or predicted status
    - Classify entities (customers, products, employees, etc.)
    - Report delivery crucial
- Data Mining
    - Often employ sophisticated statistical and mathematical techniques
    - Used for:
        - What-if analyses
        - Predictions
        - Decisions
    - Results often incorporated into some other report or system

Reporting systems summarize the current status of business activities and compare that status with past or predicted future activities. Report delivery is crucial. Reports must be delivered to the proper users on a timely basis, in the appropriate format. For example, reports may be delivered on paper, via a Web browser, or in some other format.

Data Mining Applications

Data mining applications use sophisticated statistical and mathematical techniques to perform what-if analyses, to make predictions, and to facilitate decision making. For example, data mining techniques can analyze past cell phone usage and predict which customers are likely to switch to a competing phone company. Or data mining can be used to analyze past loan behavior to determine which customers are most (or least) likely to default on a loan.

Report delivery is not as important for data mining systems as it is for reporting systems. First, most data mining applications have only a few users, and those users have sophisticated computer skills. Second, the results of a data mining analysis are usually incorporated into some other report, analysis, or information system. In the case of cell phone usage, the characteristics of customers who are in danger of switching to another company may be given to the sales department for action. Or the parameters of an equation for determining the likelihood of a loan default may be incorporated into a loan approval application.

DATA WAREHOUSES AND DATA MARTS

As shown in Figure 8-3, some BI applications read and process operational data directly from the operational database. Although this is possible for simple reporting systems and small databases, such direct reading of operational data is not feasible for more complex applications or larger databases. Operational data are difficult to use for several reasons:

- Querying data for BI applications can place a substantial burden on the DBMS and unacceptably slow the performance of operational applications.
- The creation and maintenance of BI systems require application programs, facilities, and expertise that are not normally available from operations.
- Operational data have problems that limit their use for BI applications.

Therefore, larger organizations usually process a separate database constructed from an extract of the operational database.

The Components of a Data Warehouse

A **data warehouse** is a database system that has data, programs, and personnel that specialize in the preparation of data for BI processing. Figure 8-5 shows the components of the basic data warehouse architecture. Data are read from operational databases by the **extract, transform, and load (ETL) system**. The ETL system then cleans and prepares the data for BI processing. This can be a complex process.

First, operational data often cannot be directly loaded into BI applications. Some of the problems of using operational data for BI processing include:

- "Dirty data" (for example, problematic data such as value of "G" for customer gender, a value of "213" for customer age, a value of "999-999-9999" for a U.S. phone number, or a part color of "gren")
- Missing values
- Inconsistent data (for example, data that have changed, such as a customer's phone number or address)

FIGURE 8-5

Components of a Data Warehouse

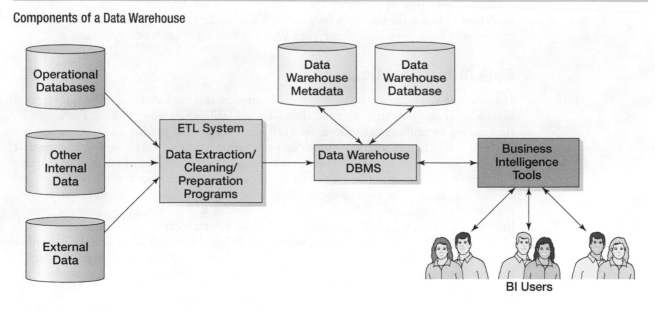

- Nonintegrated data (for example, data from two or more sources that need to be combined for BI use)
- Incorrect format (for example, data that are gathered such that there are either too many digits or not enough digits, such as time measures in either seconds or hours when they are needed in minutes for BI use)
- Too much data (for example, an excess of columns [attributes], rows [records], or both)

Second, data may need to be changed or transformed for use in a data warehouse. For example, the operational systems may store data about countries using standard two-letter country codes, such as US (United States) and CA (Canada). However, applications using the data warehouse may need to use the country names in full. Thus, the data transformation {**CountryCode** → **CountryName**} will be needed before the data can be loaded into the data warehouse.

When the data are prepared for use, the ETL system loads the data into the data warehouse database. The extracted data are stored in a data warehouse database, using a data warehouse DBMS, which may be from a different vendor than the organization's operational DBMS. For example, an organization might use Oracle Database for its operational processing but use SQL Server for its data warehouse.

BTW

Problematic operational data that have been cleaned in the ETL system can also be used to update the operational system to fix the original data problems.

Metadata concerning the data's source, format, assumptions and constraints, and other facts is kept in a **data warehouse metadata database**. The data warehouse DBMS provides extracts of its data to BI tools, such as data mining programs.

Data Warehouses Versus Data Marts

You can think of a data warehouse as a distributor in a supply chain. The data warehouse takes data from the data manufacturers (operational systems and purchased data), cleans and processes them, and locates the data on the shelves, so to speak, of the data warehouse. The people who work in a data warehouse are experts at data management, data cleaning, data transformation, and the like. However, they are not usually experts in a given business function.

A **data mart** is a collection of data that is smaller than that in the data warehouse and that addresses a particular component or functional area of the business. A data mart is like a retail store in a supply chain. Users in the data mart obtain data from the data warehouse that pertain to a particular business function. Such users do not have the data management expertise that data warehouse employees have, but they are knowledgeable analysts for a given business function.

Figure 8-6 illustrates these relationships. The data warehouse takes data from the data producers and distributes the data to three data marts. One data mart analyzes **click-stream data** for the purpose of designing Web pages. A second data mart analyzes store sales data and determines which products tend to be purchased together for the purpose of training sales staff. A third data mart analyzes customer order data for the purpose of reducing labor when picking up items at the warehouse. (Companies such as Amazon.com go to great lengths to organize their warehouses to reduce picking expenses.)

When the data mart structure shown in Figure 8-6 is combined with the data warehouse architecture shown in Figure 8-6, the combined system is known as an **enterprise data warehouse (EDW) architecture**. In this configuration, the data warehouse maintains all enterprise BI data and acts as the authoritative source for data extracts provided to the data marts. The data marts receive all their data from the data warehouse—they do not add or maintain any additional data.

Of course, it is expensive to create, staff, and operate data warehouses and data marts, and only large organizations with deep pockets can afford to operate a system such as an EDW. Smaller organizations operate subsets of such systems. For example, they may have just a single data mart for analyzing marketing and promotion data.

FIGURE 8-6

Data Warehouses and Data Marts

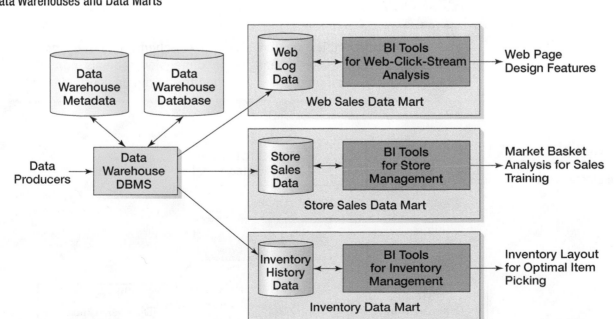

FIGURE 8-7

Characteristics of Operational and Dimensional Databases

Operational Database	Dimensional Database
Used for structured transaction data processing	Used for unstructured analytical data processing
Current data are used	Current and historical data are used
Data are inserted, updated, and deleted by users	Data are loaded and updated systematically, not by users

Dimensional Databases

The databases in a data warehouse or data mart are built to a different type of database design than the normalized relational databases used for operational systems. The data warehouse databases are built in a design called a **dimensional database** that is designed for efficient data queries and analysis. A dimensional database is used to store historical data rather than just the current data stored in an operational database. Figure 8-7 compares operational databases and dimensional databases.

Because dimensional databases are used for the analysis of historical data, they must be designed to handle data that change over time. For example, a customer may have moved from one residence to another in the same city or may have moved to a completely different city and state. This type of data arrangement is called a **slowly changing dimension**, and in order to track such changes a dimensional database must have a **date dimension** or **time dimension** as well.

The Star Schema   Rather than using the normalized database designs used in operational databases, a dimensional database uses a star schema. A **star schema**, so named because, as shown in Figure 8-8, it visually resembles a star, with a **fact table** at the center of the star and **dimension tables** radiating out from the center. The fact table is always fully normalized, but dimension tables may be non-normalized.

BTW

There is a more complex version of the star schema call the *snowflake schema*. In the snowflake schema, each dimension table is normalized, which may create additional tables attached to the dimension tables.

FIGURE 8-8

The Star Schema

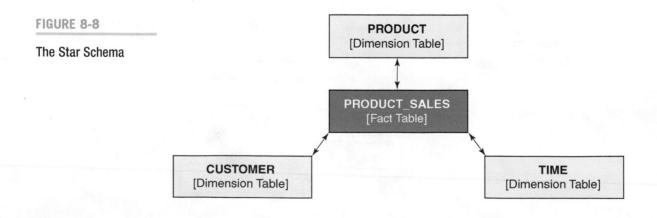

FIGURE 8-9

The HSD-DW Star Schema

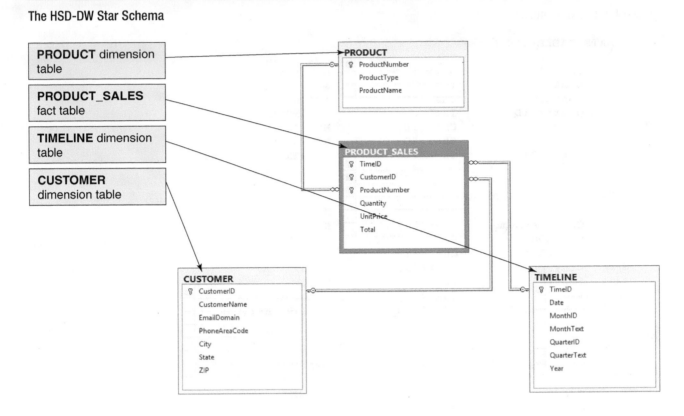

A star schema for a dimensional database named HSD-DW for BI use by Heather Sweeney Designs is shown in Figure 8-9. The SQL statements needed to create the tables in the HSD-DW database are shown in Figure 8-10, and the data in the HSD-DW database are shown in Figure 8-11. Compare this model to the HSD database diagram shown in Figure 8-2 and note how data in the HSD database have been used in the HSD-DW schema.

BTW

Note that in the HSD-DW database the CUSTOMER table uses the same surrogate primary key CustomerID, which has an integer value. Also note that we have concatenated LastName and FirstName into a single CustomerName column, and are using only the customer's area code prefix, not the entire phone number. Finally, note that we do not use individual EmailAddress values in the HSD-DW database, only values of EmailDomain, which is not unique.

A fact table is used to store **measures** of business activity, which are quantitative or factual data about the entity represented by the fact table. For example, in the HSD-DW database, the fact table is PRODUCT_SALES:

PRODUCT_SALES (TimeID, CustomerID, ProductNumber, Quantity, UnitPrice, Total)

FIGURE 8-10

The HSD-DW SQL Statements

```
CREATE TABLE TIMELINE(
    TimeID            Int             NOT NULL,
    [Date]            Date            NOT NULL,
    MonthID           Int             NOT NULL,
    MonthText         Char(15)        NOT NULL,
    QuarterID         Int             NOT NULL,
    QuarterText       Char(10)        NOT NULL,
    [Year]            Char(10)        NOT NULL,
    CONSTRAINT        TIMELINE_PK     PRIMARY KEY(TimeID)
    );

CREATE TABLE CUSTOMER(
    CustomerID        Int             NOT NULL,
    CustomerName      Char(75)        NOT NULL,
    EmailDomain       VarChar(100)    NOT NULL,
    PhoneAreaCode     Char(6)         NOT NULL,
    City              Char(35)        NULL,
    [State]           Char(2)         NULL,
    ZIP               Char(10)        NULL,
    CONSTRAINT        CUSTOMER_PK     PRIMARY KEY(CustomerID)
    );

CREATE TABLE PRODUCT(
    ProductNumber     Char(35)        NOT NULL,
    ProductType       Char(25)        NOT NULL,
    ProductName       VarChar(75)     NOT NULL,
    CONSTRAINT        PRODUCT_PK      PRIMARY KEY(ProductNumber)
    );

CREATE TABLE PRODUCT_SALES(
    TimeID            Int             NOT NULL,
    CustomerID        Int             NOT NULL,
    ProductNumber     Char(35)        NOT NULL,
    Quantity          Int             NOT NULL,
    UnitPrice         Numeric(9,2)    NOT NULL,
    Total             Numeric(9,2)    NULL,
    CONSTRAINT        PRODUCT_SALES_PK
                        PRIMARY KEY (TimeID,CustomerID,ProductNumber),
    CONSTRAINT        PS_TIMELINE_FK FOREIGN KEY(TimeID)
                        REFERENCES TIMELINE(TimeID)
                            ON UPDATE NO ACTION
                            ON DELETE NO ACTION,
    CONSTRAINT        PS_CUSTOMER_FK FOREIGN KEY(CustomerID)
                        REFERENCES CUSTOMER(CustomerID)
                            ON UPDATE NO ACTION
                            ON DELETE NO ACTION,
    CONSTRAINT        PS_PRODUCT_FK FOREIGN KEY(ProductNumber)
                        REFERENCES PRODUCT(ProductNumber)
                            ON UPDATE NO ACTION
                            ON DELETE NO ACTION
    );
```

FIGURE 8-11

The HSD-DW Table Data

	TimeID	Date	MonthID	MonthText	QuarterID	QuarterText	Year
1	41562	2013-10-15	10	October	4	Qtr4	2013
2	41572	2013-10-25	10	October	4	Qtr4	2013
3	41618	2013-12-20	12	December	4	Qtr4	2013
4	41723	2014-03-25	3	March	1	Qtr1	2014
5	41725	2014-03-27	3	March	1	Qtr1	2014
6	41729	2014-03-31	3	March	1	Qtr1	2014
7	41732	2014-04-03	4	April	2	Qtr2	2014
8	41737	2014-04-08	4	April	2	Qtr2	2014
9	41752	2014-04-23	4	April	2	Qtr2	2014
10	41766	2014-05-07	5	May	2	Qtr2	2014
11	41780	2014-05-21	5	May	2	Qtr2	2014
12	41795	2014-06-05	6	June	2	Qtr2	2014

(a) TIMELINE Dimension Table

	CustomerID	CustomerName	EmailDomain	PhoneAreaCode	City	State	ZIP
1	1	Jacobs, Nancy	somewhere.com	817	Fort Worth	TX	76110
2	2	Jacobs, Chantel	somewhere.com	817	Fort Worth	TX	76112
3	3	Able, Ralph	somewhere.com	210	San Antonio	TX	78214
4	4	Baker, Susan	elsewhere.com	210	San Antonio	TX	78216
5	5	Eagleton, Sam	elsewhere.com	210	San Antonio	TX	78218
6	6	Foxtrot, Kathy	somewhere.com	972	Dallas	TX	75220
7	7	George, Sally	somewhere.com	972	Dallas	TX	75223
8	8	Hullett, Shawn	elsewhere.com	972	Dallas	TX	75224
9	9	Pearson, Bobbi	elsewhere.com	512	Austin	TX	78710
10	10	Ranger, Terry	somewhere.com	512	Austin	TX	78712
11	11	Tyler, Jenny	somewhere.com	972	Dallas	TX	75225
12	12	Wayne, Joan	elsewhere.com	817	Fort Worth	TX	76115

(b) CUSTOMER Dimension Table

	ProductNumber	ProductType	ProductName
1	BK001	Book	Kitchen Remodeling Basics For Everyone
2	BK002	Book	Advanced Kitchen Remodeling For Everyone
3	VB001	Video Companion	Kitchen Remodeling Basics Video Companion
4	VB002	Video Companion	Advanced Kitchen Remodeling Video Companion
5	VB003	Video Companion	Kitchen Remodeling Dallas Style Video Companion
6	VK001	DVD Video	Kitchen Remodeling Basics
7	VK002	DVD Video	Advanced Kitchen Remodeling
8	VK003	DVD Video	Kitchen Remodeling Dallas Style
9	VK004	DVD Video	Heather Sweeny Seminar Live in Dallas on 25-OCT-13

(c) PRODUCT Dimension Table

	TimeID	CustomerID	ProductNumber	Quantity	UnitPrice	Total
1	41562	3	VB001	1	7.99	7.99
2	41562	3	VK001	1	14.95	14.95
3	41572	4	BK001	1	24.95	24.95
4	41572	4	VB001	1	7.99	7.99
5	41572	4	VK001	1	14.95	14.95
6	41618	7	VK004	1	24.95	24.95
7	41723	4	BK002	1	24.95	24.95
8	41723	4	VK002	1	14.95	14.95
9	41723	4	VK004	1	24.95	24.95
10	41725	6	BK002	1	24.95	24.95
11	41725	6	VB003	1	9.99	9.99
12	41725	6	VK002	1	14.95	14.95
13	41725	6	VK003	1	19.95	19.95
14	41725	6	VK004	1	24.95	24.95
15	41725	7	BK001	1	24.95	24.95
16	41725	7	BK002	1	24.95	24.95
17	41725	7	VK003	1	19.95	19.95
18	41725	7	VK004	1	24.95	24.95
19	41729	9	BK001	1	24.95	24.95
20	41729	9	VB001	1	7.99	7.99
21	41729	9	VK001	1	14.95	14.95
22	41732	11	VB003	2	9.99	19.98
23	41732	11	VK003	2	19.95	39.90
24	41732	11	VK004	2	24.95	49.90
25	41737	1	BK001	1	24.95	24.95
26	41737	1	VB001	1	7.99	7.99
27	41737	1	VK001	1	14.95	14.95
28	41737	5	BK001	1	24.95	24.95
29	41737	5	VB001	1	7.99	7.99
30	41737	5	VK001	1	14.95	14.95
31	41752	3	BK001	1	24.95	24.95
32	41766	9	VB002	1	7.99	7.99
33	41766	9	VK002	1	14.95	14.95
34	41780	8	VB003	1	9.99	9.99
35	41780	8	VK003	1	19.95	19.95
36	41780	8	VK004	1	24.95	24.95
37	41795	3	BK002	1	24.95	24.95
38	41795	3	VB001	1	7.99	7.99
39	41795	3	VB002	2	7.99	15.98
40	41795	3	VK001	1	14.95	14.95
41	41795	3	VK002	2	14.95	29.90
42	41795	11	VB002	2	7.99	15.98
43	41795	11	VK002	2	14.95	29.90
44	41795	12	BK002	1	24.95	24.95
45	41795	12	VB003	1	9.99	9.99
46	41795	12	VK002	1	14.95	14.95
47	41795	12	VK003	1	19.95	19.95
48	41795	12	VK004	1	24.95	24.95

(d) PRODUCT_SALES Fact Table

In this table:

- Quantity is quantitative data that record how many of the item were sold.
- UnitPrice is quantitative data that record the dollar price of each item sold.
- Total (= Quantity * UnitPrice) is quantitative data that record the total dollar value of the sale of this item.

The measures in the PRODUCT_SALES table are for *units of product per day*. We do not use individual sale data (which would be based on InvoiceNumber), but rather data summed for each customer for each day. For example, if you compare the HSD database INVOICE data in Figure 3-29 for Ralph Able for 6/5/14, you will see that Ralph made two purchases on that date (InvoiceNumber 35013 and InvoiceNumber 35016). In the HSD-DW database, however, these two purchases are summed into the PRODUCT_SALES data for Ralph (CustomerID = 3) for 6/5/14 (TimeID = 42160).

BTW

The TimeID values are the sequential *serial values* used in Microsoft Excel to represent dates. Starting with 01-JAN-1900 as date value 1, the date value is increased by 1 for each calendar day. Thus, 05-JUN-2014 = 42160. For more information, search "Date formats" in the Microsoft Excel help system.

A dimension table is used to record values of attributes that describe the fact measures in the fact table, and these attributes are used in queries to select and group the measures in the fact table. Thus, CUSTOMER records data about the customers referenced by CustomerID in the SALES table, TIMELINE provides data that can be used to interpret the SALES event in time (which month? which quarter?), and so on. A query to summarize product units sold by Customer (CustomerName) and Product (ProductName) would be:

```
/* *** SQL-QUERY-CH08-01 *** */
SELECT    C.CustomerID, C.CustomerName,
          P.ProductNumber, P.ProductName,
          SUM(PS.Quantity) AS TotalQuantity
FROM      CUSTOMER C, PRODUCT_SALES PS, PRODUCT P
WHERE     C.CustomerID = PS.CustomerID
   AND    P.ProductNumber = PS.ProductNumber
GROUP BY  C.CustomerID, C.CustomerName,
          P.ProductNumber, P.ProductName
ORDER BY  C.CustomerID, P.ProductNumber;
```

The results of this query are shown in Figure 8-12.

In Chapter 5, we discussed how an N:M relationship is created in a database as two 1:N relationships by use of an intersection table. We also discussed how additional attributes can be added to the intersection table in an association relationship. Similarly, the fact table is an intersection table for the relationships between the dimension tables with additional measures also stored in it. And, as with all other intersection tables, the key of the fact table is a composite key made up of all the foreign keys to the dimension tables.

Illustrating the Dimensional Model

When you think of the word *dimension*, you might think of "two dimensional" or "three dimensional." The dimensional models can be illustrated by using a two-dimensional matrix and a three-dimensional cube. Figure 8-13 shows the SQL query results from Figure 8-12 displayed as a two-dimensional matrix of Product (using ProductNumber) and Customer (using CustomerID), with each cell showing the number of units of each product purchased by each customer. Note how ProductNumber and CustomerID define the two dimensions of the matrix CustomerID labels what would be the x-axis and ProductNumber labels the y-axis of the chart.

Figure 8-14 shows a three-dimensional cube with the same ProductNumber and CustomerID dimensions, but now with the added Time dimension on the z-axis. Now, instead of occupying a two-dimensional box, the total quantity of products purchased by each customer on each day occupies a small three-dimensional cube, and all these small cubes are combined to form a large cube.

As human beings, we can visualize two-dimensional matrices and three-dimensional cubes. Although we cannot picture models with four, five, and more dimensions, BI systems and dimensional databases can handle such models.

Multiple Fact Tables and Conformed Dimensions

Data warehouse systems build dimensional models, as needed, to analyze BI questions, and the HSD-DW star schema in Figure 8-9 would be just one schema in a set of schemas. Figure 8-15 shows an extended HSD-DW schema.

In Figure 8-14, a second fact table named SALES_FOR_RFM has been added:

SALES_FOR_RFM (TimeID, CustomerID, InvoiceNumber, PreTaxTotalSale)

This table shows that fact table primary keys do not need to be composed solely of foreign keys that link to dimension tables. In SALES_FOR_RFM, the primary key includes the

FIGURE 8-12

The HSD-DW Query Results

	CustomerID	CustomerName	ProductNumber	ProductName	TotalQuantity
1	1	Jacobs, Nancy	BK001	Kitchen Remodeling Basics For Everyone	1
2	1	Jacobs, Nancy	VB001	Kitchen Remodeling Basics Video Companion	1
3	1	Jacobs, Nancy	VK001	Kitchen Remodeling Basics	1
4	3	Able, Ralph	BK001	Kitchen Remodeling Basics For Everyone	1
5	3	Able, Ralph	BK002	Advanced Kitchen Remodeling For Everyone	1
6	3	Able, Ralph	VB001	Kitchen Remodeling Basics Video Companion	2
7	3	Able, Ralph	VB002	Advanced Kitchen Remodeling Video Companion	2
8	3	Able, Ralph	VK001	Kitchen Remodeling Basics	2
9	3	Able, Ralph	VK002	Advanced Kitchen Remodeling	2
10	4	Baker, Susan	BK001	Kitchen Remodeling Basics For Everyone	1
11	4	Baker, Susan	BK002	Advanced Kitchen Remodeling For Everyone	1
12	4	Baker, Susan	VB001	Kitchen Remodeling Basics Video Companion	1
13	4	Baker, Susan	VK001	Kitchen Remodeling Basics	1
14	4	Baker, Susan	VK002	Advanced Kitchen Remodeling	1
15	4	Baker, Susan	VK004	Heather Sweeny Seminar Live in Dallas on 25-OCT-13	1
16	5	Eagleton, Sam	BK001	Kitchen Remodeling Basics For Everyone	1
17	5	Eagleton, Sam	VB001	Kitchen Remodeling Basics Video Companion	1
18	5	Eagleton, Sam	VK001	Kitchen Remodeling Basics	1
19	6	Foxtrot, Kathy	BK002	Advanced Kitchen Remodeling For Everyone	1
20	6	Foxtrot, Kathy	VB003	Kitchen Remodeling Dallas Style Video Companion	1
21	6	Foxtrot, Kathy	VK002	Advanced Kitchen Remodeling	1
22	6	Foxtrot, Kathy	VK003	Kitchen Remodeling Dallas Style	1
23	6	Foxtrot, Kathy	VK004	Heather Sweeny Seminar Live in Dallas on 25-OCT-13	1
24	7	George, Sally	BK001	Kitchen Remodeling Basics For Everyone	1
25	7	George, Sally	BK002	Advanced Kitchen Remodeling For Everyone	1
26	7	George, Sally	VK003	Kitchen Remodeling Dallas Style	1
27	7	George, Sally	VK004	Heather Sweeny Seminar Live in Dallas on 25-OCT-13	2
28	8	Hullett, Shawn	VB003	Kitchen Remodeling Dallas Style Video Companion	1
29	8	Hullett, Shawn	VK003	Kitchen Remodeling Dallas Style	1
30	8	Hullett, Shawn	VK004	Heather Sweeny Seminar Live in Dallas on 25-OCT-13	1
31	9	Pearson, Bobbi	BK001	Kitchen Remodeling Basics For Everyone	1
32	9	Pearson, Bobbi	VB001	Kitchen Remodeling Basics Video Companion	1
33	9	Pearson, Bobbi	VB002	Advanced Kitchen Remodeling Video Companion	1
34	9	Pearson, Bobbi	VK001	Kitchen Remodeling Basics	1
35	9	Pearson, Bobbi	VK002	Advanced Kitchen Remodeling	1
36	11	Tyler, Jenny	VB002	Advanced Kitchen Remodeling Video Companion	2
37	11	Tyler, Jenny	VB003	Kitchen Remodeling Dallas Style Video Companion	2
38	11	Tyler, Jenny	VK002	Advanced Kitchen Remodeling	2
39	11	Tyler, Jenny	VK003	Kitchen Remodeling Dallas Style	2
40	11	Tyler, Jenny	VK004	Heather Sweeny Seminar Live in Dallas on 25-OCT-13	2
41	12	Wayne, Joan	BK002	Advanced Kitchen Remodeling For Everyone	1
42	12	Wayne, Joan	VB003	Kitchen Remodeling Dallas Style Video Companion	1
43	12	Wayne, Joan	VK002	Advanced Kitchen Remodeling	1
44	12	Wayne, Joan	VK003	Kitchen Remodeling Dallas Style	1
45	12	Wayne, Joan	VK004	Heather Sweeny Seminar Live in Dallas on 25-OCT-13	1

FIGURE 8-13

The Two-Dimensional ProductNumber–CustomerID Matrix

Each cell shows the total quantity of each product that has been purchased by each customer

ProductNumber	CustomerID 1	2	3	4	5	6	7	8	9	10	11	12
BK001	1		1	1			1		1			
BK002			1	1		1	1					1
VB001	1		2	1	1				1			
VB002			2						1		2	
VB003						1		1			2	1
VK001	1		2	1	1				1			
VK002			2	1		1			1		2	1
VK003						1	1	1			2	1
VK004				1			1	2	1		2	1

FIGURE 8-14

The Three-Dimensional Time–ProductNumber–CustomerID Cube

Each cell will show the total quantity of each product that has been purchased by each customer on a specific date

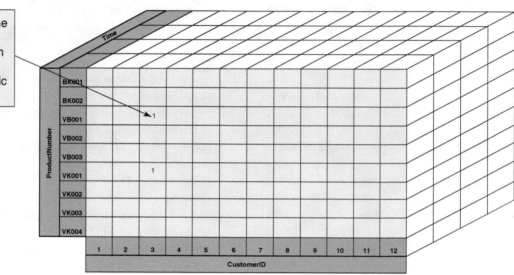

InvoiceNumber attribute. This attribute is necessary because the composite key (TimeID, CustomerID) will not be unique and cannot be the primary key. Note that SALES_FOR_RFM links to the same CUSTOMER and TIMELINE dimension tables as PRODUCT_SALES. This is done to maintain consistency within the data warehouse. When a dimension table links to two or more fact tables, it is called a **conformed dimension**.

Why would we add a fact table named SALES_FOR_RFM? This table would be used to collect and process data for an **RFM analysis**, which analyzes and ranks customers according to their purchasing patterns. It is a simple customer classification technique that considers how *recently* (R) a customer orders, how *frequently* (F) a customer orders, and *how much money* (M) the customer spends per order. RFM analysis is a commonly used BI report, and it is discussed in detail in online Appendix J.

OLAP

For an example of a BI report, we will look at OLAP, which provides the ability to sum, count, average, and perform other simple arithmetic operations on groups of data. OLAP systems produce **OLAP reports**. An OLAP report is also called an **OLAP cube**. This is a reference to the dimensional data model, and some OLAP products show OLAP displays using three axes, like a geometric cube. The remarkable characteristic of an OLAP report is that it is dynamic: The format of an OLAP report can be changed by the viewer, hence the term *online* in the name Online Analytical Processing.

FIGURE 8-15

The Extended HSD-DW Star Schema

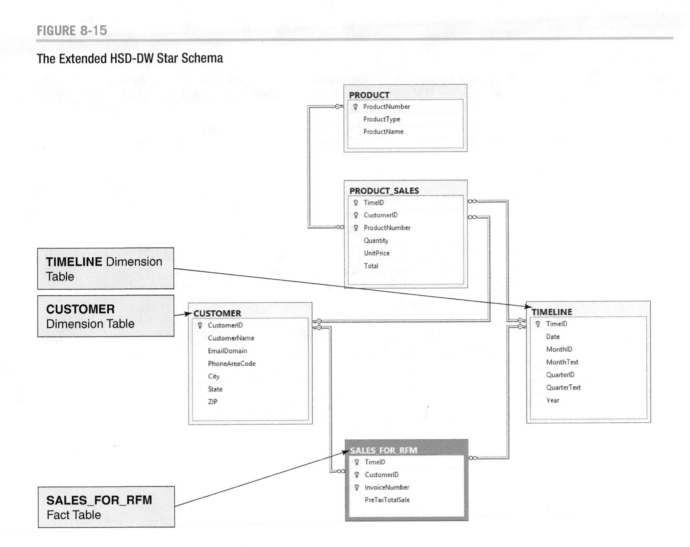

OLAP uses the dimensional database model discussed earlier in this chapter, so it is not surprising to learn that an OLAP report has measures and dimensions. A measure is a dimensional model *fact*—the data item of interest that is to be summed or averaged or otherwise processed in the OLAP report. For example, sales data may be summed to produce Total Sales or averaged to produce Average Sales. The term *measure* is used because you are dealing with quantities that have been or can be measured and recorded. A dimension, as you have already learned, is an attribute or a characteristic of a measure. Purchase date (TimeID), customer location (City), and sales region (ZIP or State) are all examples of dimensions, and in the HSD-DW database you saw how the time dimension is important.

In this section, we will generate an OLAP report by using an SQL query from the HSD-DW database and a Microsoft Excel **PivotTable**.

BTW

We use Microsoft SQL Server and Microsoft Excel to illustrate this discussion of OLAP reports and PivotTables. For other DBMS products, such as MySQL, you can use the DataPilot feature of the Calc spreadsheet application in the LibreOffice or Apache OpenOffice product suites.

Now we:

Either:

- Create a Microsoft Excel formatted table in a Microsoft Excel worksheet:
  - ➤ Copy the SQL query results into a Microsoft Excel worksheet.
  - ➤ Add column names to the results.
  - ➤ Format the query results as a Microsoft Excel table (optional).
  - ➤ Select the Microsoft Excel range containing the results with column names.

or:

- Connect to a DBMS data source.

Then:

- Click the PivotTable button in the Tables group of the Insert ribbon.
- Specify that the PivotTable should be in a new worksheet.
- Select the column variables (Column Labels), row variables (Row Labels), and the measure to be displayed (Values).

We can use an SQL query if we copy the data into a Microsoft Excel worksheet. The SQL query, as used in SQL Server, is:

```
/* *** SQL-QUERY-CH08-02 *** */
SELECT      C.CustomerID, CustomerName, C.City,
            P.ProductNumber, P.ProductName,
            T.[Year], T.QuarterText,
            SUM(PS.Quantity) AS TotalQuantity
FROM        CUSTOMER C, PRODUCT_SALES PS, PRODUCT P,
            TIMELINE T
WHERE       C.CustomerID = PS.CustomerID
    AND     P.ProductNumber = PS.ProductNumber
    AND     T.TimeID = PS.TimeID
GROUP BY    C.CustomerID, C.CustomerName, C.City,
            P.ProductNumber, P.ProductName,
            T.QuarterText, T.[Year]
ORDER BY    C.CustomerName, T.[Year], T.QuarterText;
```

However, because SQL Server (and other SQL-based DBMS products, such as Oracle Database and MySQL) can store views but not queries, we need to create and use an SQL view if we are going to use a Microsoft Excel data connection. The SQL query to create the HSDDWProductSalesView, as used in SQL Server, is:

```
/* *** SQL-CREATE-VIEW-CH08-01 *** */
CREATE VIEW HSDDWProductSalesView AS
    SELECT      C.CustomerID, C.CustomerName, C.City,
                P.ProductNumber, P.ProductName,
                T.[Year], T.QuarterText,
                SUM(PS.Quantity) AS TotalQuantity
    FROM        CUSTOMER C, PRODUCT_SALES PS, PRODUCT P,
                TIMELINE T
```

```
WHERE       C.CustomerID = PS.CustomerID
   AND      P.ProductNumber = PS.ProductNumber
   AND      T.TimeID = PS.TimeID
GROUP BY    C.CustomerID, C.CustomerName, C.City,
            P.ProductNumber, P.ProductName,
            T.QuarterText, T.[Year];
```

Figure 8-16 shows the results of SQL-QUERY-CH08-02 (which can also be obtained by using the HSDDWProductSalesView).

FIGURE 8-16

The HSD-DW-Query for OLAP Results

	CustomerID	CustomerName	City	ProductNumber	ProductName	Year	QuarterText	TotalQuantity
1	3	Able, Ralph	San Antonio	VK001	Kitchen Remodeling Basics	2013	Qtr3	1
2	3	Able, Ralph	San Antonio	VB001	Kitchen Remodeling Basics Video Companion	2013	Qtr3	1
3	3	Able, Ralph	San Antonio	VB002	Advanced Kitchen Remodeling Video Companion	2014	Qtr2	2
4	3	Able, Ralph	San Antonio	VK001	Kitchen Remodeling Basics	2014	Qtr2	1
5	3	Able, Ralph	San Antonio	VK002	Advanced Kitchen Remodeling	2014	Qtr2	2
6	3	Able, Ralph	San Antonio	BK001	Kitchen Remodeling Basics For Everyone	2014	Qtr2	1
7	3	Able, Ralph	San Antonio	BK002	Advanced Kitchen Remodeling For Everyone	2014	Qtr2	1
8	3	Able, Ralph	San Antonio	VB001	Kitchen Remodeling Basics Video Companion	2014	Qtr2	1
9	4	Baker, Susan	San Antonio	BK001	Kitchen Remodeling Basics For Everyone	2013	Qtr3	1
10	4	Baker, Susan	San Antonio	VB001	Kitchen Remodeling Basics Video Companion	2013	Qtr3	1
11	4	Baker, Susan	San Antonio	VK001	Kitchen Remodeling Basics	2013	Qtr3	1
12	4	Baker, Susan	San Antonio	VK002	Advanced Kitchen Remodeling	2014	Qtr1	1
13	4	Baker, Susan	San Antonio	VK004	Heather Sweeny Seminar Live in Dallas on 25-OCT-13	2014	Qtr1	1
14	4	Baker, Susan	San Antonio	BK002	Advanced Kitchen Remodeling For Everyone	2014	Qtr1	1
15	5	Eagleton, Sam	San Antonio	BK001	Kitchen Remodeling Basics For Everyone	2014	Qtr2	1
16	5	Eagleton, Sam	San Antonio	VB001	Kitchen Remodeling Basics Video Companion	2014	Qtr2	1
17	5	Eagleton, Sam	San Antonio	VK001	Kitchen Remodeling Basics	2014	Qtr2	1
18	6	Foxtrot, Kathy	Dallas	BK002	Advanced Kitchen Remodeling For Everyone	2014	Qtr1	1
19	6	Foxtrot, Kathy	Dallas	VB003	Kitchen Remodeling Dallas Style Video Companion	2014	Qtr1	1
20	6	Foxtrot, Kathy	Dallas	VK002	Advanced Kitchen Remodeling	2014	Qtr1	1
21	6	Foxtrot, Kathy	Dallas	VK003	Kitchen Remodeling Dallas Style	2014	Qtr1	1
22	6	Foxtrot, Kathy	Dallas	VK004	Heather Sweeny Seminar Live in Dallas on 25-OCT-13	2014	Qtr1	1
23	7	George, Sally	Dallas	VK004	Heather Sweeny Seminar Live in Dallas on 25-OCT-13	2013	Qtr3	1
24	7	George, Sally	Dallas	BK001	Kitchen Remodeling Basics For Everyone	2014	Qtr1	1
25	7	George, Sally	Dallas	BK002	Advanced Kitchen Remodeling For Everyone	2014	Qtr1	1
26	7	George, Sally	Dallas	VK003	Kitchen Remodeling Dallas Style	2014	Qtr1	1
27	7	George, Sally	Dallas	VK004	Heather Sweeny Seminar Live in Dallas on 25-OCT-13	2014	Qtr1	1
28	8	Hullett, Shawn	Dallas	VB003	Kitchen Remodeling Dallas Style Video Companion	2014	Qtr2	1
29	8	Hullett, Shawn	Dallas	VK003	Kitchen Remodeling Dallas Style	2014	Qtr2	1
30	8	Hullett, Shawn	Dallas	VK004	Heather Sweeny Seminar Live in Dallas on 25-OCT-13	2014	Qtr2	1
31	1	Jacobs, Nancy	Fort Worth	BK001	Kitchen Remodeling Basics For Everyone	2014	Qtr2	1
32	1	Jacobs, Nancy	Fort Worth	VB001	Kitchen Remodeling Basics Video Companion	2014	Qtr2	1
33	1	Jacobs, Nancy	Fort Worth	VK001	Kitchen Remodeling Basics	2014	Qtr2	1
34	9	Pearson, Bobbi	Austin	VK001	Kitchen Remodeling Basics	2014	Qtr1	1
35	9	Pearson, Bobbi	Austin	BK001	Kitchen Remodeling Basics For Everyone	2014	Qtr1	1
36	9	Pearson, Bobbi	Austin	VB001	Kitchen Remodeling Basics Video Companion	2014	Qtr1	1
37	9	Pearson, Bobbi	Austin	VB002	Advanced Kitchen Remodeling Video Companion	2014	Qtr2	1
38	9	Pearson, Bobbi	Austin	VK002	Advanced Kitchen Remodeling	2014	Qtr2	1
39	11	Tyler, Jenny	Dallas	VB002	Advanced Kitchen Remodeling Video Companion	2014	Qtr2	2
40	11	Tyler, Jenny	Dallas	VB003	Kitchen Remodeling Dallas Style Video Companion	2014	Qtr2	2
41	11	Tyler, Jenny	Dallas	VK002	Advanced Kitchen Remodeling	2014	Qtr2	2
42	11	Tyler, Jenny	Dallas	VK003	Kitchen Remodeling Dallas Style	2014	Qtr2	2
43	11	Tyler, Jenny	Dallas	VK004	Heather Sweeny Seminar Live in Dallas on 25-OCT-13	2014	Qtr2	2
44	12	Wayne, Joan	Fort Worth	BK002	Advanced Kitchen Remodeling For Everyone	2014	Qtr2	1
45	12	Wayne, Joan	Fort Worth	VB003	Kitchen Remodeling Dallas Style Video Companion	2014	Qtr2	1
46	12	Wayne, Joan	Fort Worth	VK002	Advanced Kitchen Remodeling	2014	Qtr2	1
47	12	Wayne, Joan	Fort Worth	VK003	Kitchen Remodeling Dallas Style	2014	Qtr2	1
48	12	Wayne, Joan	Fort Worth	VK004	Heather Sweeny Seminar Live in Dallas on 25-OCT-13	2014	Qtr2	1

FIGURE 8-17

OLAP ProductNumber by City Report

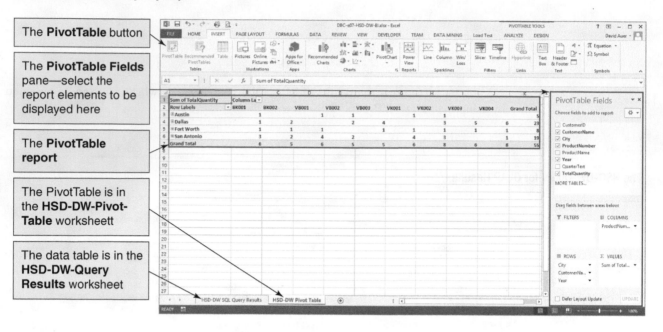

The **PivotTable** button

The **PivotTable Fields** pane—select the report elements to be displayed here

The **PivotTable report**

The PivotTable is in the **HSD-DW-Pivot-Table** worksheett

The data table is in the **HSD-DW-Query Results** worksheet

Figure 8-17 shows the OLAP report as a Microsoft Excel PivotTable. Here the measure is quantity sold, and the dimensions are ProductNumber and City. This report shows how quantity varies by product and city. For example, four copies of VB003 (Kitchen Remodeling Dallas Style Video Companion) were sold in Dallas, but none were sold in Austin.

We have generated the OLAP report in Figure 8-17 by using a simple SQL query and Microsoft Excel, but many DBMS and BI products include more powerful and sophisticated tools. For example, SQL Server includes SQL Server Analysis Services.[4] It is possible to display OLAP cubes in many ways besides with Microsoft Excel. Some third-party vendors provide more sophisticated graphical displays, and OLAP reports can be delivered just like any of the other reports described for report management systems.

The distinguishing characteristic of an OLAP report is that the user can alter the format of the report. Figure 8-18 shows an alteration in which the user added two additional dimensions, customer and year, to the horizontal display. Quantity sold is now broken out by customer and, in one case, by year. With an OLAP report, it is possible to **drill down** into the data; that is, to further divide the data into more detail. In Figure 8-18, for example, the user has drilled down into the San Antonio data to display all customer data for that city and to display year sales data for Ralph Able.

In an OLAP report, it is also possible to change the order of the dimensions. Figure 8-19 shows city quantities as vertical data and ProductID quantities as horizontal data. This OLAP report shows quantity sold by city, by product, by customer, and by year.

Both displays are valid and useful, depending on the user's perspective. A product manager might like to see product families first (ProductID) and then location data (city). A sales manager might like to see location data first and then product data. OLAP reports provide both perspectives, and the user can switch between them while viewing a report.

---

[4]Up to this point in this book, we have been using SQL Server 2014 Express, and we have been able to do all the tasks discussed on that version of SQL Server. Unfortunately, SQL Server 2014 Express does not include SQL Server Analysis Services, so you will have to use the SQL Server Standard Edition or better if you want to use the SQL Server Analysis Services. Although OLAP reports *can* be done without SQL Server Analysis Services, Analysis Services adds a lot of functionality, and the Microsoft SQL Server Data Mining Add-ins for Microsoft Office Excel 2013 (used in this text) will not function without it. Search the Microsoft Web site (**www.microsoft.com**) for more information.

FIGURE 8-18

OLAP ProductNumber by City, Customer, and Year Report

The City = San Antonio data are also showing customer data

The Customer = Able, Ralph data are also showing year data

Sum of TotalQuantity	BK001	BK002	VB001	VB002	VB003	VK001	VK002	VK003	VK004	Grand Total
Row Labels										
Austin	1		1	1		1	1			5
Pearson, Bobbi	1		1	1		1	1			5
Dallas	1	2		2	4		3	5	6	23
Foxtrot, Kathy		1			1		1	1	1	5
George, Sally	1	1						1	2	5
Hullett, Shawn					1			1	1	3
Tyler, Jenny				2	2		2	2	2	10
Fort Worth	1	1	1		1	1	1	1	1	8
Jacobs, Nancy	1		1			1	1			3
Wayne, Joan		1			1		1	1	1	5
San Antonio	3	2	4	2		4	3		1	19
Able, Ralph	1	1	2	2		2	2			10
2013			1			1				2
2014	1	1	1	2		1	2			8
Baker, Susan	1	1	1			1	1		1	6
Eagleton, Sam	1		1			1				3
Grand Total	6	5	6	5	5	6	8	6	8	55

FIGURE 8-19

OLAP City by ProductNumber, Customer, and Year Report

The city variable is on the column designator

The ProductID variable is on the primary row designator

The ProductID = VB001 data are also showing **Customer** data

The Customer = Able, Ralph data are also showing year data

Sum of TotalQuantity	Austin	Dallas	Fort Worth	San Antonio	Grand Total
Row Labels					
BK001	1	1	1	3	6
Able, Ralph				1	1
2014				1	1
Baker, Susan				1	1
Eagleton, Sam				1	1
George, Sally		1			1
Jacobs, Nancy			1		1
Pearson, Bobbi	1				1
BK002		2	1	2	5
Able, Ralph				1	1
2014				1	1
Baker, Susan				1	1
Foxtrot, Kathy		1			1
George, Sally		1			1
Wayne, Joan			1		1
VB001	1		1	4	6
Able, Ralph				2	2
2013				1	1
2014				1	1
Baker, Susan				1	1
Eagleton, Sam				1	1
Jacobs, Nancy			1		1
Pearson, Bobbi	1				1
VB002	1	2		2	5
VB003		4	1		5
VK001	1		1	4	6
VK002	1	3	1	3	8
VK003		5	1		6
VK004		6	1	1	8
Grand Total	5	23	8	19	55

DISTRIBUTED DATABASE PROCESSING

One of the first solutions to increase the amount of data that could be stored by a DBMS system was to simply spread the data among several database servers instead of just one. A group of associated servers are known as a **server cluster**,[5] and the database shared between them is called a distributed database. A **distributed database** is a database that is stored and processed on more than one computer. Depending on the type of database and

---

[5]For more information on computer clusters, see the Wikipedia article **Computer Cluster**.

the processing that is allowed, distributed databases can present significant problems. Let us consider the types of distributed databases.

Types of Distributed Databases

A database can be distributed by **partitioning**, which means breaking the database into pieces and storing the pieces on multiple computers; by **replication**, which means storing the copies of the database on multiple computers; or by a combination of replication and partitioning. Figure 8-20 illustrates these alternatives.

Figure 8-20(a) shows a nondistributed database with four pieces labeled W, X, Y, and Z. In Figure 8-20(b), the database has been partitioned but not replicated. Portions W and X are stored and processed on Computer 1, and portions Y and Z are stored and processed on Computer 2. Figure 8-20(c) shows a database that has been replicated but not partitioned. The entire database is stored and processed on Computers 1 and 2. Finally, Figure 8-20(d) shows a database that is partitioned and replicated. Portion Y of the database is stored and processed on Computers 1 and 2.

The portions to be partitioned or replicated can be defined in many different ways. A database that has five tables (for example, CUSTOMER, SALESPERSON, INVOICE, LINE_ITEM, and PART) could be partitioned by assigning CUSTOMER to portion W, SALESPERSON to portion X, INVOICE and LINE_ITEM to portion Y, and PART to portion Z. Alternatively, different rows of each of these five tables could

FIGURE 8-20

Types of Distributed Databases

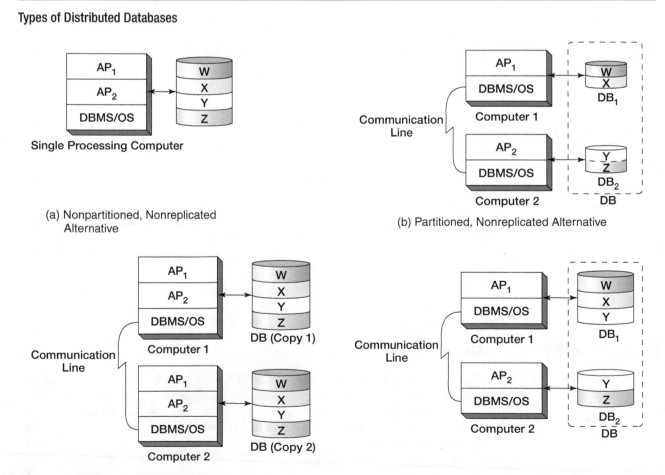

(a) Nonpartitioned, Nonreplicated Alternative

(b) Partitioned, Nonreplicated Alternative

(c) Nonpartitioned, Replicated Alternative

(d) Partitioned, Replicated Alternative

be assigned to different computers, or different columns of each of these tables could be assigned to different computers.

Databases are distributed for two major reasons: performance and control. Having a database on multiple computers can improve throughput, either because multiple computers are sharing the workload or because communications delays can be reduced by placing the computers closer to their users. Distributing the database can improve control by segregating different portions of the database to different computers, each of which can have its own set of authorized users and permissions.

Challenges of Distributed Databases

Significant challenges must be overcome when distributing a database, and those challenges depend on the type of distributed database and the activity that is allowed. In the case of a fully replicated database, if only one computer is allowed to make updates on one of the copies, then the challenges are not too great. All update activity occurs on that single computer, and copies of that database are periodically sent to the replication sites. The challenge is to ensure that only a logically consistent copy of the database is distributed (no partial or uncommitted transactions, for example) and to ensure that the sites understand that they are processing data that might not be current because changes could have been made to the updated database after the local copy was made.

If multiple computers can make updates to a replicated database, then difficult problems arise. Specifically, if two computers are allowed to process the same row at the same time, they can cause three types of error: They can make inconsistent changes, one computer can delete a row that another computer is updating, or the two computers can make changes that violate uniqueness constraints.

To prevent these problems, some type of record locking is required. Because multiple computers are involved, standard record locking does not work. Instead, a far more complicated locking scheme, called **distributed two-phase locking**, must be used. The specifics of the scheme are beyond the scope of this discussion; for now, just know that implementing this algorithm is difficult and expensive. If multiple computers can process multiple replications of a distributed database, then significant problems must be solved.

If the database is partitioned but not replicated [Figure 8-20(b)], then problems will occur if any transaction updates data that span two or more distributed partitions. For example, suppose the CUSTOMER and SALESPERSON tables are placed on a partition on one computer and that INVOICE, LINE_ITEM, and PART tables are placed on a second computer. Further suppose that when recording a sale all five tables are updated in an atomic transaction. In this case, a transaction must be started on both computers, and it can be allowed to commit on one computer only if it can be allowed to commit on both computers. In this case, distributed two-phase locking also must be used.

If the data are partitioned in such a way that no transaction requires data from both partitions, then regular locking will work. However, in this case the databases are actually two separate databases, and some would argue that they should not be considered a distributed database.

If the data are partitioned in such a way that no transaction updates data from both partitions but that one or more transactions read data from one partition and update data on a second partition, then problems might or might not result with regular locking. If dirty reads are possible, then some form of distributed locking is required; otherwise, regular locking should work.

If a database is partitioned and at least one of those partitions is replicated, then locking requirements are a combination of those just described. If the replicated portion is updated, if transactions span the partitions, or if dirty reads are possible, then distributed two-phase locking is required; otherwise, regular locking might suffice.

Distributed processing is complicated and can create substantial problems. Except in the case of replicated, read-only databases, only experienced teams with a substantial budget and significant time to invest should attempt distributed databases. Such databases also require data communications expertise. Distributed databases are not for the faint of heart.

OBJECT-RELATIONAL DATABASES

Object-oriented programming (OOP) is a technique for designing and writing computer programs. Today, most new program development is done using OOP techniques. Java, C++, C#, and Visual Basic.NET are object-oriented programming languages.

Objects are data structures that have both **methods**, which are computer programs that perform some task, and **properties**, which are data items particular to an object. All objects of a given class have the same methods, but each has its own set of data items. When using an OOP, the properties of the object are created and stored in main memory. Storing the values of properties of an object is called **object persistence**. Many different techniques have been used for object persistence. One of them is to use some variation of database technology.

Although relational databases can be used for object persistence, using this method requires substantial work on the part of the programmer. The problem is that, in general, object data structures are more complicated than the row of a table. Typically, several, or even many, rows of several different tables are required to store object data. This means the OOP programmer must design a mini-database just to store objects. Usually, many objects are involved in an information system, so many different mini-databases need to be designed and processed. This method is so undesirable that it is seldom used.

In the early 1990s, several vendors developed special-purpose DBMS products for storing object data. These products, which were called **object-oriented DBMSs (OODBMSs)**, never achieved commercial success. The problem was that by the time they were introduced, billions of bytes of data were already stored in relational DBMS format, and no organization wanted to convert its data to OODBMS format to be able to use an OODBMS. Consequently, such products failed in the marketplace.

However, the need for object persistence did not disappear. Some vendors, most notably Oracle, added features and functions to their relational database DBMS products to create **object-relational databases**. These features and functions are basically add-ons to a relational DBMS that facilitate object persistence. With these features, object data can be stored more readily than with a purely relational database. However, an object-relational database can still process relational data at the same time.[6]

Although OODBMSs have not achieved commercial success, OOP is here to stay, and modern programming languages are object-based. This is important because these are the programming languages that are being used to create the latest technologies that are dealing with Big Data.

BIG DATA AND THE NOT ONLY SQL MOVEMENT

We have used the relational database model and SQL throughout this book. However, there is another school of thought that has led to what was originally known as the **NoSQL** movement but now is usually referred as the **Not only SQL** movement.[7] It has been noted that most, but not all, DBMSs associated with the NoSQL movement are nonrelational DBMSs.

A NoSQL DBMS is often a distributed, replicated database, as described earlier in this chapter, and used where this type of a DBMS is needed to support large datasets. There have

---

[6]To learn more about object-relational databases, see the Wikipedia article **Object Database**.

[7]For a good overview, see the Wikipedia article **NoSQL**.

been several classification systems proposed for grouping and classifying NoSQL databases.[8] For our purposes, we will adopt and use a set of four categories of NoSQL databases:[9]

- **Key-Value**— Examples are Dynamo and MemcacheDB
- **Document**—Examples are Couchbase and MongoDB
- **Column Family**—Examples are Appache Cassandra and HBase
- **Graph**—Examples are Neo4J and AllegroGraph

NoSQL databases are used by widely recognized Web applications—both Facebook and Twitter use the Apache Software Foundation's **Cassandra** database. In this chapter we discuss column family databases, and we discuss the other three types in Appendix K—"Big Data".

Column Family Databases

The basis for much of the development of column family databases was a structured storage mechanism developed by Google named **Bigtable**, and column family databases are now widely available, with a good example being the Apache Software Foundation's Cassandra project. Facebook did the original development work on Cassandra and then turned it over to the open-source development community in 2008.

A generalized column family database storage system is shown in Figure 8-21. The column family database storage equivalent of a relational DBMS (RDBMS) table has a very different construction. Although similar terms are used, they do *not mean* the same thing that they mean in a relational DBMS.

The smallest unit of storage is called a **column**, but is really the equivalent of an RDBMS table cell (the intersection of an RDMBS row and column). A column consists of three elements: the *column name*, the *column value* or datum, and a *timestamp* to record when the value was stored in the column. This is shown in Figure 8-21(a) by the LastName column, which stores the LastName value Able.

FIGURE 8-21

A Generalized Column Family Database Storage System

Name: LastName
Value: Able
Timestamp: 40324081235

(a) A Column

Super Column Name:	CustomerName	
Super Column Values:	Name: FirstName	Name: LastName
	Value: Ralph	Value: Able
	Timestamp: 40324081235	Timestamp: 40324081235

(b) A Super Column

(*continued*)

---

[8]Wikipedia article **NoSQL** (accessed April 16, 2014).

[9]This set of categories corresponds to the four categories used in the Wikipedia article NoSQL as Wikipedia's taxonomy of NoSQL databases, and is also used in Ian Robinson, Jim Webber, and Emil Eifrem, *Graph Databases* (Sebastopol, CA: O'Reilly Media, 2013).

FIGURE 8-21   Continued

Column Family Name:	Customer			
RowKey001	Name: FirstName Value: Ralph Timestamp: 40324081235	Name: LastName Value: Able Timestamp: 40324081235		
RowKey002	Name: FirstName Value: Nancy Timestamp: 40335091055	Name: LastName Value: Jacobs Timestamp: 40335091055	Name: Phone Value: 817-871-8123 Timestamp: 40335091055	Name: City Value: Fort Worth Timestamp: 40335091055
RowKey003	Name: LastName Value: Baker Timestamp: 40340103518	Name: EmailAddress Value: Susan.Baker@elswhere.com Timestamp: 40340103518		

(c) A Column Family

Super Column Family Name:	Customer			
Rowkey001	**Customer Name**		**CustomerPhone**	
	Name: FirstName Value: Ralph Timestamp: 40324081235	Name: LastName Value: Able Timestamp: 40324081235	Name: AreaCode Value: 210 Timestamp: 40335091055	Name: PhoneNumber Value: 281–7987 Timestamp: 40335091055
Rowkey002	**Customer Name**		**CustomerPhone**	
	Name: FirstName Value: Nancy Timestamp: 40335091055	Name: LastName Value: Jacobs Timestamp: 40335091055	Name: AreaCode Value: 817 Timestamp: 40335091055	Name: PhoneNumber Value: 871–8123 Timestamp: 40335091055
Rowkey003	**Customer Name**		**CustomerPhone**	
	Name: FirstName Value: Susan Timestamp: 40340103518	Name: LastName Value: Baker Timestamp: 40340103518	Name: AreaCode Value: 210 Timestamp: 40340103518	Name: PhoneNumber Value: 281–7876 Timestamp: 40340103518

(d) A Super Column Family

Columns can be grouped into sets referred to as **super columns**. This is shown in Figure 8-21(a) by the CustomerName super column, which consists of a FirstName column and a LastName column and which stores the CustomerName value Ralph Able.

Columns and super columns are grouped to create **column families**, which are the column family database storage equivalent of RDBMS tables. In a column family we have rows of grouped columns, and each row has RowKey, which is similar to the primary key used in an RDBMS table. However, unlike an RDBMS table, a row in a column family does not have to have the same number of columns as another row in the same column family. This is illustrated in Figure 8-21(c) by the Customer column family, which consists of three rows of data on customers.

Figure 8-21(c) clearly illustrates the difference between structured storage column families and RDBMS tables: Column families can have variable columns and data stored in each row in a way that is impossible in an RDBMS table. This storage column structure is definitely *not* in 1NF as defined in Chapter 2, let alone BCNF! For example, note that the first row has no Phone or City columns, while the third row not only has no FirstName, Phone, or City columns, but also contains an EmailAddress column that does not exist in the other rows.

All the column families are contained in a **keyspace**, which provides the set of RowKey values that can be used in the data store. RowKey values from the keyspace are shown being used in Figure 8-21(c) to identify each row in a column family. While this structure may seem odd at first, in practice it allows for great flexibility because columns to contain new data may be introduced at any time without modifying an existing table structure.

As shown in Figure 8-21(d), a **super column family** is similar to a column family, but uses super columns (or a combination of columns and super columns) instead of columns. Of course, there is more to column family database storage than discussed here, but now you should have an understanding of the basic principles of column family databases.

MapReduce

While column family and other storage provides the means to store data in a Big Data system, the data themselves are analyzed using the **MapReduce** process. Because Big Data involves extremely large data sets, it is difficult for one computer to process data by itself. Therefore, a set of clustered computers is used using a distributed processing system similar to the distributed database system discussed previously in this chapter.

The MapReduce process is used to break a large analytical task into smaller tasks, assign each smaller task to a separate computer in the cluster, gather the results of each of those tasks, and combine them in the final product of the original tasks. The term *Map* refers to the work done on each individual computer, and the term *Reduce* refers to the combining of the individual results into the final result.

A commonly used example of the MapReduce process is counting how many times each word is used in a document. This is illustrated in Figure 8-22, where we can see how the original document is broken into sections and then each section is passed to a separate computer in the cluster for processing by the Map process. The output from each of the Map processes is then passed to one computer, which uses the Reduce process to combine the results from each Map process into the final output, which is the list of the words in the document and how many times each word appears in the document.

Hadoop

Another Apache Software Foundation project that is becoming a fundamental Big Data development platform is the **Hadoop Distributed File System (HDFS)**, which provides standard file services to clustered servers so that their file systems can function as one distributed file system. Hadoop originated as part of Cassandra, but the Hadoop project has spun off a nonrelational data store of its own called **HBase** and a query language named **Pig**.

Further, all the major DBMS players are supporting Hadoop. Microsoft is planning a Microsoft Hadoop distribution (see **http://social.technet.microsoft.com/wiki/contents/ articles/microsoft-hadoop-distribution-documentation-plan.aspx**) and has teamed up with HP and Dell to offer the **SQL Server Parallel Data Warehouse** (see **http://www.microsoft .com/sqlserver/en/us/solutions-technologies/data-warehousing/pdw.aspx**. Oracle has developed the **Oracle Big Data Appliance** that uses Hadoop (see **www.oracle.com/us/ corporate/press/512001**). A search of the Web on the term "MySQL Hadoop" quickly reveals that a lot is being done by the MySQL team as well.

FIGURE 8-22

MapReduce

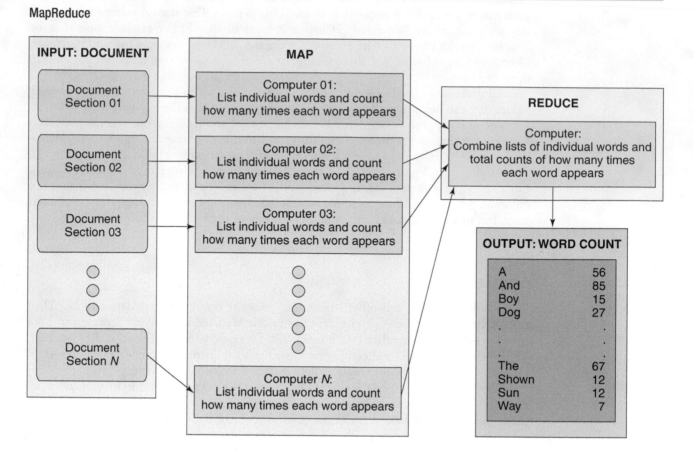

For more information on Big Data, and particularly on the various types of NoSQL databases, see Appendix K, "Big Data." The usefulness and importance of these Big Data products to organizations such as Facebook demonstrate that we can look forward to the development of not only improvements to the relational DBMSs, but also to a very different approach to data storage and information processing. Big Data and products associated with Big Data are rapidly changing and evolving, and you should expect many developments in this area in the near future.

BTW

The Not only SQL world is an exciting one, but you should be aware that if you want to participate in it you will need to sharpen your OOP programming skills. Whereas we can develop and manage databases in Microsoft Access, Microsoft SQL Server, Oracle Database, and Oracle MySQL using management and application development tools that are very user-friendly (Microsoft Access itself, Microsoft SQL Server Management Studio, Oracle SQL Developer, and MySQL Workbench), application development in the NoSQL world is currently done in programming languages.

This, of course, may change, and we look forward to seeing the future developments in the Not only SQL realm. For now, you'll need to sign up for that programming course!

THE ACCESS WORKBENCH

Section 8

Business Intelligence Systems Using Microsoft Access

In Chapter 7's section of "The Access Workbench," we built a Web site and a Web database application for the Wallingford Motors CRM. This Web site is part of a reporting system for Wallingford Motors, and updating Web pages directly from Web-based database queries is one way to deliver such reports.

In this section, we will explore how to produce an OLAP report by using the Microsoft Excel 2013 PivotTable feature. We will build an OLAP report in Microsoft Excel 2013 based on data in a Microsoft Access 2013 database. We will start by creating an OLAP report for the WMCRM database. We will continue to use the copy of the WMCRM.accdb database file that we placed in the C:\Inetpub\wwwroot\DBC\WM folder in Chapter 7's section of "The Access Workbench." This will make anything we add to the database easily available for possible use on the Wallingford Motors Web site.

Creating a View Query for an OLAP Report

To create an OLAP report, we need to create a new view, one that is a slight variant of the view named viewCustomerContacts that we created earlier in Appendix E's section of "The Access Workbench." In the new view, we need to concatenate the customer's first and last names into a single customer name, and we need to add a quantitative measure so that we can easily analyze the number of contacts made by the Wallingford Motors sales staff. We will call the new view viewCustomerContactCount.

Creating the viewCustomerContactCount Query

1. Start Microsoft Access 2013 and open the copy of the **WMCRM.accdb** database file in the **C:\Inetpub\wwwroot\DBC\WM** folder.
2. Right-click the **viewCustomerContacts** query. A shortcut menu is displayed.
3. In the shortcut menu, click the **Copy** button. The Paste As dialog box appears.
4. As shown in Figure AW-8-1, in the Paste As dialog box change the new object name to **viewCustomerContactsCount**.
5. Click the **OK** button in the Save As dialog box. As shown in Figure AW-8-2, the new object is created and displayed in Datasheet view.
6. Click the **Design View** button in the Views group of the Home ribbon to switch the query to Design view.
7. Click the **Totals** button in the Show/Hide group of the Query Tools Design ribbon to display the Total row in the fields pane.
8. Right-click the LastName field name in the LastName column to display the shortcut menu, as shown in Figure AW-8-3.
9. Click the **Build** button in the shortcut menu to display the Expression Builder.
10. Create an expression that concatenates LastName and FirstName data into a combined attribute named CustomerName as:

    CustomerName:[CUSTOMER]![LastName]&", "&[CUSTOMER]![FirstName].

    Figure AW-8-4 shows the completed expression.

11. Create the expression in Expression Builder as shown in Figure AW-8-4, and then click the **OK** button in the Expression Builder.
12. Delete the **FirstName** column from the query design.

(Continued)

FIGURE AW-8-1

The Paste As Dialog Box

The **Paste As** dialog box
The new object name has been typed into this text box
The **OK** button

FIGURE AW-8-2

The Unmodified viewCustomerContactsCount Query

The **Design View** button
The new query name
The new query object

FIGURE AW-8-3

The Shortcut Menu

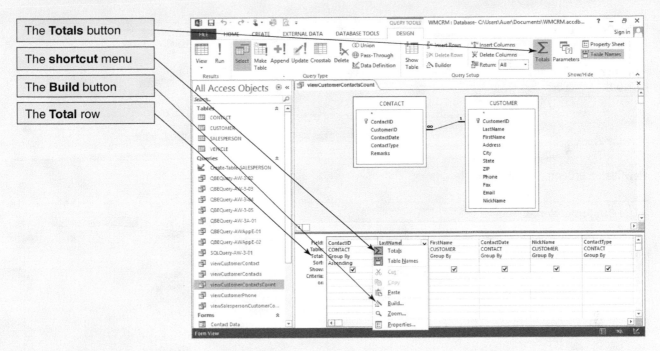

FIGURE AW-8-4

The Completed Expression in the Expression Builder

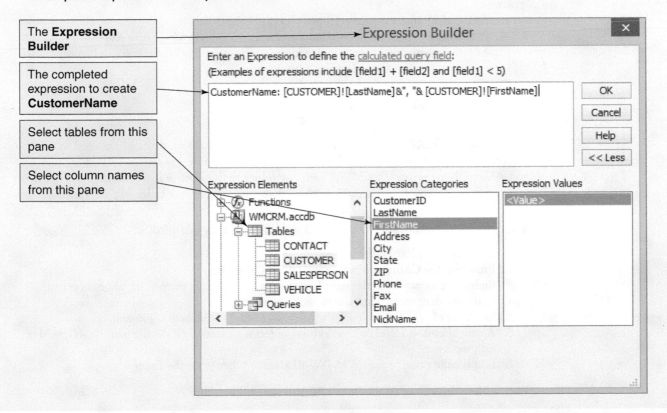

(Continued)

The ContactCount Column

The **ContactCount** expression

Set the Total setting to **Count**

viewCustomerContactCount Query Results

The **CustomerName** data

The **ContactCount** data

viewCustomerContactsCount

ContactID	CustomerName	ContactDate	NickName	ContactType	ContactCount
1	Griffey, Ben	7/7/2014	Big Bill	Phone	1
2	Griffey, Ben	7/7/2014	Big Bill	Email	1
3	Griffey, Ben	7/12/2014	Big Bill	Phone	1
4	Griffey, Ben	7/14/2014	Big Bill	Meeting	1
5	Christman, Jessica	7/19/2014	Billy	Phone	1
6	Griffey, Ben	7/21/2014	Big Bill	Email	1
7	Christman, Rob	7/27/2014	Tina	Phone	1
8	Christman, Jessica	7/27/2014	Billy	Meeting	1
9	Christman, Rob	8/2/2014	Tina	Meeting	1
10	Christman, Jessica	8/3/2014	Billy	Email	1
11	Christman, Rob	8/10/2014	Tina	Email	1
12	Hayes, Judy	8/15/2014	Tina	Phone	1

13. Delete the **Remarks** column from the query design.
14. Add a column named **ContactCount** to the query, as shown in Figure AW-8-5.
15. Save the changes to the query and then run it. The query results are shown in Figure AW-8-6.
16. Close the viewCustomerContactCount query.
17. Close the WMCRM database and Microsoft Access.

Creating a Microsoft Excel Worksheet for an OLAP Report

Because the OLAP report will be in a Microsoft Excel 2013 workbook, we need to create a new workbook to hold the OLAP report. We will continue to use the Wallingford Motors C:\Inetpub\wwwroot\DBC\WM Web site folder as the storage location, and now we need to create a Microsoft Excel 2013 workbook named WM-DW-BI.xlsx in that folder.

Creating the Microsoft Excel 2013 WM-DW-BI.xlsx Workbook

1. Start Windows Explorer.
2. Browse to the **C:\Inetpub\wwwroot\DBC\WM** folder.
3. Right-click anywhere in the right-hand folder and file pane to open the shortcut menu.
4. In the shortcut menu, click the **New** command.
5. In the list of new objects, click the **Microsoft Excel Worksheet** command.
6. A new Microsoft Excel 2013 workbook object is created, with the file name highlighted in Edit mode.
7. Edit the file name to read **WM-DW-BI.xlsx**, and then press the **Enter** key.

Now you can open the WM-DW-BI.xlsx workbook.

FIGURE AW-8-7

The WM-DW-BI.xlsx Workbook

The **DATA** command tab

The **WM-DW-BI.xlsx** workbook file

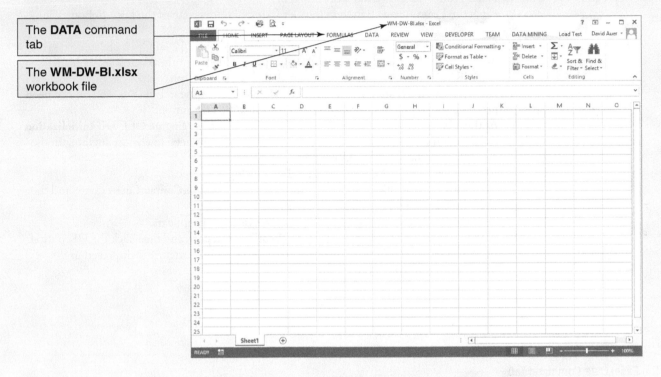

Opening the Microsoft Excel 2013 WM-DW-BI.xlsx Workbook

1. Start Microsoft Excel 2013.
2. Click the **File** command tab, and then click the **Open** button.
3. In the Open dialog box, browse to the **C:\inetpub\wwwroot\DBC\WM** folder and open the **WM-DW-BI.xlsx** file. The **WM-DW-BI.xlsx** workbook is displayed, as shown in Figure AW-8-7.

Creating a Basic OLAP Report

We can now create an OLAP report in the Microsoft Excel 2013 WM-DW-BI.xlsx workbook. Fortunately, Microsoft has made it possible to link directly to Microsoft Access 2013 to obtain the data needed for the report. We will connect the Microsoft Excel workbook to the Microsoft Access database and create the basic, blank OLAP report PivotTable.

BTW

Microsoft Excel 2013 uses the same Microsoft Office fluent user interface that you have learned to use in Microsoft Access 2013. Because you should already be familiar with the Microsoft Office fluent user interface, we do not discuss the Microsoft Excel variant of this interface.

(Continued)

Creating the Basic OLAP Report PivotTable

1. In the WM-DW-BI.xlsx workbook, click the **Data** command tab to display the Data command groups, as shown in Figure AW-8-8.
2. Click the **From Access** button in the Get External Data group of the Data ribbon. The Select Data Source dialog box appears.
3. In the Select Data Source dialog box, which functions just like an Open dialog box, browse to the **C:\inetpub\wwwroot\DBC\WM** folder. Select the Microsoft Access **WMCRM.accdb** database file, and then click the **Open** button.
4. At this point, the **Data Link Properties** dialog box *may* appear. If it does, you do not need to change anything in the dialog box, so just click the **OK** button.
5. At this point, the **Please Enter Microsoft Access Database Engine OLE DB Initialization Information** dialog box *may* appear. If it does, you do not need to change anything in the dialog box, so just click the **OK** button.
6. As shown in Figure AW-8-9, the Select Table dialog box appears.
7. In the Select Table dialog box, select the new **viewCustomerContactCount** query and then click the **OK** button.
8. As shown in Figure AW-8-10, the Import Data dialog box appears.
9. In the Import Data dialog box, select the **PivotTable Report**, and then click the **OK** button.
10. As shown in Figure AW-8-11, the basic PivotTable report structure is displayed in the Microsoft Excel worksheet.

FIGURE AW-8-8

The Excel Data Command Tab

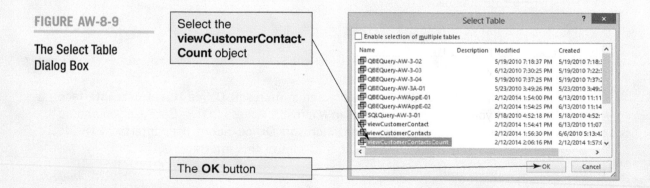

The **DATA** command tab

The **Get External Data** drop-down list arrow button

The **From Access** button

FIGURE AW-8-9

The Select Table Dialog Box

Select the **viewCustomerContact-Count** object

The **OK** button

FIGURE AW-8-10

The Import Data Dialog Box

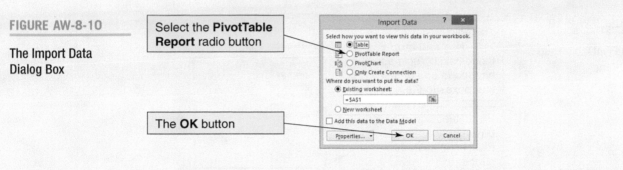

Select the **PivotTable Report** radio button

The **OK** button

11. Click the **Save** button on Microsoft Excel Quick Access Toolbar to save your work to this point.

   ■ **NOTE:** From now on, when you open the WM-DW-BI.xlsx workbook a Security Warning bar will appear, warning that data connections have been disabled. This is similar to the Microsoft Access 2013 Security Warning bar you have already learned to use, and essentially the same action is necessary: Click the **Enable Options** button.

Structuring an OLAP Report

We can now create the structure of the OLAP report. We do this by using the Microsoft Excel PivotTable Field List pane, shown in Figures AW-8-11 and AW-8-12. To build the structure of the PivotTable, we drag and drop the field objects from the field object list. We drag the measures we want displayed to the Values box. We drag the dimension attributes we want as column structure to the Column Labels box, and we drag the dimension attributes we want as row structure to the Row Labels box.

For the Wallingford Motors Customer Contact PivotTable, we will use ContactCount as the measure, so it needs to go in the Values box. The column structure will have customer

FIGURE AW-8-11

The Basic PivotTable Report Structure

The **Save** button

The **PivotTable Tools** tab

The initial **PivotTable** area

The **PivotTable Field List** pane—the structure of the PivotTable is built using these controls

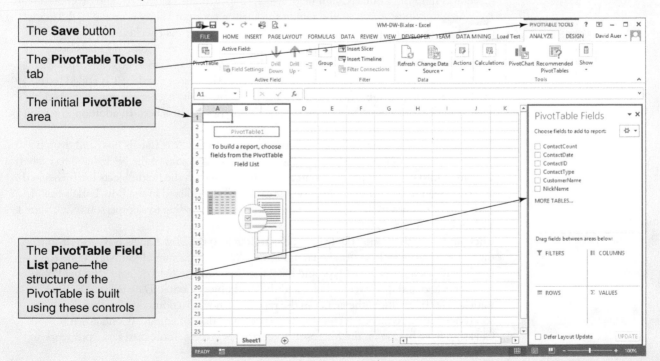

(Continued)

FIGURE AW-8-12

The PivotTable Field List Pane

The field object list—drag-and-drop these field objects as needed to one of the four boxes to the right

Field objects in this box appear as the PivotTable column structure

Field objects in this box appear in the PivotTable cell structure

Field objects in this box appear as the PivotTable row structure

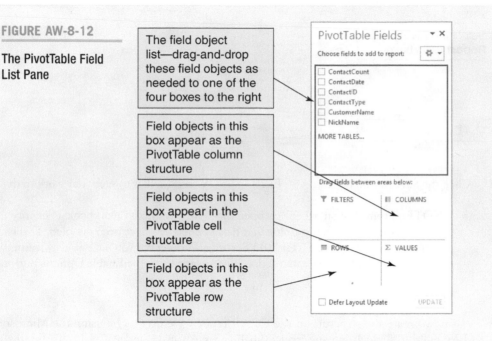

attributes, in this case only CustomerName. Finally, the row structure will have contact attributes—NickName (for SalesPerson) first, followed by ContactType and then Contact Date.

Creating the OLAP Report's PivotTable Structure

1. Click-and-hold the **CustomerName** field object, drag it to the Column Labels box, and drop it there. As shown in Figure AW-8-13, the CustomerName labels and a GrandTotal label are added to the worksheet columns, the CustomerName field object in the field objects list is checked and displayed in bold, and the field object CustomerName is listed in the Column Labels box.
2. Click-and-hold the **ContactCount** field object, drag it to the Values box, and drop it there. As shown in Figure AW-8-14, the sum of the CustomerCount values is added to the worksheet, the CustomerCount field object in the field objects list is checked and displayed in bold, and the field object Sum of CustomerCount is listed in the Column Labels box.
3. Click-and-hold the **NickName** field object, drag it to the Row Labels box, and drop it there. As shown in Figure AW-8-15, the sum of the NickName row labels is added to the worksheet, the NickName field object in the field objects list is checked and displayed in bold, and the field object NickName is listed in the Row Labels box. In addition, the values in the report are starting to show up.
4. Click-and-hold the **ContactType** field object, drag it to the Row Labels box, and drop it there, *below* NickName. As shown in Figure AW-8-16, the sum of the NickName row labels is divided into contact type, the ContactType field object in the field objects list is checked and displayed in bold, and the field object ContactType is listed in the Row Labels box. In addition, the values in the report are now distributed according to salesperson (NickName) and type of contact (ContactType).
5. Click-and-hold the **ContactDate** field object, drag it to the Row Labels box, and drop it there, *below* ContactType. As shown in Figure AW-8-17, the sum of the NickName row labels is divided into contact type and date, the ContactDate field object in the field objects list is checked and displayed in bold, and the field object ContactDate is listed in the Row Labels box. In addition, the values in the report are now distributed according to salesperson (NickName), type of contact (ContactType), and date of contact (ContactDate).
6. Click the **Save** button on the Microsoft Excel Quick Access Toolbar to save your work to this point.

FIGURE AW-8-13

The CustomerName Column Labels

The PivotTable Column Labels

The **CustomerName** field object is checked and displayed in bold

The **CustomerName** field object is displayed in the Column Labels box

FIGURE AW-8-14

The CustomerCount Values

The PivotTable cell values are now displayed—at this point only the sum for each column is shown

The **ContactCount** object is checked and displayed in bold

The **Sum of ContactCount** object is displayed in the Values box

(Continued)

FIGURE AW-8-15

The NickName Row Labels

> The NickName row labels are displayed, and now the PivotTable cell values are displayed

> The **NickName** field object is checked and displayed in bold

> The **NickName** field object is displayed in the Row Labels box

FIGURE AW-8-16

The ContactType Row Labels

> The NickName row labels are divided by **ContactType**

> The **ContactType** field object is checked and displayed in bold

> The **ContactType** field object is displayed in the Row Labels box

FIGURE AW-8-17

The ContactDate Row Labels

The NickName row labels are divided by ContactType, and ContactType is divided by ContactDate

The **ContactDate field** object is checked and displayed in bold

The **ContactDate field** object is displayed in the Row Labels box

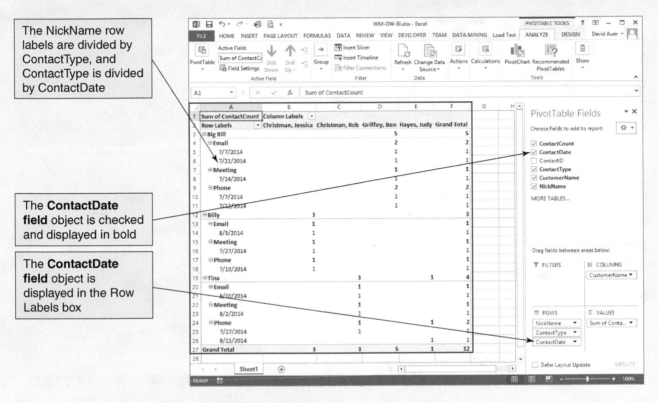

Modifying an OLAP Report

We have finished building our OLAP report. We can modify it as needed by moving the field objects in the PivotTable Field List pane. We can also format the OLAP report to make it look the way we want it.

Modifying the OLAP Report PivotTable Structure

1. Click-and-hold the **ContactDate** field object in the Row Labels box, drag it within the box to between the NickName and Type field objects' Column Labels box, and drop it there. As shown in Figure AW-8-18, the order of the row labels in the OLAP report changes, and the data move, too.
2. As shown in Figure AW-8-18, you can contract and expand various portions of the OLAP report. In that figure, the data for Big Bill are shown fully expanded, while Billy's data are completely contracted. The data for Tina are shown at the Date level of detail, but without Type detail.

Formatting the OLAP Report

1. Click the PivotTable Tools **Design** command tab to display the Design command groups, as shown in Figure AW-8-19.
2. Click the **Banded Columns** check box in the PivotTable Style Options command group.
3. Click the **PivotTable Styles Gallery** drop-down arrow button to display the PivotTable Styles Gallery, as shown in Figure AW-8-20.
4. Select the PivotTable style shown in Figure AW-8-20 to format the OLAP report.

(Continued)

FIGURE AW-8-18

The Rearranged Row Labels

The NickName row labels are divided by ContactDate, and ContactDate is divided by ContactType

Big Bill's data fully expanded, Billy's data fully contracted, and Tina's data displayed at the ContactDate level of detail

The **ContactDate field** object is now displayed between the NickName and Type field objects

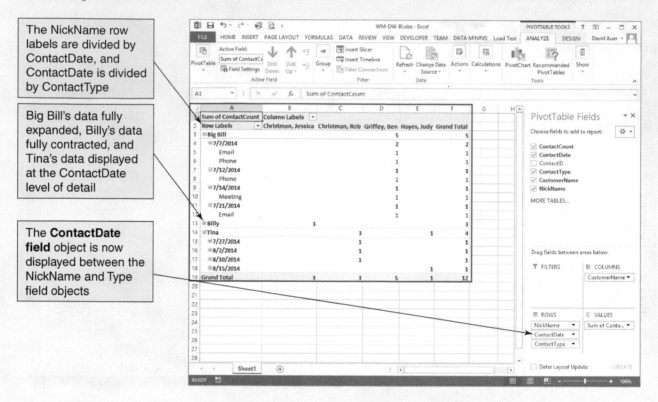

5. Adjust the column widths of columns B, C, D, E, and F so that they are uniform and the entire table is visible on the worksheet when the PivotTable Field List pane is visible.
6. The final, formatted PivotTable OLAP report is shown in Figure AW-8-21.
7. Click the **Save** button on the Microsoft Excel Quick Access Toolbar.
8. Close the WM-DW-BI.xlsx workbook.
9. Close Microsoft Excel.

In Closing

Our work is done. In "The Access Workbench," you have learned the essentials of working with Microsoft Access (and just a bit about working with Microsoft Excel). You have not learned everything there is to know, but now you know how to create and populate Microsoft

---

FIGURE AW-8-19

The Excel PivotTable Tools Design Command Tab

The **Banded Columns** checkbox

The **PivotTable Styles** gallery drop-down arrow button

FIGURE AW-8-20

The Excel PivotTable Styles Gallery

The columns in the OLAP report now have borders

The **PivotTable Styles** gallery

Click this style to format the OLAP report

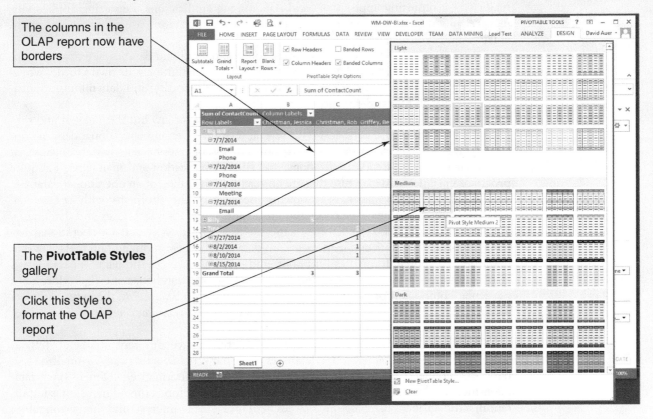

Access databases; build and use Microsoft Access queries (including view-equivalent queries), forms, and reports; secure a Microsoft Access database; connect to a Microsoft Access database from a Web page; and create a PivotTable OLAP report. You now have a solid foundation to build on, which was, after all, the overall goal of "The Access Workbench."

FIGURE AW-8-21

The Final PivotTable OLAP Report

Big Bill's data fully expanded, Billy's data fully contracted, and Tina's data displayed at the Date level of detail

	A	B	C	D	E	F
1	Sum of ContactCount	Column Labels				
2	Row Labels	Christman, Jessica	Christman, Rob	Griffey, Ben	Hayes, Judy	Grand Total
3	⊟ Big Bill			5		5
4	⊟ 7/7/2014		2			2
5	Email		1			1
6	Phone		1			1
7	⊟ 7/12/2014		1			1
8	Phone		1			1
9	⊟ 7/14/2014		1			1
10	Meeting		1			1
11	⊟ 7/21/2014		1			1
12	Email		1			1
13	⊞ Billy	3				5
14	⊟ Tina		3		1	4
15	⊞ 7/27/2014		1			1
16	⊞ 8/2/2014		1			1
17	⊞ 8/10/2014		1			1
18	⊞ 8/15/2014				1	1
19	Grand Total	3	3	5	1	12

SUMMARY

Business intelligence (BI) systems assist managers and other professionals in the analysis of current and past activities and in the prediction of future events. BI applications are of two major types: reporting applications and data mining applications. Reporting applications make elementary calculations on data; data mining applications use sophisticated mathematical and statistical techniques.

BI applications obtain data from three sources: operational databases, extracts of operational databases, and purchased data. A BI system sometimes has its own DBMS, which may or not be the operational DBMS. Characteristics of reporting and data mining applications are listed in Figure 8-4.

Direct reading of operational databases is not feasible for any but the smallest and simplest BI applications and databases—for several reasons. Querying operational data can unacceptably slow the performance of operational systems, operational data have problems that limit their usefulness for BI applications, and BI system creation and maintenance require programs, facilities, and expertise that are normally not available for an operational database.

Operational data may have problems. Because of the problems with operational data, many organizations have chosen to create and staff data warehouses and data marts. Extract, transform, and load (ETL) systems are used to extract data from operational systems; transform the data and load them into data warehouses; and maintain metadata that describes the source, format, assumptions, and constraints about the data. A data mart is a collection of data that is smaller than that held in a data warehouse and that addresses a particular component or functional area of the business. In Figure 8-6, the enterprise data warehouse distributes data to three smaller data marts, each of which services the needs of a different aspect of the business.

Operational databases and dimensional databases have different characteristics, as shown in Figure 8-7. Dimensional databases use a star schema with a fully normalized fact table that connects to dimension tables that may be non-normalized. Dimensional databases must deal with slowly changing dimensions, and therefore a time dimension is important in a dimensional database. Fact tables hold measures of interest, and dimension tables hold attribute values used in queries. The star schema can be extended with additional fact tables, dimension tables, and conformed dimensions.

The purpose of a reporting system is to create meaningful information from disparate data sources and to deliver that information to the proper users on a timely basis. Reports are produced by sorting, filtering, grouping, and making simple calculations on the data. RFM analysis is a typical reporting application. Customers are grouped and classified according to how recently they have placed an order (R), how frequently they order (F), and how much money (M) they spend on orders. An RFM report can be produced using SQL statements.

Online Analytical Processing (OLAP) reporting applications enable users to dynamically restructure reports. A measure is a data item of interest. A dimension is a characteristic of a measure. An OLAP report, or OLAP cube, is an arrangement of measures and dimensions. With OLAP, users can drill down and exchange the order of dimensions.

A distributed database is a database that is stored and processed on more than one computer. A replicated database is one in which multiple copies of some or all of the database are stored on different computers. A partitioned database is one in which different pieces of the database are stored on different computers. A distributed database can be replicated and distributed.

Distributed databases pose processing challenges. If a database is updated on a single computer, then the challenge is simply to ensure that the copies of the database are logically consistent when they are distributed. However, if updates are to be made on more than one computer, the challenges become significant. If the database is partitioned and not replicated, then challenges occur if transactions span data on more than one computer. If the database is replicated and if updates occur to the replicated portions, then a special locking algorithm called distributed two-phase locking is required. Implementing this algorithm can be difficult and expensive.

Objects consist of methods and properties or data values. All objects of a given class have the same methods, but they have different property values. Object persistence is the process of storing object property values. Relational databases are difficult to use for object persistence. Some specialized products called object-oriented DBMSs were developed in the 1990s but never received commercial acceptance. Oracle and others have extended the capabilities of their relational DBMS products to provide support for object persistence. Such databases are referred to as object-relational databases.

The NoSQL movement (now often read as "not only SQL") is built upon the need to meet the Big Data storage needs of companies such as Amazon.com, Google, and Facebook. The tools used to do this are nonrelational DBMSs know as structured storage. An early example was Bigtable, and a more recent popular example is Cassandra. These products use a non-normalized table structure built on columns, super columns, column families, and super column families tied together by rowkey values from a keyspace. Data processing of the very large data sets found in Big Data is done by the MapReduce process, which breaks a data processing task in many parallel tasks done by many computers in the cluster and then combines these results to produce a final result. An emerging product that is supported by Microsoft and Oracle Corporation is the Hadoop Distributed File System (HDFS), with its spinoffs HBase, a nonrelational storage component, and Pig, a query language.

KEY TERMS

Big Data
Bigtable
business intelligence (BI) system
Cassandra
click-stream data
column
column family
conformed dimension
data mart
data mining application
data warehouse
data warehouse metadata
    database
date dimension
dimension table
dimensional database
distributed database
distributed two-phase locking
document
drill down
enterprise data warehouse (EDW)
    architecture

extract, transform, and load (ETL)
    system
fact table
Graph
Hadoop Distributed File System
    (HDFS)
HBase
keyspace
Key-Value
measure
method
MapReduce
NoSQL
Not only SQL
object
object-oriented DBMS (OODBMS)
object-oriented programming
    (OOP)
object persistence
object-relational database
OLAP cube
OLAP report

Online Analytical Processing
    (OLAP)
online transaction processing
    (OLTP) system
operational system
Oracle Big Data Appliance
partitioning
Pig
PivotTable
property
replication
reporting system
RFM analysis
server cluster
slowly changing dimension
SQL Server Parallel Data
    Warehouse
star schema
super column
super column family
time dimension
transactional system

REVIEW QUESTIONS

8.1   What are BI systems?

8.2   How do BI systems differ from transaction processing systems?

8.3   Name and describe the two main categories of BI systems.

8.4   What are the three sources of data for BI systems?

8.5   Summarize the problems with operational databases that limit their usefulness for BI applications.

8.6   What is an ETL system, and what functions does it perform?

8.7   What problems in operational data create the need to clean data before loading the data into a data warehouse?

8.8   What does it mean to transform data? Give an example other than the ones used in this book.

8.9   Why are data warehouses necessary?

8.10   Give examples of data warehouse metadata.

8.11   Explain the difference between a data warehouse and a data mart. Give an example other than the ones used in this book.

8.12   What is the enterprise data warehouse (EDW) architecture?

8.13   Describe the differences between operational databases and dimensional databases.

8.14   What is a star schema?

8.15   What is a fact table? What types of data are stored in fact tables?

8.16   What is a measure?

8.17   What is a dimension table? What types of data are stored in dimension tables?

8.18   What is a slowly changing dimension?

8.19   Why is the time dimension important in a dimensional model?

8.20   What is a conformed dimension?

8.21   What does OLAP stand for?

8.22   What is the distinguishing characteristic of OLAP reports?

8.23   Define *measure*, *dimension*, and *cube*.

8.24   Give an example, other than ones in this text, of a measure, two dimensions related to your measure, and a cube.

8.25   What is drill down?

8.26   Explain two ways that the OLAP report in Figure 8-19 differs from that in Figure 8-18.

8.27   Define *distributed database*.

8.28   Explain one way to partition a database that has three tables: T1, T2, and T3.

8.29   Explain one way to replicate a database that has three tables: T1, T2, and T3.

8.30   Explain what must be done when fully replicating a database but allowing only one computer to process updates.

8.31   If more than one computer can update a replicated database, what three problems can occur?

8.32   What solution is used to prevent the problems in question 8.31?

8.33   Explain what problems can occur in a distributed database that is partitioned but not replicated.

8.34   What organizations should consider using a distributed database?

8.35   Explain the meaning of the term *object persistence*.

8.36   In general terms, explain why relational databases are difficult to use for object persistence.

8.37   What does *OODBMS* stand for, and what is its purpose?

8.38   According to this chapter, why were OODBMSs not successful?

8.39   What is an object-relational database?

8.40   What is *Big Data*?

8.41 What is the relationship between 1 MB of storage and 1 EB of storage?

8.42 What is the *NoSQL movement*?

8.43 What was the first nonrelational data store to be developed, and who developed it?

8.44 What is *Cassandra*, and what is the history of the development of Cassandra to its current state?

8.45 As illustrated in Figure 8-21, what is column family database storage and how are such systems organized? How do column family database storage systems compare to RDBMS systems?

8.46 Explain *MapReduce* processing.

8.47 What is *Hadoop*, and what is the history of the development of Hadoop to its current state? What are *HBase* and *Pig*?

EXERCISES

8.48 Based on the discussion of the Heather Sweeney Designs operational database (HSD) and dimensional database (HSD-DW) in the text, answer the following questions.

   A. Using the SQL statements shown in Figure 8-10, create the HSD-DW database in a DBMS.

   B. What transformations of data were made before HSD-DW was loaded with data? List all the transformations, showing the original format of the HSD data and how they appear in the HSD-DW database.

   C. Write the complete set of SQL statements necessary to load the transformed data into the HSD-DW database.

   D. Populate the HSD-DW database, using the SQL statements you wrote to answer part C.

   E. Figure 8-23 shows the SQL code to create the SALES_FOR_RFM fact table shown in Figure 8-15. Using those statements, add the SALES_FOR_RFM table to your HSD-DW database.

FIGURE 8-23

The HSD-DW SALES_FOR_RFM SQL Statements

```
CREATE TABLE SALES_FOR_RFM(
        TimeID              Int                 NOT NULL,
        CustomerID          Int                 NOT NULL,
        InvoiceNumber       Int                 NOT NULL,
        PreTaxTotalSale     Numeric(9,2)        NOT NULL,
        CONSTRAINT          SALES_FOR_RFM_PK
                            PRIMARY KEY (TimeID, CustomerID, InvoiceNumber),
        CONSTRAINT          SRFM_TIMELINE_FK FOREIGN KEY(TimeID)
                            REFERENCES TIMELINE(TimeID)
                                ON UPDATE NO ACTION
                                ON DELETE NO ACTION,
        CONSTRAINT          SRFM_CUSTOMER_FK FOREIGN KEY(CustomerID)
                            REFERENCES CUSTOMER(CustomerID)
                                ON UPDATE NO ACTION
                                ON DELETE NO ACTION
    );
```

F. What transformations of data are necessary to load the SALES_FOR_RFM table? List any needed transformations, showing the original format of the HSD data and how they appear in the HSD-DW database.

G. What data will be used to load the SALES_FOR_RFM fact table? Write the complete set of SQL statements necessary to load this data.

H. Populate the SALES_FOR_RFM fact table, using the SQL statements you wrote to answer part G.

I. Write an SQL query similar to the one shown on page 456 that uses the total dollar amount of each day's product sales as the measure (instead of the number of products sold each day).

J. Write the SQL view equivalent of the SQL query you wrote to answer part I.

K. Create the SQL view you wrote to answer part J in your HSD-DW database.

L. Create a Microsoft Excel 2013 workbook named HSD-DW-BI-Exercises .xlsx.

M. Using either the results of your SQL query from part K (copy the results of the query into a worksheet in the HSD-DW-BI.xlsx workbook and then format this range as a worksheet table) or your SQL view from part L (create a Microsoft Excel data connection to the view), create an OLAP report similar to the OLAP report shown in Figure 8-17. (*Hint:* If you need help with the needed Microsoft Excel actions, search in the Microsoft Excel help system for more information.)

N. Heather Sweeney is interested in the effects of payment type on sales in dollars.
    1. Modify the design of the HSD-DW dimensional database to include a PAYMENT_TYPE dimension table.
    2. Modify the HSD-DW database to include the PAYMENT_TYPE dimension table.
    3. What data will be used to load the PAYMENT_TYPE dimension table? What data will be used to load foreign key data into the PRODUCT_SALES fact table? Write the complete set of SQL statements necessary to load these data.
    4. Populate the PAYMENT_TYPE and PRODUCT_SALES tables, using the SQL statements you wrote to answer part 3.
    5. Create the SQL queries or SQL views needed to incorporate the PaymentType attribute.
    6. Create a Microsoft Excel 2013 OLAP report to show the effect of payment type on product sales in dollars.

ACCESS WORKBENCH EXERCISES

AW.8.1   Using the discussion of dimensional models and OLAP reports in the text and the specific discussion of OLAP reports based on a Microsoft Access 2013 database in this chapter's section of "The Access Workbench" as your reference, complete exercise 8.48 (excluding part N) for Heather Sweeney Designs. Create your HSD-DW database in Microsoft Access 2013 and your OLAP report in Microsoft Excel 2013.

MARCIA'S DRY CLEANING CASE QUESTIONS

Ms. Marcia Wilson owns and operates Marcia's Dry Cleaning, which is an upscale dry cleaner in a well-to-do suburban neighborhood. Marcia makes her business stand out from the competition by providing superior customer service. She wants to keep track of each of her customers and their orders. Ultimately, she wants to notify them that their clothes are ready via email.

Assume that Marcia has hired you as a database consultant to develop an operational database named MDC that has the following four tables:

CUSTOMER (<u>CustomerID</u>, FirstName, LastName, Phone, Email)

INVOICE (<u>InvoiceNumber</u>, *CustomerID*, DateIn, DateOut, Subtotal, Tax, TotalAmount)

INVOICE_ITEM (<u>*InvoiceNumber*</u>, <u>ItemNumber</u>, *ServiceID*, Quantity, UnitPrice, ExtendedPrice)

SERVICE (<u>ServiceID</u>, ServiceDescription, UnitPrice)

A Microsoft Access 2013 version of the MDC database and SQL scripts to create and populate the MDC database are available for Microsoft SQL Server 2014, Oracle Database Express Edition 11*g* Release 2, and MySQL 5.6 Community Server at the Database Concepts Web site at **www.pearsonhighered.com/kroenke**. Sample data for the CUSTOMER table are shown in Figure 7-37, for the SERVICE table in Figure 7-38, for the INVOICE table in Figure 7-39, and for the INVOICE_ITEM table in Figure 7-40.

A. Create a database in your DBMS named MDC, and use the MDC SQL scripts for your DBMS to create and populate the database tables. Create a user named MDC-User with the password MDC-User+password. Assign this user to database roles so that the user can read, insert, delete, and modify data.

B. Create an appropriate ODBC data source for your database.

C. You need about 20 INVOICE transactions with supporting INVOICE_ITEMs in the database. Write the needed SQL statements for any needed additional INVOICE transactions and insert the data into your database.

D. Design a data warehouse star schema for a dimensional database named MDC-DW. The fact table measure will be ExtendedPrice.

E. Create the MDC-DW database in your DBMS product.

F. What transformations of data will need to be made before the MDC-DW database can be loaded with data? List all the transformations, showing the original format of the MDC data and how it appears in the MDC-DW database.

G. Write the complete set of SQL statements necessary to load the transformed data into the MDC-DW database.

H. Populate the MDC-DW database, using the SQL statements you wrote to answer part G.

I. Write an SQL query similar to the one shown in the text on page 456 that uses the ExtendedPrice as the measure.

J. Write the SQL view equivalent of the SQL query you wrote to answer part I.

K. Create the SQL view you wrote to answer part J in your MDC-DW database.

L. Create the Microsoft Excel 2013 workbook named MDC-DW-BI-Exercises.xlsx.

M. Using either the results of your SQL query from part I (copy the results of the query into a worksheet in the MDC-DW-BI.xlsx workbook and then format this range as a worksheet table) or your SQL view from part I (create a Microsoft Excel data connection to the view), create an OLAP report similar to the OLAP report shown in Figure 8-17. (*Hint:* If you need help with the needed Microsoft Excel actions, search in the Microsoft Excel help system for more information.)

GARDEN GLORY PROJECT QUESTIONS

If you have not already implemented the Garden Glory database shown in Chapter 3 in a DBMS product, create and populate the Garden Glory database now in the DBMS of your choice (or as assigned by your instructor).

A. You need about 20 SERVICE transactions in the database. Write the needed SQL statements for any needed additional SERVICE transactions and insert the data into your database.

B. Design a data warehouse star schema for a dimensional database named GG-DW. The fact table measure will be HoursWorked.

C. Create the GG-DW database in a DBMS product.

D. What transformations of data will need to be made before the GG-DW database can be loaded with data? List all the transformations, showing the original format of the GARDEN_GLORY data and how it appears in the GG-DW database.

E. Write the complete set of SQL statements necessary to load the transformed data into the GG-DW database.

F. Populate the GG-DW database, using the SQL statements you wrote to answer part A.

G. Write an SQL query similar to the one shown in the text on page 000 that uses the hours worked per day as the measure.

H. Write the SQL view equivalent of the SQL query you wrote to answer part G.

I. Create the SQL view you wrote to answer part H in your GG-DW database.

J. Create the Microsoft Excel 2013 workbook named GG-DW-BI-Exercises.xlsx.

K. Using either the results of your SQL query from part G (copy the results of the query into a worksheet in the GG-DW-BI.xlsx workbook and then format this range as a worksheet table) or your SQL view from part I (create a Microsoft Excel data connection to the view), create an OLAP report similar to the OLAP report shown in Figure 8-17. (*Hint:* If you need help with the needed Microsoft Excel actions, search in the Microsoft Excel help system for more information.)

JAMES RIVER JEWELRY PROJECT QUESTIONS

The James River Jewelry project questions are available in online Appendix D, which can be downloaded from the textbook's Web site: **www.pearsonhighered.com/kroenke**.

THE QUEEN ANNE CURIOSITY SHOP PROJECT QUESTIONS

If you have not already implemented The Queen Anne Curiosity Shop database shown in Chapter 3 in a DBMS product, create and populate the QACS database now in the DBMS of your choice (or as assigned by your instructor).

A. You need about 30 PURCHASE transactions in the database. Write the needed SQL statements for any needed additional PURCHASE transactions and insert the data into your database.

B. Design a data warehouse star schema for a dimensional database named QACS-DW. The fact table measure will be ItemPrice.

C. Create the QACS-DW database in a DBMS product.

D. What transformations of data will need to be made before the QACS-DW database can be loaded with data? List all the transformations, showing the original format of the QACS and how it appears in the QACS-DW database.

E. Write the complete set of SQL statements necessary to load the transformed data into the QACS-DW database.

F. Populate the QACS-DW database, using the SQL statements you wrote to answer part A.

G. Write an SQL query similar to the one shown in the text on page 456 that uses retail price as the measure.

H. Write the SQL view equivalent of the SQL query you wrote to answer part G.

I. Create the SQL view you wrote to answer part H in your QACS-DW database.

J. Create a Microsoft Excel 2013 workbook named QACS-DW-BI-Exercises.xlsx.

K. Using either the results of your SQL query from part G (copy the results of the query into a worksheet in the QACS-DW-BI.xlsx workbook and then format this range as a worksheet table) or your SQL view from part I (create a Microsoft Excel data connection to the view), create an OLAP report similar to the OLAP report shown in Figure 8-17. (*Hint:* If you need help with the needed Microsoft Excel actions, search in the Microsoft Excel help system for more information.)

Online Appendices

Complete versions of these appendices are available on the textbook's Web site:
www.pearsonhighered.com/kroenke

Appendix A

Getting Started with Microsoft SQL Server 2014 Express Edition

Appendix B

Getting Started with Oracle Database Express Edition 11*g* Release 2

Appendix C

Getting Started with MySQL 5.6 Community Server

Appendix D

James River Jewelry Project Questions

Appendix E

SQL Views, SQL/PSM, and Importing Data

Appendix F

Getting Started in Systems Analysis and Design

Appendix G

Getting Started with Microsoft Visio 2013

Appendix H

The Access Workbench—Section H—Microsoft Access 2013 Switchboards

Appendix I

Getting Started with Web Servers, PHP, and the NetBeans IDE

Appendix J

Business Intelligence Systems

Appendix K

Big Data

Glossary

Although this section defines many of the key terms in the book, it is not meant to be exhaustive. Terms related to a specific DBMS product, for example, should be referenced in the chapter or appendix dedicated to that product. These references can be found in the index. Similarly, SQL concepts are included, but details of SQL commands and syntax should be referenced in the chapter that discusses those details, and Microsoft Access 2013 terms should be referenced in the sections of "The Access Workbench."

.NET Framework (.NET): Microsoft's comprehensive application development platform. It includes such components as ADO.NET and ASP.NET.

<?php and?>: The symbols used to indicate blocks of PHP code in Web pages.

ACID transaction: A transaction that is *atomic, consistent, isolated,* and *durable.* An atomic transaction is one in which a set of database changes are committed as a unit; either all of them are completed or none of them are. A consistent transaction is one in which all actions are taken against rows in the same logical state. An isolated transaction is one that is protected from changes by other users. A durable transaction is one that, once committed to a database, is permanent regardless of subsequent failure. There are different levels of consistency and isolation. *See* **transaction-level consistency** and **statement-level consistency**. *See also* **transaction isolation level**.

Active Server Pages (ASP): A combination of HTML and scripting language statements. Any statement included in <% ... %> is processed on the server. Used with Internet Information Server (IIS).

Active Data Objects (ADO): An implementation of OLE DB that is accessible via object- and non-object-oriented languages. It is used primarily as a scripting-language (JScript, VBScript) interface to OLE DB.

ADO.NET: A data access technology that is part of Microsoft's .NET initiative. ADO.NET provides the capabilities of ADO, but with a different object structure. ADO.NET also includes new capabilities for the processing of datasets.

After-image: A record of a database entity (normally a row or a page) after a change. Used in recovery to perform rollforward.

American National Standards Institute (ANSI): The American standards organization that creates and publishes the SQL standards.

AMP: An abbreviation for Apache, MySQL, and PHP/Pearl/Python. *See* **Apache Web Server** and **PHP**.

Anomaly: In normalization, an undesirable consequence of a data modification. With an insertion anomaly, facts about two or more different themes must be added to a single row of a relation. With a deletion anomaly, facts about two or more themes are lost when a single row is deleted.

Apache Web Server: A popular Web server that runs on most operating systems, particularly Windows and Linux.

Application program interface (API): The set of objects, methods, and properties that is used to access the functionality of a program such as a DBMS.

Association relationship: In database design, a table pattern where an intersection table contains additional attributes beyond the attributes that make up the composite primary key.

Associative entity: Also called an association entity, this is an entity that represents the combination of at least two other objects and that contains data about that combination. It is often used in contracting and assignment applications.

Asterisk (*): A wildcard character used in Microsoft Access queries to represent one or more unspecified characters. *See* **SQL percent sign (%) wildcard character**.

Atomic transaction: A group of logically related database operations that are performed as a unit. Either all the operations are performed or none of them are.

Attribute: (1) A value that represents a characteristic of an entity. (2) A column of a relation.

Before-image: A record of a database entity (normally a row or a page) before a change. Used in recovery to perform rollback.

Big data: The current term for the enormous datasets created by Web applications, such as search tools (e.g., Google and Bing), and by Web 2.0 social networks, such as Facebook, LinkedIn, and Twitter.

Bigtable: A nonrelational unstructured data store developed by Google.

Binary relationship: A relationship between exactly two entities or tables.

Boyce-Codd Normal Form (BCNF): A relation in third normal form in which every determinant is a candidate key.

Business intelligence (BI) systems: Information systems that assist managers and other professionals in analyzing current and past activities and in predicting future events. Two major categories of BI systems are reporting systems and data mining systems.

Business rule: A statement of a policy in a business that restricts the ways in which data can be inserted, updated, or deleted in the database.

Candidate key: An attribute or a group of attributes that identifies a unique row in a relation. One of the candidate keys is chosen to be the primary key.

Cardinality: In a binary relationship, the maximum or minimum number of elements allowed on each side of the relationship. The maximum cardinality can be 1:1, 1:N, N:1, or N:M. The minimum cardinality can be optional/optional, optional/mandatory, mandatory/optional, or mandatory/mandatory.

Cascading deletion: A property of a relationship that indicates that when one row is deleted, related rows should be deleted as well.

Cascading update: A referential integrity action specifying that when the key of a parent row is updated, the foreign keys of matching child rows should be updated as well.

Cassandra: A nonrelational unstructured data store from the Apache Software Foundation.

Checkpoint: The point of synchronization between a database and a transaction log. At the checkpoint, all buffers are written to external storage. (This is the standard definition of *checkpoint*, but DBMS vendors sometimes use this term in other ways.)

Child: A row, record, or node on the many side of a one-to-many relationship. *See also* **parent**.

Click-stream data: Data about a customer's clicking behavior on a Web page; such data are often analyzed by e-commerce companies.

Column: A logical group of bytes in a row of a relation or a table. The meaning of a column is the same for every row of the relation.

Commit: A command issued to a DBMS to make database modifications permanent. After the command has been processed, the changes are written to the database and to a log in such a way that they will survive system crashes and other failures. A commit is usually used at the end of an atomic transaction. Contrast this with **rollback**.

Composite identifier: An identifier of an entity that consists of two or more attributes.

Composite key: A key of a relation that consists of two or more columns.

Computed value: A column of a table that is computed from other column values. Values are not stored but are computed when they are to be displayed.

Concurrent transactions: A condition in which two or more transactions are processed against a database at the same time. In a single-CPU system, the changes are interleaved; in a multi-CPU system, the transactions can be processed simultaneously, and the changes on the database server are interleaved.

Concurrent update problem: An error condition in which one user's data changes are overwritten by another user's data changes. Also called *lost update problem*.

Confidence: In market basket analysis, the probability of a customer's buying one product, given that the customer has purchased another product.

Conformed dimension: In a dimensional database design, a dimension table that has relationships to two or more fact tables.

Consistency: Two or more concurrent transactions are consistent if the result of their being processed is the same as it would have been had they been processed in some sequential order.

Consistent: In an ACID transaction, either statement-level or transaction-level consistency. *See* **ACID transaction**, **consistency**, **statement-level consistency**, and **transaction-level consistency**.

COUNT: In SQL, a function that counts the number of rows in a query result. *See* **SQL built-in functions**.

Cube: *See* **OLAP cube**.

Data administration: An enterprisewide function that concerns the effective use and control of an organization's data assets. A person can perform it, but more often it is performed by a group. Specific functions include setting data standards and policies and providing a forum for conflict resolution. *See also* **database administration** and **DBA**.

Data definition language (DDL): A language used to describe the structure of a database.

Data manipulation language (DML): A language used to describe the processing of a database.

Data mart: A facility similar to a data warehouse, but with a restricted domain. Often, the data are restricted to particular types, business functions, or business units.

Data mining application: The use of statistical and mathematical techniques to find patterns in database data.

Data model: (1) A model of users' data requirements, usually expressed in terms of the entity-relationship model. It is sometimes called a users' data model. (2) A language for describing the structure and processing of a database.

Data sublanguage: A language for defining and processing a database intended to be embedded in programs written in another language—in most cases, a procedural language such as COBOL, C#, or Visual Basic. A data sublanguage is an incomplete programming language because it contains only constructs for data definition and processing.

Data warehouse: A store of enterprise data that is designed to facilitate management decision making. A data warehouse includes not only data, but also metadata, tools, procedures, training, personnel information, and other resources that make access to the data easier and more relevant to decision makers.

Data warehouse metadata database: The database used to store the data warehouse metadata.

Database: A self-describing collection of related records or, for relational databases, of related tables.

Database administration (DBA): A function that concerns the effective use and control of a particular database and its related applications.

Database administrator (DBA): A person or group responsible for establishing policies and procedures to control and protect a database. They work within guidelines set by data administration to control the database structure, manage data changes, and maintain DBMS programs.

Database backup: A copy of database files that can be used to restore a database to some previous, consistent state.

Database design: A graphical display of tables (files) and their relationships. The tables are shown in rectangles, and the relationships are shown using lines. A many relationship is shown with a crow's foot on the end of the line, an optional relationship is depicted by an oval, and a mandatory relationship is shown with hash marks.

Database management system (DBMS): A set of programs used to define, administer, and process a database and its applications.

Database schema: A complete logical view of a database.

Deadlock: A condition that can occur during concurrent processing in which each of two (or more) transactions is waiting to access data that the other transaction has locked. It also is called the *deadly embrace*.

Deadly embrace: *See* **deadlock**.

Decision support system (DSS): One or more applications designed to help managers make decisions.

Degree: In the entity-relationship model, the number of entities participating in a relationship.

Deletion anomaly: In a relation, the situation in which the removal of one row of a table deletes facts about two or more themes.

Denormalization: The process of intentionally designing a relation that is not normalized. Denormalization is done to improve performance or security.

Determinant: One or more attributes that functionally determine another attribute or attributes. In the functional dependency $(A, B) \rightarrow D, C$, the attributes (A, B) are the determinant.

Dimension table: In a star schema dimensional database, the tables that connect to the central fact table. Dimension tables hold attributes used in the organizing queries in analyses such as those of OLAP cubes.

Dimensional database: A database design that is used for data warehouses and is designed for efficient queries and analysis. It contains a central fact table connected to one or more dimension tables.

Dirty read: A read of data that have been changed but not yet committed to a database. Such changes may later be rolled back and removed from the database.

Discriminator: In the entity-relationship model, an attribute of a supertype entity that determines which subtype pertains to the supertype.

Distributed database: A database that is stored and processed on two or more computers.

Distributed two-phase locking: A sophisticated form of record locking that must be used when database transactions are processed on two or more machines.

Document type declaration (DTD): A set of markup elements that defines the structure of an XML document.

Domain: (1) The set of all possible values an attribute can have. (2) A description of the format (data type, length) and the semantics (meaning) of an attribute.

Domain key/normal form (DK/NF): A relation in which all constraints are logical consequences of domains and keys. In this text, this definition has been simplified to a relation in which the determinants of all functional dependencies are candidate keys.

Drill down: User-directed disaggregation of data used to break higher-level totals into components.

Durable: In an ACID transaction, the database changes are permanent. *See* **ACID transaction**.

Dynamo: A nonrelational unstructured data store developed by Amazon.com.

Dynamic cursor: A fully featured cursor. All inserts, updates, deletions, and changes in row order are visible to a dynamic cursor.

Enterprise-class database system: A DBMS product capable of supporting the operating requirement of large organizations.

Enterprise data warehouse (EDW) architecture: A data warehouse architecture that links specialized data marts to a central data warehouse for data consistency and efficient operations.

Entity: Something of importance to a user that needs to be represented in a database. In the entity-relationship model, entities are restricted to things that can be represented by a single table. *See also* **strong entity** and **weak entity**.

Entity class: A set of entities of the same type; two examples are EMPLOYEE and DEPARTMENT.

Entity instance: A particular occurrence of an entity; for example, Employee 100 (an EMPLOYEE) and Accounting Department (a DEPARTMENT).

Entity-relationship diagram (E-R diagram): A graphic used to represent entities and their relationships. Entities are normally shown in squares or rectangles, and relationships are shown in diamonds. The cardinality of the relationship is shown inside the diamond.

Entity-relationship model (E-R model): The constructs and conventions used to create a model of users' data. The things in the users' world are represented by entities, and the associations among those things are represented by relationships. The results are usually documented in an entity-relationship diagram. *See also* **data model**.

Exclusive lock: A lock on a data resource that no other transaction can read or update.

Explicit lock: A lock requested by a command from an application program.

Export: A function of a DBMS that writes a file of data in bulk. The file is intended to be read by another DBMS or program.

Extended entity-relationship (E-R) model: A set of constructs and conventions used to create data models. The things in the users' world are represented by entities, and the associations among those things are represented by relationships. The results are usually documented in an entity-relationship (E-R) diagram.

Extensible Markup Language (XML): A markup language whose tags can be extended by document designers.

Extract, transform, and load (ETL) system: The portion of a data warehouse that converts operation data to data warehouse data.

Fact table: The central table in a dimensional database. Its attributes are called measures. *See also* **measure**.

Field: (1) A logical group of bytes in a record used with file processing. (2) In the context of the relational model, a synonym for *attribute*.

Fifth normal form (5NF): A normal form necessary to eliminate an anomaly where a table can be split apart but not correctly joined back together. Also known as Project-Join Normal Form (PJ/NF).

File data source: An ODBC data source stored in a file that can be emailed or otherwise distributed among users.

First normal form (1NF): Any table that fits the definition of a relation.

Foreign key: An attribute that is a key of one or more relations other than the one in which it appears.

Form: A structured on-screen presentation of selected data from a database. Forms are used for both data input and data reading. A form is part of a database application. Compare this with a report.

Fourth normal form (4NF): A relation in BCNF in which every multivalued dependency is a functional dependency.

Functional dependency: A relationship between attributes in which one attribute or group of attributes determines the value of another. The expressions $X \rightarrow Y$, "X determines Y," and "Y is functionally dependent on X" mean that given a value of X, we can determine the value of Y.

HAS-A relationship: A relationship between two entities or objects that are of different logical types; for example, EMPLOYEE HAS-A(n) AUTO. Contrast this with an IS-A relationship.

Hadoop: *See* **Hadoop Distributed File System (HDFS)**.

Hadoop Distributed File System (HDFS): An open-source file distribution system that provides standard file services to clustered servers so that their file systems can function as one distributed file system.

HBase: A nonrelational unstructured data store developed as part of the Apache Software Foundation's Hadoop project. *See* **Hadoop Distributed File System (HDFS)**.

HTML document tags: The tags in HTML documents that indicate the structure of the document.

HTML syntax rules: The standards that are used to create HTML documents.

Http://localhost: For a Web server, a reference to the user's computer.

Hypertext Markup Language (HTML): A standardized set of text tags for formatting text, locating images and other nontext files, and placing links or references to other documents.

Hypertext Transfer Protocol (HTTP): A standardized means for using TCP/IP to communicate over the Internet.

ID-dependent entity: An entity that cannot logically exist without the existence of another entity. APPOINTMENT, for example, cannot exist without CLIENT to make the appointment. To be an ID-dependent entity, the identifier of the entity must contain the identifier of the entity on which it depends. Such entities are a subset of a weak entity. *See also* **existence-dependent entity**, **strong entity**, and **weak entity**.

Identifier: In an entity, a group of one or more attributes that determine entity instances. *See also* **nonunique identifier** and **unique identifier**.

Identifying relationship: A relationship that is used when the child entity is ID-dependent upon the parent entity.

IE Crow's Foot model: Formally known as the Information Engineering (IE) Crow's Foot model, it is a system of symbology used to construct E-R diagrams in data modeling and database design.

Implicit lock: A lock that is placed automatically by a DBMS.

Inconsistent backup: A backup file that contains uncommitted changes.

Inconsistent read problem: An anomaly that occurs in concurrent processing in which transactions execute a series of reads that are inconsistent with one another. This problem can be prevented by using two-phase locking and other strategies.

Index.html: A default Web page name provided by most Web servers.

Inetpub folder: In Windows operating systems, the root folder for the IIS Web server.

Information: (1) Knowledge derived from data, (2) data presented in a meaningful context, or (3) data processed by summing, ordering, averaging, grouping, comparing, or other similar operations.

Information Engineering (IE) model: An E-R model developed by James Martin.

Inner join: *See* join.

Integrated Definition 1, Extended (IDEF1X): A version of the entity-relationship model, adopted as a national standard, but difficult to understand and use. Most organizations use a simpler E-R version like the crow's foot model.

Integrated Development Environment (IDE): An application that provides a programmer or application developer with a complete set of development tools in one package.

Insertion anomaly: In a relation, a condition that exists when, to add a complete row to a table, one must add facts about two or more logically different themes.

Internet Information Server (IIS): A Windows Web server product that processes Active Server Pages (ASP).

Intersection table: A table (also called a relation) used to represent a many-to-many relationship. It contains the keys of the relations in the relationship. When used to represent entities having a many-to-many relationship, it may have nonkey data if the relationship contains data.

IS-A relationship: A relationship between a supertype and a subtype. For example, EMPLOYEE and ENGINEER have an IS-A relationship.

Isolation level: *See* transaction isolation level.

Java Database Connectivity (JDBC): A standard means for accessing DBMS products from Java. With JDBC, the unique API of a DBMS is hidden, and the programmer writes to the standard JDBC interface.

Java Server Pages (JSP): A combination of HTML and Java that is compiled into a servlet.

Join operation: A relational algebra operation on two relations, A and B, that produces a third relation, C. A row of A is concatenated with a row of B to form a new row in C if the rows in A and B meet restrictions concerning their values. For example, A1 is an attribute in A, and B1 is an attribute in B. The join of A with B in which (A1 = B1) will result in a relation, C, having the concatenation of rows in A and B in which the value of A1 is equal to the value of B1. In theory, restrictions other than equality are allowed—a join could be made in which A1 < B1. However, such non-equal joins are not used in practice. Also known as inner join. *See also* **natural join**.

Key: (1) A group of one or more attributes that identify a unique row in a relation. Because relations cannot have duplicate rows, every relation must have at least one key that is the composite of all the attributes in the relation. A key is sometimes called a logical key. (2) With some relational DBMS products, an index on a column used to improve access and sorting speed. It is sometimes called a physical key. *See also* **nonunique key**, **unique key**, and **physical key**.

LAMP: A version of AMP that runs on Linux. *See* **AMP**.

Lock: To allocate a database resource to a particular transaction in a concurrent-processing system. The size at which the resource can be locked is known as the lock granularity. *See also* **exclusive lock** and **shared lock**.

Lock granularity: The detail possible with a lock.

Log: A file that contains a record of database changes. The log contains before-images and after-images.

Logical unit of work (LUW): An equivalent term for transaction. *See* **Transaction**.

Logistic regression: A form of supervised data mining that estimates the parameters of an equation to calculate the odds that a given event will occur.

Lost update problem: Same as concurrent update problem.

MapReduce: A big data processing technique that breaks a data analysis into many parallel processes (the Map function) and then combines the results of these processes into one final result (the Reduce function).

MAX: In SQL, a function that determines the largest value in a set of numbers. *See* **SQL built-in functions**.

Maximum cardinality: (1) The maximum number of values that an attribute can have within a semantic object. (2) In a relationship between tables, the maximum number of rows to which a row of one table can relate in the other table.

Measure: In OLAP, a data value that is summed, averaged, or processed in some simple arithmetic manner.

Metadata: Data concerning the structure of data in a database stored in the data dictionary. Metadata are used to describe tables, columns, constraints, indexes, and so forth. *See also* **application metadata**.

MIN: In SQL, a function that determines the smallest value in a set of numbers. *See* **SQL built-in functions**.

Minimum cardinality: In a relationship between tables, the minimum number of rows to which a row of one table can relate in the other table.

Modification anomaly: A situation that exists when the storing of one row in a table records facts about two themes or the deletion of a row removes facts about two themes, or when a data change must be made in multiple rows for consistency.

Multiple-tier driver: In ODBC, a two-part driver, usually for a client-server database system. One part of the driver resides on the client and interfaces with the application; the second part resides on the server and interfaces with the DBMS.

Multivalued dependency: A condition in a relation with three or more attributes in which independent attributes appear to have relationships they do not have. Formally, in a relation R (A, B, C), having key (A, B, C) where A is matched with multiple values of B (or of C or of both), B does not determine C, and C does not determine B. An example is the relation EMPLOYEE (EmpNumber, EmpSkill, DependentName), where an employee can have multiple values of EmpSkill and DependentName. EmpSkill and DependentName do not have any relationship, but they do appear to in the relation.

N:M: An abbreviation for a many-to-many relationship between the rows of two tables.

Natural join: A join of a relation A having attribute A1 with relation B having attribute B1, where A1 = B1. The joined relation, C, contains either column A1 or B1 but not both.

NetBeans: A popular open-source integrated development environment (IDE).

Nonidentifying relationship: In data modeling, a relationship between two entities such that one is *not* ID-dependent on the other. *See* **Identifying relationship**.

Nonrepeatable reads: A situation that occurs when a transaction reads data it has previously read and finds modifications or deletions caused by a committed transaction.

Nonunique identifier: An identifier that determines a group of entity instances. *See also* **unique identifier**.

Nonunique key: A key that potentially identifies more than one row.

Normal form: A rule or set of rules governing the allowed structure of relations. The rules apply to attributes, functional dependencies, multivalued dependencies, domains, and constraints. The most important normal forms are 1NF, 2NF, 3NF, BCNF, 4NF, 5NF, and DK/NF.

Normalization process: The process of evaluating a relation to determine whether it is in a specified normal form and, if necessary, of converting it to relations in that specified normal form.

Null value: An attribute value that has never been supplied. Such values are ambiguous and can mean the value is unknown, the value is not appropriate, or the value is known to be blank.

Object persistence: The storage of object data values.

Object-oriented DBMS (OODBMS): A type of DBMS that provides object persistence. OODBMSs have not received commercial acceptance.

Object-oriented programming (OOP): A programming methodology that defines objects and the interactions between them to create application programs.

Object-relational database: A database created by a DBMS that provides a relational model interface as well as structures for object persistence. Oracle Database is the leading object-relational DBMS.

ODBC conformance level: In ODBC, definitions of the features and functions that are made available through the driver's application program interface (API). A driver API is a set of functions that the application can call to receive services. There are three conformance levels: Core API, Level 1 API, and Level 2 API.

ODBC data source: In the ODBC standard, a database and its associated DBMS, operating system, and network platform.

ODBC Data Source Administrator: The application used to create ODBC data sources.

ODBC Driver: In ODBC, a program that serves as an interface between the ODBC driver manager and a particular DBMS product. Runs on the client machines in a client-server architecture.

ODBC Driver Manager: In ODBC, a program that serves as an interface between an application program and an ODBC driver. It determines the required driver, loads it into memory, and coordinates activity between the application and the driver. On Windows systems, it is provided by Microsoft.

OLAP cube: In OLAP, a set of measures and dimensions arranged, normally, in the format of a table.

OLAP report: The output of an OLAP analysis in tabular format. For example, this can be a Microsoft Excel PivotTable. *See* **OLAP Cube**.

OLE DB: The COM-based foundation of data access in the Microsoft world. OLE DB objects support the OLE object standard. ADO is based on OLE DB.

1:1: An abbreviation for a one-to-one relationship between the rows of two tables.

1:N: An abbreviation for a one-to-many relationship between the rows of two tables.

Online Analytical Processing (OLAP): A technique for analyzing data values, called measures, against characteristics associated with those data values, called dimensions.

Online Transaction processing (OLTP) system: An operational database system available for, and dedicated to, transaction processing.

Open Database Connectivity (ODBC): A standard means for accessing DBMS products. Using ODBC, the unique API of a DBMS is hidden, and the programmer writes to the standard ODBC interface.

Operational system: A database system in use for the operations of the enterprise, typically an OLTP system. *See* **Online Transaction processing (OLTP) system**.

Optimistic locking: A locking strategy that assumes no conflict will occur, processes a transaction, and then checks to determine whether conflict did occur. If so, the transaction is aborted. *See also* **deadlock** and **pessimistic locking**.

Outer join: A join in which all the rows of a table appear in the resulting relation, regardless of whether they have a match in the join condition. In a left outer join, all the rows in the left-hand relation appear; in a right outer join, all the rows in the right-hand relation appear.

Parent: A row, record, or node on the one side of a one-to-many relationship. *See also* **child**.

Parent mandatory and child mandatory (M-M): A relationship where the minimum cardinality of the parent is 1 and the minimum cardinality of the child is 1.

Parent mandatory and child optional (M-O): A relationship where the minimum cardinality of the parent is 1 and the minimum cardinality of the child is 0.

Parent optional and child mandatory (O-M): A relationship where the minimum cardinality of the parent is 0 and the minimum cardinality of the child is 1.

Parent optional and child optional (O-O): A relationship where the minimum cardinality of the parent is 0 and the minimum cardinality of the child is 0.

Partitioned database: A database in which portions of the database are distributed to two or more computers.

Personal database system: A DBMS product intended for use by an individual or small workgroup. Such products typically include application development tools such as form and report generators in addition to the DBMS. For example, Microsoft Access 2013.

Pessimistic locking: A locking strategy that prevents conflict by placing locks before processing database read and write requests. *See also* **deadlock** and **optimistic locking**.

Phantom read: A situation that occurs when a transaction reads data it has previously read and then finds new rows that were inserted by a committed transaction.

PHP: *See* **PHP: Hypertext Processor**.

PHP: Hypertext Processor: A Web page scripting language used to create dynamic Web pages. It now includes an object-oriented programming component and PHP Data Objects (PDO).

Pig: A query language for nonrelational unstructured data stores developed as part of the Apache Software Foundation's Hadoop project. *See* **Hadoop Distributed File System (HDFS)**.

Primary key: A candidate key selected to be the key of a relation.

Processing rights and responsibilities: Organizational policies regarding which groups can take which actions on specified data items or other collections of data.

Properties: Same as attributes.

Query by Example (QBE): A style of query interface, first developed by IBM but now used by other vendors, that enables users to express queries by providing examples of the results they seek.

Question mark (?) wildcard character: A character used in Microsoft Access 2013 queries to represent a single unspecified character. *See* **SQL underscore (_) wildcard character**.

Read committed isolation: A level of transaction isolation that prohibits dirty reads but allows nonrepeatable reads and phantom reads.

Read uncommitted isolation: A level of transaction isolation that allows dirty reads, nonrepeatable reads, and phantom reads to occur.

Record: (1) A group of fields pertaining to the same entity; used in file-processing systems. (2) In the relational model, a synonym for row and tuple. *See also* **row**.

Recovery via reprocessing: Recovering a database by restoring the last full backup, and then recreating each transaction since the backup.

Recovery via rollback/rollforward: Recovering a database by restoring the last full backup, and then using data stored in a transaction log to modify the database as needed by either adding transactions (roll forward) or removing erroneous transactions (rollback).

Recursive relationship: A relationship among entities, objects, or rows of the same type. For example, if CUSTOMERs refer other CUSTOMERs, the relationship is recursive.

Referential integrity constraint: A relationship constraint on foreign key values. A referential integrity constraint specifies that the values of a foreign key must be a proper subset of the values of the primary key to which it refers.

Relation: A two-dimensional array that contains single-value entries and no duplicate rows. The meaning of the columns is the same in every row. The order of the rows and columns is immaterial.

Relational model: A data model in which data are stored in relations and relationships between rows are represented by data values.

Relational database: A database that consists of relations. In practice, relational databases contain relations with duplicate rows. Most DBMS products include a feature that removes duplicate rows when necessary and appropriate. Such removal is not done as a matter of course because it can be time-consuming and expensive.

Relational schema: A set of relations with referential integrity constraints.

Relationship: An association between two entities, objects, or rows of relations.

Relationship cardinality constraint: A constraint on the number of rows that can participate in a relationship. Minimum cardinality constraints determine the number of rows that must participate; maximum cardinality constraints specify the largest number of rows that can participate.

Relationship class: An association between entity classes.

Relationship instance: (1) An association between entity instances, (2) a specific relationship between two tables in a database.

Repeatable reads isolation: A level of transaction isolation that disallows dirty reads and nonrepeatable reads. Phantom reads can occur.

Replicated database: A database in which portions of the database are copied to two or more computers.

Report: A formatted set of information created to meet a user's need.

Reporting systems: Business intelligence (BI) systems that process data by filtering, sorting, and making simple calculations. OLAP is a type of reporting system.

Resource locking: *See* **lock**.

RFM analysis: A type of reporting system in which customers are classified according to how recently (R), how frequently (F), and how much money (M) they spend on their orders.

Rollback: A process that involves recovering a database in which before-images are applied to the database to return to an earlier checkpoint or other point at which the database is logically consistent.

Rollforward: A process that involves recovering a database by applying after-images to a saved copy of the database to bring it to a checkpoint or other point at which the database is logically consistent.

Row: A group of columns in a table. All the columns in a row pertain to the same entity. Also known as tuple or record.

Schema-valid document: An XML document that conforms to XML Schema.

Scrollable cursor: A cursor type that enables forward and backward movement through a recordset. Three scrollable cursor types discussed in this text are snapshot, keyset, and dynamic.

Second normal form (2NF): A relation in first normal form in which all non-key attributes are dependent on all the keys.

Serializable isolation level: A level of transaction isolation that disallows dirty reads, nonrepeatable reads, and phantom reads.

Shared lock: A lock against a data resource in which only one transaction can update the data but many transactions can concurrently read those data.

SQL: *See* **Structured Query Language (SQL)**.

SQL AND operator: The SQL operator used to combine conditions in an SQL WHERE clause.

SQL built-in function: In SQL, any of the functions COUNT, SUM, AVG, MAX, or MIN.

SQL CREATE TABLE statement: The SQL command used to create a database table.

SQL CREATE VIEW statement: The SQL command used to create a database view.

SQL FROM clause: The part of an SQL SELECT statement that specifies conditions used to determine which tables are used in a query.

SQL GROUP BY clause: The part of an SQL SELECT statement that specifies conditions for grouping rows when determining the query results.

SQL HAVING clause: The part of an SQL SELECT statement that specifies conditions used to determine which rows are in the groupings in GROUP BY clause.

SQL OR operator: The SQL operator used to specify alternate conditions in an SQL WHERE clause.

SQL ORDER BY clause: The part of an SQL SELECT statement that specifies how the query results should be sorted when they are displayed.

SQL percent sign (%) wildcard character: The standard SQL wildcard character used to specify multiple characters. Microsoft Access uses an asterisk (*) character instead of the underscore character.

SQL SELECT clause: The part of an SQL SELECT statement that specifies which columns are in the query results.

SQL SELECT/FROM/WHERE framework: The basic structure of an SQL query. *See* **SQL SELECT clause**, **SQL FROM clause**, **SQL WHERE clause**, **SQL ORDER BY clause**, **SQL GROUP BY clause**, **SQL HAVING clause**, **SQL AND operator**, and **SQL OR operator**.

SQL SELECT * statement: A variant of an SQL SELECT query that returns all columns for all tables in the query.

SQL SELECT...FOR XML statement: A variant of an SQL SELECT query that returns the query results in XML format.

SQL underscore (_) wildcard character: The standard SQL wildcard character used to specify a single character. Microsoft Access uses a question mark (?) character instead of the underscore character.

SQL view: A relation that is constructed from a single SQL SELECT statement. SQL views have at most one multivalued path. The term *view* in most DBMS products, including Microsoft Access, SQL Server, Oracle Database, and MySQL, means SQL view.

SQL WHERE clause: The part of an SQL SELECT statement that specifies conditions used to determine which rows are in the query results.

Star schema: In a dimensional database and as used in an OLAP database, the structure of a central fact table linked to dimension tables.

Statement-level consistency: A situation in which all rows affected by a single SQL statement are protected from changes made by other users during the execution of the statement. *See also* **transaction-level consistency**.

Static cursor: A cursor that takes a snapshot of a relation and processes that snapshot.

Stored procedure: A collection of SQL statements stored as a file that can be invoked by a single command. Usually, DBMS products provide a language for creating stored procedures that augments SQL with programming language constructs. Oracle provides PL/SQL for this purpose, and SQL Server provides Transact-SQL (T-SQL). With some products, stored procedures can be written in a standard language such as Java. Stored procedures are often stored within the database.

Strong entity: In the entity-relationship model, any entity whose existence in the database does not depend on the existence of any other entity. *See also* **ID-dependent entity** and **weak entity**.

Structured Query Language (SQL): A language for defining the structure and processing of a relational database. It can be used as a stand-alone query language, or it can be embedded in application programs. SQL was developed by IBM and is accepted as a national standard by the American National Standards Institute.

Subquery: A SELECT statement that appears in the WHERE clause of an SQL statement. Subqueries can be nested within each other.

Subtype entity: In generalization hierarchies, an entity or object that is a subspecies or subcategory of a higher-level type, called a supertype. For example, ENGINEER is a subtype of EMPLOYEE.

Surrogate key: A unique, system-supplied identifier used as the primary key of a relation. The values of a surrogate key have no meaning to the users and usually are hidden on forms and reports.

SUM: In SQL, a function that adds up a set of numbers. *See* **SQL built-in functions**.

Supertype entity: In generalization hierarchies, an entity or object that logically contains subtypes. For example, EMPLOYEE is a supertype of ENGINEER, ACCOUNTANT, and MANAGER.

Table: A database structure of rows and columns to create cells that hold data values. Also known as a *relation* in a relational database, although strictly only tables that meet specific conditions can be called relations. *See* **relation**.

Ternary relationship: A relationship between three entities.

Third normal form (3NF): A relation in second normal form that has no transitive dependencies.

Three-tier architecture: A Web database processing architecture in which the DBMS and the Web server reside on separate computers.

Time dimension: A required dimension table in a dimensional database. The time dimension allows the data to be analyzed over time.

Transaction: (1) A group of actions that is performed on the database atomically; either all actions are committed to the database or none of them are. (2) In the business world, the record of an event. *See also* **ACID transaction** and **atomic transaction**.

Transaction isolation level: The degree to which a database transaction is protected from actions by other transactions. The 1992 SQL standard specifies four isolation levels: read uncommitted, read committed, repeatable read, and serializable.

Transaction-level consistency: A situation in which all rows affected by any of the SQL statements in a transaction are protected from changes during the entire transaction. This level of consistency is expensive to enforce and is likely to reduce throughput. It might also prevent a transaction from seeing its own changes. *See also* **statement-level consistency**.

Transactional system: A database dedicated to processing transactions such as product sales and orders. It is designed to make sure that only complete transactions are recorded in the database.

Transitive dependency: In a relation having at least three attributes, such as R (A, B, C), the situation in which A determines B and B determines C, but B does not determine A.

Trigger: A special type of stored procedure that is invoked by the DBMS when a specified condition occurs. BEFORE triggers are executed before a specified database action, AFTER triggers are executed after a specified database action, and INSTEAD OF triggers are executed in place of a specified database action. INSTEAD OF triggers are normally used to update data in SQL views.

Tuple: *See* **row**.

Two-phase locking: A procedure in which locks are obtained and released in two phases. During the growing phase, the locks are obtained; during the shrinking phase, the locks are released. After a lock is released, no other lock will be granted that transaction. Such a procedure ensures consistency in database updates in a concurrent-processing environment.

Two-tier architecture: A Web database processing architecture in which the DBMS and the Web server reside on the same computer.

UML: *See* **Unified Modeling Language (UML)**.

Unified Modeling Language (UML): A set of structures and techniques for modeling and designing object-oriented programs and applications. UML is a methodology and a set of tools for such development. UML incorporates the entity-relationship model for data modeling.

Unique identifier: An identifier that determines exactly one entity instance. *See also* **nonunique identifier**.

Unique key: A key that identifies a unique row.

User: A person using an application.

User data source: An ODBC data source that is available only to the user who created it.

User group: A group of users. *See* **user**.

WAMP: AMP running on a Windows operating system. *See* **AMP**.

Weak entity: In the entity-relationship model, an entity whose logical existence in a database depends on the existence of another entity. *See also* **ID-dependent entity** and **strong entity**.

Web Services: A set of XML standards that enable applications to consume each other's services using Internet technology.

World Wide Web Consortium (W3C): The group that creates, maintains, revises, and publishes standards for the World Wide Web including HTML, XML, and XHMTL.

wwwroot folder: The root folder or directory of a Web site on a Microsoft IIS Web server.

XHTML: The Extensible Hypertext Markup Language. A reformulation of HTML to XML standards of well-formed documents.

Index